Chicago Kett (H. F.) and company

The Past and Present of Boone County, Illinois,

Containing a History of the County ... a Biographical Directory of its Citizens

Chicago Kett (H. F.) and company

The Past and Present of Boone County, Illinois,
Containing a History of the County ... a Biographical Directory of its Citizens

ISBN/EAN: 9783337209025

Printed in Europe, USA, Canada, Australia, Japan

Cover: Foto ©ninafisch / pixelio.de

More available books at **www.hansebooks.com**

T 45 N

T 46 N

MAP OF
BOONE
COUNTY

REFERENCE

Church
School House
Cemetery
Road
Railroad
Proposed Railroad
Timber
Swamp
Creek

T. 44 N

T. 43 N.

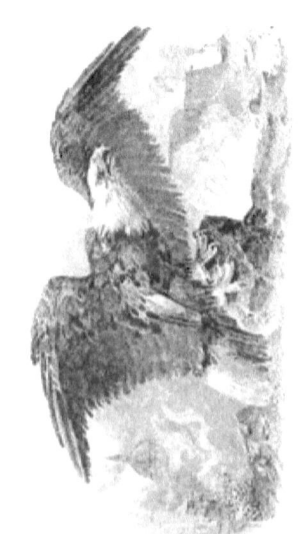

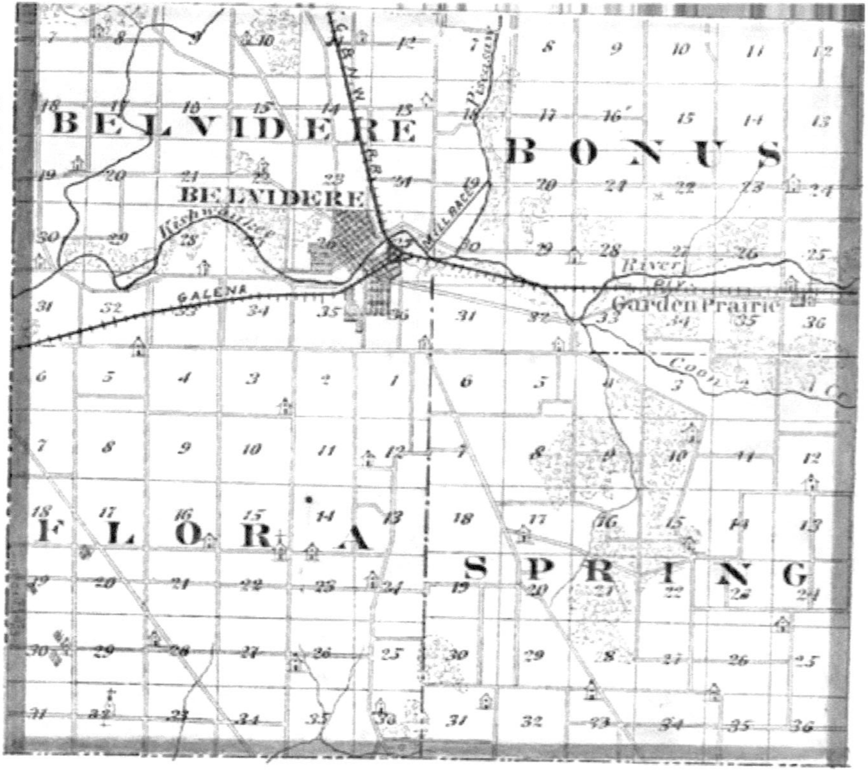

THE

PAST AND PRESENT

OF

BOONE COUNTY, ILLINOIS,

CONTAINING

A History of the County—Its Cities, Towns, &c., A Biographical Directory of its Citizens, War Record of its Volunteers in the late Rebellion, Portraits of Early Settlers and Prominent Men, General and Local Statistics, History of the Northwest, History of Illinois, Constitution of the United States, Map of Boone County, Miscellaneous Matters, Etc., Etc.

ILLUSTRATED.

CHICAGO:
H. F. KETT & CO., Cor. 5th Ave. and Washington St.
1877.

OTTAWAY & COLBERT,
PRINTERS,
147 & 149 Fifth Av., Chicago, Ill.

Preface.

We herewith present to the public THE PAST AND PRESENT OF BOONE COUNTY, in historical form. That this volume will be closely criticised by some, approved by others, and read by all, we entertain no doubt. The first we expect, the second we ardently hope for, and the last we earnestly request. It has been our purpose to collect in detail all the incidents relating to the early history of the county, as well as the later events, and to arrange them in such order as to make them not only readable, but interesting, and thus preserve the annals pertinent to pioneer life on the beautiful prairies of the Kishwaukee—on the old council grounds—the favorite resort of the Pottawatomies. Only in book form could they be thus preserved and handed down to those who will come to succeed the present population in the not far distant "by and by."

The time and labor necessary to the accomplishment of this undertaking, has been an arduous, although not an unpleasant duty. It has been full of interest to us, as well as pleasure, by having brought us in contact and acquaintance with a people whom it is an honor to know, from all of whom we received valuable information, and to all of whom we acknowledge our obligations for words of encouragement, courtesy and uniform kindness.

In this work we present a feature that is new in works of this character—the compilation of a list of the county officers, the judiciary, representatives and senators in the State Legislature, etc., their names, when elected, and all the other minutiae pertaining to a complete record of the civil officers chosen from time to time by the people, and extending over a period of forty years. This department will be invaluable as a source of reference in time to come, and is a feature that we feel assured will be appreciated by the people in whose interest this book is published. This record will date back to the first election for county officers, on the first Monday in May, 1837, and will extend up to and include the last regular election in November, 1876.

That some inaccuracies will be noted must be expected, but we trust they will prove to be few and of minor importance. We have sought to avoid such subjects of objection and criticism by every possible means, and wherever such errors may be detected, we hope they will be attributed to the proper cause. In some instances no records could be found relating to certain facts that we desired to incorporate. In seeking to obtain them by "interviewing" the "oldest living settlers," we would sometimes receive conflicting, though honest statements, from different individuals. To sift these statements and arrive at the most reasonable conclusions has been a delicate task, but we have tried to discharge that duty with the single purpose to write of things as they actually transpired. The passage of forty years in the onward flight of time wastes the energy and vigor of men's minds, as well as the strength and vigor of their physical organizations. Circumstances that were fresh in their memories ten and twenty years after their occurrence, are almost forgotten when forty years have gone; and when attention is directed to them, their memory recalls them as more like a midnight dream than actual occurrences in which they were partial, if not full participants. The foot print of time leaves its impressions on everything.

In some instances the reader will observe that we seem to get ahead of incidents as they occurred in the regular order of time and the official records of the county, but this was necessary in order to follow out and dispose of a particular subject. The seeming falling back in such instances as those to which we refer, is only taking up the date or subject from where we digressed. In other words, "resuming when we got ready to resume."

The incidents related under the caption of POLITICAL AND PERSONAL RECOLLECTIONS, are gathered from Old Settlers and a series of letters written by Dr. Daniel H. Whitney, and published by the Belvidere press a few years ago.

Our undertaking to preserve the PAST AND PRESENT OF BOONE COUNTY is completed, and it only remains for us to return our thanks to the intelligent, kind and courteous people of "Little Boone" for their words of approval, the information they have given us, as well as for their generous and liberal patronage, and to assure them that whatever of merit this offering may deserve, is due in some measure to them and the interest they have manifested in a desire to perpetuate in this form the annals of a county which their enterprise and energy has made to rank second to no other county in the state in all that goes to make a community prosperous, dignified and refined.

Respectfully,

H. F. KETT & CO.,

OCTOBER, 1877. *Publishers.*

HISTORICAL.

	Page.		Page.		Page.
History Northwest Territory	19	History Northwest Territory:		History of Boone Co.	
Geographical Position	19	Nebraska	107	County Schools	472
Early Explorations	20	History of Illinois	109	Geological Formations	222
Discovery of the Ohio	34	Coal	125	General History	225
English Explorations and Settlements	35	Compact of 1787	117	Old People	296
American Settlements	69	Chicago	132	Physical Geography	224
Division of the Northwest Territory	66	Early Discoveries	93	Political and Personal Recollections	325
Tecumseh and the War of 1812	70	Early Settlements	115	Property Statement	340
Black Hawk and the Black Hawk War	71	Education	129	Railroads	270
Other Indian Troubles	79	French Occupation	112	Senators and Representatives	319
Present Condition of the Northwest	87	Genius of La Salle	113	Vote of Boone Co.	329
Illinois		Material Resources	124	History of Towns:	
Indiana	101	Massacre at Ft. Dearborn	131	Belvidere	273
Iowa	102	Physical Features	121	Bonus	307
Michigan	104	Progress of Development	123	Boone	308
Wisconsin	104	Religion and Morals	128	Caledonia	312
Minnesota	106	War Record	130	Flora	314
		History of Boone Co.	221	Leroy	316
		Agricultural	367	Manchester	317
		Circuit Judges	320	Spring	317
		County and Town Officers, etc.	321		

ILLUSTRATIONS.

	Page.		Page.		Page.
Mouth of the Mississippi	21	Indians Attacking a Stockade		and P. R. R. Crossing the Mississippi at Davenport, Iowa	96
Source of the Mississippi	23	Black Hawk, the Sac Chieftain	75	A Western Dwelling	100
Wild Prairie	23	Big Eagle	80	Hunting Prairie Wolves at an Early Day	108
La Salle Landing on the Shore of Green Bay	25	Captain Jack, the Modoc Chieftain	83	Starved Rock, on the Illinois River, La Salle Co. Ill.	110
Buffalo Hunt	27	Kinzie House	85	An Early Settlement	116
Trapping	29	Village Residence	86	Chicago in 1830	136
Hunting	32	A Representative Pioneer	87	Old Fort Dearborn, 1860	136
Iroquois Chief	34	Lincoln Monument, Springfield Ill.		Present Site Lake St. Bridge Chicago, 1833	136
Pontiac, the Ottawa Chieftain	43	A Pioneer School House	89	Ruins of Chicago	142
Indians Attacking Frontiersmen	46	Farm View in the Winter	90	View of the City of Chicago	144
A Prairie Storm	59	Sugar Scene	91	Shabbona	
A Pioneer Dwelling	61	Pioneers' First Winter	92		
Breaking Prairie	65	Apple Harvest	94		
Tecumseh, the Shawnee Chieftain	69	Great Iron Bridge of C. B. & Q.			

LITHOGRAPHIC PORTRAITS.

	Page.		Page.		Page.
Bowley, H. F.	291	Fuller, Allen C.	249	Lawrence, L. W.	59
Brooks, W. H.	304	Fuller, Chas. E.	305	Moss, E. L.	237
Coon, R. W.	301	Foote, Jno. J.	345	May, Ezra	273
Cornwell, B.	309	Gardner, Cephas	311	Pettit, D. B.	337
Doty, S. P.	82	Harbinn, S. A.	235	Sawyer, Jas. W.	137
Drake, Abram	281	Jenner, A. E.	183	Wilt, C. F.	309

BOONE COUNTY WAR RECORD.

	Page.		Page.		Page.
Infantry	254	Infantry.		Infantry.	
11th	254	58th	259	146th	265
12th	254	65th	259	Cavalry	265
15th	254	9th	259	9th	265
17th	258	88th	259	15th	266
37th	258	105th	261	17th	266
39th	258	116th	264	Artillery	266
45th	258	142d	264	1st	266
48th	259	153d	264	2d	266

CONTENTS.

TOWNSHIP DIRECTORY.

	Page		Page		Page
Belvidere	341	Caledonia	386	Manchester	405
Boone	371	Flora	390	Spring	408
Bonus	378	Leroy	403		

ABSTRACT OF ILLINOIS STATE LAWS.

	Page		Page		Page
Adoption of Children	160	Forms: Bonds	176	Game	158
Bills of Exchange and Prom. Notes	151	Chattel Mortgages	177	Interest	151
County Courts	155	Codicil	189	Jurisdiction of Courts	154
Conveyances	164	Lease of Farm and Bld'gs	179	Limitation of Action	155
Church Organization	159	Lease of House	180	Landlord and Tenant	159
Descent	171	Landlord's Agreement	180	Liens	152
Deeds and Mortgages	207	Notes	174	Married Women	156
Drainage	163	Notice Tenant to Quit	181	Millers	159
Damages from Trespass	167	Orders	174	Marks and Brands	159
Definition of Commercial Terms	153	Quit Claim Deed	185	Paupers	164
Exemptions from Forced Sale, To.		Receipt	174	Roads and Bridges	161
Estrays	157	Real Estate Mortgage to secure paym't of Money	181	Surveyors and Surveys	160
Fences	168	Release	186	Superintendent census purchasing Books by Subscription	160
Forms: Articles of Agreement	175	Tenant's Agreement	180	Taxes	154
Bills of Purchase	174	Tenant's Notice to Quit	181	Wills and Estates	172
Bills of Sale	176	Warranty Deed	182	Weights and Measures	158
		Will	177	Wolf Scalps	164

MISCELLANEOUS.

	Page		Page		Page
Map of Boone Co.	Front.	Illinois by Counties 1870	218	Population of Fifty Principal Cities of the U. S.	214
Constitution of United States	192	Surveyors Measure	211	Population and Area of the United States	215
Electors of President and Vice-President, 1876	28	How to keep accounts	211	Population of the Principal Countries in the World	215
Practical Rules for every day use	207	Interest Table	212	Population Illinois	216 & 217
U. S. Government Land Measure	210	Miscellaneous Table	212	Vote of Boone County	339
Agricultural Productions of		Names of the States of the Union and their Significations	213		
		Population of the U. S.	214		

THE NORTHWEST TERRITORY.

GEOGRAPHICAL POSITION.

When the Northwestern Territory was ceded to the United States by Virginia in 1784, it embraced only the territory lying between the Ohio and the Mississippi Rivers, and north to the northern limits of the United States. It coincided with the area now embraced in the States of Ohio, Indiana, Michigan, Illinois, Wisconsin, and that portion of Minnesota lying on the east side of the Mississippi River. The United States itself at that period extended no farther west than the Mississippi River; but by the purchase of Louisiana in 1803, the western boundary of the United States was extended to the Rocky Mountains and the Northern Pacific Ocean. The new territory thus added to the National domain, and subsequently opened to settlement, has been called the "New Northwest," in contradistinction from the old "Northwestern Territory."

In comparison with the old Northwest this is a territory of vast magnitude. It includes an area of 1,887,850 square miles; being greater in extent than the united areas of all the Middle and Southern States, including Texas. Out of this magnificent territory have been erected eleven sovereign States and eight Territories, with an aggregate population, at the present time, of 13,000,000 inhabitants, or nearly one third of the entire population of the United States.

Its lakes are fresh-water seas, and the larger rivers of the continent flow for a thousand miles through its rich alluvial valleys and far-stretching prairies, more acres of which are arable and productive of the highest percentage of the cereals than of any other area of like extent on the globe.

For the last twenty years the increase of population in the Northwest has been about as three to one in any other portion of the United States.

EARLY EXPLORATIONS.

In the year 1541, DeSoto first saw the Great West in the New World. He, however, penetrated no farther north than the 35th parallel of latitude. The expedition resulted in his death and that of more than half his army, the remainder of whom found their way to Cuba, thence to Spain, in a famished and demoralized condition. DeSoto founded no settlements, produced no results, and left no traces, unless it were that he awakened the hostility of the red man against the white man, and disheartened such as might desire to follow up the career of discovery for better purposes. The French nation were eager and ready to seize upon any news from this extensive domain, and were the first to profit by DeSoto's defeat. Yet it was more than a century before any adventurer took advantage of these discoveries.

In 1616, four years before the pilgrims "moored their bark on the wild New England shore," Le Caron, a French Franciscan, had penetrated through the Iroquois and Wyandots (Hurons) to the streams which run into Lake Huron; and in 1634, two Jesuit missionaries founded the first mission among the lake tribes. It was just one hundred years from the discovery of the Mississippi by DeSoto (1541) until the Canadian envoys met the savage nations of the Northwest at the Falls of St. Mary, below the outlet of Lake Superior. This visit led to no permanent result; yet it was not until 1659 that any of the adventurous fur traders attempted to spend a Winter in the frozen wilds about the great lakes, nor was it until 1660 that a station was established upon their borders by Mesnard, who perished in the woods a few months after. In 1665, Claude Allouez built the earliest lasting habitation of the white man among the Indians of the Northwest. In 1668, Claude Dablon and James Marquette founded the mission of Sault Ste. Marie at the Falls of St. Mary, and two years afterward, Nicholas Perrot, as agent for M. Talon, Governor General of Canada, explored Lake Illinois (Michigan) as far south as the present City of Chicago, and invited the Indian nations to meet him at a grand council at Sault Ste. Marie the following Spring, where they were taken under the protection of the king, and formal possession was taken of the Northwest. This same year Marquette established a mission at Point St. Ignatius, where was founded the old town of Michillimackinac.

During M. Talon's explorations and Marquette's residence at St. Ignatius, they learned of a great river away to the west, and fancied —as all others did then—that upon its fertile banks whole tribes of God's children resided, to whom the sound of the Gospel had never come. Filled with a wish to go and preach to them, and in compliance with a

THE NORTHWEST TERRITORY. 21

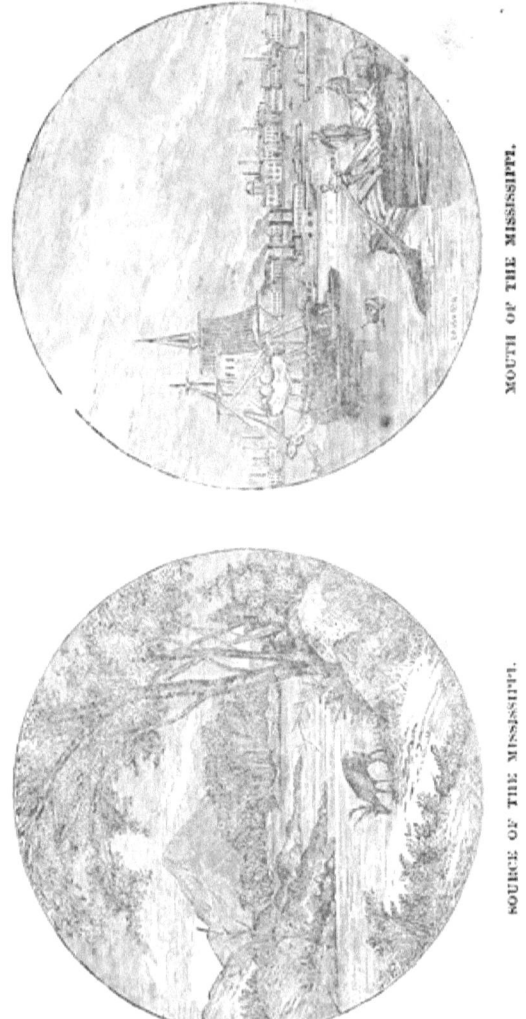

MOUTH OF THE MISSISSIPPI.

SOURCE OF THE MISSISSIPPI.

request of M. Talon, who earnestly desired to extend the domain of his king, and to ascertain whether the river flowed into the Gulf of Mexico or the Pacific Ocean, Marquette with Joliet, as commander of the expedition, prepared for the undertaking.

On the 13th of May, 1673, the explorers, accompanied by five assistant French Canadians, set out from Mackinaw on their daring voyage of discovery. The Indians, who gathered to witness their departure, were astonished at the boldness of the undertaking, and endeavored to dissuade them from their purpose by representing the tribes on the Mississippi as exceedingly savage and cruel, and the river itself as full of all sorts of frightful monsters ready to swallow them and their canoes together. But, nothing daunted by these terrific descriptions, Marquette told them he was willing not only to encounter all the perils of the unknown region they were about to explore, but to lay down his life in a cause in which the salvation of souls was involved; and having prayed together they separated. Coasting along the northern shore of Lake Michigan, the adventurers entered Green Bay, and passed thence up the Fox River and Lake Winnebago to a village of the Miamis and Kickapoos. Here Marquette was delighted to find a beautiful cross planted in the middle of the town ornamented with white skins, red girdles and bows and arrows, which these good people had offered to the Great Manitou, or God, to thank him for the pity he had bestowed on them during the Winter in giving them an abundant "chase." This was the farthest outpost to which Dablon and Allouez had extended their missionary labors the year previous. Here Marquette drank mineral waters and was instructed in the secret of a root which cures the bite of the venomous rattlesnake. He assembled the chiefs and old men of the village, and, pointing to Joliet, said: "My friend is an envoy of France, to discover new countries, and I am an ambassador from God to enlighten them with the truths of the Gospel." Two Miami guides were here furnished to conduct them to the Wisconsin River, and they set out from the Indian village on the 10th of June, amidst a great crowd of natives who had assembled to witness their departure into a region where no white man had ever yet ventured. The guides, having conducted them across the portage, returned. The explorers launched their canoes upon the Wisconsin, which they descended to the Mississippi and proceeded down its unknown waters. What emotions must have swelled their breasts as they struck out into the broadening current and became conscious that they were now upon the bosom of the Father of Waters. The mystery was about to be lifted from the long-sought river. The scenery in that locality is beautiful, and on that delightful seventeenth of June must have been clad in all its primeval loveliness as it had been adorned by the hand of

Nature. Drifting rapidly, it is said that the bold bluffs on either hand "reminded them of the castled shores of their own beautiful rivers of France." By-and-by, as they drifted along, great herds of buffalo appeared on the banks. On going to the heads of the valley they could see a country of the greatest beauty and fertility, apparently destitute of inhabitants yet presenting the appearance of extensive manors, under the fastidious cultivation of lordly proprietors.

THE WILD PRAIRIE.

On June 25, they went ashore and found some fresh traces of men upon the sand, and a path which led to the prairie. The men remained in the boat, and Marquette and Joliet followed the path till they discovered a village on the banks of a river, and two other villages on a hill, within a half league of the first, inhabited by Indians. They were received most hospitably by these natives, who had never before seen a white person. After remaining a few days they re-embarked and descended the river to about latitude 33°, where they found a village of the Arkansas, and being satisfied that the river flowed into the Gulf of Mexico, turned their course up the river, and ascending the stream to the mouth of the Illinois, rowed up that stream to its source, and procured guides from that point to the lakes. "Nowhere on this journey," says Marquette, "did we see such grounds, meadows, woods, stags, buffaloes, deer, wildcats, bustards, swans, ducks, parroquets, and even beavers, as on the Illinois River." The party, without loss or injury, reached Green Bay in September, and reported their discovery—one of the most important of the age, but of which no record was preserved save Marquette's, Joliet losing his by the upsetting of his canoe on his way to Quebec. Afterward Marquette returned to the Illinois Indians by their request, and ministered to them until 1675. On the 18th of May, in that year, as he was passing the mouth of a stream—going with his boatmen up Lake Michigan—he asked to land at its mouth and celebrate Mass. Leaving his men with the canoe, he retired a short distance and began his devotions. As much time passed and he did not return, his men went in search of him, and found him upon his knees, dead. He had peacefully passed away while at prayer. He was buried at this spot. Charlevoix, who visited the place fifty years after, found the waters had retreated from the grave, leaving the beloved missionary to repose in peace. The river has since been called Marquette.

While Marquette and his companions were pursuing their labors in the West, two men, differing widely from him and each other, were preparing to follow in his footsteps and perfect the discoveries so well begun by him. These were Robert de La Salle and Louis Hennepin.

After La Salle's return from the discovery of the Ohio River (see the narrative elsewhere), he established himself again among the French trading posts in Canada. Here he mused long upon the pet project of those ages—a short way to China and the East, and was busily planning an expedition up the great lakes, and so across the continent to the Pacific, when Marquette returned from the Mississippi. At once the vigorous mind of LaSalle received from his and his companions' stories the idea that by following the Great River northward, or by turning up some of the numerous western tributaries, the object could easily be gained. He applied to Frontenac, Governor General of Canada, and laid before him the plan, dim but gigantic. Frontenac entered warmly into his plans, and saw that LaSalle's idea to connect the great lakes by a chain of forts with the Gulf of Mexico would bind the country so wonderfully together, give unmeasured power to France, and glory to himself, under whose administration he earnestly hoped all would be realized.

LaSalle now repaired to France, laid his plans before the King, who warmly approved of them, and made him a Chevalier. He also received from all the noblemen the warmest wishes for his success. The Chevalier returned to Canada, and busily entered upon his work. He at once rebuilt Fort Frontenac and constructed the first ship to sail on these fresh-water seas. On the 7th of August, 1679, having been joined by Hennepin, he began his voyage in the Griffin up Lake Erie. He passed over this lake, through the straits beyond, up Lake St. Clair and into Huron. In this lake they encountered heavy storms. They were some time at Michillimackinac, where LaSalle founded a fort, and passed on to Green Bay, the "Baie des Puans" of the French, where he found a large quantity of furs collected for him. He loaded the Griffin with these, and placing her under the care of a pilot and fourteen sailors,

LA SALLE LANDING ON THE SHORE OF GREEN BAY.

started her on her return voyage. The vessel was never afterward heard of. He remained about these parts until early in the Winter, when, hearing nothing from the Griffin, he collected all his men—thirty working men and three monks—and started again upon his great undertaking.

By a short portage they passed to the Illinois or Kankakee, called by the Indians, "Theakeke," *wolf*, because of the tribes of Indians called by that name, commonly known as the Mahingans, dwelling there. The French pronounced it *Kiakiki*, which became corrupted to Kankakee. "Falling down the said river by easy journeys, the better to observe the country," about the last of December they reached a village of the Illinois Indians, containing some five hundred cabins, but at that moment no inhabitants. The Seur de LaSalle being in want of some breadstuffs, took advantage of the absence of the Indians to help himself to a sufficiency of maize, large quantities of which he found concealed in holes under the wigwams. This village was situated near the present village of Utica in LaSalle County, Illinois. The corn being securely stored, the voyagers again betook themselves to the stream, and toward evening, on the 4th day of January, 1680, they came into a lake which must have been the lake of Peoria. This was called by the Indians *Pim-i-te-wi*, that is, *a place where there are many fat beasts*. Here the natives were met with in large numbers, but they were gentle and kind, and having spent some time with them, LaSalle determined to erect another fort in that place, for he had heard rumors that some of the adjoining tribes were trying to disturb the good feeling which existed, and some of his men were disposed to complain, owing to the hardships and perils of the travel. He called this fort "*Crevecœur*" (broken-heart), a name expressive of the very natural sorrow and anxiety which the pretty certain loss of his ship, Griffin, and his consequent impoverishment, the danger of hostility on the part of the Indians, and of mutiny among his own men, might well cause him. His fears were not entirely groundless. At one time poison was placed in his food, but fortunately was discovered.

While building this fort, the Winter wore away, the prairies began to look green, and LaSalle, despairing of any reinforcements, concluded to return to Canada, raise new means and new men, and embark anew in the enterprise. For this purpose he made Hennepin the leader of a party to explore the head waters of the Mississippi, and he set out on his journey. This journey was accomplished with the aid of a few persons, and was successfully made, though over an almost unknown route, and in a bad season of the year. He safely reached Canada, and set out again for the object of his search.

Hennepin and his party left Fort Crevecœur on the last of February, 1680. When LaSalle reached this place on his return expedition, he found the fort entirely deserted, and he was obliged to return again to Canada. He embarked the third time, and succeeded. Seven days after leaving the fort, Hennepin reached the Mississippi, and paddling up the icy stream as best he could, reached no higher than the Wisconsin River by the 11th of April. Here he and his followers were taken prisoners by a band of Northern Indians, who treated them with great kindness. Hennepin's comrades were Anthony Auguel and Michael Ako. On this voyage they found several beautiful lakes, and "saw some charming prairies." Their captors were the Isaute or Sauteurs, Chippewas, a tribe of the Sioux nation, who took them up the river until about the first of May, when they reached some falls, which Hennepin christened Falls of St. Anthony in honor of his patron saint. Here they took the land, and traveling nearly two hundred miles to the northwest, brought them to their villages. Here they were kept about three months, were treated kindly by their captors, and at the end of that time, were met by a band of Frenchmen,

BUFFALO HUNT.

headed by one Seur de Luth, who, in pursuit of trade and game, had penetrated thus far by the route of Lake Superior; and with these fellow-countrymen Hennepin and his companions were allowed to return to the borders of civilized life in November, 1680, just after LaSalle had returned to the wilderness on his second trip. Hennepin soon after went to France, where he published an account of his adventures.

The Mississippi was first discovered by De Soto in April, 1541, in his vain endeavor to find gold and precious gems. In the following Spring, De Soto, weary with hope long deferred, and worn out with his wanderings, he fell a victim to disease, and on the 21st of May died. His followers, reduced by fatigue and disease to less than three hundred men, wandered about the country nearly a year, in the vain endeavor to rescue themselves by land, and finally constructed seven small vessels, called brigantines, in which they embarked, and descending the river, supposing it would lead them to the sea, in July they came to the sea (Gulf of Mexico), and by September reached the Island of Cuba.

They were the first to see the great outlet of the Mississippi; but, being so weary and discouraged, made no attempt to claim the country, and hardly had an intelligent idea of what they had passed through.

To La Salle, the intrepid explorer, belongs the honor of giving the first account of the mouths of the river. His great desire was to possess this entire country for his king, and in January, 1682, he and his band of explorers left the shores of Lake Michigan on their third attempt, crossed the portage, passed down the Illinois River, and on the 6th of February, reached the banks of the Mississippi.

On the 13th they commenced their downward course, which they pursued with but one interruption, until upon the 6th of March they discovered the three great passages by which the river discharges its waters into the gulf. La Salle thus narrates the event:

"We landed on the bank of the most western channel, about three leagues (nine miles) from its mouth. On the seventh, M. de LaSalle went to reconnoiter the shores of the neighboring sea, and M. de Tonti meanwhile examined the great middle channel. They found the main outlets beautiful, large and deep. On the 8th we reascended the river, a little above its confluence with the sea, to find a dry place beyond the reach of inundations. The elevation of the North Pole was here about twenty-seven degrees. Here we prepared a column and a cross, and to the column were affixed the arms of France with this inscription:

Louis Le Grand, Roi De France et de Navarre, regne; Le neuvieme Avril, 1682.

The whole party, under arms, chanted the *Te Deum*, and then, after a salute and cries of "*Vive le Roi*," the column was erected by M. de LaSalle, who, standing near it, proclaimed in a loud voice the authority of the King of France. LaSalle returned and laid the foundations of the Mississippi settlements in Illinois, thence he proceeded to France, where another expedition was fitted out, of which he was commander, and in two succeeding voyages failed to find the outlet of the river by sailing along the shore of the gulf. On his third voyage he was killed, through the treachery of his followers, and the object of his expeditions was not accomplished until 1699, when D'Iberville, under the authority of the crown, discovered, on the second of March, by way of the sea, the mouth of the "Hidden River." This majestic stream was called by the natives "*Malbouchia*," and by the Spaniards, "*la Palissade*," from the great

TRAPPING.

number of trees about its mouth. After traversing the several outlets, and satisfying himself as to its certainty, he erected a fort near its western outlet, and returned to France.

An avenue of trade was now opened out which was fully improved. In 1718, New Orleans was laid out and settled by some European colonists. In 1762, the colony was made over to Spain, to be regained by France under the consulate of Napoleon. In 1803, it was purchased by the United States for the sum of fifteen million dollars, and the territory of Louisiana and commerce of the Mississippi River came under the charge of the United States. Although LaSalle's labors ended in defeat and death, he had not worked and suffered in vain. He had thrown open to France and the world an immense and most valuable country; had established several ports, and laid the foundations of more than one settlement there. "Peoria, Kaskaskia and Cahokia, are to this day monuments of LaSalle's labors; for, though he had founded neither of them (unless Peoria, which was built nearly upon the site of Fort Crevecœur,) it was by those whom he led into the West that these places were peopled and civilized. He was, if not the discoverer, the first settler of the Mississippi Valley, and as such deserves to be known and honored."

The French early improved the opening made for them. Before the year 1698, the Rev. Father Gravier began a mission among the Illinois, and founded Kaskaskia. For some time this was merely a missionary station, where none but natives resided, it being one of three such villages, the other two being Cahokia and Peoria. What is known of these missions is learned from a letter written by Father Gabriel Marest, dated "Aux Cascaskias, autrement dit de l'Immaculate Conception de la Sainte Vierge, le 9 Novembre, 1712." Soon after the founding of Kaskaskia, the missionary, Pinet, gathered a flock at Cahokia, while Peoria arose near the ruins of Fort Crevecœur. This must have been about the year 1700. The post at Vincennes on the Oubache river, (pronounced Wä-bä, meaning *summer cloud moving swiftly*) was established in 1702, according to the best authorities.* It is altogether probable that on LaSalle's last trip he established the stations at Kaskaskia and Cahokia. In July, 1701, the foundations of Fort Ponchartrain were laid by De la Motte Cadillac on the Detroit River. These stations, with those established further north, were the earliest attempts to occupy the Northwest Territory. At the same time efforts were being made to occupy the Southwest, which finally culminated in the settlement and founding of the City of New Orleans by a colony from England in 1718. This was mainly accomplished through the efforts of the famous Mississippi Company, established by the notorious John Law, who so quickly arose into prominence in France, and who with his scheme so quickly and so ignominiously passed away.

From the time of the founding of these stations for fifty years the French nation were engrossed with the settlement of the lower Mississippi, and the war with the Chicasaws, who had, in revenge for repeated

---

* There is considerable dispute about this date, some asserting it was founded as late as 1742. When the new court house at Vincennes was erected, all authorities on the subject were carefully examined, and 1702 fixed upon as the correct date. It was accordingly engraved on the corner-stone of the court house.

injuries, cut off the entire colony at Natchez. Although the company did little for Louisiana, as the entire West was then called, yet it opened the trade through the Mississippi River, and started the raising of grains indigenous to that climate. Until the year 1750, but little is known of the settlements in the Northwest, as it was not until this time that the attention of the English was called to the occupation of this portion of the New World, which they then supposed they owned. Vivier, a missionary among the Illinois, writing from "Aux Illinois," six leagues from Fort Chartres, June 8, 1750, says: "We have here whites, negroes and Indians, to say nothing of cross-breeds. There are five French villages, and three villages of the natives, within a space of twenty-one leagues situated between the Mississippi and another river called the Karkadaid (Kaskaskias). In the five French villages are, perhaps, eleven hundred whites, three hundred blacks and some sixty red slaves or savages. The three Illinois towns do not contain more than eight hundred souls all told. Most of the French till the soil; they raise wheat, cattle, pigs and horses, and live like princes. Three times as much is produced as can be consumed; and great quantities of grain and flour are sent to New Orleans." This city was now the seaport town of the Northwest, and save in the extreme northern part, where only furs and copper ore were found, almost all the products of the country found their way to France by the mouth of the Father of Waters. In another letter, dated November 7, 1750, this same priest says: "For fifteen leagues above the mouth of the Mississippi one sees no dwellings, the ground being too low to be habitable. Thence to New Orleans, the lands are only partially occupied. New Orleans contains black, white and red, not more, I think, than twelve hundred persons. To this point come all lumber, bricks, salt-beef, tallow, tar, skins and bear's grease; and above all, pork and flour from the Illinois. These things create some commerce, as forty vessels and more have come hither this year. Above New Orleans, plantations are again met with; the most considerable is a colony of Germans, some ten leagues up the river. At Point Coupee, thirty-five leagues above the German settlement, is a fort. Along here, within five or six leagues, are not less than sixty habitations. Fifty leagues farther up is the Natchez post, where we have a garrison, who are kept prisoners through fear of the Chickasaws. Here and at Point Coupee, they raise excellent tobacco. Another hundred leagues brings us to the Arkansas, where we have also a fort and a garrison for the benefit of the river traders. * * * From the Arkansas to the Illinois, nearly five hundred leagues, there is not a settlement. There should be, however, a fort at the Oubache (Ohio), the only path by which the English can reach the Mississippi. In the Illinois country are numberless mines, but no one to work them as they deserve." Father Marest, writing from the post at Vincennes in 1812, makes the same observation. Vivier also says: "Some individuals dig lead near the surface and supply the Indians and Canada. Two Spaniards now here, who claim to be adepts, say that our mines are like those of Mexico, and that if we would dig deeper, we should find silver under the lead; and at any rate the lead is excellent. There is also in this country, beyond doubt, copper ore, as from time to time large pieces are found in the streams."

HUNTING.

At the close of the year 1750, the French occupied, in addition to the lower Mississippi posts and those in Illinois, one at Du Quesne, one at the Maumee in the country of the Miamis, and one at Sandusky in what may be termed the Ohio Valley. In the northern part of the Northwest they had stations at St. Joseph's on the St. Joseph's of Lake Michigan, at Fort Ponchartrain (Detroit), at Michillimackanac or Massillimacanac, Fox River of Green Bay, and at Sault Ste. Marie. The fondest dreams of LaSalle were now fully realized. The French alone were possessors of this vast realm, basing their claim on discovery and settlement. Another nation, however, was now turning its attention to this extensive country, and hearing of its wealth, began to lay plans for occupying it and for securing the great profits arising therefrom.

The French, however, had another claim to this country, namely, the

DISCOVERY OF THE OHIO.

This "Beautiful" river was discovered by Robert Cavalier de LaSalle in 1669, four years before the discovery of the Mississippi by Joliet and Marquette.

While LaSalle was at his trading post on the St. Lawrence, he found leisure to study nine Indian dialects, the chief of which was the Iroquois. He not only desired to facilitate his intercourse in trade, but he longed to travel and explore the unknown regions of the West. An incident soon occurred which decided him to fit out an exploring expedition.

While conversing with some Senecas, he learned of a river called the Ohio, which rose in their country and flowed to the sea, but at such a distance that it required eight months to reach its mouth. In this statement the Mississippi and its tributaries were considered as one stream. LaSalle believing, as most of the French at that period did, that the great rivers flowing west emptied into the Sea of California, was anxious to embark in the enterprise of discovering a route across the continent to the commerce of China and Japan.

He repaired at once to Quebec to obtain the approval of the Governor. His eloquent appeal prevailed. The Governor and the Intendant, Talon, issued letters patent authorizing the enterprise, but made no provision to defray the expenses. At this juncture the seminary of St. Sulpice decided to send out missionaries in connection with the expedition, and LaSalle offering to sell his improvements at LaChine to raise money, the offer was accepted by the Superior, and two thousand eight hundred dollars were raised, with which LaSalle purchased four canoes and the necessary supplies for the outfit.

On the 6th of July, 1669, the party, numbering twenty-four persons, embarked in seven canoes on the St. Lawrence; two additional canoes carried the Indian guides. In three days they were gliding over the bosom of Lake Ontario. Their guides conducted them directly to the Seneca village on the bank of the Genesee, in the vicinity of the present City of Rochester, New York. Here they expected to procure guides to conduct them to the Ohio, but in this they were disappointed.

The Indians seemed unfriendly to the enterprise. LaSalle suspected that the Jesuits had prejudiced their minds against his plans. After waiting a month in the hope of gaining their object, they met an Indian from the Iroquois colony at the head of Lake Ontario, who assured them that they could there find guides, and offered to conduct them thence.

On their way they passed the mouth of the Niagara River, when they heard for the first time the distant thunder of the cataract. Arriving

IROQUOIS CHIEF.

among the Iroquois, they met with a friendly reception, and learned from a Shawanee prisoner that they could reach the Ohio in six weeks. Delighted with the unexpected good fortune, they made ready to resume their journey; but just as they were about to start they heard of the arrival of two Frenchmen in a neighboring village. One of them proved to be Louis Joliet, afterwards famous as an explorer in the West. He had been sent by the Canadian Government to explore the copper mines on Lake Superior, but had failed, and was on his way back to Quebec. He gave the missionaries a map of the country he had explored in the lake region, together with an account of the condition of the Indians in that quarter. This induced the priests to determine on leaving the expedition and going to Lake Superior. LaSalle warned them that the Jesuits were probably occupying that field, and that they would meet with a cold reception. Nevertheless they persisted in their purpose, and after worship on the lake shore, parted from LaSalle. On arriving at Lake Superior, they found, as LaSalle had predicted, the Jesuit Fathers, Marquette and Dablon, occupying the field.

These zealous disciples of Loyola informed them that they wanted no assistance from St. Sulpice, nor from those who made him their patron saint; and thus repulsed, they returned to Montreal the following June without having made a single discovery or converted a single Indian.

After parting with the priests, LaSalle went to the chief Iroquois village at Onondaga, where he obtained guides, and passing thence to a tributary of the Ohio south of Lake Erie, he descended the latter as far as the falls at Louisville. Thus was the Ohio discovered by LaSalle, the persevering and successful French explorer of the West, in 1669.

The account of the latter part of his journey is found in an anonymous paper, which purports to have been taken from the lips of LaSalle himself during a subsequent visit to Paris. In a letter written to Count Frontenac in 1667, shortly after the discovery, he himself says that he discovered the Ohio and descended it to the falls. This was regarded as an indisputable fact by the French authorities, who claimed the Ohio Valley upon another ground. When Washington was sent by the colony of Virginia in 1753, to demand of Gordeur de St. Pierre why the French had built a fort on the Monongahela, the haughty commandant at Quebec replied: "We claim the country on the Ohio by virtue of the discoveries of LaSalle, and will not give it up to the English. Our orders are to make prisoners of every Englishman found trading in the Ohio Valley."

ENGLISH EXPLORATIONS AND SETTLEMENTS.

When the new year of 1750 broke in upon the Father of Waters and the Great Northwest, all was still wild save at the French posts already described. In 1749, when the English first began to think seriously about sending men into the West, the greater portion of the States of Indiana, Ohio, Illinois, Michigan, Wisconsin, and Minnesota were yet under the dominion of the red men. The English knew, however, pretty conclusively of the nature of the wealth of these wilds. As early as 1710, Governor Spotswood, of Virginia, had commenced movements to secure the country west of the Alleghenies to the English crown. In Pennsylvania, Governor Keith and James Logan, secretary of the province, from 1719 to 1731, represented to the powers of England the necessity of securing the Western lands. Nothing was done, however, by that power save to take some diplomatic steps to secure the claims of Britain to this unexplored wilderness.

England had from the outset claimed from the Atlantic to the Pacific, on the ground that the discovery of the seacoast and its possession was a discovery and possession of the country, and, as is well known, her grants to the colonies extended "from sea to sea." This was not all her claim. She had purchased from the Indian tribes large tracts of land. This latter was also a strong argument. As early as 1684, Lord Howard, Governor of Virginia, held a treaty with the six nations. These were the great Northern Confederacy, and comprised at first the Mohawks, Oneidas, Onondagas, Cayugas, and Senecas. Afterward the Tuscaroras were taken into the confederacy, and it became known as the SIX NATIONS. They came under the protection of the mother country, and again in 1701, they repeated the agreement, and in September, 1726, a formal deed was drawn up and signed by the chiefs. The validity of this claim has often been disputed, but never successfully. In 1744, a purchase was made at Lancaster, Pennsylvania, of certain lands within the "Colony of Virginia," for which the Indians received £200 in gold and a like sum in goods, with a promise that, as settlements increased, more should be paid. The Commissioners from Virginia were Colonel Thomas Lee and Colonel William Beverly. As settlements extended, the promise of more pay was called to mind, and Mr. Conrad Weiser was sent across the mountains with presents to appease the savages. Col. Lee, and some Virginians accompanied him with the intention of sounding the Indians upon their feelings regarding the English. They were not satisfied with their treatment, and plainly told the Commissioners why. The English did not desire the cultivation of the country, but the monopoly of the Indian trade. In 1748, the Ohio Company was formed, and petitioned the king for a grant of land beyond the Alleghenies. This was granted, and the government of Virginia was ordered to grant to them a half million acres, two hundred thousand of which were to be located at once. Upon the 12th of June, 1749, 800,000 acres from the line of Canada north and west was made to the Loyal Company, and on the 29th of October, 1751, 100,000 acres were given to the Greenbriar Company. All this time the French were not idle. They saw that, should the British gain a foothold in the West, especially upon the Ohio, they might not only prevent the French settling upon it, but in time would come to the lower posts and so gain possession of the whole country. Upon the 10th of May, 1774, Vaudreuil, Governor of Canada and the French possessions, well knowing the consequences that must arise from allowing the English to build trading posts in the Northwest, seized some of their frontier posts, and to further secure the claim of the French to the West. he, in 1749, sent Louis Celeron with a party of soldiers to plant along the Ohio River, in the mounds and at the mouths of its principal tributaries, plates of lead, on which were inscribed the claims of France. These were heard of in 1752, and within the memory of residents now living along the "Oyo," as the beautiful river was called by the French. One of these plates was found with the inscription partly defaced. It bears date August 16, 1749, and a copy of the inscription with particular account of the discovery of the plate, was sent by DeWitt Clinton to the American Antiquarian Society, among whose journals it may now be found.* These measures did not, however, deter the English from going on with their explorations, and though neither party resorted to arms, yet the conflict was gathering, and it was only a question of time when the storm would burst upon the frontier settlements. In 1750, Christopher Gist was sent by the Ohio Company to examine its lands. He went to a village of the Twigtwees, on the Miami, about one hundred and fifty miles above its mouth. He afterward spoke of it as very populous. From there he went down the Ohio River nearly to the falls at the present City of Louisville, and in November he commenced a survey of the Company's lands. During the Winter, General Andrew Lewis performed a similar work for the Greenbriar Company. Meanwhile the French were busy in preparing their forts for defense, and in opening roads, and also sent a small party of soldiers to keep the Ohio clear. This party, having heard of the English post on the Miami River, early in 1652, assisted by the Ottawas and Chippewas, attacked it, and, after a severe battle, in which fourteen of the natives were killed and others wounded, captured the garrison. (They were probably garrisoned in a block house). The traders were carried away to Canada, and one account says several were burned. This fort or post was called by the English Pickawillany. A memorial of the king's ministers refers to it as "Pickawillanes, in the center of the territory between the Ohio and the Wabash. The name is probably some variation of Pickaway or Piequa in 1773, written by Rev. David Jones Pickaweke."

* The following is a translation of the inscription on the plate: "In the year 1749, reign of Louis XV., King of France, we, Celeron, commandant of a detachment by Monsieur the Marquis of Gallissoniere, commander-in-chief of New France, to establish tranquility in certain Indian villages of these cautons, have buried this plate at the confluence of the Toradakoin, this twenty-ninth of July, near the river Ohio, otherwise Beautiful River, as a monument of renewal of possession which we have taken of the said river, and all its tributaries; inasmuch as the preceding Kings of France have enjoyed it, and maintained it by their arms and treaties; especially by those of Ryswick, Utrecht, and Aix La Chapelle."

This was the first blood shed between the French and English, and occurred near the present City of Piqua, Ohio, or at least at a point about forty-seven miles north of Dayton. Each nation became now more interested in the progress of events in the Northwest. The English determined to purchase from the Indians a title to the lands they wished to occupy, and Messrs. Fry (afterward Commander-in-chief over Washington at the commencement of the French War of 1775–1763), Lomax and Patton were sent in the Spring of 1752 to hold a conference with the natives at Logstown to learn what they objected to in the treaty of Lancaster already noticed, and to settle all difficulties. On the 9th of June, these Commissioners met the red men at Logstown, a little village on the north bank of the Ohio, about seventeen miles below the site of Pittsburgh. Here had been a trading point for many years, but it was abandoned by the Indians in 1750. At first the Indians declined to recognize the treaty of Lancaster, but, the Commissioners taking aside Montour, the interpreter, who was a son of the famous Catharine Montour, and a chief among the six nations, induced him to use his influence in their favor. This he did, and upon the 13th of June they all united in signing a deed, confirming the Lancaster treaty in its full extent, consenting to a settlement of the southeast of the Ohio, and guaranteeing that it should not be disturbed by them. These were the means used to obtain the first treaty with the Indians in the Ohio Valley.

Meanwhile the powers beyond the sea were trying to out-manœuvre each other, and were professing to be at peace. The English generally outwitted the Indians, and failed in many instances to fulfill their contracts. They thereby gained the ill-will of the red men, and further increased the feeling by failing to provide them with arms and ammunition. Said an old chief, at Easton, in 1758: " The Indians on the Ohio left you because of your own fault. When we heard the French were coming, we asked you for help and arms, but we did not get them. The French came, they treated us kindly, and gained our affections. The Governor of Virginia settled on our lands for his own benefit, and, when we wanted help, forsook us."

At the beginning of 1653, the English thought they had secured by title the lands in the West, but the French had quietly gathered cannon and military stores to be in readiness for the expected blow. The English made other attempts to ratify these existing treaties, but not until the Summer could the Indians be gathered together to discuss the plans of the French. They had sent messages to the French, warning them away; but they replied that they intended to complete the chain of forts already begun, and would not abandon the field.

Soon after this, no satisfaction being obtained from the Ohio regarding the positions and purposes of the French, Governor Dinwiddie of Virginia determined to send to them another messenger and learn from them, if possible, their intentions. For this purpose he selected a young man, a surveyor, who, at the early age of nineteen, had received the rank of major, and who was thoroughly posted regarding frontier life. This personage was no other than the illustrious George Washington, who then held considerable interest in Western lands. He was at this time just twenty-two years of age. Taking Gist as his guide, the two, accompanied by four servitors, set out on their perilous march. They left Will's Creek on the 10th of November, 1753, and on the 22d reached the Monongahela, about ten miles above the fork. From there they went to Logstown, where Washington had a long conference with the chiefs of the Six Nations. From them he learned the condition of the French, and also heard of their determination not to come down the river till the following Spring. The Indians were non-committal, as they were afraid to turn either way, and, as far as they could, desired to remain neutral. Washington, finding nothing could be done with them, went on to Venango, an old Indian town at the mouth of French Creek. Here the French had a fort, called Fort Machault. Through the rum and flattery of the French, he nearly lost all his Indian followers. Finding nothing of importance here, he pursued his way amid great privations, and on the 11th of December reached the fort at the head of French Creek. Here he delivered Governor Dinwiddie's letter, received his answer, took his observations, and on the 16th set out upon his return journey with no one but Gist, his guide, and a few Indians who still remained true to him, notwithstanding the endeavors of the French to retain them. Their homeward journey was one of great peril and suffering from the cold, yet they reached home in safety on the 6th of January, 1754.

From the letter of St. Pierre, commander of the French fort, sent by Washington to Governor Dinwiddie, it was learned that the French would not give up without a struggle. Active preparations were at once made in all the English colonies for the coming conflict, while the French finished the fort at Venango and strengthened their lines of fortifications, and gathered their forces to be in readiness.

The Old Dominion was all alive. Virginia was the center of great activities; volunteers were called for, and from all the neighboring colonies men rallied to the conflict, and everywhere along the Potomac men were enlisting under the Governor's proclamation—which promised two hundred thousand acres on the Ohio. Along this river they were gathering as far as Will's Creek, and far beyond this point, whither Trent had come for assistance for his little band of forty-one men, who were working away in hunger and want, to fortify that point at the fork of the Ohio, to which both parties were looking with deep interest.

"The first birds of Spring filled the air with their song; the swift river rolled by the Allegheny hillsides, swollen by the melting snows of Spring and the April showers. The leaves were appearing; a few Indian scouts were seen, but no enemy seemed near at hand; and all was so quiet, that Frazier, an old Indian scout and trader, who had been left by Trent in command, ventured to his home at the mouth of Turtle Creek, ten miles up the Monongahela. But, though all was so quiet in that wilderness, keen eyes had seen the low intrenchment rising at the fork, and swift feet had borne the news of it up the river; and upon the morning of the 17th of April, Ensign Ward, who then had charge of it, saw upon the Allegheny a sight that made his heart sink—sixty batteaux and three hundred canoes filled with men, and laden deep with cannon and stores. * * * That evening he supped with his captor, Contrecœur, and the next day he was bowed off by the Frenchman, and with his men and tools, marched up the Monongahela."

The French and Indian war had begun. The treaty of Aix la Chapelle, in 1748, had left the boundaries between the French and English possessions unsettled, and the events already narrated show the French were determined to hold the country watered by the Mississippi and its tributaries; while the English laid claims to the country by virtue of the discoveries of the Cabots, and claimed all the country from Newfoundland to Florida, extending from the Atlantic to the Pacific. The first decisive blow had now been struck, and the first attempt of the English, through the Ohio Company, to occupy these lands, had resulted disastrously to them. The French and Indians immediately completed the fortifications begun at the Fork, which they had so easily captured, and when completed gave to the fort the name of DuQuesne. Washington was at Will's Creek when the news of the capture of the fort arrived. He at once departed to recapture it. On his way he entrenched himself at a place called the "Meadows," where he erected a fort called by him Fort Necessity. From there he surprised and captured a force of French and Indians marching against him, but was soon after attacked in his fort by a much superior force, and was obliged to yield on the morning of July 4th. He was allowed to return to Virginia.

The English Government immediately planned four campaigns; one against Fort DuQuesne; one against Nova Scotia; one against Fort Niagara, and one against Crown Point. These occurred during 1755-6, and were not successful in driving the French from their possessions. The expedition against Fort DuQuesne was led by the famous General Braddock, who, refusing to listen to the advice of Washington and those acquainted with Indian warfare, suffered such an inglorious defeat. This occurred on the morning of July 9th, and is generally known as the battle of Monongahela, or "Braddock's Defeat." The war continued with various vicissitudes through the years 1756-7; when, at the commencement of 1758, in accordance with the plans of William Pitt, then Secretary of State, afterwards Lord Chatham, active preparations were made to carry on the war. Three expeditions were planned for this year: one, under General Amherst, against Louisburg; another, under Abercrombie, against Fort Ticonderoga; and a third, under General Forbes, against Fort DuQuesne. On the 26th of July, Louisburg surrendered after a desperate resistance of more than forty days, and the eastern part of the Canadian possessions fell into the hands of the British. Abercrombie captured Fort Frontenac, and when the expedition against Fort DuQuesne, of which Washington had the active command, arrived there, it was found in flames and deserted. The English at once took possession, rebuilt the fort, and in honor of their illustrious statesman, changed the name to Fort Pitt.

The great object of the campaign of 1759, was the reduction of Canada. General Wolfe was to lay siege to Quebec; Amherst was to reduce Ticonderoga and Crown Point, and General Prideaux was to capture Niagara. This latter place was taken in July, but the gallant Prideaux lost his life in the attempt. Amherst captured Ticonderoga and Crown Point without a blow; and Wolfe, after making the memorable ascent to the Plains of Abraham, on September 13th, defeated Montcalm, and on the 18th, the city capitulated. In this engagement Montcalm and Wolfe both lost their lives. De Levi, Montcalm's successor, marched to Sillery, three miles above the city, with the purpose of defeating the English, and there, on the 28th of the following April, was fought one of the bloodiest battles of the French and Indian War. It resulted in the defeat of the French, and the fall of the City of Montreal. The Governor signed a capitulation by which the whole of Canada was surrendered to the English. This practically concluded the war, but it was not until 1763 that the treaties of peace between France and England were signed. This was done on the 10th of February of that year, and under its provisions all the country east of the Mississippi and north of the Iberville River, in Louisiana, were ceded to England. At the same time Spain ceded Florida to Great Britain.

On the 13th of September, 1760, Major Robert Rogers was sent from Montreal to take charge of Detroit, the only remaining French post in the territory. He arrived there on the 19th of November, and summoned the place to surrender. At first the commander of the post, Beletre, refused, but on the 29th, hearing of the continued defeat of the

French arms, surrendered. Rogers remained there until December 23d under the personal protection of the celebrated chief, Pontiac, to whom, no doubt, he owed his safety. Pontiac had come here to inquire the purposes of the English in taking possession of the country. He was assured that they came simply to trade with the natives, and did not desire their country. This answer conciliated the savages, and did much to insure the safety of Rogers and his party during their stay, and while on their journey home.

Rogers set out for Fort Pitt on December 23, and was just one month on the way. His route was from Detroit to Maumee, thence across the present State of Ohio directly to the fort. This was the common trail of the Indians in their journeys from Sandusky to the fork of the Ohio. It went from Fort Sandusky, where Sandusky City now is, crossed the Huron river, then called Bald Eagle Creek, to "Mohickon John's Town" on Mohickon Creek, the northern branch of White Woman's River, and thence crossed to Beaver's Town, a Delaware town on what is now Sandy Creek. At Beaver's Town were probably one hundred and fifty warriors, and not less than three thousand acres of cleared land. From there the track went up Sandy Creek to and across Big Beaver, and up the Ohio to Logstown, thence on to the fork.

The Northwest Territory was now entirely under the English rule. New settlements began to be rapidly made, and the promise of a large trade was speedily manifested. Had the British carried out their promises with the natives none of those savage butcheries would have been perpetrated, and the country would have been spared their recital.

The renowned chief, Pontiac, was one of the leading spirits in these atrocities. We will now pause in our narrative, and notice the leading events in his life. The earliest authentic information regarding this noted Indian chief is learned from an account of an Indian trader named Alexander Henry, who, in the Spring of 1761, penetrated his domains as far as Missillimacnac. Pontiac was then a great friend of the French, but a bitter foe of the English, whom he considered as encroaching on his hunting grounds. Henry was obliged to disguise himself as a Canadian to insure safety, but was discovered by Pontiac, who bitterly reproached him and the English for their attempted subjugation of the West. He declared that no treaty had been made with them; no presents sent them, and that he would resent any possession of the West by that nation. He was at the time about fifty years of age, tall and dignified, and was civil and military ruler of the Ottawas, Ojibwas and Pottawatamies.

The Indians, from Lake Michigan to the borders of North Carolina, were united in this feeling, and at the time of the treaty of Paris, ratified February 10, 1763, a general conspiracy was formed to fall suddenly

PONTIAC, THE OTTAWA CHIEFTAIN.

upon the frontier British posts, and with one blow strike every man dead. Pontiac was the marked leader in all this, and was the commander of the Chippewas, Ottawas, Wyandots, Miamis, Shawanese, Delawares and Mingoes, who had, for the time, laid aside their local quarrels to unite in this enterprise.

The blow came, as near as can now be ascertained, on May 7, 1763. Nine British posts fell, and the Indians drank, "scooped up in the hollow of joined hands," the blood of many a Briton.

Pontiac's immediate field of action was the garrison at Detroit. Here, however, the plans were frustrated by an Indian woman disclosing the plot the evening previous to his arrival. Everything was carried out, however, according to Pontiac's plans until the moment of action, when Major Gladwyn, the commander of the post, stepping to one of the Indian chiefs, suddenly drew aside his blanket and disclosed the concealed musket. Pontiac, though a brave man, turned pale and trembled. He saw his plan was known, and that the garrison were prepared. He endeavored to exculpate himself from any such intentions; but the guilt was evident, and he and his followers were dismissed with a severe reprimand, and warned never to again enter the walls of the post.

Pontiac at once laid siege to the fort, and until the treaty of peace between the British and the Western Indians, concluded in August, 1764, continued to harass and besiege the fortress. He organized a regular commissariat department, issued bills of credit written out on bark, which, to his credit, it may be stated, were punctually redeemed. At the conclusion of the treaty, in which it seems he took no part, he went further south, living many years among the Illinois.

He had given up all hope of saving his country and race. After a time he endeavored to unite the Illinois tribe and those about St. Louis in a war with the whites. His efforts were fruitless, and only ended in a quarrel between himself and some Kaskaskia Indians, one of whom soon afterwards killed him. His death was, however, avenged by the northern Indians, who nearly exterminated the Illinois in the wars which followed.

Had it not been for the treachery of a few of his followers, his plan for the extermination of the whites, a masterly one, would undoubtedly have been carried out.

It was in the Spring of the year following Rogers' visit that Alexander Henry went to Missillimacnac, and everywhere found the strongest feelings against the English, who had not carried out their promises, and were doing nothing to conciliate the natives. Here he met the chief, Pontiac, who, after conveying to him in a speech the idea that their French father would awake soon and utterly destroy his enemies, said: "Englishman, although you have conquered the French, you have not yet conquered us! We are not your slaves! These lakes, these woods, these mountains, were left us by our ancestors. They are our inheritance, and we will part with them to none. Your nation supposes that we, like the white people, can not live without bread and pork and beef. But you ought to know that He, the Great Spirit and Master of Life, has provided food for us upon these broad lakes and in these mountains."

He then spoke of the fact that no treaty had been made with them, no presents sent them, and that he and his people were yet for war. Such were the feelings of the Northwestern Indians immediately after the English took possession of their country. These feelings were no doubt encouraged by the Canadians and French, who hoped that yet the French arms might prevail. The treaty of Paris, however, gave to the English the right to this vast domain, and active preparations were going on to occupy it and enjoy its trade and emoluments.

In 1762, France, by a secret treaty, ceded Louisiana to Spain, to prevent it falling into the hands of the English, who were becoming masters of the entire West. The next year the treaty of Paris, signed at Fontainbleau, gave to the English the domain of the country in question. Twenty years after, by the treaty of peace between the United States and England, that part of Canada lying south and west of the Great Lakes, comprehending a large territory which is the subject of these sketches, was acknowledged to be a portion of the United States; and twenty years still later, in 1803, Louisiana was ceded by Spain back to France, and by France sold to the United States.

In the half century, from the building of the Fort of Crevecœur by LaSalle, in 1680, up to the erection of Fort Chartres, many French settlements had been made in that quarter. These have already been noticed, being those at St. Vincent (Vincennes), Kohokia or Cahokia, Kaskaskia and Prairie du Rocher, on the American Bottom, a large tract of rich alluvial soil in Illinois, on the Mississippi, opposite the site of St. Louis.

By the treaty of Paris, the regions east of the Mississippi, including all these and other towns of the Northwest, were given over to England; but they do not appear to have been taken possession of until 1765, when Captain Stirling, in the name of the Majesty of England, established himself at Fort Chartres bearing with him the proclamation of General Gage, dated December 30, 1764, which promised religious freedom to all Catholics who worshiped here, and a right to leave the country with their effects if they wished, or to remain with the privileges of Englishmen. It was shortly after the occupancy of the West by the British that the war with Pontiac opened. It is already noticed in the sketch of that chieftain. By it many a Briton lost his life, and many a frontier settlement in its infancy ceased to exist. This was not ended until the year 1764, when, failing to capture Detroit, Niagara and Fort Pitt, his confederacy became disheartened, and, receiving no aid from the French, Pontiac abandoned the enterprise and departed to the Illinois, among whom he afterward lost his life.

As soon as these difficulties were definitely settled, settlers began rapidly to survey the country and prepare for occupation. During the year 1770, a number of persons from Virginia and other British provinces explored and marked out nearly all the valuable lands on the Monongahela and along the banks of the Ohio as far as the Little Kanawha. This was followed by another exploring expedition, in which George Washington was a party. The latter, accompanied by Dr. Craik, Capt. Crawford and others, on the 20th of October, 1770, descended the Ohio from Pittsburgh to the mouth of the Kanawha; ascended that stream about fourteen miles, marked out several large tracts of land, shot several buffalo, which were then abundant in the Ohio Valley, and returned to the fort.

Pittsburgh was at this time a trading post, about which was clustered a village of some twenty houses, inhabited by Indian traders. This same year, Capt. Pittman visited Kaskaskia and its neighboring villages. He found there about sixty-five resident families, and at Cahokia only forty-five dwellings. At Fort Chartres was another small settlement, and at Detroit the garrison were quite prosperous and strong. For a year or two settlers continued to locate near some of these posts, generally Fort Pitt or Detroit, owing to the fears of the Indians, who still maintained some feelings of hatred to the English. The trade from the posts was quite good, and from those in Illinois large quantities of pork and flour found their way to the New Orleans market. At this time the policy of the British Government was strongly opposed to the extension of the colonies west. In 1763, the King of England forbade, by royal proclamation, his colonial subjects from making a settlement beyond the sources of the rivers which fall into the Atlantic Ocean. At the instance of the Board of Trade, measures were taken to prevent the settlement without the limits prescribed, and to retain the commerce within easy reach of Great Britain.

The commander-in-chief of the king's forces wrote in 1769: "In the course of a few years necessity will compel the colonists, should they extend their settlements west, to provide manufactures of some kind for themselves, and when all connection upheld by commerce with the mother country ceases, an *independency* in their government will soon follow."

In accordance with this policy, Gov. Gage issued a proclamation in 1772, commanding the inhabitants of Vincennes to abandon their settlements and join some of the Eastern English colonies. To this they strenuously objected, giving good reasons therefor, and were allowed to remain. The strong opposition to this policy of Great Britain led to its change, and to such a course as to gain the attachment of the French population. In December, 1773, influential citizens of Quebec petitioned the king for an extension of the boundary lines of that province, which was granted, and Parliament passed an act on June 2, 1774, extending the boundary so as to include the territory lying within the present States of Ohio, Indiana, Illinois and Michigan.

In consequence of the liberal policy pursued by the British Government toward the French settlers in the West, they were disposed to favor that nation in the war which soon followed with the colonies; but the early alliance between France and America soon brought them to the side of the war for independence.

In 1774, Gov. Dunmore, of Virginia, began to encourage emigration to the Western lands. He appointed magistrates at Fort Pitt under the pretense that the fort was under the government of that commonwealth. One of these justices, John Connelly, who possessed a tract of land in the Ohio Valley, gathered a force of men and garrisoned the fort, calling it Fort Dunmore. This and other parties were formed to select sites for settlements, and often came in conflict with the Indians, who yet claimed portions of the valley, and several battles followed. These ended in the famous battle of Kanawha in July, where the Indians were defeated and driven across the Ohio.

During the years 1775 and 1776, by the operations of land companies and the perseverance of individuals, several settlements were firmly established between the Alleghanies and the Ohio River, and western land speculators were busy in Illinois and on the Wabash. At a council held in Kaskaskia on July 5, 1773, an association of English traders, calling themselves the "Illinois Land Company," obtained from ten chiefs of the Kaskaskia, Cahokia and Peoria tribes two large tracts of land lying on the east side of the Mississippi River south of the Illinois. In 1775, a merchant from the Illinois Country, named Viviat, came to Post Vincennes as the agent of the association called the "Wabash Land Company." On the 8th of October he obtained from eleven Piankeshaw chiefs, a deed for 37,497,600 acres of land. This deed was signed by the grantors, attested by a number of the inhabitants of Vincennes, and afterward recorded in the office of a notary public at Kaskaskia. This and other land companies had extensive schemes for the colonization of the West; but all were frustrated by the breaking out of the Revolution. On the 20th of April, 1780, the two companies named consolidated under the name of the "United Illinois and Wabash Land Company." They afterward made strenuous efforts to have these grants sanctioned by Congress, but all signally failed.

When the War of the Revolution commenced, Kentucky was an unorganized country, though there were several settlements within her borders.

In Hutchins' Topography of Virginia, it is stated that at that time "Kaskaskia contained 80 houses, and nearly 1,000 white and black inhabitants — the whites being a little the more numerous. Cahokia contains 50 houses and 300 white inhabitants, and 80 negroes. There were east of the Mississippi River, about the year 1771"—"when these observations were made — "300 white men capable of bearing arms, and 230 negroes."

From 1775 until the expedition of Clark, nothing is recorded and nothing known of these settlements, save what is contained in a report made by a committee to Congress in June, 1778. From it the following extract is made:

"Near the mouth of the River Kaskaskia, there is a village which appears to have contained nearly eighty families from the beginning of the late revolution. There are twelve families in a small village at la Prairie du Rochers, and near fifty families at the Kahokia Village. There are also four or five families at Fort Chartres and St. Philips, which is five miles further up the river."

St. Louis had been settled in February, 1764, and at this time contained, including its neighboring towns, over six hundred whites and one hundred and fifty negroes. It must be remembered that all the country west of the Mississippi was now under French rule, and remained so until ceded again to Spain, its original owner, who afterwards sold it and the country including New Orleans to the United States. At Detroit there were, according to Capt. Carver, who was in the Northwest from 1766 to 1768, more than one hundred houses, and the river was settled for more than twenty miles, although poorly cultivated—the people being engaged in the Indian trade. This old town has a history, which we will here relate.

It is the oldest town in the Northwest, having been founded by Antoine de Lamotte Cadillac, in 1701. It was laid out in the form of an oblong square, of two acres in length, and an acre and a half in width. As described by A. D. Frazer, who first visited it and became a permanent resident of the place, in 1778, it comprised within its limits that space between Mr. Palmer's store (Conant Block) and Capt. Perkins' house (near the Arsenal building), and extended back as far as the public barn, and was bordered in front by the Detroit River. It was surrounded by oak and cedar pickets, about fifteen feet long, set in the ground, and had four gates — east, west, north and south. Over the first three of these gates were block houses provided with four guns apiece, each a six-pounder. Two six-gun batteries were planted fronting the river and in a parallel direction with the block houses. There were four streets running east and west, the main street being twenty feet wide and the rest fifteen feet, while the four streets crossing these at right angles were from ten to fifteen feet in width.

At the date spoken of by Mr. Frazer, there was no fort within the enclosure, but a citadel on the ground corresponding to the present northwest corner of Jefferson Avenue and Wayne Street. The citadel was inclosed by pickets, and within it were erected barracks of wood, two stories high, sufficient to contain ten officers, and also barracks sufficient to contain four hundred men, and a provision store built of brick. The citadel also contained a hospital and guard-house. The old town of Detroit, in 1778, contained about sixty houses, most of them one story, with a few a story and a half in height. They were all of logs, some hewn and some round. There was one building of splendid appearance, called the "King's Palace," two stories high, which stood near the east gate. It was built for Governor Hamilton, the first governor commissioned by the British. There were two guard-houses, one near the west gate and the other near the Government House. Each of the guards consisted of twenty-four men and a subaltern, who mounted regularly every morning between nine and ten o'clock. Each furnished four sentinels, who were relieved every two hours. There was also an officer of the day, who performed strict duty. Each of the gates was shut regularly at sunset; even wicket gates were shut at nine o'clock, and all the keys were delivered into the hands of the commanding officer. They were opened in the morning at sunrise. No Indian or squaw was permitted to enter town with any weapon, such as a tomahawk or a knife. It was a standing order that the Indians should deliver their arms and instruments of every kind before they were permitted to pass the sentinel, and they were restored to them on their return. No more than twenty-five Indians were allowed to enter the town at any one time, and they were admitted only at the east and west gates. At sundown the drums beat, and all the Indians were required to leave town instantly. There was a council house near the water side for the purpose of holding council with the Indians. The population of the town was about sixty families, in all about two hundred males and one hundred females. This town was destroyed by fire, all except one dwelling, in 1805. After which the present "new" town was laid out.

On the breaking out of the Revolution, the British held every post of importance in the West. Kentucky was formed as a component part of Virginia, and the sturdy pioneers of the West, alive to their interests, and recognizing the great benefits of obtaining the control of the trade in this part of the New World, held steadily to their purposes, and those within the commonwealth of Kentucky proceeded to exercise their civil privileges, by electing John Todd and Richard Gallaway, burgesses to represent them in the Assembly of the parent state. Early in September of that year (1777) the first court was held in Harrodsburg, and Col. Bowman, afterwards major, who had arrived in August, was made the commander of a militia organization which had been commenced the March previous. Thus the tree of loyalty was growing. The chief spirit in this far-out colony, who had represented her the year previous east of the mountains, was now meditating a move unequaled in its boldness. He had been watching the movements of the British throughout the Northwest, and understood their whole plan. He saw it was through their possession of the posts at Detroit, Vincennes, Kaskaskia, and other places, which would give them constant and easy access to the various Indian tribes in the Northwest, that the British intended to penetrate the country from the north and south, and annihilate the frontier fortresses. This moving, energetic man was Colonel, afterwards General, George Rogers Clark. He knew the Indians were not unanimously in accord with the English, and he was convinced that, could the British be defeated and expelled from the Northwest, the natives might be easily awed into neutrality; and by spies sent for the purpose, he satisfied himself that the enterprise against the Illinois settlements might easily succeed. Having convinced himself of the certainty of the project, he repaired to the Capital of Virginia, which place he reached on November 5th. While he was on his way, fortunately, on October 17th, Burgoyne had been defeated, and the spirits of the colonists greatly encouraged thereby. Patrick Henry was Governor of Virginia, and at once entered heartily into Clark's plans. The same plan had before been agitated in the Colonial Assemblies, but there was no one until Clark came who was sufficiently acquainted with the condition of affairs at the scene of action to be able to guide them.

Clark, having satisfied the Virginia leaders of the feasibility of his plan, received, on the 2d of January, two sets of instructions—one secret, the other open—the latter authorized him to proceed to enlist seven companies to go to Kentucky, subject to his orders, and to serve three months from their arrival in the West. The secret order authorized him to arm these troops, to procure his powder and lead of General Hand at Pittsburgh, and to proceed at once to subjugate the country.

With these instructions Clark repaired to Pittsburgh, choosing rather to raise his men west of the mountains, as he well knew all were needed in the colonies in the conflict there. He sent Col. W. B. Smith to Hol-

BONUS.

ston for the same purpose, but neither succeeded in raising the required number of men. The settlers in these parts were afraid to leave their own firesides exposed to a vigilant foe, and but few could be induced to join the proposed expedition. With three companies and several private volunteers, Clark at length commenced his descent of the Ohio, which he navigated as far as the Falls, where he took possession of and fortified Corn Island, a small island between the present Cities of Louisville, Kentucky, and New Albany, Indiana. Remains of this fortification may yet be found. At this place he appointed Col. Bowman to meet him with such recruits as had reached Kentucky by the southern route, and as many as could be spared from the station. Here he announced to the men their real destination. Having completed his arrangements, and chosen his party, he left a small garrison upon the island, and on the 24th of June, during a total eclipse of the sun, which to them augured no good, and which fixes beyond dispute the date of starting, he with his chosen band, fell down the river. His plan was to go by water as far as Fort Massac or Massacre, and thence march direct to Kaskaskia. Here he intended to surprise the garrison, and after its capture go to Cahokia, then to Vincennes, and lastly to Detroit. Should he fail, he intended to march directly to the Mississippi River and cross it into the Spanish country. Before his start he received two good items of information: one that the alliance had been formed between France and the United States; and the other that the Indians throughout the Illinois country and the inhabitants, at the various frontier posts, had been led to believe by the British that the "Long Knives" or Virginians, were the most fierce, bloodthirsty and cruel savages that ever scalped a foe. With this impression on their minds, Clark saw that proper management would cause them to submit at once from fear, if surprised, and then from gratitude would become friendly if treated with unexpected leniency.

The march to Kaskaskia was accomplished through a hot July sun, and the town reached on the evening of July 4. He captured the fort near the village, and soon after the village itself by surprise, and without the loss of a single man or by killing any of the enemy. After sufficiently working upon the fears of the natives, Clark told them they were at perfect liberty to worship as they pleased, and to take whichever side of the great conflict they would, also he would protect them from any barbarity from British or Indian foe. This had the desired effect, and the inhabitants, so unexpectedly and so gratefully surprised by the unlooked for turn of affairs, at once swore allegiance to the American arms, and when Clark desired to go to Cahokia on the 6th of July, they accompanied him, and through their influence the inhabitants of the place surrendered, and gladly placed themselves under his protection. Thus the two important posts in Illinois passed from the hands of the English into the possession of Virginia.

In the person of the priest at Kaskaskia, M. Gibault, Clark found a powerful ally and generous friend. Clark saw that, to retain possession of the Northwest and treat successfully with the Indians within its boundaries, he must establish a government for the colonies he had taken. St. Vincent, the next important post to Detroit, remained yet to be taken before the Mississippi Valley was conquered. M. Gibault told him that he would alone, by persuasion, lead Vincennes to throw off its connection with England. Clark gladly accepted his offer, and on the 14th of July, in company with a fellow-townsman, M. Gibault started on his mission of peace, and on the 1st of August returned with the cheerful intelligence that the post on the "Oubache" had taken the oath of allegiance to the Old Dominion. During this interval, Clark established his courts, placed garrisons at Kaskaskia and Cahokia, successfully re-enlisted his men, sent word to have a fort, which proved the germ of Louisville, erected at the Falls of the Ohio, and dispatched Mr. Rocheblave, who had been commander at Kaskaskia, as a prisoner of war to Richmond. In October the County of Illinois was established by the Legislature of Virginia, John Todd appointed Lieutenant Colonel and Civil Governor, and in November General Clark and his men received the thanks of the Old Dominion through their Legislature.

In a speech a few days afterward, Clark made known fully to the natives his plans, and at its close all came forward and swore allegiance to the Long Knives. While he was doing this Governor Hamilton, having made his various arrangements, had left Detroit and moved down the Wabash to Vincennes intending to operate from that point in reducing the Illinois posts, and then proceed on down to Kentucky and drive the rebels from the West. Gen. Clark had, on the return of M. Gibault, dispatched Captain Helm, of Fauquier County, Virginia, with an attendant named Henry, across the Illinois prairies to command the fort. Hamilton knew nothing of the capitulation of the post, and was greatly surprised on his arrival to be confronted by Capt. Helm, who, standing at the entrance of the fort by a loaded cannon ready to fire upon his assailants, demanded upon what terms Hamilton demanded possession of the fort. Being granted the rights of a prisoner of war, he surrendered to the British General, who could scarcely believe his eyes when he saw the force in the garrison.

Hamilton, not realizing the character of the men with whom he was contending, gave up his intended campaign for the Winter, sent his four hundred Indian warriors to prevent troops from coming down the Ohio, and to annoy the Americans in all ways, and sat quietly down to pass the Winter. Information of all these proceedings having reached Clark, he saw that immediate and decisive action was necessary, and that unless he captured Hamilton, Hamilton would capture him. Clark received the news on the 29th of January, 1779, and on February 4th, having sufficiently garrisoned Kaskaskia and Cahokia, he sent down the Mississippi a " battoe," as Major Bowman writes it, in order to ascend the Ohio and Wabash, and operate with the land forces gathering for the fray.

On the next day, Clark, with his little force of one hundred and twenty men, set out for the post, and after incredible hard marching through much mud, the ground being thawed by the incessant spring rains, on the 22d reached the fort, and being joined by his " battoe," at once commenced the attack on the post. The aim of the American backwoodsman was unerring, and on the 24th the garrison surrendered to the intrepid boldness of Clark. The French were treated with great kindness, and gladly renewed their allegiance to Virginia. Hamilton was sent as a prisoner to Virginia, where he was kept in close confinement. During his command of the British frontier posts, he had offered prizes to the Indians for all the scalps of Americans they would bring to him, and had earned in consequence thereof the title " Hair-buyer General," by which he was ever afterward known.

Detroit was now without doubt within easy reach of the enterprising Virginian, could he but raise the necessary force. Governor Henry being apprised of this, promised him the needed reinforcement, and Clark concluded to wait until he could capture and sufficiently garrison the posts. Had Clark failed in this bold undertaking, and Hamilton succeeded in uniting the western Indians for the next Spring's campaign, the West would indeed have been swept from the Mississippi to the Allegheny Mountains, and the great blow struck, which had been contemplated from the commencement, by the British.

" But for this small army of dripping, but fearless Virginians, the union of all the tribes from Georgia to Maine against the colonies might have been effected, and the whole current of our history changed."

At this time some fears were entertained by the Colonial Governments that the Indians in the North and Northwest were inclining to the British, and under the instructions of Washington, now Commander-in-Chief of the Colonial army, and so bravely fighting for American independence, armed forces were sent against the Six Nations, and upon the Ohio frontier, Col. Bowman, acting under the same general's orders, marched against Indians within the present limits of that State. These expeditions were in the main successful, and the Indians were compelled to sue for peace.

During this same year (1779) the famous "Land Laws" of Virginia were passed. The passage of these laws was of more consequence to the pioneers of Kentucky and the Northwest than the gaining of a few Indian conflicts. These laws confirmed in main all grants made, and guaranteed to all actual settlers their rights and privileges. After providing for the settlers, the laws provided for selling the balance of the public lands at forty cents per acre. To carry the Land Laws into effect, the Legislature sent four Virginians westward to attend to the various claims, over many of which great confusion prevailed concerning their validity. These gentlemen opened their court on October 13, 1779, at St. Asaphs, and continued until April 26, 1780, when they adjourned, having decided three thousand claims. They were succeeded by the surveyor, who came in the person of Mr. George May, and assumed his duties on the 10th day of the month whose name he bore. With the opening of the next year (1780) the troubles concerning the navigation of the Mississippi commenced. The Spanish Government exacted such measures in relation to its trade as to cause the overtures made to the United States to be rejected. The American Government considered they had a right to navigate its channel. To enforce their claims, a fort was erected below the mouth of the Ohio on the Kentucky side of the river. The settlements in Kentucky were being rapidly filled by emigrants. It was during this year that the first seminary of learning was established in the West in this young and enterprising Commonwealth.

The settlers here did not look upon the building of this fort in a friendly manner, as it aroused the hostility of the Indians. Spain had been friendly to the Colonies during their struggle for independence, and though for a while this friendship appeared in danger from the refusal of the free navigation of the river, yet it was finally settled to the satisfaction of both nations.

The Winter of 1779–80 was one of the most unusually severe ones ever experienced in the West. The Indians always referred to it as the "Great Cold." Numbers of wild animals perished, and not a few pioneers lost their lives. The following Summer a party of Canadians and Indians attacked St. Louis, and attempted to take possession of it in consequence of the friendly disposition of Spain to the revolting colonies. They met with such a determined resistance on the part of the inhabitants, even the women taking part in the battle, that they were compelled to abandon the contest. They also made an attack on the settlements in Kentucky, but, becoming alarmed in some unaccountable manner, they fled the country in great haste.

About this time arose the question in the Colonial Congress concerning the western lands claimed by Virginia, New York, Massachusetts and Connecticut. The agitation concerning this subject finally led New York, on the 19th of February, 1780, to pass a law giving to the delegates of that State in Congress the power to cede her western lands for the benefit of the United States. This law was laid before Congress during the next month, but no steps were taken concerning it until September 6th, when a resolution passed that body calling upon the States claiming western lands to release their claims in favor of the whole body. This basis formed the union, and was the first after all of those legislative measures which resulted in the creation of the States of Ohio, Indiana, Illinois, Michigan, Wisconsin and Minnesota. In December of the same year, the plan of conquering Detroit again arose. The conquest might have easily been effected by Clark had the necessary aid been furnished him. Nothing decisive was done, yet the heads of the Government knew that the safety of the Northwest from British invasion lay in the capture and retention of that important post, the only unconquered one in the territory.

Before the close of the year, Kentucky was divided into the Counties of Lincoln, Fayette and Jefferson, and the act establishing the Town of Louisville was passed. This same year is also noted in the annals of American history as the year in which occurred Arnold's treason to the United States.

Virginia, in accordance with the resolution of Congress, on the 2d day of January, 1781, agreed to yield her western lands to the United States upon certain conditions, which Congress would not accede to, and the Act of Cession, on the part of the Old Dominion, failed, nor was anything farther done until 1783. During all that time the Colonies were busily engaged in the struggle with the mother country, and in consequence thereof but little heed was given to the western settlements. Upon the 16th of April, 1781, the first birth north of the Ohio River of American parentage occurred, being that of Mary Heckewelder, daughter of the widely known Moravian missionary, whose band of Christian Indians suffered in after years a horrible massacre by the hands of the frontier settlers, who had been exasperated by the murder of several of their neighbors, and in their rage committed, without regard to humanity, a deed which forever afterwards cast a shade of shame upon their lives. For this and kindred outrages on the part of the whites, the Indians committed many deeds of cruelty which darken the years of 1771 and 1772 in the history of the Northwest.

During the year 1782 a number of battles among the Indians and frontiersmen occurred, and between the Moravian Indians and the Wyandots. In these, horrible acts of cruelty were practised on the captives, many of such dark deeds transpiring under the leadership of the notorious frontier outlaw, Simon Girty, whose name, as well as those of his brothers, was a terror to women and children. These occurred chiefly in the Ohio valleys. Cotemporary with them were several engagements in Kentucky, in which the famous Daniel Boone engaged, and who, often by his skill and knowledge of Indian warfare, saved the outposts from cruel destruc-

INDIANS ATTACKING FRONTIERSMEN.

tion. By the close of the year victory had perched upon the American banner, and on the 30th of November, provisional articles of peace had been arranged between the Commissioners of England and her unconquerable colonies. Cornwallis had been defeated on the 19th of October preceding, and the liberty of America was assured. On the 19th of April following, the anniversary of the battle of Lexington, peace was proclaimed to the army of the United States, and on the 3d of the next September, the definite treaty which ended our revolutionary struggle was concluded. By the terms of that treaty, the boundaries of the West were as follows: On the north the line was to extend along the center of the Great Lakes; from the western point of Lake Superior to Long Lake; thence to the Lake of the Woods; thence to the head of the Mississippi River; down its center to the 31st parallel of latitude, then on that line east to the head of the Appalachicola River; down its center to its junction with the Flint; thence straight to the head of St. Mary's River, and thence down along its center to the Atlantic Ocean.

Following the cessation of hostilities with England, several posts were still occupied by the British in the North and West. Among these was Detroit, still in the hands of the enemy. Numerous engagements with the Indians throughout Ohio and Indiana occurred, upon whose lands adventurous whites would settle ere the title had been acquired by the proper treaty.

To remedy this latter evil, Congress appointed commissioners to treat with the natives and purchase their lands, and prohibited the settlement of the territory until this could be done. Before the close of the year another attempt was made to capture Detroit, which was, however, not pushed, and Virginia, no longer feeling the interest in the Northwest she had formerly done, withdrew her troops, having on the 20th of December preceding authorized the whole of her possessions to be deeded to the United States. This was done on the 1st of March following, and the Northwest Territory passed from the control of the Old Dominion. To Gen. Clark and his soldiers, however, she gave a tract of one hundred and fifty thousand acres of land, to be situated any where north of the Ohio wherever they chose to locate them. They selected the region opposite the falls of the Ohio, where is now the dilapidated village of Clarksville, about midway between the Cities of New Albany and Jeffersonville, Indiana.

While the frontier remained thus, and Gen. Haldimand at Detroit refused to evacuate alleging that he had no orders from his King to do so, settlers were rapidly gathering about the inland forts. In the Spring of 1784, Pittsburgh was regularly laid out, and from the journal of Arthur Lee, who passed through the town soon after on his way to the Indian council at Fort McIntosh, we suppose, it was not very prepossessing in appearance. He says:

"Pittsburgh is inhabited almost entirely by Scots and Irish, who live in paltry log houses, and are as dirty as if in the north of Ireland or even Scotland. There is a great deal of trade carried on, the goods being bought at the vast expense of forty-five shillings per pound from Philadelphia and Baltimore. They take in the shops flour, wheat, skins and money. There are in the town four attorneys, two doctors, and not a priest of any persuasion, nor church nor chapel."

Kentucky at this time contained thirty thousand inhabitants, and was beginning to discuss measures for a separation from Virginia. A land office was opened at Louisville, and measures were adopted to take defensive precaution against the Indians who were yet, in some instances, incited to deeds of violence by the British. Before the close of this year, 1784, the military claimants of land began to occupy them, although no entries were recorded until 1787.

The Indian title to the Northwest was not yet extinguished. They held large tracts of lands, and in order to prevent bloodshed Congress adopted means for treaties with the original owners and provided for the surveys of the lands gained thereby, as well as for those north of the Ohio, now in its possession. On January 31, 1786, a treaty was made with the Wabash Indians. The treaty of Fort Stanwix had been made in 1784. That at Fort McIntosh in 1785, and through these much land was gained. The Wabash Indians, however, afterward refused to comply with the provisions of the treaty made with them, and in order to compel their adherence to its provisions, force was used. During the year 1786, the free navigation of the Mississippi came up in Congress, and caused various discussions, which resulted in no definite action, only serving to excite speculation in regard to the western lands. Congress had promised bounties of land to the soldiers of the Revolution, but owing to the unsettled condition of affairs along the Mississippi respecting its navigation, and the trade of the Northwest, that body had, in 1783, declared its inability to fulfill these promises until a treaty could be concluded between the two Governments. Before the close of the year 1786, however, it was able, through the treaties with the Indians, to allow some grants and the settlement thereon, and on the 14th of September Connecticut ceded to the General Government the tract of land known as the "Connecticut Reserve," and before the close of the following year a large tract of land north of the Ohio was sold to a company, who at once took measures to settle it. By the provisions of this grant, the company were to pay the United States one dollar per acre, subject to a deduction of one-third for bad lands and other contingencies. They received 750,000 acres, bounded on the south by the Ohio, on the east by the seventh range of townships, on the west by the sixteenth range, and on the north by a line so drawn as to make the grant complete without the reservations. In addition to this, Congress afterward granted 100,000 acres to actual settlers, and 214,285 acres as army bounties under the resolutions of 1789 and 1790.

While Dr. Cutler, one of the agents of the company, was pressing its claims before Congress, that body was bringing into form an ordinance for the political and social organization of this Territory. When the cession was made by Virginia, in 1784, a plan was offered, but rejected. A motion had been made to strike from the proposed plan the prohibition of slavery, which prevailed. The plan was then discussed and altered, and finally passed unanimously, with the exception of South Carolina. By this proposition, the Territory was to have been divided into states

A PRAIRIE STORM.

by parallels and meridian lines. This, it was thought, would make ten states, which were to have been named as follows — beginning at the northwest corner and going southwardly: Sylvania, Michigania, Chersonesus, Assenisipia, Metropotamia, Illenoia, Saratoga, Washington, Polypotamia and Pelisipia.

There was a more serious objection to this plan than its category of names,— the boundaries. The root of the difficulty was in the resolution of Congress passed in October, 1780, which fixed the boundaries of the ceded lands to be from one hundred to one hundred and fifty miles square. These resolutions being presented to the Legislatures of Virginia and Massachusetts, they desired a change, and in July, 1786, the subject was taken up in Congress, and changed to favor a division into not more than five states, and not less than three. This was approved by the State Legislature of Virginia. The subject of the Government was again taken up by Congress in 1786, and discussed throughout that year and until July, 1787, when the famous "Compact of 1787" was passed, and the foundation of the government of the Northwest laid. This compact is fully discussed and explained in the history of Illinois in this book, and to it the reader is referred.

The passage of this act and the grant to the New England Company was soon followed by an application to the Government by John Cleves Symmes, of New Jersey, for a grant of the land between the Miamis. This gentleman had visited these lands soon after the treaty of 1786, and, being greatly pleased with them, offered similar terms to those given to the New England Company. The petition was referred to the Treasury Board with power to act, and a contract was concluded the following year. During the Autumn the directors of the New England Company were preparing to occupy their grant the following Spring, and upon the 23d of November made arrangements for a party of forty-seven men, under the superintendency of Gen. Rufus Putnam, to set forward. Six boat-builders were to leave at once, and on the first of January the surveyors and their assistants, twenty-six in number, were to meet at Hartford and proceed on their journey westward; the remainder to follow as soon as possible. Congress, in the meantime, upon the 3d of October, had ordered seven hundred troops for defense of the western settlers, and to prevent unauthorized intrusions; and two days later appointed Arthur St. Clair Governor of the Territory of the Northwest.

AMERICAN SETTLEMENTS.

The civil organization of the Northwest Territory was now complete, and notwithstanding the uncertainty of Indian affairs, settlers from the East began to come into the country rapidly. The New England Company sent their men during the Winter of 1787-8 pressing on over the Alleghenies by the old Indian path which had been opened into Braddock's road, and which has since been made a national turnpike from Cumberland westward. Through the weary winter days they toiled on, and by April were all gathered on the Yohiogany, where boats had been built, and at once started for the Muskingum. Here they arrived on the 7th of that month, and unless the Moravian missionaries be regarded as the pioneers of Ohio, this little band can justly claim that honor.

Gen. St. Clair, the appointed Governor of the Northwest, not having yet arrived, a set of laws were passed, written out, and published by being nailed to a tree in the embryo town, and Jonathan Meigs appointed to administer them.

Washington in writing of this, the first American settlement in the Northwest, said: "No colony in America was ever settled under such favorable auspices as that which has just commenced at Muskingum. Information, property and strength will be its characteristics. I know many of its settlers personally, and there never were men better calculated to promote the welfare of such a community."

A PIONEER DWELLING.

On the 2d of July a meeting of the directors and agents was held on the banks of the Muskingum, "for the purpose of naming the newborn city and its squares." As yet the settlement was known as the "Muskingum," but that was now changed to the name Marietta, in honor of Marie Antoinette. The square upon which the block-houses stood was called "*Campus Martius;*" square number 19, "*Capitolium;*" square number 61, "*Cecilia;*" and the great road through the covert way, "*Sacra Via.*" Two days after, an oration was delivered by James M. Varnum, who with S. H. Parsons and John Armstrong had been appointed to the judicial bench of the territory on the 16th of October, 1787. On July 9, Gov. St. Clair arrived, and the colony began to assume form. The act of 1787 provided two distinct grades of government for the Northwest, under the first of which the whole power was invested in the hands of a governor and three district judges. This was immediately formed upon the Governor's arrival, and the first laws of the colony passed on the 25th of July. These provided for the organization of the militia, and on the next day appeared the Governor's proclamation, erecting all that country that had been ceded by the Indians east of the Scioto River into the County of Washington. From that time forward, notwithstanding the doubts yet existing as to the Indians, all Marietta prospered, and on the 2d of September the first court of the territory was held with imposing ceremonies.

The emigration westward at this time was very great. The commander at Fort Harmer, at the mouth of the Muskingum, reported four thousand five hundred persons as having passed that post between February and June, 1788—many of whom would have purchased of the "Associates," as the New England Company was called, had they been ready to receive them.

On the 26th of November, 1787, Symmes issued a pamphlet stating the terms of his contract and the plan of sale he intended to adopt. In January, 1788, Matthias Denman, of New Jersey, took an active interest in Symmes' purchase, and located among other tracts the sections upon which Cincinnati has been built. Retaining one-third of this locality, he sold the other two-thirds to Robert Patterson and John Filson, and the three, about August, commenced to lay out a town on the spot, which was designated as being opposite Licking River, to the mouth of which they proposed to have a road cut from Lexington. The naming of the town is thus narrated in the "Western Annals":—"Mr. Filson, who had been a schoolmaster, was appointed to name the town, and, in respect to its situation, and as if with a prophetic perception of the mixed race that were to inhabit it in after days, he named it Losantiville, which, being interpreted, means: *ville*, the town; *anti*, against or opposite to; *os*, the mouth; *L.* of Licking."

Meanwhile, in July, Symmes got thirty persons and eight four-horse teams under way for the West. These reached Limestone (now Maysville) in September, where were several persons from Redstone. Here Mr. Symmes tried to found a settlement, but the great freshet of 1789 caused the "Point," as it was and is yet called, to be fifteen feet under water, and the settlement to be abandoned. The little band of settlers removed to the mouth of the Miami. Before Symmes and his colony left the "Point," two settlements had been made on his purchase. The first was by Mr. Stiltes, the original projector of the whole plan, who, with a colony of Redstone people, had located at the mouth of the Miami, whither Symmes went with his Maysville colony. Here a clearing had been made by the Indians owing to the great fertility of the soil. Mr. Stiltes with his colony came to this place on the 18th of November, 1788, with twenty-six persons, and, building a block-house, prepared to remain through the Winter. They named the settlement Columbia. Here they were kindly treated by the Indians, but suffered greatly from the flood of 1789.

On the 4th of March, 1789, the Constitution of the United States went into operation, and on April 30, George Washington was inaug-, urated President of the American people, and during the next Summer, an Indian war was commenced by the tribes north of the Ohio. The President at first used pacific means; but these failing, he sent General Harmer against the hostile tribes. He destroyed several villages, but

BREAKING PRAIRIE.

was defeated in two battles, near the present City of Fort Wayne, Indiana. From this time till the close of 1795, the principal events were the wars with the various Indian tribes. In 1796, General St. Clair was appointed in command, and marched against the Indians; but while he was encamped on a stream, the St. Mary, a branch of the Maumee, he was attacked and defeated with the loss of six hundred men.

General Wayne was now sent against the savages. In August, 1794, he met them near the rapids of the Maumee, and gained a complete victory. This success, followed by vigorous measures, compelled the Indians to sue for peace, and on the 30th of July, the following year, the treaty of Greenville was signed by the principal chiefs, by which a large tract of country was ceded to the United States.

Before proceeding in our narrative, we will pause to notice Fort Washington, erected in the early part of this war on the site of Cincinnati. Nearly all of the great cities of the Northwest, and indeed of the whole country, have had their *nuclei* in those rude pioneer structures, known as forts or stockades. Thus Forts Dearborn, Washington, Ponchartrain, mark the original sites of the now proud Cities of Chicago, Cincinnati and Detroit. So of most of the flourishing cities east and west of the Mississippi. Fort Washington, erected by Doughty in 1790, was a rude but highly interesting structure. It was composed of a number of strongly-built hewed log cabins. Those designed for soldiers' barracks were a story and a half high, while those composing the officers quarters were more imposing and more conveniently arranged and furnished. The whole were so placed as to form a hollow square, enclosing about an acre of ground, with a block house at each of the four angles.

The logs for the construction of this fort were cut from the ground upon which it was erected. It stood between Third and Fourth Streets of the present city (Cincinnati) extending east of Eastern Row, now Broadway, which was then a narrow alley, and the eastern boundary of of the town as it was originally laid out. On the bank of the river, immediately in front of the fort, was an appendage of the fort, called the Artificer's Yard. It contained about two acres of ground, enclosed by small contiguous buildings, occupied by workshops and quarters of laborers. Within this enclosure there was a large two-story frame house, familiarly called the "Yellow House," built for the accommodation of the Quartermaster General. For many years this was the best finished and most commodious edifice in the Queen City. Fort Washington was for some time the headquarters of both the civil and military governments of the Northwestern Territory.

Following the consummation of the treaty various gigantic land speculations were entered into by different persons, who hoped to obtain from the Indians in Michigan and northern Indiana, large tracts of lands. These were generally discovered in time to prevent the outrageous schemes from being carried out, and from involving the settlers in war. On October 27, 1795, the treaty between the United States and Spain was signed, whereby the free navigation of the Mississippi was secured.

No sooner had the treaty of 1795 been ratified than settlements began to pour rapidly into the West. The great event of the year 1796 was the occupation of that part of the Northwest including Michigan, which was this year, under the provisions of the treaty, evacuated by the British forces. The United States, owing to certain conditions, did not feel justified in addressing the authorities in Canada in relation to Detroit and other frontier posts. When at last the British authorities were called to give them up, they at once complied, and General Wayne, who had done so much to preserve the frontier settlements, and who, before the year's close, sickened and died near Erie, transferred his headquarters to the neighborhood of the lakes, where a county named after him was formed, which included the northwest of Ohio, all of Michigan, and the northeast of Indiana. During this same year settlements were formed at the present City of Chillicothe, along the Miami from Middletown to Piqua, while in the more distant West, settlers and speculators began to appear in great numbers. In September, the City of Cleveland was laid out, and during the Summer and Autumn, Samuel Jackson and Jonathan Sharpless erected the first manufactory of paper—the "Redstone Paper Mill"—in the West. St. Louis contained some seventy houses, and Detroit over three hundred, and along the river, contiguous to it, were more than three thousand inhabitants, mostly French Canadians, Indians and half-breeds, scarcely any Americans venturing yet into that part of the Northwest.

The election of representatives for the territory had taken place, and on the 4th of February, 1799, they convened at Losantiville—now known as Cincinnati, having been named so by Gov. St. Clair, and considered the capital of the Territory—to nominate persons from whom the members of the Legislature were to be chosen in accordance with a previous ordinance. This nomination being made, the Assembly adjourned until the 16th of the following September. From those named the President selected as members of the council, Henry Vandenburg, of Vincennes, Robert Oliver, of Marietta, James Findlay and Jacob Burnett, of Cincinnati, and David Vance, of Vanceville. On the 16th of September the Territorial Legislature met, and on the 24th the two houses were duly organized, Henry Vandenburg being elected President of the Council.

The message of Gov. St. Clair was addressed to the Legislature September 20th, and on October 13th that body elected as a delegate to Congress Gen. Wm. Henry Harrison, who received eleven of the votes cast, being a majority of one over his opponent, Arthur St. Clair, son of Gen. St. Clair.

The whole number of acts passed at this session, and approved by the Governor, were thirty-seven—eleven others were passed, but received his veto. The most important of those passed related to the militia, to the administration, and to taxation. On the 19th of December this protracted session of the first Legislature in the West was closed, and on the 30th of December the President nominated Charles Willing Bryd to the office of Secretary of the Territory vice Wm. Henry Harrison, elected to Congress. The Senate confirmed his nomination the next day.

DIVISION OF THE NORTHWEST TERRITORY.

The increased emigration to the Northwest, the extent of the domain, and the inconvenient modes of travel, made it very difficult to conduct the ordinary operations of government, and rendered the efficient action of courts almost impossible. To remedy this, it was deemed advisable to divide the territory for civil purposes. Congress, in 1800, appointed a committee to examine the question and report some means for its solution. This committee, on the 3d of March, reported that:

"In the three western countries there has been but one court having cognizance of crimes, in five years, and the immunity which offenders experience attracts, as to an asylum, the most vile and abandoned criminals, and at the same time deters useful citizens from making settlements in such society. The extreme necessity of judiciary attention and assistance is experienced in civil as well as in criminal cases. * * * * To minister a remedy to these and other evils, it occurs to this committee that it is expedient that a division of said territory into two distinct and separate governments should be made; and that such division be made by a line beginning at the mouth of the Great Miami River, running directly north until it intersects the boundary between the United States and Canada."

The report was accepted by Congress, and, in accordance with its suggestions, that body passed an Act extinguishing the Northwest Territory, which Act was approved May 7. Among its provisions were these:

"That from and after July 4 next, all that part of the Territory of the United States northwest of the Ohio River, which lies to the westward of a line beginning at a point on the Ohio, opposite to the mouth of the Kentucky River, and running thence to Fort Recovery, and thence north until it shall intersect the territorial line between the United States and Canada, shall, for the purpose of temporary government, constitute a separate territory, and be called the Indiana Territory."

After providing for the exercise of the civil and criminal powers of the territories, and other provisions, the Act further provides:

"That until it shall otherwise be ordered by the Legislatures of the said Territories, respectively, Chillicothe on the Scioto River shall be the seat of government of the Territory of the United States northwest of the Ohio River; and that St. Vincennes on the Wabash River shall be the seat of government for the Indiana Territory."

Gen. Wm. Henry Harrison was appointed Governor of the Indiana Territory, and entered upon his duties about a year later. Connecticut also about this time released her claims to the reserve, and in March a law was passed accepting this cession. Settlements had been made upon thirty-five of the townships in the reserve, mills had been built, and seven hundred miles of road cut in various directions. On the 3d of November the General Assembly met at Chillicothe. Near the close of the year, the first missionary of the Connecticut Reserve came, who found no township containing more than eleven families. It was upon the first of October that the secret treaty had been made between Napoleon and the King of Spain, whereby the latter agreed to cede to France the province of Louisiana.

In January, 1802, the Assembly of the Northwestern Territory chartered the college at Athens. From the earliest dawn of the western colonies, education was promptly provided for, and as early as 1787, newspapers were issued from Pittsburgh and Kentucky, and largely read throughout the frontier settlements. Before the close of this year, the Congress of the United States granted to the citizens of the Northwestern territory the formation of a State government. One of the provisions of the "compact of 1787" provided that whenever the number of inhabitants within prescribed limits exceeded 45,000, they should be entitled to a separate government. The prescribed limits of Ohio contained, from a census taken to ascertain the legality of the act, more than that number, and on the 30th of April, 1802, Congress passed the act defining its limits, and on the 29th of November the Constitution of the new State of Ohio, so named from the beautiful river forming its southern boundary, came into existence. The exact limits of Lake Michigan were not then known, but the territory now included within the State of Michigan was wholly within the territory of Indiana.

Gen. Harrison, while residing at Vincennes, made several treaties with the Indians, thereby gaining large tracts of lands. The next year is memorable in the history of the West for the purchase of Louisiana from France by the United States for $15,000,000. Thus by a peaceful mode, the domain of the United States was extended over a large tract of country west of the Mississippi, and was for a time under the jurisdiction of the Northwest government, and, as has been mentioned in the early part of this narrative, was called the "New Northwest." The limits of this history will not allow a description of its territory. The same year large grants of land were obtained from the Indians, and the House of Representatives of the new State of Ohio signed a bill respecting the College Township in the district of Cincinnati.

Before the close of the year, Gen. Harrison obtained additional grants of lands from the various Indian nations in Indiana and the present limits of Illinois, and on the 18th of August, 1804, completed a treaty at St. Louis, whereby over 51,000,000 acres of lands were obtained from the aborigines. Measures were also taken to learn the condition of affairs in and about Detroit.

C. Jouett, the Indian agent in Michigan, still a part of Indiana Territory, reported as follows upon the condition of matters at that post:

"The Town of Detroit.—The charter, which is for fifteen miles square, was granted in the time of Louis XIV. of France, and is now, from the best information I have been able to get, at Quebec. Of those two hundred and twenty-five acres, only four are occupied by the town and Fort Lenault. The remainder is a common, except twenty-four acres, which were added twenty years ago to a farm belonging to Wm. Macomb. * * * A stockade incloses the town, fort and citadel. The pickets, as well as the public houses, are in a state of gradual decay. The streets are narrow, straight and regular, and intersect each other at right angles. The houses are, for the most part, low and inelegant."

During this year, Congress granted a township of land for the support of a college, and began to offer inducements for settlers in these wilds, and the country now comprising the State of Michigan began to fill rapidly with settlers along its southern borders. This same year, also, a law was passed organizing the Southwest Territory, dividing it into two portions, the Territory of New Orleans, which city was made the seat of government, and the District of Louisiana, which was annexed to the domain of Gen. Harrison.

On the 11th of January, 1805, the Territory of Michigan was formed, Wm. Hull was appointed governor, with headquarters at Detroit, the change to take effect on June 30. On the 11th of that month, a fire occurred at Detroit, which destroyed almost every building in the place. When the officers of the new territory reached the post, they found it in ruins, and the inhabitants scattered throughout the country. Rebuilding, however, soon commenced, and ere long the town contained more houses than before the fire, and many of them much better built.

While this was being done, Indiana had passed to the second grade of government, and through her General Assembly had obtained large tracts of land from the Indian tribes. To all this the celebrated Indian, Tecumthe or Tecumseh, vigorously protested, and it was the main cause of his attempts to unite the various Indian tribes in a conflict with the settlers. To obtain a full account of these attempts, the workings of the British, and the signal failure, culminating in the death of Tecumseh at the battle of the Thames, and the close of the war of 1812 in the Northwest, we will step aside in our story, and relate the principal events of his life, and his connection with this conflict.

TECUMSEH, THE SHAWANOE CHIEFTAIN.

TECUMSEH, AND THE WAR OF 1812.

This famous Indian chief was born about the year 1768, not far from the site of the present City of Piqua, Ohio. His father, Puckeshinwa, was a member of the Kisopok tribe of the Swanoese nation, and his mother, Methontaske, was a member of the Turtle tribe of the same people. They removed from Florida about the middle of the last century to the birthplace of Tecumseh. In 1774, his father, who had risen to be chief, was slain at the battle of Point Pleasant, and not long after Tecumseh, by his bravery, became the leader of his tribe. In 1795 he was declared chief, and then lived at Deer Creek, near the site of the present City of Urbana. He remained here about one year, when he returned to Piqua, and in 1798, he went to White River, Indiana. In 1805, he and his brother, Laulewasikan (Open Door), who had announced himself as a prophet, went to a tract of land on the Wabash River, given them by the Pottawatomies and Kickapoos. From this date the chief comes into prominence. He was now about thirty-seven years of age, was five feet and ten inches in height, was stoutly built, and possessed of enormous powers of endurance. His countenance was naturally pleasing, and he was, in general, devoid of those savage attributes possessed by most Indians. It is stated he could read and write, and had a confidential secretary and adviser, named Billy Caldwell, a half-breed, who afterward became chief of the Pottawatomies. He occupied the first house built on the site of Chicago. At this time, Tecumseh entered upon the great work of his life. He had long objected to the grants of land made by the Indians to the whites, and determined to unite all the Indian tribes into a league, in order that no treaties or grants of land could be made save by the consent of this confederation.

He traveled constantly, going from north to south; from the south to the north, everywhere urging the Indians to this step. He was a matchless orator, and his burning words had their effect.

Gen. Harrison, then Governor of Indiana, by watching the movements of the Indians, became convinced that a grand conspiracy was forming, and made preparations to defend the settlements. Tecumseh's plan was similar to Pontiac's, elsewhere described, and to the cunning artifice of that chieftain was added his own sagacity.

During the year 1809, Tecumseh and the prophet were actively preparing for the work. In that year, Gen. Harrison entered into a treaty with the Delawares, Kickapoos, Pottawatomies, Miamis, Eel River Indians and Weas, in which these tribes ceded to the whites certain lands upon the Wabash, to all of which Tecumseh entered a bitter protest, averring as one principal reason that he did not want the Indians to give up any lands north and west of the Ohio River.

Tecumseh, in August, 1810, visited the General at Vincennes and held a council relating to the grievances of the Indians. Becoming unduly angry at this conference he was dismissed from the village, and soon after departed to incite the southern Indian tribes to the conflict.

Gen. Harrison determined to move upon the chief's headquarters at Tippecanoe, and for this purpose went about sixty-five miles up the Wabash, where he built Fort Harrison. From this place he went to the prophet's town, where he informed the Indians he had no hostile intentions, provided they were true to the existing treaties. He encamped near the village early in October, and on the morning of November 7, he was attacked by a large force of the Indians, and the famous battle of Tippecanoe occurred. The Indians were routed and their town broken up. Tecumseh returning not long after, was greatly exasperated at his brother, the prophet, even threatening to kill him for rashly precipitating the war, and foiling his (Tecumseh's) plans.

Tecumseh sent word to Gen. Harrison that he was now returned from the South, and was ready to visit the President as had at one time previously been proposed. Gen. Harrison informed him he could not go as a chief, which method Tecumseh desired, and the visit was never made.

In June of the following year, he visited the Indian agent at Fort Wayne. Here he disavowed any intention to make a war against the United States, and reproached Gen. Harrison for marching against his people. The agent replied to this; Tecumseh listened with a cold indifference, and after making a few general remarks, with a haughty air drew his blanket about him, left the council house, and departed for Fort Malden, in Upper Canada, where he joined the British standard.

He remained under this Government, doing effective work for the Crown while engaged in the war of 1812 which now opened. He was, however, always humane in his treatment of the prisoners, never allowing his warriors to ruthlessly mutilate the bodies of those slain, or wantonly murder the captive.

In the Summer of 1813, Perry's victory on Lake Erie occurred, and shortly after active preparations were made to capture Malden. On the 27th of September, the American army, under Gen. Harrison, set sail for the shores of Canada, and in a few hours stood around the ruins of Malden, from which the British army, under Proctor, had retreated to Sandwich, intending to make its way to the heart of Canada by the Valley of the Thames. On the 29th Gen. Harrison was at Sandwich, and Gen. McArthur took possession of Detroit and the territory of Michigan.

On the 2d of October, the Americans began their pursuit of Proctor, whom they overtook on the 5th, and the battle of the Thames followed. Early in the engagement, Tecumseh who was at the head of the column of Indians was slain, and they, no longer hearing the voice of their chieftain, fled. The victory was decisive, and practically closed the war in the Northwest.

INDIANS ATTACKING A STOCKADE.

Just who killed the great chief has been a matter of much dispute; but the weight of opinion awards the act to Col. Richard M. Johnson, who fired at him with a pistol, the shot proving fatal.

In 1805 occurred Burr's Insurrection. He took possession of a beautiful island in the Ohio, after the killing of Hamilton, and is charged by many with attempting to set up an independent government. His plans were frustrated by the general government, his property confiscated and he was compelled to flee the country for safety.

In January, 1807, Governor Hull, of Michigan Territory, made a treaty with the Indians, whereby all that peninsula was ceded to the United States. Before the close of the year, a stockade was built about Detroit. It was also during this year that Indiana and Illinois endeavored to obtain the repeal of that section of the compact of 1787, whereby slavery was excluded from the Northwest Territory. These attempts, however, all signally failed.

In 1809 it was deemed advisable to divide the Indiana Territory. This was done, and the Territory of Illinois was formed from the western part, the seat of government being fixed at Kaskaskia. The next year, the intentions of Tecumseh manifested themselves in open hostilities, and then began the events already narrated.

While this war was in progress, emigration to the West went on with surprising rapidity. In 1811, under Mr. Roosevelt of New York, the first steamboat trip was made on the Ohio, much to the astonishment of the natives, many of whom fled in terror at the appearance of the "monster." It arrived at Louisville on the 10th day of October. At the close of the first week of January, 1812, it arrived at Natchez, after being nearly overwhelmed in the great earthquake which occurred while on its downward trip.

The battle of the Thames was fought on October 6, 1813. It effectually closed hostilities in the Northwest, although peace was not fully restored until July 22, 1814, when a treaty was formed at Greenville, under the direction of General Harrison, between the United States and the Indian tribes, in which it was stipulated that the Indians should cease hostilities against the Americans if the war were continued. Such, happily, was not the case, and on the 24th of December the treaty of Ghent was signed by the representatives of England and the United States. This treaty was followed the next year by treaties with various Indian tribes throughout the West and Northwest, and quiet was again restored in this part of the new world.

On the 18th of March, 1816, Pittsburgh was incorporated as a city. It then had a population of 8,000 people, and was already noted for its manufacturing interests. On April 19, Indiana Territory was allowed to form a state government. At that time there were thirteen counties organized, containing about sixty-three thousand inhabitants. The first election of state officers was held in August, when Jonathan Jennings was chosen Governor. The officers were sworn in on November 7, and on December 11, the State was formally admitted into the Union. For some time the seat of government was at Corydon, but a more central location being desirable, the present capital, Indianapolis (City of Indiana), was laid out January 1, 1825.

On the 28th of December the Bank of Illinois, at Shawneetown, was chartered, with a capital of $300,000. At this period all banks were under the control of the States, and were allowed to establish branches at different convenient points.

Until this time Chillicothe and Cincinnati had in turn enjoyed the privileges of being the capital of Ohio. But the rapid settlement of the northern and eastern portions of the State demanded, as in Indiana, a more central location, and before the close of the year, the site of Columbus was selected and surveyed as the future capital of the State. Banking had begun in Ohio as early as 1808, when the first bank was chartered at Marietta, but here as elsewhere it did not bring to the state the hoped-for assistance. It and other banks were subsequently unable to redeem their currency, and were obliged to suspend.

In 1818, Illinois was made a state, and all the territory north of her northern limits was erected into a separate territory and joined to Michigan for judicial purposes. By the following year, navigation of the lakes was increasing with great rapidity and affording an immense source of revenue to the dwellers in the Northwest, but it was not until 1826 that the trade was extended to Lake Michigan, or that steamships began to navigate the bosom of that inland sea.

Until the year 1832, the commencement of the Black Hawk War, but few hostilities were experienced with the Indians. Roads were opened, canals were dug, cities were built, common schools were established, universities were founded, many of which, especially the Michigan University, have achieved a world wide-reputation. The people were becoming wealthy. The domains of the United States had been extended, and had the sons of the forest been treated with honesty and justice, the record of many years would have been that of peace and continuous prosperity.

BLACK HAWK AND THE BLACK HAWK WAR.

This conflict, though confined to Illinois, is an important epoch in the Northwestern history, being the last war with the Indians in this part of the United States.

Ma-ka-tai-me-she-kia-kiah, or Black Hawk, was born in the principal Sac village, about three miles from the junction of Rock River with the Mississippi, in the year 1767. His father's name was Py-e-sa or Pahaes; his grandfather's, Na-na-ma-kee, or the Thunderer. Black Hawk early distinguished himself as a warrior, and at the age of fifteen was permitted to paint and was ranked among the braves. About the year 1783, he went on an expedition against the enemies of his nation, the Osages, one

BLACK HAWK, THE SAC CHIEFTAIN.

of whom he killed and scalped, and for this deed of Indian bravery he was permitted to join in the scalp dance. Three or four years after he, at the head of two hundred braves, went on another expedition against the Osages, to avenge the murder of some women and children belonging to his own tribe. Meeting an equal number of Osage warriors, a fierce battle ensued, in which the latter tribe lost one-half their number. The Sacs lost only about nineteen warriors. He next attacked the Cherokees for a similar cause. In a severe battle with them, near the present City of St. Louis, his father was slain, and Black Hawk, taking possession of the "Medicine Bag," at once announced himself chief of the Sac nation. He had now conquered the Cherokees, and about the year 1800, at the head of five hundred Sacs and Foxes, and a hundred Iowas, he waged war against the Osage nation and subdued it. For two years he battled successfully with other Indian tribes, all of whom he conquered.

Black Hawk does not at any time seem to have been friendly to the Americans. When on a visit to St. Louis to see his "Spanish Father," he declined to see any of the Americans, alleging, as a reason, he did not want *two* fathers.

The treaty at St. Louis was consummated in 1804. The next year the United States Government erected a fort near the head of the Des Moines Rapids, called Fort Edwards. This seemed to enrage Black Hawk, who at once determined to capture Fort Madison, standing on the west side of the Mississippi above the mouth of the Des Moines River. The fort was garrisoned by about fifty men. Here he was defeated. The difficulties with the British Government arose about this time, and the War of 1812 followed. That government, extending aid to the Western Indians, by giving them arms and ammunition, induced them to remain hostile to the Americans. In August, 1812, Black Hawk, at the head of about five hundred braves, started to join the British forces at Detroit, passing on his way the site of Chicago, where the famous Fort Dearborn Massacre had a few days before occurred. Of his connection with the British Government but little is known. In 1813 he with his little band descended the Mississippi, and attacking some United States troops at Fort Howard was defeated.

In the early part of 1815, the Indian tribes west of the Mississippi were notified that peace had been declared between the United States and England, and nearly all hostilities had ceased. Black Hawk did not sign any treaty, however, until May of the following year. He then recognized the validity of the treaty at St. Louis in 1804. From the time of signing this treaty in 1816, until the breaking out of the war in 1832, he and his band passed their time in the common pursuits of Indian life.

Ten years before the commencement of this war, the Sac and Fox

Indians were urged to join the Iowas on the west bank of the Father of Waters. All were agreed, save the band known as the British Band, of which Black Hawk was leader. He strenuously objected to the removal, and was induced to comply only after being threatened with the power of the Government. This and various actions on the part of the white settlers provoked Black Hawk and his band to attempt the capture of his native village now occupied by the whites. The war followed. He and his actions were undoubtedly misunderstood, and had his wishes been acquiesced in at the beginning of the struggle, much bloodshed would have been prevented.

Black Hawk was chief now of the Sac and Fox nations, and a noted warrior. He and his tribe inhabited a village on Rock River, nearly three miles above its confluence with the Mississippi, where the tribe had lived many generations. When that portion of Illinois was reserved to them, they remained in peaceable possession of their reservation, spending their time in the enjoyment of Indian life. The fine situation of their village and the quality of their lands incited the more lawless white settlers, who from time to time began to encroach upon the red men's domain. From one pretext to another, and from one step to another, the crafty white men gained a foothold, until through whisky and artifice they obtained deeds from many of the Indians for their possessions. The Indians were finally induced to cross over the Father of Waters and locate among the Iowas. Black Hawk was strenuously opposed to all this, but as the authorities of Illinois and the United States thought this the best move, he was forced to comply. Moreover other tribes joined the whites and urged the removal. Black Hawk would not agree to the terms of the treaty made with his nation for their lands, and as soon as the military, called to enforce his removal, had retired, he returned to the Illinois side of the river. A large force was at once raised and marched against him. On the evening of May 14, 1832, the first engagement occurred between a band from this army and Black Hawk's band, in which the former were defeated.

This attack and its result aroused the whites. A large force of men was raised, and Gen. Scott hastened from the seaboard, by way of the lakes, with United States troops and artillery to aid in the subjugation of the Indians. On the 24th of June, Black Hawk, with 200 warriors, was repulsed by Major Demont between Rock River and Galena. The American army continued to move up Rock River toward the main body of the Indians, and on the 21st of July came upon Black Hawk and his band, and defeated them near the Blue Mounds.

Before this action, Gen. Henry, in command, sent word to the main army by whom he was immediately rejoined, and the whole crossed the

Wisconsin in pursuit of Black Hawk and his band who were fleeing to the Mississippi. They were overtaken on the 2d of August, and in the battle which followed the power of the Indian chief was completely broken. He fled, but was seized by the Winnebagoes and delivered to the whites.

On the 21st of September, 1832, Gen. Scott and Gov. Reynolds concluded a treaty with the Winnebagoes, Sacs and Foxes by which they ceded to the United States a vast tract of country, and agreed to remain peaceable with the whites. For the faithful performance of the provisions of this treaty on the part of the Indians, it was stipulated that Black Hawk, his two sons, the prophet Wabokieshiek, and six other chiefs of the hostile bands should be retained as hostages during the pleasure of the President. They were confined at Fort Barracks and put in irons.

The next Spring, by order of the Secretary of War, they were taken to Washington. From there they were removed to Fortress Monroe, "there to remain until the conduct of their nation was such as to justify their being set at liberty." They were retained here until the 4th of June, when the authorities directed them to be taken to the principal cities so that they might see the folly of contending against the white people. Everywhere they were observed by thousands, the name of the old chief being extensively known. By the middle of August they reached Fort Armstrong on Rock Island, where Black Hawk was soon after released to go to his countrymen. As he passed the site of his birthplace, now the home of the white man, he was deeply moved. His village where he was born, where he had so happily lived, and where he had hoped to die, was now another's dwelling place, and he was a wanderer.

On the next day after his release, he went at once to his tribe and his lodge. His wife was yet living, and with her he passed the remainder of his days. To his credit it may be said that Black Hawk always remained true to his wife, and served her with a devotion uncommon among the Indians, living with her upward of forty years.

Black Hawk now passed his time hunting and fishing. A deep melancholy had settled over him from which he could not be freed. At all times when he visited the whites he was received with marked attention. He was an honored guest at the old settlers' reunion in Lee County, Illinois, at some of their meetings, and received many tokens of esteem. In September, 1838, while on his way to Rock Island to receive his annuity from the Government, he contracted a severe cold which resulted in a fatal attack of bilious fever which terminated his life on October 3. His faithful wife, who was devotedly attached to him, mourned deeply during his sickness. After his death he was dressed in the uniform presented to him by the President while in Washington. He was buried in a grave six feet in depth, situated upon a beautiful eminence. "The body was placed in the middle of the grave, in a sitting posture, upon a seat constructed for the purpose. On his left side, the cane, given him by Henry Clay, was placed upright, with his right hand resting upon it. Many of the old warrior's trophies were placed in the grave, and some Indian garments, together with his favorite weapons."

No sooner was the Black Hawk war concluded than settlers began rapidly to pour into the northern parts of Illinois, and into Wisconsin, now free from Indian depredations. Chicago, from a trading post, had grown to a commercial center, and was rapidly coming into prominence. In 1835, the formation of a State Government in Michigan was discussed, but did not take active form until two years later, when the State became a part of the Federal Union.

The main attraction to that portion of the Northwest lying west of Lake Michigan, now included in the State of Wisconsin, was its alluvial wealth. Copper ore was found about Lake Superior. For some time this region was attached to Michigan for judiciary purposes, but in 1836 was made a territory, then including Minnesota and Iowa. The latter State was detached two years later. In 1848, Wisconsin was admitted as a State, Madison being made the capital. We have now traced the various divisions of the Northwest Territory (save a little in Minnesota) from the time it was a unit comprising this vast territory, until circumstances compelled its present division.

OTHER INDIAN TROUBLES.

Before leaving this part of the narrative, we will narrate briefly the Indian troubles in Minnesota and elsewhere by the Sioux Indians.

In August, 1862, the Sioux Indians living on the western borders of Minnesota fell upon the unsuspecting settlers, and in a few hours massacred ten or twelve hundred persons. A distressful panic was the immediate result, fully thirty thousand persons fleeing from their homes to districts supposed to be better protected. The military authorities at once took active measures to punish the savages, and a large number were killed and captured. About a year after, Little Crow, the chief, was killed by a Mr. Lampson near Scattered Lake. Of those captured, thirty were hung at Mankato, and the remainder, through fears of mob violence, were removed to Camp McClellan, on the outskirts of the City of Davenport. It was here that Big Eagle came into prominence and secured his release by the following order:

BIG EAGLE.

"Special Order, No. 430.   "WAR DEPARTMENT,
         "ADJUTANT GENERAL'S OFFICE, WASHINGTON, Dec. 3, 1864.
    "Big Eagle, an Indian now in confinement at Davenport, Iowa, will, upon the receipt of this order, be immediately released from confinement and set at liberty.
    "By order of the President of the United States.
"Official: "E. D. TOWNSEND, Ass't Adj't Gen.
"CAPT. JAMES VANDERVENTER, Com'y Sub. Vols.
"Through Com'g Gen'l, Washington, D. C."

Another Indian who figures more prominently than Big Eagle, and who was more cowardly in his nature, with his band of Modoc Indians, is noted in the annals of the New Northwest: we refer to Captain Jack. This distinguished Indian, noted for his cowardly murder of Gen. Canby, was a chief of a Modoc tribe of Indians inhabiting the border lands between California and Oregon. This region of country comprises what is known as the "Lava Beds," a tract of land described as utterly impenetrable, save by those savages who had made it their home.

The Modocs are known as an exceedingly fierce and treacherous race. They had, according to their own traditions, resided here for many generations, and at one time were exceedingly numerous and powerful. A famine carried off nearly half their numbers, and disease, indolence and the vices of the white man have reduced them to a poor, weak and insignificant tribe.

Soon after the settlement of California and Oregon, complaints began to be heard of massacres of emigrant trains passing through the Modoc country. In 1847, an emigrant train, comprising eighteen souls, was entirely destroyed at a place since known as "Bloody Point." These occurrences caused the United States Government to appoint a peace commission, who, after repeated attempts, in 1864, made a treaty with the Modocs, Snakes and Klamaths, in which it was agreed on their part to remove to a reservation set apart for them in the southern part of Oregon.

With the exception of Captain Jack and a band of his followers, who remained at Clear Lake, about six miles from Klamath, all the Indians complied. The Modocs who went to the reservation were under chief Schonchin. Captain Jack remained at the lake without disturbance until 1869, when he was also induced to remove to the reservation. The Modocs and the Klamaths soon became involved in a quarrel, and Captain Jack and his band returned to the Lava Beds.

Several attempts were made by the Indian Commissioners to induce them to return to the reservation, and finally becoming involved in a difficulty with the commissioner and his military escort, a fight ensued, in which the chief and his band were routed. They were greatly enraged, and on their retreat, before the day closed, killed eleven inoffensive whites.

The nation was aroused and immediate action demanded. A commission was at once appointed by the Government to see what could be done. It comprised the following persons: Gen. E. R. S. Canby, Rev. Dr. E. Thomas, a leading Methodist divine of California; Mr. A. B. Meacham, Judge Rosborough, of California, and a Mr. Dyer, of Oregon. After several interviews, in which the savages were always aggressive, often appearing with scalps in their belts, Bogus Charley came to the commission on the evening of April 10, 1873, and informed them that Capt. Jack and his band would have a "talk" to-morrow at a place near Clear Lake, about three miles distant. Here the Commissioners, accompanied by Charley, Riddle, the interpreter, and Boston Charley repaired. After the usual greeting the council proceedings commenced. On behalf of the Indians there were present: Capt. Jack, Black Jim, Schnac Nasty Jim, Ellen's Man, and Hooker Jim. They had no guns, but carried pistols. After short speeches by Mr. Meacham, Gen. Canby and Dr. Thomas, Chief Schonchin arose to speak. He had scarcely proceeded when, as if by a preconcerted arrangement, Capt. Jack drew his pistol and shot Gen. Canby dead. In less than a minute a dozen shots were fired by the savages, and the massacre completed. Mr. Meacham was shot by Schonchin, and Dr. Thomas by Boston Charley. Mr. Dyer barely escaped, being fired at twice. Riddle, the interpreter, and his squaw escaped. The troops rushed to the spot where they found Gen. Canby and Dr. Thomas dead, and Mr. Meacham badly wounded. The savages had escaped to their impenetrable fastnesses and could not be pursued.

The whole country was aroused by this brutal massacre; but it was not until the following May that the murderers were brought to justice. At that time Boston Charley gave himself up, and offered to guide the troops to Capt. Jack's stronghold. This led to the capture of his entire gang, a number of whom were murdered by Oregon volunteers while on their way to trial. The remaining Indians were held as prisoners until July when their trial occurred, which led to the conviction of Capt. Jack, Schonchin, Boston Charley, Hooker Jim, Broncho, *alias* One-Eyed Jim, and Slotuck, who were sentenced to be hanged. These sentences were approved by the President, save in the case of Slotuck and Broncho whose sentences were commuted to imprisonment for life. The others were executed at Fort Klamath, October 3, 1873.

These closed the Indian troubles for a time in the Northwest, and for several years the borders of civilization remained in peace. They were again involved in a conflict with the savages about the country of the

BELVIDERE.

CAPTAIN JACK, THE MODOC CHIEFTAIN.

Black Hills, in which war the gallant Gen. Custer lost his life. Just now the borders of Oregon and California are again in fear of hostilities; but as the Government has learned how to deal with the Indians, they will be of short duration. The red man is fast passing away before the march of the white man, and a few more generations will read of the Indians as one of the nations of the past.

The Northwest abounds in memorable places. We have generally noticed them in the narrative, but our space forbids their description in detail, save of the most important places. Detroit, Cincinnati, Vincennes, Kaskaskia and their kindred towns have all been described. But ere we leave the narrative we will present our readers with an account of the Kinzie house, the old landmark of Chicago, and the discovery of the source of the Mississippi River, each of which may well find a place in the annals of the Northwest.

Mr. John Kinzie, of the Kinzie house, represented in the illustration, established a trading house at Fort Dearborn in 1804. The stockade had been erected the year previous, and named Fort Dearborn in honor of the Secretary of War. It had a block house at each of the two angles, on the southern side a sallyport, a covered way on the north side, that led down to the river, for the double purpose of providing means of escape, and of procuring water in the event of a siege.

Fort Dearborn stood on the south bank of the Chicago River, about half a mile from its mouth. When Major Whistler built it, his soldiers hauled all the timber, for he had no oxen, and so economically did he work that the fort cost the Government only fifty dollars. For a while the garrison could get no grain, and Whistler and his men subsisted on acorns. Now Chicago is the greatest grain center in the world.

Mr. Kinzie bought the hut of the first settler, Jean Baptiste Point au Sable, on the site of which he erected his mansion. Within an inclosure in front he planted some Lombardy poplars, seen in the engraving, and in the rear he soon had a fine garden and growing orchard.

In 1812 the Kinzie house and its surroundings became the theater of stirring events. The garrison of Fort Dearborn consisted of fifty-four men, under the charge of Capt. Nathan Heald, assisted by Lieutenant Lenai T. Helm (son-in-law to Mrs. Kinzie), and Ensign Ronan. The surgeon was Dr. Voorhees. The only residents at the post at that time were the wives of Capt. Heald and Lieutenant Helm and a few of the soldiers, Mr. Kinzie and his family, and a few Canadian voyagers with their wives and children. The soldiers and Mr. Kinzie were on the most friendly terms with the Pottawatomies and the Winnebagoes, the principal tribes around them, but they could not win them from their attachment to the British.

After the battle of Tippecanoe it was observed that some of the leading chiefs became sullen, for some of their people had perished in that conflict with American troops.

One evening in April, 1812, Mr. Kinzie sat playing his violin and his children were dancing to the music, when Mrs. Kinzie came rushing into the house pale with terror, and exclaiming, "The Indians! the Indians!" "What? Where?" eagerly inquired Mr. Kinzie. "Up at Lee's, killing and scalping," answered the frightened mother, who, when the alarm was given, was attending Mrs. Burns, a newly-made mother, living not far off.

KINZIE HOUSE.

Mr. Kinzie and his family crossed the river in boats, and took refuge in the fort, to which place Mrs. Burns and her infant, not a day old, were conveyed in safety to the shelter of the guns of Fort Dearborn, and the rest of the white inhabitants fled. The Indians were a scalping party of Winnebagoes, who hovered around the fort some days, when they disappeared, and for several weeks the inhabitants were not disturbed by alarms.

Chicago was then so deep in the wilderness, that the news of the declaration of war against Great Britain, made on the 19th of June, 1812, did not reach the commander of the garrison at Fort Dearborn till the 7th of August. Now the fast mail train will carry a man from New York to Chicago in twenty-seven hours, and such a declaration might be sent, every word, by the telegraph in less than the same number of minutes.

VILLAGE RESIDENCE.

PRESENT CONDITION OF THE NORTHWEST.

Preceding chapters have brought us to the close of the Black Hawk war, and we now turn to the contemplation of the growth and prosperity of the Northwest under the smile of peace and the blessings of our civilization. The pioneers of this region date events back to the deep snow

A REPRESENTATIVE PIONEER.

of 1831, no one arriving here since that date taking first honors. The inciting cause of the immigration which overflowed the prairies early in the '30s was the reports of the marvelous beauty and fertility of the region distributed through the East by those who had participated in the Black Hawk campaign with Gen. Scott. Chicago and Milwaukee then had a few hundred inhabitants, and Gurdon S. Hubbard's trail from the former city to Kaskaskia led almost through a wilderness. Vegetables and clothing were largely distributed through the regions adjoining the lakes by steamers from the Ohio towns. There are men now living in Illinois who came to the state when barely an acre was in cultivation, and a man now prominent in the business circles of Chicago looked over the swampy, cheerless site of that metropolis in 1818 and went southward into civilization. Emigrants from Pennsylvania in 1830 left behind

LINCOLN MONUMENT, SPRINGFIELD, ILLINOIS.

them but one small railway in the coal regions, thirty miles in length, and made their way to the Northwest mostly with ox teams, finding in Northern Illinois petty settlements scores of miles apart, although the southern portion of the state was fairly dotted with farms. The water courses of the lakes and rivers furnished transportation to the second great army of immigrants, and about 1850 railroads were pushed to that extent that the crisis of 1857 was precipitated upon us, from the effects of which the Western country had not fully recovered at the outbreak of the war. Hostilities found the colonists of the prairies fully alive to the demands of the occasion, and the honor of recruiting

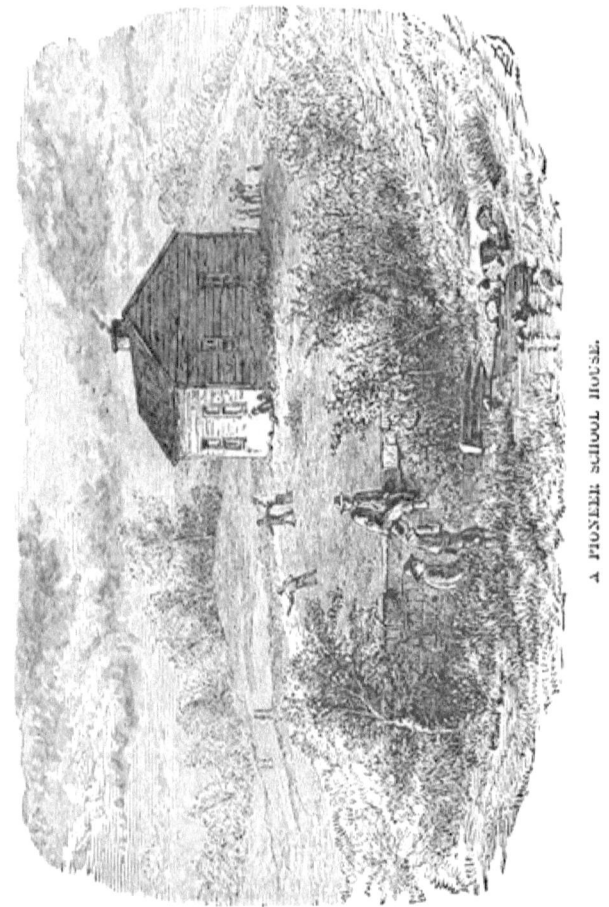

A PIONEER SCHOOL HOUSE.

the vast armies of the Union fell largely to Gov. Yates, of Illinois, and Gov. Morton, of Indiana. To recount the share of the glories of the campaign won by our Western troops is a needless task, except to mention the fact that Illinois gave to the nation the President who saved it, and sent out at the head of one of its regiments the general who led its armies to the final victory at Appomattox. The struggle, on the

FARM VIEW IN WINTER.

whole, had a marked effect for the better on the new Northwest, giving it an impetus which twenty years of peace would not have produced. In a large degree this prosperity was an inflated one, and with the rest of the Union we have since been compelled to atone therefor by four

SPRING SCENE.

PIONEERS' FIRST WINTER.

years of depression of values, of scarcity of employment, and loss of fortune. To a less degree, however, than the manufacturing or mining regions has the West suffered during the prolonged panic now so near its end. Agriculture, still the leading feature in our industries, has been quite prosperous through all these dark years, and the farmers have cleared away many incumbrances resting over them from the period of fictitious values. The population has steadily increased, the arts and sciences are gaining a stronger foothold, the trade area of the region is becoming daily more extended, and we have been largely exempt from the financial calamities which have nearly wrecked communities on the seaboard dependent wholly on foreign commerce or domestic manufacture.

At the present period there are no great schemes broached for the Northwest, no propositions for government subsidies or national works of improvement, but the capital of the world is attracted hither for the purchase of our products or the expansion of our capacity for serving the nation at large. A new era is dawning as to transportation, and we bid fair to deal almost exclusively with the increasing and expanding lines of steel rail running through every few miles of territory on the prairies. The lake marine will no doubt continue to be useful in the warmer season, and to serve as a regulator of freight rates; but experienced navigators forecast the decay of the system in moving to the seaboard the enormous crops of the West. Within the past five years it has become quite common to see direct shipments to Europe and the West Indies going through from the second-class towns along the Mississippi and Missouri.

As to popular education, the standard has of late risen very greatly, and our schools would be creditable to any section of the Union.

More and more as the events of the war pass into obscurity will the fate of the Northwest be linked with that of the Southwest, and the next Congressional apportionment will give the valley of the Mississippi absolute control of the legislation of the nation, and do much toward securing the removal of the Federal capitol to some more central location.

Our public men continue to wield the full share of influence pertaining to their rank in the national autonomy, and seem not to forget that for the past sixteen years they and their constituents have dictated the principles which should govern the country.

In a work like this, destined to lie on the shelves of the library for generations, and not doomed to daily destruction like a newspaper, one can not indulge in the same glowing predictions, the sanguine statements of actualities that fill the columns of ephemeral publications. Time may bring grief to the pet projects of a writer, and explode castles erected on a pedestal of facts. Yet there are unmistakable indications before us of

94 THE NORTHWEST TERRITORY.

APPLE HARVEST.

the same radical change in our great Northwest which characterizes its history for the past thirty years. Our domain has a sort of natural geographical border, save where it melts away to the southward in the cattle raising districts of the southwest.

Our prime interest will for some years doubtless be the growth of the food of the world, in which branch it has already outstripped all competitors, and our great rival in this duty will naturally be the fertile plains of Kansas, Nebraska and Colorado, to say nothing of the new empire so rapidly growing up in Texas. Over these regions there is a continued progress in agriculture and in railway building, and we must look to our laurels. Intelligent observers of events are fully aware of the strides made in the way of shipments of fresh meats to Europe, many of these ocean cargoes being actually slaughtered in the West and transported on ice to the wharves of the seaboard cities. That this new enterprise will continue there is no reason to doubt. There are in Chicago several factories for the canning of prepared meats for European consumption, and the orders for this class of goods are already immense. English capital is becoming daily more and more dissatisfied with railway loans and investments, and is gradually seeking mammoth outlays in lands and live stock. The stock yards in Chicago, Indianapolis and East St. Louis are yearly increasing their facilities, and their plant steadily grows more valuable. Importations of blooded animals from the progressive countries of Europe are destined to greatly improve the quality of our beef and mutton. Nowhere is there to be seen a more enticing display in this line than at our state and county fairs, and the interest in the matter is on the increase.

To attempt to give statistics of our grain production for 1877 would be useless, so far have we surpassed ourselves in the quantity and quality of our product. We are too liable to forget that we are giving the world its first article of necessity — its food supply. An opportunity to learn this fact so it never can be forgotten was afforded at Chicago at the outbreak of the great panic of 1873, when Canadian purchasers, fearing the prostration of business might bring about an anarchical condition of affairs, went to that city with coin in bulk and foreign drafts to secure their supplies in their own currency at first hands. It may be justly claimed by the agricultural community that their combined efforts gave the nation its first impetus toward a restoration of its crippled industries, and their labor brought the gold premium to a lower depth than the government was able to reach by its most intense efforts of legislation and compulsion. The hundreds of millions about to be disbursed for farm products have already, by the anticipation common to all commercial nations, set the wheels in motion, and will relieve us from the perils so long shadowing our efforts to return to a healthy tone.

Manufacturing has attained in the chief cities a foothold which bids fair to render the Northwest independent of the outside world. Nearly

GREAT IRON BRIDGE OF C. R. I. & P. R.R., CROSSING MISSISSIPPI RIVER AT DAVENPORT.

our whole region has a distribution of coal measures which will in time support the manufactures necessary to our comfort and prosperity. As to transportation, the chief factor in the production of all articles except food, no section is so magnificently endowed, and our facilities are yearly increasing beyond those of any other region.

The period from a central point of the war to the outbreak of the panic was marked by a tremendous growth in our railway lines, but the depression of the times caused almost a total suspension of operations. Now that prosperity is returning to our stricken country we witness its anticipation by the railroad interest in a series of projects, extensions, and leases which bid fair to largely increase our transportation facilities. The process of foreclosure and sale of incumbered lines is another matter to be considered. In the case of the Illinois Central road, which formerly transferred to other lines at Cairo the vast burden of freight destined for the Gulf region, we now see the incorporation of the tracks connecting through to New Orleans, every mile co-operating in turning toward the northwestern metropolis the weight of the inter-state commerce of a thousand miles or more of fertile plantations. Three competing routes to Texas have established in Chicago their general freight and passenger agencies. Four or five lines compete for all Pacific freights to a point as as far as the interior of Nebraska. Half a dozen or more splendid bridge structures have been thrown across the Missouri and Mississippi Rivers by the railways. The Chicago and Northwestern line has become an aggregation of over two thousand miles of rail, and the Chicago, Milwaukee and St. Paul is its close rival in extent and importance. The three lines running to Cairo *via* Vincennes form a through route for all traffic with the states to the southward. The chief projects now under discussion are the Chicago and Atlantic, which is to unite with lines now built to Charleston, and the Chicago and Canada Southern, which line will connect with all the various branches of that Canadian enterprise. Our latest new road is the Chicago and Lake Huron, formed of three lines, and entering the city from Valparaiso on the Pittsburgh, Fort Wayne and Chicago track. The trunk lines being mainly in operation, the progress made in the way of shortening tracks, making air-line branches, and running extensions does not show to the advantage it deserves, as this process is constantly adding new facilities to the established order of things. The panic reduced the price of steel to a point where the railways could hardly afford to use iron rails, and all our northwestern lines report large relays of Bessemer track. The immense crops now being moved have given a great rise to the value of railway stocks, and their transportation must result in heavy pecuniary advantages.

Few are aware of the importance of the wholesale and jobbing trade of Chicago. One leading firm has since the panic sold $24,000,000 of dry goods in one year, and they now expect most confidently to add seventy per cent. to the figures of their last year's business. In boots and shoes and in clothing, twenty or more great firms from the east have placed here their distributing agents or their factories; and in groceries

Chicago supplies the entire Northwest at rates presenting advantages over New York.

Chicago has stepped in between New York and the rural banks as a financial center, and scarcely a banking institution in the grain or cattle regions but keeps its reserve funds in the vaults of our commercial institutions. Accumulating here throughout the spring and summer months, they are summoned home at pleasure to move the products of the prairies. This process greatly strengthens the northwest in its financial operations, leaving home capital to supplement local operations on behalf of home interests.

It is impossible to forecast the destiny of this grand and growing section of the Union. Figures and predictions made at this date might seem ten years hence so ludicrously small as to excite only derision.

ILLINOIS.

Length, 380 miles, mean width about 156 miles. Area, 55,410 square miles, or 35,462,400 acres. Illinois, as regards its surface, constitutes a table-land at a varying elevation ranging between 350 and 800 feet above the sea level; composed of extensive and highly fertile prairies and plains. Much of the south division of the State, especially the river-bottoms, are thickly wooded. The prairies, too, have oasis-like clumps of trees scattered here and there at intervals. The chief rivers irrigating the State are the Mississippi—dividing it from Iowa and Missouri—the Ohio (forming its south barrier), the Illinois, Wabash, Kaskaskia, and Sangamon, with their numerous affluents. The total extent of navigable streams is calculated at 4,000 miles. Small lakes are scattered over various parts of the State. Illinois is extremely prolific in minerals, chiefly coal, iron, copper, and zinc ores, sulphur and limestone. The coal-field alone is estimated to absorb a full third of the entire coal-deposit of North America. Climate tolerably equable and healthy; the mean temperature standing at about 51° Fahrenheit As an agricultural region, Illinois takes a competitive rank with neighboring States, the cereals, fruits, and root-crops yielding plentiful returns; in fact, as a grain-growing State, Illinois may be deemed, in proportion to her size, to possess a greater area of lands suitable for its production than any other State in the Union. Stock-raising is also largely carried on, while her manufacturing interests in regard of woolen fabrics, etc., are on a very extensive and yearly expanding scale. The lines of railroad in the State are among the most extensive of the Union. Inland water-carriage is facilitated by a canal connecting the Illinois River with Lake Michigan, and thence with the St. Lawrence and Atlantic. Illinois is divided into 102 counties; the chief towns being Chicago, Springfield (capital), Alton, Quincy, Peoria, Galena, Bloomington, Rock Island, Vandalia, etc. By the new Constitution, established in 1870, the State Legislature consists of 51 Senators, elected for four years, and 153 Representatives, for two years; which numbers were to be decennially increased thereafter to the number of six per every additional half-million of inhabitants. Religious and educational institutions are largely diffused throughout, and are in a very flourishing condition. Illinois has a State Lunatic and a Deaf and Dumb Asylum at Jacksonville; a State Penitentiary at Joliet; and a Home for

Soldiers' Orphans at Normal. On November 30, 1870, the public debt of the State was returned at $4,870,937, with a balance of $1,808,833 unprovided for. At the same period the value of assessed and equalized property presented the following totals: assessed, $840,031,703; equalized $480,664,058. The name of Illinois, through nearly the whole of the eighteenth century, embraced most of the known regions north and west of Ohio. French colonists established themselves in 1673, at Cahokia and Kaskaskia, and the territory of which these settlements formed the nucleus was, in 1763, ceded to Great Britain in conjunction with Canada, and ultimately resigned to the United States in 1787. Illinois entered the Union as a State, December 3, 1818; and now sends 19 Representatives to Congress. Population, 2,539,891, in 1870.

A WESTERN DWELLING.

INDIANA.

The profile of Indiana forms a nearly exact parallelogram, occupying one of the most fertile portions of the great Mississippi Valley. The greater extent of the surface embraced within its limits consists of gentle undulations rising into hilly tracts toward the Ohio bottom. The chief rivers of the State are the Ohio and Wabash, with their numerous affluents. The soil is highly productive of the cereals and grasses—most particularly so in the valleys of the Ohio, Wabash, Whitewater, and White Rivers. The northeast and central portions are well timbered with virgin forests, and the west section is notably rich in coal, constituting an offshoot of the great Illinois carboniferous field. Iron, copper, marble, slate, gypsum, and various clays are also abundant. From an agricultural point of view, the staple products are maize and wheat, with the other cereals in lesser yields; and besides these, flax, hemp, sorghum, hops, etc., are extensively raised. Indiana is divided into 92 counties, and counts among her principal cities and towns, those of Indianapolis (the capital), Fort Wayne, Evansville, Terre Haute, Madison, Jeffersonville, Columbus, Vincennes, South Bend, etc. The public institutions of the State are many and various, and on a scale of magnitude and efficiency commensurate with her important political and industrial status. Upward of two thousand miles of railroads permeate the State in all directions, and greatly conduce to the development of her expanding manufacturing interests. Statistics for the fiscal year terminating October 31, 1870, exhibited a total of receipts, $3,896,541 as against disbursements, $3,532,406, leaving a balance, $364,135 in favor of the State Treasury. The entire public debt, January 5, 1871, $3,971,000. This State was first settled by Canadian voyageurs in 1702, who erected a fort at Vincennes; in 1763 it passed into the hands of the English, and was by the latter ceded to the United States in 1783. From 1788 till 1791, an Indian warefare prevailed. In 1800, all the region west and north of Ohio (then formed into a distinct territory) became merged in Indiana. In 1809, the present limits of the State were defined, Michigan and Illinois having previously been withdrawn. In 1811, Indiana was the theater of the Indian War of Tecumseh, ending with the decisive battle of Tippecanoe. In 1816 (December 11), Indiana became enrolled among the States of the American Union. In 1834, the State passed through a monetary crisis owing to its having become mixed up with railroad, canal, and other speculations on a gigantic scale, which ended, for the time being, in a general collapse of public credit, and consequent bankruptcy. Since that time, however, the greater number of the public works which had brought about that imbroglio — especially the great Wabash and Erie Canal — have been completed, to the great benefit of the State, whose subsequent progress has year by year been marked by rapid strides in the paths of wealth, commerce, and general social and political prosperity. The constitution now in force was adopted in 1851. Population, 1,680,637.

IOWA.

In shape, Iowa presents an almost perfect parallelogram; has a length, north to south, of about 300 miles, by a pretty even width of 208 miles, and embraces an area of 55,045 square miles, or 35,228,800 acres. The surface of the State is generally undulating, rising toward the middle into an elevated plateau which forms the "divide" of the Missouri and Mississippi basins. Rolling prairies, especially in the south section, constitute a regnant feature, and the river bottoms, belted with woodlands, present a soil of the richest alluvion. Iowa is well watered: the principal rivers being the Mississippi and Missouri, which form respectively its east and west limits, and the Cedar, Iowa, and Des Moines, affluents of the first named. Mineralogically, Iowa is important as occupying a section of the great Northwest coal field, to the extent of an area estimated at 25,000 square miles. Lead, copper, zinc, and iron, are also mined in considerable quantities. The soil is well adapted to the production of wheat, maize, and the other cereals; fruits, vegetables, and esculent roots; maize, wheat, and oats forming the chief staples. Wine, tobacco, hops, and wax, are other noticeable items of the agricultural yield. Cattle-raising, too, is a branch of rural industry largely engaged in. The climate is healthy, although liable to extremes of heat and cold. The annual gross product of the various manufactures carried on in this State approximate, in round numbers, a sum of $20,000,000. Iowa has an immense railroad system, besides over 500 miles of water-communication by means of its navigable rivers. The State is politically divided into 99 counties, with the following centers of population: Des Moines (capital), Iowa City (former capital), Dubuque, Davenport, Burlington, Council Bluffs, Keokuk, Muscatine, and Cedar Rapids. The State institutions of Iowa — religious, scholastic, and philanthropic — are on a par, as regards number and perfection of organization and operation, with those of her Northwest sister States, and education is especially well cared for, and largely diffused. Iowa formed a portion of the American territorial acquisitions from France, by the so-called Louisiana purchase in 1803, and was politically identified with Louisiana till 1812, when it merged into the Missouri Territory; in 1834 it came under the Michigan organization, and, in 1836, under that of Wisconsin. Finally, after being constituted an independent Territory, it became a State of the Union, December 28, 1846. Population in 1860, 674,913; in 1870, 1,191,792, and in 1875, 1,353,118.

MICHIGAN.

United area, 56,243 square miles, or 35,995,520 acres. Extent of the Upper and smaller Peninsula — length, 316 miles; breadth, fluctuating between 36 and 120 miles. The south division is 416 miles long, by from 50 to 300 miles wide. Aggregate lake-shore line, 1,400 miles. The Upper, or North, Peninsula consists chiefly of an elevated plateau, expanding into the Porcupine mountain-system, attaining a maximum height of some 2,000 feet. Its shores along Lake Superior are eminently bold and picturesque, and its area is rich in minerals, its product of copper constituting an important source of industry. Both divisions are heavily wooded, and the South one, in addition, boasts of a deep, rich, loamy soil, throwing up excellent crops of cereals and other agricultural produce. The climate is generally mild and humid, though the Winter colds are severe. The chief staples of farm husbandry include the cereals, grasses, maple sugar, sorghum, tobacco, fruits, and dairy-stuffs. In 1870, the acres of land in farms were: improved, 5,096,939; unimproved woodland, 4,080,146; other unimproved land, 842,057. The cash value of land was $398,240,578; of farming implements and machinery, $13,711,979. In 1869, there were shipped from the Lake Superior ports, 874,582 tons of iron ore, and 45,762 of smelted pig, along with 14,188 tons of copper (ore and ingot). Coal is another article largely mined. Inland communication is provided for by an admirably organized railroad system, and by the St. Mary's Ship Canal, connecting Lakes Huron and Superior. Michigan is politically divided into 78 counties; its chief urban centers are Detroit, Lansing (capital), Ann Arbor, Marquette, Bay City, Niles, Ypsilanti, Grand Haven, etc. The Governor of the State is elected biennially. On November 30, 1870, the aggregate bonded debt of Michigan amounted to $2,385,028, and the assessed valuation of land to $266,929,278, representing an estimated cash value of $800,000,000. Education is largely diffused and most excellently conducted and provided for. The State University at Ann Arbor, the colleges of Detroit and Kalamazoo, the Albion Female College, the State Normal School at Ypsilanti, and the State Agricultural College at Lansing, are chief among the academic institutions. Michigan (a term of Chippeway origin, and

signifying "Great Lake), was discovered and first settled by French
Canadians, who, in 1670, founded Detroit, the pioneer of a series of trad-
ing-posts on the Indian frontier. During the "Conspiracy of Pontiac,"
following the French loss of Canada, Michigan became the scene of a
sanguinary struggle between the whites and aborigines. In 1796, it
became annexed to the United States, which incorporated this region
with the Northwest Territory, and then with Indiana Territory, till 1803,
when it became territorially independent. Michigan was the theater of
warlike operations during the war of 1812 with Great Britain, and in
1819 was authorized to be represented by one delegate in Congress; in
1837 she was admitted into the Union as a State, and in 1869 ratified the
15th Amendment to the Federal Constitution. Population, 1,184,059.

WISCONSIN.

It has a mean length of 260 miles, and a maximum breadth of 215.
Land area, 53,924 square miles, or 34,511,360 acres. Wisconsin lies at a
considerable altitude above sea-level, and consists for the most part of an
upland plateau, the surface of which is undulating and very generally
diversified. Numerous local eminences called mounds are interspersed
over the State, and the Lake Michigan coast-line is in many parts characterized by lofty escarped cliffs, even as on the west side the banks of
the Mississippi form a series of high and picturesque bluffs. A group of
islands known as The Apostles lie off the extreme north point of the
State in Lake Superior, and the great estuary of Green Bay, running far
inland, gives formation to a long, narrow peninsula between its waters
and those of Lake Michigan. The river-system of Wisconsin has three
outlets — those of Lake Superior, Green Bay, and the Mississippi, which
latter stream forms the entire southwest frontier, widening at one point
into the large watery expanse called Lake Pepin. Lake Superior receives
the St. Louis, Burnt Wood, and Montreal Rivers; Green Bay, the
Menomonee, Peshtigo, Oconto, and Fox; while into the Mississippi
empty the St. Croix, Chippewa, Black, Wisconsin, and Rock Rivers.
The chief interior lakes are those of Winnebago, Horicon, and Court
Oreilles, and smaller sheets of water stud a great part of the surface.
The climate is healthful, with cold Winters and brief but very warm
Summers. Mean annual rainfall 31 inches. The geological system
represented by the State, embraces those rocks included between the
primary and the Devonian series, the former containing extensive
deposits of copper and iron ore. Besides these minerals, lead and zinc
are found in great quantities, together with kaolin, plumbago, gypsum,

and various clays. Mining, consequently, forms a prominent industry, and one of yearly increasing dimensions. The soil of Wisconsin is of varying quality, but fertile on the whole, and in the north parts of the State heavily timbered. The agricultural yield comprises the cereals, together with flax, hemp, tobacco, pulse, sorgum, and all kinds of vegetables, and of the hardier fruits. In 1870, the State had a total number of 102,904 farms, occupying 11,715,321 acres, of which 5,899,343 consisted of improved land, and 3,437,442 were timbered. Cash value of farms, $300,414,064; of farm implements and machinery, $14,239,364. Total estimated value of all farm products, including betterments and additions to stock, $78,027,032; of orchard and dairy stuffs, $1,045,933; of lumber, $1,327,618; of home manufactures, $338,423; of all live-stock, $45,310,882. Number of manufacturing establishments, 7,136, employing 39,055 hands, and turning out productions valued at $85,624,966. The political divisions of the State form 61 counties, and the chief places of wealth, trade, and population, are Madison (the capital), Milwaukee, Fond du Lac, Oshkosh, Prairie du Chien, Janesville, Portage City, Racine, Kenosha, and La Crosse. In 1870, the total assessed valuation reached $333,209,838, as against a true valuation of both real and personal estate aggregating $602,207,329. Treasury receipts during 1870, $886,-696; disbursements, $906,329. Value of church property, $4,749,983. Education is amply provided for. Independently of the State University at Madison, and those of Galesville and of Lawrence at Appleton, and the colleges of Beloit, Racine, and Milton, there are Normal Schools at Platteville and Whitewater. The State is divided into 4,802 common school districts, maintained at a cost, in 1870, of $2,094,160. The charitable institutions of Wisconsin include a Deaf and Dumb Asylum, an Institute for the Education of the Blind, and a Soldiers' Orphans' School. In January, 1870, the railroad system ramified throughout the State totalized 2,779 miles of track, including several lines far advanced toward completion. Immigration is successfully encouraged by the State authorities, the larger number of yearly new-comers being of Scandinavian and German origin. The territory now occupied within the limits of the State of Wisconsin was explored by French missionaries and traders in 1639, and it remained under French jurisdiction until 1763, when it became annexed to the British North American possessions. In 1796, it reverted to the United States, the government of which latter admitted it within the limits of the Northwest Territory, and in 1809, attached it to that of Illinois, and to Michigan in 1818. Wisconsin became independently territorially organized in 1836, and became a State of the Union, March 3, 1847. Population in 1870, 1,064,985, of which 2,113 were of the colored race, and 11,521 Indians, 1,206 of the latter being out of tribal relations.

MINNESOTA.

Its length, north to south, embraces an extent of 380 miles; its breadth one of 250 miles at a maximum. Area, 84,000 square miles, or 54,760,000 acres. The surface of Minnesota, generally speaking, consists of a succession of gently undulating plains and prairies, drained by an admirable water-system, and with here and there heavily-timbered bottoms and belts of virgin forest. The soil, corresponding with such a superfices, is exceptionally rich, consisting for the most part of a dark, calcareous sandy drift intermixed with loam. A distinguishing physical feature of this State is its riverine ramifications, expanding in nearly every part of it into almost innumerable lakes—the whole presenting an aggregate of water-power having hardly a rival in the Union. Besides the Mississippi — which here has its rise, and drains a basin of 800 miles of country — the principal streams are the Minnesota (334 miles long), the Red River of the North, the St. Croix, St. Louis, and many others of lesser importance; the chief lakes are those called Red, Cass, Leech, Mille Lacs, Vermillion, and Winibigosh. Quite a concatenation of sheets of water fringe the frontier line where Minnesota joins British America, culminating in the Lake of the Woods. It has been estimated, that of an area of 1,200,000 acres of surface between the St. Croix and Mississippi Rivers, not less than 73,000 acres are of lacustrine formation. In point of minerals, the resources of Minnesota have as yet been very imperfectly developed; iron, copper, coal, lead — all these are known to exist in considerable deposits; together with salt, limestone, and potter's clay. The agricultural outlook of the State is in a high degree satisfactory; wheat constitutes the leading cereal in cultivation, with Indian corn and oats in next order. Fruits and vegetables are grown in great plenty and of excellent quality. The lumber resources of Minnesota are important; the pine forests in the north region alone occupying an area of some 21,000 square miles, which in 1870 produced a return of scaled logs amounting to 313,116,416 feet. The natural industrial advantages possessed by Minnesota are largely improved upon by a railroad system. The political divisions of this State number 78 counties; of which the chief cities and towns are: St. Paul (the capital), Stillwater, Red Wing, St. Anthony, Fort Snelling, Minneapolis, and Mankato. Minnesota has already assumed an attitude of high importance as a manufacturing State; this is mainly due to the wonderful command of water-power she possesses, as before spoken of. Besides her timber-trade, the milling of flour, the distillation of whisky, and the tanning of leather, are prominent interests, which, in 1869, gave returns to the amount of $14,831,043.

Education is notably provided for on a broad and catholic scale, the entire amount expended scholastically during the year 1870 being $857,-816; while on November 30 of the preceding year the permanent school fund stood at $2,476,222. Besides a University and Agricultural College, Normal and Reform Schools flourish, and with these may be mentioned such various philanthropic and religious institutions as befit the needs of an intelligent and prosperous community. The finances of the State for the fiscal year terminating December 1, 1870, exhibited a balance on the right side to the amount of $136,164, being a gain of $44,000 over the previous year's figures. The earliest exploration of Minnesota by the whites was made in 1680 by a French Franciscan, Father Hennepin, who gave the name of St. Antony to the Great Falls on the Upper Mississippi. In 1763, the Treaty of Versailles ceded this region to England. Twenty years later, Minnesota formed part of the Northwest Territory transferred to the United States, and became herself territorialized independently in 1849. Indian cessions in 1851 enlarged her boundaries, and, May 11, 1857, Minnesota became a unit of the great American federation of States. Population, 439,706.

NEBRASKA.

Maximum length, 412 miles; extreme breadth, 208 miles. Area, 75,905 square miles, or 48,636,800 acres. The surface of this State is almost entirely undulating prairie, and forms part of the west slope of the great central basin of the North American Continent. In its west division, near the base of the Rocky Mountains, is a sandy belt of country, irregularly defined. In this part, too, are the "dunes," resembling a wavy sea of sandy billows, as well as the Mauvaises Terres a tract of singular formation, produced by eccentric disintegrations and denudations of the land. The chief rivers are the Missouri, constituting its entire east line of demarcation; the Nebraska or Platte, the Niobrara, the Republican Fork of the Kansas, the Elkhorn, and the Loup Fork of the Platte. The soil is very various, but consisting chiefly of rich, bottomy loam, admirably adapted to the raising of heavy crops of cereals. All the vegetables and fruits of the temperate zone are produced in great size and plenty. For grazing purposes Nebraska is a State exceptionally well fitted, a region of not less than 23,000,000 acres being adaptable to this branch of husbandry. It is believed that the, as yet, comparatively infertile tracts of land found in various parts of the State are susceptible of productivity by means of a properly conducted system of irrigation. Few minerals of moment have so far been found within the limits of

Nebraska, if we may except important saline deposits at the head of Salt Creek in its southeast section. The State is divided into 57 counties, independent of the Pawnee and Winnebago Indians, and of unorganized territory in the northwest part. The principal towns are Omaha, Lincoln (State capital), Nebraska City, Columbus, Grand Island, etc. In 1870, the total assessed value of property amounted to $53,000,000, being an increase of $11,000,000 over the previous year's returns. The total amount received from the school-fund during the year 1869-70 was $77,999. Education is making great onward strides, the State University and an Agricultural College being far advanced toward completion. In the matter of railroad communication, Nebraska bids fair to soon place herself on a par with her neighbors to the east. Besides being intersected by the Union Pacific line, with its off-shoot, the Fremont and Blair, other tracks are in course of rapid construction. Organized by Congressional Act into a Territory, May 30, 1854, Nebraska entered the Union as a full State, March 1, 1867. Population, 122,993.

HUNTING PRAIRIE WOLVES IN AN EARLY DAY.

EARLY HISTORY OF ILLINOIS.

The name of this beautiful Prairie State is derived from *Illini*, a Delaware word signifying Superior Men. It has a French termination, and is a symbol of how the two races—the French and the Indians—were intermixed during the early history of the country.

The appellation was no doubt well applied to the primitive inhabitants of the soil whose prowess in savage warfare long withstood the combined attacks of the fierce Iroquois on the one side, and the no less savage and relentless Sacs and Foxes on the other. The Illinois were once a powerful confederacy, occupying the most beautiful and fertile region in the great Valley of the Mississippi, which their enemies coveted and struggled long and hard to wrest from them. By the fortunes of war they were diminished in numbers, and finally destroyed. "Starved Rock," on the Illinois River, according to tradition, commemorates their last tragedy, where, it is said, the entire tribe starved rather than surrender.

EARLY DISCOVERIES.

The first European discoveries in Illinois date back over two hundred years. They are a part of that movement which, from the beginning to the middle of the seventeenth century, brought the French Canadian missionaries and fur traders into the Valley of the Mississippi, and which, at a later period, established the civil and ecclesiastical authority of France from the Gulf of St. Lawrence to the Gulf of Mexico, and from the foot-hills of the Alleghanies to the Rocky Mountains.

The great river of the West had been discovered by DeSoto, the Spanish conqueror of Florida, three quarters of a century before the French founded Quebec in 1608, but the Spanish left the country a wilderness, without further exploration or settlement within its borders, in which condition it remained until the Mississippi was discovered by the agents of the French Canadian government, Joliet and Marquette, in 1673. These renowned explorers were not the first white visitors to Illinois. In 1671—two years in advance of them—came Nicholas Perrot to Chicago. He had been sent by Talon as an agent of the Canadian government to

STARVED ROCK, ON THE ILLINOIS RIVER, LA SALLE CO., ILL.

call a great peace convention of Western Indians at Green Bay, preparatory to the movement for the discovery of the Mississippi. It was deemed a good stroke of policy to secure, as far as possible, the friendship and co-operation of the Indians, far and near, before venturing upon an enterprise which their hostility might render disastrous, and which their friendship and assistance would do so much to make successful; and to this end Perrot was sent to call together in council the tribes throughout the Northwest, and to promise them the commerce and protection of the French government. He accordingly arrived at Green Bay in 1671, and procuring an escort of Pottawattamies, proceeded in a bark canoe upon a visit to the Miamis, at Chicago. Perrot was therefore the first European to set foot upon the soil of Illinois.

Still there were others before Marquette. In 1672, the Jesuit missionaries, Fathers Claude Allouez and Claude Dablon, bore the standard of the Cross from their mission at Green Bay through western Wisconsin and northern Illinois, visiting the Foxes on Fox River, and the Masquotines and Kickapoos at the mouth of the Milwaukee. These missionaries penetrated on the route afterwards followed by Marquette as far as the Kickapoo village at the head of Lake Winnebago, where Marquette, in his journey, secured guides across the portage to the Wisconsin.

The oft-repeated story of Marquette and Joliet is well known. They were the agents employed by the Canadian government to discover the Mississippi. Marquette was a native of France, born in 1637, a Jesuit priest by education, and a man of simple faith and of great zeal and devotion in extending the Roman Catholic religion among the Indians. Arriving in Canada in 1666, he was sent as a missionary to the far Northwest, and, in 1668, founded a mission at Sault Ste. Marie. The following year he moved to La Pointe, in Lake Superior, where he instructed a branch of the Hurons till 1670, when he removed south, and founded the mission at St. Ignace, on the Straits of Mackinaw. Here he remained, devoting a portion of his time to the study of the Illinois language under a native teacher who had accompanied him to the mission from La Pointe, till he was joined by Joliet in the Spring of 1673. By the way of Green Bay and the Fox and Wisconsin Rivers, they entered the Mississippi, which they explored to the mouth of the Arkansas, and returned by the way of the Illinois and Chicago Rivers to Lake Michigan.

On his way up the Illinois, Marquette visited the great village of the Kaskaskias, near what is now Utica, in the county of LaSalle. The following year he returned and established among them the mission of the Immaculate Virgin Mary, which was the first Jesuit mission founded in Illinois and in the Mississippi Valley. The intervening winter he had spent in a hut which his companions erected on the Chicago River, a few leagues from its mouth. The founding of this mission was the last act of Marquette's life. He died in Michigan, on his way back to Green Bay, May 18, 1675.

FIRST FRENCH OCCUPATION.

The first French occupation of the territory now embraced in Illinois was effected by LaSalle in 1680, seven years after the time of Marquette and Joliet. LaSalle, having constructed a vessel, the "Griffin," above the falls of Niagara, which he sailed to Green Bay, and having passed thence in canoes to the mouth of the St. Joseph River, by which and the Kankakee he reached the Illinois, in January, 1680, erected Fort *Crevecœur*, at the lower end of Peoria Lake, where the city of Peoria is now situated. The place where this ancient fort stood may still be seen just below the outlet of Peoria Lake. It was destined, however, to a temporary existence. From this point, LaSalle determined to descend the Mississippi to its mouth, but did not accomplish this purpose till two years later—in 1682. Returning to Fort Frontenac for the purpose of getting materials with which to rig his vessel, he left the fort in charge of Tonti, his lieutenant, who during his absence was driven off by the Iroquois Indians. These savages had made a raid upon the settlement of the Illinois, and had left nothing in their track but ruin and desolation. Mr. Davidson, in his History of Illinois, gives the following graphic account of the picture that met the eyes of LaSalle and his companions on their return:

"At the great town of the Illinois they were appalled at the scene which opened to their view. No hunter appeared to break its death-like silence with a salutatory whoop of welcome. The plain on which the town had stood was now strewn with charred fragments of lodges, which had so recently swarmed with savage life and hilarity. To render more hideous the picture of desolation, large numbers of skulls had been placed on the upper extremities of lodge-poles which had escaped the devouring flames. In the midst of these horrors was the rude fort of the spoilers, rendered frightful by the same ghastly relics. A near approach showed that the graves had been robbed of their bodies, and swarms of buzzards were discovered glutting their loathsome stomachs on the reeking corruption. To complete the work of destruction, the growing corn of the village had been cut down and burned, while the pits containing the products of previous years, had been rifled and their contents scattered with wanton waste. It was evident the suspected blow of the Iroquois had fallen with relentless fury."

Tonti had escaped LaSalle knew not whither. Passing down the lake in search of him and his men, LaSalle discovered that the fort had been destroyed, but the vessel which he had partly constructed was still on the stocks, and but slightly injured. After further fruitless search, failing to find Tonti, he fastened to a tree a painting representing himself and party sitting in a canoe and bearing a pipe of peace, and to the painting attached a letter addressed to Tonti.

Tonti had escaped, and, after untold privations, taken shelter among the Pottawattamies near Green Bay. These were friendly to the French. One of their old chiefs used to say, "There were but three great captains in the world, himself, Tonti and LaSalle."

GENIUS OF LaSALLE.

We must now return to LaSalle, whose exploits stand out in such bold relief. He was born in Rouen, France, in 1643. His father was wealthy, but he renounced his patrimony on entering a college of the Jesuits, from which he separated and came to Canada a poor man in 1666. The priests of St. Sulpice, among whom he had a brother, were then the proprietors of Montreal, the nucleus of which was a seminary or convent founded by that order. The Superior granted to LaSalle a large tract of land at LaChine, where he established himself in the fur trade. He was a man of daring genius, and outstripped all his competitors in exploits of travel and commerce with the Indians. In 1669, he visited the headquarters of the great Iroquois Confederacy, at Onondaga, in the heart of New York, and, obtaining guides, explored the Ohio River to the falls at Louisville.

In order to understand the genius of LaSalle, it must be remembered that for many years prior to his time the missionaries and traders were obliged to make their way to the Northwest by the Ottawa River (of Canada) on account of the fierce hostility of the Iroquois along the lower lakes and Niagara River, which entirely closed this latter route to the Upper Lakes. They carried on their commerce chiefly by canoes, paddling them through the Ottawa to Lake Nipissing, carrying them across the portage to French River, and descending that to Lake Huron. This being the route by which they reached the Northwest, accounts for the fact that all the earliest Jesuit missions were established in the neighborhood of the Upper Lakes. LaSalle conceived the grand-idea of opening the route by Niagara River and the Lower Lakes to Canadian commerce by sail vessels, connecting it with the navigation of the Mississippi, and thus opening a magnificent water communication from the Gulf of St. Lawrence to the Gulf of Mexico. This truly grand and comprehensive purpose seems to have animated him in all his wonderful achievements and the matchless difficulties and hardships he surmounted. As the first step in the accomplishment of this object he established himself on Lake Ontario, and built and garrisoned Fort Frontenac, the site of the present city of Kingston, Canada. Here he obtained a grant of land from the French crown and a body of troops by which he beat back the invading Iroquois and cleared the passage to Niagara Falls. Having by this masterly stroke made it safe to attempt a hitherto untried expedition, his next step, as we have seen, was to advance to the Falls with all his outfit for building a ship with which to sail the lakes. He was successful in this undertaking, though his ultimate purpose was defeated by a strange combination of untoward circumstances. The Jesuits evidently hated LaSalle and plotted against him, because he had abandoned them and co-operated with a rival order. The fur traders were also jealous of his superior success in opening new channels of commerce. At LaChine he had taken the trade of Lake Ontario, which but for his presence there would have gone to Quebec. While they were plodding with their bark canoes through the Ottawa he was constructing sailing vessels to command the trade of the lakes and the Mississippi. These great plans excited the jealousy and envy of the small traders, introduced treason and revolt into the ranks of his own companions, and finally led to the foul assassination by which his great achievements were prematurely ended.

In 1682, LaSalle, having completed his vessel at Peoria, descended the Mississippi to its confluence with the Gulf of Mexico. Erecting a standard on which he inscribed the arms of France, he took formal possession of the whole valley of the mighty river, in the name of Louis XIV., then reigning, in honor of whom he named the country LOUISIANA.

LaSalle then went to France, was appointed Governor, and returned with a fleet and immigrants, for the purpose of planting a colony in Illinois. They arrived in due time in the Gulf of Mexico, but failing to find the mouth of the Mississippi, up which LaSalle intended to sail, his supply ship, with the immigrants, was driven ashore and wrecked on Matagorda Bay. With the fragments of the vessel he constructed a stockade and rude huts on the shore for the protection of the immigrants, calling the post Fort St. Louis. He then made a trip into New Mexico, in search of silver mines, but, meeting with disappointment, returned to find his little colony reduced to forty souls. He then resolved to travel on foot to Illinois, and, starting with his companions, had reached the valley of the Colorado, near the mouth of Trinity river, when he was shot by one of his men. This occurred on the 19th of March, 1687.

Dr. J. W. Foster remarks of him: "Thus fell, not far from the banks of the Trinity, Robert Cavalier de la Salle, one of the grandest characters that ever figured in American history—a man capable of originating the vastest schemes, and endowed with a will and a judgment capable of carrying them to successful results. Had ample facilities been placed by the King of France at his disposal, the result of the colonization of this continent might have been far different from what we now behold."

BELVIDERE.

EARLY SETTLEMENTS.

A temporary settlement was made at Fort St. Louis, or the old Kaskaskia village, on the Illinois River, in what is now LaSalle County, in 1682. In 1690, this was removed, with the mission connected with it, to Kaskaskia, on the river of that name, emptying into the lower Mississippi in St. Clair County. Cahokia was settled about the same time, or at least, both of these settlements began in the year 1690, though it is now pretty well settled that Cahokia is the older place, and ranks as the oldest permanent settlement in Illinois, as well as in the Mississippi Valley. The reason for the removal of the old Kaskaskia settlement and mission, was probably because the dangerous and difficult route by Lake Michigan and the Chicago portage had been almost abandoned, and travelers and traders passed down and up the Mississippi by the Fox and Wisconsin River route. They removed to the vicinity of the Mississippi in order to be in the line of travel from Canada to Louisiana, that is, the lower part of it, for it was all Louisiana then south of the lakes.

During the period of French rule in Louisiana, the population probably never exceeded ten thousand, including whites and blacks. Within that portion of it now included in Indiana, trading posts were established at the principal Miami villages which stood on the head waters of the Maumee, the Wea villages situated at Ouiatenon, on the Wabash, and the Piankeshaw villages at Post Vincennes; all of which were probably visited by French traders and missionaries before the close of the seventeenth century.

In the vast territory claimed by the French, many settlements of considerable importance had sprung up. Biloxi, on Mobile Bay, had been founded by D'Iberville, in 1699; Antoine de Lamotte Cadillac had founded Detroit in 1701; and New Orleans had been founded by Bienville, under the auspices of the Mississippi Company, in 1718. In Illinois also, considerable settlements had been made, so that in 1730 they embraced one hundred and forty French families, about six hundred "converted Indians," and many traders and voyageurs. In that portion of the country, on the east side of the Mississippi, there were five distinct settlements, with their respective villages, viz.: Cahokia, near the mouth of Cahokia Creek and about five miles below the present city of St. Louis; St. Philip, about forty-five miles below Cahokia, and four miles above Fort Chartres; Fort Chartres, twelve miles above Kaskaskia; Kaskaskia, situated on the Kaskaskia River, five miles above its confluence with the Mississippi; and Prairie du Rocher, near Fort Chartres. To these must be added St. Genevieve and St. Louis, on the west side of the Mississippi. These, with the exception of St. Louis, are among

AN EARLY SETTLEMENT.

the oldest French towns in the Mississippi Valley. Kaskaskia, in its best days, was a town of some two or three thousand inhabitants. After it passed from the crown of France its population for many years did not exceed fifteen hundred. Under British rule, in 1773, the population had decreased to four hundred and fifty. As early as 1721, the Jesuits had established a college and a monastery in Kaskaskia.

Fort Chartres was first built under the direction of the Mississippi Company, in 1718, by M. de Boisbraint, a military officer, under command of Bienville. It stood on the east bank of the Mississippi, about eighteen miles below Kaskaskia, and was for some time the headquarters of the military commandants of the district of Illinois.

In the Centennial Oration of Dr. Fowler, delivered at Philadelphia, by appointment of Gov. Beveridge, we find some interesting facts with regard to the State of Illinois, which we appropriate in this history:

In 1682 Illinois became a possession of the French crown, a dependency of Canada, and a part of Louisiana. In 1765 the English flag was run up on old Fort Chartres, and Illinois was counted among the treasures of Great Britain.

In 1779 it was taken from the English by Col. George Rogers Clark. This man was resolute in nature, wise in council, prudent in policy, bold in action, and heroic in danger. Few men who have figured in the history of America are more deserving than this colonel. Nothing short of first-class ability could have rescued Vincens and all Illinois from the English. And it is not possible to over-estimate the influence of this achievement upon the republic. In 1779 Illinois became a part of Virginia. It was soon known as Illinois County. In 1784 Virginia ceded all this territory to the general government, to be cut into States, to be republican in form, with "the same right of sovereignty, freedom, and independence as the other States."

In 1787 it was the object of the wisest and ablest legislation found in any merely human records. No man can study the secret history of

THE "COMPACT OF 1787,"

and not feel that Providence was guiding with sleepless eye these unborn States. The ordinance that on July 13, 1787, finally became the incorporating act, has a most marvelous history. Jefferson had vainly tried to secure a system of government for the northwestern territory. He was an emancipationist of that day, and favored the exclusion of slavery from the territory Virginia had ceded to the general government; but the South voted him down as often as it came up. In 1787, as late as July 10, an organizing act without the anti-slavery clause was pending. This concession to the South was expected to carry it. Congress was in session in New York City. On July 5, Rev. Dr. Manasseh Cutler, of Massachusetts, came into New York to lobby on the northwestern territory. Everything seemed to fall into his hands. Events were ripe.

The state of the public credit, the growing of Southern prejudice, the basis of his mission, his personal character, all combined to complete one of those sudden and marvelous revolutions of public sentiment that once in five or ten centuries are seen to sweep over a country like the breath of the Almighty. Cutler was a graduate of Yale—received his A.M. from Harvard, and his D.D. from Yale. He had studied and taken degrees in the three learned professions, medicine, law, and divinity. He had thus America's best indorsement. He had published a scientific examination of the plants of New England. His name stood second only to that of Franklin as a scientist in America. He was a courtly gentleman of the old style, a man of commanding presence, and of inviting face. The Southern members said they had never seen such a gentleman in the North. He came representing a company that desired to purchase a tract of land now included in Ohio, for the purpose of planting a colony. It was a speculation. Government money was worth eighteen cents on the dollar. This Massachusetts company had collected enough to purchase 1,500,000 acres of land. Other speculators in New York made Dr. Cutler their agent (lobbyist). On the 12th he represented a demand for 5,500,000 acres. This would reduce the national debt. Jefferson and Virginia were regarded as authority concerning the land Virginia had just ceded. Jefferson's policy wanted to provide for the public credit, and this was a good opportunity to do something.

Massachusetts then owned the territory of Maine, which she was crowding on the market. She was opposed to opening the northwestern region. This fired the zeal of Virginia. The South caught the inspiration, and all exalted Dr. Cutler. The English minister invited him to dine with some of the Southern gentlemen. He was the center of interest.

The entire South rallied round him. Massachusetts could not vote against him, because many of the constituents of her members were interested personally in the western speculation. Thus Cutler, making friends with the South, and, doubtless, using all the arts of the lobby, was enabled to command the situation. True to deeper convictions, he dictated one of the most compact and finished documents of wise statesmanship that has ever adorned any human law book. He borrowed from Jefferson the term "Articles of Compact," which, preceding the federal constitution, rose into the most sacred character. He then followed very closely the constitution of Massachusetts, adopted three years before. Its most marked points were:

1. The exclusion of slavery from the territory forever.
2. Provision for public schools, giving one township for a seminary,

and every section numbered 16 in each township; that is, one-thirty-sixth of all the land, for public schools.

3. A provision prohibiting the adoption of any constitution or the enactment of any law that should nullify pre-existing contracts.

Be it forever remembered that this compact declared that "Religion, morality, and knowledge being necessary to good government and the happiness of mankind, schools and the means of education shall always be encouraged."

Dr. Cutler planted himself on this platform and would not yield. Giving his unqualified declaration that it was that or nothing—that unless they could make the land desirable they did not want it—he took his horse and buggy, and started for the constitutional convention in Philadelphia. On July 13, 1787, the bill was put upon its passage, and was unanimously adopted, every Southern member voting for it, and only one man, Mr. Yates, of New York, voting against it. But as the States voted as States, Yates lost his vote, and the compact was put beyond repeal.

Thus the great States of Ohio, Indiana, Illinois, Michigan and Wisconsin—a vast empire, the heart of the great valley—were consecrated to freedom, intelligence, and honesty. Thus the great heart of the nation was prepared for a year and a day and an hour. In the light of these eighty-nine years I affirm that this act was the salvation of the republic and the destruction of slavery. Soon the South saw their great blunder, and tried to repeal the compact. In 1803 Congress referred it to a committee of which John Randolph was chairman. He reported that this ordinance was a compact, and opposed repeal. Thus it stood a rock, in the way of the on-rushing sea of slavery.

With all this timely aid it was, after all, a most desperate and protracted struggle to keep the soil of Illinois sacred to freedom. It was the natural battle-field for the irrepressible conflict. In the southern end of the State slavery preceded the compact. It existed among the old French settlers, and was hard to eradicate. The southern part of the State was settled from the slave States, and this population brought their laws, customs, and institutions with them. A stream of population from the North poured into the northern part of the State. These sections misunderstood and hated each other perfectly. The Southerners regarded the Yankees as a skinning, tricky, penurious race of peddlers, filling the country with tinware, brass clocks, and wooden nutmegs. The Northerner thought of the Southerner as a lean, lank, lazy creature, burrowing in a hut, and rioting in whisky, dirt and ignorance. These causes aided in making the struggle long and bitter. So strong was the sympathy with slavery that, in spite of the ordinance of 1787, and in spite of the deed of cession, it was determined to allow the old French settlers to retain their slaves. Planters from the slave States might bring their slaves, if they would give them a chance to choose freedom or years of service and bondage for their children till they should become thirty years of age. If they chose freedom they must leave the State in sixty days or be sold as fugitives. Servants were whipped for offenses for which white men are fined. Each lash paid forty cents of the fine. A negro ten miles from home without a pass was whipped. These famous laws were imported from the slave States just as they imported laws for the inspection of flax and wool when there was neither in the State.

These Black Laws are now wiped out. A vigorous effort was made to protect slavery in the State Constitution of 1817. It barely failed. It was renewed in 1825, when a convention was asked to make a new constitution. After a hard fight the convention was defeated. But slaves did not disappear from the census of the State until 1850. There were mobs and murders in the interest of slavery. Lovejoy was added to the list of martyrs—a sort of first-fruits of that long life of immortal heroes who saw freedom as the one supreme desire of their souls, and were so enamored of her that they preferred to die rather than survive her.

The population of 12,282 that occupied the territory in A.D. 1800, increased to 45,000 in A.D. 1818, when the State Constitution was adopted, and Illinois took her place in the Union, with a star on the flag and two votes in the Senate.

Shadrach Bond was the first Governor, and in his first message he recommended the construction of the Illinois and Michigan Canal.

The simple economy in those days is seen in the fact that the entire bill for stationery for the first Legislature was only $13.50. Yet this simple body actually enacted a very superior code.

There was no money in the territory before the war of 1812. Deer skins and coon skins were the circulating medium. In 1821, the Legislature ordained a State Bank on the credit of the State. It issued notes in the likeness of bank bills. These notes were made a legal tender for every thing, and the bank was ordered to loan to the people $100 on personal security, and more on mortgages. They actually passed a resolution requesting the Secretary of the Treasury of the United States to receive these notes for land. The old French Lieutenant Governor, Col. Menard, put the resolution as follows: "Gentlemen of the Senate: It is moved and seconded *dat de notes of dis bank* be made land-office money. All in favor of dat motion say aye; all against it say no. It is decided in de affirmative. Now, gentlemen, I bet you one hundred dollar he never be land-office money!" Hard sense, like hard money, is always above par.

This old Frenchman presents a fine figure up against the dark background of most of his nation. They made no progress. They clung to their earliest and simplest implements. They never wore hats or caps

They pulled their blankets over their heads in the winter like the Indians, with whom they freely intermingled.

Demagogism had an early development. One John Grammar (only in name), elected to the Territorial and State Legislatures of 1816 and 1836, invented the policy of opposing every new thing, saying, "If it succeeds, no one will ask who voted against it. If it proves a failure, he could quote its record." In sharp contrast with Grammar was the character of D. P. Cook, after whom the county containing Chicago was named. Such was his transparent integrity and remarkable ability that his will was almost the law of the State. In Congress, a young man, and from a poor State, he was made Chairman of the Ways and Means Committee. He was pre-eminent for standing by his committee, regardless of consequences. It was his integrity that elected John Quincy Adams to the Presidency. There were four candidates in 1824, Jackson, Clay, Crawford, and John Quincy Adams. There being no choice by the people, the election was thrown into the House. It was so balanced that it turned on his vote, and that he cast for Adams, electing him; then went home to face the wrath of the Jackson party in Illinois. It cost him all but character and greatness. It is a suggestive comment on the times, that there was no legal interest till 1830. It often reached 150 per cent., usually 50 per cent. Then it was reduced to 12, and now to 10 per cent.

PHYSICAL FEATURES OF THE PRAIRIE STATE.

In area the State has 55,410 square miles of territory. It is about 150 miles wide and 400 miles long, stretching in latitude from Maine to North Carolina. It embraces wide variety of climate. It is tempered on the north by the great inland, saltless, tideless sea, which keeps the thermometer from either extreme. Being a table land, from 600 to 1,600 feet above the level of the sea, one is prepared to find on the health maps, prepared by the general government, an almost clean and perfect record. In freedom from fever and malarial diseases and consumptions, the three deadly enemies of the American Saxon, Illinois, as a State, stands without a superior. She furnishes one of the essential conditions of a great people—sound bodies. I suspect that this fact lies back of that old Delaware word, Illini, superior men.

The great battles of history that have been determinative of dynasties and destinies have been strategical battles, chiefly the question of position. Thermopylæ has been the war-cry of freemen for twenty-four centuries. It only tells how much there may be in position. All this advantage belongs to Illinois. It is in the heart of the greatest valley in the world, the vast region between the mountains—a valley that could feed mankind for one thousand years. It is well on toward the center of the continent. It is in the great temperate belt, in which have been found nearly all the aggressive civilizations of history. It has sixty-five miles of frontage on the head of the lake. With the Mississippi forming the western and southern boundary, with the Ohio running along the southeastern line, with the Illinois River and Canal dividing the State diagonally from the lake to the Lower Mississippi, and with the Rock and Wabash Rivers furnishing altogether 2,000 miles of water-front, connecting with, and running through, in all about 12,000 miles of navigable water.

But this is not all. These waters are made most available by the fact that the lake and the State lie on the ridge running into the great valley from the east. Within cannon-shot of the lake the water runs away from the lake to the Gulf. The lake now empties at both ends, one into the Atlantic and one into the Gulf of Mexico. The lake thus seems to hang over the land. This makes the dockage most serviceable; there are no steep banks to damage it. Both lake and river are made for use.

The climate varies from Portland to Richmond; it favors every product of the continent, including the tropics, with less than half a dozen exceptions. It produces every great nutriment of the world except bananas and rice. It is hardly too much to say that it is the most productive spot known to civilization. With the soil full of bread and the earth full of minerals; with an upper surface of food and an under layer of fuel; with perfect natural drainage, and abundant springs and streams and navigable rivers; half way between the forests of the North and the fruits of the South; within a day's ride of the great deposits of iron, coal, copper, lead, and zinc; containing and controlling the great grain, cattle, pork, and lumber markets of the world, it is not strange that Illinois has the advantage of position.

This advantage has been supplemented by the character of the population. In the early days when Illinois was first admitted to the Union, her population were chiefly from Kentucky and Virginia. But, in the conflict of ideas concerning slavery, a strong tide of emigration came in from the East, and soon changed this composition. In 1870 her non-native population were from colder soils. New York furnished 133,290; Ohio gave 162,623; Pennsylvania sent on 98,352; the entire South gave us only 206,734. In all her cities, and in all her German and Scandinavian and other foreign colonies, Illinois has only about one-fifth of her people of foreign birth.

PROGRESS OF DEVELOPMENT.

One of the greatest elements in the early development of Illinois is the Illinois and Michigan Canal, connecting the Illinois and Mississippi Rivers with the lakes. It was of the utmost importance to the State. It was recommended by Gov. Bond, the first governor, in his first message. In 1821, the Legislature appropriated $10,000 for surveying the route. Two bright young engineers surveyed it, and estimated the cost at $600,000 or $700,000. It finally cost $8,000,000. In 1825, a law was passed to incorporate the Canal Company, but no stock was sold. In 1826, upon the solicitation of Cook, Congress gave 800,000 acres of land on the line of the work. In 1828, another law—commissioners appointed, and work commenced with new survey and new estimates. In 1834-35, George Farquhar made an able report on the whole matter. This was, doubtless, the ablest report ever made to a western legislature, and it became the model for subsequent reports and action. From this the work went on till it was finished in 1848. It cost the State a large amount of money; but it gave to the industries of the State an impetus that pushed it up into the first rank of greatness. It was not built as a speculation any more than a doctor is employed on a speculation. But it has paid into the Treasury of the State an average annual net sum of over $111,000.

Pending the construction of the canal, the land and town-lot fever broke out in the State, in 1834-35. It took on the malignant type in Chicago, lifting the town up into a city. The disease spread over the entire State and adjoining States. It was epidemic. It cut up men's farms without regard to locality, and cut up the purses of the purchasers without regard to consequences. It is estimated that building lots enough were sold in Indiana alone to accommodate every citizen then in the United States.

Towns and cities were exported to the Eastern market by the ship-load. There was no lack of buyers. Every up-ship came freighted with speculators and their money.

This distemper seized upon the Legislature in 1836-37, and left not one to tell the tale. They enacted a system of internal improvement without a parallel in the grandeur of its conception. They ordered the construction of 1,300 miles of railroad, crossing the State in all directions. This was surpassed by the river and canal improvements. There were a few counties not touched by either railroad or river or canal, and those were to be comforted and compensated by the free distribution of $200,000 among them. To inflate this balloon beyond credence it was ordered that work should be commenced on both ends of each of these railroads and rivers, and at each river-crossing, all at the same time. The appropriations for these vast improvements were over $12,000,000, and commissioners were appointed to borrow the money on the credit of the State. Remember that all this was in the early days of railroading, when railroads were luxuries; that the State had whole counties with scarcely a cabin; and that the population of the State was less than 400,000, and you can form some idea of the vigor with which these brave men undertook the work of making a great State. In the light of history I am compelled to say that this was only a premature throb of the power that actually slumbered in the soil of the State. It was Hercules in the cradle.

At this juncture the State Bank loaned its funds largely to Godfrey Gilman & Co., and to other leading houses, for the purpose of drawing trade from St. Louis to Alton. Soon they failed, and took down the bank with them.

In 1840, all hope seemed gone. A population of 480,000 were loaded with a debt of $14,000,000. It had only six small cities, really only towns, namely: Chicago, Alton, Springfield, Quincy, Galena, Nauvoo. This debt was to be cared for when there was not a dollar in the treasury, and when the State had borrowed itself out of all credit, and when there was not good money enough in the hands of all the people to pay the interest of the debt for a single year. Yet, in the presence of all these difficulties, the young State steadily refused to repudiate. Gov. Ford took hold of the problem and solved it, bringing the State through in triumph.

Having touched lightly upon some of the more distinctive points in the history of the development of Illinois, let us next briefly consider the

MATERIAL RESOURCES OF THE STATE.

It is a garden four hundred miles long and one hundred and fifty miles wide. Its soil is chiefly a black sandy loam, from six inches to sixty feet thick. On the American bottoms it has been cultivated for one hundred and fifty years without renewal. About the old French towns it has yielded corn for a century and a half without rest or help. It produces nearly everything green in the temperate and tropical zones. She leads all other States in the number of acres actually under plow. Her products from 25,000,000 of acres are incalculable. Her mineral wealth is scarcely second to her agricultural power. She has coal, iron, lead, copper, zinc, many varieties of building stone, fire clay, cuma clay, common brick clay, sand of all kinds, gravel, mineral paint—every thing needed for a high civilization. Left to herself, she has the elements of all greatness. The single item of coal is too vast for an appreciative handling in figures. We can handle it in general terms like algebraical signs, but long before we get up into the millions and billions the human mind drops down from comprehension to mere symbolic apprehension.

When I tell you that nearly four-fifths of the entire State is underlaid with a deposit of coal more than forty feet thick on the average (now estimated, by recent surveys, at seventy feet thick), you can get some idea of its amount, as you do of the amount of the national debt. There it is! 41,000 square miles—one vast mine into which you could put any of the States; in which you could bury scores of European and ancient empires, and have room enough all round to work without knowing that they had been sepulchered there.

Put this vast coal-bed down by the other great coal deposits of the world, and its importance becomes manifest. Great Britain has 12,000 square miles of coal; Spain, 3,000; France, 1,719; Belgium, 578; Illinois about twice as many square miles as all combined. Virginia has 20,000 square miles; Pennsylvania, 16,000; Ohio, 12,000. Illinois has 41,000 square miles. One-seventh of all the known coal on this continent is in Illinois.

Could we sell the coal in this single State for one-seventh of one cent a ton it would pay the national debt. Converted into power, even with the wastage in our common engines, it would do more work than could be done by the entire race, beginning at Adam's wedding and working ten hours a day through all the centuries till the present time, and right on into the future at the same rate for the next 600,000 years.

Great Britain uses enough mechanical power to-day to give to each man, woman, and child in the kingdom the help and service of nineteen untiring servants. No wonder she has leisure and luxuries. No wonder the home of the common artisan has in it more luxuries than could be found in the palace of good old King Arthur. Think, if you can conceive of it, of the vast army of servants that slumber in the soil of Illinois, impatiently awaiting the call of Genius to come forth to minister to our comfort.

At the present rate of consumption England's coal supply will be exhausted in 250 years. When this is gone she must transfer her dominion either to the Indies, or to British America, which I would not resist; or to some other people, which I would regret as a loss to civilization.

COAL IS KING.

At the same rate of consumption (which far exceeds our own) the deposit of coal in Illinois will last 120,000 years. And her kingdom shall be an everlasting kingdom.

Let us turn now from this reserve power to the *annual products* of the State. We shall not be humiliated in this field. Here we strike the secret of our national credit. Nature provides a market in the constant appetite of the race. Men must eat, and if we can furnish the provisions we can command the treasure. All that a man hath will he give for his life.

According to the last census Illinois produced 30,000,000 of bushels of wheat. That is more wheat than was raised by any other State in the Union. She raised In 1875, 130,000,000 of bushels of corn—twice as much as any other State, and one-sixth of all the corn raised in the United States. She harvested 2,747,000 tons of hay, nearly one-tenth of all the hay in the Republic. It is not generally appreciated, but it is true, that the hay crop of the country is worth more than the cotton crop. The hay of Illinois equals the cotton of Louisiana. Go to Charleston, S. C., and see them peddling handfuls of hay or grass, almost as a curiosity, as we regard Chinese gods or the cryolite of Greenland; drink your coffee and *condensed milk;* and walk back from the coast for many a league through the sand and burs till you get up into the better atmosphere of the mountains, without seeing a waving meadow or a grazing herd; then you will begin to appreciate the meadows of the Prairie State, where the grass often grows sixteen feet high.

The value of her farm implements is $211,000,000, and the value of her live stock is only second to the great State of New York. In 1875 she had 25,000,000 hogs, and packed 2,113,845, about one-half of all that were packed in the United States. This is no insignificant item. Pork is a growing demand of the old world. Since the laborers of Europe have gotten a taste of our bacon, and we have learned how to pack it dry in boxes, like dry goods, the world has become the market.

The hog is on the march into the future. His nose is ordained to uncover the secrets of dominion, and his feet shall be guided by the star of empire.

Illinois marketed $57,000,000 worth of slaughtered animals—more than any other State, and a seventh of all the States.

Be patient with me, and pardon my pride, and I will give you a list of some of the things in which Illinois excels all other States.

Depth and richness of soil; per cent. of good ground; acres of improved land; large farms—some farms contain from 40,000 to 60,000 acres of cultivated land, 40,000 acres of corn on a single farm; number of farmers; amount of wheat, corn, oats and honey produced; value of animals for slaughter; number of hogs; amount of pork; number of horses —three times as many as Kentucky, the horse State.

Illinois excels all other States in miles of railroads and in miles of postal service, and in money orders sold per annum, and in the amount of lumber sold in her markets.

Illinois is only second in many important matters. This sample list comprises a few of the more important: Permanent school fund (good for a young state); total income for educational purposes; number of publishers of books, maps, papers, etc.; value of farm products and implements, and of live stock; in tons of coal mined.

The shipping of Illinois is only second to New York. Out of one port during the business hours of the season of navigation she sends forth a vessel every ten minutes. This does not include canal boats, which go one every five minutes. No wonder she is only second in number of bankers and brokers or in physicians and surgeons.

She is third in colleges, teachers and schools; cattle, lead, hay, flax, sorghum and beeswax.

She is fourth in population, in children enrolled in public schools, in law schools, in butter, potatoes and carriages.

She is fifth in value of real and personal property, in theological seminaries and colleges exclusively for women, in milk sold, and in boots and shoes manufactured, and in book-binding.

She is only seventh in the production of wood, while she is the twelfth in area. Surely that is well done for the Prairie State. She now has much more wood and growing timber than she had thirty years ago.

A few leading industries will justify emphasis. She manufactures $205,000,000 worth of goods, which places her well up toward New York and Pennsylvania. The number of her manufacturing establishments increased from 1860 to 1870, 300 per cent.; capital employed increased 350 per cent., and the amount of product increased 400 per cent. She issued 5,500,000 copies of commercial and financial newspapers—only second to New York. She has 6,759 miles of railroad, thus leading all other States, worth $636,458,000, using 3,245 engines, and 67,712 cars, making a train long enough to cover one-tenth of the entire roads of the State. Her stations are only five miles apart. She carried last year 15,795,000 passengers, an average of 36½ miles, or equal to taking her entire population twice across the State. More than two-thirds of her land is within five miles of a railroad, and less than two per cent. is more than fifteen miles away.

The State has a large financial interest in the Illinois Central railroad. The road was incorporated in 1850, and the State gave each alternate section for six miles on each side, and doubled the price of the remaining land, so keeping herself good. The road received 2,595,000 acres of land, and pays to the State one-seventh of the gross receipts. The State receives this year $350,000, and has received in all about $7,000,000. It is practically the people's road, and it has a most able and gentlemanly management. Add to this the annual receipts from the canal, $111,000, and a large per cent. of the State tax is provided for.

THE RELIGION AND MORALS

of the State keep step with her productions and growth. She was born of the missionary spirit. It was a minister who secured for her the ordinance of 1787, by which she has been saved from slavery, ignorance, and dishonesty. Rev. Mr. Wiley, pastor of a Scotch congregation in Randolph County, petitioned the Constitutional Convention of 1818 to recognize Jesus Christ as king, and the Scriptures as the only necessary guide and book of law. The convention did not act in the case, and the old Covenanters refused to accept citizenship. They never voted until 1824, when the slavery question was submitted to the people; then they all voted against it and cast the determining votes. Conscience has predominated whenever a great moral question has been submitted to the people.

But little mob violence has ever been felt in the State. In 1817 regulators disposed of a band of horse-thieves that infested the territory. The Mormon indignities finally awoke the same spirit. Alton was also the scene of a pro-slavery mob, in which Lovejoy was added to the list of martyrs. The moral sense of the people makes the law supreme, and gives to the State unruffled peace.

With $22,300,000 in church property, and 4,298 church organizations, the State has that divine police, the sleepless patrol of moral ideas, that alone is able to secure perfect safety. Conscience takes the knife from the assassin's hand and the bludgeon from the grasp of the highwayman. We sleep in safety, not because we are behind bolts and bars—these only fence against the innocent; not because a lone officer drowses on a distant corner of a street; not because a sheriff may call his posse from a remote part of the county; but because *conscience* guards the very portals of the air and stirs in the deepest recesses of the public mind. This spirit issues within the State 9,500,000 copies of religious papers annually, and receives still more from without. Thus the crime of the State is only one-fourth that of New York and one-half that of Pennsylvania.

Illinois never had but one duel between her own citizens. In Belleville, in 1820, Alphonso Stewart and William Bennett arranged to vindicate injured honor. The seconds agreed to make it a sham, and make them shoot blanks. Stewart was in the secret. Bennett mistrusted something, and, unobserved, slipped a bullet into his gun and killed Stewart. He then fled the State. After two years he was caught, tried, convicted, and, in spite of friends and political aid, was hung. This fixed the code of honor on a Christian basis, and terminated its use in Illinois.

The early preachers were ignorant men, who were accounted eloquent according to the strength of their voices. But they set the style for all public speakers. Lawyers and political speakers followed this rule. Gov.

Ford says: "Nevertheless, these first preachers were of incalculable benefit to the country. They inculcated justice and morality. To them are we indebted for the first Christian character of the Protestant portion of the people."

In education Illinois surpasses her material resources. The ordinance of 1787 consecrated one thirty-sixth of her soil to common schools, and the law of 1818, the first law that went upon her statutes, gave three per cent. of all the rest to

EDUCATION.

The old compact secures this interest forever, and by its yoking morality and intelligence it precludes the legal interference with the Bible in the public schools. With such a start it is natural that we should have 11,050 schools, and that our illiteracy should be less than New York or Pennsylvania, and only about one-half of Massachusetts. We are not to blame for not having more than one-half as many idiots as the great States. These public schools soon made colleges inevitable. The first college, still flourishing, was started in Lebanon in 1828, by the M. E. church, and named after Bishop McKendree. Illinois College, at Jacksonville, supported by the Presbyterians, followed in 1830. In 1832 the Baptists built Shurtleff College, at Alton. Then the Presbyterians built Knox College, at Galesburg, in 1838, and the Episcopalians built Jubilee College, at Peoria, in 1847. After these early years colleges have rained down. A settler could hardly encamp on the prairie but a college would spring up by his wagon. The State now has one very well endowed and equipped university, namely, the Northwestern University, at Evanston, with six colleges, ninety instructors, over 1,000 students, and $1,500,000 endowment.

Rev. J. M. Peck was the first educated Protestant minister in the State. He settled at Rock Spring, in St. Clair County, 1820, and left his impress on the State. Before 1837 only party papers were published, but Mr. Peck published a Gazetteer of Illinois. Soon after John Russell, of Bluffdale, published essays and tales showing genius. Judge James Hall published *The Illinois Monthly Magazine* with great ability, and an annual called *The Western Souvenir*, which gave him an enviable fame all over the United States. From these beginnings Illinois has gone on till she has more volumes in public libaaries even than Massachusetts, and of the 44,500,000 volumes in all the public libraries of the United States, she has one-thirteenth. In newspapers she stands fourth. Her increase is marvelous. In 1850 she issued 5,000.000 copies; in 1860, 27,590,000; in 1870, 113,140,000. In 1860 she had eighteen colleges and seminaries; in 1870 she had eighty. That is a grand advance for the war decade.

This brings us to a record unsurpassed in the history of any age,

THE WAR RECORD OF ILLINOIS.

I hardly know where to begin, or how to advance, or what to say. I can at best give you only a broken synopsis of her deeds, and you must put them in the order of glory for yourself. Her sons have always been foremost on fields of danger. In 1832-33, at the call of Gov. Reynolds, her sons drove Blackhawk over the Mississippi.

When the Mexican war came, in May, 1846, 8,370 men offered themselves when only 3,720 could be accepted. The fields of Buena Vista and Vera Cruz, and the storming of Cerro Gordo, will carry the glory of Illinois soldiers along after the infamy of the cause they served has been forgotten. But it was reserved till our day for her sons to find a field and cause and foemen that could fitly illustrate their spirit and heroism. Illinois put into her own regiments for the United States government 256,000 men, and into the army through other States enough to swell the number to 290,000. This far exceeds all the soldiers of the federal government in all the war of the revolution. Her total years of service were over 600,000. She enrolled men from eighteen to forty-five years of age when the law of Congress in 1864—the test time—only asked for those from twenty to forty-five. Her enrollment was otherwise excessive. Her people wanted to go, and did not take the pains to correct the enrollment. Thus the basis of fixing the quota was too great, and then the quota itself, at least in the trying time, was far above any other State.

Thus the demand on some counties, as Monroe, for example, took every able-bodied man in the county, and then did not have enough to fill the quota. Moreover, Illinois sent 20,844 men for ninety or one hundred days, for whom no credit was asked. When Mr. Lincoln's attention was called to the inequality of the quota compared with other States, he replied, "The country needs the sacrifice. We must put the whip on the free horse." In spite of all these disadvantages Illinois gave to the country 73,000 years of service above all calls. With one-thirteenth of the population of the loyal States, she sent regularly one-tenth of all the soldiers, and in the peril of the closing calls, when patriots were few and weary, she then sent one-eighth of all that were called for by her loved and honored son in the white house. Her mothers and daughters went into the fields to raise the grain and keep the children together, while the fathers and older sons went to the harvest fields of the world. I knew a father and four sons who agreed that one of them must stay at home; and they pulled straws from a stack to see who might go. The father was left. The next day he came into the camp, saying: "Mother says she can get the crops in, and I am going, too." I know large Methodist churches from which every male member went to the army. Do you want to know what these heroes from Illinois did in the field? Ask any soldier with a good record of his own, who is thus able to judge, and he will tell you that the Illinois men went in to win. It is common history that the greater victories were won in the West. When everything else looked dark Illinois was gaining victories all down the river, and dividing the confederacy. Sherman took with him on his great march forty-five regiments of Illinois infantry, three companies of artillery, and one company of cavalry. He could not avoid

GOING TO THE SEA.

If he had been killed, I doubt not the men would have gone right on. Lincoln answered all rumors of Sherman's defeat with, "It is impossible; there is a mighty sight of fight in 100,000 Western men." Illinois soldiers brought home 300 battle-flags. The first United States flag that floated over Richmond was an Illinois flag. She sent messengers and nurses to every field and hospital, to care for her sick and wounded sons. She said, "These suffering ones are my sons, and I will care for them."

When individuals had given all, then cities and towns came forward with their credit to the extent of many millions, to aid these men and their families.

Illinois gave the country the great general of the war—Ulysses S. Grant—since honored with two terms of the Presidency of the United States.

One other name from Illinois comes up in all minds, embalmed in all hearts, that must have the supreme place in this story of our glory and of our nation's honor; that name is Abraham Lincoln, of Illinois.

The analysis of Mr. Lincoln's character is difficult on account of its symmetry.

In this age we look with admiration at his uncompromising honesty. And well we may, for this saved us. Thousands throughout the length and breadth of our country who knew him only as "Honest Old Abe," voted for him on that account; and wisely did they choose, for no other man could have carried us through the fearful night of the war. When his plans were too vast for our comprehension, and his faith in the cause too sublime for our participation; when it was all night about us, and all dread before us, and all sad and desolate behind us; when not one ray shone upon our cause; when traitors were haughty and exultant at the South, and fierce and blasphemous at the North; when the loyal men here seemed almost in the minority; when the stoutest heart quailed, the bravest cheek paled; when generals were defeating each other for place, and contractors were leeching out the very heart's blood of the prostrate republic: when every thing else had failed us, we looked at this calm, patient man standing like a rock in the storm, and said: "Mr. Lincoln is honest, and we can trust him still." Holding to this single point with the energy of faith and despair we held together, and, under God, he brought us through to victory.

His practical wisdom made him the wonder of all lands. With such certainty did Mr. Lincoln follow causes to their ultimate effects, that his foresight of contingencies seemed almost prophetic.

He is radiant with all the great virtues, and his memory shall shed a glory upon this age that shall fill the eyes of men as they look into history. Other men have excelled him in some point, but, taken at all points, all in all, he stands head and shoulders above every other man of 6,000 years. An administrator, he saved the nation in the perils of unparalleled civil war. A statesman, he justified his measures by their success. A philanthropist, he gave liberty to one race and salvation to another. A moralist, he bowed from the summit of human power to the foot of the Cross, and became a Christian. A mediator, he exercised mercy under the most absolute abeyance to law. A leader, he was no partisan. A commander, he was untainted with blood. A ruler in desperate times, he was unsullied with crime. A man, he has left no word of passion, no thought of malice, no trick of craft, no act of jealousy, no purpose of selfish ambition. Thus perfected, without a model, and without a peer, he was dropped into these troubled years to adorn and embellish all that is good and all that is great in our humanity, and to present to all coming time the representative of the divine idea of free government.

It is not too much to say that away down in the future, when the republic has fallen from its niche in the wall of time; when the great war itself shall have faded out in the distance like a mist on the horizon; when the Anglo-Saxon language shall be spoken only by the tongue of the stranger; then the generations looking this way shall see the great president as the supreme figure in this vortex of history

CHICAGO.

It is impossible in our brief space to give more than a meager sketch of such a city as Chicago, which is in itself the greatest marvel of the Prairie State. This mysterious, majestic, mighty city, born first of water, and next of fire; sown in weakness, and raised in power; planted among the willows of the marsh, and crowned with the glory of the mountains; sleeping on the bosom of the prairie, and rocked on the bosom of the sea; the youngest city of the world, and still the eye of the prairie, as Damascus, the oldest city of the world, is the eye of the desert. With a commerce far exceeding that of Corinth on her isthmus, in the highway to the East; with the defenses of a continent piled around her by the thousand miles, making her far safer than Rome on the banks of the Tiber;

HISTORY OF THE STATE OF ILLINOIS. 133

CHICAGO IN 1833.

with schools eclipsing Alexandria and Athens; with liberties more conspicuous than those of the old republics; with a heroism equal to the first Carthage, and with a sanctity scarcely second to that of Jerusalem—set your thoughts on all this, lifted into the eyes of all men by the miracle of its growth, illuminated by the flame of its fall, and transfigured by the divinity of its resurrection, and you will feel, as I do, the utter impossibility of compassing this subject as it deserves. Some impression of her importance is received from the shock her burning gave to the civilized world.

When the doubt of her calamity was removed, and the horrid fact was accepted, there went a shudder over all cities, and a quiver over all lands. There was scarcely a town in the civilized world that did not shake on the brink of this opening chasm. The flames of our homes reddened all skies. The city was set upon a hill, and could not be hid. All eyes were turned upon it. To have struggled and suffered amid the scenes of its fall is as distinguishing as to have fought at Thermopylae, or Salamis, or Hastings, or Waterloo, or Bunker Hill.

Its calamity amazed the world, because it was felt to be the common property of mankind.

The early history of the city is full of interest, just as the early history of such a man as Washington or Lincoln becomes public property, and is cherished by every patriot.

Starting with 560 acres in 1833, it embraced and occupied 23,000 acres in 1869, and, having now a population of more than 500,000, it commands general attention.

The first settler—Jean Baptiste Pointe au Sable, a mulatto from the West Indies—came and began trade with the Indians in 1796. John Kinzie became his successor in 1804, in which year Fort Dearborn was erected.

A mere trading-post was kept here from that time till about the time of the Blackhawk war, in 1832. It was not the city. It was merely a cock crowing at midnight. The morning was not yet. In 1833 the settlement about the fort was incorporated as a town. The voters were divided on the propriety of such corporation, twelve voting for it and one against it. Four years later it was incorporated as a city, and embraced 560 acres.

The produce handled in this city is an indication of its power. Grain and flour were imported from the East till as late as 1837. The first exportation by way of experiment was in 1839. Exports exceeded imports first in 1842. The Board of Trade was organized in 1848, but it was so weak that it needed nursing till 1855. Grain was purchased by the wagon-load in the street.

I remember sitting with my father on a load of wheat, in the long line of wagons along Lake street, while the buyers came and untied the bags, and examined the grain, and made their bids. That manner of business had to cease with the day of small things. Now our elevators will hold 15,000,000 bushels of grain. The cash value of the produce handled in a year is $215,000,000, and the produce weighs 7,000,000 tons or 700,000 car loads. This handles thirteen and a half ton each minute, all the year round. One tenth of all the wheat in the United States is handled in Chicago. Even as long ago as 1853 the receipts of grain in Chicago exceeded those of the goodly city of St. Louis, and in 1854 the exports of grain from Chicago exceeded those of New York and doubled those of St. Petersburg, Archangel, or Odessa, the largest grain markets in Europe.

The manufacturing interests of the city are not contemptible. In 1873 manufactories employed 45,000 operatives; in 1876, 60,000. The manufactured product in 1875 was worth $177,000,000.

No estimate of the size and power of Chicago would be adequate that did not put large emphasis on the railroads. Before they came thundering along our streets canals were the hope of our country. But who ever thinks now of traveling by canal packets? In June, 1852, there were only forty miles of railroad connected with the city. The old Galena division of the Northwestern ran out to Elgin. But now, who can count the trains and measure the roads that seek a terminus or connection in this city? The lake stretches away to the north, gathering in to this center all the harvests that might otherwise pass to the north of us. If you will take a map and look at the adjustment of railroads, you will see, first, that Chicago is the great railroad center of the world, as New York is the commercial city of this continent; and, second, that the railroad lines form the iron spokes of a great wheel whose hub is this city. The lake furnishes the only break in the spokes, and this seems simply to have pushed a few spokes together on each shore. See the eighteen trunk lines, exclusive of eastern connections.

Pass round the circle, and view their numbers and extent. There is the great Northwestern, with all its branches, one branch creeping along the lake shore, and so reaching to the north, into the Lake Superior regions, away to the right, and on to the Northern Pacific on the left, swinging around Green Bay for iron and copper and silver, twelve months in the year, and reaching out for the wealth of the great agricultural belt and isothermal line traversed by the Northern Pacific. Another branch, not so far north, feeling for the heart of the Badger State. Another pushing lower down the Mississippi—all these make many connections, and tapping all the vast wheat regions of Minnesota, Wisconsin, Iowa, and all the regions this side of sunset. There is that elegant road, the Chicago, Burlington & Quincy, running out a goodly number of

136 HISTORY OF THE STATE OF ILLINOIS.

OLD FORT DEARBORN, 1830.

PRESENT SITE OF LAKE STREET BRIDGE, CHICAGO, IN 1833.

branches, and reaping the great fields this side of the Missouri River. I can only mention the Chicago, Alton & St. Louis, *our* Illinois Central, described elsewhere, and the Chicago & Rock Island. Further around we come to the lines connecting us with all the eastern cities. The Chicago, Indianapolis & St. Louis, the Pittsburgh, Fort Wayne & Chicago, the Lake Shore & Michigan Southern, and the Michigan Central and Great Western, give us many highways to the seaboard. Thus we reach the Mississippi at five points, from St. Paul to Cairo and the Gulf itself by two routes. We also reach Cincinnati and Baltimore, and Pittsburgh and Philadelphia, and New York. North and south run the water courses of the lakes and the rivers, broken just enough at this point to make a pass. Through this, from east to west, run the long lines that stretch from ocean to ocean.

This is the neck of the glass, and the golden sands of commerce must pass into our hands. Altogether we have more than 10,000 miles of railroad, directly tributary to this city, seeking to unload their wealth in our coffers. All these roads have come themselves by the infallible instinct of capital. Not a dollar was ever given by the city to secure one of them, and only a small per cent. of stock taken originally by her citizens, and that taken simply as an investment. Coming in the natural order of events, they will not be easily diverted.

There is still another showing to all this. The connection between New York and San Francisco is by the middle route. This passes inevitably through Chicago. St. Louis wants the Southern Pacific or Kansas Pacific, and pushes it out through Denver, and so on up to Cheyenne. But before the road is fairly under way, the Chicago roads shove out to Kansas City, making even the Kansas Pacific a feeder, and actually leaving St. Louis out in the cold. It is not too much to expect that Dakota, Montana, and Washington Territory will find their great market in Chicago.

But these are not all. Perhaps I had better notice here the ten or fifteen new roads that have just entered, or are just entering, our city. Their names are all that is necessary to give. Chicago & St. Paul, looking up the Red River country to the British possessions; the Chicago, Atlantic & Pacific; the Chicago, Decatur & State Line; the Baltimore & Ohio; the Chicago, Danville & Vincennes; the Chicago & LaSalle Railroad; the Chicago, Pittsburgh & Cincinnati; the Chicago and Canada Southern; the Chicago and Illinois River Railroad. These, with their connections, and with the new connections of the old roads, already in process of erection, give to Chicago not less than 10,000 miles of new tributaries from the richest land on the continent. Thus there will be added to the reserve power, to the capital within reach of this city, not less than $1,000,000,000.

Add to all this transporting power the ships that sail one every nine minutes of the business hours of the season of navigation; add, also, the canal boats that leave one every five minutes during the same time—and you will see something of the business of the city.

THE COMMERCE OF THIS CITY

has been leaping along to keep pace with the growth of the country around us. In 1852, our commerce reached the hopeful sum of $20,000,000. In 1870 it reached $400,000,000. In 1871 it was pushed up above $450,000,000. And in 1875 it touched nearly double that.

One-half of our imported goods come directly to Chicago. Grain enough is exported directly from our docks to the old world to employ a semi-weekly line of steamers of 3,000 tons capacity. This branch is not likely to be greatly developed. Even after the great Welland Canal is completed we shall have only fourteen feet of water. The great ocean vessels will continue to control the trade.

The banking capital of Chicago is $24,431,000. Total exchange in 1875, $659,000,000. Her wholesale business in 1875 was $294,000,000. The rate of taxes is less than in any other great city.

The schools of Chicago are unsurpassed in America. Out of a population of 300,000 there were only 186 persons between the ages of six and twenty-one unable to read. This is the best known record.

In 1831 the mail system was condensed into a half-breed, who went on foot to Niles, Mich., once in two weeks, and brought back what papers and news he could find. As late as 1846 there was often only one mail a week. A post-office was established in Chicago in 1833, and the postmaster nailed up old boot-legs on one side of his shop to serve as boxes for the nabobs and literary men.

It is an interesting fact in the growth of the young city that in the active life of the business men of that day the mail matter has grown to a daily average of over 6,500 pounds. It speaks equally well for the intelligence of the people and the commercial importance of the place, that the mail matter distributed to the territory immediately tributary to Chicago is seven times greater than that distributed to the territory immediately tributary to St. Louis.

The improvements that have characterized the city are as startling as the city itself. In 1831, Mark Beaubien established a ferry over the river, and put himself under bonds to carry all the citizens free for the privilege of charging strangers. Now there are twenty-four large bridges and two tunnels.

In 1833 the government expended $30,000 on the harbor. Then commenced that series of manœuvers with the river that has made it one

of the world's curiosities. It used to wind around in the lower end of
the town, and make its way rippling over the sand into the lake at the
foot of Madison street. They took it up and put it down where it now
is. It was a narrow stream, so narrow that even moderately small crafts
had to go up through the willows and cat's tails to the point near Lake
street bridge, and back up one of the branches to get room enough in
which to turn around.

In 1844 the quagmires in the streets were first pontooned by plank
roads, which acted in wet weather as public squirt-guns. Keeping you
out of the mud, they compromised by squirting the mud over you. The
wooden-block pavements came to Chicago in 1857. In 1840 water was
delivered by peddlers in carts or by hand. Then a twenty-five horse-
power engine pushed it through hollow or bored logs along the streets
till 1854, when it was introduced into the houses by new works. The
first fire-engine was used in 1835, and the first steam fire-engine in 1859.
Gas was utilized for lighting the city in 1850. The Young Men's Christian Association was organized in 1858, and horse railroads carried them
to their work in 1859. The museum was opened in 1863. The alarm
telegraph adopted in 1864. The opera-house built in 1865. The city
grew from 560 acres in 1833 to 23,000 in 1869. In 1834, the taxes
amounted to $48.90, and the trustees of the town borrowed $60 more for
opening and improving streets. In 1835, the legislature authorized a loan
of $2,000, and the treasurer and street commissioners resigned rather than
plunge the town into such a gulf.

Now the city embraces 36 square miles of territory, and has 30 miles
of water front, besides the outside harbor of refuge, of 400 acres, inclosed
by a crib sea-wall. One-third of the city has been raised up an average
of eight feet, giving good pitch to the 263 miles of sewerage. The water
of the city is above all competition. It is received through two tunnels
extending to a crib in the lake two miles from shore. The closest analysis fails to detect any impurities, and, received 35 feet below the surface,
it is always clear and cold. The first tunnel is five feet two inches in
diameter and two miles long, and can deliver 50,000,000 of gallons per
day. The second tunnel is seven feet in diameter and six miles long,
running four miles under the city, and can deliver 100,000,000 of gallons per day. This water is distributed through 410 miles of water-
mains.

The three grand engineering exploits of the city are: First, lifting
the city up on jack-screws, whole squares at a time, without interrupting
the business, thus giving us good drainage; second, running the tunnels
under the lake, giving us the best water in the world; and third, the
turning the current of the river in its own channel, delivering us from the
old abominations, and making decency possible. They redound about

equally to the credit of the engineering, to the energy of the people, and to the health of the city.

That which really constitutes the city, its indescribable spirit, its soul, the way it lights up in every feature in the hour of action, has not been touched. In meeting strangers, one is often surprised how some homely women marry so well. Their forms are bad, their gait uneven and awkward, their complexion is dull, their features are misshapen and mismatched, and when we see them there is no beauty that we should desire them. But when once they are aroused on some subject, they put on new proportions. They light up into great power. The real person comes out from its unseemly ambush, and captures us at will. They have power. They have ability to cause things to come to pass. We no longer wonder why they are in such high demand. So it is with our city.

There is no grand scenery except the two seas, one of water, the other of prairie. Nevertheless, there is a spirit about it, a push, a breadth, a power, that soon makes it a place never to be forsaken. One soon ceases to believe in impossibilities. Balaams are the only prophets that are disappointed. The bottom that has been on the point of falling out has been there so long that it has grown fast. It can not fall out. It has all the capital of the world itching to get inside the corporation.

The two great laws that govern the growth and size of cities are, first, the amount of territory for which they are the distributing and receiving points; second, the number of medium or moderate dealers that do this distributing. Monopolists build up themselves, not the cities. They neither eat, wear, nor live in proportion to their business. Both these laws help Chicago.

The tide of trade is eastward—not up or down the map, but across the map. The lake runs up a wingdam for 500 miles to gather in the business. Commerce can not ferry up there for seven months in the year, and the facilities for seven months can do the work for twelve. Then the great region west of us is nearly all good, productive land. Dropping south into the trail of St. Louis, you fall into vast deserts and rocky districts, useful in holding the world together. St. Louis and Cincinnati, instead of rivaling and hurting Chicago, are her greatest sureties of dominion. They are far enough away to give sea-room,—farther off than Paris is from London,—and yet they are near enough to prevent the springing up of any other great city between them.

St. Louis will be helped by the opening of the Mississippi, but also hurt. That will put New Orleans on her feet, and with a railroad running over into Texas and so West, she will tap the streams that now crawl up the Texas and Missouri road. The current is East, not North, and a seaport at New Orleans can not permanently help St. Louis.

Chicago is in the field almost alone, to handle the wealth of one-fourth of the territory of this great republic. This strip of seacoast divides its margins between Portland, Boston, New York, Philadelphia, Baltimore and Savannah, or some other great port to be created for the South in the next decade. But Chicago has a dozen empires casting their treasures into her lap. On a bed of coal that can run all the machinery of the world for 500 centuries; in a garden that can feed the race by the thousand years; at the head of the lakes that give her a temperature as a summer resort equaled by no great city in the land; with a climate that insures the health of her citizens; surrounded by all the great deposits of natural wealth in mines and forests and herds, Chicago is the wonder of to-day, and will be *the city of the future.*

MASSACRE AT FORT DEARBORN.

During the war of 1812, Fort Dearborn became the theater of stirring events. The garrison consisted of fifty-four men under command of Captain Nathan Heald, assisted by Lieutenant Helm (son-in-law of Mrs. Kinzie) and Ensign Ronan. Dr. Voorhees was surgeon. The only residents at the post at that time were the wives of Captain Heald and Lieutenant Helm, and a few of the soldiers, Mr. Kinzie and his family, and a few Canadian *voyageurs*, with their wives and children. The soldiers and Mr. Kinzie were on most friendly terms with the Pottawattamies and Winnebagos, the principal tribes around them, but they could not win them from their attachment to the British.

One evening in April, 1812, Mr. Kinzie sat playing on his violin and his children were dancing to the music, when Mrs. Kinzie came rushing into the house, pale with terror, and exclaiming: "The Indians! the Indians!" "What? Where?" eagerly inquired Mr. Kinzie. "Up at Lee's, killing and scalping," answered the frightened mother, who, when the alarm was given, was attending Mrs. Barnes (just confined) living not far off. Mr. Kinzie and his family crossed the river and took refuge in the fort, to which place Mrs. Barnes and her infant not a day old were safely conveyed. The rest of the inhabitants took shelter in the fort. This alarm was caused by a scalping party of Winnebagos, who hovered about the fort several days, when they disappeared, and for several weeks the inhabitants were undisturbed.

On the 7th of August, 1812, General Hull, at Detroit, sent orders to Captain Heald to evacuate Fort Dearborn, and to distribute all the United States property to the Indians in the neighborhood—a most insane order. The Pottawattamie chief, who brought the dispatch, had more wisdom than the commanding general. He advised Captain Heald not to make the distribution. Said he: "Leave the fort and stores as they are, and let the Indians make distribution for themselves; and while they are engaged in the business, the white people may escape to Fort Wayne."

RUINS OF CHICAGO.

Captain Heald held a council with the Indians on the afternoon of the 12th, in which his officers refused to join, for they had been informed that treachery was designed—that the Indians intended to murder the white people in the council, and then destroy those in the fort. Captain Heald, however, took the precaution to open a port-hole displaying a cannon pointing directly upon the council, and by that means saved his life.

Mr. Kinzie, who knew the Indians well, begged Captain Heald not to confide in their promises, nor distribute the arms and munitions among them, for it would only put power into their hands to destroy the whites. Acting upon this advice, Heald resolved to withhold the munitions of war; and on the night of the 13th, after the distribution of the other property had been made, the powder, ball and liquors were thrown into the river, the muskets broken up and destroyed.

Black Partridge, a friendly chief, came to Captain Heald, and said: "Linden birds have been singing in my ears to-day: be careful on the march you are going to take." On that dark night vigilant Indians had crept near the fort and discovered the destruction of their promised booty going on within. The next morning the powder was seen floating on the surface of the river. The savages were exasperated and made loud complaints and threats.

On the following day when preparations were making to leave the fort, and all the inmates were deeply impressed with a sense of impending danger, Capt. Wells, an uncle of Mrs. Heald, was discovered upon the Indian trail among the sand-hills on the borders of the lake, not far distant, with a band of mounted Miamis, of whose tribe he was chief, having been adopted by the famous Miami warrior, Little Turtle. When news of Hull's surrender reached Fort Wayne, he had started with this force to assist Heald in defending Fort Dearborn. He was too late. Every means for its defense had been destroyed the night before, and arrangements were made for leaving the fort on the morning of the 15th.

It was a warm bright morning in the middle of August. Indications were positive that the savages intended to murder the white people; and when they moved out of the southern gate of the fort, the march was like a funeral procession. The band, feeling the solemnity of the occasion, struck up the Dead March in Saul.

Capt. Wells, who had blackened his face with gun-powder in token of his fate, took the lead with his band of Miamis, followed by Capt. Heald, with his wife by his side on horseback. Mr. Kinzie hoped by his personal influence to avert the impending blow, and therefore accompanied them, leaving his family in a boat in charge of a friendly Indian, to be taken to his trading station at the site of Niles, Michigan, in the event of his death.

VIEW OF THE CITY OF CHICAGO.

The procession moved slowly along the lake shore till they reached the sand-hills between the prairie and the beach, when the Pottawattamie escort, under the leadership of Blackbird, filed to the right, placing those hills between them and the white people. Wells, with his Miamis, had kept in the advance. They suddenly came rushing back, Wells exclaiming, "They are about to attack us; form instantly." These words were quickly followed by a storm of bullets, which came whistling over the little hills which the treacherous savages had made the covert for their murderous attack. The white troops charged upon the Indians, drove them back to the prairie, and then the battle was waged between fifty-four soldiers, twelve civilians and three or four women (the cowardly Miamis having fled at the outset) against five hundred Indian warriors. The white people, hopeless, resolved to sell their lives as dearly as possible. Ensign Ronan wielded his weapon vigorously, even after falling upon his knees weak from the loss of blood. Capt. Wells, who was by the side of his niece, Mrs. Heald, when the conflict began, behaved with the greatest coolness and courage. He said to her, "We have not the slightest chance for life. We must part to meet no more in this world. God bless you." And then he dashed forward. Seeing a young warrior, painted like a demon, climb into a wagon in which were twelve children, and tomahawk them all, he cried out, unmindful of his personal danger, "If that is your game, butchering women and children, I will kill too." He spurred his horse towards the Indian camp, where they had left their squaws and papooses, hotly pursued by swift-footed young warriors, who sent bullets whistling after him. One of these killed his horse and wounded him severely in the leg. With a yell the young braves rushed to make him their prisoner and reserve him for torture. He resolved not to be made a captive, and by the use of the most provoking epithets tried to induce them to kill him instantly. He called a fiery young chief a *squaw*, when the enraged warrior killed Wells instantly with his tomahawk, jumped upon his body, cut out his heart, and ate a portion of the warm morsel with savage delight!

In this fearful combat women bore a conspicuous part. Mrs. Heald was an excellent equestrian and an expert in the use of the rifle. She fought the savages bravely, receiving several severe wounds. Though faint from the loss of blood, she managed to keep her saddle. A savage raised his tomahawk to kill her, when she looked him full in the face, and with a sweet smile and in a gentle voice said, in his own language, "Surely you will not kill a squaw!" The arm of the savage fell, and the life of the heroic woman was saved.

Mrs. Helm, the step-daughter of Mr. Kinzie, had an encounter with a stout Indian, who attempted to tomahawk her. Springing to one side, she received the glancing blow on her shoulder, and at the same instant seized the savage round the neck with her arms and endeavored to get hold of his scalping knife, which hung in a sheath at his breast. While she was thus struggling she was dragged from her antagonist by another powerful Indian, who bore her, in spite of her struggles, to the margin of the lake and plunged her in. To her astonishment she was held by him so that she would not drown, and she soon perceived that she was in the hands of the friendly Black Partridge, who had saved her life.

The wife of Sergeant Holt, a large and powerful woman, behaved as bravely as an Amazon. She rode a fine, high-spirited horse, which the Indians coveted, and several of them attacked her with the butts of their guns, for the purpose of dismounting her; but she used the sword which she had snatched from her disabled husband so skillfully that she foiled them; and, suddenly wheeling her horse, she dashed over the prairie, followed by the savages shouting. " The brave woman! the brave woman! Don't hurt her!" They finally overtook her, and while she was fighting them in front, a powerful savage came up behind her, seized her by the neck and dragged her to the ground. Horse and woman were made captives. Mrs. Holt was a long time a captive among the Indians, but was afterwards ransomed.

In this sharp conflict two-thirds of the white people were slain and wounded, and all their horses, baggage and provision were lost. Only twenty-eight straggling men now remained to fight five hundred Indians rendered furious by the sight of blood. They succeeded in breaking through the ranks of the murderers and gaining a slight eminence on the prairie near the Oak Woods. The Indians did not pursue, but gathered on their flanks, while the chiefs held a consultation on the sand-hills, and showed signs of willingness to parley. It would have been madness on the part of the whites to renew the fight; and so Capt. Heald went forward and met Blackbird on the open prairie, where terms of surrender were soon agreed upon. It was arranged that the white people should give up their arms to Blackbird, and that the survivors should become prisoners of war, to be exchanged for ransoms as soon as practicable. With this understanding captives and captors started for the Indian camp near the fort, to which Mrs. Helm had been taken bleeding and suffering by Black Partridge, and had met her step-father and learned that her husband was safe.

A new scene of horror was now opened at the Indian camp. The wounded, not being included in the terms of surrender, as it was interpreted by the Indians, and the British general, Proctor, having offered a liberal bounty for American scalps, delivered at Malden, nearly all the wounded men were killed and scalped, and the price of the trophies was afterwards paid by the British government.

CIRCUIT CLERK AND RECORDER.
BELVIDERE

SHABBONA.

This celebrated Indian chief, whose portrait appears in this work, deserves more than a passing notice. Although Shabbona was not so conspicuous as Tecumseh or Black Hawk, yet in point of merit he was superior to either of them.

Shabbona was born at an Indian village on the Kankakee River, now in Will County, about the year 1775. While young he was made chief of the band, and went to Shabbona Grove, now DeKalb County, where they were found in the early settlement of the county.

In the war of 1812 Shabbona with his warriors joined Tecumseh, was aid to that great chief, and stood by his side when he fell at the battle of the Thames. At the time of the Winnebago war, in 1827, he visited almost every village among the Pottawatomies, and by his persuasive arguments prevented them from taking part in the war. By request of the citizens of Chicago, Shabbona, accompanied by Billy Caldwell (Sauganash), visited Big Foot's village at Geneva Lake, in order to pacify the warriors, as fears were entertained that they were about to raise the tomahawk against the whites. Here Shabbona was taken prisoner by Big Foot, and his life threatened, but on the following day was set at liberty. From that time the Indians (through reproach) styled him "the white man's friend," and many times his life was endangered.

Before the Black Hawk war, Shabbona met in council at two different times, and by his influence prevented his people from taking part with the Sacs and Foxes. After the death of Black Partridge and Senachwine, no chief among the Pottawatomies exerted so much influence as Shabbona. Black Hawk, aware of this influence, visited him at two different times, in order to enlist him in his cause, but was unsuccessful. While Black Hawk was a prisoner at Jefferson Barracks, he said, had it not been for Shabbona the whole Pottawatomie nation would have joined his standard, and he could have continued the war for years.

To Shabbona many of the early settlers of Illinois owe the preservation of their lives, for it is a well-known fact, had he not notified the people of their danger, a large portion of them would have fallen victims to the tomahawk of savages. By saving the lives of whites he endangered his own, for the Sacs and Foxes threatened to kill him, and made two attempts to execute their threats. They killed Pypeogee, his son, and Pyps, his nephew, and hunted him down as though he was a wild beast.

Shabbona had a reservation of two sections of land at his Grove, but by leaving it and going west for a short time, the Government declared the reservation forfeited, and sold it the same as other vacant land. On Shabbona's return, and finding his possessions gone, he was very sad and broken down in spirit, and left the Grove for ever. The citizens of Ottawa raised money and bought him a tract of land on the Illinois River, above Seneca, in Grundy County, on which they built a house, and supplied him with means to live on. He lived here until his death, which occurred on the 17th of July, 1859, in the eighty-fourth year of his age, and was buried with great pomp in the cemetery at Morris. His squaw, Pokanoka, was drowned in Mazen Creek, Grundy County, on the 30th of November, 1864, and was buried by his side.

In 1861 subscriptions were taken up in many of the river towns, to erect a monument over the remains of Shabbona, but the war breaking out, the enterprise was abandoned. Only a plain marble slab marks the resting-place of this friend of the white man.

Abstract of Illinois State Laws.

BILLS OF EXCHANGE AND PROMISSORY NOTES.

No *promissory note, check, draft, bill of exchange, order, or note, negotiable instrument* payable at sight, or on demand, or on presentment, shall be entitled to *days of grace*. All other *bills of exchange, drafts or notes* are entitled to *three days of grace*. All the above mentioned paper falling due on *Sunday, New Years' Day, the Fourth of July, Christmas*, or any day appointed or recommended by the *President of the United States* or the *Governor of the State* as a day of *fast or thanksgiving*, shall be deemed as due on the day previous, and should two or more of these days come together, then such instrument shall be treated as due on the day *previous* to the first of said days. No *defense* can be made against a *negotiable instrument* (*assigned before due*) in the hands of the assignee without notice, *except fraud was used* in obtaining the same. To hold an *indorser*, due *diligence* must be used *by suit*, in collecting of the maker, unless suit would have been unavailing. Notes payable to *person named* or to order, in order to absolutely *transfer title*, must be indorsed by the *payee*. Notes payable to *bearer* may be *transferred by delivery*, and when so payable *every indorser* thereon is held as a *guarantor of payment* unless otherwise expressed.

In *computing interest* or discount on negotiable instruments, a *month* shall be considered a *calendar month or twelfth of a year*, and for less than a month, a day shall be figured a *thirtieth* part of a month. Notes *only bear interest* when so expressed, but after due they draw the legal interest, even if not stated.

INTEREST.

The *legal rate* of interest is *six per cent*. Parties *may agree in writing* on a rate not exceeding *ten per cent*. If a rate of interest greater than ten per cent. is contracted for, it works a *forfeiture of the whole of said interest*, and only the principal can be recovered.

DESCENT.

When *no will is made*, the property of a deceased person is distributed as follows:

First. To his or her children and their descendants in equal parts; the descendants of the deceased *child or grandchild* taking the share of their deceased parents in equal parts among them.

Second. Where there is no child, nor descendant of such child, and no widow or surviving husband, then to the parents, brothers and sisters of the deceased, and their descendants, in equal parts, the surviving parent, if either be dead, taking a double portion; and if there is no parent living, then to the brothers and sisters of the intestate and their descendants.

Third. When there is *a widow* or *surviving husband, and no child or children*, or descendants of the same, then one-half of the real estate and the whole of the personal estate shall *descend* to *such widow* or *surviving husband*, absolutely, and the other half of the real estate shall descend as in other cases where there is no child or children or descendants of the same.

Fourth. When there *is a widow or surviving husband* and *also a child or children*, or descendants of the latter, then *one third* of all the personal estate to the *widow* or *surviving husband* absolutely.

Fifth. If there is *no child, parent, brother or sister*, or descendants of either of them, and no widow or surviving husband, then in *equal* parts to the *next of kin* to the intestate in equal degree. Collaterals shall not be represented except with the descendants of brothers and sisters of the intestate, and there shall be no *distinction between kindred of the whole and the half blood*.

Sixth. If any intestate leaves a *widow or surviving husband* and *no kindred*, then to *such widow or surviving husband;* and if there is no such widow or surviving husband, it shall escheat to and vest in the county where the same, or the greater portion thereof, is situated.

WILLS AND ESTATES OF DECEASED PERSONS.

No exact form of words are necessary in order to make a will good at law. *Every male* person of the age of *twenty-one years*, and every *female of the age of eighteen years, of sound mind and memory*, can make a valid will; it must be in *writing*, signed by the testator or by some one in his or her presence and by his or her direction, and *attested by two* or more *credible witnesses*. Care should be taken that the *witnesses are not interested* in the will. *Persons knowing themselves to have been named in the will* or appointed executor, must within *thirty days* of the death of deceased cause the will to be proved and recorded in the proper county, or present it, and *refuse to accept;* on failure to do so are *liable* to forfeit the sum of *twenty dollars per month. Inventory* to be made by executor or administrator within *three months* from date of letters testamentary or of administration. Executors' and administrators' *compensation* not to exceed six per cent. on amount of personal estate, and three per cent. on money realized from real estate, with such additional allowance as shall be reasonable for extra services. *Appraisers' compensation* $2 per day.

Notice requiring all claims to be presented against the estate shall be given by the executor or administrator *within six months* of being qualified. Any person having a claim *and not presenting it* at the time fixed by said notice is required to have summons issued notifying the executor or administrator of his having filed his claim in court; in such cases the costs have to be paid by the claimant. *Claims* should be filed within *two* years from the time *administration* is granted on an estate, as after that time they are *forever barred*, unless *other estate is found* that was not inventoried. *Married women, infants, persons insane, imprisoned* or without the United States, in the employment of the United States, or of this State, have *two years* after their disabilities are removed to file claims.

Claims are *classified* and *paid out* of the *estate* in the following manner:

First. Funeral expenses.

Second. The *widow's award*, if there is a widow; or *children* if there are children, *and no widow.*

Third. Expenses attending the *last illness*, not including physician's bill.

Fourth. Debts due the *common school* or *township fund.*

Fifth. All expenses of *proving the will* and taking out letters testamentary or administration, and settlement of the estate, and the *physician's bill* in the last illness of deceased.

Sixth. Where the *deceased* has received *money in trust* for any purpose, his executor or administrator shall pay out of his estate the amount received and not accounted for.

Seventh. All other debts and demands of whatsoever kind, without regard to *quality or dignity*, which shall be exhibited to the court within *two years* from the granting of letters.

Award to Widow and Children, exclusive of debts and legacies or bequests, except funeral expenses:

First. The *family pictures* and *wearing apparel, jewels* and *ornaments* of *herself* and *minor children.*

Second. School books and the *family library of the value of* $100.

Third. One *sewing machine.*

Fourth. Necessary beds, bedsteads and *bedding* for herself and family.

Fifth. The *stoves* and *pipe* used in the family, with the necessary *cooking utensils*, or in case they have none, $50 in money.

Sixth. Household and *kitchen furniture to the value of* $100.

Seventh. One *milch cow and calf for every four members of her family.*

Eighth. Two *sheep* for each member of her family, and the fleeces taken from the same, and *one horse, saddle and bridle.*
Ninth. Provisions for herself and family for one year.
Tenth. Food for the stock above specified for six months.
Eleventh. Fuel for herself and family for three months.
Twelfth. One hundred dollars worth of other property suited to her condition in life, to be *selected by the widow.*

The *widow if she elects* may have in lieu of the said award, the same personal property or money in place thereof as is or may be *exempt from execution* or attachment against the *head of a family.*

TAXES.

The owners of real and personal property, on the *first day of May* in each year, are *liable for the taxes* thereon.

Assessments should be completed before the *fourth Monday in June,* at which time the town board of review meets to examine assessments, *hear objections,* and make such *changes* as ought to be made. The county board have also power *to correct or change assessments.*

The tax books are placed in the hands of the town collector on or before the tenth day of December, who retains them until the tenth day of March following, when he is required to return them to the county treasurer, who then *collects all delinquent taxes.*

No *costs accrue* on real estate taxes *till advertised,* which takes place the first day of April, when three weeks' notice is required before judgment. Cost of advertising, twenty cents each tract of land, and ten cents each lot.

Judgment is usually obtained at *May term* of County Court. Costs six cents each tract of land, and five cents each lot. Sale takes place in June. Costs in addition to those before mentioned, twenty-eight cents each tract of land, and twenty-seven cents each town lot.

Real estate sold for taxes may be *redeemed* any time before the *expiration of two years* from the date of sale, by *payment* to the *County Clerk* of the amount for which it was sold and twenty-five per cent. thereon if redeemed within six months, fifty per cent. if between six and twelve months, if between twelve and eighteen months seventy-five per cent., and if between eighteen months and two years one hundred per cent., and in addition, all subsequent taxes paid by the purchaser, with ten per cent. interest thereon, also one dollar each tract if notice is given by the purchaser of the sale, and a fee of twenty-five cents to the clerk for his certificate.

JURISDICTION OF COURTS.

Justices have jurisdiction in all civil cases on *contracts* for the *recovery of moneys for damages for injury to real property,* or taking, detaining, or *injuring personal property; for rent;* for all cases to recover damages done real or personal property by railroad companies, in actions of *replevin,* and in actions for damages for *fraud* in the *sale, purchase,* or *exchange of personal property,* when the amount claimed as due is not over $200. They have also *jurisdiction* in all cases for *violation* of the *ordinances* of *cities, towns* or *villages.* A *justice of the peace* may *orally* order an *officer or a private person* to *arrest* any one committing or attempting to commit a *criminal offense. He also* upon complaint can issue his warrant for the arrest of any person *accused of having committed a crime,* and have him brought before him for examination.

COUNTY COURTS

Have jurisdiction in all *matters of probate* (except in counties having a population of one hundred thousand or over), settlement of estates of *deceased persons,* appointment of *guardians* and *conservators,* and settlement of their accounts; all matters relating to *apprentices;* proceedings for the *collection* of *taxes* and *assessments,* and in proceedings of *executors, administrators, guardians* and *conservators for the sale of real estate.* In *law* cases they have concurrent jurisdiction with Circuit Courts in all cases where justices of the peace now have, or hereafter may have, jurisdiction when the amount claimed shall not exceed $1,000, and in all criminal offenses where the punishment *is not imprisonment in the penitentiary, or death,* and in all cases of appeals from justices of the peace and police magistrates; *excepting* when the county judge is sitting as a justice of the peace. *Circuit Courts* have unlimited jurisdiction.

LIMITATION OF ACTION.

Accounts five years. Notes and written contracts *ten years. Judgments twenty years. Partial payments* or new promise in writing, within or after said period, will *revive the debt.* Absence from the State deducted, and when the cause of action is barred by the law of another State, it has the same effect here. *Slander and libel, one year. Personal injuries, two years. To recover* land or make entry thereon, *twenty years. Action to foreclose mortgage* or trust deed, or make a sale, *within ten years.*

All persons in *possession of land,* and *paying taxes for seven* consecutive *years,* with color of title, and all persons paying taxes for seven consecutive years, with color of title, on vacant land, shall be held to be the *legal owners to the extent of their paper title.*

MARRIED WOMEN

May sue and be sued. Husband and wife not liable for each other's debts, either before or after marriage, but both are liable for expenses and education of the family.

4

She may contract the same as if unmarried, except that in a partnership business she can not, without consent of her husband, *unless he has abandoned or deserted her*, or is idiotic or insane, or confined in penitentiary; she is entitled and can recover her own earnings, but neither husband nor wife is entitled to compensation for any services rendered for the other. At the death of the husband, in addition to widow's award, a married woman has a dower interest (one-third) in all real estate owned by her husband after their marriage, and which has not been released by her, and the husband has the same interest in the real estate of the wife at her death.

EXEMPTIONS FROM FORCED SALE.

Home worth $1,000, *and the following Personal Property:* Lot of ground and buildings thereon, occupied as a residence by the debtor, being a householder and having a family, to the value of $1,000. *Exemption continues after the death* of the householder for the benefit of widow and family, some one of them occupying the homestead until *youngest child shall become twenty-one years of age, and until death of widow.* There is *no exemption from sale for taxes,* assessments, debt or liability incurred for the *purchase or improvement of said homestead.* No release or waiver of exemption is valid, unless in writing, and subscribed by such householder and wife (if he have one), and acknowledged as conveyances of real estate are required to be acknowledged. The *following articles of personal property* owned by the debtor, are exempt from *execution, writ of attachment, and distress for rent:* The necessary *wearing apparel*, Bibles, school books and family pictures of every person; and, 2d, one hundred dollars worth of other property to be selected by the debtor, and, in addition, when the debtor is the head of a family and resides with the same, three hundred dollars worth of other property to be selected by the debtor; provided that such selection and exemption shall not be made by the debtor or allowed to him or her from any money, salary or wages due him or her from any person or persons or corporations whatever.

When the head of a family shall die, desert or not reside with the same, the family shall be entitled to and receive all the benefit and privileges which are by this act conferred upon the head of a family residing with the same. No personal property is exempt from execution when judgment is obtained for the *wages* of *laborers or servants.* Wages of a laborer who is the head of a family can not be garnisheed, except the sum due him be in excess of $25.

DEEDS AND MORTGAGES.

To be valid there must be a valid consideration. Special care should be taken to have them signed, sealed, delivered, and properly acknowledged, with the proper seal attached. *Witnesses* are not required. The *acknowledgement* must be made in this state, before *Master in Chancery, Notary Public, United States Commissioner, Circuit or County Clerk, Justice of Peace,* or any *Court of Record* having a seal, or any *Judge, Justice, or Clerk of any such* Court. When taken before a *Notary Public, or United States Commissioner,* the same shall be *attested* by his *official seal*, when taken before a *Court or the Clerk* thereof, the same shall be attested by the *seal* of such *Court*, and when taken before a *Justice of the Peace* residing out of the county where the real estate to be conveyed lies, there shall be added a certificate of the *County Clerk* under his seal of office, *that he was a Justice of the Peace* in the county at the time of taking the same. A deed is good without such certificate attached, but can not be used in evidence unless such a certificate is produced or other competent evidence introduced. Acknowledgements made out of the state must either be executed according to the laws of this state, or there should be attached a certificate that it is in conformity with the laws of the state or country where executed. Where this is not done the same may be proved by any other legal way. Acknowledgments where the *Homestead* rights are to be waived must state as follows: "Including the release and waiver of the right of homestead."

Notaries Public can take acknowledgements any where in the state.

Sheriffs, if authorized by the mortgagor of real or personal property in his mortgage, may sell the property mortgaged.

In the case of the *death of grantor or holder of the equity of redemption* of real estate mortgaged, or conveyed by deed of trust where equity of redemption is waived, and it contains power of sale, must be foreclosed in the same manner as a common mortgage in court.

ESTRAYS.

Horses, mules, asses, neat cattle, swine, sheep, or goats found straying at any time during the year, in counties where such animals are not allowed to run at large, or between the last day of October and the 15th day of April in other counties, *the owner thereof being unknown, may be taken up as estrays.*

No person *not a householder* in the county where estray is found can lawfully take up an estray, and then only *upon or about his farm* or place of residence. *Estrays should not be used before advertised*, except animals giving milk, which may be milked for their benefit.

Notices must be posted up within five (5) days in three (3) of the most public places in the town or precinct in which estray was found, giving the residence of the taker up, and a particular description of the estray, its age, color, and marks natural and artificial, and stating before what justice of the peace in such town or precinct, and at what time, not less than ten (10) nor more than fifteen (15) days from the time of posting such notices, he will apply to have the estray appraised.

A copy of such notice should be filed by the taker up with the *town clerk*, whose duty it is to enter the same at large, *in a book* kept by him for that purpose.

If the *owner* of estray shall not have appeared and *proved ownership*, and taken the same away, first paying the taker up his reasonable charges for taking up, keeping, and advertising the same, the taker up shall appear before the justice of the peace mentioned in above mentioned notice, and make an affidavit as required by law.

As the *affidavit has to be made before the justice*, and all other steps as to appraisement, etc., are before him, who is familiar therewith, they are therefore omitted here.

Any person taking up an estray at any other place than about or upon his farm or residence, or *without complying with the law, shall forfeit and pay a fine of ten dollars with costs.*

Ordinary diligence is required in *taking care of estrays*, but in case they die or get away the taker is not liable for the same.

GAME.

It is *unlawful* for any person to kill, or attempt to kill or destroy, in any manner, any *prairie hen or chicken* or *woodcock* between the 15th day of January and the 1st day of September; or any *deer, fawn, wild-turkey, partridge* or *pheasant* between the 1st day of February and the 1st day of October; or any quail between the 1st day of February and 1st day of November; or any wild goose, duck, snipe, brant or other water fowl between the 1st day of May and 15th day of August in each year. Penalty: Fine not less than $5 nor more than $25, for each bird or animal, and costs of suit, and stand committed to county jail until fine is paid, but not exceeding ten days. *It is unlawful* to hunt with *gun, dog or net* within the inclosed grounds or lands of another *without permission.* Penalty: Fine not less than $3 nor more than $100, to be paid into school fund.

WEIGHTS AND MEASURES.

Whenever any of the following articles shall be contracted for, or sold or delivered, and no special contract or agreement shall be made to the contrary, the weight per bushel shall be as follows, to-wit:

	Pounds.		Pounds.
Stone Coal,	80	Buckwheat,	52
Unslacked Lime,	80	Coarse Salt,	50
Corn in the ear,	70	Barley,	48
Wheat,	60	Corn Meal,	48
Irish Potatoes,	60	Castor Beans,	46
White Beans,	60	Timothy Seed,	45
Clover Seed,	60	Hemp Seed,	44
Onions,	57	Malt,	38
Shelled Corn,	56	Dried Peaches,	33
Rye,	56	Oats,	32
Flax Seed,	56	Dried Apples,	24
Sweet Potatoes,	55	Bran,	20
Turnips,	55	Blue Grass Seed,	14
Fine Salt,	55	Hair (plastering),	8

Penalty for giving less than the above standard is double the amount of property wrongfully not given, and ten dollars addition thereto.

MILLERS.

The owner or occupant of every public grist mill in this state shall grind all grain brought to his mill in its turn. The *toll* for both *steam* and *water* mills, is, for grinding and bolting *wheat, rye,* or *other grain,* one *eighth part;* for grinding *Indian corn, oats, barley* and *buckwheat* not required to be *bolted,* one *seventh part;* for grinding *malt,* and *chopping* all kinds of grain, one *eighth part.* It is the duty of every miller when his mill is in repair, to *aid* and *assist* in *loading* and *unloading* all grain brought to him to be ground, and he is also required to keep an accurate *half bushel measure,* and an accurate set of *toll dishes* or *scales* for weighing the grain. The *penalty* for neglect or refusal to comply with the law is $5, to the use of any person to sue for the same, to be recovered before any justice of the peace of the county where penalty is incurred. Millers are accountable for the safe keeping of all grain left in his mill for the purpose of being ground, with bags or casks containing same (except it results from unavoidable accidents), provided that such bags or casks are distinctly marked with the initial letters of the owner's name.

MARKS AND BRANDS.

Owners of cattle, horses, hogs, sheep or goats may have *one ear mark* and one brand, but which shall be *different* from his *neighbor's,* and may be *recorded* by the county clerk of the county in which such property is kept. The *fee* for such record is fifteen cents. The *record* of such shall be *open* to examination free of charge. In cases of *disputes* as to marks or brands, such *record* is *prima facie evidence.* Owners of cattle, horses, hogs, sheep or goats that may have been branded by the *former owner,* may be re-branded in presence of one or more of his neighbors, who shall certify to the facts of the marking or branding being done, when done, and in what brand or mark they were re-branded or re-marked, which certificate may also be recorded as before stated.

ADOPTION OF CHILDREN.

Children may be adopted by any resident of this state, by filing a petition in the Circuit or County Court of the county in which he resides, asking leave to do so, and if desired may ask that the name of the child be changed. Such petition, if made by a person having a husband or wife, will not be granted, unless the husband or wife joins therein, as the adoption must be by them jointly.

The petition shall state name, sex, and age of the child, and the new name, if it is desired to change the name. Also the name and residence of the parents of the child, if known, and of the guardian, if any, and whether the parents or guardians consent to the adoption.

The court must find, before granting decree, that the *parents of the child*, or the survivors of them, have *deserted his or her family* or such child for one year next preceding the application, or if neither are living, the guardian; if no guardian, the next of kin in this state capable of giving consent, has had notice of the presentation of the petition and consents to such adoption. If the child is of the *age* of *fourteen years* or upwards, the adoption *can not* be made *without its consent*.

SURVEYORS AND SURVEYS.

There is in every county elected a surveyor known as county surveyor, who has power to appoint deputies, for whose official acts he is responsible. It is the *duty* of the *county surveyor*, either by himself or his deputy, to make *all surveys* that he may be called upon to make within his county as soon as may be after application is made. The necessary chainmen and other assistance must be employed by the person requiring the same to be done, and to be by him paid, unless otherwise agreed; but the chainmen must be disinterested persons and approved by the surveyor and sworn by him to measure justly and impartially.

The County Board in each county is required by law to provide a copy of the United States field notes and plats of their surveys of the lands in the county to be kept in the recorder's office subject to examination by the public, and the county surveyor is required to make his surveys in conformity to said notes, plats and the laws of the United States governing such matters. The surveyor is also required to keep a record of all surveys made by him, which shall be subject to inspection by any one interested, and shall be delivered up to his successor in office. A certified copy of the said surveyor's record shall be *prima facie* evidence of its contents.

The fees of county surveyors are six dollars per day. The county surveyor is also *ex officio inspector of mines*, and as such, assisted by some practical miner selected by him, shall once each year inspect all the mines in the county, for which they shall each receive such compensation as may be fixed by the County Board, not exceeding $5 a day, to be paid out of the county treasury.

ROADS AND BRIDGES.

Where practicable from the nature of the ground, persons traveling in any kind of vehicle, *must turn to the right* of the center of the road, so as to permit each carriage to pass without interfering with each other. The *penalty* for a violation of this provision is $5 for every offense, to be recovered by the *party injured;* but to recover, there must have occurred some injury to person or property resulting from the violation. The *owners* of any carriage traveling upon any road in this State for the conveyance of passengers who shall *employ* or continue in his employment as driver any person who is addicted to *drunkenness*, or the excessive use of spiritous liquors, after he has had notice of the same, *shall forfeit*, at the rate of $5 per day, and if any *driver* while actually engaged in driving any such carriage, shall be guilty of *intoxication* to such a degree as to *endanger* the safety of *passengers*, it shall be the duty of the owner, on receiving *written notice* of the fact, signed by one of the *passengers*, and *certified* by him *on oath*, forthwith to discharge such driver. If such owner shall have such driver in his *employ within three months* after such notice, he is liable for $5 per day for the time he shall keep said driver in his employment after receiving such notice.

Persons *driving* any *carriage* on any public highway are prohibited from *running their horses* upon any occasion under a *penalty* of a fine not exceeding $10, or imprisonment not exceeding sixty days, at the discretion of the court. Horses *attached* to any *carriage* used to convey *passengers* for hire must be *properly hitched* or the lines placed in the hands of some other person before the driver leaves them for any purpose. For violation of this provision each driver shall *forfeit twenty dollars*, to be recovered by action, to be commenced within six months. It is understood by the *term carriage* herein to mean any carriage or vehicle used for the transportation of passengers or goods or either of them.

The commissioners of highways in the different towns have the care and superintendence of highways and bridges therein. They have all the powers necessary to lay out, vacate, regulate and repair all roads, build and repair bridges. In addition to the above, it is their duty to erect and keep in repair at the forks or crossing-place of the most important roads post and guide boards with plain inscriptions, giving directions and distances to the most noted places to which such road may lead; also to make provisions to prevent thistles, burdock, and cockle burrs, mustard, yellow dock, Indian mallow and jimson weed from seeding, and to extirpate the same as far as practicable, and to prevent all rank growth of vegetation on the public highways so far as the same may obstruct public travel, and it is in their discretion to erect watering places for public use for watering teams at such points as may be deemed advisable.

The Commissioners, on or before the 1st day of May of each year, shall make out and deliver to their treasurer a list of all able-bodied men in their town, *excepting* paupers, idiots, lunatics, and such others as are exempt by law, and assess against each the sum of two dollars as a poll tax for highway purposes. Within thirty days after such list is delivered they shall cause a written or printed notice to be given to each person so assessed, notifying him of the time when and place where such tax must be paid, or its equivalent in labor performed; they may contract with persons owing such poll tax to perform a certain amount of labor on any road or bridge in payment of the same, and if such tax is not paid nor labor performed by the first Monday of July of such year, or within ten days after notice is given after that time, they shall bring suit therefor against such person before a justice of the peace, who shall hear and determine the case according to law for the offense complained of, and shall forthwith issue an execution, directed to any constable of the county where the delinquent shall reside, who shall forthwith collect the moneys therein mentioned.

The Commissioners of Highways of each town shall annually ascertain, as near as practicable, how much money must be raised by tax on real and personal property for the making and repairing of roads, only, to any amount they may deem necessary, not exceeding forty cents on each one hundred dollars' worth, as valued on the assessment roll of the previous year. The tax so levied on property lying within an incorporated village, town or city, shall be paid over to the corporate authorities of such town, village or city. Commissioners shall receive $1.50 for each day necessarily employed in the discharge of their duty.

Overseers. At the first meeting the Commissioners shall choose one of their number to act General Overseer of Highways in their township, whose duty it shall be to take charge of and safely keep all tools, implements and machinery belonging to said town, and shall, by the direction of the Board, have general supervision of all roads and bridges in their town.

As all township and county officers are familiar with their duties, it is only intended to give the points of the law that the public should be familiar with. The manner of laying out, altering or vacating roads, etc., will not be here stated, as it would require more space than is contemplated in a work of this kind. It is sufficient to state that, the first step is by petition, addressed to the Commissioners, setting out what is prayed for, giving the names of the owners of lands if known, if not known so state, over which the road is to pass, giving the general course, its place of beginning, and where it terminates. It requires not less than twelve *freeholders* residing within three miles of the road who shall sign the petition. Public roads must not be less than fifty feet wide, nor more than sixty feet wide. Roads not exceeding two miles in length, if petitioned for, may be laid out, not less than forty feet. Private roads for private and public use, may be laid out of the width of three rods, on petition of the person directly interested; the damage occasioned thereby shall be paid by the premises benefited thereby, and before the road is opened. If not opened in two years, the order shall be considered rescinded. Commissioners in their discretion may permit persons who live on or have private roads, to work out their road tax thereon. Public roads must be opened in five days from date of filing order of location, or be deemed vacated.

DRAINAGE.

Whenever one or more owners or occupants of land *desire to construct a drain* or ditch across the land of others for *agricultural, sanitary or mining purposes*, the proceedings are as follows:

File a petition in the Circuit or County Court of the county in which the proposed ditch or drain is to be constructed, setting forth the necessity for the same, with a description of its proposed starting point, route and terminus, and if it shall be necessary for the drainage of the land or coal mines or for sanitary purposes, that a drain, ditch, levee or similar work be constructed, a description of the same. It shall also set forth the names of all persons owning the land over which such drain or ditch shall be constructed, or if unknown stating that fact.

No private property shall be taken or damaged for the purpose of constructing a ditch, drain or levee, without compensation, if claimed by the owner, the same to be ascertained by a jury; but if the construction of such ditch, drain or levee shall be a benefit to the owner, the same shall be a set off against such compensation.

If the proceedings seek to affect the property of a minor, lunatic or married woman, the guardian, conservator or husband of the same shall be made party defendant. The petition may be amended and parties made defendants at any time when it is necessary to a fair trial.

When the petition is presented to the judge, he shall note thereon when he will hear the same, and order the issuance of summonses and the publication of notice to each non-resident or unknown defendant.

The petition may be heard by such judge in vacation as well as in term time. Upon the trial, the jury shall ascertain the just compensation to each owner of the property sought to be damaged by the construction of such ditch, drain or levee, and truly report the same.

As it is only contemplated in a work of this kind to give an abstract of the laws, and as the parties who have in charge the execution of the further proceedings are likely to be familiar with the requirements of the statute, the necessary details are not here inserted.

WOLF SCALPS.

The County Board of any county in this State may hereafter allow such bounty on *wolf scalps* as the board may deem reasonable.

Any person claiming a bounty shall produce the scalp or scalps with the ears thereon, within sixty days after the wolf or wolves shall have been caught, to the Clerk of the County Board, who shall administer to said person the following oath or affirmation, to-wit: "You do solemnly swear (or affirm, as the case may be), that the scalp or scalps here produced by you was taken from a wolf or wolves killed and first captured by yourself within the limits of this county, and within the sixty days last past."

CONVEYANCES.

When the reversion expectant on a lease of any tenements or hereditaments of any tenure shall be surrendered or merged, the estate which shall for the time being confer as against the tenant under the same lease the next vested right to the same tenements or hereditaments, shall, to the extent and for the purpose of preserving such incidents to and obligations on the same reversion, as but for the surrender or merger thereof, would have subsisted, be deemed the reversion expectant on the same lease.

PAUPERS.

Every poor person who shall be unable to earn a livelihood in consequence of any *bodily infirmity, idiocy, lunacy* or *unavoidable cause*, shall be supported by the father, grand-father, mother, grand-mother, children, grand-children, brothers or sisters of such poor person, if they or either of them be of sufficient ability; but if any of such dependent class shall have become so from *intemperance* or other *bad conduct*, they shall not be entitled to support from any relation except parent or child.

STATES ATTORNEY
BELVIDERE.

The children shall first be called on to support their parents, if they are able; but if not, the parents of such poor person shall then be called on, if of sufficient ability; and if there be no parents or children able, then the brothers and sisters of such dependent person shall be called upon; and if there be no brothers or sisters of sufficient ability, the grand-children of such person shall next be called on; and if they are not able, then the grand-parents. Married females, while their husbands live, shall not be liable to contribute for the support of their poor relations except out of their separate property. It is the duty of the state's (county) attorney, to make complaint to the County Court of his county against all the relatives of such paupers in this state liable to his support and prosecute the same. In case the state's attorney neglects, or refuses, to complain in such cases, then it is the duty of the overseer of the poor to do so. The person called upon to contribute shall have at least ten days' notice of such application by summons. The court has the power to determine the kind of support, depending upon the circumstances of the parties, and may also order two or more of the different degrees to maintain such poor person, and prescribe the proportion of each, according to their ability. The court may specify the time for which the relative shall contribute—in fact has control over the entire subject matter, with power to enforce its orders. Every county (except those in which the poor are supported by the towns, and in such cases the towns are liable) is required to relieve and support all poor and indigent persons *lawfully* resident therein. Residence means the *actual* residence of the party, or the place where he was employed; or in case he was in no employment, then it shall be the place where he made his home. When any person becomes chargeable as a pauper in any county or town who did not reside at the commencement of six months immediately preceding his becoming so, but did at that time reside in some other county or town in this state, then the county or town, as the case may be, becomes liable for the expense of taking care of such person until removed, and it is the duty of the overseer to notify the proper authorities of the fact. If any person shall bring and leave any pauper in any county in this state where such pauper had no legal residence, knowing him to be such, he is liable to a fine of $100. In counties under township organization, the supervisors in each town are ex-officio overseers of the poor. The overseers of the poor act under the directions of the County Board in taking care of the poor and granting of temporary relief; also, providing for non-resident persons not paupers who may be taken sick and not able to pay their way, and in case of death cause such person to be decently buried.

The residence of the inmates of poorhouses and other charitable institutions for voting purposes is their former place of abode.

FENCES.

In counties under township organization, the *town assessor* and commissioner of highways are the fence-viewers in their respective towns. In other counties the County Board appoints three in each precinct annually. A *lawful fence* is *four and one-half feet high*, in good repair, consisting of rails, timber, boards, stone, hedges, or whatever the fence-viewers of the town or precinct where the same shall lie, shall consider equivalent thereto, but in counties under township organization the annual town meeting may establish any other kind of fence as such, or the County Board in other counties may do the same. Division fences shall be made and maintained in just proportion by the adjoining owners, except when the owner shall choose to let his land lie open, but after a division fence is built by agreement or otherwise, neither party can remove his part of such fence so long as he may crop or use such land for farm purposes, or without giving the other party one year's notice in writing of his intention to remove his portion. When any person shall enclose his land upon the enclosure of another, he shall refund the owner of the adjoining lands a just proportion of the value at that time of such fence. The value of fence and the just proportion to be paid or built and maintained by each is to be ascertained by two fence-viewers in the town or precinct. Such fence-viewers have power to settle all disputes between different owners as to fences built or to be built, as well as to repairs to be made. Each party chooses one of the viewers, but if the other party neglects, after eight days' notice in writing, to make his choice, then the other party may select both. It is sufficient to notify the tenant or party in possession, when the owner is not a resident of the town or precinct. The two fence-viewers chosen, after viewing the premises, shall hear the statements of the parties, in case they can't agree, they shall select another fence-viewer to act with them, and the decision of any two of them is final. The decision must be reduced to writing, and should plainly set out description of fence and all matters settled by them, and must be filed in the office of the town clerk in counties under township organization, and in other counties with the county clerk.

Where any person is liable to contribute to the erection or the repairing of a division fence, neglects or refuses so to do, the party injured, after giving sixty days notice in writing when a fence is to be erected, or ten days when it is only repairs, may proceed to have the work done at the expense of the party whose duty it is to do it, to be recovered from him with costs of suit, and the party so neglecting shall also be liable to the party injured for all damages accruing from such neglect or refusal, to be determined by any two fence-viewers selected as before provided, the appraisement to be reduced to writing and signed.

Where a person shall conclude to remove his part of a division fence, and let his land lie open, and having given the year's notice required, the adjoining owner may cause the value of said fence to be ascertained by fence-viewers as before provided, and on payment or tender of the amount of such valuation to the owner, it shall prevent the removal. A party removing a division fence without notice is liable for the damages accruing thereby.

Where a fence has been built on the land of another through mistake, the owner may enter upon such premises and remove his fence and material within six months after the division line has been ascertained. Where the material to build such a fence has been taken from the land on which it was built, then before it can be removed, the person claiming must first pay for such material to the owner of the land from which it was taken, nor shall such a fence be removed at a time when the removal will throw open or expose the crops of the other party; a reasonable time must be given beyond the six months to remove crops.

The compensation of fence-viewers is one dollar and fifty cents a day each, to be paid in the first instance by the party calling them, but in the end all expenses, including amount charged by the fence-viewers, must be paid equally by the parties, except in cases where a party neglects or refuses to make or maintain a just proportion of a division fence, when the party in default shall pay them.

DAMAGES FROM TRESPASS.

Where stock of any kind breaks into any person's enclosure, the fence being *good* and *sufficient*, the owner is liable for the damage done; but where the damage is done by stock *running at large, contrary to law*, the owner is liable where there is not such a fence. Where stock is found trespassing on the enclosure of another as aforesaid, the owner or occupier of the premises may take possession of such stock and keep the same until damages, with reasonable charges for keeping and feeding and all costs of suit, are paid. Any person taking or rescuing such stock so held without his consent, shall be liable to a fine of not less than three nor more than five dollars for each animal rescued, to be recovered by suit before a justice of the peace for the use of the school fund. Within twenty-four hours after taking such animal into his possession, the person taking it up must give notice of the fact to the owner, if known, or if unknown, notices must be posted in some public place near the premises.

LANDLORD AND TENANT.

The owner of lands, or his legal representatives, can sue for and recover rent therefor, in any of the following cases:

First. When rent is due and in arrears on a lease for life or lives.

Second. When lands are held and occupied by any person without any special agreement for rent.

Third. When possession is obtained under an agreement, written or verbal, for the purchase of the premises and before deed given, the right to possession is terminated by forfeiture on con-compliance with the agreement, and possession is wrongfully refused or neglected to be given upon demand made in writing by the party entitled thereto. Provided that all payments made by the vendee or his representatives or assigns, may be set off against the rent.

Fourth. When land has been sold upon a judgment or a decree of court, when the party to such judgment or decree, or person holding under him, wrongfully refuses, or neglects, to surrender possession of the same, after demand in writing by the person entitled to the possession.

Fifth. When the lands have been sold upon a mortgage or trust deed, and the mortgagor or grantor or person holding under him, wrongfully refuses or neglects to surrender possession of the same, after demand in writing by the person entitled to the possession.

If any tenant, or any person who shall come into possession from or under or by collusion with such tenant, shall willfully hold over any lands, etc., after the expiration the term of their lease, and *after demand made in writing* for the possession thereof, is liable to pay *double rent*. A tenancy from year to year requires sixty days notice in writing, to terminate the same at the end of the year; such notice can be given at any time within four months preceding the last sixty days of the year.

A tenancy by the month, or less than a year, where the tenant holds over without any special agreement, the landlord may terminate the tenancy, by thirty days notice in writing.

When rent is due, the landlord may serve a notice upon the tenant, stating that unless the rent is paid within not less than five days, his lease will be terminated; if the rent is not paid, the landlord may consider the lease ended. When default is made in any of the terms of a lease, it shall not be necessary to give more than ten days notice to quit or of the termination of such tenancy; and the same may be terminated on giving such notice to quit, at any time after such default in any of the terms of such lease; which notice may be substantially in the following form, viz:

To ———, You are hereby notified that, in consequence of your default in (here insert the character of the default), of the premises now occupied by you, being etc. (here describe the premises), I have elected to determine your lease, and you are hereby notified to quit and deliver up possession of the same to me within ten days of this date (dated, etc.)

The above to be signed by the lessor or his agent, and no other notice or demand of possession or termination of such tenancy is necessary.

Demand may be made, or notice served, by delivering a written or printed, or partly either, copy thereof to the tenant, or leaving the same with some person above the age of twelve years residing on or in possession of the premises; and in case no one is in the actual possession of the said premises, then by posting the same on the premises. When the tenancy is for a certain time, and the term expires by the terms of the lease, the tenant is then bound to surrender possession, and no notice to quit or demand of possession is necessary.

Distress for rent.—In all cases of distress for rent, the landlord, by himself, his agent or attorney, may seize for rent any personal property of his tenant that may be found in the county where the tenant resides; the property of any other person, even if found on the premises, is not liable.

An inventory of the property levied upon, with a statement of the amount of rent claimed, should be at once filed with some justice of the peace, if not over $200; and if above that sum, with the clerk of a court of record of competent jurisdiction. Property may be released, by the party executing a satisfactory bond for double the amount.

The landlord may distrain for rent, any time within *six months* after the expiration of the term of the lease, or when terminated.

In all cases where the premises rented shall be sub-let, or the lease assigned, the landlord shall have the same right to enforce lien against such lessee or assignee, that he has against the tenant to whom the premises were rented.

When a tenant abandons or removes from the premises or any part thereof, the landlord, or his agent or attorney, may seize upon any grain or other crops grown or growing upon the premises, or part thereof so abandoned, whether the rent is due or not. If such grain, or other crops, or any part thereof, is not fully grown or matured, the landlord, or his agent or attorney, shall cause the same to be properly cultivated, harvested or gathered, and may sell the same, and from the proceeds pay all his labor, expenses and rent. The tenant may, before the sale of such property, redeem the same by tendering the rent and reasonable compensation for work done, or he may replevy the same.

Exemption.—The same articles of personal property which are by law exempt from execution, except the crops as above stated, is also exempt from distress for rent.

If any tenant is about to or shall permit or attempt to sell and remove from the premises, without the consent of his landlord, such portion of the crops raised thereon as will endanger the lien of the landlord upon such crops, for the rent, it shall be lawful for the landlord to distress before rent is due.

LIENS.

Any person who shall by *contract*, express or implied, or partly both, with the owner of any lot or tract of land, furnish labor or material, or services as an architect or superintendent, in building, altering, repairing or ornamenting any house or other building or appurtenance thereto on such lot, or upon any street or alley, and connected with such improvements, shall have a lien upon the whole of such lot or tract of land, and upon such house or building and appurtenances, for the amount due to him for such labor, material or services. If the contract is *expressed*, and the time for the *completion* of the work is *beyond three years* from the commencement thereof; or, if the time of payment is beyond one year from the time stipulated for the completion of the work, then no lien exists. If the contract is *implied*, then no lien exists, unless the work be done or material is furnished within one year from the commencement of the work or delivery of the materials. As between different creditors having liens, no preference is given to the one whose contract was first made; but each shares pro-rata. Incumbrances existing on the lot or tract of the land at the time the contract is made, do not operate on the improvements, and are only preferred to the extent of the value of the land at the *time of making the contract*. The above lien can not be enforced *unless suit is commenced* within *six months* after the last payment for labor or materials shall have become due and payable. Sub-contractors, mechanics, workmen and other persons furnishing any material, or performing any labor for a contractor as before specified, have a lien to the extent of the amount due the contractor at the time the following notice is served upon the owner of the land who made the contract:

To ———, You are hereby notified, that I have been employed by ——— (here state whether to labor or furnish material, and substantially the nature of the demand) upon your (here state in general terms description and situation of building), and that I shall hold the (building, or as the case may be), and your interest in the ground, liable for the amount that may (is or may become) due me on account thereof. Signature, ———
Date, ———

If there is a contract in writing between contractor and sub-contractor, a copy of it should be served with above notice, and said notice must be served within forty days from the completion of such sub-contract, if there is one; if not, then from the time payment should have been made to the person performing the labor or furnishing the material. If the owner is not a resident of the county, or can not be found therein, then the above notice must be filed with the clerk of the Circuit Court, with his fee, fifty cents, and a copy of said notice must be published in a newspaper published in the county, for four successive weeks.

When the owner or agent is notified as above, he can retain any money due the contractor sufficient to pay such claim; if more than one claim, and not enough to pay all, they are to be paid pro rata.

The owner has the right to demand in writing, a statement of the contractor, of what he owes for labor, etc., from time to time as the work progresses, and on his failure to comply, forfeits to the owner $50 for every offense.

The liens referred to cover any and all estates, whether in fee for life, for years, or any other interest which the owner may have.

To enforce the lien of *sub-contractors*, suit must be commenced within *three months* from the time of the performance of the sub-contract, or during the work or furnishing materials.

Hotel, inn and *boarding-house keepers*, have a lien upon the baggage and other valuables of their guests or boarders, brought into such hotel, inn or boarding-house, by their guests or boarders, for the proper charges due from such guests or boarders for their accommodation, board and lodgings, and such *extras* as are furnished at their request.

Stable-keepers and other persons have a lien upon the horses, carriages and harness kept by them, for the proper charges due for the keeping thereof and expenses bestowed thereon at the request of the owner or the person having the possession of the same.

Agisters (persons who take care of cattle belonging to others), and persons keeping, yarding, feeding or pasturing domestic animals, shall have a lien upon the animals agistered, kept, yarded or fed, for the proper charges due for such service.

All persons who may furnish any railroad corporation in this state with fuel, ties, material, supplies or any other article or thing necessary for the construction, maintenance, operation or repair of its road by contract, or may perform work or labor on the same, is entitled to be paid as part of the current expenses of the road, and have a lien upon all its property. Sub-contractors or laborers have also a lien. The conditions and limitations both as to contractors and sub-contractors, are about the same as herein stated as to general liens.

DEFINITION OF COMMERCIAL TERMS.

$—— means *dollars*, being a contraction of U. S., which was formerly placed before any denomination of money, and meant, as it means now, United States Currency.

£—— means *pounds*, English money.

@ stands for *at* or *to*. ℔ for *pound*, and bbl. for *barrel*; ℔ for *per* or *by the*. Thus, Butter sells at 20@30c ℔ ℔, and Flour at $8@12 ℔ bbl.

% for *per cent* and # for *number*.

May 1.—Wheat sells at $1.20@1.25, "seller June." *Seller June* means that the person who sells the wheat has the privilege of delivering it at any time during the month of June.

Selling *short*, is contracting to deliver a certain amount of grain or stock, at a fixed price, within a certain length of time, when the seller has not the stock on hand. It is for the interest of the person selling "short," to depress the market as much as possible, in order that he may buy and fill his contract at a profit. Hence the "shorts" are termed "bears."

Buying *long*, is to contract to purchase a certain amount of grain or shares of stock at a fixed price, deliverable within a stipulated time, expecting to make a profit by the rise of prices. The "longs" are termed "bulls," as it is for their interest to "operate" so as to "toss" the prices upward as much as possible.

NOTES.

Form of note is legal, worded in the simplest way, so that the amount and time of payment are mentioned.

$100.   Chicago, Ill., Sept. 15, 1876.

Sixty days from date I promise to pay to E. F. Brown, or order, One Hundred dollars, for value received.

L. D. LOWRY.

A note to be payable in any thing else than money needs only the facts substituted for money in the above form.

ORDERS.

Orders should be worded simply, thus:

Mr. F. H. COATS: Chicago, Sept. 15, 1876.

Please pay to H. Birdsall, Twenty-five dollars, and charge to

F. D. SILVA.

RECEIPTS.

Receipts should always state when received and what for, thus:

$100.   Chicago, Sept. 15, 1876.

Received of J. W. Davis, One Hundred dollars, for services rendered in grading his lot in Fort Madison, on account.

THOMAS BRADY.

If receipt is in full it should be so stated.

BILLS OF PURCHASE.

W. N. MASON,   Salem, Illinois, Sept. 15, 1876.

Bought of A. A. GRAHAM.

4 Bushels of Seed Wheat, at $1.50		$6.00
2 Seamless Sacks " .30		.60
Received payment,		$6.60

A. A. GRAHAM.

ARTICLES OF AGREEMENT.

An agreement is where one party promises to another to do a certain thing in a certain time for a stipulated sum. Good business men always reduce an agreement to writing, which nearly always saves misunderstandings and trouble. No particular form is necessary, but the facts must be clearly and explicitly stated, and there must, to make it valid, be a reasonable consideration.

GENERAL FORM OF AGREEMENT.

THIS AGREEMENT, made the Second day of October, 1876, between John Jones, of Aurora, County of Kane, State of Illinois, of the first part, and Thomas Whiteside, of the same place, of the second part—

WITNESSETH, that the said John Jones, in consideration of the agreement of the party of the second part, hereinafter contained, contracts and agrees to and with the said Thomas Whiteside, that he will deliver, in good and marketable condition, at the Village of Batavia, Ill., during the month of November, of this year, One Hundred Tons of Prairie Hay, in the following lots, and at the following specified times; namely, twenty-five tons by the seventh of November, twenty-five tons additional by the fourteenth of the month, twenty-five tons more by the twenty-first, and the entire one hundred tons to be all delivered by the thirtieth of November.

And the said Thomas Whiteside, in consideration of the prompt fulfillment of this contract, on the part of the party of the first part, contracts to and agrees with the said John Jones, to pay for said hay five dollars per ton, for each ton as soon as delivered.

In case of failure of agreement by either of the parties hereto, it is hereby stipulated and agreed that the party so failing shall pay to the other, One Hundred Dollars, as fixed and settled damages.

In witness whereof, we have hereunto set our hands the day and year first above written.
JOHN JONES,
THOMAS WHITESIDE.

AGREEMENT WITH CLERK FOR SERVICES.

THIS AGREEMENT, made the first day of May, one thousand eight hundred and seventy-six, between Reuben Stone, of Chicago, County of Cook, State of Illinois, party of the first part, and George Barclay, of Englewood, County of Cook, State of Illinois, party of the second part—

WITNESSETH, that said George Barclay agrees faithfully and diligently to work as clerk and salesman for the said Reuben Stone, for and during the space of one year from the date hereof, should both live such length of time, without absenting himself from his occupation;

during which time he, the said Barclay, in the store of said Stone, of Chicago, will carefully and honestly attend, doing and performing all duties as clerk and salesman aforesaid, in accordance and in all respects as directed and desired by the said Stone.

In consideration of which services, so to be rendered by the said Barclay, the said Stone agrees to pay to said Barclay the annual sum of one thousand dollars, payable in twelve equal monthly payments, each upon the last day of each month; provided that all dues for days of absence from business by said Barclay, shall be deducted from the sum otherwise by the agreement due and payable by the said Stone to the said Barclay.

Witness our hands.   REUBEN STONE.
        GEORGE BARCLAY.

BILLS OF SALE.

A bill of sale is a written agreement to another party, for a consideration to convey his right and interest in the personal property. The purchaser must take actual possession of the property. Juries have power to determine upon the fairness or unfairness of a bill of sale.

COMMON FORM OF BILL OF SALE.

KNOW ALL MEN by this instrument, that I, Louis Clay, of Princeton, Illinois, of the first part, for and in consideration of Five Hundred and Ten dollars, to me paid by John Floyd, of the same place, of the second part, the receipt whereof is hereby acknowledged, have sold, and by this instrument do convey unto the said Floyd, party of the second part, his executors, administrators, and assigns, my undivided half of ten acres of corn, now growing on the farm of Thomas Tyrrell, in the town above mentioned; one pair of horses, sixteen sheep, and five cows, belonging to me, and in my possession at the farm aforesaid; to have and to hold the same unto the party of the second part, his executors and assigns, forever. And I do, for myself and legal representatives, agree with the said party of the second part, and his legal representatives, to warrant and defend the sale of the afore-mentioned property and chattels unto the said party of the second part, and his legal representatives, against all and every person whatsoever.

In witness whereof, I have hereunto affixed my hand, this tenth day of October, one thousand eight hundred and seventy-six.

        LOUIS CLAY.

BONDS.

A bond is a written admission on the part of the maker in which he pledges a certain sum to another, at a certain time.

COMMON FORM OF BOND.

KNOW ALL MEN by this instrument, that I, George Edgerton, of Watseka, Iroquois County, State of Illinois, am firmly bound unto Peter Kirchoff, of the place aforesaid, in the sum of five hundred dollars, to be paid to the said Peter Kirchoff, or his legal representatives; to which payment, to be made, I bind myself, or my legal representatives, by this instrument.

Sealed with my seal, and dated this second day of November, one thousand eight hundred and sixty-four.

The condition of this bond is such that if I, George Edgerton, my heirs, administrators, or executors, shall promptly pay the sum of two hundred and fifty dollars in three equal annual payments from the date hereof, with annual interest, then the above obligation to be of no effect; otherwise to be in full force and valid.

Sealed and delivered in
    presence of   GEORGE EDGERTON. [L.S.]
WILLIAM TURNER.

CHATTEL MORTGAGES.

A chattel mortgage is a mortgage on personal property for payment of a certain sum of money, to hold the property against debts of other creditors. The mortgage must describe the property, and must be acknowledged before a justice of the peace in the township or precinct where the mortgagee resides, and entered upon his docket, and must be recorded in the recorder's office of the county.

GENERAL FORM OF CHATTEL MORTGAGE.

THIS INDENTURE, made and entered into this first day of January, in the year of our Lord one thousand eight hundred and seventy-five, between Theodore Lottinville, of the town of Geneseo in the County of Henry, and State of Illinois, party of the first part, and Paul Henshaw, of the same town, county, and State, party of the second part.

Witnesseth, that the said party of the first part, for and in consideration of the sum of one thousand dollars, in hand paid, the receipt whereof is hereby acknowledged, does hereby grant, sell, convey, and confirm unto the said party of the second part, his heirs and assigns forever, all and singular the following described goods and chattels, to wit:

Two three-year old roan-colored horses, one Burdett organ, No. 987, one Brussels carpet, 15x20 feet in size, one marble-top center table, one Home Comfort cooking stove, No. 8, one black walnut bureau with mirror attached, one set of parlor chairs (six in number), upholstered in green rep, with lounge corresponding with same in style and color of upholstery, now in possession of said Lottinville, at No. 4 Prairie Ave., Geneseo, Ill.;

Together with all and singular, the appurtenances thereunto belonging, or in any wise appertaining; to have and to hold the above described goods and chattels, unto the said party of the second part, his heirs and assigns, forever.

Provided, always, and these presents are upon this express condition, that if the said Theodore Lottinville, his heirs, executors, administrators, or assigns, shall, on or before the first day of January, A.D., one thousand eight hundred and seventy-six, pay, or cause to be paid, to the said Paul Ranslow, or his lawful attorney or attorneys, heirs, executors, administrators, or assigns, the sum of One Thousand dollars, together with the interest that may accrue thereon, at the rate of ten per cent. per annum, from the first day of January, A.D. one thousand eight hundred and seventy-five, until paid, according to the tenor of one promissory note bearing even date herewith for the payment of said sum of money, that then and from thenceforth, these presents, and everything herein contained, shall cease, and be null and void, anything herein contained to the contrary notwithstanding.

Provided, also, that the said Theodore Lottinville may retain the possession of and have the use of said goods and chattels until the day of payment aforesaid; and also, at his own expense, shall keep said goods and chattels; and also at the expiration of said time of payment, if said sum of money, together with the interest as aforesaid, shall not be paid, shall deliver up said goods and chattels, in good condition, to said Paul Ranslow, or his heirs, executors, administrators, or assigns.

And provided, also, that if default in payment as aforesaid, by said party of the first part, shall be made, or if said party of the second part shall at any time before said promissory note becomes due, feel himself unsafe or insecure, that then the said party of the second part, or his attorney, agent, assigns, or heirs, executors, or administrators, shall have the right to take possession of said goods and chattels, wherever they may or can be found, and sell the same at public or private sale, to the highest bidder for cash in hand, after giving ten days' notice of the time and place of said sale, together with a description of the goods and chattels to be sold, by at least four advertisements, posted up in public places in the vicinity where said sale is to take place, and proceed to make the sum of money and interest promised as aforesaid, together with all reasonable costs, charges, and expenses in so doing; and if there shall be any overplus, shall pay the same without delay to the said party of the first part, or his legal representatives.

In testimony whereof, the said party of the first part has hereunto set his hand and affixed his seal, the day and year first above written.
Signed, sealed and delivered in
    presence of   THEODORE LOTTINVILLE. [L.S.]
SAMUEL J. TILDEN.

LEASE OF FARM AND BUILDINGS THEREON.

THIS INDENTURE, made this second day of June, 1875, between David Patton of the Town of Bisbee, State of Illinois, of the first part, and John Doyle of the same place, of the second part,

Witnesseth, that the said David Patton, for and in consideration of the covenants hereinafter mentioned and reserved, on the part of the said John Doyle, his executors, administrators, and assigns, to be paid, kept, and performed, hath let, and by these presents doth grant, demise, and let, unto the said John Doyle, his executors, administrators, and assigns, all that parcel of land situate in Bisbee aforesaid, bounded and described as follows, to wit:

[*Here describe the land.*]

Together with all the appurtenances appertaining thereto. To have and to hold the said premises, with appurtenances thereto belonging, unto the said Doyle, his executors, administrators, and assigns, for the term of five years, from the first day of October next following, at a yearly rent of Six Hundred dollars, to be paid in equal payments, semi-annually, as long as said buildings are in good tenantable condition.

And the said Doyle, by these presents, covenants and agrees to pay all taxes and assessments, and keep in repair all hedges, ditches, rail, and other fences; (the said David Patton, his heirs, assigns and administrators, to furnish all timber, brick, tile, and other materials necessary for such repairs.)

Said Doyle further covenants and agrees to apply to said land, in a farmer-like manner, all manure and compost accumulating upon said farm, and cultivate all the arable land in a husbandlike manner, according to the usual custom among farmers in the neighborhood; he also agrees to trim the hedges at a seasonable time, preventing injury from cattle to such hedges, and to all fruit and other trees on the said premises. That he will seed down with clover and timothy seed twenty acres yearly of arable land, ploughing the same number of acres each Spring of land now in grass, and hitherto unbroken.

It is further agreed, that if the said Doyle shall fail to perform the whole or any one of the above mentioned covenants, then and in that case the said David Patton may declare this lease terminated, by giving three months' notice of the same, prior to the first of October of any year, and may distrain any part of the stock, goods, or chattels, or other property in possession of said Doyle, for sufficient to compensate for the non-performance of the above written covenants, the same to be determined, and amounts so to be paid to be determined, by three arbitrators, chosen as follows: Each of the parties to this instrument to choose one, and the two so chosen to select a third ; the decision of said arbitrators to be final.

In witness whereof, we have hereto set our hands and seals.

Signed, sealed, and delivered
    in presence of   DAVID PATTON. [L.S.]
JAMES WALDRON.   JOHN DOYLE. [L.S.]

FORM OF LEASE OF A HOUSE.

THIS INSTRUMENT, made the first day of October, 1875, witnesseth that Amos Griest of Yorkville, County of Kendall, State of Illinois, hath rented from Aaron Young of Logansport aforesaid, the dwelling and lot No. 13 Ohio Street, situated in said City of Yorkville, for five years from the above date, at the yearly rental of Three Hundred dollars, payable monthly, on the first day of each month, in advance, at the residence of said Aaron Young.

At the expiration of said above mentioned term, the said Griest agrees to give the said Young peaceable possession of the said dwelling, in as good condition as when taken, ordinary wear and casualties excepted.

In witness whereof, we place our hands and seals the day and year aforesaid.

Signed, sealed and delivered   AMOS GRIEST. [L.S.]
    in presence of
NICKOLAS SCHUTZ,   AARON YOUNG. [L.S.]
        Notary Public.

LANDLORD'S AGREEMENT.

THIS certifies that I have let and rented, this first day of January, 1876, unto Jacob Schmidt, my house and lot, No. 15 Erie Street, in the City of Chicago, State of Illinois, and its appurtenances ; he to have the free and uninterrupted occupation thereof for one year from this date, at the yearly rental of Two Hundred dollars, to be paid monthly in advance ; rent to cease if destroyed by fire, or otherwise made untenantable.

                                                   PETER FUNK.

TENANT'S AGREEMENT.

THIS certifies that I have hired and taken from Peter Funk, his house and lot, No. 15 Erie Street, in the City of Chicago, State of Illinois, with appurtenances thereto belonging, for one year, to commence this day, at a yearly rental of Two Hundred dollars, to be paid monthly in advance ; unless said house becomes untenantable from fire or other causes, in which case rent ceases ; and I further agree to give and yield said premises one year from this first day of January 1876, in as good condition as now, ordinary wear and damage by the elements excepted.

Given under my hand this day.   JACOB SCHMIDT.

NOTICE TO QUIT.

To F. W. ARLEN.

Sir: Please observe that the term of one year, for which the house and land, situated at No. 6 Indiana Street, and now occupied by you, were rented to you, expired on the first day of October, 1875, and as I desire to repossess said premises, you are hereby requested and required to vacate the same. Respectfully Yours,

P. T. BARNUM.

LINCOLN, NEB., October 4, 1875.

TENANT'S NOTICE OF LEAVING.

DEAR SIR:

The premises I now occupy as your tenant, at No. 6 Indiana Street, I shall vacate on the first day of November, 1875. You will please take notice accordingly.

Dated this tenth day of October, 1875. F. W. ARLEN.

To P. T. BARNUM, ESQ.

REAL ESTATE MORTGAGE TO SECURE PAYMENT OF MONEY.

THIS INDENTURE, made this sixteenth day of May, in the year of our Lord, one thousand eight hundred and seventy-two, between William Stocker, of Peoria, County of Peoria, and State of Illinois, and Olla, his wife, party of the first part, and Edward Singer, party of the second part.

Whereas, the said party of the first part is justly indebted to the said party of the second part, in the sum of Two Thousand dollars, secured to be paid by two certain promissory notes (bearing even date herewith) the one due and payable at the Second National Bank in Peoria, Illinois, with interest, on the sixteenth day of May, in the year one thousand eight hundred and seventy-three; the other due and payable at the Second National Bank at Peoria, Ill., with interest, on the sixteenth day of May, in the year one thousand eight hundred and seventy-four.

Now, therefore, this indenture witnesseth, that the said party of the first part, for the better securing the payment of the money aforesaid, with interest thereon, according to the tenor and effect of the said two promissory notes above mentioned; and, also in consideration of the further sum of one dollar to them in hand paid by the said party of the second part, at the delivery of these presents, the receipt whereof is hereby acknowledged, have granted, bargained, sold, and conveyed, and by these presents do grant, bargain, sell, and convey, unto the said party of the second part, his heirs and assigns, forever, all that certain parcel of land, situate, etc.

[*Describing the premises.*]

To have and to hold the same, together with all and singular the Tenements, Hereditaments, Privileges and Appurtenances thereunto belonging or in any wise appertaining. And also, all the estate, interest, and claim whatsoever, in law as well as in equity which the party of the first part have in and to the premises hereby conveyed unto the said party of the second part, his heirs and assigns, and to their only proper use, benefit and behoof. And the said William Stocker, and Olla, his wife, party of the first part, hereby expressly waive, relinquish, release, and convey unto the said party of the second part, his heirs, executors, administrators, and assigns, all right, title, claim, interest, and benefit whatever, in and to the above described premises, and each and every part thereof, which is given by or results from all laws of this state pertaining to the exemption of homesteads.

Provided always, and these presents are upon this express condition, that if the said party of the first part, their heirs, executors, or administrators, shall well and truly pay, or cause to be paid, to the said party of the second part, his heirs, executors, administrators, or assigns, the aforesaid sums of money, with such interest thereon, at the time and in the manner specified in the above mentioned promissory notes, according to the true intent and meaning thereof, then in that case, these presents and every thing herein expressed, shall be absolutely null and void.

In witness whereof, the said party of the first part hereunto set their hands and seals the day and year first above written.

Signed, sealed and delivered in presence of

  JAMES WHITEHEAD,   WILLIAM STOCKER. [L.S.]
  FRED. SAMUELS.   OLLA STOCKER. [L.S.]

WARRANTY DEED WITH COVENANTS.

THIS INDENTURE, made this sixth day of April, in the year of our Lord one thousand eight hundred and seventy-two, between Henry Best of Lawrence, County of Lawrence, State of Illinois, and Belle, his wife, of the first part, and Charles Pearson of the same place, of the second part.

Witnesseth, that the said party of the first part, for and in consideration of the sum of Six Thousand dollars in hand paid by the said party of the second part, the receipt whereof is hereby acknowledged, have granted, bargained, and sold, and by these presents do grant, bargain, and sell, unto the said party of the second part, his heirs and assigns, all the following described lot, piece, or parcel of land, situated in the City of Lawrence, in the County of Lawrence, and State of Illinois, to wit:

[*Here describe the property.*]

Together with all and singular the hereditaments and appurtenances thereunto belonging or in any wise appertaining, and the reversion and reversions, remainder and remainders, rents, issues, and profits thereof; and all the estate, right, title, interest, claim, and demand whatsoever, of the said party of the first part, either in law or equity, of, in, and to the

JUSTICE OF THE PEACE
BELVIDERE.

above bargained premises, with the hereditaments and appurtenances. To have and to hold the said premises above bargained and described, with the appurtenances, unto the said party of the second part, his heirs and assigns, forever. And the said Henry Best, and Belle, his wife, parties of the first part, hereby expressly waive, release, and relinquish unto the said party of the second part, his heirs, executors, administrators, and assigns, all right, title, claim, interest, and benefit whatever, in and to the above described premises, and each and every part thereof, which is given by or results from all laws of this state pertaining to the exemption of homesteads.

And the said Henry Best, and Belle, his wife, party of the first part, for themselves and their heirs, executors, and administrators, do covenant, grant, bargain, and agree, to and with the said party of the second part, his heirs and assigns, that at the time of the ensealing and delivery of these presents they were well seized of the premises above conveyed, as of a good, sure, perfect, absolute, and indefeasible estate of inheritance in law, and in fee simple, and have good right, full power, and lawful authority to grant, bargain, sell, and convey the same, in manner and form aforesaid, and that the same are free and clear from all former and other grants, bargains, sales, liens, taxes, assessments, and encumbrances of what kind or nature soever; and the above bargained premises in the quiet and peaceable possession of the said party of the second part, his heirs and assigns, against all and every person or persons lawfully claiming or to claim the whole or any part thereof, the said party of the first part shall and will warrant and forever defend.

In testimony whereof, the said parties of the first part have hereunto set their hands and seals the day and year first above written.

Signed, sealed and delivered
    in presence of   HENRY BEST, [L.S.]
    JERRY LINKLATER.   BELLE BEST. [L.S.]

QUIT-CLAIM DEED.

THIS INDENTURE, made the eighth day of June, in the year of our Lord one thousand eight hundred and seventy-four, between David Tour, of Plano, County of Kendall, State of Illinois, party of the first part, and Larry O'Brien, of the same place, party of the second part,

Witnesseth, that the said party of the first part, for and in consideration of Nine Hundred dollars in hand paid by the said party of the second part, the receipt whereof is hereby acknowledged, and the said party of the second part forever released and discharged therefrom, has remised, released, sold, conveyed, and quit-claimed, and by these presents does remise, release, sell, convey, and quit-claim, unto the said party of the second part, his heirs and assigns, forever, all the right, title, interest,

claim, and demand, which the said party of the first part has in and to the following described lot, piece, or parcel of land, to wit:
[*Here describe the land.*]

To have and to hold the same, together with all and singular the appurtenances and privileges thereunto belonging, or in any wise thereunto appertaining, and all the estate, right, title, interest, and claim whatever, of the said party of the first part, either in law or equity, to the only proper use, benefit, and behoof of the said party of the second part, his heirs and assigns forever.

In witness whereof the said party of the first part hereunto set his hand and seal the day and year above written.

Signed, sealed and delivered   DAVID TOUR. [L.S.]
   in presence of
THOMAS ASHLEY.

The above forms of Deeds and Mortgage are such as have heretofore been generally used, but the following are much shorter, and are made equally valid by the laws of this state.

WARRANTY DEED.

The grantor (here insert name or names and place of residence), for and in consideration of (here insert consideration) in hand paid, conveys and warrants to (here insert the grantee's name or names) the following described real estate (here insert description), situated in the County of ―― in the State of Illinois.

Dated this ―― day of ―― A. D. 18――.

QUIT CLAIM DEED.

The grantor (here insert grantor's name or names and place of residence), for the consideration of (here insert consideration) convey and quit-claim to (here insert grantee's name or names) all interest in the following described real estate (here insert description), situated in the County of ―― in the State of Illinois.

Dated this ―― day of ―― A. D. 18――.

MORTGAGE.

The mortgagor (here insert name or names) mortgages and warrants to (here insert name or names of mortgagee or mortgagees), to secure the payment of (here recite the nature and amount of indebtedness, showing when due and the rate of interest, and whether secured by note or otherwise), the following described real estate (here insert description thereof), situated in the County of ―― in the State of Illinois.

Dated this ―― day of ―― A. D. 18――.

RELEASE.

KNOW ALL MEN by these presents, that I, Peter Ahlund, of Chicago, of the County of Cook, and State of Illinois, for and in consideration of One dollar, to me in hand paid, and for other good and valuable considerations, the receipt whereof is hereby confessed, do hereby grant, bargain, remise, convey, release, and quit-claim unto Joseph Carlin of Chicago, of the County of Cook, and State of Illinois, all the right, title, interest, claim, or demand whatsoever, I may have acquired in, through, or by a certain Indenture or Mortgage Deed, bearing date the second day of January, A. D. 1871, and recorded in the Recorder's office of said county, in book A of Deeds, page 46, to the premises therein described, and which said Deed was made to secure one certain promissory note, bearing even date with said deed, for the sum of Three Hundred dollars.

Witness my hand and seal, this second day of November, A. D. 1874.

PETER AHLUND. [L.S.]

State of Illinois, } ss.
Cook County.

I, George Saxton, a Notary Public in and for said county, in the state aforesaid, do hereby certify that Peter Ahlund, personally known to me as the same person whose name is subscribed to the foregoing Release, appeared before me this day in person, and acknowledged that he signed, sealed, and delivered the said instrument of writing as his free and voluntary act, for the uses and purposes therein set forth.

[NOTARIAL SEAL]

Given under my hand and seal, this second day of November, A. D. 1874.

GEORGE SAXTON, N. P.

GENERAL FORM OF WILL FOR REAL AND PERSONAL PROPERTY.

I, Charles Mansfield, of the Town of Salem, County of Jackson, State of Illinois, being aware of the uncertainty of life, and in failing health, but of sound mind and memory, do make and declare this to be my last will and testament, in manner following, to wit:

First. I give, devise and bequeath unto my oldest son, Sidney H. Mansfield, the sum of Two Thousand Dollars, of bank stock, now in the Third National Bank of Cincinnati, Ohio, and the farm owned by myself in the Town of Buskirk, consisting of one hundred and sixty acres, with all the houses, tenements, and improvements thereunto belonging; to have and to hold unto my said son, his heirs and assigns, forever.

Second. I give, devise and bequeath to each of my daughters, Anna Louise Mansfield and Ida Clara Mansfield, each Two Thousand dollars in bank stock, in the Third National Bank of Cincinnati, Ohio, and also each one quarter section of land, owned by myself, situated in the Town of Lake, Illinois, and recorded in my name in the Recorder's office in the county where such land is located. The north one hundred and sixty acres of said half section is devised to my eldest daughter, Anna Louise.

Third. I give, devise and bequeath to my son, Frank Alfred Mansfield, Five shares of Railroad stock in the Baltimore and Ohio Railroad, and my one hundred and sixty acres of land and saw mill thereon, situated in Manistee, Michigan, with all the improvements and appurtenances thereunto belonging, which said real estate is recorded in my name in the county where situated.

Fourth. I give to my wife, Victoria Elizabeth Mansfield, all my household furniture, goods, chattels, and personal property, about my home, not hitherto disposed of, including Eight Thousand dollars of bank stock in the Third National Bank of Cincinnati, Ohio, Fifteen shares in the Baltimore and Ohio Railroad, and the free and unrestricted use, possession, and benefit of the home farm, so long as she may live, in lieu of dower, to which she is entitled by law; said farm being my present place of residence.

Fifth. I bequeath to my invalid father, Elijah H. Mansfield, the income from rents of my store building at 145 Jackson Street, Chicago, Illinois, during the term of his natural life. Said building and land therewith to revert to my said sons and daughters in equal proportion, upon the demise of my said father.

Sixth. It is also my will and desire that, at the death of my wife, Victoria Elizabeth Mansfield, or at any time when she may arrange to relinquish her life interest in the above mentioned homestead, the same may revert to my above named children, or to the lawful heirs of each.

And lastly. I nominate and appoint as executors of this my last will and testament, my wife, Victoria Elizabeth Mansfield, and my eldest son, Sidney H. Mansfield.

I further direct that my debts and necessary funeral expenses shall be paid from moneys now on deposit in the Savings Bank of Salem, the residue of such moneys to revert to my wife, Victoria Elizabeth Mansfield, for her use forever.

In witness whereof, I, Charles Mansfield, to this my last will and testament, have hereunto set my hand and seal, this fourth day of April, eighteen hundred and seventy-two.

Signed, sealed, and declared by Charles Mansfield, as and for his last will and testament, in the presence of us, who, at his request, and in his presence, and in the presence of each other, have subscribed our names hereunto as witnesses thereof. PETER A. SCHENCK, Sycamore, Ills. FRANK E. DENT, Salem, Ills.	CHARLES MANSFIELD. [L.S.]

CODICIL.

Whereas I, Charles Mansfield, did, on the fourth day of April, one thousand eight hundred and seventy-two, make my last will and testament, I do now, by this writing, add this codicil to my said will, to be taken as a part thereof.

Whereas, by the dispensation of Providence, my daughter, Anna Louise, has deceased November fifth, eighteen hundred and seventy-three, and whereas, a son has been born to me, which son is now christened Richard Albert Mansfield, I give and bequeath unto him my gold watch, and all right, interest, and title in lands and bank stock and chattels bequeathed to my deceased daughter, Anna Louise, in the body of this will.

In witness whereof, I hereunto place my hand and seal, this tenth day of March, eighteen hundred and seventy-five.

Signed, sealed, published, and declared to us by the testator, Charles Mansfield, as and for a codicil to be annexed to his last will and testament. And we, at his request, and in his presence, and in the presence of each other, have subscribed our names as witnesses thereto, at the date hereof.

CHARLES MANSFIELD. [L.S.]

FRANK E. DENT, Salem, Ills.
JOHN C. SHAY, Salem, Ills.

CHURCH ORGANIZATIONS

May be legally made by *electing* or *appointing*, according to the *usages* or *customs* of the body of which it is a part, at any meeting held for that purpose, *two* or *more* of its *members* as trustees, wardens or vestrymen, and may adopt a *corporate* name. The chairman or secretary of such meeting shall, as soon as possible, make and file in the office of the recorder of deeds of the county, an affidavit substantially in the following form:

STATE OF ILLINOIS, }
———— County. } ss.

I, ————, do solemnly swear (or affirm, as the case may be), that at a meeting of the members of the (here insert the name of the church, society or congregation as known before organization), held at (here insert place of meeting), in the County of ————, and State of Illinois, on the ———— day of ————, A.D. 18—, for that purpose, the following persons were elected (or appointed) [*here insert their names*] trustees, wardens, vestrymen, (or officers by whatever name they may choose to adopt, with powers similar to trustees) according to the rules and usages of such (church, society or congregation), and said ————

ABSTRACT OF ILLINOIS STATE LAWS.

adopted as its corporate name (here insert name), and at said meeting this affiant acted as (chairman or secretary, as the case may be).

Subscribed and sworn to before me, this —— day of ——, A.D. 18—. Name of Affiant —— ——

which affidavit must be recorded by the recorder, and shall be, or a certified copy made by the recorder, received as evidence of such an incorporation.

No certificate of election after the first need be filed for record.

The term of office of the trustees and the general government of the society can be determined by the rules or by-laws adopted. Failure to elect trustees at the time provided does not work a dissolution, but the old trustees hold over. A trustee or trustees may be removed, in the same manner by the society as elections are held by a meeting called for that purpose. The property of the society vests in the corporation. The corporation may hold, or acquire by purchase or otherwise, land not exceeding ten acres, for the purpose of the society. The trustees have the care, custody and control of the property of the corporation, and can, *when directed* by the society, erect houses or improvements, and repair and alter the same, and may also when so directed by the society, mortgage, encumber, sell and convey any real or personal estate belonging to the corporation, and make all proper contracts in the name of such corporation. But they are prohibited by law from encumbering or interfering with any property so as to destroy the effect of any gift, grant, devise or bequest to the corporation; but such gifts, grants, devises or bequests, must in all cases be used so as to carry out the object intended by the persons making the same. Existing societies may organize in the manner herein set forth, and have all the advantages thereof.

SUGGESTIONS TO THOSE PURCHASING BOOKS BY SUBSCRIPTION.

The business of *publishing books by subscription* having so often been brought into disrepute by agents making representations and declarations *not authorized by the publisher;* in order to prevent that as much as possible, and that there may be more general knowledge of the relation such agents bear to their principal, and the law governing such cases, the following statement is made:

A *subscription* is in the *nature of a contract* of mutual promises, by which the subscriber agrees to *pay a certain sum* for the work described; the *consideration is concurrent* that the publisher shall *publish the book named*, and deliver the same, for which the subscriber is to pay the price named. *The nature and character of the work is described in the prospectus and by the sample shown. These should be carefully examined before subscribing,* as they are the basis and consideration of the promise to pay, and not the too *often exaggerated statements of the agent*, who is *merely employed* to *solicit subscriptions*, for which he is usually *paid a commission* for each subscriber, and has *no authority* to *change or alter* the conditions upon which the subscriptions are authorized to be made by the publisher. Should the *agent assume* to agree to make the subscription conditional or *modify or change the agreement of the publisher*, as set out by prospectus and sample, in order to *bind the principal*, the *subscriber* should see that such conditions or changes are stated *over or in connection with his signature*, so that the publisher may have notice of the same.

All persons making contracts in reference to matters of this kind, or any other business, should remember *that the law as to written contracts is*, that they can *not be varied, altered or rescinded verbally, but if done at all, must be done in writing*. It is therefore *important* that all *persons contemplating subscribing should distinctly understand that all talk before or after the subscription is made, is not admissible as evidence, and is no part of the contract*.

Persons employed to solicit subscriptions are known to the trade as canvassers. They are agents *appointed to do a particular business in a prescribed mode*, and *have no authority* to do it in any other way to the prejudice of their principal, nor can they bind their principal in any other matter. They *can not collect money*, or agree that payment may be made in *anything else but money*. They *can not extend* the time of payment *beyond the time of delivery*, nor bind their principal for the *payment of expenses* incurred in their buisness.

It would save a great deal of trouble, and often serious loss, if persons, *before signing* their names to any subscription book, or any written instrument, would *examine carefully what it is;* if they can not read themselves, should call on some one disinterested who can.

CONSTITUTION OF THE UNITED STATES OF AMERICA, AND ITS AMENDMENTS.

We, the people of the United States, in order to form a more perfect union, establish justice, insure domestic tranquillity, provide for the common defense, promote the general welfare, and secure the blessings of liberty to ourselves and our posterity, do ordain and establish this Constitution for the United States of America.

ARTICLE I.

SECTION 1. All legislative powers herein granted shall be vested in a Congress of the United States, which shall consist of a Senate and House of Representatives.

SEC. 2. The House of Representatives shall be composed of members chosen every second year by the people of the several states, and the electors in each state shall have the qualifications requisite for electors of the most numerous branch of the State Legislature.

No person shall be a representative who shall not have attained to the age of twenty-five years, and been seven years a citizen of the United States, and who shall not, when elected, be an inhabitant of that state in which he shall be chosen.

Representatives and direct taxes shall be apportioned among the several states which may be included within this Union, according to their respective numbers, which shall be determined by adding to the whole number of free persons, including those bound to service for a term of years, and excluding Indians not taxed, three-fifths of all other persons. The actual enumeration shall be made within three years after the first meeting of the Congress of the United States, and within every subsequent term of ten years, in such manner as they shall by law direct. The number of Representatives shall not exceed one for every thirty thousand, but each state shall have at least one Representative; and until such enumeration shall be made the State of New Hampshire shall be entitled to choose three, Massachusetts eight, Rhode Island and Providence Plantations one, Connecticut five, New York six, New Jersey four, Pennsylvania eight, Delaware one, Maryland six, Virginia ten, North Carolina five, and Georgia three.

When vacancies happen in the representation from any state, the Executive authority thereof shall issue writs of election to fill such vacancies.

The House of Representatives shall choose their Speaker and other officers, and shall have the sole power of impeachment.

SEC. 3. The Senate of the United States shall be composed of two Senators from each state, chosen by the Legislature thereof for six years; and each Senator shall have one vote.

Immediately after they shall be assembled in consequence of the first election, they shall be divided as equally as may be into three classes. The seats of the Senators of the first class shall be vacated at the expiration of the second year, of the second class at the expiration of the fourth year, and of the third class at the expiration of the sixth year, so that one-third may be chosen every second year; and if vacancies happen by resignation or otherwise, during the recess of the Legislature of any state, the Executive thereof may make temporary appointments until the next meeting of the Legislature, which shall then fill such vacancies.

No person shall be a Senator who shall not have attained to the age of thirty years and been nine years a citizen of the United States, and who shall not, when elected, be an inhabitant of that state for which he shall be chosen.

The Vice-President of the United States shall be President of the Senate, but shall have no vote unless they be equally divided.

The Senate shall choose their other officers, and also a President *pro tempore*, in the absence of the Vice-President, or when he shall exercise the office of President of the United States.

The Senate shall have the sole power to try all impeachments. When sitting for that purpose they shall be on oath or affirmation. When the President of the United States is tried the Chief Justice shall preside. And no person shall be convicted without the concurrence of two-thirds of the members present.

Judgment, in cases of impeachment, shall not extend further than to removal from office, and disqualification to hold and enjoy any office of honor, trust, or profit under the United States; but the party convicted shall nevertheless be liable and subject to indictment, trial, judgment, and punishment according to law.

SEC. 4. The times, places and manner of holding elections for Senators and Representatives shall be prescribed in each state by the Legislature thereof; but the Congress may at any time by law make or alter such regulations, except as to the places of choosing Senators.

The Congress shall assemble at least once in every year, and such meeting shall be on the first Monday in December, unless they shall by law appoint a different day.

SEC. 5. Each house shall be the judge of the election, returns, and qualifications of its own members, and a majority of each shall constitute a quorum to do business; but a smaller number may adjourn from day to day, and may be authorized to compel the attendance of absent members in such manner and under such penalties as each house may provide.

Each house may determine the rules of its proceedings, punish its members for disorderly behavior, and, with the concurrence of two-thirds, expel a member.

Each house shall keep a journal of its proceedings, and from time to time publish the same, excepting such parts as may, in their judgment, require secrecy; and the yeas and nays of the members of either house on any question shall, at the desire of one-fifth of those present, be entered on the journal.

Neither house, during the session of Congress, shall, without the consent of the other, adjourn for more than three days, nor to any other place than that in which the two houses shall be sitting.

SEC. 6. The Senators and Representatives shall receive a compensation for their services, to be ascertained by law, and paid out of the treasury of the United States. They shall in all cases, except treason, felony, and breach of the peace, be privileged from arrest during their attendance at the session of their respective houses, and in going to and returning from the same; and for any speech or debate in either house they shall not be questioned in any other place.

No Senator or Representative shall, during the time for which he was elected, be appointed to any civil office under the authority of the United States, which shall have been created, or the emoluments whereof shall have been increased during such time; and no person holding any office under the United States, shall be a member of either house during his continuance in office.

SEC. 7. All bills for raising revenue shall originate in the House of Representatives; but the Senate may propose or concur with amendments as on other bills.

Every bill which shall have passed the House of Representatives and the Senate, shall, before it becomes a law, be presented to the President of the United States; if he approve he shall sign it; but if not he shall return it, with his objections, to that house in which it shall have originated, who shall enter the objections at large on their journal, and proceed to reconsider it. If, after such reconsideration two-thirds of that house shall agree to pass the bill, it shall be sent, together with the objections, to the other house, by which it shall likewise be reconsidered, and if approved by two-thirds of that house, it shall become a law. But in all such cases the votes of both houses shall be determined by yeas and nays, and the names of the persons voting for and against the bill shall be entered on the journal of each house respectively. If any bill shall not be returned by the President within ten days (Sundays excepted), after it shall have been presented to him, the same shall be a law, in like manner as if he had signed it, unless the Congress, by their adjournment, prevent its return, in which case it shall not be a law.

Every order, resolution, or vote to which the concurrence of the Senate and House of Representatives may be necessary (except on a question of adjournment), shall be presented to the President of the United States, and before the same shall take effect shall be approved by him, or, being disapproved by him, shall be re-passed by two-thirds of the Senate and House of Representatives, according to the rules and limitations prescribed in the case of a bill.

SEC. 8. The Congress shall have power—

To lay and collect taxes, duties, imposts and excises, to pay the debts, and provide for the common defense and general welfare of the United States; but all duties, imposts, and excises shall be uniform throughout the United States;

To borrow money on the credit of the United States;

To regulate commerce with foreign nations, and among the several States, and with the Indian tribes;

To establish a uniform rule of naturalization, and uniform laws on the subject of bankruptcies throughout the United States;

To coin money, regulate the value thereof, and of foreign coin, and fix the standard of weights and measures;

To provide for the punishment of counterfeiting the securities and current coin of the United States;

To establish post offices and post roads;

To promote the progress of sciences and useful arts, by securing, for limited times, to authors and inventors, the exclusive right to their respective writings and discoveries;

To constitute tribunals inferior to the Supreme Court;

To define and punish piracies and felonies committed on the high seas, and offenses against the law of nations;

To declare war, grant letters of marque and reprisal, and make rules concerning captures on land and water;

To raise and support armies, but no appropriation of money to that use shall be for a longer term than two years;

To provide and maintain a navy;

To make rules for the government and regulation of the land and naval forces;

To provide for calling forth the militia to execute the laws of the Union, suppress insurrections, and repel invasions;

To provide for organizing, arming and disciplining the militia, and for governing such part of them as may be employed in the service of the United States, reserving to the states respectively the appointment of the officers, and the authority of training the militia according to the discipline prescribed by Congress;

To exercise legislation in all cases whatsoever over such district (not exceeding ten miles square) as may, by cession of particular states, and the acceptance of Congress, become the seat of the government of the United States, and to exercise like authority over all places purchased by the consent of the Legislature of the state in which the same shall be, for the erection of forts, magazines, arsenals, dock yards, and other needful buildings; and

To make all laws which shall be necessary and proper for carrying into execution the foregoing powers, and all other powers vested by this Constitution in the government of the United States, or in any department or officer thereof.

SEC. 9. The migration or importation of such persons as any of the states now existing shall think proper to admit, shall not be prohibited by the Congress prior to the year one thousand eight hundred and eight, but a tax or duty may be imposed on such importation, not exceeding ten dollars for each person.

The privilege of the writ of habeas corpus shall not be suspended, unless when in cases of rebellion or invasion the public safety may require it.

No bill of attainder or *ex post facto* law shall be passed.

No capitation or other direct tax shall be laid, unless in proportion to the census or enumeration hereinbefore directed to be taken.

No tax or duty shall be laid on articles exported from any state.

No preference shall be given by any regulation of commerce or revenue to the ports of one state over those of another; nor shall vessels bound to or from one state be obliged to enter, clear, or pay duties in another.

No money shall be drawn from the Treasury, but in consequence of appropriations made by law; and a regular statement and account of the receipts and expeditures of all public money shall be published from time to time.

No title of nobility shall be granted by the United States: and no person holding any office of profit or trust under them, shall, without the consent of the Congress, accept of any present, emolument, office, or title of any kind whatever, from any king, prince, or foreign state.

SEC. 10. No state shall enter into any treaty, alliance, or confederation; grant letters of marque and reprisal; coin money; emit bills of credit; make anything but gold and silver coin a tender in payment of debts; pass any bill of attainder, *ex post facto* law, or law impairing the obligation of contracts, or grant any title of nobility.

No state shall, without the consent of the Congress, lay any imposts or duties on imports or exports, except what may be absolutely necessary for executing its inspection laws, and the net produce of all duties and imposts laid by any state on imports or exports, shall be for the use of the Treasury of the United States; and all such laws shall be subject to the revision and control of the Congress.

No state shall, without the consent of Congress, lay any duty on tonnage, keep troops or ships of war in time of peace, enter into any agreement or compact with another state, or with a foreign power, or engage in war, unless actually invaded, or in such imminent danger as will not admit of delay.

ARTICLE II.

SECTION 1. The Executive power shall be vested in a President of the United States of America. He shall hold his office during the term of four years, and, together with the Vice-President chosen for the same term, be elected as follows:

Each state shall appoint, in such manner as the Legislature thereof may direct, a number of Electors, equal to the whole number of Senators and Representatives to which the state may be entitled in the Congress; but no Senator or Representative, or person holding an office of trust or profit under the United States, shall be appointed an Elector.

[* The Electors shall meet in their respective states, and vote by ballot for two persons, of whom one at least shall not be an inhabitant of the same state with themselves. And they shall make a list of all the persons voted for, and of the number of votes for each; which list they shall sign and certify, and transmit, sealed, to the seat of the government of the United States, directed to the President of the Senate. The President of the Senate shall, in the presence of the Senate and House of Representatives, open all the certificates, and the votes shall then be counted. The person having the greatest number of votes shall be the President, if such number be a majority of the whole number of Electors appointed; and if there be more than one who have such majority, and have an equal number of votes, then the House of Representatives shall immediately choose by ballot one of them for President; and if no person have a majority, then from the five highest on the list the said House shall in like manner choose the President. But in choosing the President, the vote shall be taken by states, the representation from each state having one vote; a quorum for this purpose shall consist of a member or members from two-thirds of the states, and a majority of all the states shall be necessary to a choice. In every case, after the choice of the President,

---

* This clause between brackets has been superseded and annulled by the Twelfth amendment.

the person having the greatest number of votes of the Electors shall be the Vice-President. But if there should remain two or more who have equal votes, the Senate shall choose from them by ballot the Vice-President.]

The Congress may determine the time of choosing the Electors, and the day on which they shall give their votes; which day shall be the same throughout the United States.

No person except a natural born citizen, or a citizen of the United States at the time of the adoption of this Constitution, shall be eligible to the office of President; neither shall any person be eligible to that office who shall not have attained the age of thirty-five years, and been fourteen years a resident within the United States.

In case of the removal of the President from office, or of his death, resignation, or inability to discharge the powers and duties of the said office, the same shall devolve on the Vice-President, and the Congress may by law provide for the case of removal, death, resignation, or inability, both of the President and Vice-President, declaring what officer shall then act as President, and such officer shall act accordingly, until the disability be removed, or a President shall be elected.

The President shall, at stated times, receive for his services a compensation which shall neither be increased nor diminished during the period for which he shall have been elected, and he shall not receive within that period any other emolument from the United States or any of them.

Before he enters on the execution of his office, he shall take the following oath or affirmation:

"I do solemnly swear (or affirm) that I will faithfully execute the office of President of the United States, and will, to the best of my ability, preserve, protect, and defend the Constitution of the United States."

SEC. 2. The President shall be commander in chief of the army and navy of the United States, and of the militia of the several states, when called into the actual service of the United States; he may require the opinion, in writing, of the principal officer in each of the executive departments, upon any subject relating to the duties of their respective offices, and he shall have power to grant reprieves and pardon for offenses against the United States, except in cases of impeachment.

He shall have power, by and with the advice and consent of the Senate, to make treaties, provided two-thirds of the Senators present concur; and he shall nominate, and by and with the advice of the Senate, shall appoint ambassadors, other public ministers and consuls, judges of the Supreme Court, and all other officers of the United States whose appointments are not herein otherwise provided for, and which shall be established by law; but the Congress may by law vest the appointment of such inferior officers as they think proper in the President alone, in the courts of law, or in the heads of departments.

The President shall have power to fill up all vacancies that may happen during the recess of the Senate, by granting commissions which shall expire at the end of their next session.

SEC. 3. He shall from time to time give to the Congress information of the state of the Union, and recommend to their consideration such measures as he shall judge necessary and expedient; he may on extraordinary occasions convene both houses, or either of them, and in case of disagreement between them, with respect to the time of adjournment, he may adjourn them to such time as he shall think proper; he shall receive ambassadors and other public ministers; he shall take care that the laws be faithfully executed, and shall commission all the officers of the United States.

Sec. 4. The President, Vice-President, and all civil officers of the United States, shall be removed from office on impeachment for, and conviction of, treason, bribery, or other high crimes and misdemeanors.

Article III.

Section I. The judicial power of the United States shall be vested in one Supreme Court, and such inferior courts as the Congress may from time to time ordain and establish. The Judges, both of the Supreme and inferior courts, shall hold their offices during good behavior, and shall, at stated times, receive for their services a compensation, which shall not be diminished during their continuance in office.

Sec. 2. The judicial power shall extend to all cases, in law and equity, arising under this Constitution, the laws of the United States, and treaties made, or which shall be made, under their authority; to all cases affecting ambassadors, other public ministers, and consuls; to all cases of admiralty and maritime jurisdiction; to controversies to which the United States shall be a party; to controversies between two or more states; between a state and citizens of another state; between citizens of different states; between citizens of the same state claiming lands under grants of different states, and between a state or the citizens thereof, and foreign states, citizens, or subjects.

In all cases affecting ambassadors, other public ministers, and consuls, and those in which a state shall be a party, the Supreme Court shall have original jurisdiction.

In all the other cases before mentioned, the Supreme Court shall have appellate jurisdiction, both as to law and fact, with such exceptions and under such regulations as the Congress shall make.

The trial of all crimes, except in cases of impeachment, shall be by jury; and such trial shall be held in the state where the said crimes shall have been committed; but when not committed within any state, the trial shall be at such place or places as the Congress may by law have directed.

Sec. 3. Treason against the United States shall consist only in levying war against them, or in adhering to their enemies, giving them aid and comfort. No person shall be convicted of treason unless on the testimony of two witnesses to the same overt act, or on confession in open court.

The Congress shall have power to declare the punishment of treason, but no attainder of treason shall work corruption of blood, or forfeiture, except during the life of the person attainted.

Article IV.

Section 1. Full faith and credit shall be given in each state to the public acts, records, and judicial proceedings of every other state. And the Congress may, by general laws, prescribe the manner in which such acts, records, and proceedings shall be proved, and the effect thereof.

SEC. 2. The citizens of each state shall be entitled to all privileges and immunities of citizens in the several states.

A person charged in any state with treason, felony, or other crime, who shall flee from justice and be found in another state, shall, on demand of the executive authority of the state from which he fled, be delivered up, to be removed to the state having jurisdiction of the crime.

No person held to service or labor in one state, under the laws thereof escaping into another, shall, in consequence of any law or regulation therein, be discharged from such service or labor, but shall be delivered up on the claim of the party to whom such service or labor may be due.

SEC. 3. New states may be admitted by the Congress into this Union; but no new state shall be formed or erected within the jurisdiction of any other state; nor any state be formed by the junction of two or more states, or parts of states, without the consent of the Legislatures of the states concerned, as well as of the Congress.

The Congress shall have power to dispose of and make all needful rules and regulations respecting the territory or other property belonging to the United States; and nothing in this Constitution shall be so construed as to prejudice any claims of the United States or of any particular state.

SEC. 4. The United States shall guarantee to every state in this Union a republican form of government, and shall protect each of them against invasion, and on application of the Legislature, or of the Executive (when the Legislature can not be convened), against domestic violence.

ARTICLE V.

The Congress, whenever two-thirds of both houses shall deem it necessary, shall propose amendments to this Constitution, or, on the application of the Legislatures of two-thirds of the several states, shall call a convention for proposing amendments, which, in either case, shall be valid to all intents and purposes as part of this Constitution, when ratified by the Legislatures of three fourths of the several states, or by conventions in three-fourths thereof, as the one or the other mode of ratification may be proposed by the Congress. Provided that no amendment which may be made prior to the year one thousand eight hundred and eight shall in any manner affect the first and fourth clauses in the ninth section of the first article; and that no state, without its consent, shall be deprived of its equal suffrage in the Senate.

ARTICLE VI.

All debts contracted and engagements entered into before the adoption of this Constitution shall be as valid against the United States under this Constitution as under the Confederation.

This Constitution, and the laws of the United States which shall be made in pursuance thereof, and all treaties made, or which shall be made, under the authority of the United States, shall be the supreme law of the land; and the Judges in every state shall be bound thereby, anything in the Constitution or laws of any state to the contrary notwithstanding.

The Senators and Representatives before mentioned, and the members of the several state Legislatures, and all executive and judicial officers, both of the United States and of the several states, shall be bound by oath or affirmation to support this Constitution; but no religious test shall ever be required as a qualification to any office or public trust under the United States.

ARTICLE VII.

The ratification of the Conventions of nine states shall be sufficient for the establishment of this Constitution between the states so ratifying the same.

Done in convention by the unanimous consent of the states present, the seventeenth day of September, in the year of our Lord one thousand seven hundred and eighty-seven, and of the independence of the United States of America the twelfth. In witness whereof we have hereunto subscribed our names.

GEO. WASHINGTON,
President and Deputy from Virginia.

New Hampshire.
JOHN LANGDON,
NICHOLAS GILMAN.

Massachusetts.
NATHANIEL GORHAM,
RUFUS KING.

Connecticut.
WM. SAM'L JOHNSON,
ROGER SHERMAN.

New York.
ALEXANDER HAMILTON.

New Jersey.
WIL. LIVINGSTON,
WM. PATERSON,
DAVID BREARLEY,
JONA. DAYTON.

Pennsylvania.
B. FRANKLIN,
ROBT. MORRIS,
THOS. FITZSIMONS,
JAMES WILSON,
THOS. MIFFLIN,
GEO. CLYMER,
JARED INGERSOLL,
GOUV. MORRIS.

Delaware.
GEO. READ,
JOHN DICKINSON,
JACO. BROOM,
GUNNING BEDFORD, JR.,
RICHARD BASSETT.

Maryland.
JAMES M'HENRY,
DANL. CARROLL,
DAN. OF ST. THOS. JENIFER.

Virginia.
JOHN BLAIR,
JAMES MADISON, JR.

North Carolina.
WM. BLOUNT,
HU. WILLIAMSON,
RICH'D DOBBS SPAIGHT.

South Carolina.
J. RUTLEDGE,
CHARLES PINCKNEY,
CHAS. COTESWORTH PINCKNEY,
PIERCE BUTLER.

Georgia.
WILLIAM FEW,
ABR. BALDWIN.

WILLIAM JACKSON, *Secretary.*

EDITOR "NORTHWESTERN"
BELVIDERE.

ARTICLES IN ADDITION TO AND AMENDATORY OF THE CONSTITUTION OF THE UNITED STATES OF AMERICA.

Proposed by Congress and ratified by the Legislatures of the several states, pursuant to the fifth article of the original Constitution.

ARTICLE I.

Congress shall make no law respecting an establishment of religion, or prohibiting the free exercise thereof; or abridging the freedom of speech, or of the press; or the right of the people peaceably to assemble, and to petition the Government for a redress of grievances.

ARTICLE II.

A well regulated militia being necessary to the security of a free state, the right of the people to keep and bear arms shall not be infringed.

ARTICLE III.

No soldier shall, in time of peace, be quartered in any house without the consent of the owner, nor in time of war but in a manner to be prescribed by law.

ARTICLE IV.

The right of the people to be secure in their persons, houses, papers, and effects against unreasonable searches and seizures, shall not be violated; and no warrants shall issue but upon probable cause, supported by oath or affirmation, and particularly describing the place to be searched and the persons or things to be seized.

ARTICLE V.

No person shall be held to answer for a capital or otherwise infamous crime, unless on a presentment or indictment of a Grand Jury, except in cases arising in the land or naval forces, or in the militia when in actual service in time of war or public danger; nor shall any person be subject for the same offense to be twice put in jeopardy of life or limb; nor shall be compelled in any criminal case to be a witness against himself, nor be deprived of life, liberty, or property, without due process of law; nor shall private property be taken for public use, without just compensation.

ARTICLE VI.

In all criminal prosecutions, the accused shall enjoy the right to a speedy and public trial, by an impartial jury of the state and district wherein the crime shall have been committed, which district shall have been previously ascertained by law, and to be informed of the nature and cause of the accusation; to be confronted with the witnesses against him; to have compulsory process for obtaining witnesses in his favor; and to have the assistance of counsel for his defense.

ARTICLE VII.

In suits at common law, where the value in controversy shall exceed twenty dollars, the right of trial by jury shall be preserved, and no fact tried by a jury shall be otherwise re-examined in any court of the United States than according to the rules of the common law.

ARTICLE VIII.

Excessive bail shall not be required, nor excessive fines imposed, nor cruel and unusual punishments inflicted.

ARTICLE IX.

The enumeration, in the Constitution, of certain rights, shall not be construed to deny or disparage others retained by the people.

ARTICLE X.

The powers not delegated to the United States by the Constitution, nor prohibited by it to the states, are reserved to the states respectively, or to the people.

ARTICLE XI.

The judicial power of the United States shall not be construed to extend to any suit in law or equity commenced or prosecuted against one of the United States by citizens of another state, or by citizens or subjects of any foreign state.

ARTICLE XII.

The Electors shall meet in their respective states and vote by ballot for President and Vice-President, one of whom, at least, shall not be an inhabitant of the same state with themselves; they shall name in their ballots the person to be voted for as president, and in distinct ballots the person voted for as Vice-President, and they shall make distinct lists of all persons voted for as President, and of all persons voted for as Vice-President, and of the number of votes for each, which list they shall sign and certify, and transmit sealed to the seat of the government of the United States, directed to the President of the Senate. The President of the Senate shall, in presence of the Senate and House of Representatives, open all the certificates, and the votes shall then be counted. The person having the greatest number of votes for President shall be the President, if such number be a majority of the whole number of Electors appointed; and if no person have such majority, then from the persons having the highest number not exceeding three on the list of those voted for as President, the House of Representatives shall choose immediately, by ballot, the President. But in choosing the President, the votes shall be taken by States, the representation from each state having one vote; a quorum for this purpose shall consist of a member or members from two-thirds of the states, and a majority of all the states shall be necessary to a choice. And if the House of Representatives shall not choose a President whenever the right of choice shall devolve upon them, before the fourth day of March next following, then the Vice-President shall act as President, as in the case of the death or other constitutional disability of the President. The person having the greatest number of votes as Vice-President, shall be the Vice-President, if such number be the majority of the whole number of electors appointed, and if no person have a majority then from the two highest numbers on the list, the Senate shall choose the Vice-President; a quorum for the purpose shall consist of two-thirds of the whole number of Senators, and a majority of the whole number shall be necessary to a choice. But no person constitutionally ineligible to the office of President shall be eligible to that of Vice-President of the United States.

ARTICLE XIII.

SECTION 1. Neither slavery nor involuntary servitude, except as a punishment for crime, whereof the party shall have been duly convicted, shall exist within the United States, or any place subject to their jurisdiction.

SEC. 2. Congress shall have power to enforce this article by appropriate legislation.

ARTICLE XIV.

SECTION 1. All persons born or naturalized in the United States and subject to the jurisdiction thereof, are citizens of the United States, and of the state wherein they reside. No state shall make or enforce any law which shall abridge the privileges or immunities of citizens of the United States; nor shall any state deprive any person of life, liberty, or property, without due process of law, nor deny to any person within its jurisdiction the equal protection of the laws.

SEC. 2. Representatives shall be appointed among the several states according to their respective numbers, counting the whole number of persons in each state, excluding Indians not taxed; but when the right to vote at any election for the choice of Electors for President and Vice-President of the United States, Representatives in Congress, the executive and judicial officers of a state, or the members of the Legislature thereof, is denied to any of the male inhabitants of such state, being twenty-one years of age and citizens of the United States, or in any way abridged except for participation in rebellion or other crimes, the basis of representation therein shall be reduced in the proportion which the number of such male citizens shall bear to the whole number of male citizens twenty-one years of age in such state.

SEC. 3. No person shall be a Senator or Representative in Congress, or Elector of President and Vice-President, or hold any office, civil or military, under the United States, or under any state, who, having previously taken an oath as a Member of Congress, or as an officer of the United States, or as a member of any state Legislature, or as an executive or judicial officer of any state to support the Constitution of the United States, shall have engaged in insurrection or rebellion against the same, or given aid or comfort to the enemies thereof. But Congress may, by a vote of two-thirds of each house, remove such disability.

SEC. 4. The validity of the public debt of the United States authorized by law, including debts incurred for payment of pensions and bounties for services in suppressing insurrection or rebellion, shall not be questioned. But neither the United States nor any state shall pay any debt or obligation incurred in the aid of insurrection or rebellion against the United States, or any loss or emancipation of any slave, but such debts, obligations, and claims shall be held illegal and void.

SEC. 5. The Congress shall have power to enforce, by appropriate legislation, the provisions of this act.

ARTICLE XV.

SECTION 1. The right of citizens of the United States to vote shall not be denied or abridged by the United States, or by any state, on account of race, color, or previous condition of servitude.

SEC. 2. Congress shall have power to enforce this article by appropriate legislation.

ELECTORS OF PRESIDENT AND VICE-PRESIDENT.

November 7, 1876.

COUNTIES.	Hayes and Wheeler, Republican.	Tilden and Hendricks, Democrat.	Peter Cooper, Greenback.	Smith, Prohibition.	Anti-Secret Societies.	COUNTIES.	Hayes and Wheeler, Republican.	Tilden and Hendricks, Democrat.	Peter Cooper, Greenback.	Smith, Prohibition.	Anti-Secret Societies.
Adams	4853	6368	43	17		Livingston	3550	2134	1170		3
Alexander	1219	1286				Logan	4798	2598	37		
Bond	1530	1142	77			McDonough	3140	2782	268	16	
Boone	1965	863	43	2		Macoupin	3567	4076	114		
Brown	944	1195	185	1		Madison	4554	4730	39	1	
Bureau	3719	2218	145	2	11	Marion	2009	2444	218		
Calhoun	441	900				Marshall	1554	1430	135		1
Carroll	2243	918	111	1	3	Mason	1566	1949	86	3	
Cass	1209	1618	75	7		Massac	1231	794	20		
Champaign	4530	3103	604		1	McDonough	2952	2811	347		
Christian	2501	3282	207	1	5	McHenry	3465	1874	34		5
Clark	1814	2187	210		9	McLean	6390	4410	518	8	7
Clay	1416	1547	112			Menard	1115	1657	10		
Clinton	1829	1988	132			Mercer	2208	1428	90		3
Coles	2957	2822	102			Monroe	815	1651	7		
Cook	36518	39240	221			Montgomery	2486	3014	201		
Crawford	1355	1641	38			Morgan	3069	3174	109		3
Cumberland	1145	1407	129			Moultrie	1245	1672	28		
De Kalb	3679	1413	65		3	Ogle	3833	1921	104		8
De Witt	1928	1515	716	10	3	Peoria	4655	5443	95		
Douglas	1631	1557	94			Pope	1319	800	5		
DuPage	2129	1276	25		8	Perry	1541	1389	48		
Edgar	2715	2884	161			Piatt	1807	1816	117		
Edwards	970	466	61			Pike	3055	4040	35	1	4
Effingham	1145	2265	13			Pulaski	1043	775			
Fayette	1884	2421	2			Putnam	646	455	14		
Ford	1601	712	204			Randolph	2357	2389	2		
Franklin	966	1802	391			Richland	1410	1552	55		
Fulton	4187	4660	89		1	Rock Island	3912	2838	67		
Gallatin	703	1160	282	2		Saline	989	1087	649		
Greene	1695	3160	7		9	Sangamon	4851	5841	29		
Grundy	1996	1142	108			Schuyler	1522	1804	115		
Hamilton	627	1488	770		4	Scott	910	1269	192		
Hancock	3456	4257				Shelby	2009	3551	343		
Hardin	540	671	134			Stark	1140	786	96		
Henderson	1815	1015				St. Clair	4706	5801	99		1
Henry	4177	1928	340	4	6	Stephenson	3198	2758	26		3
Iroquois	3768	2578	249	14	1	Tazewell	2889	3171	44	2	2
Jackson	2040	2071	106			Union	978	2155	3		
Jasper						Vermilion	4372	3031	288		9
Jefferson	1346	1667	547			Wabash	850	936	207		
Jersey	1335	2168		12		Warren	2795	1984	178		1
Jo Daviess	2907	2276	140	2	3	Washington	1911	1671	39		
Johnson	1367	893	81			Wayne	1570	1751	482		
Kane	5396	2850	172		5	White	1297	2056	469		4
Kankakee	2627	1308	26		2	Whiteside	3851	2133	133	8	1
Kendall	1809	524	308			Will	4770	3999	617		
Knox	5235	2632	141		1	Williamson	1672	1644	41		
Lake	2619	1615	55			Winnebago	4505	1568	70	13	2
La Salle	6277	6301	514		15	Woodford	1733	2105	237	1	4
Lawrence	1198	1529	27								
Lee	3087	2080	100	2	6	Total	275958	257099	16951	130	157

Practical Rules for Every Day Use.

How to find the gain or loss per cent. when the cost and selling price are given.

RULE.—Find the difference between the cost and selling price, which will be the gain or loss.

Annex two ciphers to the gain or loss, and divide it by the cost price; the result will be the gain or loss per cent.

How to change gold into currency.

RULE.—Multiply the given sum of gold by the price of gold.

How to change currency into gold.

Divide the amount in currency by the price of gold.

How to find each partner's share of the gain or loss in a copartnership business.

RULE.—Divide the whole gain or loss by the entire stock, the quotient will be the gain or loss per cent.

Multiply each partner's stock by this per cent., the result will be each one's share of the gain or loss.

How to find gross and net weight and price of hogs.

A short and simple method for finding the net weight, or price of hogs, when the gross weight or price is given, and vice versa.

NOTE.—It is generally assumed that the gross weight of hogs diminished by 1-5 or 20 per cent. of itself gives the net weight, and the net weight increased by ¼ or 25 per cent. of itself equals the gross weight.

To find the net weight or gross price.

Multiply the given number by .8 (tenths.)

To find the gross weight or net price.

Divide the given number by .8 (tenths.)

How to find the capacity of a granary, bin, or wagon-bed.

RULE.—Multiply (by short method) the number of cubic feet by 6308, and point off ONE decimal place—the result will be the correct answer in bushels and tenths of a bushel.

For only an approximate answer, multiply the cubic feet by 8, and point off one decimal place.

How to find the contents of a corn-crib.

RULE.—Multiply the number of cubic feet by 54, short method, or by 4½ ordinary method, and point off ONE decimal place—the result will be the answer in bushels.

NOTE.—In estimating corn in the ear, the **quality** and the **time it has been cribbed** must be taken into consideration, since corn will shrink considerably during the Winter and Spring. This rule generally holds good for corn measured at the time it is cribbed, provided it is sound and clean.

How to find the contents of a cistern or tank.

RULE.—Multiply the square of the mean diameter by the depth (all in feet) and this product by 5681 (short method), and point off ONE decimal place—the result will be the contents in barrels of 31½ gallons.

How to find the contents of a barrel or cask.

RULE.—Under the square of the mean diameter, write the length (all in inches) in REVERSED order, so that its UNITS will fall under the TENS; multiply by short method, and this product again by 430; point off one decimal place, and the result will be the answer in wine gallons.

How to measure boards.

RULE.—Multiply the length (in feet) by the width (in inches) and divide the product by 12—the result will be the contents in square feet.

How to measure scantlings, joists, planks, sills, etc.

RULE.—Multiply the width, the thickness, and the length together (the width and thickness in inches, and the length in feet), and divide the product by 12—the result will be square feet.

How to find the number of acres in a body of land.

RULE.—Multiply the length by the width (in rods), and divide the product by 160 (carrying the division to 2 decimal places if there is a remainder); the result will be the answer in acres and hundredths.

When the opposite sides of a piece of land are of unequal length, add them together and take one-half for the mean length or width.

How to find the number of square yards in a floor or wall.

RULE.—Multiply the length by the width or height (in feet), and divide the product by 9, the result will be square yards.

How to find the number of bricks required in a building.

RULE.—Multiply the number of cubic feet by 22½.

The number of cubic feet is found by multiplying the length, height and thickness (in feet) together.

Bricks are usually made 8 inches long, 4 inches wide, and two inches thick; hence, it requires 27 bricks to make a cubic foot without mortar, but it is generally assumed that the mortar fills 1-6 of the space.

How to find the number of shingles required in a roof.

RULE.—Multiply the number of square feet in the roof by 8, if the shingles are exposed 4½ inches, or by 7 1-5 if exposed 5 inches.

To find the number of square feet, multiply the length of the roof by twice the length of the rafters.

To find the length of the rafters, at ONE-FOURTH pitch, multiply the width of the building by .56 (hundredths); at ONE-THIRD pitch, by .6 (tenths); at TWO-FIFTHS pitch, by .64 (hundredths); at ONE-HALF pitch, by .71 (hundredths). This gives the length of the rafters from the apex to the end of the wall, and whatever they are to project must be taken into consideration.

NOTE. By ¼ or ½ pitch is meant that the apex or comb of the roof is to be ¼ or ½ the width of the building higher than the walls or base of the rafters.

How to reckon the cost of hay.

RULE.—Multiply the number of pounds by half the price per ton, and remove the decimal point three places to the left.

How to measure grain.

RULE.—Level the grain; ascertain the space it occupies in cubic feet; multiply the number of cubic feet by 8, and point off one place to the left.

NOTE.—Exactness requires the addition to every three hundred bushels of one extra bushel.

The foregoing rule may be used for finding the number of gallons, by multiplying the number of bushels by 8.

If the corn in the box is in the ear, divide the answer by 2, to find the number of bushels of shelled corn, because it requires 2 bushels of ear corn to make 1 of shelled corn.

Rapid rules for measuring land without instruments.

In measuring land, the first thing to ascertain is the contents of any given plot in square yards; then, given the number of yards, find out the number of rods and acres.

The most ancient and simplest measure of distance is a step. Now, an ordinary-sized man can train himself to cover one yard at a stride, on the average, with sufficient accuracy for ordinary purposes.

To make use of this means of measuring distances, it is essential to walk in a straight line; to do this, fix the eye on two objects in a line straight ahead, one comparatively near, the other remote; and, in walking, keep these objects constantly in line.

Farmers and others by adopting the following simple and ingenious contrivance, may always carry with them the scale to construct a correct yard measure.

Take a foot rule, and commencing at the base of the little finger of the left hand, mark the quarters of the foot on the outer borders of the left arm, pricking in the marks with indelible ink.

To find how many rods in length will make an acre, the width being given.

RULE.—Divide 160 by the width, and the quotient will be the answer.

How to find the number of acres in any plot of land, the number of rods being given.

RULE.—Divide the number of rods by 8, multiply the quotient by 5, and remove the decimal point two places to the left.

The diameter being given, to find the circumference.

RULE.—Multiply the diameter by 3 1-7.

How to find the diameter, when the circumference is given.

RULE.—Divide the circumference by 3 1-7.

To find how many solid feet a round stick of timber of the same thickness throughout will contain when squared.

RULE.—Square half the diameter in inches, multiply by 2, multiply by the length in feet, and divide the product by 144.

General rule for measuring timber, to find the solid contents in feet.

RULE.—Multiply the depth in inches by the breadth in inches, and then multiply by the length in feet, and divide by 144.

To find the number of feet of timber in trees with the bark on.

RULE.—Multiply the square of one-fifth of the circumference in inches, by twice the length, in feet, and divide by 144. Deduct 1-10 to 1-15 according to the thickness of the bark.

Howard's new rule for computing interest.

RULE.—The reciprocal of the rate is the time for which the interest on any sum of money will be shown by simply removing the decimal point two places to the left; for ten times that time, remove the point one place to the left; for 1-10 of the same time, remove the point three places to the left.

Increase or diminish the results to suit the time given.

NOTE.—The reciprocal of the rate is found by **inverting** the rate; thus 3 per cent. per month, inverted, becomes ⅓ of a month, or 10 days.

When the rate is expressed by one figure, always write it thus: 3-1, three ones.

Rule for converting English into American currency.

Multiply the pounds, with the shillings and pence stated in decimals, by 400 plus the premium in fourths, and divide the product by 90.

U. S. GOVERNMENT LAND MEASURE.

A township—36 sections each a mile square.

A section—640 acres.

A quarter section, half a mile square—160 acres.

An eighth section, half a mile long, north and south, and a quarter of a mile wide—80 acres.

A sixteenth section, a quarter of a mile square—40 acres.

The sections are all numbered 1 to 36, commencing at the north-east corner.

The sections are divided into quarters, which are named by the cardinal points. The quarters are divided in the same way. The description of a forty acre lot would read: The south half of the west half of the south-west quarter of section 1 in township 24, north of range 7 west, or as the case might be; and sometimes will fall short and sometimes overrun the number of acres it is supposed to contain.

The nautical mile is 795 4-5 feet longer than the common mile.

SURVEYORS' MEASURE.

7 92-100 inches	make	1 link.
25 links	"	1 rod.
4 rods	"	1 chain.
80 chains	"	1 mile.

NOTE.—A chain is 100 links, equal to 4 rods or 66 feet.

Shoemakers formerly used a subdivision of the inch called a barleycorn; three of which made an inch.

Horses are measured directly over the fore feet, and the standard of measure is four inches—called a hand.

In Biblical and other old measurements, the term span is sometimes used, which is a length of nine inches.

The sacred cubit of the Jews was 24.024 inches in length.

The common cubit of the Jews was 21.704 inches in length.

A pace is equal to a yard or 36 inches.

A fathom is equal to 6 feet.

A league is three miles, but its length is variable, for it is strictly speaking a nautical term, and should be three geographical miles, equal to 3.15 statute miles, but when used on land, three statute miles are said to be a league.

In cloth measure an aune is equal to 1¼ yards, or 45 inches.

An Amsterdam ell is equal to 26.796 inches.

A Trieste ell is equal to 25.284 inches.

A Brabant ell is equal to 27.116 inches.

HOW TO KEEP ACCOUNTS.

Every farmer and mechanic, whether he does much or little business, should keep a record of his transactions in a clear and systematic manner. For the benefit of those who have not had the opportunity of acquiring a primary knowledge of the principles of book-keeping, we here present a simple form of keeping accounts which is easily comprehended, and well adapted to record the business transactions of farmers, mechanics and laborers.

1875.		A. H. JACKSON.	Dr.		Cr.	
Jan.	10	To 7 bushels Wheat..................at $1.25	$8	75		
"	17	By shoeing span of Horses..................			$2	50
Feb.	4	To 14 bushels Oats....................at $ .45	6	30		
"	4	To 5 lbs. Butter....................at .25	1	25		
March	8	By new Harrow...........................			18	00
"	8	By sharpening 2 Plows....................				40
"	13	By new Double-Tree......................			2	25
"	27	To Cow and Calf.........................	48	00		
April	9	To half ton of Hay.......................	6	25		
"	9	By Cash.................................			25	00
May	6	By repairing Corn-Planter................			4	75
"	24	To one Sow with Pigs....................	17	50		
July	4	By Cash, to balance account..............			35	15
			$88	05	$88	05

1875.		CASSA MASON.	Dr.		Cr.	
March	21	By 3 days' labor..............at $1.25			$3	75
"	21	To 2 Shoats...................at 3.00	$6	00		
"	23	To 18 bushels Corn............at .45	8	10		
May	1	By 1 month's Labor.....................			25	00
"	1	To Cash................................	10	00		
June	19	By 8 days' Mowing............at $1.50			12	00
"	26	To 50 lbs. Flour........................	2	75		
July	10	To 27 lbs. Meat..............at $ .10	2	70		
"	29	By 9 days' Harvesting.........at 2.00			18	00
Aug.	12	By 6 days' Labor.............at 1.50			9	00
"	12	To Cash................................	20	00		
Sept.	1	To Cash to balance account.............	18	20		
			$67	75	$67	75

INTEREST TABLE.

A SIMPLE RULE FOR ACCURATELY COMPUTING INTEREST AT ANY GIVEN PER CENT. FOR ANY LENGTH OF TIME.

Multiply the *principal* (amount of money at interest) by the *time reduced to days*; then divide this product by the *quotient* obtained by dividing 360 (the number of days in the interest year) by the *per cent* of interest, and the *quotient thus obtained* will be the required Interest.

ILLUSTRATION.   Solution.

Require the interest of $462.50 for one month and eighteen days at 6 per cent. An interest month is 30 days; one month and eighteen days equal 48 days. $462.50 multiplied by 48 gives $222.0000; 360 divided by 6 (the per cent of interest) gives 60, and $222.0000 divided by 60 will give you the exact interest, which is $3.70. If the rate of interest in the above example were 12 per cent., we would divide the $222.0000 by 30 (because 360 divided by 12 gives 30); if 4 per cent. we would divide by 90; if 8 per cent., by 45; and in like manner for any other per cent.

$462.50
.48

3700000
185000

60 / $222.0000; $3.70
180

420
420

00

MISCELLANEOUS TABLE.

12 units, or things, 1 Dozen. | 196 pounds, 1 Barrel of Flour. | 24 sheets of paper, 1 Quire.
12 dozen, 1 Gross. | 200 pounds, 1 Barrel of Pork. | 20 quires paper 1 Ream
20 things, 1 score. | 56 pounds, 1 Firkin of Butter. | 4 ft. wide, 1 ft. high, and 8 ft. long, 1 Cord Wood.

NAMES OF THE STATES OF THE UNION, AND THEIR SIGNIFICATIONS.

Virginia.—The oldest of the States, was so called in honor of Queen Elizabeth, the "Virgin Queen," in whose reign Sir Walter Raleigh made his first attempt to colonize that region.

Florida.—Ponce de Leon landed on the coast of Florida on Easter Sunday, and called the country in commemoration of the day, which was the Pasqua Florida of the Spaniards, or "Feast of Flowers."

Louisiana was called after Louis the Fourteenth, who at one time owned that section of the country.

Alabama was so named by the Indians, and signifies "Here we Rest."

Mississippi is likewise an Indian name, meaning "Long River."

Arkansas, from Kansas, the Indian word for "smoky water." Its prefix was really *arc*, the French word for "bow."

The *Carolinas* were originally one tract, and were called "Carolana," after Charles the Ninth of France.

Georgia owes its name to George the Second of England, who first established a colony there in 1732.

Tennessee is the Indian name for the "River of the Bend," *i. e.*, the Mississippi which forms its western boundary.

Kentucky is the Indian name for "at the head of the river."

Ohio means "beautiful;" *Iowa*, "drowsy ones;" *Minnesota*, "cloudy water," and *Wisconsin*, "wild-rushing channel."

Illinois is derived from the Indian word *illini*, men, and the French suffix *ois*, together signifying "tribe of men."

Michigan was called by the name given the lake, *fish-weir*, which was so styled from its fancied resemblance to a fish trap.

Missouri is from the Indian word "muddy," which more properly applies to the river that flows through it.

Oregon owes its Indian name also to its principal river.

Cortes named *California*.

Massachusetts is the Indian for "The country around the great hills."

Connecticut, from the Indian Quon-eh-ta-Cut, signifying "Long River."

Maryland, after Henrietta Maria, Queen of Charles the First, of England.

New York was named by the Duke of York.

Pennsylvania means "Penn's woods," and was so called after William Penn, its original owner.

Delaware after Lord De La Ware.

New Jersey, so called in honor of Sir George Carteret, who was Governor of the Island of Jersey, in the British Channel.

Maine was called after the province of Maine in France, in compliment of Queen Henrietta of England, who owned that province.

Vermont, from the French word *Vert Mont*, signifying Green Mountain.

New Hampshire, from Hampshire county in England. It was formerly called Laconia.

The little State of *Rhode Island* owes its name to the Island of Rhodes in the Mediterranean, which domain it is said to greatly resemble.

Texas is the American word for the Mexican name by which all that section of the country was called before it was ceded to the United States.

POPULATION OF THE UNITED STATES.

STATES AND TERRITORIES.	Total Population.
Alabama	996,992
Arkansas	484,471
California	560,247
Connecticut	537,454
Delaware	125,015
Florida	187,748
Georgia	1,184,109
Illinois	2,539,891
Indiana	1,680,637
Iowa	1,191,792
Kansas	364,399
Kentucky	1,321,011
Louisiana	726,915
Maine	626,915
Maryland	780,894
Massachusetts	1,457,351
Michigan	1,184,059
Minnesota	439,706
Mississippi	827,922
Missouri	1,721,295
Nebraska	122,993
Nevada	42,491
New Hampshire	318,300
New Jersey	906,096
New York	4,382,759
North Carolina	1,071,361
Ohio	2,665,260
Oregon	90,923
Pennsylvania	3,521,791
Rhode Island	217,353
South Carolina	705,606
Tennessee	1,258,520
Texas	818,579
Vermont	330,551
Virginia	1,225,163
West Virginia	442,014
Wisconsin	1,054,670
Total States	**38,113,253**
Arizona	9,658
Colorado	39,864
Dakota	14,181
District of Columbia	131,700
Idaho	14,999
Montana	20,595
New Mexico	91,871
Utah	86,786
Washington	23,955
Wyoming	9,118
Total Territories	**442,730**
Total United States	**38,555,983**

POPULATION OF FIFTY PRINCIPAL CITIES.

CITIES.	Aggregate Population.
New York, N. Y.	942,292
Philadelphia, Pa.	674,022
Brooklyn, N. Y.	396,099
St. Louis, Mo.	310,864
Chicago, Ill.	298,977
Baltimore, Md.	267,354
Boston, Mass.	250,526
Cincinnati, Ohio	216,239
New Orleans, La.	191,418
San Francisco, Cal.	149,473
Buffalo, N. Y.	117,714
Washington, D. C.	109,199
Newark, N. J.	105,059
Louisville, Ky.	100,753
Cleveland, Ohio	92,829
Pittsburg, Pa.	86,076
Jersey City, N. J.	82,546
Detroit, Mich.	79,577
Milwaukee, Wis.	71,440
Albany, N. Y.	69,422
Providence, R. I.	68,904
Rochester, N. Y.	62,386
Allegheny, Pa.	53,180
Richmond, Va.	51,038
New Haven, Conn.	50,840
Charleston, S. C.	48,956
Indianapolis, Ind.	48,244
Troy, N. Y.	46,465
Syracuse, N. Y.	43,051
Worcester, Mass.	41,105
Lowell, Mass.	40,928
Memphis, Tenn.	40,226
Cambridge, Mass.	39,634
Hartford, Conn.	37,180
Scranton, Pa.	35,092
Reading, Pa.	33,930
Paterson, N. J.	33,579
Kansas City, Mo.	32,260
Mobile, Ala.	32,034
Toledo, Ohio	31,584
Portland, Me.	31,413
Columbus, Ohio	31,274
Wilmington, Del.	30,841
Dayton, Ohio	30,473
Lawrence, Mass.	28,921
Utica, N. Y.	28,804
Charlestown, Mass.	28,323
Savannah, Ga.	28,235
Lynn, Mass.	28,243
Fall River, Mass.	26,766

POPULATION OF THE UNITED STATES.

States and Territories	Area in square Miles	Population 1870	Population 1875	Miles R. R. 1872	States and Territories	Area in square Miles	Population 1870	Population 1875	Miles R. R. 1872
States.					*States.*				
Alabama	50,722	996,992		1,671	Pennsylvania	46,000	3,521,791		5,113
Arkansas	52,198	484,471		25	Rhode Island	1,306	217,353	258,239	136
California	188,981	560,247		1,013	South Carolina	29,385	705,606	925,145	1,391
Connecticut	4,674	537,454		820	Tennessee	45,600	1,258,520		1,520
Delaware	2,120	125,015		227	Texas	237,504	818,579		865
Florida	59,268	187,748		466	Vermont	10,212	330,551		675
Georgia	58,000	1,184,109		2,108	Virginia	40,904	1,225,163		1,489
Illinois	55,410	2,539,891		5,904	West Virginia	23,000	442,014		585
Indiana	33,809	1,680,637		3,529	Wisconsin	53,924	1,054,670	1,236,799	1,725
Iowa	55,045	1,191,792	1,350,544	3,160					
Kansas	81,318	364,399	528,349	1,760	*Total States*	1,950,171	38,113,253		59,587
Kentucky	37,680	1,321,011		1,124	*Territories.*				
Louisiana	41,346	726,915	857,039	539	Arizona	113,916	9,658		
Maine	31,776	626,915		871	Colorado	104,500	39,864		392
Maryland	11,184	780,894		820	Dakota	147,490	14,181		
Massachusetts	7,800	1,457,351	1,651,912	1,696	Dist. of Columbia	60	131,700		
Michigan	56,451	1,184,059	1,334,031	2,215	Idaho	90,932	14,999		
Minnesota	83,531	439,706	558,429	1,612	Montana	143,776	20,595		
Mississippi	47,156	827,922		990	New Mexico	121,201	91,874		
Missouri	65,350	1,721,295		2,503	Utah	80,056	86,786		
Nebraska	75,995	123,993	246,280	828	Washington	69,944	23,955		375
Nevada	112,090	42,491	52,540	593	Wyoming	93,107	9,118		498
New Hampshire	9,280	318,300		780					
New Jersey	8,320	906,096	1,026,502	1,265	*Total Territories*	965,032	442,730		1,265
New York	47,000	4,382,759	4,705,208	4,450					
North Carolina	50,704	1,071,361		1,160	Aggregate of U. S.	2,915,203	38,555,983		60,852
Ohio	39,964	2,665,260		3,740					
Oregon	95,244	90,923		159					

* Last Census of Michigan taken in 1874.   † Included in the Railroad Mileage of Maryland.

PRINCIPAL COUNTRIES OF THE WORLD;
Population and Area.

Countries	Population	Date of Census	Area in Square Miles	Inhabitants to Square Mile	Capitals	Population
China	446,500,000	1871	3,741,846	119.3	Pekin	1,648,800
British Empire	226,817,108	1871	4,677,432	48.8	London	3,251,800
Russia	81,925,480	1871	8,003,778	10.2	St. Petersburg	667,000
United States with Alaska	38,925,000	1870	4,664,884	7.78	Washington	109,199
France	36,469,800	1866	204,091	178.7	Paris	1,825,300
Austria and Hungary	35,904,400	1869	240,348	149.4	Vienna	833,900
Japan	33,785,300	1871	149,399	232.8	Yeddo	1,554,900
Great Britain and Ireland	31,817,100	1871	121,315	262.3	London	3,251,800
German Empire	39,906,092	1871	160,207	187	Berlin	825,400
Italy	27,482,174	1871	118,847	230.9	Rome	244,484
Spain	16,642,000	1867	195,775	85	Madrid	332,000
Brazil	10,000,000		3,254,029	3.07	Rio Janeiro	420,000
Turkey	16,463,000		672,621	24.4	Constantinople	1,075,000
Mexico	9,173,000	1868	761,526		Mexico	210,300
Sweden and Norway	5,937,560	1870	292,871	20.	Stockholm	139,900
Persia	5,000,000	1870	635,964	7.8	Teheran	120,000
Belgium	5,021,300	1869	11,374	441.5	Brussels	314,100
Bavaria	4,861,400	1871	29,292	165.9	Munich	169,500
Portugal	3,995,200	1868	34,494	115.8	Lisbon	224,054
Holland	3,688,300	1870	12,680	290.9	Hague	90,100
New Granada	3,000,000	1870	357,157	8.4	Bogota	45,500
Chili	2,000,000	1869	132,616	15.1	Santiago	115,400
Switzerland	2,669,100	1870	15,992	166.9	Berne	36,000
Peru	2,500,000	1871	471,838	5.3	Lima	160,100
Bolivia	2,000,000		497,324	4.	Chuquisaca	23,000
Argentine Republic	1,812,000	1869	871,848	2.1	Buenos Ayres	177,800
Wirtemberg	1,818,500	1871	7,533	241.4	Stuttgart	91,600
Denmark	1,784,700	1870	14,753	120.9	Copenhagen	182,012
Venezuela	1,500,000		368,238	4.2	Caraccas	42,000
Baden	1,461,400		5,912	247.	Carlsruhe	36,600
Greece	1,457,900	1870	19,353	75.3	Athens	43,400
Guatemala	1,180,000	1871	40,879	28.9	Guatemala	40,000
Ecuador	1,300,000		218,928	5.9	Quito	70,000
Paraguay	1,000,000	1871	85,787	13.6	Asuncion	48,000
Hesse	823,138		2,969	277.	Darmstadt	30,000
Liberia	718,000	1871	9,576	74.9	Monrovia	3,000
San Salvador	600,000	1871	7,335	81.8	Sal Salvador	15,500
Hayti	572,000		10,205	56.	Port au Prince	20,000
Nicaragua	350,000	1871	58,171	6.	Managua	10,000
Uruguay	300,000	1871	66,722	6.5	Monte Video	44,500
Honduras	350,000	1871	47,092	7.4	Comayagua	12,000
San Domingo	1,300,000		17,867	7.7	San Domingo	15,000
Costa Rica	185,000	1870	21,495	7.7	San Jose	2,000
Hawaii	62,950		7,634	80.	Honolulu	7,633

POPULATION OF ILLINOIS,
By Counties.

COUNTIES.	AGGREGATE.					
	1870.	1860.	1850.	1840.	1830.	1820.
Adams	56362	41323	26508	14476	2186	....
Alexander	10564	4707	2484	3313	1390	626
Bond	13152	9815	6144	5060	3124	2931
Boone	12942	11678	7624	1705	....	....
Brown	12205	9935	7198	4183	....	....
Bureau	32415	26426	8841	3067	....	....
Calhoun	6562	5144	3231	1741	1090	....
Carroll	16705	11733	4586	1023	....	....
Cass	11580	11325	7253	2981	....	....
Champaign	32737	14629	2649	1475	....	....
Christian	20363	10492	3203	1878	....	....
Clark	18719	14987	9532	7453	3940	931
Clay	15875	9336	4289	3228	755	....
Clinton	16285	10941	5139	3718	2330	....
Coles	25235	14203	9335	9616	....	....
Cook	349966	144954	43385	10201	....	*23
Crawford	13889	11551	7135	4422	3117	2999
Cumberland	12223	8311	3718	....	....	....
De Kalb	23265	19086	7540	1697	....	....
De Witt	14768	10820	5002	3247	....	....
Douglas	13484	7140	....	....	....	....
Du Page	16685	14701	9290	3535	....	....
Edgar	21450	16925	10692	8225	4071	....
Edwards	7565	5454	3524	3070	1649	3444
Effingham	15653	7816	3799	1675	....	....
Fayette	19638	11189	8075	6328	2704	....
Ford	9103	1979	....	....	....	....
Franklin	12652	9393	5681	3682	4083	1763
Fulton	38291	33338	22508	13142	1841	....
Gallatin	11134	8055	5448	10760	7405	3155
Greene	20277	16093	12429	11951	7674	....
Grundy	14938	10379	3023	....	....	....
Hamilton	13014	9915	6362	3945	2616	....
Hancock	35935	29061	14652	9946	483	....
Hardin	5113	3759	2887	1378	....	....
Henderson	12582	9501	4612	....	....	....
Henry	35506	20660	3807	1260	41	....
Iroquois	25782	12325	4149	1695	....	....
Jackson	19634	9589	5862	3566	1828	1542
Jasper	11234	8364	3220	1472	....	....
Jefferson	17864	12965	8109	5762	2555	691
Jersey	15054	12051	7354	4535	....	....
Jo Daviess	27820	27325	18604	6180	2111	....
Johnson	11248	9342	4114	3626	1596	843
Kane	39091	30062	16703	6501	....	....
Kankakee	24352	15412	....	....	....	....
Kendall	12399	13074	7730	....	....	....
Knox	39522	28663	13279	7060	274	....
Lake	21014	18257	14226	2634	....	....
La Salle	60792	48332	17815	9348	....	....
Lawrence	12533	9214	6181	7092	3668	....
Lee	27171	17651	5900	2035	....	....
Livingston	31471	11637	1553	759	....	....
Logan	23053	14272	5128	2333	....	....

POPULATION OF ILLINOIS—Concluded.

COUNTIES.	AGGREGATE.					
	1870.	1860.	1850.	1840.	1830.	1820.
Macon	26481	13738	3988	3039	1122	
Macoupin	32726	24602	12355	7926	1990	
Madison	44131	31251	20441	14433	6221	13550
Marion	20622	12739	6720	4742	2125	
Marshall	16950	13437	5180	1849		
Mason	16184	10931	5921			
Massac	9581	6213	4092			
McDonough	26509	20069	7616	5308	(b)	
McHenry	23762	22089	14978	2578		
McLean	53988	28772	10163	6565		
Menard	11735	9584	6349	4431		
Mercer	18769	15042	5246	2352	26	*21
Monroe	12982	12832	7679	4481	2000	1516
Montgomery	25314	13979	6277	4490	2953	
Morgan	28463	22113	16064	19547	12714	
Moultrie	10385	6385	3234			
Ogle	27492	22888	10020	3479		
Peoria	47540	36601	17547	6153	(c)	
Perry	13723	9552	5278	3222	1215	
Piatt	10953	6127	1606			
Pike	30768	27249	18819	11728	2396	
Pope	11437	6742	3975	4094	3316	2610
Pulaski	8752	3943	2265			
Putnam	6280	5587	3924	2131	d1310	
Randolph	20859	17205	11079	7944	4429	3492
Richland	12803	9711	4012			
Rock Island	29783	21005	6937	2610		
Saline	12714	9331	5588			
Sangamon	46352	32274	19228	14716	12960	
Schuyler	17419	14684	10573	6972	b2959	
Scott	10530	9069	7914	6215		
Shelby	25476	14613	7807	6659	2972	
Stark	10751	9004	3710	1573		*5
St. Clair	51068	37694	20180	13631	7078	5248
Stephenson	30608	25112	11666	2800		
Tazewell	27903	21470	12052	7221	4716	
Union	16518	11181	7615	5524	3239	2362
Vermilion	30388	19800	11492	9303	5836	
Wabash	8841	7313	4690	4240	2710	
Warren	23174	18336	8176	6739	308	
Washington	17599	13731	6953	4810	1675	1517
Wayne	19758	12223	6825	5133	2553	1114
White	16846	12403	8925	7919	6091	4828
Whitesides	27503	18737	5361	2514		
Will	43013	29321	16703	10167		
Williamson	17329	12205	7216	4457		
Winnebago	29301	24491	11773	4609		
Woodford	18956	13282	4415			
Total	2539891	1711951	851470	476183	157445	*49 55162

PRODUCTIONS OF AGRICULTURE, STATE OF ILLINOIS, BY COUNTIES.—1870.

COUNTIES.	Improved Land.	Woodl'nd	Other unimproved	Spring Wheat.	Winter Wheat.	Rye.	Indian Corn.	Oats.
	Number.	Number.	Number.	Bushels.	Bushels.	Bushels.	Bushels.	Bushels.
Total	19,329,952	5,061,578	1,491,331	10,133,207	19,995,198	2,456,578	129,921,395	42,780,851
Adams	287,926	112,576	19,370	16,191	947,616	20,989	1,452,905	759,074
Alexander	13,836	17,761	…	…	42,658	30	244,220	21,627
Bond	145,015	42,613	1,915	700	368,625	6,210	1,064,052	461,097
Boone	137,397	28,886	2,658	241,042	599	35,871	466,985	579,127
Brown	57,062	35,491	25,608	13,276	117,362	4,712	337,769	70,852
Bureau	398,611	41,866	15,808	465,236	724	43,811	3,010,404	987,426
Calhoun	37,681	63,443	2,754	75	221,298	186	241,041	26,231
Carroll	186,861	29,793	33,402	418,073	260	25,721	1,367,965	775,100
Cass	92,902	33,495	6,604	12,165	127,054	2,772	1,148,990	168,784
Champaign	419,368	16,789	58,502	102,577	123,091	45,752	3,921,720	721,875
Christian	241,472	19,803	19,174	18,360	504,041	10,722	1,883,336	383,821
Clark	118,594	102,201	5,420	…	195,118	7,308	614,582	212,628
Clay	146,922	80,612	5,225	1,894	85,747	3,221	1,019,994	269,915
Clinton	150,177	48,868	8,722	500	610,888	1,619	813,257	456,321
Coles	208,337	45,914	3,274	2,651	154,485	8,825	2,133,111	315,951
Cook	348,824	18,635	17,337	144,296	4,904	20,171	570,427	1,581,225
Crawford	105,505	78,430	27,185	69	212,924	15,497	581,963	136,255
Cumberland	75,312	40,331	5,601	550	84,697	14,798	403,075	171,880
DeKalb	334,502	17,722	6,551	398,059	190	21,018	1,023,849	1,087,074
DeWitt	168,539	29,518	17,638	106,463	11,695	11,540	1,311,635	216,756
Douglas	147,633	11,897	7,316	7,683	65,161	9,017	1,680,225	225,074
DuPage	164,874	17,213	3,851	106,096	693	7,532	331,981	860,809
Edgar	265,158	66,808	14,282	13,283	247,360	37,508	2,107,615	290,679
Edwards	58,912	57,585	860	…	122,709	528	352,371	129,152
Effingham	120,313	56,310	28,206	77	195,716	19,759	620,247	386,073
Fayette	187,196	93,460	16,786	…	351,310	25,328	962,525	497,395
Ford	141,228	2,996	63,976	42,571	1,008	11,577	565,673	154,589
Franklin	80,749	3,994	86,710	365	111,324	5,195	653,205	222,426
Fulton	278,142	123,823	4,076	193,669	223,930	131,711	1,508,763	261,390
Gallatin	49,572	68,750	2,565	…	83,092	515	509,494	27,164
Greene	175,408	93,212	29,653	…	577,606	415	1,051,313	61,029
Grundy	193,995	6,256	4,505	21,700	156	4,969	295,974	269,342
Hamilton	88,996	93,878	3,313	129	92,317	11,672	735,952	203,164
Hancock	311,517	13,385	18,489	181,378	232,750	133,533	1,510,401	579,599
Hardin	28,117	14,771	107	13	32,300	865	172,651	25,991
Henderson	130,951	34,705	14,215	161,112	69,062	96,410	1,712,901	229,286
Henry	263,901	12,626	31,459	462,379	445	35,768	2,541,680	668,367
Iroquois	322,510	22,478	63,498	57,160	10,480	23,257	799,811	430,746
Jackson	78,518	87,042	5,993	890	329,036	521	611,951	149,931
Jasper	94,867	67,023	12,250	…	87,808	9,167	461,345	149,214
Jefferson	118,957	94,888	776	…	100,551	5,934	887,981	385,919
Jersey	94,145	51,127	1,364	…	558,367	…	519,129	71,770
JoDaviess	156,517	82,076	45,778	282,758	555	7,185	1,286,326	874,016
Johnson	57,820	3	79,141	…	92,191	2,468	343,298	74,525
Kane	240,126	31,640	399	188,629	325	23,618	674,33[illegible]	785,608
Kankakee	312,182	10,978	10,598	103,466	480	12,93[illegible]	637,391	774,408
Kendall	161,004	14,241	2,283	90,681	1,249	5,116	981,267	468,890
Knox	330,829	31,566	25,153	267,764	7,654	113,587	2,708,311	787,952
Lake	207,779	21,072	21,399	168,914	221	5,871	517,355	699,069
Lasalle	533,724	38,117	2,356	271,181	2,193	48,408	3,077,023	1,569,642
Lawrence	87,828	72,738	3,273	…	264,131	1,121	656,886	131,388
Lee	342,212	12,071	7,109	450,792	2,260	14,825	1,656,978	903,197
Livingston	377,505	12,462	41,788	120,206	1,335	26,162	1,182,690	659,100
Logan	221,708	17,391	408	198,056	40,962	37,252	4,221,648	490,226
Macon	205,259	18,153	9,115	55,238	156,613	29,225	2,314,461	454,648
Macoupin	231,055	81,221	7,343	160	861,398	2,101	1,051,541	459,417
Madison	257,082	89,450	13,675	550	1,207,184	3,687	2,127,540	475,252
Marion	173,081	61,579	4,112	…	173,652	14,517	1,034,052	389,446
Marshall	166,057	28,260	2,976	106,128	900	36,135	1,182,907	362,604
Mason	209,251	31,739	31,013	73,261	125,628	49,182	2,618,729	272,660
Massac	25,151	33,390	30	…	72,416	541	133,120	22,097
McDonough	261,635	52,517	14,035	273,871	36,140	52,403	1,362,498	280,717
McHenry	230,566	53,293	57,998	401,790	270	29,267	1,145,005	910,397
McLean	491,978	40,364	49,087	211,861	10,957	39,824	4,724,379	911,127
Menard	134,173	31,941	13,952	36,152	45,791	4,28[illegible]	1,973,88[illegible]	235,091
Mercer	222,805	45,977	22,598	289,291	13,201	40,778	2,054,965	452,889
Monroe	92,816	84,369	666	…	651,767	1,427	543,712	152,251
Montgomery	276,682	47,804	8,495	59	744,891	3,260	1,527,899	668,425
Morgan	294,150	60,217	1,876	18,196	357,527	5,547	3,198,835	198,724
Moultrie	144,220	24,785	13,112	17,128	196,430	6,676	1,757,141	263,992
Ogle	316,883	43,643	14,913	497,038	5,580	157,501	1,787,066	141,510
Peoria	170,726	48,666	2,516	92,361	31,813	99,502	969,224	334,892
Perry	94,754	68,474	220	…	350,446	1,044	384,446	358,760
Piatt	94,154	5,978	13,897	26,382	39,762	9,248	1,079,725	193,610
Pike	243,785	128,958	9,302	130	1,057,497	25,303	1,399,188	161,419
Pope	55,980	87,733	…	…	70,457	2,305	315,958	67,886
Pulaski	19,419	12,518	…	…	44,922	222	195,735	16,511
Putnam	37,271	17,181	4,174	28,137	796	7,705	331,258	86,519
Randolph	140,761	102,274	1,170	450	1,031,022	3,235	510,080	414,487
Richland	75,078	50,618	2,025	…	150,268	3,305	482,594	201,631
Rock Island	155,214	31,239	20,755	243,541	2,279	20,090	1,459,653	276,575
Saline	72,309	70,393	809	200	84,011	568	531,510	69,763
Sangamon	421,748	51,085	19,932	89,301	217,658	23,074	4,388,761	397,218
Schuyler	96,195	62,477	21,294	56,221	165,724	20,843	410,975	119,559
Scott	85,331	34,633	1,610	18	266,105	930	752,771	18,402
Shelby	310,179	74,908	9,314	15,526	452,015	23,086	2,082,578	637,812
Stark	138,129	12,375	2,783	124,630	…	30,534	1,149,878	316,726
St. Clair	231,117	76,591	2,016	2,550	1,562,621	1,608	1,423,121	476,851
Stephenson	251,857	18,167	13,701	527,394	2,118	135,302	1,615,679	960,620
Tazewell	229,126	45,268	14,846	132,417	72,110	59,027	2,062,053	505,841
Union	75,852	83,608	5,900	…	180,231	1,745	679,753	124,473
Vermilion	360,251	53,078	31,122	44,806	249,558	52,476	2,818,027	436,051
Wabash	54,063	37,558	509	…	202,201	…	421,361	110,798
Warren	256,187	27,294	14,583	186,290	5,712	72,212	2,982,853	601,054
Washington	177,582	55,852	1,931	…	672,496	2,526	836,115	533,398
Wayne	117,352	116,794	10,486	266	164,689	8,665	1,179,291	401,182
White	92,998	78,157	869	…	184,321	418	870,521	119,654
Whiteside	289,809	21,925	37,310	457,455	264	31,658	2,162,943	880,848
Will	419,442	24,261	6,335	195,260	1,996	8,030	1,131,458	1,868,682
Williamson	128,128	116,949	1,618	176	170,787	6,228	655,710	180,986
Winnebago	211,373	37,238	15,237	408,606	2,468	137,985	1,237,406	868,903
Woodford	225,504	25,217	23,135	178,139	108,307	20,426	2,154,185	744,581

GEN. ALLEN C. FULLER
BELVIDERE.

HISTORY OF BOONE COUNTY.

PHYSICAL GEOGRAPHY.

The physical geography of Boone County is not remarkable, the general face of its surface being not dissimilar to that of the counties by which it is immediately surrounded. The townships of Spring and Flora, and all that part of the county south of the Kishwaukee is, properly speaking, (Shattuck's Grove excepted,) a treeless prairie—not level, however, but a series of long, low, undulating rolls, and low ranges of hills and ridges. In some places there are swales and sloughs of limited extent, between moist marshes and black, fat meadow lands. A few trees skirt along Coon creek in the southwest part of the county, and scattered patches of timber in one or two other places relieve the level landscape. A broad, rich comparatively level prairie, these sections still preserve some of that primitive beauty from which Spring and Flora townships derived their names. In the report of Prof. A. H. Worthen, State Geologist, published in 1873, he says of this section: "Before the busy, teeming millions of the sons of toil swarmed over the fertile West, prairie flowers, in spring-like beauty and autumnal glory, bloomed where now the glancing plow-share turns the spring furrow, and the golden-ripened wheat fields dally with the fugitive winds. The purple and golden clouds of flowers that used to lie on these prairies are now no more; but in their place, the ta-selled Indian corn waves its head, and men are growing rich from the cultivation in useful crops of these old flower-beds of nature."

North of the Kishwaukee the country changes in appearance, becoming more rolling; and, although still good for agricultural purposes, the soil becomes thinner and lighter colored. More streams are found. These are margined with hills, to some extent, and hilly barrens. There "are wide stretches of rather light timber and brushwood that extend for miles along these streams and over the intervening highlands. Occasionally a better grove of timber may be found. Small prairies, prairie openings, and long stretches of prairie still exist in every direction." The same general remarks apply to this portion of the county, except that wet and swampy land, in which many of the streams of the county take their origin. The northwestern part of the county has considerable prairie, as well as much wet land; the northeastern has more timber, and is higher and dryer, and on towards the "Big Foot" prairie, in Wisconsin, contains good farming lands.

The timber for the most part consists of black, white, burr, red, yellow and some other rarer varieties of the oak, black walnut and butternut, shell bark and common hickory, cottonwood, sugar maple, honey locust, sycamore, water and slippery elm, haw, dogwood, common poplar, white and red ash, red cedar, white pine, linden or basswood, common swamp willow, and a few other shrubs and plants. The groves in this part of the county are made up principally of the common black and white oaks to be met with in the poorer-timbered regions of northern Illinois. The alluvial lands skirting the larger streams are the only places where many of the above species of trees are to be found.

For the most part the county is well watered, and most admirably adapted to stock raising and agricultural purposes, for which it has become so noted, her products being second to no county in the northwest in proportion to her size. The Kishwaukee enters it on the east, not far from the centre of the eastern line of Bonus township, and crosses in long, easy-flowing curves, entering Winnebago County at the village of Cherry Valley. The water is reasonably clear and of moderate current. Coon Creek comes in from the southeast, and falls into it near the centre of Bonus township. On the north is the Piscasaw, which discharges its waters into the Kishwaukee above the Big Thunder Mills, a short distance east of Belvidere. Beaver Creek comes in at the northeastern corner of the county, flows in a direction west of south, and joins the Kishwaukee a short distance above the village of Cherry Valley. Some smaller streams, having their sources in the township of Manchester, find their way towards Rock river.

GEOLOGICAL FORMATIONS.

[Compiled from the Geological Survey of Illinois.]

The Cincinnati group and the upper division of the Trenton limestones are the only rocks which outcrop, or in any manner show themselves, in this county. About the northwestern corner, extending to even some distance within its borders, the middle and lower Trenton limestones doubtless are the underlying rocks; but they nowhere outcrop, that could be noticed by the surveyor. The deposits of the Quaternary system are extensive in the county, covering it over in many places to a great depth. It will thus be seen that the geological formations of Boone County are few, and its geology comparatively simple. The following sections of the rocks exposed and the superficial deposits, is comparatively correct, although nothing but an approximation to the thickness of the latter can be given:

SECTION OF FORMATION IN BOONE COUNTY.

Alluvial, principally partially stratified clays, sands and fine gravels, along the Kishwaukee, with loams and surface soils—20 feet.
Light-colored, velvety, tough, tenacious, impervious potter's clay—30 feet.
Ordinary drift deposits, consisting of the usual sands, gravels, hard pan and clays—35 feet.
Cincinnati shales; the formation much deeper, but worked to a depth of—18 feet.
The Galena limestone, worked—35 feet.
Lower Trenton limestones—unknown.

SURFACE GEOLOGY.

The surface geology consists of the usual Quaternary deposits, except that the loess is perhaps entirely wanting. The alluvial deposits along the small streams are narrow, rich and black. On the Kishwaukee they are wider and deeper, intermingled with sands and fine gravels, and bear, in places, a heavy growth of bottom timber. The usual thin prairie soils, swamp mucks and peats of various degrees of purity and ripeness, make up the rest.

The drift proper is a heavy body of abraded and transported materials. Over that part of the county underlaid by the Cincinnati shales, there is a thinner superficial deposit of a fine, laminated, comminuted clay, of a light ashy or blue color, bearing mingled evidence of deposition in still waters and the dissolving *in situ* of the underlying clayey shale rocks. No extensive gravel beds exist; but occasional large boulders may be noticed, more especially lying about the low, springy places.

But leaving the gently rolling prairies, and going northward to the region underlaid by the Galena limestone, the reddish clays, hard-pan and coarse gravel beds of the upper members of the drift largely predominate. A few miles west of Capron are localities where boulders of the average size of a man's head lay thickly strewn over the ground. These were noticed to lie thickest where boggy and springy places were met with, surrounded by rougher and more rolling land. The boulders are all from the metamorphic regions of the north, and consist of granite, gneiss, hornblende, trap, and some other varieties, with their various combinations. Across the whole northern part of the county, these boulders were noticed in greater or less abundance, associated with clays, and sometimes clayey sands. Across the central part of the county the coarse gravel beds, unstratified hard-pan and partially stratified clays, make up the surface coverings of the rocks. Under these, all over this region, laminated clays rest upon the indurated rocks below. Some of the gravel beds northwest of Caledonia are almost a mile long, and several feet deep. They are made up of materials very much rounded and abraded, are partially stratified and the gravel is of all sizes, intermingled with clean sand. A low drift hill of gravelly clay lies close to Belvidere, on which the court-house stands. In the banks of the Kishwaukee, a short distance below the bridge between the north and south parts of the city, on the north side of the stream, are outcrops of the bank of tenacious potter's clay, before referred to. It runs under at least a part of the city, and in one place, borings for some public work showed it to be some seventy feet in thickness. At another locality, some workmen were sinking a well, when after going through this deposit, which was there much thinner, water rushed into the well so fast that the men could hardly get out in safety.

The traditional stories of nuggets of copper having been found among the gravel and boulders were not confirmed by the survey. In prosecuting his work, Prof. Worthen, the geologist, says that in connection with his observations upon the drift, he watched closely in order to detect indications of glacial action, but that he was forced, somewhat reluctantly, to admit that atmospheric and chemical agencies and aqueous forces probably explained most of the phenomena connected with these superficial deposits. In the moraine-like hillocks of Ogle county, in his opinion, glacial action was more manifest.

The Cincinnati Shales.—The shaley rocks of this deposit underlie nearly all that part of the county south of the Kishwaukee. Coon Creek, doubtless, cuts down to the Galena: but all the prairie ridges show the outcroppings of the former rocks, although worked exposures are rare. In fact, says the report, there are but two good stone quarries in Boone County: one in the Cincinnati shales, five or six miles south of Belvidere, and one in the Galena limestone, three or four miles northwest of the city. The former of these is opened in the brow of a low hill. A few feet of clay and subsoil is stripped from the surface of the shingly rocks. The formation is quarried into about eighteen feet in depth, and great quantities of stone have been removed and hauled for many miles over the surrounding country, and into the city of Belvidere. The quarry, or rather series of quarries, is a source of profit, not so much on account of the valuable properties of the stone, as on account of the ease with which they can be quarried and the scarcity of all kinds of stone in the county. We noticed here flagging stones twelve by twenty-one feet and three or four inches thick, without an apparent crack. In some parts of the rocky walls, where exposed to the air, the rock is crumbling and decaying rapidly. About Garden Prairie, this formation is quarried and hauled north and northwest for a distance of seven and eight miles, for purposes of ordinary stone masonry. It is not worked at any other place in the county. No natural outcrops exist, on account of the ease with which it disintegrates and covers up its natural outcrops; but it is not difficult to trace its boundaries by the gently undulating elevations, the marshy springs along their base, the color of the waters that trickle down the slopes, and the nature of the overlying clays themselves.

The formation here is unfossiliferous to a high degree. Nothing but a few indistinct tracings of fucoids or sea weeds were noticed.

The Galena Limestone.—Two-thirds of the county, perhaps, is underlaid by the lead-bearing rocks of the Trenton limestone. And yet in all this extent of superficial area, there is but one good outcrop, and one place where the Galena is worked to any extent or advantage. This is at the exposure on Beaver Creek, three and a half miles west of Belvidere. The quarry is worked to a depth of thirty-five feet. The stone is massive and solid. Some of the bottom layers are from six to eight feet in thickness. Much stone has been quarried for the railroad bridge at Belvidere, and for building purposes in the surrounding country.

The country round the quarry is barrens and oak openings, with brushwood and a thin, whitish soil. The upper strata of this outcrop are thin enough to be readily removed with pick and wedge and crow-bar; but the lower ones can only be displaced by patient blasting. Here Prof. Worthen found many of the characteristic fossils, such as *Receptaculites sulcata, Murchisonia gracilis, M. gigas, Pleurotomaria angulata, Ambonychia, Bellerophon,* and fragments of *Orthocera.*

"My examinations," continues Prof. Worthen, "indicate that both Beaver Creek and the Piscasaw, for their whole length in this county, are underlaid by the Galena limestone. From Belvidere, on a line east of north, in the townships of Bonus, Boone and Leroy to Capron, and on nearly to the State line; thence west a few miles; thence south along the center township line of the county through Poplar Grove, to the starting point; thence northwest to Caledonia, and a few miles north of the same; thence back on any convenient road to the starting point; thence west on the North Rockford road to the county line, and on all this extent of country gone over, I only saw indications of this limestone. Only a few imperfect, crumbly outcrops were seen in the faces of some of the little hills—not such as would pay to work."

On the Upper Beaver and round the feeding springs of one of the Kinnikinniks, some poor specimens of stone are quarried, such as are used for the foundations of houses about Capron and in that part of the county.

Blue Limestone.—In the northwestern part of the county were found indications of the existence of the lower divisions of the Trenton formation. Its close proximity to Roscoe and Beloit, with some surface indications, lead to the opinion that these would be the surface rocks if the superincumbent clays were removed.

ECONOMICAL GEOLOGY.

Building Stone.—Building stones are scarce in Boone County. The quarry on Beaver Creek furnishes a solid, massive, hard stone, very suitable for bridge piers, culverts and other solid work, but requires a good deal of labor to adapt it to the lighter kinds of masonry. Most of the heavy building stones used in Belvidere, such as church foundations, and other like work, are obtained at this quarry. For the lighter kinds of work, the quarry in the Cincinnati shales, south of Belvidere, furnishes most of the stone used, and enters largely into cellar walls, foundations of ordinary houses, etc., etc. The stone is easily quarried and broken into blocks of any required superficial area, and are consequently well adapted to the uses named. At Gen. Hurlbut's residence in Belvidere, some of the stone from this quarry have been in use for over twenty years, and are but little disturbed by the action of time. For flagging stone they can be quarried of any desired size and shape. They are used for this purpose in some instances in Belvidere, and serve the purpose admirably. For solid work the stone from this quarry is not recommended.

Lime.—A limekiln has been successfully operated at the Galena quarry (heretofore mentioned) for some years. The lime made at this kiln is of good quality, but builders at Belvidere find it more economical to use lime shipped by railroad. A perpetual limekiln at the Beaver quarry would be a good investment.

Minerals.—There are no mineral deposits in the county, although bog iron ore has been noticed in considerable abundance in some of the bogs west of Capron. Pieces of float copper are said to have been found in the gravels of the drift. A few traces of lead have been found in the Galena limestone. Springs of chalybeate water exist in places. These are matters of curiosity and interest, rather than sources of economical value.

Sands and Clays.—From the ordinary clay and sand banks almost everywhere abounding in more or less purity, sand for building purposes, and clay for ordinary red brick, may be obtained in great abundance. The subsoil over most of the Galena rocks makes a good common brick. The bed of potters' clay, heretofore mentioned, deserves more than a passing notice. When ground and mixed with sand, it makes a hard, handsome, cream-colored brick, quite as beautiful, and, as is generally believed, more enduring than the far-famed Milwaukee brick. For this purpose alone this bed of clay is valuable. For any article of common crockery it would also be very valuable, and even queensware of fair quality might be made from this deposit. When first dug this clay is tough and tenacious. The color is between a milk-white and chocolate brown. When dry it breaks with a somewhat conchoidal fracture; has a fat, unctious feel to the fingers, and becomes lighter in color. Its chemical composition is not given in the report from which we quote.

Peat.—In the township of Bonus, near the residence of Mr. Dan'l Chapman, and partly owned by him, there is a peat bog of about twenty acres in extent. Messrs. Brown and Dana also own peat land in the same slough. In all, there is about forty acres. This deposit is located in a swale running down into the Piscasaw creek in an east and west direction, and is susceptible of easy drainage. It is covered with a dense growth of sedgy grass, and quakes and shakes as one walks over it. Beneath its carpet of sphagnum mosses, it seems soft and easy of penetration. A common pole can be easily forced down to a depth of seven and eight feet. The quality of the peat is a little fibrous, and is recognized as grass peat rather than moss peat, but both grass and moss enter into its composition, but when the report was made pronounced to be in its formative stage, consequently unripe, good for purposes of fertilization, but hardly adapted to a successful fuel. Peat deposits of good quality are also said to exist in the towns of Manchester and Leroy.

GENERAL HISTORY.

Although the territory embraced in the State of Illinois was occupied by the French under LaSalle as early as 1680, nearly three hundred years ago, but little progress towards the occupancy of the country by white people was made until about the beginning of the present century. About that time public attention and the attention of the people of the older states began to be attracted to the rich prairies and fertile valleys of the territory, and immigrants from the states of Virginia, Kentucky, Tennessee, and North Carolina—the largest proportion from the latter state—began coming in and settling down to the work of making farms. These settlements were confined, as a general rule, to the lands along the rivers—the Ohio, above Cairo, the Wabash, the Mississippi, and to some extent along the Illinois. Growing year by year, immigration gradually increasing, every accession made another innovation upon the uncultivated domain, and so, still pushing onward and outward, the southern part of the state came to be settled first.

As the great natural fertility and productiveness of the soil became known, its easy subjection to cultivation to be understood, *Illini* came to be looked upon from one end of our common country to the other as a very paradise—as a land where, with common industry, prudence, and ordinary economy, any man might grow rich in a very few years, as compared with life in the older and timbered states.

For many years the settlements in Illinois were thus confined to the more southern part of the state, but about the years 1832-3, the beautiful valleys of Fox and Rock Rivers and their tributaries began to attract attention in the New England and more northerly of the Middle States, and a tide of immigration set in from that direction. These immigrants brought with them that thrift and economy, enterprise and judgment, that had enabled them and their fathers by closest industry to make an humble living among the rocks and timber, the hillsides and mountain tops of their native states. Here, on these rich prairies—lands free from rocks and boulders, already cleared and waiting for the plow, with half the toil expended, would produce fourfold more than could ever be realized in the lands left behind. Thrift, prosperity, and independence have followed their steps and rewarded their energy. Almost every house is a palace in finish and surroundings. The wild prairies of less than half a century ago have been reduced to a garden of beauty and made to blossom with the rose. Want is comparatively unknown, and intelligence and refinement prevail.

Less than half a century ago, the eight townships composing the county of Boone were a part of the unbroken wild of which we have written. But naturally grand and rich, the territory it embraces could not long fail to attract the attention of immigrants, and in 1835 a few settlers found their way hitherwards, and settled down in the immediate vicinity of the town of Belvidere. At that time there were but two organized counties in this part of the state, Jo Daviess and Cook. They extended from the Lake on the east to the Mississippi on the west.

In this part of Illinois, as in all other parts of the state, and, in fact, as is always the practice in the settlement of new territories (unless there are peculiar local considerations), the first settlements were invariably made along the rivers or creeks, or in groves of timber. Rock River, a stream of attractive beauty and great power (if fully developed) for manufacturing purposes, had drawn to its rich lands a sufficient number of settlers anterior to this date (1835) to render them ambitious for a county organization, and at the session of the legislature at Vandalia, in 1835-6, an act was passed creating the county of Winnebago, and defining the boundaries as follows:

Commencing at the southeast corner of township number 43, range number 4, east of the third principal meridian, and running thence west to the said meridian; thence north along the line of said meridian to the southeast corner of township number 46, in range number 11, east of the fourth principal meridian; thence west to the dividing line between ranges numbers 7 and 8; thence north along said dividing line to the northern boundary line of the state; thence east along said boundary line to the northeast corner of range number 4, east of the third principal meridian; thence south to the place of beginning.—Approved Jan. 16, 1836.

After the passage of the act creating the county of Winnebago, and sometime previous to the organization, Charles Reed had occupied a tract of land on the west side of Rock river, and about two miles above the present site of the city of Rockford, by covering it with an Indian "float." He named his place Winnebago, and sought to have it made the county seat. About the same time Germanicus Kent, Dr. Haskell, Selden M. Church and Daniel S. Haight, and some others, had also taken claims where the city of Rockford has since grown up. They, also, had county seat aspirations, and between them and Mr. Reed a rivalry sprang up that, suffice it to say without entering into details, resulted finally in fixing their county seat at Rockford and establishing the county of Boone.

At the first election in Winnebago county, Aug. 1, 1836 (before the erection of Boone), Simon P. Doty was elected County Commissioner for the Belvidere district, and William E. Dunbar and Thomas B. Talcott for the other two districts into which the county had been divided. The first meeting of the County Commissioners' Court was held at the house of Daniel S. Haight (called the Rockford Hotel). Don Alonzo Spaulding was appointed as Clerk of their court. At that session of their court the Belvidere precinct was established, and an order entered providing for the election of two Justices of the Peace and two Constables therein. James Sayne, John K. Towner, and Charles Payne were appointed to be judges or inspectors of the election. The time of holding the election was set for Saturday, Aug. 27, 1836, and the house of Simon P. Doty named as the place of holding the election, which, for a number of years, continued to be the voting place in the Belvidere precinct. At that election, John K. Towner and John S. King were elected Justices of the Peace, and Mason Sherburne and Abel Thurston chosen as Constables. These were the first civil officers elected in what is now Boone County.

During the session of the legislature of 1836-7, an act was passed providing for the erection of the county of Boone, and defining its boundaries as follows:

Be it enacted by the people of the State of Illinois, represented in the General Assembly, That all that tract of country beginning at the northeast corner of township 46 north, range 4 east; thence south with the line dividing ranges 4 and 5 east, to the southwest corner of township 43 north; thence west on said line to the southeast corner of Winnebago County; thence north to the place of beginning on the north boundary of the state, shall form a county to be called Boone, in honor of Col. Daniel Boone, the first settler of the State of Kentucky.—Approved March 4, 1837.

The following winter Legislative attention was directed to the matter, and an act was passed correcting the boundary lines and defining them as follows:

That the boundary lines of Boone County shall be as follows, to-wit: Beginning at the northeast corner of Winnebago County, and running thence east on the State line to the northeast corner of township forty-six north, range five, east of the third principal meridian; thence south on the range line to the line dividing townships forty-two and forty-three north; thence west on said line to the southeast corner of Winnebago County; thence north with the line of Winnebago to the place of beginning; *Provided, however,* that if a majority of the legal voters residing within the limits of townships forty-three, forty-four, forty-five, and forty-six, north of range five east of the third principal meridian, shall, on the first Monday in August next, vote against the above named townships forming a part of the County of Boone, then the line dividing ranges four and five east shall continue to form the eastern boundary of Boone County.—Approved March 2, 1839, p. 242, Acts '38-9.

Thus established, Boone County was eleven miles wide and twenty-four miles long, leaving a strip one mile in width, including sections 6, 7, 18, 19, 30, and 31, in town 46, range 3, and the same number of sections each in towns 45, 44, and 43, that, under Government survey, clearly belonged to Boone County. But this was a measure of compromise to conciliate and reconcile the conflicting interests in Winnebago County. At a later period, the question of annexing the western tier of sections in range 3, to Boone County, began to be agitated, and finally culminated in the passage of an enabling act by the Legislature of 1842-3, to allow the settlers on the "strip" to elect to which county they would belong. No one but those immediately interested as settlers were allowed to vote. The interest became warm. As a natural consequence, the people of Boone County favored the scheme. They could not vote, but they could talk, and their best talkers were set to work "where they could do the most good," and they worked earnestly. None were more interested than the people of Belvidere. The eastern part of Winnebago County, the settlers on the strip excepted, opposed the scheme, for, if it prevailed, it would involve the establishment of their county seat in some doubt, and weaken their chances of securing the seat of justice at East Rockford. The people of the western part of Winnebago County favored the scheme, because, if successful, it would strengthen their chances for securing the county seat at West Rockford, or on the west side of Rock River.

During the session of the Legislature in the winter of 1843, an act entitled "An Act to define the bounds of Boone County," was passed, providing as follows:

Be it enacted by the People of the State of Illinois, represented in General Assembly, That sections 6, 7, 18, 19, 30, and 31, in each of the townships 43, 44, 45, and 46, in range 3 east of the 3d principal meridian, are hereby attached to and shall form a part of the county of Boone; *Provided,* an election shall be held at the house of Samuel Keith, in the village of Newburg, in Winnebago County, on the fourth day of May next (1843), under the inspection of Benjamin Hoyt and Samuel Keith, as judges, and A. W. Canfield, as clerk of said election, whose duty it shall be to attend at the time and place aforesaid and hold said election. A poll book shall be opened with columns headed "for" and "against" being attached to the County of Boone, and the legal voters residing on the aforesaid sections shall be permitted to vote for or against being so attached. The poll shall be kept open from 10 o'clock A. M. to 5 o'clock P. M., of said day, and, upon closing the poll, the judges and clerk shall certify the result on the poll book and seal up and deliver the same to the clerk of the County Commissioners' Court of Winnebago County within five days thereafter, and the clerk of said court shall, within two days, in the presence of two Justices of the Peace of his county, open and examine said poll book, and compare the certificate with the votes given, and thereupon make out a certificate of the result of said election, which shall be signed by said clerk and justices, and the same shall be entered upon the records of the Commissioners' Court for Winnebago County; and if it shall appear, by the result of said election, that a majority of said voters are in favor of being attached to the county of Boone, then and in that case, the aforesaid sections shall be and remain a part of Boone County, otherwise, they shall remain as heretofore; *Provided, further,* that if either of said judges or clerk shall fail to attend and act at said election, then the voters present shall choose others to act in their place, who shall be governed by the provisions of this act.—Approved Feb. 28, 1843, p. 92 Laws of '42–3.

As the day of the election drew nigh, the interest, especially among the people of Belvidere, grew in intensity. Every man of influence, character and intelligence, that could be made available in any way, was sent over to work among the settlers on the strip. Those of the Winnebago people who were unfriendly to the "annexation" scheme were equally earnest in their efforts. "Noses were counted," and so equally divided did the settlers seem to be that neither party felt assured of success. The drift of public sentiment among the settlers on the strip, however, seemed to settle towards Boone County, and this imbued the Belvidere people with renewed energy. Argument, entreaty, figures, advantages, and every sort of inducement were held out to the settlers. Finally the day that was to decide the issue came. Every settler entitled to a vote was brought out. When the polls were declared closed and the ballots counted, the tally sheet showed that 95 votes had been cast, of which 51 votes were "for" annexation to Boone County, and 44 votes "against"—a majority of 7 in favor of annexation.

This election and its result settled the status of Boone County and quieted all agitation incident to the organization of all new counties. It added twenty-five sections of valuable land, capable of supporting a thousand people, to the domain, and increasing the taxable property many thousands of dollars.

In section 10 of an act entitled "An Act to create certain counties therein named," passed by the Legislature of 1837, it was provided that elections for county officers should be held in Boone and DeKalb Counties on the first Monday of the following May.

Section 11 of the same act provided that it should be the duty of the clerks of the Commissioners' Courts of the counties thereby organized to give notice at least ten days previous to the elections to be held "as is above provided in said counties, and in case there shall be no clerk in said counties, it shall be the duty of the clerk of the Commissioners' Court of Winnebago County to give notice of the elections to be held in the counties of Boone and DeKalb."

Section 13 provided that the counties of Stephenson and Boone should continue to form a part of the county of Jo Daviess, until organized, and "when organized according to this act, shall continue attached to the county of Jo Daviess in all general elections, until otherwise provided by law."

In pursuance of the provisions of section 11, above quoted, there being no clerk of the Commissioners' Court in Boone County, the county not yet having been fully organized, a warrant for the election provided for in section 10, issued from the clerk of the Commissioners' Court of Winnebago County.

The law providing for this election also provided that it should be held at the house of Simon P. Doty in the Belvidere precinct, which at that time included all of Boone County.

The first Monday of May, A. D. 1837, was a day of interest to the people of "Belvidere precinct." The county of Boone had been established, and by the election of county officers they were to be enrolled among the other fully organized counties of the State and clothed with "all the rights and privileges" of the other counties. In those days printed or written ballots were not in use, but citizens voted *viva voce*. The polls were opened with great *eclat*, and midst jest and good nature, the election continued until the hour provided by law for closing the polls in the evening. Milton S. Mason, Cornelius Cline, and John Q. A. Rollins, were elected County Commissioners, Simon P. Doty, Sheriff, and John Handy, Coroner. On the 3d of May, the County Commissioners elect met, and organized the first Commissioners' Court held in Boone County. Milton S. Mason administered the oath of office to Cornelius Cline and John Q. A. Rollins, and Mr. Rollins administered the oath of office to Milton S. Mason. Dr. Daniel H. Whitney was appointed and qualified as clerk of the Commissioners' Court, and the transaction of county business commenced. Belvidere precinct was divided, and an additional precinct established, called the Lambertsburg precinct, taking in all the territory embraced in the four north townships of the county, and so named in honor of two brothers, James B. and Jeremiah Lambert, who had taken claims in what is now Leroy township. At this session it was also "ordered that John K. Towner be and he is hereby appointed County Treasurer for the county of Boone" (no Treasurer having been elected). Benjamin Sweet was appointed School Commissioner and Agent for the inhabitants of Boone, and Erastus A. Nixon, David Caswell, and George D. Hicks, were appointed trustees of the school lands in Congressional township 44 north, range 3 east of the third principal meridian, and William Dresser, John K. Towner, and Milton S. Mason, were appointed judges of all elections to be held in Belvidere precinct.

The erection of road districts and appointment of road supervisors appears next on record, and a further order providing that all county roads should be "opened fifty feet in the clear, and that each able-bodied man should work on some road five days in each year." This constituted one day's work for the court, when it adjourned without day.

Thus it may be assumed that the history of Boone County, as an organized body, dates from May 3, 1837—the date of the first meeting of the County Commissioners' Court, or in less than two years from the time when the first white settlements were made at Belvidere and Shattuck's Grove, in what is now Spring township, in 1835. If previous to that time there were any white settlers here, their identity is lost. No records are to be found of their presence, and hence it is concluded that the first settlements date from June or July of that year. When Simon P. Doty and Dr. Daniel H. Whitney arrived here, in August, 1835, they found Archibald Metcalf and David Dunham, encamped in a shanty on the west bank of the Kishwaukee (Indian for Sycamore), about eighty rods below where the State street bridge in Belvidere spans that stream.

A note on a county map, published by Messrs. William McVickar and

D. Kelsey, in 1858, under the heading of "First Settlers of Boone County, A. D. 1835," gives a list of the settlers at that period, saying that "Oliver Robbins and Brothers made the first claims in Boone County. Archibald Metcalf, David Dunham, Timothy Caswell and family, Charles H. Payne and family, John K. Towner and family, Cornelius Cline, Erastus A. Nixon, Erastus Shattuck and family, John Handy and family, Simon P. Doty and wife, Dr. Daniel H. Whitney, Charles Watkins, Abel Thurston, Milton S. Mason and family, David Elliott, Asahel Daggett and family."

The same authority gives the population of the county in 1858 at 12,860. Oliver Hale, of Bonus township, who settled at his present residence Oct. 1, 1836, is of the opinion that the list of settlers here in 1835, as quoted above, is not fully correct. He cites Christopher Payne and family as an addition that ought to be made. When Mr. Hale came, he found Mr. Payne occupying a claim of several thousand acres on Squaw Prairie, of whom he bought one claim of 400 acres. Payne had settled there in the fall of 1835. Mr. Andrew F. Moss, who came in May, 1836, makes a further correction by adding the names of David Caswell and family and Moses Blood and family. Mr. Hale is now a man of nearly eighty years, but is remarkably well preserved, intellectually and physically, and has a clear memory of the scenes and incidents of those early days, and his statements may be taken as conclusively correct. Mr. Moss, while a younger man by some years, has always been a close observer, and carries in his mind the names of all the pioneers he found here on his coming, in 1836, so that at least two families are added by their corrections. These families represented a population all told of only thirty-seven persons, as reported by a census-taker in the latter part of October of that year. In 1840, the population had increased to 1,705; in 1850, to 7,624; in 1860, to 11,678; in 1870, to 12,942; and is now estimated at 14,000. Real estate at that date was not taxable, by reason of the non-expiration of the three years' exemption from taxation after purchase or entry. In 1850, the assessed valuation of real and personal property was $828,714; in 1860, $1,511,376; in 1870, $1,790,218.

Until about 1840, the increase by immigration was comparatively slow. After that period, until the government land was all taken, the immigration was large and rapid. In September, 1836, the government surveyors established the township lines, and during the following winter subdivided them into sections. The lands were not open to sale or entry, however, until October, 1839. The lands in Boone county were divided between the Galena and Chicago land districts. The lands in range 3 comprised a part of the Galena district, while those in range 4 belonged to the Chicago district, and were subject to purchase or entry at that office. From the time the lands were opened to purchase and entry, claims were rapidly confirmed.

Who made the first purchase or first entry, has long since been forgotten, and there are no records immediately accessible that will supply the data to justify an opinion on this subject.

Between 1835 and October, 1839, when the land in this district was opened to sale, claims had been taken in almost all parts of the county. In this time a good commencement had been made towards reducing their wild sward to farm tillage, and in most cases they were yielding large enough returns to maintain the families occupying them, in comparative comfort, and in some instances they had been so productive and remunerative as to yield a sufficient surplus to enable their owners to provide against the day of purchase or entry, thus making their claims pay for themselves. From 1835 to 1840-41, might justly be called the "log cabin" age. But after the latter date the log cabins and shanties began to give way to a better class of houses, and prairie barns, with their grassy coverings, went down, to make room for more pretentious and convenient structures. Now, in 1877, there is scarcely a quarter section of land in the county that does not boast its large and handsome brick or frame residence, with tastefully arranged grounds, fine large barns and substantial fencings. The ox-wagon has given place to more modern vehicles, and fine carriages and well-trained horses are among the possessions of a large majority of the citizens. But little land, as compared with many other western counties, was entered for speculative purposes. The largest, and it may be said the only lands so purchased, was by William Taylor, as agent for the Aberdeen Bank of Scotland, in 1839. That agency purchased very largely in the counties of Winnebago, McHenry and Boone, 4,640 acres of it being selected, in different sections, in Boone. But that and all other lands so purchased long since passed into the hands of actual settlers and sturdy farmers, who, by cheerful industry and prudent economy, have made homes of which any people might be justly proud. Taylor, the agent referred to, some time after he made the entry, was going down the Mississippi river on the steamboat "War Eagle," and when near St. Louis was drowned from the boat. It has been said he jumped into the river, but there were no reasons to justify a suspicion of suicide.

In 1835, when the first settlers came, post-offices were unknown in the bounds of what is now Boone county, and for a large district of country outside. That was long before the days of cheap postage or the prepaid system, and for many months when a settler went to Chicago, the nearest post-office, his pockets were filled with quarters to pay the postage on letters from friends and relatives in the "old homes." Ottawa was the nearest point for milling purposes until a mill was built at the Napier settlement, now Napierville. Later, a mill was built at Belvidere, stores and trading places were licensed, and gradually the hardships of pioneer life gave way before the advancement of civilization and the better things of more modern achievements. Indians had never been troublesome to the settlers, except as beggars, and soon after were all removed to new hunting grounds on the plains and prairies of the further west—to Iowa, and afterwards to Kansas, and a future opened out before this people that has grown brighter and brighter, until the brightest hopes of the hardy and sturdy pioneers of 1835 are left deeply shaded. Many of these early settlers have been gathered with their fathers on the brighter shores of the Great Beyond. A few are left awaiting the summons to join those who have gone before, but who shared with them the hardships and privations incident to pioneer life in this country of the Kish-wau-kee, erst the home of the Pottawatomie chief, Big Thunder, and his people. But all those who have gone before and all those who are waiting the summons to follow, made noble records for honesty, morality, industry, and all else that goes to make up noble lives. A record is left their descendants that will serve as a beacon light to guide them in paths of peace, pleasantness, happiness, and prosperity.

Before resuming the history proper of Boone county from where we left the organization of the county and the proceedings of the County Commissioners' Court in May, 1837, we may be pardoned by the reader for a slight digression relative to Big Thunder and his burial, and incidents relative thereto. Big Thunder was a noted character among his people, not from his stature, however, which was rather under the medium average of his race, but from his influence among them. His voice, perhaps, gave him the name he bore, as it is a prevailing practice with nearly all Indian tribes to name any object after that of which it most reminds them. Big Thunder, no doubt, when he laid aside the bow and arrow for the more effective rifle, tomahawk and scalping knife, was possessed of a strong, stentorian voice that in councils or giving words of command reminded his tribe or followers of a deep, distant thunder, and hence the name. But be this as it may, some time previous to the removal of his tribe to the west, he sickened and was taken over to the "happy hunting grounds." His burial place was selected on the highest point of ground on the mound where the court house has since been built. As was their custom no grave was dug, but wrapped in his blankets, and seated on a rude stool or bench, with his feet placed on an Indian-made rug, with his face turned towards the West, a direction in which a battle was expected to take place between his tribe and another, a structure made of split white ash logs, from which the bark was pealed, was erected around his body and covered with bark. The expected battle never came off, and consequently the war spirit of Big Thunder did not re-enter his mouldering body and join the victorious "whoops" of his braves as their vanquished foes fell beneath their tomahawks and scalping knives. In those days Belvidere was on a stage route from Chicago to Galena. The travel was heavy, and here the horses were changed, and sometimes for other causes a delay of from half an hour to an hour would occur. For many miles in all directions, the Indian "sarcophagus" that surrounded the body of Big Thunder could be distinctly seen. The logs or slabs from which the bark had been pealed had bleached and whitened in the sun, until they were almost as white as snow. To travelers and land hunters from the East, those who had never seen an Indian or an Indian grave, this "last abode" of Big Thunder was an object of curiosity. And while the stage would be delayed, passengers would betake themselves to the mound on which he was buried to view his "coop" and perhaps scratch their names and date of their visit on the logs, or may be, when the flesh had mouldered and fallen from the bones, leaving only a dried skeleton, a gather up a bone and carry it home as a trophy of their visit out in the "Indian country." His head was the first part of his anatomy to be carried away. That was taken to Chicago, and finally found its way into the possession of a noted phrenologist. Next another bone would be taken, and then another and another, until the bones composing the human frame were nearly all gone. Appreciating and wishing to gratify the curiosity of travelers some of the "wags" of Belvidere would secretly gather up the dried bones of hogs and as secretly throw them into Big Thunder's "coop." None the wiser of this little trick, travelers and curiosity gatherers would stop and pick out such bones as their fancy liked, pocket them and carry them away. This little joke of the "boys" of Belvidere was kept up as long as the grounds around the "coop" were left open, and it is pretty safe to assume that many a museum of curiosities in the eastern states has hog bones labeled "Thigh bone of Big Thunder, an Indian chief of the Pottawatomie Indians, buried at Belvidere, Illinois;" or a "forearm," a "middle finger," a "rib," a "spinal joint," or something else.

Another incident connected with Big Thunder's "coop" may not be amiss in this connection. It is told of Simon P. Doty. He does not deny it, but laughs over it when the matter is spoken of, as heartily as any one. Like hundreds of other people, especially sailors (of whom he was one in his earlier years), Mr. Doty likes tobacco. Very often in the early settlement of Boone County, the supply of tobacco hereabouts would give out, and "chewers of the weed" would, per force of circumstance, be compelled to go without for days at a time, sometimes for a week or more. Indians are proverbial for their use of tobacco, and whenever they chanced to pass by the "coop" of Big Thunder, they would throw a piece of chewing, or pouch of smoking tobacco at his feet or into his lap. On one of the occasions when tobacco among the white settlers had given out, Mr. Doty and Erastus A. Nixon were engaged in scoring and hewing timber. Doty had suffered and agonized for some time for a "chew." Finally he could endure it no longer, and passing up to Big Thunder's "coop," he reached in and abstracted a small supply. Mr. Nixon was equally suffering and longing for some tobacco. To his requests of Mr. Doty for a "chew," the latter protested that he had none. This, however, was before Doty had visited the "coop" on the mound, and of course he was honest and truthful when he protested he "was out." After that visit, his friend and co-laborer noticed him expectorate, and his suspicions were aroused. He picked up the chip upon which the spittle had fallen, and exclaimed, "Doty, you have tobacco!" Doty had to own up—to acknowledge the truth of the charge, and pledging Mr. Nixon to secrecy, he told him where and how he obtained it. But it was too good to keep—the joke, and not the tobacco—and it had to be told. It has been the occasion of many a laugh at Doty's expense, but he takes it in good part, and in speaking of it even at this day, in his eighty-first year, will laugh as heartily over it as any of the "boys," who always know where and how to get tobacco without going to the "coop" of a dead Indian chieftain for it.

Turning back to the proceedings of the County Commissioners' Court, May 3, 1837, and resuming a review of the record, we find that Charles McDougal was appointed Supervisor of Road, district No. 1; Ira Haskins of No. 2; David Caswell of No. 3, and Cornelius Cline of No. 4. These, then, were the first Road Supervisors appointed in Boone County, and divided into four districts, it may be assumed that the increase of population from the number of settlers in 1835, as already stated, had been pretty large. The wild lands had been surveyed, township and section lines defined, and the country mapped out and started on the high road to wealth and opulence.

On the 4th day of May, 1837, D. H. Whitney, Clerk of the County Commissioners' Court, made a transcript of the returns of the election held on the Monday previous, which transcript we copy from the records:

Made a transcript of the returns of the election in which Simon P. Doty was declared duly elected to the office of sheriff.

John Handy was declared duly elected to the office of coroner.

Seth S. Whitman was declared duly elected to the office of recorder.

And S. P. Hyde was declared duly elected to the office of county surveyor, and transmitted the same to the Secretary of State, this 4th day of May, A. D. 1837.

D. H. WHITNEY, *Clerk C. C. C., Boone County.*

The same day he "made out and delivered to the sheriff elect, certificates of appointment to Erastus A. Nixon, George D. Hicks and David Caswell, trustees of school land in T. 44, N. R. 3 E. 3 P. M. (3d principal meridian), and to Charles McDougal, as Supervisor of Road, district No. 1; David Caswell, Supervisor of Road, district No. 2, and Cornelius Cline, as Supervisor of Road, district No. 4." Mr. Whitney also recorded his appointment of William Dresser as "deputy clerk of the County Commissioners' Court."

The first session of the County Commissioners' Court was held at the house of Simon P. Doty. The next session convened at the same place, on the 5th of June following, when S. P. Doty, sheriff-elect, reported to the court that he had served notices of appointment on the several appointees of the previous session of the court, and that they all accepted.

John K. Towner, a Justice of the Peace in and for the County of Boone, reported the assessment of fines on his docket, to-wit:

"State of Illinois vs. Uriah Payne, $18.16¼, fine and cost, May 30, 1837. Execution issued to Abel Thurston, constable, returnable in 70 days." "State of Illinois vs. John Q. A. Rollins, $16.69, fine and costs, May 30, 1837. Execution issued to Abel Thurston, constable, returnable in 70 days."

The collection of these fines was the first money ever paid into the county treasury.

This term of the court adjourned on the 5th of June. On the 6th the clerk granted permission to Simon P. Doty and Charles F. H. Goodhue to "retail ardent spirits by the small measure," for which they were each charged the sum of $5. These were the first places licensed in Boone County for such purposes. In those days all business houses, of whatever character, had to secure license or permission from the county court, before they could commence operations. In almost every part of the county where settlements were made, some one would take out license for keeping a tavern or hotel, for which the charges ranged from $5 to $25. This was one source of revenue, but sometimes applicants for such permission being short of funds, would give their notes, and in some instances would afterwards take them up in full or in part, with county warrants issued to them for some kind of services rendered the county. The court also regulated the prices such hotels were allowed to charge for the entertainment of man and horse. At the September term, 1837, the court ordered that tavern rates for Boone County shall be:

Per meal, thirty-seven and a half cents.
For lodging per night, twelve and a half cents.
For horse to hay, eighteen and three-fourths cents.
Oats per peck, fifty cents.
All kinds of liquors, per drink, six cents.

In September, 1838, these rates were revised, and the following prices established:

Ordered that tavern rates for the ensuing year shall be as follows, viz.: Per meal, thirty-seven and a half cents; night's lodging twelve and a half cents; oats per peck, twenty-five cents; span of horses to hay over night, thirty-seven and a half cents; *good* brandy, rum, gin and wine, twelve and a half cents per drink; *poor* do., and whiskey, six and a fourth cents; per meal for stage passengers, fifty cents.

At the beginning of the September term of the court, the available means of the county amounted to $40, and the liabilities to $41.84. The clerk was allowed one dollar and fifty cents per day for his services, and the commissioners the same sum.

In November of that year, a special term of the Commissioners' Court was held, continuing only one day, the 6th. The act of the Legislature providing for the location of the county seat of Boone County, also appointed commissioners for that purpose, naming John M. Wilson, of Will County; James Day, of LaSalle County, and James H. Woodworth, of Cook County, as such commissioners. Pursuant to appointment, two of these commissioners, John M. Wilson and James H. Woodworth, visited Belvidere on the 30th of October to discharge the trust imposed upon them. When the Commissioners' Court met in special session on the 6th of November, and opened for business, the clerk submitted the following documents and vouchers:

OCT. 31ST, 1837.
COUNTY OF BOONE.

To James H. Woodworth and John M. Wilson.

Dr. To services in locating county seat of said county, 10 days each—20 days—at $2..$40.00.

Received payment.

JAMES H. WOODWORTH.
JOHN M. WILSON.

The court "ordered that the communication from the clerk and the accompanying documents be spread on record." The documents referred to were the following oaths, which were administered to Messrs. James H. Woodworth and John M. Wilson. Although the oaths were administered separately, the record shows that they were administered the same day (Oct. 30, 1837,) and in the same words, so that a copy of one will serve for both, excepting a change of name, to-wit:

STATE OF ILLINOIS,
BOONE COUNTY. } ss.

I, James H. Woodworth, do swear upon the Holy Evangelists of Almighty God, that I will proceed to examine and determine on a place for the permanent seat of justice for Boone County, faithfully taking into consideration the convenience of the people, the situation of the settlements, with an eye to future population, and designate the same according to law, so help me God.

(Signed) JAS. H. WOODWORTH.

Sworn and subscribed before me this 30th day of October, Anno Domini, 1837.

D. H. WHITNEY,
Justice of the Peace for Boone Co., Ill.

The report of the locating commissioners follows next of record, and is in these words:

Be it known, that we, James H. Woodworth and John M. Wilson, commissioners appointed to locate the County Seat of Boone county in the State of Illinois, under an act entitled an Act to create certain counties therein named, approved 4th March, A. D., 1837, being duly sworn, did on the (31) thirty-first day of October, A. D., 1837, proceed to examine and determine on a place for the permanent seat of justice for said county, and taking into view the convenience of the inhabitants, the situation of the settlements, the probable future population and eligibility of location, have and do locate said county seat upon the north-east quarter of section twenty-six, in township forty-four north, range three east of the third principal meridian, being in the Galena land district.

Given under our hands, this thirty-first day of October, A. D. 1837.

(Signed) JAS. H. WOODWORTH,
JOHN M. WILSON.

The commissioners then ordered that the draft of the clerk in favor of Mr. Cephas Gardner for forty dollars borrowed money for the payment of the commissioners for locating the seat of justice of this county, be paid out of the first money in the county treasury; and that eight dollars, the bill of S. P. Doty, made by said commissioners while performing said service for the county, be assumed, and that the clerk issue his draft on the treasury for the same.

The first claim made in Boone county was taken by Oliver Robbins and brothers, and included the southeast quarter of section twenty-six, township forty-four north, range three east, divided nearly equally by the

E. E. Moss

BELVIDERE.

Kishwaukee river, and was made early in the summer of 1835. These brothers subsequently sold their claim to Archibald Metcalf and David Dunham, who at a later period sold out to Dr. Goodhue, Charles Peck and Nathaniel Crosby, forming a part of what was subsequently known as the Belvidere Company. The Robbins Bros. pushed on West, probably taking other claims, selling out again as immigration followed them, and pushing on again. One of them afterwards returned to Boone county and made his home at Blood's Point, in Flora township. When the war of the rebellion came on, he enlisted in one of the companies formed in Boone county and was killed at the battle of Shiloh. Of the other brothers all trace has been lost.

The parties purchasing this claim of Dunham and Metcalf, afterwards, by purchase or otherwise, secured control of a large tract of land in the vicinity, including the northeast quarter of section twenty-six, and when the county seat question began to be agitated, proposed to relinquish to the county their claim to that particular quarter section on condition that the county seat should be located thereon. The agreement was kept, and when the land came into market in 1839, it was bid in in the name of the county commissioners, John K. Towner, Moses Blood and Robert B. Hurd. The date of purchase was October 17, 1839. November 10, 1841, a United States patent issued to them "as commissioners of Boone county, and to their successors in office forever."

The Belvidere Company, already referred to, was enlarged by the admission of other members to the number of ten, and the claims were parceled out in shares representing one thousand dollars each, and when put on the market in October, 1839, the land was purchased for and managed in the interests of the company. The company was made up of Charles Peck, Dr. Goodhue, Nathaniel Crosby, of Fredonia, N. Y., Prof. S. S. Whitman, Dr. John S. King, Jacob Whitman and others, to the number of ten.

In 1836 the town site, that part of it on the southeast quarter of section twenty-six, was partially laid off into town lots, by establishing the corners of State and Mechanic streets with an old iron carpenter's square. Lots were given to mechanics who would build on and occupy them. The first lot given away was to Simon P. Doty. His lot was at the corner of State and Mechanic streets—on the West side of State street and south of Mechanic street to the Kishwaukee. Having previously built a house a short distance west of the town site, he moved it up on to his lot, where he soon afterwards opened a hotel, calling it the "Belvidere House."

The commissioners locating the seat of justice designated where the county seat should be on the land selected by driving a stake in the ground on the *mound* where the court-house has since been built, within one-fourth of a mile of which, by the then existing laws, the county offices should be kept. At a later period in the progress of events (December, 1838,) it was discovered that Daniel H. Whitney, the county clerk, kept his office more than a quarter of a mile from the point so designated, and the commissioners declared the office vacant, and proceeded to appoint James L. Loop as clerk to fill the vacancy. Mr. Loop gave bonds in the sum of one thousand dollars and entered upon the discharge of his duties. Mr. Whitney's deputy had, as the court expressed it in an order of record, "contemptiously" taken from the table the records of the court. It was ordered and adjudged by the court that he pay a fine of twenty-five dollars, and stand committed until the fine was paid. A warrant of commitment was made out and placed in the hands of the sheriff to be executed if the fine was not paid. A writ of replevin was also sued out to procure the books, papers and records "contemptuously" carried away, and also placed in the hands of the sheriff to be executed. The writ was served, and the books, papers, records, etc., recovered and returned to court. On the 7th of December, Mr. Briggs, the deputy, by Mr. S. P. Doty as representative, appeared before the court and confessed that he was too hasty in committing the contempt on the day previous, whereupon the court ordered that one-half of the fine be remitted. The other half ($12.50) was paid by Mr. Doty, and thus subsided the first little "ripple" in the proceedings of the Commissioners' Court for the county of Boone.

The county seat having been located, the claim, donated to the county by the Belvidere Company, was surveyed into lots and blocks, a plot of ten acres being reserved on the highest point for county buildings. Daniel H. Whitney was appointed commissioner to sell and dispose of lots and blocks on the quarter section of land belonging to this county on which the seat of justice had been located, and required to enter into bonds in the sum of $2,000 for the faithful performance of the duty imposed. He was also required, as clerk, to make and transmit to the general land office and to the land office at Galena, copies of the report and all other papers received from the commissioners in reference to the location of the seat of justice of the county, and request from the general land office such information as might be necessary touching the perfecting of the title to said land.

At the December meeting of the County Commissioners' Court, Mr. Whitney reported that after advertising in the Chicago *Democrat and American*, and posting up written notices at Belvidere and other public places, giving notice of such sale, to be held on the 27th, 28th, 29th and 30th days of November, offering for sale lots on the county lands, he had on the 27th of that month sold lots to the amount of $364.75. On the 28th he adjourned the sales without day, the sales not meeting his expectations. Before making the above report, he had sold another lot at private sale, for $30, making the total of sales $394.75.

The sales made were for part cash and balance on time—sometimes one-half cash, and sometimes one-third, balance in one and two years, or six and twelve months, with mortgage on premises, or other satisfactory security, with interest on deferred payments. And thus from time to time, the lots belonging to the county continued to be disposed of until all were sold, and proceeds applied as conditioned in the donation of the "claim."

From this time forward, the sessions of the Commissioners' Court were principally occupied in looking after the interests of the county, managing its financial business, granting prayers of petitioners for roads, etc. At the March term, A. D. 1838, the first Grand and Petit Jurors were selected. James McBride, Israel Stone, Ira Haskins, William Ames, Albert Stone, Levi Hammon, Nathan Tripp, John Lawrence, Peter Payne, Thos. O. Davis, John K. Towner, Alexander Neely, Alfred Shattuck, Benjamin S. Lawrence, James Shinn, Hiram Waterman, Oliver Hale, John Wright, Frederick W. Crosby, Cephas Gardner, Edward E. Moss, John Sponable and Milton S. Mason were selected as grand jurors.

Erastus A. Nixon, Arthur Blood, James Gooch, Loudy Stephenson, Hiram Stow, John H. Herbert, Ebenezer Tuttle, David Caswell, James B. Lambert, Pearson B. Crosby, Z. H. Sawtell, William Dresser, Thomas Hartwell, Benjamin Sweet, Chas. H. Payne, Elias Congdon, William S.

Stewart, Frederick Sheldon, Jacob Fisk, A. D. Bishop, Joseph Briggs, Cornelius Cline, and John Q. A. Rollins " were the petit jurors for the first term of the Circuit Court to be held in and for said county."

Of the above selection for grand jurors, Albert Stone, Alexander Neely, Oliver Hale, John Wright, Cephas Gardner, and Edward E. Moss are still living, and all residents of the county except Mr. Neely, who, some years since, moved to Waterloo, Iowa. Of the petit jurors, John Q. A. Rollins and John H. Herbert are still living. Mr. Herbert resides in Belvidere, and Mr. Rollins at Denver, Colorado, where he is extensively engaged in mining operations.

At this term of the Commissioners' Court, Dr. D. H. Whitney resigned his position as Commissioner of Sales for Boone County, and Hiram Waterman was appointed to the vacancy.

April 17, 1838, the Commissioners convened in special session, and among other things, ordered that the clerk advertise for sealed proposals, to be received until the first Monday in June, for the erection of a court house, " forty by thirty feet, with a basement story of stone, the basement story to be finished one-half for a jail, the other half into a room for a family ; the first story to be finished with three offices and a hall and one room for a family's occupancy ; the second story to be finished with a court room and two jury-rooms ; the house when finished to be worth five or six thousand dollars." Proposals were also to be " received until the first Monday in June, for the purchase of the whole or any part of the county lands, and payment to be made by the erection of the court house, or the furnishing of materials for the same, or erecting any portion of the same."

At the June term, 1838, it was " ordered that the north room of S. P. Doty's house be used for the use and purposes of a county jail until otherwise ordered." Until this time, there had been no place for the imprisonment of violators of law and offenders against the peace and dignity of the State. Hence it is written on the records of Boone County that the "north room of S. P. Doty's house " was the first place " used for the uses and purposes of a county jail." At the same session of the Court, however, a contract was made and entered into with Simon P. Doty for the erection of a county jail, for $250.00, to be completed in four months. The jail so contracted for was a " block jail," which was subsequently removed to another location and used for other purposes, and finally, in 1877, made into fire wood and fence posts. The contract price was paid in full (in notes) at the time, and the jail completed within the time specified.

The financial panic of 1837 laid a heavy hand on Boone County and its people, and in June, 1838, Mr. Whitney was authorized to negotiate a loan of one thousand dollars " with any individual, or with the Chicago Branch Bank, of the State of Illinois, or with any bank in the State of Michigan, on the faith and credit of said county of Boone," at such rate of interest as could be had, and on such time, not less than six months nor exceeding two years, as could be agreed upon.

August 16, 1838, the first tax list or assessment roll, returned or delivered by the treasurer, showed the whole amount of taxable personal property (no land at that time being taxable) to be valued at $31,204.03. On this valuation, a tax of $234.03 had been assessed. The list was delivered to S. P. Doty, as collector. At the December term of the Court, Mr. Doty made a settlement, the entry of the clerk showing the following statement :

Amount charged to sheriff (Aug. 10) on page 97	$234.03
Amount deducted for errors	1.89
Amount to collect	$232.14
Deduct sheriff's commission 7½ per cent. on whole	17.41
Leaves due county	$214.73
Credit by amount paid into treasury in orders, as appears by receipts filed in the office of the clerk	196.42
Yet due the county, from which no commission is to be deducted	$18.31

The first money paid into the treasury was twenty-five dollars for fines assessed and collected by Justice of the Peace Towner, in two assault and battery cases, and for licenses collected by the clerk of the Commissioners' Court, in September, 1837.

In August, 1838, a new Board of Commissioners was elected. The new board was composed of Moses Blood, Orris Crosby and John K. Towner. At the same election, Houghton C. Walker (Democrat) and S. P. Doty (Whig) had been pitted against each other for sheriff. Walker was elected by a majority of six. John Handy was elected coroner. The first meeting of the new Board of Commissioners was held in September. Meeting for organization, they drew for terms. Mr. Towner drew the ticket on which "three years" was written, and was thus chosen to serve for three years; Mr. Blood drew the ticket on which "two years" was written, and was thereby entitled to serve two years, and Mr. Crosby drew the one-year ticket. Taking the oath of office, the new court proceeded to business. At their March term, 1839, the second grand and petit jurors were selected. The term of court for which the former jurors were selected, for some reason was never held, and consequently they were never sworn as jurors. The second selection was made and their names entered on record, but, for cause not appearing of record, a special term of the Commissioners' Court, held on the 23d of the same month, entered an order revoking the selection of jurors, as made in order 59 of the regular session, and a third selection made, as follows:

GRAND JURORS.—James McBride, Israel Stone, Ira Haskins, S. P. Hyde, Albert Stow, Levi Hammon, Nathan Tripp, John Lawrence, Peter Payne, William Brett, Nathaniel Crosby, Alexander Neely, Alfred E. Ames, Benjamin F. Lawrence, James Shinn, Daniel S. Brooks, Oliver Hale, John Wright, John Langdon, Cephas Gardner, Edward E. Moss, John Sponable, and Milton S. Mason. The court fixed their pay at seventy-five cents per day, and no mileage.

PETIT JURORS.—Horace Piersall, Allen Baldwin, Arthur Blood, James C. Gooch, Landy Stephenson, John Tinker, John H. Herbert, Ebenezer Tuttle, James B. Lambert, Albert Neely, Austin Gardner, Thomas Hartwell, Benjamin Sweet, Charles H. Payne, Elias Congdon, William Stewart, Frederick Sheldon, David Drake, Robert B. Hurd, Dewey Walker, Stephen M. Jenner, William P. Molony, Henry Loop and Daniel Bliss.

Of the grand jurors above selected, Alexander Neely, Oliver Hale, John Wright, Cephas Gardner and Edward E. Moss are still living and all residents of the county, except Alexander Neely, who is now a citizen of Iowa. Of the petit jurors, John H. Herbert and Dewey Walker are still living and citizens of the county.

The term of the Circuit Court for which the above named jurors were selected was set for the Thursday after the fourth Monday in April, 1839.

The place of holding the court was designated by the County Commissioners' Court as "the Baptist House of worship," and although these jurors were the *third* selection, they were the *first* to qualify and discharge jurors' duties. The building in which the court met had been erected by the Baptist people, on the corner of what is now East and Van Buren streets (the lot now being occupied by the residence of Mr. E. H. Reynolds), and for a number of years was used as a house of worship, school house, Circuit Court room, and a place for holding political and other public meetings. It was afterwards removed to the opposite side of Van Buren street, and used as a house of worship by the Universalist Society until about 1861, when it was sold to Gray Brothers, and removed to another location and used as a paint shop. Later, it was removed to the western part of town, and is now occupied as a residence by Mr. Ira D. Hill.

At the first term of the court, commencing on the 25th of April, 1839, that being the Thursday after the fourth Monday in that month, Judge Dan. Stone presided. Seth S. Whitman, who had been previously commissioned by Judge Stone, served as clerk, and H. C. Walker (now a merchant in Belvidere), was the Sheriff. There was but little business, and that nearly all of a civil character. The docket for that term only shows four cases of a criminal character—assault and battery cases, etc., all appeal cases from the different Justices of the Peace. Only forty-one cases had been docketed, and were disposed of in three days, the court adjourning on Saturday, the 27th of April, until the next term in course, April, 1840. When that term came on, Sheldon L. Hall appeared as prosecutor on the part of the people, Judge Stone again presiding. Mr. Walker had resigned the office of Sheriff, and was succeeded by B. F. Lawrence. The Sheriff of Winnebago County appeared in open court and presented Martin Thompson, who had been indicted by the Grand Jury of Winnebago County for passing counterfeit money and sent here for trial. He asked for and obtained a continuance. This case was not disposed of until April, 1841, when he was found guilty and sentenced to the Penitentiary for one year, one month of which was to be spent in solitary confinement. The charge upon which he was indicted was for passing a two-dollar counterfeit bill. He was not regarded as a bad man, and after his conviction, he was taken out to the residence and farm of Albert Stone, who was then Sheriff, where he was kept at work some two or three weeks, until Mr. Stone could get ready to take him to Alton. He was fully trusted, and allowed to go unattended all about the farm. Conversing with Mr. Stone about the case, during the writing of this book, he said he had the most implicit confidence in Thompson's faith and honesty, and believes if he had told him immediately after his conviction to go where he pleased until a certain day, and then meet him at Peru, from whence in those days travel to Alton and St. Louis went by boat, his prisoner would have been there. Thompson was never manacled or handcuffed, and when he was turned over to the Warden of the prison, the Sheriff told that gentleman that the prisoner was not a bad man, that he would make no attempt to escape, and that he could be fully trusted around the open yard and gates of the prison. The Warden expressed surprise to see a convict brought to the doors of the prison unfettered by handcuffs and shackles, and remarked that it was the first instance of the kind in his experience as Warden. Thompson served out his time, and subsequently came back to the county and called to visit the Sheriff who had treated him so kindly. That was the first conviction in the Circuit Court of Boone County.

Returning to the September (1840) term of the Circuit Court, we find that the first application for citizenship was made at that term. Charles McDougal, now living in Belvidere, was the applicant. The application was placed on record, and the necessary papers ordered to be issued.

At the same term of court the first divorce case was disposed of, and the marriage relations between Rosiel Campbell and his wife, Sally J. Campbell, declared to be dissolved.

Since that time to date (September, 1877), a period of thirty-seven years, there have only been forty-nine convictions for criminal offenses, as follows:

Forgery, 1; larceny, 32; burglary, 7; rape, 2; manslaughter, 3; counterfeiting, 2; mayhem, 1; robbery, 1. Nearly one-half of these convictions were for crimes committed in other counties and sent here on a change of venue, or for crimes committed by transient persons passing through the county. The criminal docket shows fewer cases, perhaps, than any other county in the State, or probably in any county of any of the adjoining States — a fact that speaks volumes for the intelligence, morality, virtue and honesty of the people.

At a special term of the Commissioners' Court, held on the 15th of April, 1839, the jail built by Simon P. Doty was inspected and accepted, and the keys handed over to the Sheriff, H. C. Walker, who was directed to "procure two sets of shackles for hands, and put a ring, bolt and chain for the use of said jail." The north room of Simon P. Doty's residence, which had previously been designated as a jail, was given up, and the new jail put in order for the "reception" of such as might be sentenced to incarceration within its walls. The first use made of the new jail for the purposes for which it was built seems to have been between April and June of that year, two persons having been incarcerated therein, one of them a notorious character and horse-thief, and the other on a similar charge, but a charge made without sufficient grounds on which to sustain an indictment or conviction. The facts in the case were that he had hired a horse to ride to Rockford, but went beyond and was gone longer than the time he specified, and the owner of the horse, becoming uneasy, went in pursuit. He met the man coming back, but preferred a charge of horse-stealing against him, and had him arrested and put in jail. When his case was called for trial at Rockford, where it had been transferred, and the circumstances stated to the court, he was acquitted. The other character, giving his name as J. H. Hartwell, was taken to Freeport, and thence to Galena, for safe keeping, but, a desperado by nature and education, and used to all sorts of jails and prisons in all parts of the country, the West Indies included, if his story was to be believed, and used to breaking out of jail as often as he was put in, he did not remain long in the Galena prison, but laid a plan and carried it out by which himself and some half dozen other scapegraces got away. From that day to this, he has never been seen or heard of in this part of the country. While confined in jail here he managed to break out once, but was soon overhauled and taken back, and in a few days thereafter taken to Freeport, and thence to Galena, for "safer keeping." How safely he was kept has been shown.

The records of the June (1838) session of the Commissioners' Court do not show that any proposals were submitted for building the Court House, as advertised for in April, but following the records up to March, 1839, they show that Hiram Waterman was appointed commissioner and agent for the County Commissioners, for the purpose of letting jobs, making contracts, etc., "for the purpose of building a Court House at Belvidere." At the same session of the court, in order 58, it was declared that a Court House should be built, the order further specifying that it should be 40 feet in length and 30 feet in width; posts 25 feet long, with entry for stairs on each side of front door; hall five feet wide through lower story, with back door and two rooms on each side of the hall—the upper room to be arched overhead and arranged in a plain, neat and convenient manner for holding court. In December following, the clerk was ordered to "draw a contract with Wm. B. Page for brick for Court House, said brick to be ready for delivery on or before the 1st of July next; one hundred thousand brick at $4 per thousand." At a special session, in the same month, the clerk was directed to contract with "Robert B. Hurd for finding all materials excepting the brick, and laying the walls for the Court House, the price agreed upon, $5 per thousand, payable $290 in county bonds and the balance in cash after the job is commenced." The same session the clerk was directed to advertise for proposals for the lumber for the Court House building—bids to be received on the 6th of January. On James Johnson, some time previous, had taken a contract for doing certain work on the Court House, to commence work on the 1st of June, 1840, but the lumber not being delivered, the time was extended to the time when the lumber would be in readiness, etc. In July (1840) the clerk was further directed to contract with John Bruce for delivering stone for the foundation, "and that the said Bruce be allowed $10 per cord for what stone were necessary, supposed to be about nine cords—the stone to be measured after the wall of it is laid up—the stone to be delivered before the 1st day of August next." When all was in readiness to commence the foundation walls of the Court House, it was found that the jail erected by Doty had been built on the site intended for the Court House, and it was ordered to be removed to a site selected for it. The work commenced in 1840, progressed slowly, and in February, 1842, the contract between James Johnson and the commissioners was deemed to have been forfeited on the part of Johnson, and was pronounced null and void by the court, and the clerk directed to advertise for sealed proposals for "framing and finishing the outside of the Court House in Belvidere—the proposals to be handed in one week previous to the March term of the Commissioners' Court." Little by little the work on the Court House was prosecuted, and it was not until some time in 1843—six years after the organization of the county—that it was completed and ready for occupancy. For a period of ten years it served the purpose for which it was erected. But the progress and development of the county was rapid. Population had increased, and with the increase of population came an increase of county business, demanding enlarged and better arranged quarters, and, in 1853, arrangements were made for tearing down the old structure and erecting a new one, which would include a substantial and secure jail, as well. In March, 1854, an order was passed to borrow $5,000 to aid in the construction, and five county bonds of $1,000 each ordered to be issued for that purpose, and Allen C. Fuller and Alexander Neely appointed to negotiate the sale of the bonds. In 1851, the subject of building a new jail was agitated, but no definite action was taken until it was determined to build Court House and jail in one, and about May 20, 1854, the County Board entered into a contract with Mr. John Higby, as contractor, for the erection of the present Court House and jail, for the sum of $9,900, Mr. Higby taking the material in the old Court House in part payment. S. W. Smith, architect, of Chicago, was employed to furnish the plans and specifications. Isaac Miller, Samuel Rockwell and John L. Curtis, had previously been appointed as a building committee, to superintend and manage the construction. At the September meeting of the Board of Supervisors, they tendered their resignation as such committee, which resignation was accepted, and Allen C. Fuller, L. M. Beebe, and John M. Vanhoesen, appointed to succeed them. Vanhoesen soon after removed from the State, and Messrs. Fuller and Beebe were left to the duty for which the committee had been raised. On September 12, 1855, this committee reported the Court House finished, and the Board directed the clerk to enter upon the record a resolution of thanks to Messrs. Fuller and Beebe for the faithful, honest and impartial manner in which they had discharged their duty as a building committee. At the same meeting of the Board, Fuller and Beebe were instructed to procure furniture for the new temple of county justice and the several offices, that would be in keeping with its character, architecture and finish. This trust discharged, on the 11th of March, 1856, they were discharged from further duty. The Court House had been accepted and occupied, since when the debts contracted in the course of its erection have been fully paid; and carefully managed, the county is entirely free from debt and its county orders considered as good as gold.

In 1845, the Legislature passed an act providing as follows: "That it shall be lawful for the County Commissioners' Court of the county of Boone, by an order to be entered upon the records of said court, to require the Recorder of the county of Winnebago, and the Clerk of the Commissioners' Court of said county, to transcribe into a book, to be provided for that purpose by the County Commis-ioners' Court of the said county of Boone, all records of said offices relating to the following described territory of land, to-wit: Sections 6, 7, 8, 19, 30, and 31, in each of the townships of 43, 44, 45, and 46, in range 3 east of the third principal meridian."

This act related to the lands included in the mile strip, that, when the law creating Boone County was passed, had been left as a part of Winnebago County, as a compromise measure to conciliate the conflicting interests in that county. The provisions of the law were carried out. The Commissioners' Court of Boone, for the purpose of perfecting a record of the lands, roads, etc., on that strip, provided the necessary books, and required the Recorder and Clerk, as aforesaid, to transcribe all records and orders relating to the said lands, roads, etc. The transcript was made, and, when completed and properly certified, was forwarded to Boone and placed among the recorded proceedings of the county, thus perfecting and completing the county's record.

From the date of the organization of the county of Boone, and the election of the first board of county officers, in May, 1837, the management of the affairs of the county were vested in a board of three county commissioners, as provided under the original constitution of the state, adopted A. D. 1818. The law under which these commissioners were elected provided that one of them should serve for one year, one for two years, and one for three years. Each county was divided into three commissioners' districts, and each district voted only for its own commissioner. At the first meeting of the Board after its election, the members drew for terms—that is, three tickets were prepared, on one of which was written "one year," on another, "two years," and on the other one, "three years." These tickets were placed in a box, or may be a hat, and each commissioner drew out one, the one drawing the ticket with the words "three years" upon it was entitled to serve three years; the one drawing the "two years'" ticket would serve two years, and the other one would serve one year, it being intended by the law that one commissioner should be elected every year after the first election for a term of three years. This law governed in the election of commissioners in each county in the state up to and succeeding the adoption of the constitution of 1847, and its ratification by the people, March 6, 1848. After the latter date, and until the township organization system was adopted by the people of Boone—among the first in the state to adopt it—the management of county affairs was conducted by a county judge and two associate justices. A law was passed under and by virtue of the constitution of 1847, however, providing that the people of the several townships throughout the state should, on the first Monday in April, 1850, vote "for" or "against" the township organization system.

While the people of Boone adopted the system, several other counties in the state, particularly in the more southern part, voted against it, and are still under the old system of management by a board of county commissioners. The same constitutional enactments, and the laws thereunder, changed the time of holding elections from August to November. In November, 1849, the first election after the change was held; Daniel H. Whitney was elected county judge, Edward Hawley and Lucius Fuller associate justices, and John Jackson clerk of the county court. This court succeeded the county commissioners in the management of county affairs until the adoption and carrying into effect of the township organization system, in 1850. The first Board of Supervisors was elected in April, 1850, and held their first meeting June 11 following, in response to a notice issued to them from Hon. D. H. Whitney, county judge. They were: Frederick P. Low, Fairfield (now Flora) Township; Nathaniel Crosby, Belvidere Township; Henry Jenks, Caledonia Township; Charles W. Libby, Manchester Township; William Raymond, Leroy Township; Hiram C. Miller, Boone Township; Isaac Miller, Bonus Township; Charles B. Lord, Concord (now Spring) Township.

At that meeting, H. C. Miller, of Boone, was elected chairman *pro tem*. Allen C. Fuller was elected county attorney. After the transaction of some unimportant business, the Board adjourned until the 11th of November, the time fixed by law for their regular meeting. At that meeting the full management of the affairs of the county was turned over to them. Their first transactions were a change of voting places in the several townships, etc. Thus commenced a new, but perhaps not better, era in the management of the public affairs of the county. Soon after this, the subject of building a new jail and court house commenced to be discussed, resulting, as already shown, in the erection of the present county buildings.

Thus far it has been the purpose to follow as minutely as possible all the more important incidents pertinent to the history of the county. They have been pretty closely followed from the time the Robbins claim was taken, in May or June 1835, to the completion of a second court house, in 1855. Since that date the county has steadily grown in population, wealth and importance, and public affairs have been so well managed that the faith and credit of the county ranks among the first in the state. No bonds in aid of railroad or other public enterprises were ever voted by the people, the consequence of which is that no debt hangs over the tax payers. Free from debt, with money in the treasury, Boone County orders or warrants are good at their face in any home market, and as readily taken in business transactions as National Bank Notes.

Passing over a period of some years, in which we find no absorbing incidents of importance, we come to that period in the Nation's history which is equally a part of the history of every county—the War of the Rebellion—and the part borne in that ever-to-be-remembered conflict by the brave and patriotic men of Boone.

When the peace and tranquillity of the North was disturbed by intelligence borne along the electric wires that Fort Sumter had been fired upon by the enemies of the Union of our fathers, there was awakened a sentiment of patriotism and unanimity that knew no limit until an army was raised and equipped that brooked no obstacle—that swept from the lakes on the north to the gulf on the south—wherever an armed hand was raised against the government—that, with one voice reiterated and re-affirmed the declaration of the soldier statesman, President Jackson, that "by the Great Eternal, this Union must and shall be preserved." Imbued with the spirit of the men of '76, they pledged their lives, their fortunes, and their sacred honors in defense of the government of their homes. Homes and their pleasures and comforts were given up for the hardships and privations of a soldier's life on the tented field of danger, carnage and strife. Such an uprising the civilized world had never known before. But the cause was just, and the triumph of victory only a question of time.

When this people were startled by the call "to arms," patriotic words from Dr. Daniel H. Whitney, always a true and noble, as well as a generous, public spirited and patriotic citizen, Gen. S. A. Hurlbut, A. C. Fuller, L. W. Lawrence, Wm. Haywood, D. L. Baker, Dr. Molony, and others, without regard to previous political opinions, needed no interpretation to inspire their fellow citizens to respond to their country's call. Men by hundreds offered their services, and their lives, if need be, in defense of the Nation's integrity and unity. Money by tens of thousands of dollars was placed at the disposal of the government, and thus it came that no county in all the counties of the patriotic North made a bolder or more honorable record of devotion to the Union than the noble one made by "Little Boone." Among the smallest in the state, not one of all the others more clearly defined its position. There was no halting between two opinions. Party lines that had sometimes been closely drawn were obliterated, harsh and bitter words previously spoken in moments of political excitement were forgotten and forgiven, and joining hands in a common cause, with a sincerity of motive, they united in a oneness of purpose, the remembrance of which will live as a monument grander, if not more enduring, than any ever fashioned out of granite or marble.

On the pages of Holy Writ it is inscribed that "he that provideth not for his own household is worse than an infidel." The influence of this text was not lost upon those in authority in this county, and measures were inaugurated and carried out to secure the families—the wives and little ones—of those who went out with their lives in their hands to meet the foes of the government, against want. Never was there a grander spirit evinced; never was there a more eloquent sermon preached from the text above quoted than when the county treasury was made the source from whence the supplies were drawn that secured soldiers' "loved ones" at home the necessary comforts of life. There was no grumbling about high taxes to keep the treasury full, nor were they grudgingly paid. Every one was glad of an opportunity to help in so noble a cause. Because of this knowledge that wives and little ones, aged fathers and mothers, were thus provided for, though their beds were made upon mother earth, their covering only that of the azured canopy above, the dreams of Boone's boys in blue were none the less sweet, nor their slumbers less refreshing. The records of the official proceedings of Boone County show that during the war the sum of $161,011.56 was appropriated for the purpose of paying bounties and aiding in the support of soldiers' families. When it is considered that there are only eight townships in the county—that it is only twelve miles from east to west and twenty-four miles from north to south (less the fractional sections along the Wisconsin state line), and containing only two hundred and eighty-four square miles, this sum seems almost fabulous. Basing the population at 11,678, as reported by the census of 1860, this sum was equal to $13.78 to each man, woman and child in the county. In addition, each of the eight townships were equally as wise, generous and patriotically benevolent. Belvidere appropriated $38,422.58; Spring, $6,250.97; Flora, $6,124.10; Bonus, $9,212.50; Boone, $7,641.63; Manchester, $9,498.22; Caledonia, $4,629.86; Leroy, $10,912.83.

These appropriations swelled the aggregate to $252,704.25, increasing the proportion to $21.64 to each man, woman and child in the county. Add to the above total the sum of $63,176.06—(a sum equal to one-fourth of the amount raised by county and town taxation)—voluntarily contributed by the people and paid on the spot whenever occasion or circumstances seemed to demand, and we find a grand total of $315,880.31, appropriated by the patriots of Boone for bounties, etc., and increasing the total proportion to $27.05 to each man, woman and child in the county. Add the still further fact that, from first to last, nearly two thousand men* had enlisted from this county, and justice demands that Boone be recorded as the *Banner County of Illinois* in the great and final conflict between Freedom and Slavery!

Fort Sumter had been fired upon, and was surrendered to the rebels, April 13,1861. President Lincoln's proclamation calling for 75,000 men was issued April 15, 1861. But already had S. A. Hurlbut, Esq., made a movement to organize a regiment of minute men in the northern counties. He had just returned to Belvidere from a trip to Washington and the South. He expressed his belief that the rebellion would prove a more formidable affair than the people of the North generally anticipated, because the trouble had passed beyond the range of compromise, if, indeed, it ever was confined to that limit, and that no possible mode except stern force existed by which the supremacy of the constitution and laws could be vindicated, and the Union maintained. A war meeting was called to meet at the court house at two o'clock, Saturday, April 20. The meeting was the largest congregation of people ever seen in Belvidere. Dr. D. H. Whitney was chosen to preside, making a stirring speech on taking the chair. Dr. Molony followed, taking strong grounds against the traitors. Mr. Hurlbut, chairman of the committee appointed for that purpose, reported a series of resolutions, which were adopted as the sentiment of the meeting, "after which," said the Belvidere *Standard* of April 23, "he made one of

---

*This estimate includes men who enlisted in regiments raised in other States, as in Wisconsin, and other counties, of which there were a large number, and who were not all credited to Boone county.

the most ringing and soul-stirring speeches that ever electrified an audience." Such excitement was never witnessed. "Mr. Hurlbut," the *Standard* continues, "opened the muster roll with his signature.

"Judge Fuller then came forward with a resolution calling for the raising of a Citizens' War Fund, the subscriptions to be applied towards the support of the families of the volunteers during their absence in the war. The resolution was accompanied with his check for five hundred dollars. The meeting gave the Judge three cheers, and called for a speech. He took the floor, and for half an hour the meeting was swayed with an eloquence which we cannot describe. Strong men wept like children, and the Judge, himself, was agitated with emotions so strong as to almost preclude speech. We never saw an audience so completely under the spell thrown over them by a speaker. * * * The call was now for money. In less than an hour the following sums had been subscribed and paid on the spot, either by cash or check:

Allen C. Fuller	$500	L. Foster	$ 25
M. G. Leonard	100	J. V. Wing	25
A. H. Bradley*	50	W. H. Wood	50
D. H. Whitney*	100	D. E. Ellis	25
I. R. Mudge	100	R. Roberts	25
Asa Baldwin*	100	R. D. Rix*	25
W. R. Cornell	100	L. H. March	25
R. S. Molony	100	E. H. Reynolds	25
Jas. Jaffray	100	Wm. Corning	15
I. T. Witbeck	100	D. Wallin	25
James Bennett*	250	F. A. Hull	25
Montgomery Smith	100	Big Thunder Mill	50
H. D. Waterman	100	E. Gore*	25
H. N. Bush	50	John Yonrt	100
L. W. Lawrence	50	S. W. Bristol*	25
H. C. DeMunn	50	Geo. Waterman*	100
Albert Stone	50	E. K. F. Randolph	100
Dan'l E. Foote	50	A. F. Moss	50
Geo. Dean	50	W. Thompson*	25
A. W. Burnside	50	J. M. Glasner	25
Cephas Gardner	50	B. Ames, 1st in'st.	50
Dan'l Mabie	50	Geo. W. Downs	50
Hiram Jones	50	Thos. Lillibridge*	50
J. K. Soule*	15	S. Lovett	25
S. Terwilliger	50	G. Lacey*	20
Geo. Chafee	50	W. Sunderlin	20
Horatio Sage	50	Mrs. M. Doty	5
D. C. Wolverton	25	Isaac Miller*	25
T. D. Walker	25	Lewis Wilson	25
John Servaty	25	John Hannah	25
Wm. Coultrup	25	L. L. Lake	25
M. Reiss	25	W. Cunningham	5
D. T. Olney	200	J. H. Robbins	5
Geo. W. March	25		
Total			$3,935.

*Dead.

"The enlistment roll," continues the *Standard*, "was then opened, and fifteen or twenty men came forward and affixed their names. A meeting was fixed for the evening, in the basement of the Presbyterian church, which was packed full, a large number of ladies being present. * * * The meeting was called to order and brief speeches made by the chairman (Dr. Whitney), S. A. Hurlbut, W. Thompson, Wales W. Wood, and Dr. Molony. The subscription proceeded briskly during the intervals, and stopped a little short of $4,000!"

At this meeting fifty-eight names were signed to the muster roll, up to the time the report was made to the *Standard*, and additions constantly being made. The enlistments were as follows:

S. A. Hurlbut,
Wm. Haywood,
David L. Baker,
J. W. Harper,
J. W. Batchelder,
Geo. W. Drake,
L. O. Gilman,
J. W. H. Stoner,
W. W. Jones,
Martin Derthick,
Forrester Clark,
S. S. Stoner,
R. S. Hambridge,
Hiram F. Howe,
N. Vanalstine,
Wm. Baker,
John J. Norton,
Plummer F. Robinson,
R. D. Woodruff,
Alonzo Powers,
James Barker,
Orrin Whipple,
Richard A. Gould,
Albert Wheeler,
Joel Danavie,
E. B. White,
Beverly W. Whitney,
James M. Tisdel,
Daniel L. Tuttle,

Nelson Payne,
Frank Neely,
Chas. Outcalt,
Chas. Rayner,
C. N. Case,
James O. Greytren,
Nicholas Butler,
W. R. Coe,
H. W. Avery,
Z. H. Pratt,
Thos. Tobey,
Amos Bates,
Wm. Ward,
N. A. Gallagher,
A. D. Carpenter,
Jas. M. Smith,
John Patrick,
A. J. McElhany,
Walter Miles,
Robert Giles,
C. A. Crocker,
J. J. M. Chamberlain,
H. F. Hovey,
P. M. Eighmy,
E. F. Morley,
G. H. Merrill,
Geo. W. Rodgers,
Wm. Derthick,
E. A. Wallace.—58.

By the 30th of April, one hundred and fifteen men had enrolled their names, elected officers and drilled daily and nightly. The officers elected were: S. A. Hurlbut, Captain; William Haywood, First Lieutenant, and D. L. Baker, Second Lieutenant.

"The Governor was telegraphed," continues the *Standard*, of May 11th, "that the company desired to be accepted as a part of the six regiments; but the unwelcome answer was returned that the six regiments were full, and over fourteen had offered their services who could not be accepted. A bill having been introduced into the legislature, then in session, to authorize the Governor to accept ten additional regiments, who should go into camp, for instruction, thirty days, unless sooner called for by the President, our company decided to keep up their drill for a few days. There was some delay in the legislature acting upon this bill and some doubt in relation to its passage. The company, on the 4th, adjourned until the 8th, to determine what they would do. On Monday morning, the 6th, the Adjutant General telegraphed Captain Hurlbut to put his company in marching order and report himself and company at Freeport, last Saturday, the 11th inst. A citizens' meeting was immediately called for Tuesday evening, and it was then resolved that the company should be presented with a uniform military dress. A committee was appointed and left for Chicago on the night train, and on Wednesday at three o'clock telegraphed that the cloth was bought and would arrive at nine o'clock that evening. At ten o'clock that evening the goods were received and unpacked, the tailor shops in town transferred to the hall, and everything ready for action.

"Thursday morning found the hall almost crowded to suffocation, with ladies, all anxious to show their devotion to the good cause by hard work. And hard work it was. It was decided to abolish the word 'impossible' and see what could be done. And at it they went with a will. The tailors cut, the maidens basted, and the matrons put together, and at twelve o'clock Friday night the work was done. All honor to the fair ones of Belvidere. The thanks of grateful hearts and a soldier's blessing is your well-earned reward. Eighty-four men carry upon their persons the grateful evidences of your determination to act your part promptly. A few coats finished Saturday morning are not needed at present. Cloth was bought for one hundred, but owing to the uncertainty of the acceptance of the company, several volunteers who originally enlisted and went home, did not return. Several applications, however, were made on Saturday, and we have no doubt the company will be increased at Freeport to one hundred.

"At an early hour on Saturday morning, our citizens began to pour into town. At ten o'clock, as a mark of respect to our citizen soldiers, all stores and shops were closed and business in town suspended. At half-past eleven o'clock the procession was formed at the corner of State and Mechanic streets, under direction of Sheriff Garcelon, and at noon, precisely, the gallant Boone County Volunteers, in full dress and looking every inch the soldier, were escorted to the depot by from five to six thousand of their fellow citizens. Arriving at the depot a short time before the train was due, short and appropriate exercises took place.

"Doctor Whitney called the meeting to order, and after a few touching allusions to the solemnity of the occasion which had called together so many of the citizens, invited the Rev. Mr. Roe to offer up a prayer. Elder Roe then came forward and pronounced a most touching prayer. W. Thompson, Esq., addressed the soldiers and people in a short and happy speech of ten minutes. Rev. H. B. Holmes also delivered a short address. A. C. Fuller then came forward and presented a beautiful sword to Captain Hurlbut, who acknowledged its presentation as complimentary to himself and company, and on behalf of himself and company thanked the citizens of Boone county for the many acts of kindness shown them, and promised to give a good account of themselves should their active service be required by the government. Although the occasion was most solemn and imposing, nobody made a speech—nobody could make a speech—and to the credit of all, nobody tried to make a speech—the hearts of all were too full for utterance. There stood eighty-four of our citizen soldiers who had pledged themselves to maintain the honor of our flag, and if need be, to seal their devotion to the constitution and laws by their blood, the polished guns and glistening steel now in their hands to make good that pledge—and around them beat the aching hearts of fathers, mothers, sisters, brothers, neighbors and friends, pressing on their ranks to take, as it may be, a last farewell. What can be said at such a time, except to give a word of encouragement and breathe a prayer for their welfare?

"No man or woman in this county but what ought to feel a common pride in that company. We are glad to believe their gallant Captain will be made a Colonel of the regiment. If so, First Lieutenant Haywood, who has seen service in Mexico, will probably be their Captain. The officers and men are a fine, healthy, and, we have no doubt, brave set of men. There may be some five or six 'wild ones' among them, but they will make good soldiers, and in point of intelligence and character the company will compare favorably with the people of the country."

Such was the beginning made by the gallant and brave sons of "Little Boone," that responded so readily to their country's call, swelling the army by thousands, and of the patriotic citizens, fathers and mothers, that so readily gave of their substance to save the government's honor, maintain its dignity and preserve the union they loved so well—

"A union of lakes, a union of lands—
A union none can sever—
A union of hearts, a union of hands,
The American union forever."

Monuments may crumble; cities may fall into decay; the tooth of time leave its impress on all the works of man, but the memory of the gallant deeds of the army of the union in the war of the great rebellion, in which the sons of Boone bore so conspicuous a part, will live in the minds of men so long as time and civilized governments endure.

In concluding this section of the PAST AND PRESENT OF BOONE COUNTY, what more fitting tribute can be paid, what greater halo of glory cast around and about their deeds of valor, than a full and complete War Record, embracing the names, the terms of enlistment, the battles in which they engaged, and all the minutiæ of their soldier lives? It will be a wreath of glory encircling every brow, and a memento which each and every one of them earned in defense of their country's honor, integrity and unity.

BOONE COUNTY WAR RECORD.

11th Infantry.

Company D.

PRIVATES.

Marshall Wm. e. Sept. 1, '61, m. o. as Sergt., Sept. 16, '64.

Company G.

Corpl. Thos. E. Echols, e. Aug. 11, 1861, disd. July 23, 1862, wounds.

PRIVATES.

Carnes Wm. H. e. Aug. 10, 1861, m. o. July 29, 1864.
Carnes Henry W. e. Aug. 15, 1861, prmtd. Corpl., disd. Aug. 15, 1864
Hughes Wm. e. Aug. 10, 1861, disd. May 17, 1862.
Kattenback I. e. Aug. 10, 1861, m. o. July 29, 1864.
Moore Geo. W. e. Aug. 15, 1861, died Nov. 9, 1861.
McKay Jas. Aug. 10, 1861, died March 1, 1862.
Ruland John F. e. Aug. 15, 1861, killed at Yazoo City, March 5, 1864
Stivers Wm. M. e. Aug. 10, 1861, m. o. July 29, 1864.
McCullums J. e. Aug. 10, 1861, died Aug. 15, 1864.

Company I.

Corpl. Fred. M. Hanman, e. Aug. 20, 1861, disd. June 23, 1862.

12th Infantry.

Company A.

PRIVATES.

Slowey Frank, e. Sept. 17, 1861.
Van Vorce Isaac, e. Sept. 17, 1861, re-enlisted as vet.
Whiting Luther, e. Sept. 17, 1861, re-enlisted as vet.

RECRUITS.

Butt Patrick, e. Jan. 24, 1865, deserted June 19, 1865.
Henesy Jas. e. Jan. 24, 1865, deserted June 26, 1865.
Little Jos. e. Jan. 24, 1865, m. o. July 10, 1865.
Young Peter, e. Jan. 24, 1865, deserted June 26, 1865.

Company K.

First Lieutenant Francis Rutger, e. as private Aug. 1, 1861. Promoted Second Lieutenant Aug. 30, 1862. Promoted First Lieutenant Dec. 14, 1862. Term expired Oct. 21, 1864.

Sketch of 15th Infantry.

The Fifteenth Regiment Infantry Illinois Volunteers was organized at Freeport, Illinois, and mustered into the United States service May 24, 1861—being the first regiment organized from the state for the three years' service. It then proceeded to Alton, Ill., remaining there six weeks for instruction. Left Alt n for St. Charles, Mo.; thence, by rail, to Mexico, Mo. Marched 1 Hannibal, Mo.; thence, by steamboat, to Jefferson Barracks; then, by rail, to Rolla, Mo. Arrived in time to cover Gen. Siegel's retreat from Wilson's Creek; thence to Tipton, Mo., and thence joined Gen. Fremont's army. Marched from there to Springfield, Mo.; thence back to Tipton; then to Sedalia, with Gen. Pope, and assisted in the capture of 1,300 of the enemy a few miles from the latter place; from there marched to Otterville, Mo., where it went into winter quarters, Dec. 26, 1861. Remained there until Feb. 1, 1862. Then marched to Jefferson City; thence to St. Louis, by rail; embarked on transports for Fort Donelson, arriving there the day of the surrender.

The regiment was then assigned to the Fourth Division, Gen. Hurlbut commanding, and marched to Fort Henry. Then embarked on transport for Pittsburg Landing. Participated in the battles of the 6th and 7th of April, losing 252 men, killed and wounded. Among the former were Lieuten't Colonel E. T. W. Ellis, Major Goddard, Captains Bromwell and Wayne, and Lieutenant John W. Puterbaugh. Captain Adam Nase, wounded and taken prisoner. The regiment then marched to Corinth, participating in various skirmishes and the siege of that place, losing a number of men killed and wounded.

After the evacuation of Corinth, the regiment marched to Grand Junction; thence to Holly Springs, back to Grand Junction; thence to Lagrange; thence to Memphis, arriving there July 21, 1862, and remained there until September 6th. Then marched to Bolivar; thence to the Hatchie river, and participated in the battle of the Hatchie. Lost fifty killed and wounded in that engagement. Then returned to Bolivar; from thence to Lagrange; thence with Gen. Grant, down through Mississippi to Coffeeville, returning to Lagrange and Memphis; thence to Vicksburg, taking an active part in the siege of that place. After the surrender of Vicksburg, marched with Sherman to Jackson Miss.; then returned to Vicksburg and embarked for Natchez. Marched thence to Kingston; returned to Natchez; then to Harrisburg, La., crossing Fort Beauregard, on the Wachita river. Returned to Natchez, remained there until Nov. 20, 1863. Proceeded to Vicksburg and went into winter quarters. Here the regiment re-enlisted as veterans, remaining until Feb. 1, 1864, when it moved with Gen. Sherman through Mississippi. On Champion Hills had a severe engagement with rebel Carrey. Marched to Meridian; thence south to Enterprise; thence back to Vicksburg. Was then ordered to Illinois on veteran furlough. On expiration of furlough joined Seventeenth Army Corps and proceeded up the Tennessee river to Clifton; thence to Huntsville, Ala.; thence to Decatur and Rome, Ga.; thence to Kingston, and joined Gen. Sherman's army, marching on Atlanta.

At Allatoona Pass the Fifteenth and the Fourteenth Infantry were consolidated, and the organization was known as the Veteran Battalion Fourteenth and Fifteenth Illinois Infantry Volunteers and numbering 635 men. From Allatoona Pass it proceeded to Ackworth, and was then assigned to duty, guarding the Chattanooga and Atlanta Railroad. Whilst engaged in this duty, the regiment being scattered along the line of road, the rebel Gen. Hood, marching north, struck the road at Big Shanty and Ackworth, and captured about 300 of the command. The remainder retreated to Marietta, were mounted and acted as escorts for Gen. Vandever. They were afterwards transferred to Gen. F. P. Blair, and marched with Gen. Sherman through Georgia.

After the capture of Savannah, the regiment proceeded to Beaufort, South Carolina; thence to Salkahatchee river, participating in the various skirmishes in that vicinity—Columbia, S. C., Fayetteville, N. C., battle of Bentonsville—losing a number wounded; thence to Goldsboro and Raleigh. At Raleigh, recruits sufficient to fill up both regiments were received, and the organization of the Veteran Battalion discontinued, and the Fifteenth reorganized. The campaign of Gen. Sherman ended by the surrender of Gen. Johnson. The regiment then marched with the army to Washington, D. C., via Richmond and Fredericksburg, and participated in the grand review at Washington, May 24, 1865; remained there two weeks. Proceeded, by rail and steamboat, to Louisville, Ky.; remained at Louisville two weeks. The regiment was then detached from the Fourth Division, Seventeenth Army Corps, and proceeded, by steamer, to St. Louis; from thence to Fort Leavenworth, Kansas, arriving there

BELVIDERE.

BOONE COUNTY WAR RECORD.   257

July 1, 1865. Joined the army serving on the Plains. Arrived at Fort Kearney, August 14th; then ordered to return to Fort Leavenworth, Sept. 1, 1865, where the regiment was mustered out the service and placed en route for Springfield, Ill., for final payment and discharge—having served four years and four months.

Number of miles marched 4299
Number of miles by rail 2403
Number of miles by steam r 4310
    Total miles traveled 11,012
Number of men joined from organization 1963
Number of men at date of muster-out 640

15th Infantry.

Company B.

Captain Wm. Haywood, com. May 24, 1861. Resigned April 12, 1862.
Captain David L. Baker, com. First Lieutenant May 24, 1861. Promoted Captain April 12, 1862. Resigned March 4, 1863.
Captain Wesley W. Jones, e. as Sergeant May 24, 1861. Promoted Second Lieutenant April 12, 1862. Promoted First Lieutenant Jan. 5, 1863. Promoted Captain March 4, 1863. Resigned July 31, 1863.
Captain Lemuel O. Gilman, e. as Corporal May 24, 1861. Promoted First Lieutenant March 4, 1863. Promoted Captain July 31, 1863. Mustered out at consolidation.
First Lieutenant Addison N. Longcor, com. Second Lieutenant May 24, 1861. Promoted First Lieutena t April 12, 1862. Died Jan. 5, 1863.
First Lieutenant Dani. L. Clark, com. Second Lieutenant March 4, 1863. Promoted First Lieutenant July 31, 1863. Died at Natchez, Sept. 23, 1863.
First Lieutenant Joseph Develin, com. Sept. 23, 1863. (See 15 h Reorganized.)
Second Lieutenant Charles Outcult, e. as private May 24, 1861. Promoted Second Lieutenant Sept. 23, 1863. Mustered out at consolidation.
Sergt. James L. Tisdel, e. May 24, '61, disd. on writ of habeas corpus, June 5, 1861.
Sergt. Job Kenyan, e. May 24, 1861, disd. Oct. 18, 1862, disab.
Corpl. Beverly W. Whitney, e. May 24, 1861, trans. to Co. I, 46th I V. I., Oct. 31, 1863.
Corpl. Deeter S. Thomas, e. May 24, 1861, disd. Sept. 13, 1861, disab.
Corpl. Albert Wheeler, e. May 24,'61, m.o. May 24,'64.
Musician Wm. Howard, e. May 24, 1861, disd. Aug. 22, 1861, disab.
Musician Elias B. White, e. May 24, 1861, trans. to Band May 29, 1861.

PRIVATES.

Avery H. W, e. May 24, 1861, m. o. June 28, 1864.
Burke Jas. e. May 24, 1861, deserted Aug. 18, 1861, insane.
Bachelder Jas. W. e. May 24,'61, disd.Nov.22,'61,disab.
Bramlis Wm. e. May 24, 1861, re enlisted as vet. Jan. 1, 1864, m. o. Sept. 16, 1865, as Sergt.
Baker Wm. e. May 24, '61, disd. April 19, '62, disab.
Bates Amos, e. May 24, '61, disd. Oct. 18, '62, disab.
Brown Richard, e. May 24, '61, died April 6, '62, wds.
Brown Bartlett, e. May 24, 1861, re-enlisted as vet. Jan. 1, 1864, m. o. Sept. 16, 1865, as Corpl.
Carefoot H. A. e. May 24, '61, disd. Oct. 18, '62, disab.
Cline Geo. e. May 24, 1861.
Childs John, e. May 24, '61, m. o. May 24, 1864.
Childs Robt. A. e. May 24, 1861, m. o. May 24, 1864.
Callahan J. W. e. May 24, 1861, re-enlisted as vet. Jan. 1, 1864, m. o. May 30, 1865.
Christian C. M. e. May 24, 1861, killed at Shiloh, April 6, 1862.
Crocker C. A. e. May 24, 1861, m. o. Sept. 9, 1864.
Colemen Isaac, e. May 24, 1861, re-enlisted as vet. Jan. 1, 1864, m. o. Sept. 16, 1865 as 1st Sergt.
Drake Geo. W. e. May 24, 1861, m. o. June 24, 1864.
Douaire Jules, e. May 24, 1861, re-enlisted as vet. Jan. 1, 1864, on detached service.
Derthie Martin, e. May 24, 1861, trans. to Co. B, Vet. Battalion, deserted twice.
Derthie Wm. e. May 24, '61, disd. Sept. 26, '63, disab.
Dunnevan Florence,e.May24,'61,disd.Aug 21,'62,disab.
Doyle John, e. May 24, '61, killed at Shiloh, Apr. 6,'62.

Eigheney P. M. e. May 24,'61, disd. April 19,'62,disab.
Gallagher Wm. A. e. May 24, '61, m. o. May 24, 1864.
Graves Geo. H. e. May 24, 1861, m. o. May 24, 1864.
Gaines John, e. May 24, 1861, re-enlisted as vet., m. o. Sept. 16, 1865, as Sergt.
Greysrax Jas. O. e. May 24,'61, disd.Aug.21,'62, disab.
Hovey Henry F. e. May 24, 1861, re-enlisted as vet. Jan. 1, 1864, m. o. May 30, 1865.
Hambridge R. S. e. May 24, 1861, re-enlisted as vet. Jan. 1, 1864, m. o. Sept. 16, 1865.
Johnson Wm. W. e. May 24, 1861, died Jan. 15, 1862.
McElhany A. J. e. May 24, 1861, re-enlisted as vet. Jan. 1, 1864, m. o. May 30, 1865.
Morely E. T. e. May 24, 1861.
McKee Thos. e. May 24,'61, disd. Oct. 18, '62, disab.
Miles Walter, e. May 24, '61, dis . Sept. 23, '62, disab.
Miles Hiram, e. May 24, '61, disd. Oct. 22, '61, disab.
Norton Samuel, e. May 24, 1861, killed at Shiloh, April 6, 1862.
Outcult Chas. e. May 24, '61, m. o. May 24, 1864.
Payne Nelson, e. May 24, 1861, disd. Aug. 19, 1862.
Parker A. B. e. May 24, 1861, disd. July 17, '62, disab.
Powers Alonzo, e. May 24, 1861.
Pickie B. e. May 24, 1861.
Rairden John R. e. May 24, 1861, disd. Feb. 6, 1862, worthlessness.
Rogers Geo. W. e. May 24, 1861, died June 14, 1862.
Stoner John Wm. H. e. May 24, 1861, killed at Shiloh, April 6, 1862.
Smith Jas. M. e. May 24, '61, disd. Sept. 2. '61, disab.
Smith S. D. e. May 24, 1861.
Tovey Thos. e. May 24, 1861, disd. Aug. 9, '62, disab.
Vanahstine N. P. e. May 24,'61, disd. Oct.20,'62, disab.
Whitney O. e. May 24, 1861, disd. Oct. 18, '63, disab.
Wallace C. A. e. May 24, 1861, re-enlisted as vet. Jan. 1, 1864, m. o. May 30, 1864.
Worthington Geo. e. May 24, 1861, m. o. May 24, 1864.
Woodruff R. D. e. May 24, 1861, re-enlisted as vet. Jan. 1, 1864.
Ward Wm. e. May 24, 1861.
Wellington S. H. e. May 24, 1861, died July 25, 1863.
Walther Wm. e. May 24, 1861.
Webster Thos. J. e. May 24,'61, disd. Aug. 15,'62,disab.

RECRUITS.

Ainsworth Geo. e. Sept. 24, 1861, disd. Feb. 6, 1862, worthlessness.
Blakey James, e. May 24, 1861.
Clark D. N. e. May 24, 1861.
Case Chas. N. e. May 24, '61, disd. April 19,'62, disab.
Courtright G. A. e. Dec. 4, 1863, trans. to Co. B, Vet. Battalion, deserted June 26, 1865.
Clark Samuel J. e. March 10, 1862, re-enlisted as vet. March 10, 1864, m. o. June 19, 1865.
Doram Hiram, e. May 24, '61, disd. July 1, '62, disab.
Davis John G. e. May 24, 1861, re-enlisted as vet. Jan. 1, 1864, m. o. Sept. 16, 1865.
Dean O. E. e. May 24, 1861, disd. Aug. 28, '62, disab.
Greene Geo. E. e. May 24, 61, disd. April 28,'62, disab.
Herrick Ira O. e. May 24, 1861, disd. Feb.6, '62, disab.
Howe Frank O. e. May 24, 1861, re-enlisted as vet. Jan. 1, 1864, m. o. May 30, 1865.
Hathaway L. e. March 28, 1862, trans. to Co. B, Vet. Battalion, prisoner of war.
Keeler Calvin, e. May 24, 1861, killed at Corinth, May 28, 1862.
Lee Edward, e. May 24, 1861, m. o. May 24, 1864.
Minor Wesley, e. Feb. 7, 1862, re-enlisted as vet. Jan. 1, 1864, m. o. Sept 16, 1865.
Randall Jas. M. e. May 24, 1861.
Robinson Geo. W. e. Sept. 24, 1861, trans. to Co. B, Vet. Battalion, m. o. Sept. 23, 1864.
Rhulman Fred. e. March 8, 1862, re-enlisted as vet. Jan. 1, 1864, m. o. Aug. 11, 1865.
Shilber Adam, e. Jan. 24, 1862, re-enlisted as vet. Jan. 1, 1864, m. o. Sept. 16, 1865.
Smith A. C. e. Dec. 8, 1863, trans. to Co. B, Vet. Battalion, died May 27, 1865.
Thorn John G. e. May 24, 1861, re-enlisted as vet., m. o. May 30, 1865.
White Henry G. e. Sept. 24, 1861, trans. to Co. B, Vet. Battalion, m. o. Sept. 23, 1864.
White Chas. W. e. Sept. 24, 1861, re-enlisted as vet. Jan. 1, 1864, m. o. Sept. 16, 1865.
Wilson John W. e. Sept. 24,'61, disd. Aug.21,'62, disab.
Woods Wm. disd. Oct. 22, 1861, disab.

Company D.

Lillibridge H. F. e. Sept. 16, 1861, died Dec. 13, 1861.

15th Infantry Reorganized.

Lieutenant Colonel Lemuel O. Gilman, com. Captain Co. H, Vet. Battalion, 14th and 15th Regts., July 31, 1863. Promoted Lieutenant Colonel July 20, 1864. Mustered out Sept. 16, 1865.
Major Jos. Develin, com. First Lieutenant Co. H, Vet. Battalion, 14th and 15th Regts, sept. 23, 1863. Promoted Captain July 20, 1864. Promoted Major June 27, 1865. Mustered out Sept. 16, 1865.
Adjutant Saml. J. Dunham, e. as Corporal Co. B, Jan. 1, 1864. Promoted Sergeant. Promoted Adjutant Sept. 20, 1865. Mustered out (as Sergeant) Sept. 16, 1865.

Company A.

First Lieutenant Geo. W. Thompson, com. Feb. 12, 1865. Mustered out Sept. 16, 1865.
First Serg. Aaron W. McGill, e. Feb. 17, 1865. m. o. Sept. 16, 1865.
Corpl. Dennis Ahern, e. Feb. 17, '65, m.o. Sept. 16, '65.

PRIVATES.

Hegley Gottlieb, e. Feb. 16, 1865, m. o. July 31, 1865.
Jackson Jas. H. e. Feb. 16, 1865, m. o. Sept. 16, 1865.
Patten Patrick, e. Feb. 21, 1865, deserted Feb. 25, 1865.

Company B.

Captain Arthur Dawson, e. as Corpl. Jan. 1, 1864. Promoted Sergeant Major. Promoted Captain Aug. 21, 1865. Mustered out (as Sergeant Major) Sept. 16, 1865.
First Lieutenant Chas. White, e. as Sergeant Jan. 1, 1864. Promoted First Lieutenant Aug. 21, 1865. Mustered out (as Sergeant) Sept. 16, 1865.
Second Lieutenant Isaac Coleman, e. as Corporal Jan. 1, 1864. Promoted First Sergeant. Promoted Second Lieutenant Sept. 20, 1865. Mustered out (as Sergeant) Sept. 16, 1865.
First Sergeant Geo. G. Smith, e. Jan. 1, 1864, m. o. May 30, 1865.

PRIVATES.

Alkey Saml. e. Jan. 1, 1864. m. o. May 30, 1865.
Brown Robt. e. Jan. 1, 1864, vet., m. o. Sept. 16, 1865.
Clark Saml. J. e. March 10, 1864, m. o. June 19, 1865.
Kortright Jas. S. e. Sept. 6, 1864, m. o. May 23, 1865.

17th Infantry.

First Asst. Surg. Henry H. Penniman, com. 2d Asst. Surg. Dec. 26, 1862. Promoted 1st Asst. Surg. July 1, '63. Mustered out for promotion Nov. 28, '63.

29th Infantry.

Company B.

Black Saml. A. e. Sept. 6, 1864, m. o. Aug. 4, 1865.

39th Infantry.

Second Asst. Surg. Wm. Woodward, com. Dec. 9, '62, promt. Surg. 58th I, V. I.

Sketch of 45th Infantry.

The Washburne Lead Mine Regiment was organized at Chicago, Ill., Dec. 25, 1861, by Col. John E. Smith, and mustered into the United States service as the Forty-fifth Infantry Illinois Volunteers. January 15, 1862, moved to Cairo, Illinois, February 3rd assigned to Brigade of Col. W. H. L. Wallace, Division of Brig. Gen. McClernand. February 4th, landed below Fort Henry, on the Tennessee, and on the 6th marched into the fort, it having been surrendered to the gun-boats. February 11th, moved toward Fort Donelson, and during the succeeding days bore its part of the suffering and of the battle. The flag of the Forty-fifth was the first planted on the enemy's works. Loss—3 killed and 26 wounded. March 4th, moved to the Tennessee River, and 11th, arrived at Savannah. Was engaged in the expedition to Pin Hook. March 25th moved to Pittsburg Landing, and encamped near Shiloh Church.

The Forty-fifth took a conspicuous and honorable part in the two days' battle of Shiloh, losing 26 killed and 199 wounded and missing—nearly one-half of the regiment. April 12 h, Col. John E. Smith, of the Forty-fifth, took command of the Brigade. During the siege of Corinth, the regiment was in the First Brigade, Third Division, Reserve Army of the Tennessee, and bore its full share of the labors and dangers of the campaign. June 4th, the regiment was assigned to Third Brigade, and moved towards Purdy, fifteen miles. On the 5th, marched to Bethel; 7th to Montezuma, and on the 8th to Jackson, Tennessee, the enemy flying on its approach. During the months of June and July, engaged in garrison and guard duty. August 11th, assigned to guarding railroad, near Toon's Station. On the 31st, after much desperate fighting, companies C and D were captured. The remainder of the regiment, concentrated at Toon's Station, were able to resist the attack of largely outnumbering forces. Loss—3 killed, 13 wounded, and 43 taken prisoners. September 17th, moved to Jackson; Nov. 11 to Bolivar, and was assigned to First Brigade, Third Div., Right Wing, Thirteenth Army Corps. Nov. 3, 1862, marched from Bolivar to Van Buren; 4th, to Lagrange, and were assigned to provost duty; 28th, marched to Holly Springs, Dec. 31, to Waterford; 4th, to Abbeville; 5th, to Oxford, to Yocona river, near Spring Dale. Communications with the North having been cut off, foraged on the country for supplies. Dec. 17 h notice received of the promotion of Col. John E. Smith, to Brigadier General, ranking from Nov. 29th. Dec. 22d returned to Oxford; 24th moved to a camp three miles north of Abbeville, on the Tallahatchie river, where the regiment remained during the month. Mustered out July 12, 1865, at Louisville, Ky., and arrived at Chicago, July 15, 1865, for final payment and discharge.

45th Infantry.

Company A.

Sullivan John, e. Sept. 2, 1864, m. o. June 3, 1865.

Company F.

First Lieutenant Edwin L. Lawrence, com. Second Lieutenant Dec. 23, 1 61. Promoted First Lieutenant April 8, 18 2. Resigned Sept. 2, 1862.
First Lieutenant Jno. A. Rollins, e. as private Sept. 23, 1861. Promoted Second Lieutenant June 1, 1862. Promoted First Lieutenant Oct. 1, 1862. Resigned July 22, 1863.
First Lieutenant Jno. P. Jones, e. as Sergt. Oct. 7, '61. Promoted Second Lieutenant, from First Sergeant, Oct. 1, 1862. Promoted First Lieutenant July 22, 1863. Term expired Dec. 28, 1864.
Second Lieutenant Gideon S. Riley, e. as private Oct. 1, 1861. Re-enlisted as vet. Jan. 5, 1864. Com. 2d Lieut. Mustered out (as Sergt.) July 12, 1865.
First Sergt. Henry Crittendon, e. Sept. 21, 1861, died at Jackson, Tenn., Sept. 2, 1862, wounds.
Sergt. Horace B. Sears, e. Sept. 26, 1861, disd. March 13, 1862, disab.
Sergeant Jos. S. Buck, e. Oct. 14, 1861, disd. Nov. 10, 1863, wounds.
Musician Row. Tripp, e. Sept. 25, 1861, m. o. Dec. 19, 1864, term ex.

PRIVATES.

Allen Danl. M. e. Oct. 9, 1861, re-enlisted as vet. Jan. 5, 1864, m. o. July 12, 1865, as Corpl.
Brown John, e. Nov. 28, 1861, re-enlisted as vet. Dec. 19, 1863, m. o. July 12, 1865.
Buckley Jas. e. Nov. 20, 1861, disd. for promotion as Hospital Steward.
Clark Seymour, e. Dec. 10, 1861, disd. May 16, 1862.
Dalby Abner, e. Nov. 21, 1861, died at Vicksburg, Nov. 12, 1863.
Dickerson John, e. Oct. 9, 1861, killed at Vicksburg, May 23, 1863.
Francis Wm. Oct. 1, 1861, killed at Vicksburg. June 26, 1863.
Frederick John, e. Sept. 29, '61, m. o. Jan. 17, '65, term ex.
Long Timothy, e. Oct. 19, 1861, claimed as a deserter Jan. 13, 1862.
Longfield H. R. E. e. Nov. 19, 1861, dropped from rolls Aug. 18, 1862.

BOONE COUNTY WAR RECORD.   259

McMahon A. F. e. Nov 6, '61, disd. Feb. 27, '63, disab.
Nash E. J. e. Oct. 5, 1861, disd. May 16, 1862.
Primer John M. e. Nov. 14, 1861, re-e listed as vet. Dec. 18, 1863, disd. June 19, 1865, wounds.
Robbins John, e. Oct. 7, '61, m. o. Dec. 19, '64, term ex.
Robbins Henry, e. Oct. 12, 1861, disd., minor and dis b.
Smith Luther, e. Oct. 1, re-enlisted as vet. J. n. 5, '64, m. o. July 12, 1865, as Corpl.
Sullivan Dennis, e. Nov 8, 1861, re-enlisted as vet. Jan. 5, 1864, m. o. July 12, 1865.
Squier Abram, e. Nov. 8, 1861, disd. May 16, 1862.
Spackman Wm., e. Nov. 18, 1861, trans. to V. R. C., May 31, 1864.
Smedley L.D. e.Oct.1,'61, dishonorably disd. April 1,'62.
Young David, e. Sept. 21, 1861, died at St. Louis, March 24, 1862.

RECRUITS.

Buck Wm. P. e. Sept. 15, 1862, prmt. Corpl., m. o. June 5, 1865.
Baxter Leslie B. e. Sept. 29, '64, m. o. June 3, 1865.
Wynn Henry, e. Sept. 29, 1864, m. o. June 3, 1865.

48th Infantry.

Second Asst. Surg. Jno. J. Golden, e. as Hospital Steward, com. Aug. 10, 1865. Mustered out (as Hospital Steward) Aug. 15, 1865.

Company C.

Stotts Benj. e. Feb. 24, 1864, died at Scottsboro, Ala., April 10, 1864.

Company K.

Jones or James Sam'l, e. Oct. 23, '61, m.o. Nov. 16,'64.
Little Wm. B. e. Oct. 23, 1861, trans. to V. R. C. June 15, 1864.

VETERANS.

Dallas Eli, e. March 9, 1864, disd. June 25, 1865.
Golden B. J. e. March 9, 1864, disd. at Marietta, Ga., Aug. 22, 1864.

RECRUITS.

Braswell John F. e. Feb. 24, 1864, m. o. Aug. 15, 1865.
Babb Thos. J. e. Feb. 24, 1864, m. o. Aug. 15, 1865.
Baxter Ino. W. e. Feb. 12, 1864, deserted March 1, '64.
Candy J cob, e. Feb. 10, 1864, disd. July 11, 1865.
Deming Har.ey, e. Feb. 10, 1864, m. o. Aug. 15, 1865, on furlough.
Dye Isaac, e. Feb. 24, 1864, m. o. Aug. 15, 1865.
Kenner Ino. e. Feb. 24, 1864, prmt. Serge. Major.
Shive A. J. e. Nov. 1, 1861, died at Cairo, Dec. 12, '61.
Wilson Shelby, e. Feb. 10, 1864, deserted March 1, '64.

58th Infantry.

Company B.

First Lieutenant Jas. E. Moss, promoted Second Lieutenant March 26, 1862. Promoted First Lieutenant March 2, 1863. Killed May 18, 1864.
Hogan Thos. e. Dec. 11, 1861, disd. June 3, 1862.
Hogan Jno. e. Dec. 11, 1861, disd. Dec. 31, 1862.
Herron F. E. March 27, 1863, deserted July 29, 1863.
Hill Merrett, e. June 13, 1863, trans. to Co. H as consol'd, m. o. April 1, 1866.
Lawrence O. B. e. March 27, 1863, disd. April 25, 1865.

Company G.

Ramer Chas. e. Dec. 9, 1861, trans. to Co. I, Jan. 5, '62.

58th Infantry Consolidated.

Surgeon Wm. Woodward, com. April 11, 1865. Mustered out April 1, 1866.

65th Infantry.

Chaplain Chas. H. Roe, com. May 1, 1862. Resigned Jan. 10, 1863.

Company E.

VETERANS.

Barr Jas. e. March 31, 1864, trans. to Co. K as consol'd, m. o. July 13, 1865.
Lawrence Chas. e. March 31, 1864, trans. to Co. K as consol'd, m. o. July 13, 1865.
Mack R. J. e. March 31, 1864, trans. to Co. K as consol'd, m. o. July 13, 1865.
Taff Harrison, e. March 31, 1864, trans. to Co. K as consol'd, m. o. July 13, 1865.

90th Infantry.

Company I.

Captain Wm. Cunningham, com. Oct. 31, 1862. Resigned July 11, 1864.
Corpl. Thos. Julian, e. Aug. 14, 1862, private, absent without leave since April 17, 1864.
Corpl. Lawrence Donavan, e. Aug. 16, 1862, disd. Feb. 24, 1865, as Sergt., disab.

PRIVATES.

Downs M. e. Aug. 16, 1862, m.o. June 6, 1865, as Sergt.
Gallaher Hugh, e. Aug. 12, 1862, m. o. June 6, 1865.
McLaughlin B. e. Aug. 27, 1862, died July 15, 1864, No. of grave 1,634.
Rosencrans W. e. Aug. 19, 1862, m. o. June 24, 1865, as corpl., pris. war.
Shields Francis, e. Aug. 16, 1862, m. o. June 6, 1865.

RECRUITS.

Hanley Jno. e. Oct. 10, 1862, deserted June 2, 1863.
Lovell Dan. e. Oct. 8, 1862, disd. Sept. 3, 1864, disab.
Smith A. B. deserted Nov. 8, 1862.

Sketch of 95th Infantry.

The Ninety-fifth Infantry Illinois Volunteers was organized at Camp Fuller, Rockford, Illinois, in August, 1862, by Col. Lawrence S. Church, and mustered into the United States' service Sept. 4, 1862.

The Regiment moved from camp, Nov. 4th, and proceeded, via Cairo and Columbus, to Jackson, Tenn., and, afterward, to Grand Juncti-n, Tenn., where it was assigned to Gen. McArthur's Division, Army of the Tennesee. Took part in Gen. Grant's campaign in N rthern Mississippi, in the winter of 1862.

Moved from Memphis to Milliken's Bend in the spring of 1863. Participated in the march to Grand Gulf, and all the battles between that place and the rear of Vicksburg. Was in the charges of May 19th and 22d, losing 25 killed, 124 wounded, and 10 missing—a much heavier loss than that of any other Regiment in the Division.

In March, 1864, went on Red River expedition, under Gen. A. J. Smith, and was engaged in the capture of Fort DeRussey and in the battles of Old River, Cloutierville, Mansouri, Yellow Bayou, and all the movements of that advance and retreat.

In May, 1864, returned to Vicksburg, and soon after moved to Memphis and took part in the ill-fated Sturgis expedition. Was in the battle of Guntown, and fought with undaunted bravery, but was overpowered, and, with the whole of Sturgis' army, retreated in confusion to Memphis. Col. Thomas W. Humphrey was killed, and nearly the whole Regiment was k lled, wounded or made prisoners. The campaign nearly annihilated the Regiment.

After recruiting at Memphis the command, in August, joined Gen. Mower. Moved up White river, and marched from Brownsville, through Arkansas, to Missouri, in pursuit of Price. The Ninety-fifth arrived at Benton Barracks, Missouri, Nov. 1, 1864. Nov. 30th, moved to Nashville, Tenn. Took part in battle of Nashville, Dec. 15 and 16, 1864, and in pursuit of Hood's defeated army to Tennessee river. Jan. 2, 1865, moved up the river to Eastport.

In February, 1865, embarked for New Orleans, arriving Feb. 21st.

On the 14th of March, moved to Dauphin Island, at mouth of Mobile Bay. On the 18th, landed at Cedar Point, with Col. Moore's Brigade, and commenced the first offensive operations against Mobile. Took part in Gen. Canby's movement from Fish river. During the

260 BOONE COUNTY WAR RECORD.

siege of Spanish Fort, carried its trenches to within 30 yards of the enemy's works, and participated in the storming and capture of the fort, April 8, 1865, being the first Regiment to occupy what was known, in the rebel line, as the "Red Fort."

After the fall of Mobile, the Ninety-fifth marched to Montgomery, Ala., arriving April 25th. From thence, moved to Opelika, Ala.

July 18th, started home. August 3d, arrived at Vicksburg; 10th, at St. Louis, and moved to Camp Butler, Ill., where, Aug. 18, 1865, it was mustered out of service.

During the summer of 1864, the Regiment had a detachment of 100 men, with Maj. Charles B. Loop, Capt. James Nish and Capt. A. S. Stewart, in charge. They participated in the battles of Kenesaw Mountain, Chattahoochie river, Atlanta, Jonesboro and Lovejoy Station.

The Regiment has marched 1,800 miles, and moved, by rail and water, 6,460 miles. Eighty-four men have been killed in battle or died of wounds and 176 died of disease. Total number of men who have belonged to the Ninety-fifth, 1,355.

95th Infantry.

Major Chas. B. Loop, com. Captain Co. B, Sept. 4, 1862. Promoted Major June 12, 1864. Mustered out Aug. 17, 1865.
Adjutant Wales W. Wood, com. Sept. 4, 1862. Mustered out Aug. 17, 1865.
Surgeon Geo. N. Woodward, com. Oct. 10, 1862. Resigned March 24, 1864.

Company A.

Drake Albert, e. Aug. 5, 1862, dis'd. Nov. 25, 1863, for promotion in 6th Miss. Vol. A. D.
Devine J. e. Dec. 29, 1863, died. Mch. 20, 1865, disab.
Huff Matt. e. Jan. 19, '65, trans. to Co. A, 47th I. V. I.
Smith Jas. H. e. Dec. 19, 1863, trans. to Co. A, 47th I. V. I.
Tooney Jos. e. Dec. 28, '63, trans. Co. A, 47th I. V. I.
Tucker C. F. e. Dec. 5, 1863, m. o. May 18, 1865.

Company B.

Captain Jas. M. Tisdel, e. as Sergt. Aug. 7, 1862. Promoted First Sergeant. Promoted Second Lieutenant July 26, 1863. Promoted First Lieutenant April 1, 1864. Promoted Captain June 12, 1864. Mustered out Aug. 17, 1865.
First Lieutenant Milton E. Keeler, com. Sept. 4, 1862. Resigned April 1, 1864.
First Lieutenant Wm. H. H. Curtis, e. as Sergeant Aug. 5, 1862. Promoted First Sergeant. Promoted Second Lieutenant April 1, 1864. Promoted First Lieutenant June 12, 1864. Mustered out Aug. 17, 1865.
Second Lieutenant Aaron F. Randall, com. July 28, 1862. Resigned Jan. 16, 1863.
Second Lieutenant Edwin D. Pierce, e. as First Sergeant Aug. 6, 1862. Promoted Second Lieutenant Jan. 16, 1863. Resigned July 26, 1863.
Second Lieutenant Edwin H. Roseman, e. as Corporal Aug. 15, 1862. Promoted Sergeant. Promoted Second Lieutenant June 12, 1864. Mustered out Aug. 17, 1865.
Sergt. Albert E. Locke, e. Aug. 5, 1862, died at Vicksburg Oct. 25, 1863.
Corpl. Stephen A. Rollins, e. Aug. 13, 1862, Sergt., kld. Gantown, Miss., June 10, 1864.
Corpl. Solomon H. Bailey, e. Aug. 14, 1862, disd. March 6, 1863, disab.
Corpl. H. B. Bogardus, e. Aug. 15, 1862, m. o. Aug. 17, 1865, as First Sergt.
Corpl. Chas. W. Webb, e. Aug. 15, 1862, m. o. Aug. 17, 1865, as Sergt.
Corpl. Chas. B. Drake, e. Aug. 14, 1862, disd. March 23, 1863, disab.
Corpl. Jno. Horan, e. Aug. 12, '62. died at Memphis, wds.
Corpl. John G. Morey, e. Aug. 2, 1862, m. o. Aug. 17, 1865, as Sergt.
Musician Pete White, e. Aug. 10, 1862, prmt. Principal Musician.
Musician A. M. Horton, e. Aug. 4, 1862, m. o. Aug. 17, 1864, wds.
Wagoner Benj. Easton, e. Aug. 6, 1862, died at Memphis, June 19, 1863, wds.

PRIVATES.

Allen Osborn, e. Aug. 7, 1862, disd. Mch. 22, '63, disab.
Atkinson Robt. e. Aug. 9, '62, disd. Oct. 21, '63, disab.
Butler John, e. Aug. 12, 1862, m. o. Aug. 17, 1865.
Bishop J. C. e. Aug. 11, 1862, m. o. Aug. 17, 1865.
Boyce Wm. H. e. Aug. 15, '62, died at Memphis Feb. 3, 1863.
Barker Edw. e. Aug. 20, 1862, disd. Mch. 23, '63, disab.
Blatchford Geo. e. Aug. 14, 1862, m. o. Aug. 17, 1865.
Curtis Chas. e. Aug. 5, 1862, prmt. Sergt. Maj.
Chamberlin D. e. Aug. 7, 1862, m. o. May 31, '63, wds.
Chilvers W. B. e. Aug. 9, '62, m. o. Aug. 17, '65, Corpl.
Curner Isaac, e. Aug. 11, '62, disd. Jan. 14, '63, disab.
Corcoran John, e. Aug. 11, 1862, died at St. Louis, Oct. 19, 1863.
Carpenter A. D. e. Aug. 11, 1862, deserted May 24, '63.
Cox David, e. Aug. 5, 1862. m. o. May 31, 63, wds.
Carpenter G. D. e. Aug. 14, 1862, m. o. Aug. 17, 1865.
Cummings A. S. e. Aug. 15, '62, m. o. Aug. 17, '65, wds.
Coller John, e. Aug. 13, 1862, m. o. Aug. 17, 1865.
Cramer Peter, e. Aug. 15, 1862, disd. Feb. 11, '63, disab.
Draper Hiram, e. Aug. 13, '62, disd. Mch. 20, '63, disab.
Fitsimons J. e. Aug. 17, 1862, m. o. Aug. 17, 1865.
Griffin Geo. H. e. Aug. 13, '62, disd. June 22, '63, disab.
Goodman J. G. e. Aug. 11, 1862, m. o. July 22, 1865, prisoner war.
Hovey Austin, e. Aug. 7, 1862, m. o. Aug. 17, 1865.
Houck F. F. e. Aug. 7, 1862, m. o. Aug. 17, 1865, prisoner war.
Horton Thos. D. e. Aug. 14, 1862, m. o. Aug. 17, 1865.
Horan Owen, e. Aug. 12, 1862, m. o. Aug. 17, 1865.
Hill Wm. F. e. Aug. 12, 1862, m. o. Aug. 17, '65, Corpl.
Hall Ira D. e. Aug. 11, 1862, m. o. Aug. 17, 1865.
Hostrawser Paul, e. Aug. 9, '62, m. o. Aug. 17, 1865, as Corpl.
Harder Wellington, e. Aug. 6, '62, m. o. Aug. 17, 1865.
Harter Walter, e. Aug. 9, 1862, m. o. Aug. 17, 1865.
Heffin Wm. e. Aug. 6, '62, m. o. Aug. 17, '65, Sergt.
Kelly Thomas, e. Aug. 14, 1862, deserted Nov. 19, '62.
Lopez Orlando, e. Aug. 9, 1862, absent, wounded, at end of regt.
Leach F. J. e. Aug 13, 1862, died Sept. 27, 1863, disab.
Marvin Geo. e. Aug. 15, 1862, disd. Mch. 20, '63, disab.
Marion S. F. e. Aug. 14, 1862, m. o. Aug. 17, '65, Corpl.
McCoy H. e. Aug. 15, 1862, m. o. Aug. 17, 1865.
Munge H. J. e. Aug. 8, 1862, m. o. Aug. 17, 1865.
Moore Thos. e. Aug. 9, '62, m. o. Aug. 17, '65, wnd'd.
Merrill John J. e. Aug. 15, 1862, m. o. Aug. 17, 1865.
Martin Jos. M. e. Aug. 15, '62, m. o. Aug. 17, '65, wnd'd.
Manning Jas. R. e. Aug. 14, 1862, died Sept. 18, 1864, disab.
Muley I. e. Aug. 7, 1862, m. o. Aug. 17, 1865.
Newcomb W. O. e. Aug. 12, 1862, trans. to Invalid Corps, Sept. 25, 1863.
O'Donnell James, e. Aug. 7, 1862, m. o. Aug. 17, 1865.
Porter W. e. Aug. 15, 1862, disd. May 18, 1865, disab.
Park E. J. e. Aug. 15, 1862, m. o. Aug. 17, 1865.
Powell M. L. e. Aug. 6, 1862, m. o. July 22, 1865, was prisoner.
Ridge Robt. e. Aug. 12, '62, m. o. Aug. 17, '65, Corpl.
Sackett Geo. W. e. Aug. 6, 1862, m. o. Aug. 17, 1865.
Studley D. F. e. Aug. 15, 1862, died June 18, '63, wds.
Studley Chas. A. e. Aug. 15, 1862, m. o. Aug. 17, 1865, as Corpl.
Stevenson Wm. R. e. Aug. 13, 1862, m. o. Aug. 17, '65, wounded.
Stevenson S. L. e. Aug. 13, 1862, m. o. Aug. 17, 1865.
Sexton John, e. Aug. 15, 1862, died at Memphis, June 26, 1864.
Shackley E. e. Aug. 13, 1862, m. o. Aug. 17, '65, wnd'd.
Shanneman H. e. Aug. 15, 1862, m. o. Aug. 17, 1865.
Smith H. e. Aug. 5, 1862, m. o. Aug. 17, 1865, Corpl.
Sweetapple Jos. e. Aug. 5, 1862, m. o. Aug. 17, 1865, as Sergt.
Thompson Ransom, e. Aug. 15, '62, m. o. Aug. 17, '65.
Tibbals F. D. e. Aug. 15, 1862, m. o. Aug. 17, 1865.
Winegar D. G. e. Aug. 14, 1862, m. o. Aug. 17, 1865.
Westberry J. b. H. e. Aug. 14, 1862, kld. May 27, 1864.
Winegar Geo. W. e. Aug. 14, 1862, m. o. Aug. 17, 1865.

RECRUITS.

Andrews Mervin, e. Aug. 31, 1864, disd. June 10, 1865, disab.
Barnes Geo. e. Sept. 14, 1864, m. o. Aug. 17, 1865.
Bare Wm. e. Dec. 29, 1863, trans. to Co. B, 47th I. V. I.
Church Chas. e. Sept. 12, 1864, m. o. Aug. 17, 1861.
Coller Smith, e. Dec. 21, 1863, trans. Co. B, 47th I. V. I.
Curtis F. H. e. Jan. 4, 1864, trans. Co. B, 47th I. V. I.

BOONE COUNTY WAR RECORD.

Demerest Lemuel, e. Sept. 22, 1864, m. o. Aug. 17, '65.
Delany Richard, e. Sept. 19, 1864, m. o. Aug. 17, 1865.
Dupuy Garrett, e. Dec. 25, 1863, trans. to Co. B, 47th I.V.I.
Dixon M. e. Jan. 5, 1864, died at Mound City, Ill., June 26, 1864.
Fagan Lawrence, e. Dec. 22, 1863, trans. to Co. B, 47th I.V.I., absent sick.
Farnsworth Chas. e. Dec. 7, 1863, died at Memphis, Sept. 18, 1864.
Gallagher Andrew, e. Sept. 19, 1864, m. o. Aug. 17, '65.
Haight A. C. e. Jan. 2, 1864, m. o. June 5, 1865.
Hovey Edwin, e. Dec. 12, 1863, died at Montgomery, Ala., July 22, 1865.
Johnson Thore, s. Dec. 30, 1863, trans. to Co. B, 47th I. V. I.
Johnson John, e. Jan. 18, 1864, trans. to Co. B, 47th I. V. I., absent sick.
Jacobs J. A. e. March 26, 1864, trans. Co. B, 47th I.V.I.
Leach C. C. e. Nov. 26, 1863, trans. Co. B, 47th I.V.I.
Moore John, e. Sept. 14, 1864, m. o. Aug. 17, 1865.
Moore D. A. e. Sept. 3, 1864, m. o. May 23, 1865.
Marvin D. E. e. Dec. 21, 1863, m. o. June 15, 1865.
Murphy James, e Feb 8, 1864, trans. Co. B, 47th I.V.I.
Mead Wm. H. e. Dec. 16, 1863, died at Vicksburg, Feb. 24, 1864.
Miller Jas. C. e. Dec. 30, 1863, died at Vicksburg, Feb. 18, 1865.
McNelly Wm. e. Dec. 15, 1863, died at Rome, Ga., July 14, 1864.
Mikleson Kittle, e. Jan. 5, 1864, died at Memphis, July 14, 1864.
Parsons John H. e. Dec. 11, 1863.
Randolph John, e. Sept. 23, 1862.
Smith A. M. e. Sept. 12, 1864, m. o. Aug. 17, 1865.
Searls John A. e. Dec. 30, 1863, trans. to Co. B, 47th I. V. I.
Sergeant Tim, e. Nov. 18, 1863, trans. to Co. B, 47th I. V. I.
Seibert A. W. e. Dec. 28, 1863, died at Louisville, Ky., July 21, 1864.
Strong E. N. e. Dec. 1, 1863, died in Andersonville Prison, Sept. 17, 1864; No. of grave, 9,013.
Tyler Wm. N. e. Dec. 28, 1863, Veteran Recruit, paroled prisoner, m. o. July 31, 1865.
Tyler E. A. e. Dec. 28, 1863, died at Memphis, Sept. 8, 1864.
Williams Henry, e. Dec. 22, 1863, kld. at Guntown, Miss., June 10, 1864.

Company D.

Davis L. J. e. Sept. 23, 1864, m. o. Aug. 17, 1865.
Hinderman H. e. Sept. 6, 1864, m. o. Aug. 17, 1865.
Schla, Henry, e. Sept. 12, 1864, m. o. Aug. 17, 1865.

Company E.

Sergt. Wm. Andrews, e. Aug. 22, 1862, m. o. Aug. 17, 1865, as 1st Sergt.
Corpl. Geo. G. Blaze, e. Aug. 22, 1862, m. o. Aug. 17, 1865. Reduced at his own request.

PRIVATES.

Alderman John L. e. Aug. 22, 1862, died April 25, 1863.
Bassett Geo. e. Aug. 22, '62, died at Vicksburg, Dec. 8, '63.
Brown Jas. e. Aug. 22, 1862, m. o. Aug. 17, 1865.
Barnard Geo. V. e. Aug. 15, 1862, m. o. Aug. 17, 1865.
Bassett Wm. e. Aug. 22, 62 kld. at Vicksburg May 17, '63.
Holden Chas. A. e. Aug. 15, 1862, m. o. Aug. 17, 1865.
Stott Jas. e. Aug. 22, 1862, disd. March 20, 1863, as Corpl., disab.

RECRUITS.

Hall Frank G. e. Sept. 14, 1864, m. o. June 15, 1865.
Cummings Robt. e. Sept. 14, 1864, m. o. July 25, 1865.
Fitzer L. F. e. Oct. 3, 1864, died at Eastport, Miss., Jan. 28, 1865.

Company F.

RECRUIT

Brown Morris F. e. Oct. 3, 1864, trans. to Co. D, 47th Illinois Infantry.

Company G.

Captain Elliott N. Bush, com. Sept. 4, 1862. Killed in battle, June 12, 1864.

Captain Henry M. Bush, com. First Lieutenant Sept. 4, 1862. Promoted Captain June 12, 1864. Mustered out Aug. 17, 1864.
First Lieutenant Chas. W. Ives, e. as First Sergeant Aug. 4, 1862. Promoted Second Lieutenant June 24, 1863. Promoted First Lieutenant June 12, 1864. Resigned (as Second Lieutenant) Sept. 8, 1864.
First Lieutenant Jeremiah Wilcox, e. as Sergeant Aug. 5, 1862. Promoted First Sergeant. Promoted Second Lieute nant June 12, 1864. Promoted First Lieutenant Sept 8, 1864. Mustered out Aug. 17, 1865.
Second Lieutenant Joseph M. Collier, com. Sept. 4, 1862. Died June 24, 1863.
Sergt. Jas. S. Collins, e. Aug 5, 1862, died at Lagrange, Tenn., Jan. 15, 1863.
Sergt. Daniel B. Cornell, e. July 26, 1862, m. o. June 10, 1865, as First Sergt., wds.
Corpl Wm. Bryden, e. Aug. 5, 1862, disd. Feb. 24, '63, disab.
Corpl. Rich d O. Gunn, e. July 29, 1862, died at Keokuk, Iowa, Dec. 14, 1863, wds.
Corpl. Wells Briggs, e. Aug. 2, 1862, m. o. Aug. 1, '65, pris. war, wds.
Corpl. A. Quackenbuss, e. Aug. 4, 1862, died at Memphis, March 1, 1863.
Corpl. D. S. Gookins, e. July 30, 1862, m. o. Aug. 17, 1865, as S rgt. wds.
Corpl. D. E. Keeler, e. July 31, 1862, m. o. May 27, 1865, as private.
Corpl. C. N. Wilson, e. Aug 14, 1862, disd. June 6, 1863, for promotion as R. Q. M. 8th La. Col. Inf.
Musician Fred, Wood, e. July 31, 1862, m. o. Aug. 17, 1865, as private.
Musician J. Atterly Moore, e. Aug. 5, 1862, m. o. Aug. 17, 1865.
Wagoner Wm. Whitehead, e. Aug. 9, 1862, m. o. Aug. 17, 1865, as private.

PRIVATES.

Abbott Marcus R. e. Aug. 21, 1862, m. o. Aug. 17, '65, as Corpl.
Barnes Chas. e. Aug. 6, 1862, died at Vicksburg, July 17, 1863.
Barnes Orrin, e. Aug. 6, 1862, m. o. Aug. 17, 1865.
Benedict Jno. E. e. Aug. 4, '62, kld. Vicksburg, May 19, '63.
Bennett Geo. e. Aug. 7, '62, m. o. Aug. 17, '65, was pris.
Blood Albert, e. July 30, 1862, m. o. Aug. 17, '65, wds.
Borst W. S. e. Aug. 11, 1862, deserted Oct. 10, 1862.
Briggs Royal, e. Aug. 6, 1862, died at home, Aug., '64.
Brist I N. S. e. Aug. 2, 1862, m. o. Aug. 17, 1865.
Byson Peter, e. Aug 6, 1862, disd. A g. 18, 1864, wds.
Cashire A. D. J. e. Aug. 6, 1862, m. o. Aug. 17, 1865.
Caswell J. D. e. Aug. 6, 1862, disd. Jan. 15, 1863.
Chase D. F. e. Aug. 2, 1862, disd. Dec. 23, 1863, for promotion as 1st Sergt.
Caswell H. A. e. Aug. 5, '62, m. o. Aug. 29, '65, pris.war.
Collins Chas. O. e. Aug. 8, 1862, died Feb. 26, 1863.
Danforth Chas. e. Aug. 6, 1862, m. o. Aug. 17, 1865.
Douglass H. Ford, e. July 26, 1 62, disd. June 7, 1861, for promotion as Capt. Ind Co. attached to 8th La. Col. Inf.
Dible Jno. H. e. Aug. 7, 1862, m. o. Aug. 17, 1865.
Down Geo. W. e. Aug. 6, '62, disd. Feb. 24, '63, disab.
Eastman P. e. Aug. 5, 1862, m. o. Aug. 17, 1865.
Feakins Hawley, e. Aug. 6, 1862, m. o. Aug. 17, 1865.
Feakins Wm. A. e. Aug. 2, '62, died home, Sept. 10, '63.
Field M. L. e. Aug. 2, 1862, trans. to Invalid Corps, Oct. 19, 1863.
Foote E. L. e. Aug. 5, 1862, m. o. Aug. 17, '65, Corpl.
Frederick W. H. e. Aug. 6, 1862, m. o. Aug. 17, 1865.
Gilbert Pierce, e. Aug. 2, '62. disd. July 20, '63, disab.
Gile Rufus B. e. Aug. 5, 1862, died at Montgomery, Ala., July 22, 1865.
Gilkerson Wm. e. Aug 26, 1862, m. o. Jan. 24, 1865, as Sergt., prisoner of war.
Gunn Wm. E. e. Aug. 26, 1862, killed at Vicksburg, May 22, 1863.
Hamlin W. e. Aug. 22, 1862, died June 13, 1863.
Hannah R. D. e. Aug. 6, '62, m. o. May 27, '65, Corpl.
Hannah Thos. J. e. Aug. 4, 1862, m. o. Aug. 17, 1865, as Corpl., wounded.
Hanks Buel F. e. Aug. 5, 1862.
Hakes H. C. e. Aug. 5, 1862.
Hudson H. e. Aug. 2, 1862.
Hogan Michael, July 28, 1862.
Horan Robt. e. Aug. 5, 1862.
Johnson S. A. e. Aug. 5, 1862.
Lincoln E. N. e. Aug. 14, 1862.
McCormick Jos. E. e. Aug. 2, 1862.

Middleton Wm. e. Aug. 6, 1862.
Morton Jay H. e. Aug. 4, 1862, m. o. Aug. 17, 1865.
Norton Amos, e. July 26, 1862, m. o. Aug. 17, 1865.
O'Neil Henry, e. July 28, 62, m.o Aug 17, '64, was pris.
Orcutt L. A. e. Aug. 9, 1862, disd. Nov. 3, 1864.
Peebles O. C. e. Aug. 7, 1862, m. o. Aug. 17, 1865.
Pepper Samuel, e. July 28, 1862, m. o. Aug. 17, 1865.
Pierce R. D. e. Aug. 8, 1862, m. o. Aug. 17, 1865.
Pray C. J. e. Aug. 4, 1862, died at Memphis, June 9, 1862, wounds.
Ramsey John, e. Aug. 7, 1862, m. o. May 27, 1865.
Randall Geo. E. e. July 26, 1862, died at Brownsville, Ark., Sept. 29, 1864.
Riley Henry, e. Aug. 8, 1862, m. o. Aug. 17, 1865.
Saxton Jay H. e. July 28, 1861, m. o. May 28, 1865.
Seibert Jacob, e. Aug. 5, 1862, wounded, absent at m. o. of regt.
Smith John M. e. Aug. 6, '62, m. o. May 28, '65, Corpl.
Smith Wm. I., e. Aug. 6, 1862, m. o. May 28, 1865.
Snow Geo. W. e. July 30, 1862, m. o. May 28, 1865.
Stocking C. P. e. Aug. 6, 1862, m. o. May 27, 1865.
Sughrue P. F. e. Aug. 6, 1862, m. o. Aug. 17, 1865.
Thomas E. H. e. Aug. 6, 1862, m. o. Aug. 17, 1865.
Weaver Daniel, e. Aug. 12, 1862, m. o. Aug. 17, 1865.
Williams Leslie, e. Aug. 9, 1862, m. o. Aug. 17, 1865.

RECRUITS.

Allen John, e. Sept. 12, 1864, m. o. Aug. 17, 1865.
Ashlan Peter, e. Jan. 5, 1864, m. o. June 24, 1864, pris.
Bac e H. M. e. Sept. 30, 1864, m. o. Aug. 1b, 1865.
Conver James, e. Dec. 22, 1863, trans. to W. R. C.
Case Wills, e. Jan. 4, '64, trans. to Co. B, 47th I. V. I.
Childs H. F. e. Jan. 4, 1864, disd. Jan. 24, 1865, accidental wounds.
Cohorn D. W. e. Dec.11,'63, died Memphis, July 2, '64.
Downs L. L. e. Dec 24, '64, trans. to Co. B, 47th I.V.I.
Doran Thos. died May 13, 1863.
Farnsworth Chas. disd. March 24, 1863, di-ab.
Hogan John M. e. Dec. 7, 1863, m. o. Aug. 17, 1865, was prisoner.
Houghtaling John W. e. Dec. 24, 1864, trans. to Co. B, 47th I.V.I.
Lucas Eber, e. Sept. 30, 1864, m. o. Aug. 17, 1865.
Milks David, e. Jan. 5, '64, trans. to Co. B, 47th I.V.I.
Oaks Geo. A. e. Sept. 12, 1864, m.o. Aug. 17, '65, wds.
Orcutt Josiah, e. Jan. 4, 1864, died at Jefferson Barracks, Mo., July 13, 1864.
Russell D. F. e. Jan. 29, 1864, died at Vicksburg, May 29, 1864.
Ray Wm. e. Jan. 5, 1864, died at Winnebago Co., Ill.
Sweett S. W. e. Feb.29, '64, trans. to Co. B, 47th I.V.I.
Stenner Jacob, e. Jan.20,'64, trans. to Co. B 47th I.V.I.
Stafford Edgar, e. Sept.30,'64,trans to Co. B,47th I.V.I.
Wolverton R. C. e. April 8,'64,trans.to Co.H,47th I.V.I.
Wright James, e. Dec. 22, 1863, died at Memphis, July 1, 1864.

Company H.

Wright Gibson, e. Sept. 2, 1864, m. o. Aug. 17, 1865.

Company I.

Bates Amos M. e. Sept. 29, 1864, m. o. Aug. 17, 1865.
Edson Chas. e. Sept. 14, 1864, detached at m.o. of regt.
Morris John, e. Oct. 3, 1864, disd. June 10, 1865.

Company K.

Captain Gabriel E. Cornell, com. Sept. 4, 1862. Killed in battle, May 22, 1863.
Captain Almon Schellenger, com. First Lieutenant, Sept. 4, 1862. Promoted Captain, May 22, 1863. Mustered out Aug. 17, 1865.
First Lieutenant Alonzo Brooks, com. Second Lieutenant, Sept. 4, 1862. Promoted First Lieutenant, May 22, 1863. Mustered out Aug. 17, 1865.
Second Lieutenant Jno. D. Abbe, e. as First Sergeant, Aug. 20, 1862. Promoted Second Lieutenant, May 22, 1863. Resigned Sept. 19, 1864.
Second Lieutenant Alfred P. Cheney, e. as Sergeant, Aug. 7, 1862. Promoted First Sergeant, Promoted Second Lieutenant, Sept. 19, 1864. Mustered out Aug. 17, 1864.
Sergt. Sewell Valentine, e. Aug. 7, 1862, m. o. Aug. 17, 1865, as First Sergeant.
Sergt. Jos. W. Bowman, e. Aug. 7, 1862, died at Memphis, Feb. 7, 1863.

Sergt. John Van Antwerp, e. Aug. 13, 1862, m. o. Aug. 17, 1865, wounded.
Corpl. Henry B. Putnam, e. July 28, 1862, m. o. Aug 17, 1865, as private.
Corpl. F. Geng, e. Aug. 2, 1862, m. o. Aug. 8, 1865, as private.
Corpl. H. Morgan, e Aug 13, 1862, m. o. Aug. 17, 1865, as Sergt., wounded.
Corpl. Jos. P. Smith, e. Aug. 11, 1862, m. o. Aug. 17, 1865, as Sergt.
Corpl. H S Vanyerhacker, e. Aug. 15, 1862, deserted Feb. 14, 1863.
Corpl. Geo. W. Sawyer, e. Aug. 5, 1862, died at Lake Providence, La., May 3, 1863.
Corpl. L. K. Greene, e. Aug. 15, 1862, died at Memphis, Aug. 25, 1862.
Corpl. Thomas Vincent, e. Aug. 5, 1862, m. o. Aug. 17, 1865, as private, reduced at his own request.
Musician Eli Bunhck, e. Aug. 7, '62, m. o. May 21, '65.
Musician Geo. E. Hansom, e Aug 22, 1862, m. o. June 3, 1865.
Wagoner P. H. Weldon, e. Aug. 7, 1862, m. o. Aug. 1, 1865, as private.

PRIVATES.

Atkinson John H. e. July 28, '62, drowned Aug. 24,'63.
Bowman Thos. H. e. Aug. 7, 1862, m. o. Aug. 17, 1865, as Corpl.
Butterfield H. S. e. July 24, 1862, died at LaGrange, Tenn., Jan. 22, 1863.
Butler M. e. July 28, 1862, disd. June 5, 1864, wds.
Baker Wm. T. e. Aug. 7, 1862, kld at Vicksburg, May 22, 1863.
Barnes H. e. Aug. 7, 1862, disd. May 27, 1865.
Burroughs John, e. Aug. 11, 1862, Corpl. absent sick at m. o. of regt.
Bruce C. e. Aug. 9, '62, absent, wounded, at m. o. regt.
Cleman John N. e. Aug. 13, 1862, m. o. Aug. 17, 1865.
Cornwell G. J. e. Aug. 13, '62, Sergt., kld. Apl 22, '64.
Chapple Wm. H. e. Aug. 13, 1862, m. o. June 6, 1865, as Corpl.
Dymond Jas. e. Aug. 7, 1862, m. o. Aug. 1, '65, wnd'd.
Dymond Stephen, e. Aug 15, 1862, m. o. Aug. 17, '65, as Corpl.
Dullam John D. e. Aug. 13, 1862, m. o. Aug. 17, 1865.
Emmans Richard, e. Aug. 14, 1862, died in Tenn., Jan. 22, 1863.
Ellsworth Geo. O. e. Aug. 11, 1862, wounded, trans. to 2d Miss. Heavy Art., Jan. 27, 1864.
Ellis James, e. Aug. 7, 1862, m. o. Aug. 17, 1865.
Foos Chas. W. e. Aug. 15, 1862, m. o. Aug 17, 1865.
Gibbs Wm. e. Aug. 7, 1862, m. o. Aug. 17, 1865, wnd'd.
Hill Samuel H. e. Aug. 8, 1862, disd. April 1, 1865, as Corpl.
Hutchins Willard, e. Aug. 11, 1862, disd March 10, '63.
Hill Alpheus, e. Aug. 9, 1862,died Aug. 30, 1863.
Hutchins Wm. e. Aug. 11, '63, m.o. Aug. 17, '65, wnd'd.
Hill Henry, e. Aug. 9, 1862 m. o. June 21, 1865.
Kirk Chas. e. Aug. 13, 1862, m. o. Aug. 17, 1865.
Knox A. T. e. Aug. 7, 1862, kld. at Vicksburg, June 24, 1863.
Labonne Fred. e. Aug. 13, 1862, deserted Feb. 14, 1863.
Lewis Geo. e. Aug 7, 1862, m. o. June 24, 1865, was prisoner, wounded.
Lilley J. R. e. Aug 7, 1862, m. o. Aug. 17, 1865, Sergt.
Lighof N. e. Aug. 7, 1862, died Jan. 27, 1863.
Landon James, e. Aug. 21, 1862, m. o. Aug. 17, 1865.
McIntire Jarvis, e. Aug. 7, 1862, died March 25, 1863.
North H. W. e. Aug. 22, 1862, di-d. May 27, 1865.
Ouckell Sam'l, e. Aug. 14, 1865, died at home, Sept. 6, 1864.
Oleson Thos. e. Aug. 8, 1862, m. o. Aug. 17, 1865.
Ostram Jacob, e. Aug. 5, 1862, died at Memphis, Feb. 7, 1863.
Oleson Andrew, e. Aug 8, 1862, m. o. May 20, 1865.
Oleson Nelson, e. Aug. 8, 1862, di-d. April 6, '63, di-ab.
Perkins Anson, e. Aug. 11, 1862, kld. at Clanterville, April 24, 1864.
Pickard David, e. Aug. 7, 1862, m. o. July 22, 1865, was prisoner.
Robinson Robt. e. Aug. 5, '62, disd. Mch. 21,'63,disab.
Richman Robt. e. Aug. 9, '62 deserted May 24, 1863.
Rosewalt W. J. e. Aug. 21, 1862, m. o. Aug. 17, 1865.
Rasa Artemas, e. Aug. 11, 1862, disd. for disab.
Reser H. M. e. Aug. 7, 1862, m. o. Aug. 17, 1865.
Renne Jay. e. Aug. 7, 1862, m. o. Aug. 17, 1865.
Reed Wm. e. Aug. 22. 1862, m. o. Aug. 17, 1865.
Scougal Jas. B. e. Aug. 5, '62, disd. Feb. 11, '65, disable.
Sewell Jos. e. Aug. 13, 1862, m.o. Aug. 17, 1865.

Story R. G. e. Aug. 5. 1862. died Nashville, Tenn., Dec. 20, 1864.
Smith Jos. N. e. Aug. 15, 1862, Corpl., kld. Vicksburg, May 22, 1863
Stall Hans, e. Aug. 11, 1862, m. o. Aug. 17. '65, Corpl.
Stitsyer John H. e. Aug. 11, 1862, m. o. Aug. 17, 1865.
Stougal L. e. Aug. 13, 1862, m. o. Aug. 17, '65, Corpl.
Streeter Geo. W. e. Aug. 7. 1862, m. o. Aug. 17, 1865.
Sherman Sam'l D. e. Aug. 9, 1865, disd. Jan. 26, 1864, disab.
Smith Rufus, e. Aug. 11, 1862, m. o. Aug. 17, 1865.
Spencer S. W. e. Aug. 9, 1862, died at Vicksburg, July 17, 1863.
Steele H. W. e. Aug. 7, 1862, disd. Mch. 21,'63, disab.
Stockwell Abram, e. Aug. 11, 1862, trans. to V. R. C., Sept. 15, 1863.
Stockwell Wm. H. e. Aug. 11, 1862, disd. May 25, 1865, as Corpl.
Stockwell Geo. W. e. Aug. 11.'62, m.o. Aug.17,'65, wds.
Sherman Chas, E. e. Aug. 22.'62, disd. May 23,'65,wds.
Sharkle Thos. e. Aug. 7, 1862, m. o. June 20, 1865.
Smith Ira, e. Aug. 11. 1862, m. o. May 18, 1865.
Vandewacher Geo. e. Aug. 13, 1812, died at Natchez, Miss., Sept. 3, 1863.
Vincent Jas. e. Aug. 5, 1862, died at Vicksburg, Dec. 21, 1863.
Vickers Jas. P. e. Aug. 9, 1862, died at Nebraska, La., Feb. 3, 1863.
Vickers Jas. e. Aug. 11. 1862. m. o. July 8, 1865.
Warren Cyrus L. e. Aug. 15, 1862, died at Vicksburg, March 21, 1864.
Wakefield Abner, e. Aug. 11, 1862, m. o. Aug. 17, 1865.
Wilson Theo. e. Aug. 15, 1862, trans. to V. R. C., Sept. 15, 1863.
Webster L. H. E. e. Aug. 21, 1862, disd. April 5, 1865.
Wright G. C. e. Aug. 7, '62, m. o. Aug. 17, '65. Corpl.
Willey Duane. e. Aug. 5, 1862, died at Memphis, Tenn., Feb. 11, 1863.
Wakefield L. e. Aug. 7, 1862. m. o. Aug. 17. 1865.
Wakefield S. e. Aug 7. 1862, disd. at St. Louis, wds.

RECRUITS.

Blake Robt. e. Sept. 15, 1864, disd. May 23. 1865.
Booth Wm. H. e. Oct. 5, 1864. trans. to Co. F, 47th I. V. I.
Burdick Wm. A. e. Nov. 30. 1863, m. o. May 19. 1865.
Ball Thos. e. Sept. 28. 1864, died Mch. 29, 1865.
Brown S. H. e. Dec. 22, 1863, died at Cairo, Ill., Oct. 28, 1864.
Bowman Sam'l P. e. Sept. 15, 1861, m. o. Aug. 17, '65.
Desmore John, e. Oct. 5, 1864. trans. to Co. F, 47th I. V. I.
Elsworth Eugene, e. Jan. 18, 1864, trans to V. R. C., Dec. 25. 1864.
Hovey R. F. e. Oct. 5, 1864. m. o. May 17, 1865.
Joslin J. N. B. e. Oct.3,'64, trans. to Co. F, 47th I.V.I.
Klumph A. e. Dec. 30, 1864, m. o. June 7, 1865.
Lowell E. E. e. Sept. 1, 1864, m. o. Aug. 17, 1865.
La Fever Robt. e. Dec.20.'61, trans. to Co F.,7th I.V I.
Livingston John R. e. Oct. 3, 1864, trans. to Co. F, 47th I. V. I.
Lumley John W. e. Oct. 3, 1864, died at Vicksburg.
Mansfield John T. e. March 31, 1864, trans. to Co. F, 47th I. V. I.
McCarty Jno. e. Jan. 5, '64, trans. Co. K, 47th I. V. I.
Miller O. D. e. Dec. 9, 1863, m. o. May 22, 1865.
Peck A. S. e. Jan. 4, 1864. trans. Co. F, 47th I. V. I.
Rodow It S. e. Sept. 1, 1864, m. o. Aug. 17, 1865.
Reel Jas. e. Oct. 3, 1864 trans. to Co. F, 47th I. V. I.
Streeter H. A. e. Sept. 2, 1864. m. o. Aug. 17, 1865.
Stanno Geo. e. Feb. 29 '64, trans. Co. F, 47th I. V. I.
Smith Jas, P. e. Dec. 9, 63, trans. to Co. F., 47th I. V. I.
Salsbury O. A. e. Jan. 2, 64 trans. Co. F., 47th I. V. I.
Slater F. M. e. Dec 22, 1863, died at Simsport, La., May 20, 1864.
Vanderwacher F. e. Dec. 24, '63. Vet. Recruit, m. o. May 16, 1865.
Vandyke M. e. Dec. 9, 1863, died June 5, 1864.
Watts Wm. e. Oct. 3, '64, trans. to Co. F, 47th I. V. I.
Webster A. L. e. Oct. 3 '64, trans to Co. F., 47th I. V. I.
Wakefield D. Dec. 4, '63. disd. June 10, 1865.

UNASSIGNED RECRUITS.

Beauchamp A. G. e. Aug. 29, 1864, Sub.
Bridgett Newman, e. Sept. 1, 1864.
Higgins Philip, e. Sept. 28, 1864.
Hannum B. e. Sept. 12, 1864.
Johnson Thos. e. Dec. 31, 1863.

Salter Smith, e. Dec. 31, 1863.
Tyler Sam'l H. e. Dec. 28, 1863, rejected, disd.

105th Infantry.

Company G.

First Lieutenant Samuel H. Williamson, e. Aug. 7, 1862. Promoted First Sergeant, then First Lieutenant, July 17, 1864. Mustered out June 7, 1865.
Corpl. Jas. R. Williamson, e. Aug. 12, 1862, m. o. June 7, 1865, as Sergt., wds.

PRIVATES.

Burbig Theo. e. Aug. 15, 1862, m. o. June 7, 1865, wds.
McKee A. R. e. Aug. 12, 1862, died at Gallatin, Tenn., Dec. 18, 1862.
Tatilin O. H. e. Aug. 10, 1862, m. o. June 7, 1865, wds.
Williamson Thos. E. e. Aug. 7, 1862, m. o. June 7, '65, as Sergt., wds.
Hailer Gabriel, e. Sept. 29, 1864, m. o. June 7, 1865.

134th (100 days) Infantry.

Company G.

Second Lieutenant Jas. H. Roe, com. May 31, 1864, m. o. Oct. 25. 1864.
Corpl. Robt. Atkinson, e. May 13,'64, m.o. Oct. 25.'64.

PRIVATES.

Gaylord H. M. e. May 13. 1864, m. o, Oct. 25. 1864.
Hays Henry, e. May 13, 1864, m. o. Oct. 25. 1864.
Waterman H. B. e. May 6, 1864, m. o. Oct. 25, 1864.

Sketch of 142d Infantry.

The One Hundred and Forty-second Infantry Illinois Volunteers was organized at Freeport, Illinois, by Col. Rollin V. Ankney, as a Battalion of eight companies, and ordered to Camp Butler, Illinois, where two companies were added, and the Regiment mustered, June 18 1864, for 100 days.
On 21st of June, the Regiment moved for Memphis, via Cairo and Mississippi river, and arrived on the 24th. On 26th, moved to White's Station, 11 miles from Memphis, on the Memphis and Charleston railroad, where it was assigned to guarding railroad.
Mustered out of the United States' service, Oct. 27, 1864, at Chicago, Ill.

142d (100 days) Infantry.

Company C.

Captain James M. Humphrey, com. June 18. 1864. Mustered out Oct. 27, 1864.
Second Lieutenant Luther C. Lawrence, com. June 18, 1864. Mustered out Oct. 27, 1864.
First Sergt Nathan H. Wooster, e. April 30, 1864, m. o. Oct. 26, 1864.
Sergt. H. L. Bennett, e. May 17, 1864, m. o. Oct. 26, 1864 a 1st Sergt.
Sergt. Jos. B. Dustin, e. May 3, 1864, died at White Station, Tenn., Aug. 4, 1864.
Sergt. Orville E. Benn, e. May 16,'64, m. o. Oct. 26,'64.
Corpl L. L. Shattuck, e. May 11, 1864, m. o. Oct. 26, 1864, as Sergt.
Corpl. Rollin C. Park, m. o. Oct. 26, 1864.
Corpl. R. Smiley, m. o. Oct. 26, 1864.
Musician Chas. Coleman, e. May 16, 1864, m. o. Oct. 26, 1864.

PRIVATES.

Anson John W. e. May 18, 1864, m. o. Oct. 26, 1864.
Ayres Geo. e. May 6, 1864, m. o. Oct. 26. 1864.
Burdick H. S. e. April 10. 1864, m. o. Oct. 26, 1864.
Buckway Chas. O. e. May 18, 186, m. o. Oct. 26, '64.
Ballard Edward, e. May 11, 1864, m. o. Oct. 26. 1864.
Busch Chas. W. e. June 1, 1864, m. o. Oct. 2, 1864.
Briggs Chas. F. e. June 1, 1864 m. o. died Oct. 21, 1864.
Curtis Samuel. e. May 20, 1864, m. o. Oct. 26, 1864.
Cole John. e. May 3, 1864, m. o. Oct. 26, 1864.
Chambers Wm. H. e. May 17, 1864, m. o. Oct. 26, 1864.

Crocker D. e. May 18, 1864, m. o. Oct. 26, 1864.
Coleman Chas. e. May 16, 1864, m. o. Oct. 26, 1864
Conley H. N. e. May 19, 1864, m. o. Oct. 26, 1864.
Cumpston Wm. H. e. May 14, 1864, m. o. Oct. 26, 1864, as private.
Durthick D. e. May 14, 1864, m. o. Oct. 26, 1864.
Dawson Wm. M. e. May 12, 1864, m. o. Oct. 26, 1864.
Day Hiram, e. May 14, 1864, m. o. Oct. 26, 1864.
Day S. e. May 18, 1864, m. o. Oct. 26, 1864.
Farnsworth D. e. May 7, 1864, m. o. Oct. 26, '64, Corpl.
Foster S. P. e. June 1, 1864, m. o. Oct. 26, 1864.
Gorham F. e. May 16, 1864, m. o. Oct. 26, 1864.
Hyde Newton, e. May 18, 1864, m. o. Oct. 26, 1864.
Hathaway L. D. e. May 5, 1864, m. o. Oct. 26, 1864.
Hedelin E. e. May 27, 1864, m. o. Oct. 26, 1864.
Haynie W. S. e. May 1, 1864, m. o. Oct. 26, 1864.
Loper John H. e. May 9, 1864, m. o. Oct. 26, 1864.
Leonard E. e. May 25, 1864, m. o. Oct. 26, 1864.
Landon Samuel, e. May 15, 1864, m. o. Oct. 26, 1864.
Moore O. e. May 17, 1864, m. o. Oct. 26, 1864.
Markle Geo. B. e. May 20, 1864, m. o. Oct. 26, 1864.
McBurney S. e. June 1, 1864, m. o. Oct. 26, 1864.
McCallom E. W. e. May 2, 1864, m. o. Oct. 26, 1864, as Corpl.
Nash Chas. H. e. May 9, 1864, m. o. Oct. 26, 1864.
Osmanson A. e. May 5, 1864, m. o. Oct. 26, 1864
Patrick Geo. e. May 15, 1864, m. o. Oct. 26, 1864
Robbin W. D. e. May 6, 1864, m. o. Oct. 26, 1864
Rehid u Theo. e. May 2, 1864, m. o. Oct. 26, 1864.
Ray Geo. e. May 7, 1864, m. o. Oct. 26, 1864
Rayner Chas. e. May 18, 1864, m. o. Oct. 26, 1864.
Rosencrans John, e. May 9, 1864, m. o. Oct. 26, 1864
Richardson Geo. e. May 21, 1864, m. o. Oct. 26, 1864.
Rice Luther. e. May 21, 1864 m. o. Oct. 26, 1864.
Simpson John H. e. May 20, 1864, m. o. Oct. 26, 1864.
Stott John, Jr., e. May 9, 1864, m. o. Oct. 26, 1864.
Squires Abram, e. May 14, 1864, m. o. Oct. 26, 1864.
Sergeant Dexter, e. May 16, 1864, m. o. Oct. 26, 1864.
Shannon M. e. May 14, 1864, m. o. Oct. 26, 1864.
Smith Wm. e. May 1, 1864, m. o. Oct. 26, 1864.
Tuttle Wm. H. e. April 30, 1865, m. o. Oct. 26, 1864.
Taylor N. Y. e. May 20, 1864, m. o. Oct. 26, 1864.
Trowbridge H. H. e. May 6, 1864, m. o. Oct. 26, 1864
Wilcox Andrew, e. May 1, 1864, m. o. Oct. 26, 1864.
Witter L. B. e. May 20, 1864, m. o. Oct. 26, 1864.
Woodward Earl M. e. May 18, 1864, m. o. Oct. 26, '64.
Warrs Moses B. e. May 10, 1864, died at Benton Barracks, Oct. 10, 1864.
Wicks Wesley M. e. May 12, 1864, died at White Station, Tenn., Aug. 18, 1864.

Sketch of 153d Infantry.

The One Hundred and Fifty-third Infantry Illinois Volunteers was organized at Camp Fry, Illinois, by Col. Stephen Bronson, and was mustered in Feb. 27, 1865, for one year. On March 4th, moved, by rail, via Louisville and Nashville, to Tullahoma, reporting to Major General Millroy. The Regiment was assigned to the Second Brigade, Defenses of Nashville and Chattanooga Railroad, Brevet Brigadier General Dudley commanding Brigade. In the latter part of March, Major Wilson with three companies, went on a campaign into Alabama and returned. On July 1st, moved, via Nashville and Louisville to Memphis, Tenn., and was assigned to the command of Brevet Major General A. L. Chetlain. Was mustered out Sept. 15, 1865, and moved to Springfield Ill., and September 24th, received final pay and discharge.

Colonel Bronson received appointment as Brevet Brigadier General.

153d Infantry (One Year).

Company A.

Captain Giles D. Walker, com. Feb. 27, 1865. Mustered out Sept. 21, 1865.
First Lieutenant Jno. Steele, com. Feb. 27, 1865. Mustered out Sept. 21, 1865.
Second Lieutenant Luther C. Lawrence, com. Feb. 27, 1865. Mustered out Sept. 21, 1865
Sergeant Major Geo. W. Turner, e. Feb. 7, 1865, m. o. Sept. 21, 1865.
First Sergeant Franklin J. Zuck, e. Feb. 7, 1865, m. o. Sept. 21, 1865.
Sergeant Robert Porter, e. Feb. 2, '65, m.o. June 24, '65.
Sergeant Geo. W. Turner, e. Feb. 7, 1865, promoted Sergeant Major.

Corpl. A. H. Woods, e. Feb. 1, 1865, m. o. Sept. 21, 1865, as private.
Corpl. F. D. Crane, e. Feb. 1, 1865, m. o. Sept. 21, '65, as private.
Corpl. D. C. Crane, e. Feb. 16, 1865, m. o. Sept. 21, '65
Corpl. R. M. Barmore, e. Feb. 10, '65, m.o. Sept. 21, '65.
Corpl M. P. Gilmore, e. Feb. 6, '65, m.o. Sept. 21, '65
Musician Jos. Latimer, e. Feb. 6, '65, m.o. Sept. 21, '65.
Wagoner Thomas A. Wheelon, e. Feb. 11, 1865, m. o. Aug. 17, 1865.

PRIVATES.

Allen Almerson, e. Feb. 8, 1865, m. o. Sept. 21, 1865.
Buck John, e. Feb. 17, 1865, m. o. July 22, 1865.
Billings D. W. e. Feb. 16, 1865, m. o. Sept. 21, 1865.
Barney Wm. Z. e. Feb. 7, 1865, died at Camp Fry, Il., March 18, 1865.
Bruce Wm. H. e. Feb. 7, 1865, m. o. Sept. 21, 1865.
Barzley James, e. Feb. 2, 1865, m. o. Sept. 21, 1865.
Corey Simeon, e. Feb. 6, 1865, m. o. Sept. 21, 1865
Chamberlain T. e. Feb. 2, 1865, m. o. Sept. 21, 1865.
Doyle Henry, e. Feb. 6, 1865, m. o. Sept. 21, 1865.
Dammon Alonzo, e. Feb. 12, 1865, m. o. Sept. 21, 1865.
Gore F. A. e. Feb. 10, 1865, m. o. Sept. 21, 1865.
Harmon M. W. e. Feb. 17, 1865, m. o. July 31, 1865.
Hall Edw. L. e. Feb. 16, 1865, m. o. June 19, 1865.
Hepenstall James, e. Feb 2, 1865, m. o. Sept. 21, 1865.
Knox O. O. e. Feb. 7, 1865, m. o. Sept. 21, 1865.
Little Philip, e. Feb. 7, 1865, m. o. Sept. 21, 1865.
Myers C. F. e. Feb. 2, 1865, m. o. Sept. 21, '65, Corpl.
Morey M. e. Feb. 6, 1865, m. o. Sept. 21, 1865.
Nash Chas. M. e. Feb. 7, 1865, m. o. May 25, 1865.
Osmer E. B. e. Feb. 16, '65, m. p. Sept. 21, '65, Corpl.
Richard A. W. e. Feb. 1, 1865, m. o. Sept. 21, 1865.
Smith D. M. e. Feb. 6, 1865, m. o. Aug. 26, 1865.
Shannon E. e. Feb. 15, 1865, m. o. Sept. 21, 1865.
Simons Perry, e. Feb. 16, 1865, m. o. Sept. 4, 1865.
Touage E. E. e. Feb. 20, 1865, m. o. Sept. 21, 1865.
Tinker J. H. e. Feb. 1, 1864, m. o. Sept. 21, 1865.
Waddell Theo. e. Feb. 6, 1865, m. o. Sept. 21, 1865.

Company B.

Captain Jas. A. Landon, com. First. Lieutenant Feb. 27, 1865. Promoted Captain June 6, 1865. Mustered out Sept. 21, 1865
Second Lieutenant H. D. Brown, e. as First Sergeant Feb. 3, 1865. Promoted Second Lieutenant June 6, 1865. Mustered out July 15, 1865.
Sergt. Andrew Blake, e. Feb. 11, 1865, m. o. Aug. 18, 1865, as private.
Sergt. Geo. Wordruff, e. Feb. 11, '65, m. o. June 5, '65.
Sergt. John Scott co Stott, e. Feb. 12, '65, m. o. Sept. 21, '65.
Sergt. Warren Corning, e. Feb. 11, '65, m. o. Sept. 21, '65.
Corpl. John S. Ford, e. Feb. 11, 1865, Sergt., absent sick, m. o. with leave.
Corpl. Warren Russell, e. Feb. 11, '65, deserted Jul 7, '65.
Corpl. Iziah Hill, e. Feb. 11, '65, m. o. Sept. 21, '65, Sergt.
Corpl. Harrison Bailey, e. Feb. 12, '65, m. o. Sept. 21, '65.
Corpl John Cummings, e. Feb. 12, 1865, absent without leave at m. o.
Corpl. Geo W. Degraw, e. Feb. 11, '65, disd. June 19, '65
Wagoner Hiram Reed, e. Feb. 13, '65, died March 14, '65.

PRIVATES.

Backes Mickle, e. Feb. 14, 1865, died at Nashville, Tenn., April 22, 1865.
Butts H. W. e. Feb. 13, 1865, m. o. Sept. 21, 1865.
Benett Allen, e. Feb. 11, 1865, m. o. Sept. 21, 1865.
Buchanan Wm. M. e. Feb. 12, 1865, m. o. Sept. 21, '65.
Benson B. L. e. Feb. 11, 1865, m. o. Sept. 21, 1865.
Carpenter John, e. Feb. 19, '65, m. o. Sept. 21, '65, Corpl.
Camp Chester, e. Feb. 11, 1865, m. o. July 25, 1865.
Day Hiram, e. Feb. 13, 1865, m. o. Sept. 21, 1865.
Hank E. S. e. Feb. 11, 1865, m. o. July 25, 1865.
Hogan Frank, e. Sept. 13, 1865, m. o. Sept. 21, 1865.
Hammond H. S. e. Sept. 16, 1865, m. o. Sept. 21, 1865, as Corpl.
Hovey Thearon, e. Feb. 12, 1865, m. o. Sept. 21, 1865.
Hasperstead H. G. e. Feb. 11, 1865, m. o. Sept. 21, 1865.
Hye or Hyde N. e. Feb. 11, 1865, m. o. Sept 21, 1865.
Hill Simon P. e. Feb. 11, 1865, m. o. Sept. 21, 1865.
Harmonson Ile, e. Feb. 11, 1865, m. o. Sept. 21, 1865.
Johnson C. F. e. Feb. 11, 1865, m. o. Sept. 21, 1865.
Jrome F. H. e. Feb. 14, 1865, m. o. Sept. 21, 1865.
Landon Sam'l. e. Feb. 11, '65, m. o. Sept. 21, '65, Corpl.
Lower Richard, e. Feb. 11, 1865, m. o. Sept. 21, 1865.
Linderman A. S. e. Feb. 11, 1865, died at Nashville, Tenn., April 1, 1865.

McClure Jas. e. Feb. 11, 1865, m.o. Sept. 21, '65, Corpl.
Markle Geo. B. e. Feb. 16, 1865, Corpl., absent without leave at m. o.
Oleson John. e. Feb. 11, 1865, m. o. Sept. 21, 1865.
Orvis M. M. e. Feb. 12, 1865, m. o. Sept. 21, 1865.
Reed Seymour E. e. Feb. 13, 1865, m. o. Sept. 21, 1865.
Robins W. D. e. Feb. 11, 1865, m. o. Sept. 21, 1865.
Scott Sam'l F. e. Feb. 12, 1865, absent at m. o.
Stine H. O. e. Feb. 12, 1865, m. o. Sept. 21, 1865.
Scott Jas. e. Feb. 12, 1861, absent at m. o.
Simpson John H. e. Feb. 11, 1865, m. o. Sept. 21, 1865.
Thompson Conrad. e. Feb. 11, 1865, m. o. Sept. 21, '65.
Warner F. V. e. Feb. 16, 1865, m. o. Sept. 21, 1865.
Ward A. e. Feb. 11, 1865, m. o. Sept. 21, 1865.

156th (one year) Infantry.

Company F.

Hummel Jno. e. Feb. 28, 1865, m. o. Sept. 20, 1865.
Rodgers Henry. e. Feb. 17, 1865, m. o. Sept. 20, 1865.
Waters John T. e. Feb. 27, 1865, m. o. Sept. 20, 1865.

Company K.

Meyers Lester. e. Feb. 14, 1865, deserted July 12, 1865.
Williams John, e. Feb. 21, 1865, deserted March 15, '65.

Sketch of 9th Cavalry.

The Ninth Cavalry Regiment was organized at Chicago, Ill., in Nov., 1861, by Col. A. G. Brackett, and was mustered in Nov. 30th. On Feb. 17, 1862, moved to Benton Barracks, Mo., and thence to Pilot Knob. On 27th, marched to Reeves' Station, on Big Black, and was assigned, by Brig. Gen. F. Steele, to Third Brigade. On May 23d, Steele's Division joined Gen. Curtis' army, at Jacksonport, Ark. In a skirmish at Waddell's Plantation, June 12th, lost 12 wounded and 1 missing, and at Stewart's Plantation, on June 27th, lost 2 killed and 35 wounded. Among the latter were Col. Brackett, Adjt. Blackburn, and Capt. Keight. June 26th, commenced the march to Helena. During this march, five men died from hardships—water and rations being almost impossible to obtain. At Helena, the Ninth Cavalry was assigned to Third Brigade, Col. Cyrus Bussey; Fourth Division, Brig. Gen. A. P. Hovey; Gen. Steele's Army; District of Eastern Arkansas. On Sept 15th, two 12 pdr. mountain howitzers were assigned to the regiment and were commanded by Lieut. E. G. Butler, with a detail from the regiment. On Nov. 7th, at Lagrange, Lieut. Butler repulsed a charge of two regiments of Texan Rangers, killing over fifty of the enemy. Its loss was 20 killed and 6 wounded. The regiment went on an expedition under Gen. Washburn, and was engaged, Nov. 6th, at Okolona, Miss., and near Coffeyville, Nov. 7th. Jan. 9, 1863, marched, with Gen. Gorman, to Duvall's Bluff, and returned. On April 3rd, moved to Memphis, and on 14th, moved to Germantown, Tenn.

Was assigned to Brigade of Col. McCrillis, of Third Illinois Cavalry, and to the Sixteenth Corps. Engaged at Coldwater, Miss., July 28th, and at Granada, Aug. 18th, and moved to Lagrange, Tenn., Aug. 26th. Made an attack on the enemy at Sal m, Miss., Oct. 8th, and drove him from his position. Met the enemy at Wyatt, Miss. Oct. 13th, and, after fighting all day, the enemy fell back and retreated in the night. Nov. 8th, moved from Lagrange to Corinth, and soon after returned. Marched to Collierville, and was assigned to Second Brigade, Cavalry Division, Sixteenth Army Corps. Was engaged with the enemy Dec. 3, 1863, at Saulsbury, Tenn., and on the 4th, the Division, under command of Brig. Gen. B. H. Grierson, was engaged at Moscow, Tenn. In this battle, the Ninth Cavalry took a conspicuous and honorable part. On Feb. 11, 1864, marched, with the expeditions of Brig. Gen. B. H. Grierson, and Gen. W. S. Smith, into Mississippi, Met and defeated the enemy at West Point, Feb. 20th. Was engaged at Okolona, Feb 21st, and at Mount Ivy, Miss., on the 23d, and compel at Germantown, on 24th. On March 16th, the regiment was mustered as a veteran organizati n, and on the 17th, marched to Memphis, Moved to Illinois for veteran furlough. April 27th, returned to Memphis.

A detachment of the regiment was with Gen. Sturgis, on the expedition to Guntown, Miss., and was rear guard for the disorganized command on the retreat,

losing 5 killed, 23 wounded, and 12 prisoners, out of 160 men. July 7th, marched, with Generals A. J. Smith and Grierson, to Tupelo. Had a severe engagement at Pontotoc, driving the enemy, and was engaged in the two-days battle, July 14th and 15th, at Tupelo and Old Town Creek. On Aug. 3d, moved, via Holly Springs, to Abbeville, Miss., where it skirmished with the enemy. On the 11th, skirmished at Oxford. Had an engagement at Hurricane Creek, Miss., Aug. 13th, losing 4 killed and several wounded. Returned to camp, near Memphis, Sept. 4th. On Sept. 30, 1864, moved eastward, Capt. Blackburn commanding regiment. Crossed Tennessee river at Clifton. Moved, via Waynesboro, Lawrenceburg, Florence, Alabama, Waterloo, Hamburg and Savannah, to Clifton. The command moved again to Florence, and met Hood's advancing army.

Gen. Hatch's Division did hard fighting at Shoal Creek. On Nov. 19th, crossed the river and attacked the enemy—the Ninth Cavalry in advance. Two divisions of the enemy advancing, compelled it to recross the river. One Battalion of the regiment becoming detached, passed through the rebel line, and was compelled to remain in the enemy's rear until night, when it re-crossed. The command skirmished with the enemy's advance every day. At Campbellville, Nov. 24th, the regiment was very hotly engaged, but stood their ground, holding back many times their number, until their ammunition was entirely exhausted, when they fought hand to hand, clubbing their carbines. Took a prominent part in the battle of Franklin, Tenn., and the two-days' fight, Dec. 15th and 16th, at Nashville. Engaged in the pursuit of Hood, to Tennessee river, skirmishing at Brentwood, Franklin Pike, near Franklin, Rutherford's Creek, and at Ross' farm.

The command moved to Huntsville, Florence, Eastport and Gravelly Springs. On Feb. 9, 1865, moved to Eastport. On June 2nd, to Iuka, Miss. July 4th, moved to Decatur, Ala., and thence to Montgomery, Selma, and finally to Gainesville, Ala., arriving Aug. 20th. Mustered out at Selma, Ala., Oct. 31, 1865, and ordered to Springfield, Ill., where it received final payment and discharge.

9th Cavalry.

Colonel Jos. W. Harper, com. Second Lieutenant Co. 1, Oct. 23, 1861. Promoted First Lieutenant Nov. 17, 1861. Promoted Captain Oct. 3, 1862. Promoted Lieutenant Colonel Dec. 4, 1864. Promoted Co onel Dec 5, 1864. Mustered out Oct. 31, 1865.
Major Leander L. Shattuck, e. as First Sergeant Co. I, Sept. 12, 1861. Promoted Second Lieutenant Nov. 13, 1861. Promoted First Lieutenant Oct. 3, 1862. Promoted Captain Dec. 14, 1863. Promoted Major May 10, 1865. Mustered out Oct. 31, 1865.

Company I.

Captain Harvey M. Jenner, e. as Corporal Sept. 12, 1861. Promoted First Lieutenant Dec. 4, 1864. Promoted Captain May 10, 1865. Mustered out Oct. 31, 1865.
Second Lieutenant Frederick P. B. Sisson, e. as private. Promoted First Sergeant, then Second Lieutenant May 10, 1865. Mustered out Oct. 31, 1865.
Sergt. Plummer E. Robinson, e. Sept. 12, 1861, disd. Nov. 17, 1862.
Sergt. Wm. N. Tyler, e. Sept. 12, 1861, died. Sept. 20, '62.
Corpl. Milton Orton, e. Sept. 12, 1861, m. o. Oct. 31, '64, as private.
Corpl. L. L. Shattuck, e. Sept. 12, 1861, disd. Oct. 23, 1862, as Sergt.
Corpl. F. B. Hubbell, e. Sept. 12, 1861, reenlisted as Vet. m. o. Oct. 31, 1865, as 1st Sergt.
Bugler Dan. K. Bemer, e. Oct. 9, '61, rejected Jan. 24, '62.
Bugler F. P. Lander, e. Sept. 12, 1861, disd. Dec. 9, '62.

PRIVATES.

Albright Delos, e. Sept. 12, '61, Corpl., disd Oct. 1, '62.
Atkinson Eli, e. Sept. 12, 1861, die Aug. 17, 1862.
Cates J. H. e. Sept. 10, 1861, disd Aug. 28, 1862.
DeWolf Putnam, e. Sept. 28, 61, disd. Sept. 19, '62, as Farrier.
Fox J. C. e. Sept. 12, 1861, re-enlisted as Vet. Sergt., deserted Sept. 29, 1863.
Furgeson Robt. e. Sept. 16, 1861, disd. Dec. 9, 1864.
Gilbert David D. e. Sept. 12, 1861, rejected Jan. 24, '62.

Geaves Theo. W. e. Sept. 12, 1861.
Hawes Jesse, e. Sept 12,'61, prl'd pris., m.o. July 22,'65.
Hawes Byron, e. Sept. 23, 1861, trans. to 169th, Co. I, Battalion V. R. C. April 29, 1864.
Kator Chas. e. Oct. 3, 1861.
Kittor Sisson, e. Oct. 9, 1861.
King L. e. Oct. 3 1861, disd. Sept. 29, 1861.
Lenderman Alonzo, e. Oct. 1, 1861, disd. Oct. 30, 1862.
Locke Chas. A. e. Oct. 9, 1861, disd. May 29, 1862.
Ludden C. F. e. Oct. 23, '61, re-enlisted as Vet., prm't. Com. Sergt., died Dec 22, 1864, wds.
Montgomery Wm. e. Sept. 12, 1861, re-enlisted as Vet. deserted Sept. 1, 1865.
Morgan Sam'l J. e. Sept. 12, 1861, re-enlisted as Vet., m. o. Oct. 31, 1865.
Morse New. L. e. Sept. 14, 61, died at St. Louis, Oct. 26,'64.
Marshall John, e. Oct. 1, 1861.
Robinson F. e. Sept. 12, 1861, died at Helena, Ark., Sept. 1, 1862.
Rockwood Samuel, e. Sept. 12, 1861.
Rosekrans Jas. O. e. Oct. 9, 1861, m. o. Oct. 31, 1864.
Rosekrans Jacob D. e. Oct. 16, '61, disd. Oct. 11, 1862.
Storm S. S. e. Sept. 22, 1861, died at Reeves Station, Mo., April 2, 1862.
Strong H. e. Oct. 23, 1861.
Thorn W. S. e. Sept. 12, 1861, disd. Sept. 19, 1862.
Tyler Sam'l H. e. Sept. 12, 1861, rejected Nov. 28, '61.
Thomas J M. e. Sept 17, 1861, m. o. Oct. 31, 1864.
Turner H. A. e. Oct. 15, 1861, disd. Nov. 24, 1861.
Tibbits J. W. e. Oct. 16, 1861, m. o. Oct. 31, 1864.
Vale Barnett, e. Sept. 12, 1861, died at Helena, Ark., Sept. 16, 1862.
Williams Gilbert, e. Sept. 12, 1861.
Wixon Smith, e. Sept. 16, 1864, disd. Dec 9, 1864.
Walsh John, e. Sept. 14, 1861, died at Helena, Ark., Sept. 27, 1862.
Woolward J. N. e. Oct. 9, 1861.

VETERANS.

Saddler Wm. J. Twas.

PRIVATES.

Curtis Michael, e. Jan. 1, '64, m. o. Oct. 31, '65, Sergt.
McD de Alfred, e. Jan. 1, 1864, died about July 1, '65, in rebel prison.
Strong Miles H. e. Jan. 1, '64, m. o. Oct. 31, '65, Sergt.
Young Edw. R. e. Jan. 1, '64, deserted Sept. 29, 1865.

RECRUITS.

Austin Clark C. e. Jan. 4, 1864, m. o. Oct. 31,'65, Corpl.
Austin H. W. e. Oct. 3, 1864, m. o. Oct. 13, 1865.
Adams S. L. e. Oct. 3, 1864, m. o. Oct. 13, 1865.
Ayres Benj. F. e. Sept. 29, 1864, m. o. June 15, 1865.
Brewol L. F. e. Jan. 4, 1864, m. o. Oct. 31, 1865.
Baxter John S. e. Feb. 4, 1864, m. o. Jul. 25, 1865.
Basty Austin B. e. Oct. 3, 1864, m. o. Oct. 13, 1865.
Brown Caleb N. e. Oct. 3, 1864, died March 19, '65.
Butcher Isaac E. e. March 3, 1865, died at Cairo, Ill., March 24, 1865.
Branch Edwin H. e. F b. 9, 1864, kld. at Pontotoc, Miss., July 13, 1864.
Curtis M. e. Nov. 25, 1861, re-enlisted as veteran.
Comstock James A. e. Nov. 25, 1861.
Cline Jas. e. Jan. 16, 1864, m. o. Oct. 31, 1865.
Curtis Geo. e. Feb. 8 1864, died at Louisville, Ky., Jan. 1, 1865, wds.
Elis John O. e. Jan. 2, 1864, promt. Sergt. Maj.
Fox Geo. e. Jan. 16, 1864, m. o. Oct. 31, 1865.
Fox W. J. e. Sept 28 1864, m. o. June 15 1865.
Higdon J. ho D. e. Dec. 28 1863, m. o. Oct. 31, 1865.
Hare Martin, e. Sept. 23, 1864, m. o. June 15, 1865.
Jacobs J. A. e. Nov. 2, 1861, d'sd. Aug. 24, '62, disab.
Jackson Wm. F. e. March 3, '65, deserted Sept. 29, '65.
Keefe John, e. Jan. 8, 1864, m. o. Oct. 31, 1865, Corpl.
Little E. B. e. Jan. 5 1864, m. o. Oct. 31, 1865, Corpl.
Laing Geo. e. Jan. 2, '64, m. o. Oct. 31, '65, as Bugler.
Lowe E. S. e. Jan. 10, 1864, d serted Sept. 29, 1865.
Longfield H. R. E. e. Mch 8, '64, deserted Sept. 29, '65.
Mordoff F. M. e. Nov. 25, 1861, died at Cairo, Ill., Oct. 29, 1862.
Marver Alexander, e. Feb. 11, 1864, died at Nashville, Tenn., Jan. 29, 1865.
Miner Geo. e. Sept. 29, 1864, died at Jeffersonville, Ind., April 5, 1865.
Maloy Stephen, e. April 1, 1864, kld. at Campbellville, Tenn., Nov. 24, 1864.
Olney Jacob M. e. Feb. 6, '64, m. o. Oct. 31, '65, Corpl.

Peters Robt. e. Nov. 8, 1861, kld. Nov. 24, 1864.
Prindeville Thos. e. April 1, 1864, m. o. Oct. 31, 1865, as Corpl.
Raridan John R. e. Jan. 4, 1864, m. o. Oct. 31, 1864.
Raymond A. e. Feb. 9, 1864, died at Belvidere, Ill., April 24, 1864.
Shattuck Geo. M. e. Jan. 3, 1864, m. o. Oct. 31, 1865.
Shepard R. D. e. Jan. 3, 1864, m. o. Oct. 31, 1865.
Simkins Geo. e. Feb. 15, 1864, m. o. Oct. 31, 1865.
Shader Frank, e. Jan 30, '64, died Memphis, Aug 1, '64.
Shattuck M. A. e. Jan. 12, 1864, deserted Sept. 29, '65.
Tiffany L. e. Feb. 4, 1864, m. o. Oct. 31, '65, as Sergt.
Turn r Wm. E. e. March 28,'64, m. o Oct. 31,'65, Corpl.
Tibbetts Chas. e. Jan. 2, 1864, m. o. Oct. 31, 1865.
Tracy F. L. e. Jan. 25, 1864, m. o. Oct. 31, 1865, absent, sick.
Turner O. A. e. March 16, 1864, died at Nashville, Tenn., Dec. 25, 1864.
Vandyke A. B. e. Jan. 4, 1864, m. o. Oct. 31, 1865, as Co. Q. M. Sergt.
Wild Roby M. e. April 1, 1864, disd. July 25, 1864.
Whitney Saml. D. e. Oct. 3, 1864, m. o. Oct. 23, 1865.
Wilson Robt. e. Jan. 5, 1864, disd. April 18, '65, disab.

UNASSIGNED RECRUITS.

Appleton Horace, e. Jan. 18, 1864.
Barker John W. e. March 4, 1864.
Ready Wm. e Jan. 23, 1864, deserted Feb. 1, 1864.
Bevins Jacob D. e. Feb. 14, 1864.
Cody Chas. e. Jan. 4, 1865.
Dickenson J. e. Feb. 4, 1864, rejected.
Granger Henry, e. Jan. 23, 1865.
Hickey James e. Jan 29, 1865.
Howe A. V. e. Feb. 16, 1865.
Kelley Wm. e. Jan. 24, 1865.
Mawer Jno. R. e. Feb. 17, 1864, died at Camp Butler, Ill., April 21, 1864.
Williams Chas. H. e. Jan. 24, 1864.
Wright Geo. W.

13th Cavalry.

First Asst. Surgeon Leonard L. Lake, com. Dec. 31, 1861. Resigned Feb. 19, 1862.

17th Cavalry.

Company K.

Mandy Sam'l A. died at Marengo, Ill., Feb. 21, 1864.
Keeney Don A. m. o. Dec. 22, 1865.
Ostrander Geo. T. deserted July 28 1864.
Dudley Martin, deserted July 28, 1864.

1st Artillery.

Company I.

Captain John C. Ne ly, e. as Sergt. Feb. 1, 1862. Promoted Second Lieutenant Feb. 2, 1862. Promoted Sen. Second Lieutenant May 5, 1862. Promoted Sen. First Lieutenant June 16, 1862. Promoted Captain Feb. 10, 1864. Mustered out July 26, 1865.

PRIVATES.

Gowar Henry, e. Jan. 21, 1862, re-enlisted as Vet., died at Iuka, Miss., July 21, 1865.
Hadley Geo. e. Feb. 6, 1864, re-enlisted as Vet., m. o. July 26, 1864.
Nolan Michael, e. Feb. 7, 1862, disd. Feb. 17, 1862.
Parent Geo. e. Feb. 18, 1863, re enlisted as Vet., m. o. July 26, 1865.

RECRUIT.

Dale James, e. Aug. 31, 1864, m. o. June 5, 1865.

2d Artillery.

Company G.

First Lieutenant Edward Webster, e. as Sergeant, Aug. 6, 1861. Promoted Sergeant, 2d en Sen. Second Lieutenant, Sept. 22, 1863. Promoted Jr. First Lieutenant, Jan. 25, 1864. Promoted in Colored Regiment July 12, 1864.

The war ended and peace concluded, the Union preserved in its integrity, those of the sons of Boone who had volunteered their lives in defense of their government who were spared to see the Army of the Union victorious, returned to their homes to receive grand ovations and tributes of honor from friends and neighbors who had eagerly and jealously followed them wherever the fortunes of the war called them. Exchanging their soldiers' uniform for citizens' dress, they fell back to their old avocations—on the farm, at the forge, the bench, in the shop, and whatever else their hands found to do. Brave men are honorable always, and no class of Boone's citizens are entitled to greater respect than the volunteer soldiery, not alone because they were soldiers in the hour of the country's peril, but because in their associations with their fellow-citizens their walk is upright and their honesty and character without reproach.

AGRICULTURAL.

Being an agricultural community, there has been but little to disturb its tranquility since the close of the war. Falling back into the old routine of farm life, renewed energy and industry, if indeed such a thing were possible, has marked the years that have come and gone since a peace was conquered. Prosperity has continued to attend all legitimate undertakings, and, "at peace at home, with all the world and rest of mankind," there is but little left for our humble pen to add to the general history of Boone County. By-and-by the people of to-day will have passed away, and others will come after them. All will have made history, but the compilation of that history will be for other minds, and, we hope, abler and more experienced ones, than the humble one that has directed this work.

Pre-eminently an agricultural community, and one embracing some of the first and most successful farmers in the State of Illinois, the agricultural interests are of more direct importance than all others combined. Appreciating the great worth of this interest, and desiring to present it in all its importance, we know of no more reliable or correct data upon which to base a summary than the records of the Boone County Agricultural Society. In the fall and winter of 1855-6, the question of forming such a society began to be agitated among the more thinking and intelligent part of the people, and in the spring of 1856 a meeting was called to consider the subject and devise ways and means to effect such an organization. The meeting was called for the 25th of April, and Plane's Hall designated as the place for meeting and deliberation. Isaac Miller, Esq., was selected as chairman. At that meeting it was determined to organize an agricultural society, and Elias Congdon, Stephen A. Hurlbut and M. G. Leonard were appointed as a committee to draft a constitution and by-laws for the government of the society, subject to amendment. The organization was further completed by the election of the following named gentlemen as officers for the year 1855:

President, Allen C. Fuller; Vice President, John Stockham; Secretary and Treasurer, George J. Wood. Directors: Fredrick P. Low, Flora; Nijah Hotchkiss, Belvidere; Martin T. Gilbert, Caledonia; Hiram Hopkins, Manchester; E. L. Tisdell, Leroy, Willett Webster, Boone; H. W. Pier, Bonus; C. F. Witt, Spring.

In the course of the preparation of this work, the nineteenth annual fair of the society was held, commencing on Tuesday, the 4th of September, and ending on Friday, the 7th, during which time Mr. R. W. Coon, editor and publisher of the *Northwestern*, assisted by Mr. A. H. Keeler, issued a daily edition of that paper, which, though small, was filled with useful information, not the least important of which was a somewhat comprehensive history of the society, which we transfer to the pages of the PAST AND PRESENT OF BOONE COUNTY.

"The first meeting of the society was appointed to take place on the 25th and 26th of October, 1855, on the site now known to the people of Boone county as the 'Old Fair Grounds.'

"The total receipts of the Treasurer for 1855 were $624, expenditures $302.51, leaving a balance on hand of $321.49. Thus far the society regarded their effort a success, and the officers began agitating the question of purchasing a sufficient amount of land for the purpose of a fair ground. A committee was appointed to act in this matter and the old site of the fair grounds was purchased. Active preparations were then made for the improvements of the ground and a successful fair to be held on October 1st, 2d and 3d. Allen C. Fuller was elected President for the second year, and Geo. J. Wood, Secretary and Treasurer.

"The total receipts for 1856 were $983.70, against $624 in 1855, giving an increase of $359.70 for the second year.

"In 1857 the following officers were elected: President, Allen C. Fuller; Vice President, John B. Tinker; Secretary and Treasurer, Geo. J. Wood.

"The Secretary's report for 1856 shows the total receipts to be $983.70, with disbursements reaching $685.45. These amounts not including amounts on hand from previous year, or expenditures.

"From 1857 to 1867 the fair was held on the old grounds, and the society had years of reasonable success, and again seasons of depression.

"In 1860 Mr. A. E. Jenner was chosen Secretary, and in the minutes of the Board held in 1860, when Ezra May was elected President; E. E. Moss, Vice President; A. E. Jenner, Secretary, and G. W. Downs, Treasurer, is the following:

"*Resolved*, That the Board is hereby authorized to pay the Secretary for his services any amount not exceeding thirty dollars.

"In 1862, on motion of Mr. George Dean, it was voted to postpone the holding of a fair until the fall of 1863, and again at a meeting of the directors in June, 1863, it was voted to postpone holding a fair 'until after the next annual meeting of the society,' and the board then adjourned to meet on the call of the secretary. The records then show that the next meeting was held at the court-house in April, 1865, when it was voted that the secretary call a mass meeting of the members, farmers, mechanics, merchants, ladies and everybody to meet in the court-house on Saturday, June 3, 1865, 'to determine whether the society shall live or die.' At the June meeting, we infer, it was decided to try to live, for L. W. Lawrence was elected President; E. A. Jenner, Secretary, and W. R. Cornell, Treasurer, and a fair was held that year in September, and the society did very well, we judge, for at the annual meeting, held April 4, 1876, the society owed only $15.

"In 1867, at the annual meeting, E. E. Moss was elected President; J. D. Tripp, Vice President; A. E. Jenner, Secretary, and G. W. Downs,

Treasurer; and at a meeting in June of the same year, G. W. Downs moved 'that we deem it expedient to change our fair grounds,' and steps were taken for the purchase of the grounds at present occupied by the society. These grounds were purchased of J. R. Williams for $1,200, the society paying him $675, the cash received from A. C. Fuller for the old grounds, and giving notes for the balance. Steps were at once taken for the removal of buildings, etc., to the new grounds, and the fair of 1867 was held in their new home.

"The fair held on the new grounds in 1867 was probably not very profitable, for a motion was passed authorizing the treasurer and secretary to borrow money on the best terms they could to pay the indebtedness of the society. The officers of the society for the past ten years have been as follows:

"1868, D. W. Gates, Pres.; Geo. Sands, Vice Pres.; A. E. Jenner, Sec. and Treas. 1869, D. W. Gates, Pres.; Geo. Reed, Vice Pres.; A. E. Jenner, Sec. and Treas. 1870. A. C. Fuller, Pres.; L. W. Lawrence, Vice Pres.; L. O. Gilman, Sec.; G. N. Woodward, Treas. 1871, same with the exception of A. E. Jenner as Sec. 1872, John J. Foote, Pres.; Amzi Abbe, Vice Pres.; A. E. Jenner, Sec.; C. B. Loop, Treas. 1873, John J. Foote, Pres.; Luke Teeple, Vice Pres.; A. E. Jenner, Sec.; C. B. Loop, Treas. 1874, Luke Teeple, Pres.; D. R. Andrus, Vice Pres.; A. E. Jenner, Sec.; W. S. Jones, Treas. 1875, Ezra May, Pres.; D. R. Andrus, Vice Pres.; A. E. Jenner, Sec.; W. S. Jones, Treas. 1876, Ezra May, Pres.; D. R. Andrus, Vice Pres.; A. E. Jenner, Sec.; C. B. Loop, Treas. 1877, Richard Barnes, Pres.; John Hannah, Vice Pres.; A. E. Jenner, Sec. and Treas.

"Shortly after the Society moved into its new grounds it began to be bothered by debts, principally contracted by the expense of the change and the cost of new buildings. In 1867, this debt amounted to $2,490 and interest, while at the same time the amount expended on the grounds, buildings, etc., aggregated $5,740.16. In this year we find that a new departure was had in that the Treasurer was required to give bonds. Dr. G. N. Woodward was at that time Treasurer, and his bond was for $1,000, signed by P. J. Garcelon, E. R. Bishop, Ira Wilson and O. H. Wright, as sureties. This is the only bond that the records show as having ever been given by a Treasurer of the Society. In 1871, after the fair, the receipts and cash were not so large as was desirable by the friends of the Society, and the debts were pressing. While things were in this condition, at a meeting held in November, 1871, the proper officers of the Society were authorized and instructed to execute a mortgage on the property of the Society to secure certain indebtedness of the Society, said mortgage to run two years from December, 1871.

"On December 9th, of the same year, at a meeting of the Society, it was resolved to amend the Constitution so as to make the Society a joint stock company with a capital of $5,000, in shares of $10 each, the change to take effect as soon as 100 shares of stock should be subscribed, when a transfer of the property should be made to the stockholders of the joint stock company. Shortly afterwards a Constitution was adopted, and since that time the Boone County fairs have been run by the joint stock company, and we believe we are justified in saying that each year the fairs have been better and the people have become more and more interested in them until the present time. Finally, in 1876, a strong effort was made by the members of the Society to clear their indebtedness, and for that purpose stock was increased and sold up to 600 shares, and with the money thus raised the entire indebtedness was paid. Thus, at the present time, the Society, after an existence of over twenty years, is in better condition than ever before. It has fair grounds on which are first-class buildings and improvements, it has the confidence and regard of the people of the county, and is free from debt."

At the last annual election for officers, held on Wednesday, Sept. 5, 1877, the following named gentlemen were chosen:

President—Richard Barnes, Belvidere; Vice President, John Hannah, Belvidere; Secretary, Asher E. Jenner, Belvidere; Treasurer; C. H. Peck, Belvidere.

Directors—A. O. Witbeck, Flora Township; Luke Teeple, Belvidere; John Moore, Caledonia; Arthur P. Daniels, Manchester; George Reed, Spring; Joel E. Cronk, Bonus; George Sands, Boone; Silas DeMunn, LeRoy; E. T. Bellmeyer, Cherry Valley; H. P. Kimball, Rockford; W. C. Vanderook, Guilford; A. T. Ames, Marshall.

This nineteenth annual gathering of the farmers, stock growers, mechanics and artisans of Boone County was largely attended, and the display of farm and pasture products, machinery, etc., exceedingly creditable. Nor were evidences of woman's handiwork wanting. In this department the display was surprisingly fine. The Secretary's books show that there were 1,048 entries; premiums awarded, $1,291.50; special premiums, $100. The annual address was delivered by Hon. S. A. Hurlbut, and was listened to with marked attention. The Society is now said to be in better condition, financially, than it has ever been, and it is to be hoped that its success and prosperity will grow with its years. The grounds are situated about one mile and a half due west of the Court House, a part of them beautifully shaded, the grove occupying an elevated plateau of table land. The judges' stand and a portion of the driveway are situated in a kind of basin that is overlooked from the grove in the northwest corner of the grounds. The open space immediately below the grove (or the most of it) remains in the condition in which it was left by the Pottawatomie Indians. The ridges and hills they had thrown up for cultivation are sodded over, but easily traced. The grazing places of their ponies are now included as a show ground and trial track for cattle and horses of finest blood. The shady grove in which their "braves" were wont to "sleep the hours away" after a return from the hunt or the warpath, and where the squaws, maidens and papooses would betake themselves to avoid the beating rays of the midsummer's sun, the former to pursue the work of beading moccasins and other Indian gear, is now filled with halls for the display of the finer mechanism of their pale-faced brothers, and the still finer handiwork of their pale-faced sisters. What a change less than half a century has wrought!

RAILROADS.

Although Boone County is traversed by three lines of railroads, the people of the county never voted a single dollar in bonds or money in aid of their construction. When the Rockford & Kenosha Road was in contemplation some of the farmers in the vicinity of its contemplated line were prevailed upon to take stock, for which they gave mortgages on their farms and lands, with the guaranty from the company that the company would pay interest on the amount of stock so taken. The mortgages were payable in ten years.

Another contemplated road—the Racine, Janesville & Mississippi—pursued a like course in soliciting and obtaining stock subscriptions, except as to the guaranty. Quite a number were inveigled into the scheme, and mortgaged their lands for large sums. A few of these mortgages were compromised, but the larger proportion of the mortgagers filed bills in chancery, and on hearing they were cancelled by decree of court.

A number of the mortgages given in aid of the Kenosha & Rockford division were for small amounts—some of them for sums not exceeding one hundred dollars. The smaller mortgages were paid in full, and the larger ones compromised, and there is now no individual railroad indebtedness in the county.

The Galena Division of the Chicago & Northwestern Railroad enters the county near the northeast corner of section thirty-six in Bonus Township, and runs nearly due west to a point near the northwest corner of section thirty-two, when it bears to the northwest, leaving Bonus Township at the northwest corner of section thirty, and enters the town of Belvidere near the center of section twenty-five. From Belvidere it bears to the southwest, and leaves Boone County at the southwest corner of section thirty-one in Belvidere Township. This road was completed to Belvidere in December, 1852.

The Madison Branch (originally known as the Beloit Branch) of the Chicago & Northwestern Railroad, after leaving Belvidere, bears a little to the west of north, passing through sections twenty-three, fourteen, eleven, and two, in Belvidere Township, enters Caledonia Township on the southwest quarter of section thirty-five, passes up through section twenty-seven, and at the southwest corner of section twenty-two bears directly to the northwest, and passing through sections twenty-one (just touching the southwest corner of section sixteen), seventeen, and seven, leaves the county at the northwest corner of section seven. Caledonia, an important point for the shipment of grain, etc., is a station on this road. It was completed in 1853.

The Kenosha Division of the Chicago & Northwestern Railroad, running from Kenosha to Rockford, enters Boone Township at the southeast corner of section one, soon after which it turns directly southwest, passing through Capron in the northwest corner of section eleven, thence into and through sections ten and sixteen and to near the center of section twenty, when it diverges a little to the north through section nineteen, entering Caledonia Township at Poplar Grove on the northeast quarter of section twenty-four in that township, thence through section twenty-three to the northeast corner thereof, when it bears to the southwest, crossing the Madison Division at Caledonia Junction, on section twenty-one; thence again northwest to a point a little north of the center of section twenty; thence southwest and through section nineteen, leaving the county at the village of Argyle, a Scotch hamlet named after Argyle of Scotland.

The main line of the Chicago & Northwestern also passes through the extreme northeastern part of LeRoy Township, crossing only a few rods of section one.

The total number of miles of railroad in the county is returned at 40 miles and 3,463 feet; the assessed valuation for 1876 at $218,934.

GRAIN ELEVATORS.

There are two grain elevators in successful operation. The stone elevator was erected in 1851, by W. H. Gilman, Sr., at a cost of $10,000. Some years later it passed into the ownership of D. W. Reed and Deacon Congdon, who converted it into a flouring mill. As such it continued to be used until about 1860 or 1861, when M. G. Leonard, the present owner, became proprietor, by purchase. The mill machinery was taken out and the building returned to its original use as an elevator. It has a capacity of 60,000 bushels.

The Harper elevator, a wooden structure, was built in 1865, by George H. Harper. It is now operated by H. Whitehead.

The following is a monthly statement of the shipments by the car load of grain and stock from Belvidere for the year ending December 31, 1876. This is not up to the usual average of shipments. During that year the crops were light. In 1875 the business was large, and it is estimated that for the current year (1877) the business will be at least one-third larger:

	Grain.	Stock.		Grain.	Stock.
January	38	18	July	31	12
February	57	17	August	42	9
March	23	12	September	71	14
April	22	10	October	68	17
May	86	17	November	46	17
June	67	7	December	52	39
Total				603	189
Grand Total				792	

In the month of December, 1876, 61,980 pounds of poultry were shipped.

Butter is becoming quite an item in the commercial transactions of the county, and up to the 14th of September, 1877, a little over 60,000 pounds have been shipped—the largest part of it finding its way directly to the eastern markets. In addition, there are two butter factories that are holding their productions for an advance in prices.

COUNTY SCHOOLS.

Perhaps no interests of Boone County have been so carefully guarded and fostered as the educational. The care exercised by the early authorities in guarding the school lands—section sixteen in each township—was significant of a determination to maintain them intact to the purposes for which they had been set apart. The policy marked out by the first Board of County Commissioners for the preservation of these lands seems to have been strictly and rigidly adhered to by their successors until the lands were fully and completely disposed of, and the proceeds properly applied. Such care was not without its legitimate fruits. The last report of the State Superintendent of Public Instruction shows that the county has a township fund derived from this source of $14,288.00; of this amount, $13,491.17 is loaned, $11,458.74 on personal security, and $2,032.43 on real estate security. The principal of this sum was derived from the sale of township lands, and is a perpetual school fund, the principal or interest of which cannot be diverted to any other purpose. And no sane man would ever wish to appropriate it to any other use.

BELVIDERE.

We extract the following statistics from the report of the State Superintendent for the school year ending September 30, 1876:

Total receipts during the year, $42,196.14; total expenditures, $32,944.22; balance on hand, $9,251.92; total of expenditures and balance, $42,196.14; estimated value of school houses and grounds, $75,250.00; estimated value of school apparatus, $994.40; estimated value of school libraries, $231.40; number of volumes in libraries, 409; number of school houses, 74; number of males under 21 years of age, 2,264; females under 21 years of age, 2,673; whole number under 21 years of age, 5,337; males between the ages of 6 and 21, 2,042; females between the ages of 6 and 21, 1,917; whole number between 6 and 21 years of age, 3,959; number of school districts, 80; number of districts having school five months or more, 77; whole number of free public schools, 72; average number of months school sustained, 7.4; only three districts had school less than five months; the whole number of months during which school was sustained, 523, equal to 43 years and 7 months; there were enrolled for that year, 1,730 males, and 1,651 females; total, 3,381; 54 male and 123 female teachers were employed, making a total of 177 teachers employed during 1876; there are five graded schools, two public high schools, and two private schools; eight of the school houses are built of stone, six of brick, and 60 are frame; two were built during the year; the highest monthly wages paid male teachers was $122.22; the lowest, $25.00; highest monthly wages paid to female teachers, $44.00; lowest, $15.00; average monthly wages paid male teachers, $46.22, female teachers, $28.55. Twelve examinations were held during the year and 178 applicants examined; 18 first grade and 114 second grade certificates were granted; 11 male and 35 female applicants were rejected; total rejections, 46. During the year, the Superintendent spent 38 days in visiting schools, 50 days in examinations, 20 in institute work, and 20 days in other official duties, making 128 days spent in a directly official capacity.

In November, 1873, ten ladies were elected County Superintendents of schools. Mrs. Mary E. Crary was elected in this county, December 28-9, 1874. A meeting of the State Association of County Superintendents of schools was held in Chicago. Five of these lady superintendents had been appointed to read papers and lead in the discussions. The appointments were: Mrs. Sarah McIntosh, of Will County; Miss Mary Allen West, of Knox County; Miss Mary W. Whiteside, of Peoria County; Mrs. Mary E. Crary, of Boone County; and Mrs. Mary S. Carpenter, of Winnebago County. The executive committee of the association had selected a list of topics for the consideration of the Chicago meeting. In his report for 1873-4, the State Superintendent said: "Mrs. Mary E. Crary, of Boone County, in answer to the question, 'Ought certificates to be renewed without examination?' gave a decided negative, based upon the following reasons: Frequent examinations are a great help to the teachers, spurring them on to higher attainments, getting them out of the ruts of mechanical study and teaching, and raising their salaries by cutting off the supply of poor, cheap teachers." In the same report, State Superintendent Etter said of these lady superintendents: "Their excellent official record in this office warrants the belief that they acquitted themselves (in the Chicago meeting) with credit." These references are simply placed on record here as being pertinent to the "PRESENT" part of our work, for these reasons: first, the election of lady superintendents was an experiment; and second, because one of them, Mrs. Crary, was elected in Boone County.

One of the ten lady superintendents of schools, a resident of the county, and her official record a part of the history of the PRESENT, a brief personal biography of Mrs. Mary E. Crary will not be out of place in these pages:

Mrs. Crary was born in New York, in 1846. When ten years of age, her parents came West, and after a few years of study in different schools of Kansas and Missouri, she entered Lanrence University, at Appleton, Wisconsin, but was called home by the death of her mother. After that bereavement, she entered the Rockford Seminary, from which she graduated with honor. She then took a course of study in Vassar College, Poughkeepsie, New York. After a few years of successful teaching, she was married, and settled down in Belvidere, still continuing to teach, however, in both the High Schools. In the fall of 1873, her name was proposed as a candidate for the school superintendency, to which office she was elected. Her official record is good. Her reports to the State Superintendent are highly commended by that officer, while at home her official character, industry, and interest in the schools is universally praised. As a teacher she sustained an exalted reputation. She possesses an excellent education—nothing of the superficial order—but thorough and comprehensive. She is a woman of indomitable energy and industry, and as an educator she ranks among the foremost in the state.

BELVIDERE.

As stated elsewhere in the progress of this writing, Oliver Robbins and brothers made the first claim in Boone County. That claim covered the grounds now occupied in part by North Belvidere, and was divided by the Kiswaukee River, and must have been made early in the summer of 1835. This is only presumption, however, based upon subsequent events. In June of that year, the claim was found occupied by Archibald Metcalf and David Dunham, so that the Robbins Bros. either sold their claim to Messrs. Metcalf and Dunham, or abandoned it, when the latter "jumped " it.

About the 4th of June, 1835, John K. Towner, wife and eight children, with their worldly goods packed in a wagon made expressly for the occasion, turned their backs upon the village of Avoca, in the town of Bath, County of Steuben, N. Y., to find a new home in Michigan. It had been Mr. Towner's purpose to make the trip alone—to go and spy out a new home in Michigan, and then return for his family; but to this proposition Mrs. T. would not consent, and bidding relatives and friends "good-by," they started on their journey, passing through Canada, and entering Michigan at Detroit. Near Detroit they stopped with a sister of Mrs. Towner's mother (a Mrs. Mathews), until Mrs. Towner could rest up, her health being poor, and to allow Mr. Towner time to select a location for a future home. Not finding the situation and surroundings in that State to his liking, and hearing a good deal of Chicago, Mr. Towner left his wife and children among her friends, and started *via* the lake, for that city. On the way across the lake he was overtaken by sickness, and was compelled to lay up for a few days at the old Tremont House, for treatment and rest. While thus housed up it happened that two citizens of Kennedyville, Steuben County, N. Y., and acquaintances of his, were stopping at the same hotel, and hearing the name of their old New York friend and neighbor mentioned, they sought his room, to renew on the banks of Lake Michigan the acquaintanceship commenced in New York in their boyhood days. These men were Cornelius Cline and Erastus A. Nixon—men whose names have already become known to those who have followed the pages of this book.

Mr. Towner was not satisfied with the outlook of Chicago as presented at that date, and was free to express his dislike to his friends. The Rock River country at that time was a great center of attraction among people hunting new homes, and its natural beauty and wealth of soil was highly praised, and Mr. Towner determined to visit that new El Dorado. Always a man of influence and a leader among his associates in his native State, Messrs. Cline and Nixon needed no persuasion to be induced to accompany him. As soon as able to travel, the trio started on foot for Rockford, following the trail made only a few years before by the army of General Winfield Scott in his campaign against the hostile Blackhawk Indians. When Messrs. Towner, Cline and Nixon arrived at the Kishwaukee, they found Metcalf and Dunham encamped in a small shanty on the claim already described. This was in June—the month of roses. The landscape was covered with myriads of flowers, and the great natural beauty of the surroundings enlisted the admiration of Mr. Towner. Tradition relates that when the Indians first entered upon and beheld the flower-bedecked landscape of one of the Southern States, they exclaimed: "Alabama!" which being interpreted means, "Here we rest." The same sentiment seems to have filled the soul of Mr. Towner, for after a night's rest and a general survey of the beautiful landscape surrounding, examining the rich soil, etc., etc., he said to his companions: "Others, expecting to find a paradise on Rock River, may go there; as for me, I go no further." His decision was the decision of his friends, and here they rested.

His decision rendered, he purchased a part of the claim held by Messrs. Metcalf and Dunham that included some timber, and took an additional claim that covered both sides of the river, a little below the present residence of Mr. Andrew F. Moss. He arranged with Mr. Cline for the erection of a log cabin, and started back for his family, walking to Chicago, and thence by lake vessel to Detroit, arriving home with his family just four weeks from the time he left them. After a day or two of rest, their goods were re-packed and re-loaded, and the journey for the Kishwaukee country commenced. Coming by way of Chicago, Mr. Towner there bought four pairs of oxen and an old-fashioned Pennsylvania wagon, in those days called "Prairie Schooners." Laying in a small supply of provisions, such as flour, bacon, etc., and his wife taking charge of the horse team that had hauled them from New York, through Canada and Michigan to Chicago, the last end of their journey to find a new earthly habitation was commenced. At midnight of the last day of July, 1835, Mrs. Towner, with the younger children and her "carriage," arrived on the south bank of the Kishwaukee, at a point nearly opposite the present site of the Baltic (Martyn's) mills, and went into camp. The next morning, up betimes, she saw the sun arise in glory and splendor, and cast his genial rays over the ground now occupied by Belvidere—until then the favorite resort of the Pottawattomies, their council grounds, as well as a burial place for their dead.*

*Some years ago a large number of Indian skeletons were unearthed along the bluff bank on the north side of the Kishwaukee, a little below the State street bridge, of which more may be said in the course of this volume.

The erection of the house contracted for by Mr. Towner on his previous visit, had not been completed, having only been raised four "rounds"—that is, four logs high on each side, and until it was completed, the family made the best possible shift. They moved into Metcalf and Dunham's shanty, where they remained until Mr. Cline completed his cabin. The Towners then moved into that and remained there while Cline went East and returned with his own family. Soon after their own house was finished, into which they moved. While the Towners were occupying the Metcalf and Dunham shanty, Simon P. Doty and Dr. D. H. Whitney put in an appearance at their door, and claimed their hospitality, which was granted, as in those days no door was closed against the wayfarers on the wide, sparsely settled prairies. This fact fixes the date of the arrival of Messrs. Doty and Whitney at from the fifth to the tenth days of August, 1835, and not the first of that month, as we have previously stated, a discrepancy, however, of minor importance. This chain of evidence establishes beyond all doubt, if, indeed, any doubt ever existed, that Archibald Metcalf, David Dunham, John K. Towner and family, Cornelius Cline, Erastus A. Nixon, Simon P. Doty and Dr. D. H. Whitney were the pioneer settlers of Boone County, and that Mrs. Towner was the first white woman whose feet pressed the green carpet spread by nature upon these beautiful "Elysian Fields."*

Later in the month of August, Ebenezer Peck and Dr. Goodhue came here, and like all who had preceded them, were delighted with the situation and the country, and while not seeking a place for new homes, they determined to secure an interest in what they foresaw must become valuable property and a site for a thriving town. In connection with Dr. D. H. Whitney, they purchased the claims of Messrs. Dunham and Metcalf, which embraced most of the lands occupied by the north part of Belvidere. This purchase was the first step towards the formation of the Belvidere Company, subsequently organized for the purpose of increasing the capital, building a town, mills, and making such other improvements as would add to the convenience and accommodation of immigrants and settlers. On his arrival in August, Dr. Whitney was so enraptured with the beauty of the landscape, that, in his enthusiasm, he named the place "Elysian Fields." When the Metcalf and Dunham claims were purchased, the name was changed to Belvidere, in honor of Mr. Peck's native place, Belvidere, Canada. In September, Deacon Nathaniel Crosby, then of Fredonia, New York, visited the settlement and purchased an interest in these claims, and returned East to make arrangements for building a mill at Belvidere the next year. "About this time," says Dr. Whitney, in a series of letters published in the Belvidere papers, "the company bought the claims of Messrs. Payne and Wheeler, two Hoosiers of the claim-making persuasion, who resided on Fox River. They had cut logs for a cabin, and Dr. Whitney had them hauled up on the site intended for the town plot, where he used them for the erection of a double log house, which was the first building in Belvidere that could be dignified by the name of a house. It was christened the Belvidere House, and Simon P. Doty installed as landlord. Mr. Doty continued in the management of this hostelry until the fall of 1836, when he moved into his own house, the first framed building erected in Boone County. The frame buildings of those days were sided or clap-

---

*Mrs. Towner is of the opinion that the wife of a chief of the Pottawattomies, whom she found here, was a white woman, but was so painted as to conceal her identity. But of this more under the caption of POLITICAL AND PERSONAL RECOLLECTIONS.

boarded and shingled with oak lumber made by hand. An oak tree of suitable size would be selected, cut down, and sawed into "cuts" of the desired length. These "cuts" were split into "bolts," and the bolts reduced by splitting with a frow as nearly the required thickness as possible, after which they were dressed down with a drawing knife, when they were ready for use.

"The Belvidere hotel was the only 'first-class hotel in the city,' and as its landlord knew how to 'keep hotel,' and was withal a popular gentleman and an unadulterated Whig, it was a place of popular resort, and besides serving as a hotel, it was used as a place for holding public meetings.

"In the latter part of October, 1835, the Marshal for LaSalle county, for taking the census, came to number the people of Belvidere, and the entire population was returned at thirty-seven, men, women and children."

Early in 1836, Nathaniel Crosby returned from New York. The claims were divided into ten shares, representing one thousand dollars each. The shares were all taken, and Messrs. John S. King, Jacob Whitman, Josiah C. Goodhue, Simon P. Doty, Frederick W. Crosby, John P. Chapin, Joel Parker and Henry L. Crosby admitted to equal interests in the Belvidere Company. Nathaniel Crosby became the general business manager in the building of the mills, etc.

The Belvidere Company was thus fully organized, and the work of building the mills at once commenced. All the lumber used in the erection of the sawmill was made by hand from the trees of the forest near by, by cutting, sawing, splitting and shaving, as described in a previous paragraph. Among those who were employed in building this sawmill, and who have remained permanently in the county, are Andrew F. Moss and Edward E. Moss, who have become prosperous farmers. Andrew F. Moss occupies a farm made on the land he pre-empted and bought of the government, in 1839, and upon which no debt or mortgage has ever been contracted.

The mill was completed and set in operation in the fall of that year. Its gearing, machinery, etc. were a great curiosity to the Indians remaining here, as well as a great convenience, benefit and accommodation to immigrants and to settlers, and white settlers had been steadily coming in.

While the sawmill was building, timber for the gristmill was being prepared, and by the time the former was finished, the latter was ready for sawed material for its completion. Rev. Dr. John S. King and Nathaniel Crosby jointly superintended the building of this mill, and for many years after its completion settlers came from many miles distant with their corn or wheat to be ground. Sometimes there would be from twenty to forty teams around the mill at one time, each owner awaiting his turn. The later comers would sometimes be compelled to wait a day or two for their grinding, but, as they had come prepared to "stay all night," they would camp around and patiently bide their time. That old mill was succeeded by the present Baltic Mills of Jas. B. Martyn.

The completion of these mills gave a fresh and vigorous impetus to immigration, and the sawmill had all it could do to keep up with the demands for timber. About the time the building of this mill was undertaken, Col. Mahlon Sayers had commenced the erection of another one, at a point about five miles below Belvidere, at a place then known as Newburg. For a time it was "nip and tuck" as to which of these undertakings would be completed first. Col. Sayers, the proprietor of Newburg, was a rival of the Belvidere company, and was seeking to make his place the leading town in the county. When the State road between Chicago and Galena came to be located, in June, 1836, there was a lively contest between Newburg and Belvidere—Doty representing Belvidere, and Col. Sayer fighting for Newburg. But Doty was the stronger man of the two and spared no effort to have Belvidere made a point on the road, and was successful; the Newburg enterprise was abandoned, and Belvidere leaped into new life.

The commissioners to locate that road were Messrs. James Harrington and Mark Daniels, of Kane County, and John Phelps, of Ogle County. Their coming was looked for with interest. Claims along the line of that road would be valuable, and claim hunters went out to meet them and make their selections, and some amusing incidents are related of the eagerness, amounting almost to greediness, of some of these parties—incidents which we may hereafter relate. That road established, it became the stage road between Chicago and Galena. The travel was heavy in those days. In the summer and fall, four-horse coaches were employed, and in the winter four-horse sleighs. In December, 1836, a post-office was established at Belvidere, being the first on the northern route between Chicago and Galena. S. S. Whitman was appointed postmaster. "He held the office about six years," says Dr. Whitney, in his reminiscences of Boone County, "when, without a hearing, he was accused, tried and convicted of being an honest, upright and faithful public servant, and a Whig, when off went his head."

In the fall of 1836, Messrs. S. P. Doty and Deacon Crosby established the corners of State and Mechanic streets, with an old, iron, carpenter's square. State street was named from the State road, bearing a little west of north. Mechanic street was so named because the Belvidere company, in order to encourage immigration, had resolved to donate building lots to mechanics who would improve and reside upon them. The first buildings erected on these corners were: Simon P. Doty built a frame house on the corner now occupied by Williams' drug store, which was the Belvidere House, of which we have already spoken. The next house was commenced by Matt. Malony, on the corner now occupied by the Greenlee Brothers as a hardware store. That building was a two-story frame, 24x40 feet. When framed, raised and covered, further work was abandoned until 1839, when H. C. Walker took it in hand and completed it, and occupied it as a dry goods store. For a long while the upper story was used by the Presbyterian people as a house of worship, further mention of which will be made in another place. The next corner to be occupied was the one now occupied by the large grocery house of E. W. Case. A frame building had been erected in the hollow up near the present residence of Cephas Gardner, Esq., and an effort made to start the town up there, but Doty objected, and putting in a strong oar, he foiled that scheme, and the building was moved down to the corner just named, and occupied by Charles Goodhue as a dry goods house. He was soon after succeeded by Alexander Neely. The erection of another building was commenced on the remaining corner, now occupied by Jones' boot and shoe and clothing house. The building was abandoned, however, and the structure, as far as it had progressed, torn down and removed to another place. When the lands came into market, (1839) the southeast quarter of section twenty-six, where Belvidere had been commenced, was bought in by Col. Joel Walker. Soon after, a division of the lands among interested parties was decided upon, and titles confirmed by quit claim deeds from Mr. Walker. In that division of property, the last corner spoken of fell to Mr. Doty, who subsequently deeded it to McKnight, who erected thereon the present brick building, which was the first brick house built in Belvidere. Doty soon after built a brick addition to his Belvidere House, on the Williams drug store corner, which was afterwards destroyed by fire. These were the business houses of Belvidere from 1836 to 1840. Of course there were a few residence houses, but until the year of the "Log Cabin and Hard Cider" campaign (1840), the growth of Belvidere was slow. After that year, improvements commenced to be made, and in 1877 the population is estimated at 4,000, with business houses that reach into the hundreds, that in character and magnitude will compare with those of any town in the State. The town has extended across the river, and covers an area of at least four miles square. The streets are wide, smooth and handsomely shaded. The residence houses are neat, tasty and attractive in their outward finish, betokening thrift, comfort and refinement within. Churches, school-houses, banks and all the other attendants of more advanced life have followed, until the "Elysian Fields" of nature—the home of the Indians forty-two years ago—has become a delightful and attractive place for homes in 1877.

When the county seat was located on the northeast quarter of section twenty-six, railroads did not enter into consideration, and had any one been bold enough to predict that in less than a quarter of a century such an enterprise would not only be undertaken, but completed, and the time occupied in making a trip from Belvidere to Chicago reduced from six days to as many hours, the prediction would have been scouted, and the seer pronounced an idiot or lunatic. Had he predicted that in the same time railroads and telegraph lines would traverse almost every township in the county, he would have been either laughed out of the county or sent to some charitable institution as incompetent to take care of himself. But they are accomplished realities, and the whistling of locomotives and the rumbling of long trains of cars are heard almost hourly in each of the eight townships. And the man who would express the determination to travel back to New York in a wagon drawn by horses, as John K. Towner and family traveled from that State to the Kishwaukee country in 1835, would be scouted as badly as one would have been at that date to predict the railroad and telegraph realities of the present. Forty-two years have marked wonderful changes. The next forty-two will mark still greater ones.

Previous to the building and completion of the railroad from Chicago to Rockford, the growth of Belvidere had been confined to the north side of the Kishwaukee, as contemplated when the county seat was located on the mound. When this line of that road was established, however, about one-half mile south of the river, building commenced on that side, the result of which was to transfer the bulk of the business to the near vicinity of the road, and the consequent following of residences, churches and school houses, and it is now conceded that the population is about equally divided by the Kishwaukee. The river is spanned by a magnificent wrought iron bridge, by which State street connects North and South Belvidere, and, almost as level as a floor, (except the easy descent on either side of the river) affords a magnificent drive-way.

Belvidere was incorporated under the general laws of the State in 1847, but only remained under such government about one year, when, the management not proving satisfactory to the people, they voted the corporation down. Until 1857 there was no town or village government, but about that time the citizens applied for and were granted a special charter. The Act granting the charter was approved February 5, 1857. The Act provided that the inhabitants of the town of Belvidere, in Boone County, should be constituted a body politic and corporate, to be known by the name of the "President and Trustees of the Town of Belvidere," and by that name should be known to law, etc. The Act further provided that all that district of country contained in and known as all of section twenty-six and the west half of section twenty-five, in township number forty-four, north of range three east, in Boone county, and also all additions of lots, blocks and out-blocks to said town, which had been laid out and recorded in the recorder's office of Boone County, should be recognized as forming the corporation, with the proviso that the board of trustees might extend the limits of the corporation not to exceed two miles square of land. The first Monday in every month was fixed as the regular time for the meeting of the board of trustees, providing also for the holding of adjourned and special meetings, and that the first election of trustees should be held at the court-house, and be conducted in the same manner as other elections are held. The board of trustees consisted of five members, from one of which number a president is elected, who by virtue of the charter is *ex-officio* a member of the Board of Supervisors. The charter provided that the first election should be held on the second Monday in March, 1857, and annually thereafter on the first Monday in March in each and every year.

At the first election for trustees, John K. Towner, Israel Tripp, D. W. Read, Cephas Gardner and Warren Pierce were elected. Their first meeting was held at the office of Messrs. Fuller & Wood, on the evening of March 10, 1857. The certificate of the judges of election showed that John K. Turner had received 209 votes; Cephas Gardner, 213 votes; Israel Tripp, 212 votes; Warren Pierce, 212 votes; David W. Read, 203 votes. Warren Pierce was chosen as president of the board, Asher E. Jenner clerk, Mark Ramsey, treasurer, and William Haywood, assessor.

Twenty years have come and gone since the date of the election of the first board of trustees. As many changes have taken place in the selection of town officials, but the line of policy marked out by the charter and inaugurated by the first board, has been carefully and jealously followed. The finances have been economically managed, and the morals of the town jealously guarded. No debts were ever contracted that the corporation had not the ability to meet. Streets were improved, sewerage provided, sidewalks built as fast as the growth of the town demanded, the result of which is that in all these things Belvidere presents as cleanly, neat, tidy and healthy appearance as any other town of the same population in the State. Practically speaking, it has been maintained as a temperance community. Occasionally a contest as between the temperance and ante-temperance elements has sprung up, but the former have always managed to hold the balance of power within their own control. As a consequence no criminal cases, growing out of drunken brawls, have ever found their way into the courts. Sometimes the municipal regulations touching the traffic in spirituous liquors have been violated, but the violators were as promptly arrested and the evils abated. All the adjuncts of good morals have been zealously and carefully fostered and guarded. Good schools have been maintained from the earliest days of Belvidere to the present. Churches have increased with the increase of population, until the primitive building erected by the Baptist people for a house of worship, and which, in its time served as school house, court room, public hall, etc., is now succeeded by twelve* church buildings, some of which are structures that would do credit to any metropolitan congregation. Besides the congregations represented by these church edifices, there are two religious societies without any house of worship of their own. But all of these will be mentioned more at length under proper divisions. Public halls have also been built as the town has grown in population and importance, until there are now two of most ample capacity for present or future demands. These, likewise, will be more specifically noticed in another place. These notes in general upon the origin and growth of Belvidere, and we notice as next in order the

EDUCATIONAL INTERESTS.

The first schools taught were private or family schools. When these valleys began to fill up the free school system had not become general even in the older States. And if it had prevailed throughout the country, there were no sources here from which to derive revenue for their support.

Among the early teachers was Miss Harriet King, daughter of Rev. Dr. John S. King. Another of the pioneer teachers was Miss Rebecca Loop, a sister to Mrs. John K. Towner, who taught a school in the winter of 1836-7 at the Towner family residence on the south side of the Kishwaukee. These, according to our best sources of information, were the first schools taught in what is now Boone County. In the years in which they were taught, the settlements were sparse, that at Belvidere being the largest in the county, and consequently better able to support a school.

In 1836 or '37 a joint stock company was formed for the purpose of building and maintaining an academy to be known as the Newton Academy. March 4, 1838, an instrument of writing issued from Boone County, by Dr. Whitney, commissioner of sales for the county, conveying to John S. King, Hiram Waterman, A. D. Bishop, William Dresser and F. W. Crosby, trustees of the Newton Academy, and their successors in office for the use of the academy, a certain tract of land described as block 20, in the original town of Belvidere. This tract of ground cornered with the southeast corner of the public or court-house square, and is now occupied by the handsome residence of H. C. DeMunn, Esq. The academy building was commenced and so far completed as to be tenantable, and Prof. S. S. Whitman taught a school therein. He was succeeded by another teacher, says Mrs. Towner, whose name is forgotten. In August, 1843, the academy, grounds, franchises, etc., passed out of the ownership of the association, and became the property of John Walworth, in trust, to be used by him for educational purposes and none other. In the same month, Walworth conveyed the premises to Arthur B. Fuller,† subject to all the conditions named in the conveyance to Walworth. Fuller, after coming into possession of

---

*Methodist, 2; Baptist, 2; Presbyterian, 1; German Evangelical Lutheran, 1; Free Methodist, 1; Catholic, 1; Episcopal, 1; Universalist, 1; Christian, 1; German Evangelical Association, 1.--12. Two of these, the Episcopal and Christian Churches, are without pastors and have no regular services.

†The Arthur Fuller here spoken of was a brother to Miss Margaret Fuller, a noted woman of Boston. She came here in person and bought the property for her brother and had it deeded to him. Subsequently she visited the European continent, became acquainted with and married an Italian nobleman, Count D'Orsini. At a later period herself, husband and child made a visit to her friends in the East and, on the return voyage, were lost off Long Island.

the property, occupied it as teacher for about two years, when he conveyed it to John K. Towner and Eben Conant, subject to the same conditions. A son of Conant was a Unitarian minister, and employed the academy as a school room and house of worship, but his doctrines not proving satisfactory to the representatives of the other churches, neither his school nor church aspirations succeeded very well, and in January, 1852, Towner and Conant conveyed the property to Rev. Charles Hill Roe, a Baptist minister. Up to the time of Roe's purchase the building had been used for educational purposes, and consequently was the first school-house (the old Baptist church excepted) in Belvidere. After his purchase, Roe remodeled the building and occupied it as a residence until 1862, when he removed it and built a new house on the ground it had occupied, using the old academy building as a barn. In March, 1865, Roe conveyed the premises to Henry D. Waterman; in March, 1868, Waterman conveyed it to Enoch Kendall, and in July, 1869, Kendall conveyed it to H. C. DeMunn, the present owner and occupant. And thus was the Newton Academy, grounds, franchises, etc., disposed of. The old academy building is still used as a barn by DeMunn, who says he owes much of his greatness and learning to his living so long on such classical ground, around which cluster the memories of so many learned men and educators, and to which he has given the name of "Piety Hill."

In October, 1845, D. B. Pettit commenced a select school with eighty-six scholars, in the old Baptist church, of which we have repeatedly spoken. He continued this school for six months, when he went East, remained absent a few months, and, returning, resumed teaching. During Mr. Pettit's absence, his school was continued by Jeremiah Phillips, who came here in February, 1846, to visit a sister, and while making this visit engaged in teaching penmanship. After Pettit's return, he and Mr. Phillips were engaged in teaching for six years, occupying rooms wherever they could be obtained, sometimes in the court-house and sometimes in second stories of business houses; a part of the time occupying the old academy.

About this time (1842) the lands had become taxable, and the people forehanded enough to maintain public schools, and to build school-houses. In town and country the good work was prosecuted. About 1854 the stone part of the public school building in the Court-house square was undertaken, and when completed was the most pretentious school building in the county. In 1857-8 a brick addition was built, affording accommodations for 400 scholars. This building cost about $8,000. Since then the increase of population on the South side demanded the erection of school buildings over there. Besides a large brick and stone house, with accommodations for 400 scholars, two other buildings (frame) are occupied.

The present principal of the North Belvidere school is Henry J. Sherrill, formerly of Madison county, New York. He has occupied this position about eleven years in succession. As an educator, he has but few, if any, superiors in the Northwest. His discipline is thorough, and his system of teaching as nearly perfect as is generally acquired. Scholars have gone from this school to *graduate* in others with high sounding names, and after an absence of some months have returned to find themselves far behind the classes they left. He is ably assisted by the following corps of teachers:

Blanche Soule, assistant in High School department; Prudie May, grammar department; Hattie Clark and Emma Shedd, intermediate department; Susie Rix and Emma May, primary department.

Three hundred scholars are enrolled.

Mr. J. W. Gibson is principal of the South Belvidere school. He was chosen to this position in 1874, and has given the most liberal satisfaction. He is represented to be an excellent classical scholar, thoroughly practiced in his method of teaching, and his discipline without fault. His educational *aides de camp* are:

Mrs. B. M. Blackburn, assistant in High School; Miss Ida May Fry, grammar department—Nettie B. Gray, assistant grammar department; Miss Mary E. Wyman, intermediate department—Miss Carrie Bush, assistant; Miss Sina Coleson, second primary; Eva Smedley, first primary.

Such are the schools of Belvidere in 1877. In either of them better scholars can be graduated than were graduated from Yale or Harvard "when this country was new." They are the pride of the people by whom they are sustained, and an honor and a credit to the great State in which they are maintained, and whose wise and generous laws have made them equal to the colleges of fifty years ago.

RELIGIOUS INTERESTS.

BAPTIST CHURCHES.

Passing from the educational interests, we come to the Church History of Boone County, the next in importance to the history of its early settlement. In fact, these histories are so closely interwoven with each other as to be almost inseparable. From the best sources of information at our command, it appears that the Baptist people were the first to enter upon and occupy the field, and with that perseverance, industry, and earnestness for which that branch of the Christian church has ever been noted from the days when St. John the Baptist went down into the water, they have, in some degree, maintained the supremacy, as is shown both by numbers and the two elegant church edifices in which they worship. We learn, also, that in the early days of this county it was their purpose to build up here an educational and theological institution, and thus make it a great disseminating center of religious truths and instructions, but from causes not known to the writer (perhaps more liberal offers of property and other aid being tendered in other localities) the scheme was never carried out. Be this as it may, that people are none the less worthy of commendation for their early work in planting the seeds that have germinated and ripened into such fullness as is evidenced in the presence of large adult congregations, learned pastors, prosperous, well-conducted Sabbath-schools, and their two large and commodious houses of worship. The plan that has ripened into such good results appears to have been laid among the Baptists of Chautauqua County, New York. It was a worthy undertaking, and has been crowned with brilliant success. How true that bread cast upon the waters will return many days hence!

To Rev. Dr. John S. King, a very eminent Baptist divine, and a man whose name has often appeared on these pages, one whose moral, social, business and religious character was without reproach, belongs the honor and the glory of preaching the first sermon uttered in the Kishwaukee wilds. Dr. King came here in the late winter of 1835, and an earnest and zealous servant of the Lord, a faithful sentinel on the outposts of the Christian army, he soon found a place for holding religious services. The doors of the primitive home of Timothy Caswell were thrown open, and in that humble cabin, standing in what is now the eastern part of Belvidere, not far from the banks of the easy-flowing Kishwaukee, on a March Sunday, in 1836, the voice of prayer and praise first ascended heavenward, and floated out upon the air that had so short a time before been undisturbed except by savage shouts, the howling of the wolf, or songs of birds. The attendance was not large, but the words of wisdom—of glad tidings and great joy—of that peace that surpasseth all understanding—were none the less earnest. Without money and without price—no immediate earthly reward in expectancy—his sermon was none the less eloquent. Glittering jewels and flashy attire were not there for display, but hearts full of earnest resolve—resolves taken long years before in the old churches, in the old homes away back by the clear, silvery waters of Lake Chautauqua—were of more worth than all the glittering jewels and tinsels of fashion that ever flashed and shone in the temples of the unholy. The songs of prayer and praise may not have been so finished and artistically rendered as those of the present day; there may have been but one hymn-book in the congregation, and the preacher compelled to line out his selections, but a deep inspiration of holiness and solemnity filled every soul, and rendered vocal with sweetest melody every song of praise and invocation. That first religious meeting—on the banks of the far western Kishwaukee,appointed perhaps in the far east Chautauqua—was the precursor of better things—the first rays of that glorious light that has continued to grow and shine until Belvidere has become pre-eminently a city of churches and church-going people. He planted the seed, lived to see it ripen into a golden harvest, and at the advanced age of nearly ninety years—years full of usefulness—Dr. John S. King, in September, 1875, at DeKalb, DeKalb County, was called to a home in the mansions above, there to receive the fullness of his reward.

Thus commenced the Baptist work in the Kishwaukee valley. At a little later period an humble and unpretentious house (of which we have repeatedly spoken) was erected, and in its day served its purpose well, but finally gave way before the demands of an increased population, and consequently increased congregation. That, too, in time, had to give way to a larger and more commodious structure, and the present society now occupies as handsome a church edifice as any people could desire—much more elegant in architecture and finish than even the most sanguine of its Chautauqua parentage ever anticipated.

The following historical summary is compiled from the church records, and shows a degree of prosperity and usefulness rarely equalled:

The first sermon was preached here in March, 1836. There were quite a number of Baptists here at that time, and Rev. Dr. John S. King, Deacon N. Crosby, Ira Haskins and others, soon thereafter began holding regular religious meetings. Every door was kindly opened, and the house was filled every Sabbath, whether preaching or praise meeting. In July, 1836, the Baptist Society was organized, with the following named constituent members:

Rev. John S. King, M. D.; Mr. and Mrs. Ira Haskins and daughter, May; Timothy Caswell and wife, Mercy Matilda, and unmarried daughter, and Mrs. Elizabeth Payne, another daughter; Moses Blood and son, Caleb, now Rev. Caleb Blood, of Kansas; Melvin Schenck and wife, Ann; Calvin Kingsley and wife, Charlotte S.; Nathaniel Crosby, Andrew F. Moss, and Charles Whitman. Melvin Schenck was chosen church clerk.

Others soon joined the new interest. In September, 1836, Prof. Seth S. Whitman, from Hamilton, New York, became their first pastor. Their numbers rapidly increased by the coming of John Lawrence and wife, Luther W. Lawrence and wife, Asa Moss, Sr., and wife, and others.

This church was blessed with many strong and efficient members, and soon became a power. It was the first church to incorporate the adult members into the Sunday-school.

List of Pastors.—Prof. Seth S. Whitman, ten years; Rev. S. A. Estee, three years; Rev. Charles Hill Roe, D. D., thirteen years; Rev. H. J. Eddy, D. D., four and one-half years; Rev. N. W. Miner, D. D., three years; Rev. J. P. Phillips, four months (fell into ill health and resigned); and Rev. W. A. Welsher (in his fourth year) present incumbent.

The supplies have been: Revs. S. Morton, John S. King, L. W. Lawrence, N. Otis, and others. Evangelists who made a good record for the cause: Revs. Isaac T. Hinton, Thomas Powell, Jacob Knapp, Robert Boyd, D. D., W. W. Moore, Morgan Edwards, and H. G. Weston.

This society has had a total membership of nearly 1,300, numbering about 500 during the pastorate of Rev. Dr. Roe, of blessed memory. The present number is about 250.

Sabbath-school.—Present number, 80; enrolled, 120.

In 1865, about 65 members were dismissed to form the South Belvidere Baptist Church, which now numbers over 300 members, with a total membership of 480. That church has had for pastors, Revs. Horace M. Carr, J. L. Benedict, John Fulton, and the present incumbent, J. M. Whitehead. Like the parent society, this congregation has a fine house of worship, and an open door for good, dividing the Baptist interest between the two churches. The total membership of the two churches is a little over 1,700.

The first house of worship erected by this people has already been spoken of. Their second one was a brick edifice, 42x62 feet, built in 1858, at a cost of about $5,000, and occupied the lot now occupied. In 1867, this house was pulled down to make room for the present beautiful edifice, which is 65x105 feet, which was erected furnished at a cost of $30,000, the most of which cost was borne by the congregation occupying it.

In 1866, the South Belvidere church built a temporary house of worship, 24x40 feet, costing $1,000. It was afterwards used for a conference room. In 1867, they built a house on the corner now occupied by John Plane's hardware store, which cost $12,000. That building, together with the conference room, was destroyed by fire, in December, 1871, and in 1873 the present beautiful edifice, 44x70 feet, and a conference room, 24x36 feet, was built, at a cost of nearly $15,000.

S. S. Statistics of South Belvidere Baptist Church.—The School was organized in October, 1865, with about 200 members enrolled. Average Sabbath attendance, nearly 150; present enrollment, about 250. The Superintendents (in the order named) have been E. E. Moss, Henry G. Andrews, H. O. Sherman, and George B. Ames. Volumes in library, 260.

The total value of the Baptist Church property is estimated at $50,000.

FIRST PRESBYTERIAN CHURCH.

The next church in the order of organization is the First Presbyterian. For a period of time involving nearly four years from the date of the first settlement of Boone County, the only regular religious services at Belvidere were conducted under the auspices of the Baptist Church, but the services were open to all, and no member of any other church organization declined to attend because they were Baptist. As immigration increased, so increased the adherents to the different forms of worship. Presbyterianism, as industrious, earnest and zealous as the Baptist or the Methodist—always jealous of the tenets of its faith, and true to the spirit of its founders—had representatives among the immigrants, and as time grew apace, and their numbers increased, they, too, determined upon establishing a church. Their first services were held at the house of Stephen Burnet, about three miles north of Belvidere. At first, like their Baptist co-laborers, their congregations were small, but their earnestness and religious ardor were none the less sincere. The same zeal and devotion that had been the governing principles of the fathers of that branch of the Church—that had carried its tenets and truths wherever man had an abiding place—that, through evil report as well as good, had enabled it to build churches, found schools and seminaries and colleges—was present in these pioneer meetings, and sustained and encouraged its believers. Years of trial and persecution, as all Christian people were persecuted in the earlier days of the Christian era, had only tended to purify and strengthen their faith. While acknowledging all religious organizations as co-laborers in one common field, and ready to bow with them in the presence of the Most High, there is yet an independence in a true Presbyterian that will accept no compromise of his church's Articles of Faith, or to depart therefrom and give up its individuality by becoming a part of any other church organization, unless for reasons beyond possible control, such as inaccessibility to their own churches and houses of worship. Love of order and home enter largely into the hearts of Presbyterians everywhere, as much in the Kishwaukee wilds as in the densely populated cities. No matter where Presbyterians may go, they carry these attributes with them, and never feel that they are at home until worshiping beneath their own vine and fig tree—their own roof, and that free from debt. First assembled as a little band of true and steadfast worshipers at the humble pioneer home of Stephen Burnet, on Squaw Prairie, in 1838, without organization, we trace the history of their society organization, its success and prosperity, down to the present. In the compilation of this summary, we are much indebted to Henry W. Avery, Jr., clerk of the church, merchants and esteemed citizens of Belvidere.

The church is designated on the records of the Ottawa Presbytery as the "First Presbyterian Church of Belvidere, Illinois." It was organized at the log house of Stephen Burnet, above quoted, March 17, 1839, with 23 members, whose names were as follows:

Mrs. Dorcas May, Ezra May, Mrs. Abigail Burnet, Stephen Burnet, Mrs. Harriet Sheldon, Frederic S. Sheldon, Mrs. Abigail Hicks, George D. Hicks, Mrs. Mary Gardner, Austin Gardner, David Caswell, Aaron H. Billings, Mrs. Louisa Rollins, Chauncy Bristol, Mrs. Maria L. Fisk, Mrs. Mary C. Dubois, Mrs. Hannah Blood, Mrs. Juliet M. Gilman, Mrs. Nancy Hale, Mrs. Phil. McBride, Mrs. Louisa May, Mrs. R. Cunningham, Miss Adaline E. Sheldon.

At the organization, Rev. John Morrill officiated, and Ezra May and Austin Gardner were elected ruling elders. The Articles of Faith and Covenant now in use were then adopted.

Up to the arrival of Col. Joel Walker, the congregation worshipped at the residence of Mr. Burnet, and then in the former's log house across the prairie, three miles north of Belvidere, until the following year.

In 1840, the second story of the frame store-building erected by Col. Walker the previous year, on the northwest corner of State and Mechanic streets was finished off, and its use as a place of worship given the society. The hall was dedicated June 4, 1840, and occupied three years.

The church was received into the Ottawa Presbytery, when in session at Belvidere, June 23, 1841, at which time Rev. Royal Nathaniel Wright was installed as the first pastor, with a promised salary of $400 per annum, $150 of which was pledged by the Home Missionary Society.

In 1843, the first church edifice of this society, and the first building in the county used exclusively for religious purposes, was erected, on the corner of Main and Mechanic streets, the present location. It was dedicated in August of the same year. The material was white brick, its dimensions 36x48 feet, its cost $2,250, and the design plain and unpretentious.

In April, 1857, the erection of the church building now occupied as a place of worship by the society was commenced, and in February, 1858, it was dedicated. It is built of red brick, after the Corinthian order of architecture; with the addition of a spire, is 60x80 feet in dimensions, will seat 800 persons, and cost $18,000. While the new church was building, the society met for worship in the first Union Hall.

The membership record is: Original number, 23; received during various pastorates, 835; received between the pastorates, 27; total since organization, 885. Present number of members, 400. Number of original members now living, 10.

The pastors have been: Morrill (supply), commenced labor, March 17, 1839; pastorate ceased, March, 1840; duration, 1 yr.; members received, 23.

Royal Nathaniel Wright, commenced labor, June, 1841; installed, June 23, 1841; pastorate ceased, Oct. 6, 1849; cause, died, aged 38; duration, 8½ years; members received, 182.

Charles Fanning, installed, Oct. 23, 1850; pastorate ceased, April, 1854; cause, resigned, ill-health; duration, 3½ yrs.; members received, 118.

E. D. Willis (supply), commenced labor, April, 1854; pastorate ceased, May, 1855; duration, 13 months.

Eleazer T. Ball, commenced labor, May 6, 1855; installed, July 9, 1855; pastorate ceased, Aug. 9, 1855; cause, died; duration 1 month; members received, 16.

Henry B. Holmes, commenced labor, Jan. 18, 1856; installed, April 23, 1856; pastorate ceased, Dec., 1862; cause, resigned, call to Dubuque; duration, 6⅔ years; members received, 149.

David R. Eddy, commenced labor, May 10, 1863; installed, May 4, 1864; pastorate ceased, July 7, 1872; cause, resigned, call to Flint; duration, 8 1-6 years; members received, 313.

Supplys, July to December, 1872.

Thomas C. Easton, commenced labor, Dec. 15, 1872; installed, Sept. 15, 1873; now serving; members received, 57.

The Record of Eldership is as follows:

Ezra May, elected March, 1839; died Sept., 1854; served 15½ years.
Austin Gardner, elected March, 1839; died Feb., 1843; served 4 years.
Joel Walker, elected Feb., 1841; died July, 1855; served 14½ years.
Marcus White, elected April, '42; removed Sept., '50; served 8½ years.
David Dickey, elected Jan., 1846; died Dec., 1850; served 5 years.

Sidney Avery, elected January, 1846; still serving.
Jona. Mitchell, elected Sept., 1850; died Sept., 1853; served 3 years.
Theron Linsley, elected Sept., 1851; died May, 1857; served 5½ years.
Sey. Gookings, elected Sept., '51; removed April, '55; served 3½ years.
Eli Foote, elected Sept., 1851; retired Nov., 1864; served 13 years.
Eli Foote, re-elected Nov., 1869; still serving.
John Lawrie, elected Sept., 1851; retired Nov., 1860; served 9 years.
H. W. Avery, Jr., elected Sept., 1852; still serving.
James D. Tripp, elected Nov., 1854; still serving.
Warren Pierce, elected Nov., 1855; removed 1859; served 3¼ years.
Olney Nichols, elected Nov., '56; removed Aug., '62; served 5¾ years.
D. E. Foote, elected Nov., 1856; still serving.
Danl. McEwen, elected Nov., '57; removed Dec., '67; served 10 years.
Saml. Pepper, elected Nov., 1861; retired Nov., 1864; served 3 years.
Elliot Bush, elected Nov., 1861; died June, 1864; served 2½ years.
H. D. Waterman, elected Nov., 1862; retired Nov., 1865; served 3 years.
John Yourt, elected Jan., 1864; still serving.
M. C. Tomkins, elected Nov., 1864; removed Mch., 1873; served 8¼ years.
N. C. Bentley, elected Jan., 1866; still serving.
Ira Stanbro, elected Oct., 1868; retired Nov., 1872; served 4 years.
M. Linsley, elected Nov., 1872, retired Nov., 1875; served 3 years.
I. T. Witbeck, elected Oct., 1873; still serving.
H. J. Sherrill, elected March, 1876; still serving.

The system of rotary eldership was adopted November, 1851, and has been practiced since that date.

The retirements were occasioned by no causes discreditable to those withdrawing.

The Sabbath School was organized in the hall owned by Col. Walker, June 6, 1840. Deacon Austin Gardner was its first Superintendent. Mrs. Mary Gardner, Col. Walker, and Mrs. Alice Walker, were his associate teachers, and the pupils numbered about twenty-five. Additions were gradually made, and soon the names of C.C. Bristol, Bradford Dean, Mrs. Hannah Blood, Mrs. Annette S. Wright, and Mrs. Louisa M. Fisk, appear as teachers. In 1843, Deacon Gardner was removed by death. Mr. Albert Brainerd was elected his successor, but the responsibility rested upon and was borne more particularly by Col. Walker, who, from its organization to his death, in July, 1855, was zealous for the prosperity of this Sabbath-school. Mr. Brainerd was succeeded by N. C. Amsden, some time in 1844. About the first of January, 1846, H. W. Avery, Jr., was elected Superintendent, and, by re-elections, was continued until May, 1866, excepting intervals of from a few months to perhaps a year, which were filled by H. P. Woodworth, E. B. Conklin, L. B. Danforth, Seymer Gookins, and E. N. Bush. In May, 1866, Dr. D. E. Foote was elected Superintendent, and, by annual re-elections, was continued until May, 1876, when he was succeeded by D. D. Sabin. In May, 1877, Mr. Sabin declining a re-election, James R. Leonard was elected, and is at this date the acting Superintendent. There have been probably more than one hundred and fifty different teachers. The classes have increased from three or four, at first, to twenty-five, and the pupils from twenty-five to three hundred and fifty, as perhaps the highest number ever reported. A marked feature of this school is the attendance of many adults. Probably one-fourth of the members are classed as adults, who, with their own and others' children, together study the regular Bible

H. F. Bowley
MERCHANT
BELVIDERE.

lesson. Nearly all the members of the Sabbath-school are regular attendants upon the church service, and the church receives many additional members from this nursery. The library is usually replenished yearly, with such books as are considered suitable, while those which have been read and are in fair condition are gratuitously sent to more destitute schools in the farther West.

The most important and, in some respects, remarkable revival in the annals of this organization occurred during the pastorate of Rev. D. R. Eddy, in the winter of 1864–5. As its fruit sixty-seven persons were received into covenant on profession.

This church has been notably preserved from internal discord and division, and marked for its love of reformatory movements and faithfulness to the doctrines of civil and religious liberty.

Biographical.—Rev. Thomas Chalmers Easton, M. A., was born in Jedburg, Roxburghshire, Scotland, November 12, 1835. He received his classical education in the Latin School and Nest Academy, under the tuition of Burnett, and entered St. Mary's College, at St. Andrews, well qualified, and graduated with distinguished honors, class of 1855. He soon after emigrated to this country, and entered the Congregational ministry, and in 1868 had his present degree of M. A. conferred by Beloit (Wisconsin) College. He has been the pastor of three large churches—his first charge being the First Congregational Church in South Glastonbury, Connecticut; his second, the Scotch Church at Argyle, Winnebago County, Illinois, and his present charge, the First Presbyterian Church, Belvidere. During the years 1860–1, he served as Chaplain to the Legislature of New York, and was identified with the Abolition movement, debating largely the "Personal Liberty Bill," in company with Hon. Gerritt Smith, Fred. Douglass, and others, who viewed these important political subjects from the same standpoint as Mr. Easton. He is well known as a lecturer, and takes the deepest interest in all philanthropic and educational reforms, and is greatly beloved by his present congregation.

METHODIST EPISCOPAL CHURCH.

Where has Methodism not been carried? From a little class organized by John Wesley in London, England, in 1739; persecuted and hunted from place to place, their numbers increasing from month to month, from year to year, they now rank first in point of numbers among the civilized people of the world. There is no limit to the industry and earnestness of this people. Wherever it has been possible to reach mankind at home and abroad, there the truths taught by the followers of John Wesley have been carried. It has made the dark places light, and opened the pathway of peace to millions of benighted souls. No sluggard can be a Methodist. That organization tolerates no drones; and its system is so perfect, that each part of its working machinery is in full harmony with the other. These people follow their plan of evangelization as regularly as the sun follows its orbit. No plummet was ever truer to the line than are the Methodists to their work. Not only is industry a pre-requisite to a good Methodist, but courage as well, particularly to the ministry. When once one's mind is made up to enter that sacred calling, friends, kindred, home, and if needs be, country, must be sacrificed to the duty embraced, and wherever work is to be done, there must he go. It may be to missionary service in the remotest islands of the sea—a backwoods or a prairie mission or circuit, with perhaps the appointments a day's journey or a week's journey apart—the settlements sparse, the labor great and the prospect of earthly reward exceeding small. Hunger, exposure, persecution are in the way, but Methodism smiles at these as it sings its hosannas of praise, and shouts its pæans of defiance at the bulwarks of the tempter. In the character of the pioneer Methodist ministers—circuit riders, like Peter Cartright, or Kentucky's Findley, there is something grand, and touchingly sublime. But these are only two of tens of thousands, the memory of whose character, courage, self-denial and devotion to the cause of the Master and the salvation of souls, lives as a monument in the minds of every true follower of the Author and Finisher of men's faith.

Early in the field everywhere, they followed close on the heels of the early immigrants to the prairies of the Kishwaukee, chanting their songs of praise and shouting defiance at all obstacles between them and the accomplishment of the work they were commissioned to do.

As a general rule, their missionaries go ahead to spy out the land and look after the spiritual needs of the early pioneers. Later comes the circuit rider with his saddle-bags, Bible and hymn book, and thus, step by step, their good work is prosecuted.

The history of Methodism in Northern Illinois shows that the first class formed within the bounds of the Rock River Conference was at Galena, in 1829; the second at Plainfield, the same year; the third at Chicago, in 1831. At the next year's conference, Zadoc Hall was sent to explore the country, and form a new circuit west of the Illinois River and north of Peoria. His charge was called the Peoria Mission, and was larger than the entire conference is now. The Ottawa circuit was formed from the northern part of the Ottawa, in 1833, and the Belvidere circuit cut from the Ottawa circuit two or three years later.

The following list comprises the preachers in charge to the present time (September, 1877): 1838, Jesse Walker; 1839, N. Jewett; 1840, — Brayton; 1841, Jas. McKean; 1842, R. A. Blanchard; 1843, M. Decker; 1844-5, R. A. Blanchard; 1846, Wesley Latin; 1847, Geo. Lovesse; 1848, W. Wilmot; 1849, R. Beatty; 1850, M. Decker; 1852-4, Thos. North; 1856, L. Anderson; 1857, S. Stover; 1859, C. S. McReading; 1860, S. F. Denning; H. Crew, P. E.; 1861, S. F. Denning; R. A. Blanchard, P. E.; 1862, F. A. Read; 1863, H. Atchison; 1864-6 Geo. J. Bliss; H. L. Martin, P. E.

Since then the preachers have been: 1867, J. C. Stoughton, 1st church, 176 members; S. Cates, 2d church, 55 members. 1868, E. W. Adams, 1st church; S. A. Cates, 2d church, W. A. Willing, P. E. 1869, W. H. Fisher, 1st church; S. Cates, 2d church. 1870, W. H. Fisher, 1st church; W. H. Wilkinson, 2d church. 1871, W. H. Fisher, 1st church, 148 members; R. A. Blanchard, 2d church, 110 members. 1872, — Newton, 1st church; J. O. Ogden, 2d church, W. A. Gray, P. E. 1873, W. H. Haight, 1st church; J. O. Odgers, 2d church. 1874, W. H. Haight, 1st church; J. O. Odgers, 2d church; 1875, W. H. Haight, 1st church; W. T. Shaw, 2d church; 1876, N. H. Axtell, 1st and 2d churches.

April 29, 1866, the following persons took letters from the church, and organized the Second (South Belvidere) Methodist Episcopal Church:

G. Chamberlain, H. Nicholson, N. Nicholson, A. Howard, L. Howard, G. D. Smith, E. Smith, B. B. Hovey, M. J. Boyce, J. Danforth, E. Esta-Brook. M. S. Chamberlain, H. Chanahim, M. S. Bassett, S. A. Banks, P. Burton, R. Swail, H. Cornell, C. Cornell, E. Allbright, H. Bennett, H. Pastee. L. Anderson was made pastor.

In the year 1850, the brick church was dedicated, then the finest house of worship in the city. This people first occupied, as a place of worship, the second story of a frame building that had been commenced by a Mr. Fisk, on the Rockford road between Belvidere and Beaver Creek; but after being raised was pulled down and removed to Belvidere and erected at the corner of State and Perry streets, opposite the present residence of Mrs. John K. Towner. At a later period, they moved into a building erected by Dr. Whitney for a law office, on the rear end of the lot now occupied by the Presbyterian church, and which they occupied one winter, when they moved into a building that had been erected on State street (now occupied as a residence by Mrs. Wilbur) by J. G. Saxton, for a hardware store for Nijah Hotchkiss. They continued to occupy this place until they had purchased the site of their present church, and erected a small framed house thereon, where they remained until their present house of worship was built.

The interests of the town growing more favorable to the South Side, that church has become the strong one. Its Sabbath-school is the largest and most prosperous in the city. It has the singular honor of having thirty-three per cent. of its scholars entitled to diplomas for perfect lessons for the entire year. That number having been perfect also in rigid examination upon the year's study. Prof. I. B. Gibson is the superintendent at present.

Biographical.—Rev. N. H. Axtel came to take charge of the two churches, from the Park Avenue Church, Chicago. He was born in Pennsylvania, in 1836, and entered Allegheny Preparatory School in 1848. Then, after spending two years in the South and West, returned to college and graduated in 1860. Being elected to a professorship in Willoughby College, he spent one year there and the next two years in Evanston, teaching in the Northwestern University, and completing a course of Divinity in Garrett Biblical Institute. Since entering the ministry, his appointments have been Princeton, Galena, Aurora, Mendota, Elgin, Park Avenue—Chicago, and Belvidere. He is represented as a close student, a deep thinker, a ready and logical speaker, and sincere piety.

EVANGELICAL LUTHERAN IMMANUEL CHURCH.

In 1868, the Rev. A. Wagner, of Chicago, occasionally came to Belvidere, rendering sermons to the German Lutherans of the town and vicinity. Early in 1869, about twenty families were organized as a congregation, and sent a call to Rev. Phil. Estel, which was accepted. Services were held at the court house, and in private residences. In time, Mr. Estel accepted a call to another field, and services were rendered to the congregation by surrounding ministers, until in 1873, Rev. William Heinrauf accepted a call as pastor of the congregation. In 1875 the congregation succeeded in buying the former Congregational church, a frame building 50x30 feet, 20 feet high, surmounted by a steeple 40 feet in height. The church was consecrated the 25th of July, 1875, after being thoroughly repaired and refurnished. In July, 1877, Rev. Heinrauff removed to Missouri, and was succeeded in the pastorate by Rev. C. F. Th. Eissfeldt, who was installed August 12th.

The congregation has a present membership of forty-six. Services are held every other Sunday at 10:30 o'clock A. M.; Sunday-school from 12 to 1 o'clock P. M. From November to April, a school is taught by the pastor, which is sustained by the congregation.

The names of the original members of this church are: J. Suhr, J. H. Buhmeyer, Fr. Sturm, G. Gierhahn, F. Reimer, J. Watomann, John Berg, Chr. Grawe, J. Wesebaum, H. Kratt, J. Wascher, C. Johannis, John Riedel, C. Gahlbeck, A. Sander, John Sturm, C. Marske, Chr. Johannis, J. Weber, A. Lettow, S. Luhmann, J. Piehl, H. Streage—23.

THE UNIVERSALIST CHURCH.

Among the other people that settled here in the early times were a few representatives of this branch of the church. As jealous of their belief as the others were of theirs, they secured occasional preaching as opportunity offered. Rev. Seth Barnes, who was settled at Rockford, made occasional visits to Belvidere, and preached here as early as 1838. The meetings were held whenever a suitable building could be secured. Sometimes they were held in Towner's Hall, sometimes in some of the church edifices, and often in private houses, and were generally well attended. Mr. Barnes continued these meetings for about one year, when he removed from Rockford, finally locating at St. Anthony (now East Minneapolis), where he continued preaching until his death some years later. Before his removal to Minnesota, however, he assisted in establishing the *Better Covenant*, a newspaper devoted to the interests of his church. Subsequently the name of the paper was changed to the *New Covenant*, and continues to be published under that name at Chicago.

Until 1853, the Belvidere Universalists only had occasional services, conducted by different preachers. The first day of August, 1853, the first regular organization was effected. That meeting was held at the court house, and under the direction of Rev. T. S. Bartholomew, the First Universalist Society of Belvidere was fully organized. Jeremiah Phillips was chosen as church clerk, Peter Payne treasurer, and Charles McDougal, Simmons Terwilliger and Timothy Lewis, trustees for the society. The names of the parent members of the society were:

Timothy Lewis, Chas. McDougal, John W. Mack, Simmons Terwilliger, Jeremiah Phillips, Peter Payne, T. S. Bartholomew, Chas. E. Drake, Sherman E. Lewis, David Beebe, Eben Hammond, Selva Mack, Cephas Gardner, Enos Walker, J. R. Murphy, Elisha Leach, F. A. Hull, H. C. DeMunn, S. S. Stroud, W. C. Tuttle, Hannah Morse, H. J. Doolittle, Mary Curtis, Almira Lewis, Martha Drake, Emeret Lewis, Nancy Beebe, Augenett Merrill, Elizabeth White, Melissa Payne, Emily Kandy, N. A. Hull, Wm. Perkins, Fanny McDougal, Esther E. Doolittle, B. N. Fox, J. J. Waterman, L. C. Waterman, L. J. Cohoon, H. A. Cohoon, Nathaniel Bancroft, E. A. Bancroft, E. M. Rogers, S. M. Cook and N. G. Tripp—45.

After the organization of the society, their meetings were held in the old Baptist church building, (which had been purchased by Alexander Neely for a school-house) at the corner of Van Buren and East streets, and which they afterwards purchased, together with the ground on which it stood. In 1862, the society commenced to build a new house, and one in keeping with the character of the surroundings. It is a very handsome frame building, with stone foundation, and a seating capacity for two hundred persons. With the grounds, it cost about $3,000.

Mr. Bartholomew remained as pastor of the society about two years, and was succeeded by Rev. R. G. Hamilton, who remained three years. He in turn was succeeded by Rev. A. B. Ellis, who labored with them about the same length of time. Under his pastorate, in 1865, a re-organization of the society was effected. The next pastor was Rev. W. S. Ralph. The next pastors in succession were Rev. J. J. Austin, who remained two years; Rev. S. A. Holt, not quite one year, when he resigned. Until a permanent pastor could be secured, arrangements were made by which Rev. D. M. Reed, of Rockford, preached for them every alternate Sabbath. This supply continued about six months, when Rev. H. Slade, of Elgin, was called to the pastorate of the society, filling the pulpit for one year. Rev. H. W. Harrington came next, and remained two years, closing his pastorate April 1, 1876.

Since Mr. Harrington retired, the society has been without a pastor, but its organization is kept up, and the pulpit occasionally supplied by Rev. D. M. Reed.

Their Sabbath-school was first organized in 1854, by Mrs. T. S. Bartholomew, and re-organized in 1861, with Mrs. Bartholomew as superintendent. In 1865 another organization of the school was accomplished. At this time the school numbered one hundred scholars and fourteen teachers, and had a library of 300 volumes. At the last organization, Rev. Bartholomew was chosen superintendent. The present trustees of the society are D. E. Moulton, William Weed and S. Terwilliger; Charles Carpenter, clerk and treasurer.

CHRISTIAN CHURCH.

When the Towners came to the Kishwaukee, in 1835, they brought with them the doctrines and faith taught by Alexander Campbell, the founder of the Christian (often synically called the Campbellite) Church. This people, although liberal in their sympathies and regard for the other denominations, are as closely wedded to their faith as are the Methodists, the Baptists, or the Presbyterians, to theirs. And it is not strange that such representatives as Mr. and Mrs. Towner should seek the earliest opportunity to establish the doctrines of their church among the others that have grown up in Belvidere.

The first minister to proclaim the doctrines of this branch of the Church to the people of Boone County was Elder Walworth, in 1838. He is represented to have been a preacher of great power and eloquence, as well as of great worth and piety. Under his ministrations, the Christian society was organized and put in the way of usefulness. The owner at one time of the old Newton Academy building, spoken of elsewhere, he used it as a place of worship. While laboring here, he was a correspondent for the Unitarian papers, and by this means made the acquaintance of Rev. Mr. Conant, a Unitarian minister and educator. This acquaintance resulted in bringing Mr. Conant to Belvidere, and he finally succeeded Elder Walworth in the ownership of the Academy building and pastorate of the Christian society. Elder Walworth, being recognized as a great evangelist, had frequent calls to other fields, but, during such absences, his Belvidere pulpit was filled every alternate Sabbath by Mr. Conant. Elder Walworth is now located in Green County, Wisconsin.

About 1841–2, Elder William Roberts came and assumed the place Elder Walworth had filled so satisfactorily, and continued to preach the truths of his church until failing health compelled his resignation, some time in the year 1843. A writer in the *Herald of Gospel Liberty*, under date of August, 1877, in referring to the early life of Elder Roberts, holds this language: "After dedicating himself to the labor of the ministry, his labors, which were somewhat itinerant, were directed for a time to the little hamlet two miles from my father's—now DeLancy—where a blessed and extensive work of grace crowned his efforts. Much of the time, for perhaps a year or more, he labored among us, and in all his intercourse with the people his bearing was such as to hold the love and respect his first labors had won. Being still unmarried, it is somewhat remarkable, perhaps, and also a fact to be thankful for, that no shadow of flirtation was ever known of him, and no one of the many young lady converts ever betrayed the least indiscretion in relation to him that I ever heard of. The 'holy kiss,' which I fear has given too much latitude to some cordial, unsanctified natures, was limited in his case, I fully believe, to greetings of my father. This they ever exchanged on meeting after a few weeks' separation, and I wish that all who practice obedience to the Apostolic injunction in this matter could as certainly know it to be the 'holy kiss' as I believe were these greetings of my father and his 'dear little elder.' I have heard my father say he was one of the very few he had known who never, to all human appearance, had an hour's declension from his first love. * * * The last meeting he attended among us was very much like the one recorded in the last chapter of Acts. It continued five hours."

Arthur Fuller came next after Elder Roberts, and he, likewise, through the help of his sister, Miss Margaret Fuller, became the owner of the Academy building. He remained two years, as teacher and preacher. After his resignation, Rev. J. L. Towner, son of John K. Towner, who had graduated from college, preached to the Christian society; and whenever Elder Walworth could find time from other more needy fields he would come and preach to his people. Thus were the meetings kept up until Elder William Bradley came, in January, 1853. Under the ministration of this divine the church was wonderfully blessed. Until his coming, no decisive measures had been undertaken for the erection of a church building, but he soon set about this enterprise, and in June, 1856, says Mrs. Towner, their church edifice was completed and dedicated. Elder Bradley remained in this charge until 1858, when he resigned the pastorate. He is now preaching in Boston.

Next in the succession came Elder Adams, through the remainder of 1859-'60, and then went to California. Elder Watson, from New Hampshire, a young man of excellent qualifications, succeeded Mr. Adams, and remained four or five years. He is now located at Troy, Miami County, Ohio, and is recognized as one of their ablest and most worthy preachers.

About this time the society began to lose its strength and influence, by reason of the removal of members to Iowa and other new homes—sometimes as many as twenty of them going at one time.

Elder Linscott was the last regular pastor of the society. He was a most industrious and zealous worker. During his pastorate, about eighteen months, he preached to three congregations almost every Sunday—at Belvidere in the morning, to the Bonus Prairie congregation in the afternoon, and at Capron in the evening. His labors carried the society up to 1863-4, when it had become too weak to support a pastor, and it gave up the field as an organized church body. Their church building has passed into other hands, but is still occupied as a house of worship. Only a few of the old members still remain here. Among these is Mrs. Towner, relict of John K. Towner, who died November 7, 1861. Mrs. Towner, though far advanced in life, is hale and vigorous, and the last female representative of the Belvidere settlers of 1835. In fact, she is the mother—an honored and respected one—of the city. Her son, Elder John L. Towner, of whom mention has been made in the course of this church sketch, is located at Industry, McDonough County, doing a work of usefulness.

EPISCOPAL CHURCH.

This church organized in 1847. Members—Mr. and Mrs. Albert Neely, Mrs. Margaret Keith, Mr. Nijah Hotchkiss, Miss Alma Hotchkiss, Mr. George Dean, Mrs. A. F. Moss, and Mr. and Mrs. George Williams. Clergymen—Rev. Alfred Louderback, Rev. S. D. Pulford, Rev. E. B. Tuttle, Rev. Mr. Waterbury, Rev. La Bagh, Rev. W. H. Cooper, Rev. W. H. Couch, Rev. W. H. Yeator, Rev. W. H. Partmus, Rev. W. H. Eddy. Owing to loss of church records by fire a full history cannot be given.

FREE METHODIST CHURCH.

The Free Methodist congregation has a small but very neat church edifice, and regular services, by Rev. E. C. Best. Their Sabbath-school is in a prosperous condition, and the members of the society earnest, industrious workers in their church's interest. Unable to gather the data for a more extended notice of this society, we present the following lines from the pastor, which explains itself and justifies the brevity of this sketch:

"CITY, Sept. 20.—Dear Sir: I find it impossible for me to give a *full* history of our church here, as I can not get the records prior to about 1865 or 1868, for a few days at least. Respectfully yours,
"E. C. BEST."

This note was in answer to one written to Mr. Best, after two or three visits to the parsonage and finding him absent, asking for information about his church society, etc.

CATHOLIC CHURCH.

The Catholics have a very handsome church edifice and good congregation, but in consequence of the absence of the priest on a visit to Europe, it was impossible to obtain any data relating the church's history, although repeated efforts to accomplish that end were made, hence the brevity of this sketch.

GERMAN EVANGELICAL ASSOCIATION.

This people have a small church edifice, and a membership of fifty persons. Their society was organized about 1867, with not to exceed ten persons as members. Rev. L. Keller is their present pastor, who preaches to the congregation every alternate Sunday. Their Sabbath-school numbers from thirty-five to forty scholars, and six teachers; Charles Fritz, Superintendent.

PUBLIC LIBRARY.

The only library in Belvidere is that, under the management of the ladies, known as the Belvidere Library Society.

It was first organized in 1851, continued four or five years, and then, owing to some trouble with the acting librarian, was abandoned.

In May, 1874, a few ladies, feeling the need of some organization looking to literary culture and advancement, collected what books could be found belonging to the old society—some 120 volumes in all—and formed the present society.

It is, like the old one, a subscription library, and has at the present time (1877) one thousand volumes, has been tendered the use of a lot, the gift of a small building which is being fitted up, and so, struggling on by littles, the ladies hope that the time is not far distant when the voters of the town, realizing the necessities of the case, may be induced to take the matter into their hands and by a tax under the state law, make of it a free public library, to which the intelligence and general enterprise of the people entitle them.

Officers:—President, Mrs. M. G. Leonard; Secretary, Miss M. E. Dunton; Treasurer, Mrs. Dr. F. S. Whitney; Librarian, Miss N. G. Rice; Trustees, Mrs. O. H. Wright, Mrs. J. M. Glasner, Mrs. R. Roberts, Mrs. M. M. Rutger, Miss S. M. Mundy.

PUBLIC HALLS.

Public halls in the early days of Belvidere were not so much of an object as the erecting of houses and offices of immediate necessity. But as time wore on, and Belvidere increased in population and importance, halls began to be erected. Some of these were very commonplace ones, but served their purpose well in their time. Among the first to be designated by the name of a hall, was the upper part of the Big Thunder Hotel, erected by Mr. Towner, in 1838. This hall was in demand for religious meetings, lectures, public meetings, etc., until Alexander Neely prepared one in the brick block at the northwest corner of State and Mechanic streets. The Walker building, commenced by Mr. Molony and completed by Col. Joel Walker, on the corner occupied by Greenlee Brothers, also afforded a hall in its time. The memory of some other halls of early presence might be resurrected, but they have all passed away and out of usefulness, and as the people became richer and prouder, better and finer ones were planned to succeed them. Pride doeth many things, and has built two halls in Belvidere in which any people might take pride.

Union Hall.—This hall is located in Union block, at the foot of State street, North Belvidere. The erection of the block of buildings of which it forms a part, was commenced in the spring of 1868, and completed in the fall of 1869. The hall proper is the property of a joint stock company, and cost $15,000. The main floor is supplied with one thousand chairs, and the gallery is provided with raised seats for five hundred persons. Besides, there are dressing rooms, a kitchen, and other conveniences that render it one of the most popular halls west of Chicago. Its interior finish is in good taste, and in keeping with the spirit that prompted its erection.

Adelphi Hall.—This hall is situated in South Belvidere, in what is known as the "Adelphi Block." The block of buildings in which it is located was built in 1864, by a joint stock company, and cost $15,000. The hall has seating accommodations for eight hundred persons. It is well finished, and in every respect first-class.

STATE STREET BRIDGE.

The first bridge built across the Kishwaukee river at the State street crossing was a wooden structure, in 1837. In 1840 the largest freshet ever known in the Kishwaukee valley came and carried it away. Another wooden bridge was erected, which stood until 1845, when it was likewise carried away by a flood. That in time was succeeded by a covered bridge, built by the county. William H. Gilman and Cornelius Cline were the contractor and builder. That bridge was built on bents, as it was supposed at that time that in consequence of the quicksand bottom, piles would be of no avail. In 1867 that bridge was condemned as unsafe, when it was torn down and replaced by the present wrought iron bridge. The contract for its erection was awarded, August 5, 1867, to L. E. Truesdell & Co. The bridge is known as the Truesdell patent. It was completed in November, 1867, at a cost of $15,115. The cost of its construction was covered by bonds, issued by authority of the corporation of Belvidere. These bonds have since been paid off, and no debt contracted for any purpose hangs over the tax payers of the corporation.

MANUFACTURING.

This branch of industry has never been prosecuted to any great extent. The moneyed men, capitalists, and property owners—men that ought to have been more directly interested in such enterprises than any other class, seem to have been more intent upon investing their money in loans at a good rate of interest—"ten per cent.," as their terms are ironically spoken of—than in aiding enterprises that would have had a tendency not only to increase the population by attracting operatives and capital, but in centering here a large trade that the building of manufacturing enterprises at other places has taken away. The business houses of Belvidere are sustained almost exclusively by the farmers of the county. There are no manufactories of any kind that give employment to more than a half-dozen men, and of these very few. And these few manufacture only to accommodate home demand. There is no good reason why woolen mills, cotton mills, manufactories of wooden implements, wagons, and everything else needed by farmers at home and abroad should not be maintained here as well as in many other localities in the state. They would prove as profitable here as elsewhere, and it has been a great oversight not to encourage them. But it is not our province to criticise the judgment, theory, or practice of this people on this or any other subject of local economy. However, it is but truth to add that nearly every plow, wagon, harrow, hay rake, chair, table, and every other thing down to a broom used on the farm or in the house, is imported from foreign points. A large average of broom corn is annually grown in the county, but instead of being manufactured here the largest part of it is sold to other points, made into brooms, and shipped back at the cost of the final purchaser. So of wool, etc.

The nearest approaches to the establishment and maintenance of manufacturing industries have been through individual enterprise and industry, and these may be briefly summarized.

S. Longcor's Plow Works were established in 1840. He makes a specialty of Longcor's Iron Beam Plows, Longcor's Silver Medal Stirring Plows, and Sod and Stubble Plows; also, Longcor's Improved Two-horse Cultivator and Pulverizer. He is an energetic citizen, and had he received that material encouragement the moneyed men were able to bestow—such encouragement as capitalists in other places extended to other mechanics and manufacturers—would have been able to manufacture thousands of these implements where he now makes but hundreds, and to give employment to hundreds of men where he now employs but one or two.

Pump Works.—The pump works of Junia Morse were established in 1857. He manufactures all kinds of wooden pumps, which find ready purchasers among the farmers of the county. His trade is strictly local.

Carriages, Buggies, etc.—In 1857, Woodruff & Dawson commenced the manufacture of carriages, buggies, etc., and employ six operatives. Their sales are not exclusively local, the character of their workmanship and finish having established for them a good reputation abroad.

E. J. Leach, wagon maker, established himself here in June, 1864, after coming out of the army. He has given employment to six men. He is a good mechanic, and ought to have been so encouraged as to now be able to employ a large number of workmen. In connection with his wood working department, he has a blacksmith and repair shop. His shops are sufficiently capacious to employ fifteen men.

J. List is also a manufacturer of wagons and carriages, commencing in 1855. He gives employment to five men.

J. V. Wing's carriage manufacturing establishment was commenced in 1849, and is the oldest of the kind in Belvidere.

J. H. Fellows' pump and machinery repair works were established in 1856. Pump making and machinery repairs are his specialties. In busy seasons he employs five men.

These complete the list of anything approaching the dignity of manufacturing establishments, unless we include the Butter Factory. This establishment was built in 1867, by Messrs. Terwilliger & Partridge, at a cost of $6,000, and was originally intended for a cheese manufactory. It was devoted to this business about eight years, making annually about 200,000 pounds. In 1870, Mr. Terwilliger sold his interest in the establishment to the present management, who are engaged in the manufacture of Butter.

The Big Thunder Mills might also be mentioned. This mill was built in 1845, by Alexander Neely and Harvey D. May, at a cost of $20,000. It has a capacity of one hundred barrels of flour per day. This property is now owned by L. Pitkin.

The first mill built here, in 1836, of which previous mention has been made, went down, before the demands of an increased and increasing population, in a few years, and in 1845 the present Baltic Mills, of Martyn, were erected by the Crosby Company, at a cost of $12,000. O. B. Derthick had charge of the mechanism.

The Belvidere Brewery was erected in 1854, by E. Whitforth, at a cost of $10,000. Its capacity is twenty barrels per day. It is now (Sept., 1877) operated by John Waldock.

One of the most ingenious mechanics is Mr. Charles Carpenter, a cabinet maker. He had on exhibition at the county fair a small box, 14 inches long, 9 inches wide, and 7 inches deep, that was a marvel of curiosity and handiwork. Thirteen different varieties of wood, and 3,927 *distinct and separate pieces were used in its make up.*

LODGES, ASSOCIATIONS, ETC.

Belvidere Lodge No. 60, A. F. & A. Masons.—Organized in 1847. Chartered by Grand Lodge, October 4, 1848.

Charter Members.—Alfred E. Ames, First Master; Orris Crosby, Nijah Hotchkiss, Lucius Fuller, Amos Witter, Asa Williams, Hezekiah Ripley, Joseph G. Prentiss. All dead.

Present Officers.—C. B. Loop, W. M.; C. L. Smith, S. W.; G. H. Hurlbut, J. W.; George W. Downs, Treas.; S. H. Moss, Sec.; E. B. Sherman, S. D.; O. Barnes, J. D.; W. H. Bennett, S. S.; Will Williams, J. S.; D. Wilcox, Tyler. Eighty-five members. Meet first and third Mondays in each month.

Kishwaukee Chapter No. 90, R. A. Masons.—Organized in 1865. Chartered October 5, A. D. 1866.

Charter Members.—A. W. Burnside, John B. Mulliken, Nijah Hotchkiss, Cephas Gardner, Charles B. Loop, Geo. W. Downs, Stephen A. Hurlbut, George B. Ames, L. E. Benson, W. C. Detrick, Nathan Smedley, Wm. D. Avery, D. D. Sabin, A. C. Fuller. Now numbers about fifty members.

Present Officers.—A. W. Burnside, H. P.; C. B. Loop, K.; C. E. Kelsey, S.; G. H. Hurlbut, P. S.; G. B. Ames, Sec. Meet first and third Wednesdays in each month.

Both societies are in flourishing circumstances, and occupy the whole third story of the brick block, corner of State and Mechanic streets. Their hall is beautifully furnished and is spacious and pleasant.

I. O. O. F.

Big Thunder Lodge No. 28. Organized April 28, 1847. Charter members: Daniel Hornell, B. A. J. Crosby, N. W. Birge, E. G. Wolcott, J. S. Whitney. Present officers: George Williamson, N. G.; D. J. Edgecomb, V. G.; E. H. Reynolds, Sec.; Wm. Haywood, Treas.; Wm. Robinson, P. G. J.; George Davy, Warren; H. T. Lake, Conductor; Jas. Morse, R. S. N. G.; Jacob Seibert, L. S. N. G.; M. C. Morse, R. S. V. G.; John Barney, L. S. V. G.; L. C. Lewis, R. S. S.; H. W. Ames, L. S. S.; W. Manin, I. G.; Geo. W. Dean, O. G. This order has ninety members. Regular meetings, Saturday evening of each week.

GOOD TEMPLARS.

The Star in the West Lodge, No. 421, I. O. of G. T., was organized Dec. 7, 1874, with a membership of thirteen, and is the only temperance organization in successful operation in the city. This lodge has adopted the same name, and uses the same seal and fixtures which were used by the Good Templars' Lodge instituted Jan. 28, 1862, and was successfully conducted until 1868, and at one time was the most popular social organization in the city. The present lodge has a membership of fifty-nine, a number of whom have been reclaimed from the evils of intemperance, and are now respected by the community. The following are the present officers of the lodge: J. G. Stevens, L. D.; Colby M. Avery, W. C. T.; Stella Foote, W. V. T.; E. S. Pepper, W. S.; T. L. Ray, W. A. S.; Jas. Smedley, W. F. S.; Mrs. Mary A. Worf, W. T.; Chas. A. Church, W. M.; Carrie Bush, W. A. M.; Zora Graham, W. C.; Mary Tumeaure, R. H. S.; Jessie Talbot, L. H. S.; Libbie Collier, W. G.; E. Whitworth, W. S.; Wm. Robinson, P. W. C. T. Regular meetings Monday evening of each week.

THE PRESS.

The Belvidere *Republican* (Whig) was commenced in 1847, by J. W. Snow. The press and type were brought from Woodstock. It lived about two years (until 1849), when it succumbed to fast accumulating debts, like most ventures of the sort. It is a notorious fact that more money and time are lost in the attempt to establish newspapers in new country towns than in almost any other undertaking. And this in face of the fact that no other agency can be made so useful in presenting the advantages, or made so potent in advancing local interests, as a well-conducted newspaper. But we are writing history. The last number of the *Republican* was printed on brown paper.

The *Republican* was succeeded by the Belvidere *Standard*, which was commenced in 1851, by its present manager and proprietor, Ralph Roberts, Esq., and is one of the oldest papers in Northern Illinois, (except one in Galena) having remained nearly twenty-six years under one proprietorship. The *Standard* was maintained as an exponent and advocate of Democratic principles up to the organization of the Republican party in 1856, the proprietor, Mr. Roberts, being a delegate to the Bloomington Convention of that period that nominated Bissell for governor. Since its commencement, the *Standard* has had a good circulation, and fair advertising patronage. Mr. Roberts is a practical printer, of industrious habits, close economist (a rare virtue among printers), a deep thinker, and a close observer of passing events. And when fully enlisted upon any question, wields a caustic and ready pen.

In 1873, Mr. Roberts was appointed by Governor Beveridge as one of the Illinois Commissioners to the Vienna exposition, but, for reasons satisfactory to himself, did not honor the appointment by going to the exposition.

Several attempts were made to establish newspapers in Belvidere, but only two of them proved successful undertakings—the *Standard* and the *North-Western*. Of these ventures, the following is a record:

Two or three numbers of a weekly paper were issued by Prof. Gower, about 1859. These were printed in Rockford.

The Belvidere *Independent* (Rep.), by J. N. Brockway, afterwards Post-master, for some years.

The Belvidere *Union* (Rep.), by —— Jackson, which weathered the storm for a year or two.

The Boone County *Democrat*, by —— Wilson, which lived through the presidential campaign of 1864.

The Boone County *Advertiser*, by W. H. Cadwell, lived two or three years, when the office was removed to Rock Falls, where it is used by Messrs. Cadwell & Tuttle in the publication of the *Progress*.

The publication of the *Daily Index* was undertaken by W. C. Coates, in 1875. It was published two or three months, when the enterprise was abandoned.

Another small sheet, called *Students' Thought Leaves*, was undertaken by J. N. Brockway, but only two numbers were published, and it went to join its predecessors.

The *North-Western* was commenced in January, 1867, by E. H. Talbot, Esq., as editor and proprietor. In 1870, the office, good will, etc., were purchased by Mr. R. W. Coon, by whom the paper is still continued. This paper was first printed in rooms over George B. Ames' store. In 1869, the office was removed to Charles Dean's building, near the railroad track. In 1875, it was again removed, and at last found a resting place in commodious and elegant quarters in Sabin's building, at the head of State street. The business of the paper has been carefully and judiciously managed, and as a local newspaper, it ranks well among its contemporaries in Northern Illinois. It has always enjoyed a large subscription and job patronage.

The office is well fitted up with presses, type, etc. It is republican in politics.

HOTELS.

The first hotel was Doty's "Belvidere House," a small log house erected in the fall of 1835. The next season (1836) he built a larger one, on the lot occupied by Williams' drug store. The flooring used in his first house was the first sawed lumber ever hauled from Chicago to Gen. Scott's crossing of the Kishwaukee. Since then Mr. Doty has kept hotel almost continuously, following State street down to the river, and finally crossed it, and keeping the old name, is now located just south of the bridge.

In 1838, John K. Towner built a hotel near the present site of the residence left to his widow. That was christened the "Big Thunder Hotel," and the wooden sign bearing the name of the house was surmounted by a big sheet-iron Indian. The opening was a grand affair, and attended by all the elite of the city, as well as by guests from abroad. In time that gave way and others followed.

During the summer of 1842, the American House, a two-story frame, was built by William H. Gilman. In November or December it was opened with great éclat by B. F. Lawrence and H. C. Walker. At the time it was the grandest hotel between Chicago and Freeport and Galena. The opening was in keeping with the house. Guests were present from Chicago (among whom were Long John), Freeport, Elgin, Sycamore, etc. Lawrence and Walker continued as mine hosts for about a year, when they retired. The present proprietor is William Anderson, who is now under his third lease. He first occupied it in 1861, and continued its management for about one year, when, in the fall of 1862, he bought the furniture and good will of the Julien House, where he remained not quite a year, sold out and removed to Rockford. In 1864 he came back to the American and remained about three years, when he sold and went to Madison, Wis. In May, 1877, he found his way back to the old stand, and took a lease of the house for four years, refurnishing it throughout. The property is owned by Terwilliger and Perkins.

The Julien House.—About twenty-five years ago a three-story and basement brick building 20x40 feet, with an L 25x60, was built at what is now the corner of State and Main streets, South Belvidere, by a Mr. Mauler, for hotel purposes. In time, this property passed into the ownership of a Mr. Downer, of Boston. In August, 1865, Robert J. Traver came here from Iowa and purchased this property from Mr. Downer, and entered upon the hotel business. A short time after assuming charge of the Julien, R. J. Tousley married his only child and daughter, and became associated with him in business. In 1869 the popularity of the house had so increased that enlarged quarters became necessary, and the erection of the present stone front, 44x72 feet (three stories and basement), was commenced. In 1870 it was completed and opened at a cost of about $15,000. This addition gave them about seventy-five rooms and otherwise enlarged hotel conveniences. In the spring of 1875, Mr. Traver sold a half interest in the house to H. J. Sheldon, and the firm became Tousley & Sheldon, Mr Traver retiring to the shades of private life.

BANKING INTERESTS.

The First National Bank of Belvidere, Illinois, organized May, 1865. Capital, one hundred thousand dollars. Allen C. Fuller was elected President; B. F. Lawrence, elected Vice President; Newel C. Tomkins, elected Cashier; James S. Terwilliger, Teller. Allen C. Fuller, B. F. Lawrence, Mark Ramsey, Wm. S. Dunton, Ezra May, Geo. Waterman, John Yourt, Isaac T. Witbeck, Newel C. Tomkins, were elected directors.

Jan. 10, 1866, B. F. Lawrence declining a re-election to the office of vice-president, Mark Ramsey was elected to fill that office.

Feb. 26, 1866, James S. Terwilliger was appointed assistant cashier, and John C. Neely, teller.

Jan. 8, 1867, James S. Terwilliger was elected cashier in place of Newel C. Tomkins, resigned.

Jan. 11, 1867, Allen C. Fuller resigned the office of president.

Feb. 27, 1867, Mr. H. B. Sykes was appointed teller in place of John C. Neely, resigned.

At a special meeting of the directors held March 14, 1867, Mark Ramsey was unanimously elected president, Mr. Ramsey declining to accept the position. At a subsequent meeting held March 25, 1867, Wm. S. Dunton was elected president.

Sept. 28, 1868, Mr. Irving Terwilliger was appointed teller in place of H. B. Sykes, resigned, and on April 24, 1871, was appointed assistant cashier.

The present officers of the bank are: William S. Dunton, president; Mark Ramsey, vice-president; James S. Terwilliger, cashier; Irving Terwilliger, assistant cashier. Directors: Wm. S. Dunton, Mark Ramsey, James S. Terwilliger, Allen C. Fuller, Edward F. Lawrence, Isaac T. Witbeck, John M. Glasner, John Yourt, Ezra May.

The average amount of deposits of this bank are much less than they would be from the fact that the management have rigidly adhered to the rule of not paying interest on deposits. The annual amount of business done through the bank cannot be accurately stated, but since its organization has been many millions.

The stockholders have cause to congratulate themselves upon the success of the management of the bank, as the losses upon discounts since its organization have been less than one hundred dollars.

Yost, Lawrence & Co.—This banking house is located in South Belvidere. The association was organized July 15, 1874, and is composed of twenty-two members.

The business of this bank is conducted by a board of five directors. The present directors are Ezra May, J. T. Whitbeck, W. S. Duncan, Mark Ramsey and J. S. Terwilliger. This board is elected annually.

BELVIDERE CEMETERY.

If the people of Boone County are proud of any one thing more than another, it is of the order in which the Belvidere cemetery is kept. The Association was incorporated A. D. 1847—John K. Towner, Asher E. Jenner and William T. Burgess being the incorporate members. The original cemetery plot was on the north line of the original town plot of Belvidere, and included about four acres of ground. Since that time two additions have been made, increasing the area to about fifteen acres, enclosed with a substantial fence. The grounds are laid off in lots and blocks, divided by alleys and avenues, and beautifully decorated with evergreens and other shrubbery, and an experienced florist steadily employed to trim and train them and keep the grounds in order. Here is evidenced the spirit and pride of the people by whom it is maintained.

"*Hic jacet requiescat.*"

BONUS.

This is a Latin phrase, meaning good, hence the name of this township. Christopher Payne was the first settler in this township. In the fall of 1835 he came up from Dupage County, and located a claim on Squaw Prairie, a part of which claim he subsequently (in 1836) sold to Oliver Hale. Payne had erected a cabin, and broken an acre or two of prairie. This breaking was included in that part of the claim sold to Mr. Hale, and was probably the first land cultivated in the township. In September, 1836, L. W. Lawrence came in, when he found the following settlers present: Oliver Hale, O. Sands, Benjamin Sweet, Melvin Schenck, Geo. B. Ames, John Sponable, David H. Sackett, James Shinn and Christopher Payne—ten, all told, including Mr. Lawrence. At that time what is now called Bonus township was included in the Belvidere precinct. The elections were held in Belvidere, at the house of Simon P. Doty, and the citizens went there to vote. Soon after the organization of the county, territory of Bonus township was erected into a separate precinct, and named Deerfield. By this name it continued to be known until the adoption of the township organization system, when the name was changed to Bonus. The first election in the Deerfield precinct for justices of the peace, etc., was held at the house of John Herbert, and John Lawrence (father of L. W. Lawrence) and Hiram Stow were elected justices.

The first child born was William Shinn, son of James Shinn. The first death was that of Billy Ames, in August, 1837. The first school taught was by Mrs. Lydia Lawrence (mother of L. W.). She deprecated the idea of children growing up in ignorance and comparative idleness, and gathered them together in the capacity of a school. The school house was the *shade of a large white oak tree.* The seats were the ground. As the shade shifted, the school house and its furniture was moved, but always "took up" at the same place. With knitting in hand, giving her services *free*, she heard lessons recited. This was the *first* free school in Boone County. The first school house in the township was built of hewed logs, near the residence of James Shinn, on section seven, in the fall of 1838. In 1841, another school house, was built—a frame one. At a Sunday night meeting, after preaching, Mr. L. W. Lawrence gave notice that on the Monday evening following a meeting would be held to devise ways and means to build a school house. At that meeting a sufficient sum was subscribed to build the house, and in just two weeks from that Monday morning, it was completed, and Mr. Lawrence opened school with forty scholars. That was enterprize. His salary was $12.00 per month, to board himself and collect his own tuition bills—the school being maintained by private subscription.

The winter of 1837 was a hard one on the settlers in the Lawrence neighborhood. Provisions were scarce, and money a good deal scarcer. In the Lawrence cabin, all in one room, seventeen persons domiciled that winter. Their food for the most part was bean porridge, made without meat or seasoning of any kind, except a little salt. A crop of potatoes had been raised, but bread was a rarity, and flour and corn meal difficult to obtain.

Bonus Township is a Grange stronghold, and one of the most successful Granges in the State is in prosperous working condition. It was organized in the winter of 1873, and is known as Bonus Grange No. 908. The following are the officers: O. S. Nichols, Master; S. C. Fox, Overseer; M. W. Poyer, Steward; J. D. Rosekrans, Mrs. O. S. Nichols, Assistant Stewards; M. K. Avery, Lecturer; A. C. Fassett, Chaplain; J. O. Rosekrans, Gate Keeper; Mrs. M. K. Avery, Ceres; Mrs. J. Cronk, Pomona; Mrs. M. W. Poyer, Flora; J. J. Roper, Secretary; James W. Porter, Treasurer.

There are in the township eight school houses and full districts and four fractional districts. The population is about 1,300.

Garden Prairie is the only village in the township. It is situated on the Galena division of the C. & N. W. R. R., and is an outgrowth of that thoroughfare, having been laid off about the time of the completion of that road, in 1851-2, by David H. Sackett, one of the pioneer settlers. The present population is about 200. There are two stores, two blacksmith shops, one wagon shop, a lumber yard, hotel, post-office, and two churches, Methodist and Congregational. The first Methodist class was organized in 1843, by Rev. R. H. Blanchard, and was composed of Captain Boomer, a part of his family, and Parmelia Hyde. The class met with a good many crosses, although it managed to keep up its organization and had occasional preaching by Rev. Mr. Cassidy, and ministers of other denominations. In 1864, the class was re-organized by Rev. A. P. Mead. Mr. Mead was succeeded by Rev. Mr. Adams, he in turn, by conference rules, by Rev. S. Cates. In 1868, the Rock River conference, in session at Kankakee, appointed Rev. W. P. Jordan to the work. Since then the preachers in succession have been: Rev. J. A. Lovejoy, Rev. William Clark, Rev. Edwin Brown, Rev. John Bacon and the present pastor, Rev. Leonard Clifford. In 1872, the congregation built a church, at a cost of $2,250. The prime movers in this undertaking were Daniel R. Payne, Jirah Payne, and G. W. Newell.

The Congregational Church was organized May 8, 1858. Their house of worship was built in 1860, at a cost of $1,600. The pastors in succession have been: Revs. N. C. Clark, John B. Fairbank, B. M. Amsden, S. C. Hamson, and D. J. Baldwin.

The Garden Prairie Lodge of Good Templars, No. 115, was organized June 20, 1877, and bids fair for great usefulness. The lodge numbers thirty-six members. Their meetings are held on Tuesday evening of each week.

BOONE.

Under the old organization, this township was included in Beaver precinct. Our sketch of it will of necessity be brief, from the fact of our inability to find the necessary data upon which to base as extended a notice as we would like. Its settlement commenced in 1836-7. During these years, however, the immigration was light, but in the latter part of 1837 and early part of 1838, the increase was rapid. The first settlers in the township of whom we can find any trace were a Mr. Barker, Bradford Dean, and a Mr. Putney, who located at or near what is now known as Poplar Grove, on the Madison branch of the Chicago & Northwestern R. R. Mr. Dean was the first school teacher, and although the house was just across the line in what is now Caledonia Township, the most of his pupils belonged in

CAPRON.

Boone. This school is said to have been taught in the winter of 1838-9. Mr. Dean was also the first Justice of the Peace.

Poplar Grove.—This village was laid out in 1859 by I. Evi Sherman. A part of the village is in Caledonia Township, and was originally called Shermantown. The present population is about 200. The business is represented by two stores that keep a general stock of dry goods, etc., one hardware store, lumber yard, a confectionery establishment, etc., two blacksmith and wagon shops, shoemaker shop, hotel, and one grain elevator. There is a good graded school and two churches. Poplar Grove is quite an important local shipping point for grain and stock.

In 1842, a Methodist class was organized by Rev. R. A. Blanchard, and in 1864 a house of worship was erected, costing about 2,000. The church now has a membership of about sixty persons, and a flourishing Sabbath-school, of which George Dean is the Superintendent. Rev. G. L. S. Stuff is present pastor.

April 21st, 1858, a Presbyterian Church was formed in Boone Township. Rev. H. B. Holmes, Rev. Morrison Huggins, committee from the Belvidere Presbytery, and R. J. S. Emery, missionary, were present, and conducted the exercises. Bradford Dean, Mrs. Relief Dean, Mrs. Mary Cowan, Mrs. Agnes Roe, Mrs. Isabella Maskey, Mrs. Jane Robinson, Mrs. Anna Warren, Mrs. Susannah Warren, Richard Warren, William Warren, George Warren, Henry Warren, Tisdell Dean and John Warren, gave a relation of their Christian experience, which was satisfactory to the committee, and they were constituted a church society—to be known as the First Presbyterian (N. S.) of Caledonia. Dean's school house was fixed upon as a place of worship, because of its convenience to the society. In 1863, the society re-organized under the "manual, usages, principles, and doctrines of the Congregational Church." At the meeting under which this organization was effected, Rev. S. W. Champion was Moderator and George R. Warren, Clerk. That season they inaugurated measures to build a church, and by the 22d day of June, 1864, the building (30x45 feet) was completed and dedicated. The dedication services were conducted as follows: Introductory prayer, by Rev. Mr. Smith, of the M. E. Church; sermon, by Rev. Mr. Goodwin, of Rockford; dedicatory prayer, by Rev. Mr. Thompson, of Belvidere; evening sermon, by Rev. Mr. Ray, of Chicago.

On the 28th of November, Mr. Champlin preached his farewell sermon, and was succeeded by Rev. D. W. Comstock, who was followed by Rev. Levi Wheaton, who continued with the society nearly five years, but September 20th, 1871, the society "concluded to drop Mr. Wheaton, and try a student or some one else, and invite him to supply, if we had no one else." At a subsequent business meeting of the society a committee was appointed to draft resolutions of recommendation and present them to Mr. Wheaton at the close of his pastorate. The next pastor was Rev. M. S. Hall, who commenced his labors Feb. 18, 1872, and remained until Jan. 19th, 1873. Rev. Mr. Kidder came next, and remained with the society until his death, in December, 1874. His remains were taken to Beloit, Wisconsin, for burial. Samuel Kidder (son of the deceased) filled the pulpit for a few Sabbaths after the death of his father, and on May 30, 1875, he was engaged for fourteen weeks. Rev. Mr. Wadsworth succeeded Mr. Kidder. The 5th of January, 1877, their church building was destroyed by fire, but they immediately rebuilt, at a cost of $2,000, Rev. Mr. Easton, of Belvidere, preaching the dedicatory sermon, on Wednesday, September 19, 1877. The society numbers fifty-two members, with a good Sabbath-school. The society is now known as the First Congregational Church of Poplar Grove.

Capron is a village of about 300. It has six dry good stores, three grocery and provision stores, hotel, two good grain elevators, a fine school house, employing an able corps of teachers, two fine churches, with good congregations, good Sabbath-schools, etc. There is a Masonic Lodge, in good working condition. The Capron *Independent*, a weekly newspaper, was an experiment of a few years, but did not succeed satisfactorily. As a shipping point, Capron is a place of local importance. More grain and stock is shipped from Capron than from any other point in the county except Belvidere.

CALEDONIA.

Under the old-time regulations, the three present townships of Caledonia, Boone and LeRoy were known as Beaver precinct. The town of Manchester was known and designated as Manchester precinct. In August, 1838, David Drake and his brother, Abram Drake, of New Hampshire, came to the southwest part of Beaver precinct, where each of them located claims. Previous to that time, there were but few settlers in the precinct, and none in that part of it now known as Caledonia. Between the 1st of September and the 31st day of December, 1838, the following named settlers came in and settled claims: Michael S. Taplin, Abijah Story, Jas. Ramsey, Thomas Ramsey and Widow Nancy Stevens. January 1, 1839, the population was about twenty-five persons. During 1839 there were the following accessions: Enoch O. Garland and family, Allen Carpenter, Dr. Calvin Cass and family, Philemon DeGroff and family, Benjamin Guile, Robert Morgan and family, Isaac Sewell and wife, Steven Covey and family, John Bruce and family, John Picken and family, George Picken and family, and Charles Whiting and family. There may have been others, but before a record of the old settlers was made, they had moved away, and the date of their coming is lost. So far as known, the above record covers the population December 31, 1839. In 1840, immigrants began coming in large numbers. In 1839 the lands had been opened to sale, and the natural richness and beauty of the county attracted the attention of people hunting new homes. Of the settlers of 1838, Abram Drake and wife, Mrs. Stevens (now aged seventy-six years), and three sons (one of them in Wisconsin), five of the Ramsey family, and Michael S. Taplin, only, are living.

In June, 1839, a petition was presented to the County Commissioners' Court, signed by all the voters in town 45, N., R. 3 East, asking that it be set off from Beaver precinct, in consequence of the distance voters had to travel to reach the usual place of holding elections. The prayer of the petitioners was granted, and the township or precinct designated on the county record as Caledonia, a name selected by the petitioners. The first election was held at the house of David Drake, on the east half of the southeast quarter of section 34, now owned and occupied by a man named Winne.

At that election, two justices of the peace and two constables were elected—Timothy Barker and Abram Drake, and David Drake and Wm.

Streeter were elected constables. Mr. Drake served as justice of the peace for ten years in succession. During the administration of John Tyler, as President of the United States, Squire Drake was appointed post-master of Precinct P. O.—an office established some time about the latter part of 1842 or the beginning of 1843. He held that office for ten years, keeping the office in his residence, a log house, still standing, and until the Madison Division of the C. & N. W. R. R. was completed and the office removed to Caledonia Station. In September, 1841, the township was divided into four school districts, and numbered one, two, three and four. The school-trustees at that time were Abram Drake, Edward Hawley and Robert Morgan. William Frank was appointed their treasurer. The first school house was built in District No. 3, and was of logs. At the first enumeration of children of proper school age in District No. 1, there were 20; District No. 2, 11; District No. 3, 30; District No. 4, 26; all told in this township, 87. The first school taught was in 1841-2, and was supported by private subscription. It was kept at the residence of Philemon DeGroff, and Miss Axie Knox was the teacher. There are now eleven public school houses and districts in the township, and four fractional districts, that are attached to other townships for school purposes. There is one church building, the Little Bethel, in the township. It was built by the Free Methodists, in 1868, but is now owned and occupied by the American Wesleyan Methodists. Caledonia village is an outgrowth of the Madison Division of the C. & N. W. R. R. There are two stores, a few shops, etc., and a good school building, that also serves the purpose of a church. Caledonia has furnished but few criminal cases. Only one murder stains its good name. June 28, 1852, Rufus Guile shot and killed Leonard Van Alstine. Guile was arrested, tried, convicted, and sent to the penitentiary for seven years.

During the ten years that Mr. Drake served as justice of the peace, he solemnized seventeen marriages. They were in the following order:

Oct. 16, 1840, William Story to Miss Anna Outcalt. This marriage was in Belvidere township. The groom was a resident of Caledonia, and the bride lived just across the township line, in Belvidere. Fee, $1.25.

On the 22d of the same month, David R. Gardner and Miss Sarah Bruce. This was the first marriage in the township. Mr. Gardner is still living, and clerk of a county court in Nebraska.

Feb. 18, 1841, Albert Holt and Miss Laura Story. Are living at Stockbridge, Calumet Co., Wisconsin.

Feb. 8, 1845, Wm. Howard and Mrs. Mary Ann Little. These parties are still living in Caledonia township. At the same time and place, Isaac Tyson and Miss Mary Postlethwaite. Both deceased, and buried in Belvidere cemetery.

March 30, 1845, Christopher Burrell and Mrs. Elizabeth J. Irwin. Removed to Canada, and still living.

Sept. 19, 1846, Jas. C. Hammond and Miss Fannie J. Turner. Removed to Iowa, and still living.

Oct. 31, 1846, Amasa S. Ireland and Miss Cynthia Dupuy. This marriage was not a happy one, and a separation ensued. Mr. Ireland went to California, since when all trace of him has been lost. Mrs. Ireland remarried, and subsequently removed to Minnesota.

Jan. 27, 1847, Lorin Turneaure and Miss Louisa E. Cline. Removed to Iowa; subsequently returned to Boone, where Mr. Turneaure died. His wife is still living.

Jan. 25, 1848, Rufus R. Turner and Mrs. Francis R. Knight. Left Caledonia twenty years ago for the Black River country, Wisconsin; subsequently removed to Iowa, where they are still living.

Feb. 26, 1848, Davis Bates and Mrs. Clarissa Joshlin. Both died in Boone County.

April 19, 1848, Rollin G. Story and Miss Charlotte M. Knox. Mr. Story enlisted in the army, and was run over and killed by a train of cars. His widow and children removed to and are now living in Iowa.

Oct. 1, 1848, Peter Hostrawser to Miss Mary Dill. Mr. Hostrawser died a few years after marriage, and his widow removed from the State.

Nov. 15, 1848, Solomon Terwilliger and Miss Esther A. Powell. Removed to Iowa ten years ago, where they are still living.

March 27, 1849, Orville S. Stevens and Miss Caroline M. Irwin. Mrs. Stevens died in Caledonia, in the winter of 1876-7. Mr. Stevens still lives on the old place.

Aug. 12, 1849, Jas. W. Outcalt to Mrs. Electa Ann Gilbert. Mrs. Outcalt died twenty years ago. Mr. Outcalt re-married, and removed from the State about two years ago.

Nov. 17, 1849, Henry P. Seldon and Miss Jane Ellis. These parties were strangers to Mr. Justice Drake. They were en route for Wisconsin, procured their marriage license at Belvidere as they passed through, stopped at Mr. Drake's residence, five and a half miles out, and were made man and wife, started from there on their honeymoon trip, and have never since been heard of.

The first birth, according to the best sources of information, was a son to Isaac and Mary Sewell, May 20, 1840. The second was a daughter to John Erwin, Aug. 3, 1840; and the third, a son to Robt. and Eliza Morgan, Nov. 9, 1840.

The first death was that of Solomon Story, which occurred in December, 1838, a short time after his settlement in the township.

FLORA.

The name of this township is derived from the primitive beauty of the landscape. Originally, it was an open, rather undulating prairie. In spring time it was bedecked and bespangled with myriads of flowers of every conceivable hue and color—the admiration of every beholder. The first settlers were Indianans, the later ones from New York and the New England States. Arthur Blood settled in what is now the township of Flora in the fall of 1835, and was the first white settler. In 1836, a Mr. Penwell, A. M. McCoy, a large family by the name of Russell, Abel R. Blood, the Case family, and Peter Nichols, came in and settled down to the work of making homes. The first Justice of the Peace was Daniel Bliss. His successor was Walter Rice. The first Constable was Reuben Russell. The first school was taught in the winter of 1836-7, by Daniel Bliss. The building was an old log house that stood on what is now the land of R. G. Norton. It was the only school house for many miles around, and children attended from DeKalb County. Walter Lucas has the honor of being the first white child born in the township, but that was long before the adoption of the township system and while the territory was designated as a precinct. His wife, Edna Cushman, was the first female infant to put in an appearance and lay claim to recognition and citizenship, and it was only fitting that in later years Mr. Lucas should take her to wife.

The first religious society was of the Christian denomination, but the first sermon preached was by Rev. Father Gaddis, at the house of Reuben Penwell. Father Gaddis was a well known Methodist preacher in the earlier days of Methodism in this part of Illinois, and his memory is held in high esteem by *all* the early settlers of the Kishwaukee country, regardless of religious preferences.

The precinct became a township under the township organization law, and ranks among the foremost in the point of good morals, obedience to law, intelligence, etc., in Northern Illinois. It was twenty-five years after the first settlement before a single case found its way from that part of Boone County into the Circuit Court, and only three suits were sent up and docketed in forty years. What other township can say as much?

As a guard against perambulating depredators, the citizens of Flora have a vigilance association, and every man watches his neighbor's property as carefully as he does his own. Wide awake, honest, determined, intelligent and industrious people, naturally a rich garden spot, it is but reasonable that Flora should be what it is—a township of great floral beauty and attractiveness.

In 1859, the people of Flora Township, and those of North Franklin Township, DeKalb County, living adjacent to the county line, united and built a church edifice that is known as the Union Church. The building is a frame structure, and cost $1,800. The leading men in this undertaking were Alfred Banks, E. J. Pullen, Lewis Keith, John Bailey, Samuel McKee, James Farley, and Adam Klein. Elder W. P. Gray preached the dedicatory sermon. Rev. W. D. Skelton, Methodist Episcopal, at that time was laboring on that circuit, and Rev. Joseph Gifford, a preacher of the Free-Will Baptist faith, was the pastor of that people. Rev. Mr. Freeman, a Wesleyan Methodist, was also laboring among the people at the time, and occupied the building in common with the other denominations. The present pastors are, Rev. A. H. Scoonmaker, Methodist Episcopal, and Rev. Mr. Vandoren, Wesleyan Methodist.

Flora Grange, No. 526, was organized June 26, 1873. It has a good hall, and is in good working order. The officers are: F. I. Hall, W. M.; F. S. Weber, W. O.; Laura Bowen, W. L.; Samuel Robinson, Steward; W. I. Graves, W. A. Steward; Joseph Witter, W. C.; Lydia Graves, W. Treas.; G. H. Graves, W. Sec.; Edwin Dean, G. K.; Cassie M. Lambert, Ceres; Abbie Hall, Pomona; Ella Delavergne, Flora; Ellen Gallagher, Assistant Steward; Maggie Russell, Chorister. Grange meets every Saturday night.

One thing in Flora excites curiosity. When first settled bowlders or surface rocks were unknown. As the country has grown older and been subjected to cultivation, these bowlders have appeared, some of them so large and heavy that two good horses can not move them. Where did they come from? Has some internal action of the earth forced them to the surface? These are questions for scientists to answer. On the farms of Messrs. J. V. Draper, J. I. Witbeck, and J. T. Witbeck, many of these bowlders are to be seen.

LEROY.

This township in early times was first known and designated as Lambertson precinct. The first claims were made by James B. and Jeremiah A. Lambert, in the fall of 1836. These men were unmarried, and made their home in Bonus Prairie. The first actual settlers were John Langdon and family, and his brothers, who settled in a grove at the northeast corner of Long Prairie, in the fall of 1836, where they built the first cabin in the township. The wife of John Langdon died in the winter of 1837-8. This was the first death among the settlers of the township. She was buried in the corner of the grove. Soon after the Langdons came in, four brothers by the name of Chamberlain made a claim on Round Prairie, where one of them (Joseph) is still living. These brothers were all single men, and worked around wherever they could find work to do. In April, 1837, John Wright and family also made a claim in Round Prairie, and built the first house in Round Prairie. Mr. Wright is still living on the same land where he first settled, at the ripe old age of seventy-eight years. In the fall of 1837, Levi Hammon and family settled at the southwest part of Round Prairie, and here in April, 1838, the first sermon preached in the township, was delivered by Rev. L. S. Walker, of the Methodist Episcopal church. Mr. Walker continued to preach in the neighborhood every four weeks for about one year. In the winter of 1838-9 a school house was built near the residence of Mr. Hammon, in which a school was taught in the summer of 1839. This school house was also used as a place of worship for two or three years.

The first election in the precinct was held at the house of John Wright, in August, 1837. James B. Lambert, John Wright and Allen Carpenter were judges of the election. Only twelve votes were polled, but the polls were not closed till late in the evening, and it was well on towards morning of the next day before the votes were counted and the tally sheet made out. John Wright and James B. Lambert were elected justices of the peace, and Gibson Wright and Alfred Chamberlain, constables. At the next election for constables, Ormond Haydon, the owner of the only horse in the township, and that was a brindled ox, was elected. This ox had been broken to the saddle, was a fast trotter, making 3:20 in the *slough*, and because of the possession of this animal, he was chosen as constable.

The first church was built by the Methodist Episcopal society, in 1862, at Union Corners, at a cost of $2,500. It will seat about three hundred persons. It is a good building, the only church edifice in the township, a credit thereto, as well as to the people that built and maintain it.

The first post-office was established in 1839, and was called Amazon. It was located on the southwest corner of section twenty-seven. Robert B. Hurd was appointed post-master, and held the office till his death, about 1848-9. In January, 1848, another post-office was established in the northeast part of the township, and called Burton's Corners. Benjamin P. Patton was appointed post-master. Mr. Patton held this office until the completion of the C. & N. W. Railway through to Sharon, Wisconsin, when the office was removed to Sharon, and he resigned.

Three good cheese factories are in successful operation in this township, employing an aggregate capital of $30,000. The population of the township is about 1,500, and strictly agricultural in their pursuits.

MANCHESTER.

When Boone County was organized this township was designated as Manchester precinct. The first settlements were made about 1836-7, but the settlers of 1836 were but few. The first settlers of whom we can get any direct knowledge were Rolin Gray, a Mr. Hammon (whose first name is lost), Alvin Cady, William Ward and Luther Linderman. Of these, Rollin Gray and Luther Linderman are the only ones remaining in the township.

The first justices of the peace were Rossel Campbell and Hiram Hopkins; first constable, Amasa Nobles. The first school in the precinct was taught by Mary Jane Campbell, wife of Horace Campbell. It was taught in 1841, in a private house, now the property of William Peters, on section nine. Mr. A. B. Wadsworth was the first post-master, and the name of the post-office entered upon the postal records as Hunter. It was established about 1844. His successor was William Wadsworth.

The first church organized in the township was by the Methodist Episcopal people, in 1839, when Rev. Leander Walker and Nathan Jewett instituted a class. William Linderman, Luther Linderman and W. Wood were the active members of this class. Services were held in private residences until the building of school houses, since when they have been used as places of worship. At one time $1,300 had been subscribed to build a church edifice, but some dissensions arising as to the choice of a location, the enterprise fell through, and the school house at Fisher's Corners is the regular place of meeting. The present pastor is Rev. George Hobbs; membership, twenty-four. There is no other church organization in the township.

The Grange has an organization known as the Manchester Grange No. 709. It was organized Nov. 7, 1873. R. G. Farrant is Worthy Master; Thomas Bamlet, Overseer; George Swensen, Steward; Wilson Bennett and Miss Mary L. Bennett, Assistant Stewards; A. H. Manly, Secretary; Luke Cass, Treasurer; W. W. Casper, Lecturer; B. F. Linderman, Chaplain; Melvin Hill, Gate Keeper; Mrs. R. H. Farrant, Ceres; Mrs. M. E. Hinkley, Pomona; Miss Flora Marston, Flora; membership, sixty-four. Meet on Saturday of or before the full of the moon.

SPRING.

Until the adoption of the township organization system, the territory embraced in Spring township was known as Ohio precinct. The first settlement was made in 1835 by John Handy, at what is now known as Reed's corners, four and a half miles east of south from Belvidere, and two miles west of Shattuck's Grove. In the early part of 1835, Alfred Shattuck and wife and two sons (Harlyn, aged twenty years, and F. H., aged about twelve), left Painesville, Geauga county, Ohio, to find a new home in Illinois. Arriving in Dupage county, twenty-seven miles from Chicago, they rented a farm from a man named Sweet, and raised a crop of corn. In the latter part of September of that year, Alfred Shattuck and his son, Harlyn, came out to the Kishwaukee country to select claims, which they made in the grove that bears their name. The elder Shattuck returned to Dupage county to take care of his crop, and Harlyn remained to prepare a cabin, make rails for fencing purposes, etc., boarding with John Handy, who had preceded them a few weeks, and who was already settled. The first work Harlyn did was to cut and gather some old grass of the previous year's growth on which to feed a yoke of cattle he had brought up from Dupage county. A small quantity of corn meal was mixed with this old grass and thus rendered a substitute for more substantial fodder. In February following the balance of the family came up. The log cabin for which Harlyn had cut the logs was soon after raised on the grounds occupied by Harlyn's present residence, of which the family took possession before fully completed. The doors, window casings, pantry shelving, etc., were made of bass wood puncheons dressed down. The flooring was made of the same kind of material. The roofing was made of oak clapboards, made by hand, and held in place by weight-poles, between which knees were placed to separate at the proper distances. At that date there were in that settlement, John Handy and family, Erastus Shattuck, wife, three sons and one daughter, and Alfred Shattuck and family (already mentioned); Erastus Shattuck and John Handy had come together in the summer before). At the time Alfred Shattuck's family moved into their new house, the last of February or first of March, 1836, there were not to exceed fifteen persons in the settlement. In the spring of 1836 the Blatchfords, Curtis Bros. and John Baxter joined the settlers. Of the Blatchfords there were the father, mother and three sons, Stephen, James and Francis. The Curtis Bros. were unmarried, and kept "bachelor's hall." McVeigh and Bruce came soon after, and Dr. Orris Crosby was the next one to put in an appearance. During that summer and fall there was quite a rush of immigrants to that neighborhood.

At the first election in the precinct, held at the house of Alfred Shattuck, in the spring of 1838, Alfred Shattuck and William M. Britt were judges; P. S. Crittenden and William Dresser were clerks. Alfred Shattuck and P. S. Crittenden were elected justices of the peace, offices which they continued to fill for several years. Stephen DeWolf and Ira Gould were elected constables.

The first school house in the township was a log structure, built on what is now the Gleason farm, in section twenty-one. Lucy Burnett was the first teacher. She afterwards became the wife of John Q. A. Rollins. P. S. Crittenden was the next teacher.

There are now ten school houses in the township, and four fractional, or union districts—that is, territory attached to districts in adjoining townships for school purposes.

Jennette Handy, daughter of John and Celinda Handy, has the honor to be the first female child born in the township. She married William Dawson, but died four years later.

The male claimants for a similar honor were Henry Crittenden and Owen Handy. Henry Crittenden grew to manhood's estate and married Laura Rue. At the breaking out of the war he enlisted with the Galena Zouaves, and was killed in the battle of Fort Donelson.

The first marriage was between Stephen Blatchford and Maria Bump.

Dr. Orris Crosby was the first physician to locate in the precinct, but he starved out in a year or two, and sought other fields for practice. Dr. Angell, now of Belvidere, also tried it once or twice, but finally located permanently in Belvidere.

There has never been a church building erected in the township, although religious services are frequent, the several school houses being open at all times for such purposes. A majority of the people attend divine service at Belvidere. Neither has there ever been a post-office established in the township.

The name of the township is derived from its great primitive beauty in spring time, and was so christened when the township organization system was adopted.

A little episode in the pioneer experience of Harlyn Shattuck may not be ill-timed in closing this sketch. In March, 1836, his oxen got tired of their fodder, and escaping from their enclosure, strayed away. Presuming they had gone towards Dupage county, from whence they had been brought, he started in pursuit in that direction. The cattle had some hours the start. The first night out, he stayed over night at the house of John Hamilton, in Pleasant Grove, twelve miles distant. A storm of rain and snow had come on, settling down into a regular hail of sleet and cold. When he reached the south fork of the north branch of the Kishwaukee, a small stream usually, but swollen by the late rains, it was a torrent of running (anchor) ice. His cattle had crossed the evening previous. It was eight miles to the nearest house in any direction. The storm was howling fitfully, and the wind and atmosphere piercingly cold. There was but one thing for Harlyn to do—cross the icy stream. But how? That was the question. There was neither canoe, dug-out nor raft. There was but one way of crossing, and that was to wade. To do so with his clothes on was only to invite death by freezing after he had crossed. But true to the energy and determination of his nature, he stripped to the "buff," and holding his clothes above his head, plunched into the icy bath and waded across, the water and ice coming up to his chin. He made the passage in safety, and by the time he had dressed himself after crossing, he was in a perfect perspiration. In speaking of the adventure now, he says it was a cold experience, but one that left no injurious influence. Resuming his tramp, he came up with his oxen on the bank of Fox river, about half way between Elgin and Dundee, where they had taken shelter from the storm in a grove of timber and underbrush. Such were the experiences of at least one of the early settlers of Spring township, now a thickly populated and wealthy municipality.

Names and Dates of Election of

SENATORS AND REPRESENTATIVES

REPRESENTING BOONE COUNTY IN THE GENERAL ASSEMBLY OF THE STATE OF ILLINOIS.

SENATORS.

Geo. W. Harrison, elected Aug., '38.
Ira Minard, elected Aug., 1842.
Elijah Wilcox, elected Aug., 1846.
Alfred E. Ames, elected Aug., 1848.
Thos. B. Talcott, elected Nov., 1852.
Waite Talcott, elected Nov., 1856.
Zenas Applington, elected Nov., '60.
Cornelius Lansing, elected November, 1864.
A. C. Fuller, elected Nov., 1868.
John Early, elected Nov., 1872.
John Early, elected Nov., 1876.

REPRESENTATIVES.

John Phelps, elected Aug., 1838.
Robt. J. Cross, elected Aug., 1838.
Thompson Campbell, elected Aug., 1840.
Thos. Drummond, elected Aug., '40.
Henry Madden, elected Aug., 1842.
Wm. M. Jackson, elected Aug., '42.
Wm. M. Jackson, elected Aug., '44.
James S. Loop, elected Aug., 1844.
E. G. Jewell, elected Aug., 1844.
George W. Kretsinger, elected Aug., 1846.
Jas. Harrington, elected Aug., '46.
James T. Pierson, elected Aug., '46.
John F. Gray, elected Aug., 1848.
Selby Leach, elected Aug., 1848.
A. H. Nixon, elected Nov., 1850.
George Gage, elected Nov., 1850.
H. C. Miller, elected Nov., 1852.
A. H. Nixon, elected Nov., 1852.
R. C. Miller, elected Nov., 1854.
A. H. Nixon, elected Nov., 1854.
S. W. Lawrence, elected Nov., 1856.
—— Diggins, elected Nov., 1856.
L. S. Church, elected Nov., 1858.
L. W. Lawrence, elected Nov., 1858.
L. S. Church, elected Nov., 1860.
S. A. Hurlbut, elected Nov., 1860.
S. A. Hurlbut, elected Nov., 1862.
L. S. Church, elected Nov., 1862.
W. W. Sedgwick, elected Nov., '64.
L. W. Lawrence, elected Nov., '64.
Allen C. Fuller, elected Nov., 1866.
Ira V. Randall, elected Nov., 1866.
S. A. Hurlbut, elected Nov., 1868.
Robert Hampton, elected Nov., '68.
Chas. W. Marsh, elected Nov., 1870.
E. H. Talbott, elected Nov., 1870.
Robert J. Cross, elected Nov., 1872.
Jesse S. Hurlbut, elected Nov., '72.
D. J. Stewart, elected Nov., 1872.
R. F. Crawford, elected Nov., 1872.
Andrew Ashton, elected Nov., 1874.
R. F. Crawford, elected Nov., 1874.
Myron K. Avery, elected Nov., '74.
Geo. H. Hollister, elected Nov., '76.
John Budlong, elected Nov., 1876.
Andrew Ashton, elected Nov., 1876.

CIRCUIT JUDGES.

Dan Stone, 1839 to 1841.
Thomas C. Brown, 1841 to 1847.
Jesse B. Thomas, 1847 to 1849.
Hugh Henderson, 1849 to 1851.
Isaac G. Wilson, 1851 to 1861.
Allen C. Fuller, 1861 to 1862, when, having been appointed Adjt. Gen. of the State by Richard Yates, Governor, he resigned the office of judge. Theodore D. Murphy was elected circuit judge in 1862, and still holds the office.

CIRCUIT CLERKS.

Seth S. Whitman, 1839 to 1849.
Noah W. Birge, 1849 to 1850, when he departed this life, and in April, 1850, Stephen C. Gooding was appointed clerk by Hugh Henderson, then circuit judge. Gooding held the office of clerk from 1850 to 1851.
Daniel T. Olney, 1851 to 1853.
Fayette B. Hamlin, 1853 to 1857.
Daniel H. Whitney, 1857 to Feb. 12, 1864, when he died.
Horatio C. DeMunn was appointed circuit clerk Feb. 15, 1864, and held the office until December, 1876, when James W. Sawyer, the present clerk, was elected.

STATE'S ATTORNEYS.

Shelton L. Hall, 1839 to 1843.
Joseph B. Wells, 1843 to 1845.
James L. Loop, 1845 to 1846.
Thomas L. Turner, 1846 to 1847.
W. A. Boardman, 1847 to 1849.
Alonzo Platt, 1849 to 1851.
P. W. Platt, 1851 to 1852.
Amos B. Coon, 1852 to 1853.
Millard M. Boyce, 1853 to 1857.
E. L. Joslyn, 1857 to 1861.
Amos B. Coon, 1861 to 1865.
Charles Kellum, 1869 to 1873.
Wales W. Wood, 1873 to 1876.
Charles E. Fuller was elected in 1876, and now holds the office.

RECORD OF COUNTY AND TOWN OFFICERS, ETC.

The following is an official record of the public officers of Boone County, from the first election on the first Monday in May, 1837, to the last regular election in November, 1876:

May, 1837. County Commissioners—Milton S. Mason, Cornelius Cline, John Q. A. Rollins, John K. Towner was appointed Treasurer, May 3, 1837; D. H. Whitney, Clerk of the County Commissioners' Court, same date. Simon P. Doty was elected Sheriff; John Handy, Coroner; Seth S. Whitman, Recorder; and S. P. Hyde, Surveyor.

The next election was held in August, 1837. D. H. Whitney was elected County Clerk, and John K. Towner, County Treasurer.

August, 1838. County Commissioners—Moses Blood, Orris Crosby and John K. Towner. [After this date, until the adoption of the township organization system, only one commissioner was elected annually, unless vacancies occurred in the board by reason of death or resignation.] Sheriff, H. C. Walker. [He resigned in 1839, and B. F. Lawrence was elected to fill vacancy, Dec. 2, 1839.] Coroner, John Handy.

In December, 1838, the office of the Clerk of the County Court was declared vacant, and James L. Loop was appointed to the vacancy.

Aug. 5, 1839. County Commissioner, Robt. B. Hurd; County Clerk, Jas. L. Loop; Recorder, Alexander Neely; Treasurer, Cephas Gardner; Surveyor, Geo. F. Kasson. September, 1839, James M. Loop was appointed Deputy County Clerk. In September, 1840, he resigned his position, and J. Z. Saxton was appointed to the vacancy.

August, 1840. Sheriff, Albert Stone; Coroner, Edward Hawley; Commissioner, Jas. Shinn. In May, 1841, George Walker was appointed Deputy County Clerk, to fill the vacancy occasioned by the resignation of Saxton, as Deputy.

June, 1841. The office of County Clerk was declared to be vacant, and John Z. Saxton was appointed to fill the vacancy.

August, 1841. Commissioner, Orris Crosby; County Clerk, Asher E. Jenner. Nov. 13. James Shinn and Orris Crosby resigned their offices as County Commissioners. A special election was held Dec. 13, 1841, to fill the vacancies, when S. P. Doty and Nathaniel Crosby were elected, to serve two and three years, from August, 1841. Doty and Crosby drew lots for terms, Crosby drawing the three-years term.

August, 1842. Sheriff, Wm. Smith; Nahum Rice, Coroner; and Edw. Hawley, Commissioner.

August, 1843. Commissioner, Thomas Hartwell; Clerk, Ralph D. Rix; Recorder, Wm. T. Burgess; Treasurer, Samuel Bennett; Surveyor, Daniel Trowbridge.

August, 1844. Sheriff, Joel Florada; Coroner, Chas. B. Lord; Commissioner, Albert Neely.

August, 1845. Commissioner, A. L. Bush.

August, 1846. Sheriff, Joel Florada; Commissioner, Abraham Drake; Coroner, John L. Bush. October 19th, a special election for County Commissioners was held, to fill vacancy occasioned by resignation of Alexander Neely.

April 19, 1847, at a special election, M. C. Bentley was elected County Commissioner.

August, 1847. Recorder, Hezekiah Ripley; Commissioner, Sidney Avery; Clerk, Ralph D. Rix; Assessor and Treasurer, Edward Hawley; Surveyor, Daniel Trowbridge; Probate Justice, Joel Walker.

August, 1848. Sheriff, Alson L. Ames; Commissioner, Charles W. Libby; Coroner, Christopher Burrell.

Sept. 4, 1848. Special election. Noah W. Birge was elected Clerk of the Circuit Court.

November, 1849. County Judge, Daniel H. Whitney; Assessor and Treasurer, Samuel Bennett; Surveyor, Daniel Trowbridge.

April 26, 1850. John Jackson, County Clerk. Resigned, and May 17th, H. Ripley was appointed to the vacancy.

In 1850, the township organization system went into effect. The time of holding county elections was changed from August to November, and the time for the election of Supervisors fixed for April in each year. At the first election for Supervisors, the following board was chosen:*

November, 1850. Recorder, Daniel Olney; County Clerk, H. Ripley. [Died May 5, 1851, and A. J. Tanner was appointed to fill the vacancy.] Coroner, John K. Towner; Sheriff, Joel Florada.

November, 1851. County Clerk, A. J. Tanner.

November, 1852. Clerk Circuit Court, Fayette B. Hawlin; Sheriff, George I. Wood; Coroner, George Dean.

November, 1853. County Judge, Hiram C. Miller; County Clerk, Leonard M. Beebe; Treasurer, George W. Downs; Surveyor, Yates V. Beebe. Mr. Beebe died while in office, Sept. 15, 1857, and William McVicker was appointed to the vacancy.

November, 1854. County Judge, Daniel H. Whitney; Sheriff, Hanson R. Wilson; Coroner, L. L. Lake.

Nov. 6, 1855. Treasurer, A. E. Jenner; Surveyor, E. L. Lawrence.

Nov. 4, 1856. County Judge, Allen C. Fuller; Clerk Circuit Court, Daniel H. Whitney; Sheriff, Elias L. Tisdel; Coroner, L. L. Lake.

Nov. 6, 1857. County Judge, A. C. Fuller; Clerk, A. H. Bradley; Treasurer, A. E. Jenner; Surveyor, William McVicker.

Nov. 2, 1858. Sheriff, Henry F. Jennison; Coroner, L. L. Lake.

Nov. 8, 1859. Treasurer, H. C. DeMunn; Surveyor, E. L. Lawrence.

Nov. 6, 1860. Clerk Circuit Court, D. H. Whitney; Sheriff, P. J. Garcelon; Coroner, D. E. Foote.

June 3, 1861. (Special election.) M. M. Boyce was elected County Judge.

Nov. 5, 1861. County Judge, M. M. Boyce; Clerk, A. H. Bradley; Treasurer, William C. Tuttle; Surveyor, E. L. Lawrence.

Nov. 4, 1862. Sheriff, John H. Andrus; Coroner, D. E. Foote.

Nov. 3, 1863. Treasurer, Enoch Kendall; Surveyor, E. L. Lawrence.

Nov. 8, 1864. Clerk Circuit Court, H. C. DeMunn; Sheriff, P. J. Garcelon; Coroner, L. L. Lake.

Nov. 7, 1865. County Judge, L. W. Lawrence; Clerk, C. B. Loop; Surveyor, E. L. Lawrence; Treasurer, Enoch Kendall.

Nov. 6, 1866. Sheriff, L. O. Gilman; Coroner, D. E. Foote.

Nov. 5, 1867. Treasurer, Enoch Kendall; Surveyor, E. L. Lawrence.

November, 1868. Clerk Circuit Court, H. C. DeMunn; Sheriff, J. C. Styles; Coroner, D. E. Foote. (In September, 1869, L. O. Gilman was

---

*The record of the several Boards of Supervisors, from April, 1850, to April, 1877, will be found on the following pages.

appointed to fill the vacancy in the Treasurer's office caused by the removal of Enoch Kendall.)

November, 1869. Treasurer, L. O. Gilman; County Judge, L. W. Lawrence; Clerk, C. B. Loop; Surveyor, E. L. Lawrence.

November, 1870. Sheriff, R. E. Osgood; Coroner, D. E. Foote.

November, 1871. Treasurer, John Gray; Surveyor, Charles S. Moss.

November, 1872. Clerk Circuit Court, H. C. DeMunn; Sheriff, S. L. Covey; Coroner, D. E. Foote.

November, 1873. County Judge, L. W. Lawrence; Clerk, C. B. Loop. (Mr. Loop resigned March 13, 1876, and F. I. Hall was appointed to the vacancy.) Treasurer, A. E. Jenner.

November, 1874. Sheriff, S. L. Covey; Coroner, G. W. Robinson.

November, 1875. Treasurer, Daniel Wilcox; Surveyor, Charles S. Moss.

November, 1876. Clerk Circuit Court, J. W. Sawyer; Sheriff, S. L. Covey; Coroner, F. S. Whitman; Surveyor, C. S. Moss.

Wm. McVicker and D. H. Whitney were appointed Deputy County Clerks, in September, 1857, but filled that position only a short time.

Mary Boyde was appointed Deputy County Clerk in March, 1865, and filled that position six years.

Jas. S. Terwilliger was appointed Deputy County Clerk, in 1860, and held that position a year.

Simmons Terwilliger was appointed Deputy County Clerk in November, 1861, and remained in that position seven or eight months.

Chester S. Crosby was appointed Deputy County Clerk in July, 1862, and filled that position two or three years.

Geo. W. Wilbur was appointed Deputy County Clerk and filled that position for two years.

Willis H. Bennett was appointed Deputy County Clerk in July, 1875, under C. B. Loop, and afterwards under F. I. Hall, in March, 1877, and is still holding that position.

H. C. DeMunn was appointed Deputy Circuit Clerk in 1859, under D. H. Whitney, and held that position for four years. Mr. Whitney died before his term of office expired, and Mr. H. C. DeMunn was appointed to fill the vacancy. Col. L. O. Gilman and Miss Addie Whitney, now Mrs. W. S. Jones, were appointed his Deputies.

RECORD OF SUPERVISORS.

Election First Monday in April, Annually.

1850.—Frederick P. Low, Nathaniel Crosby, Henry Jenks, Charles W. Libby, William Raymond, Hiram C. Miller, Isaac Miller, Charles B. Lord.

1851.—Cephas Gardner, Martin G. Gilbert, Isaac Mitchell, Isaac Miller, Mason Smith, F. P. Low, M. C. Manley, M. C. Bentley.

1852.—Cephas Gardner, M. Y. Gilbert, M. C. Manley, John Kerr, James C. Gooch, Isaac Miller, John L. Curtis, F. B. Bement.

1853.—Samuel Rockwood, R. D. Rix, M. Y. Gilbert, M. C. Manley, John Prindle, Joseph P. Woods, Isaac Miller, J. L. Curtis.

1854.—Isaac R. Miller, Joseph P. Woods, Amos Older, F. P. Low, R. D. Rix, M. C. Manley, Abram Drake, C. F. Witt.

1855.—R. D. Rix, M. Y. Gilbert, F. P. Low, Isaac Miller, Bradford Dean, C. F. Witt, Hiram Hopkins, Amos Older.

1856.—C. F. Witt, Daniel Mabie, Joseph P. Woods, M. C. Bentley, Stephen Lambert, R. D. Rix, M. Y. Gilbert, Hiram Hopkins.

1857.—Theo. Grant, M. Y. Gilbert, B. P. Patten, A. M. Miller, Daniel Mabie, F. P. Low, C. F. Witt, R. D. Rix.

1858.—Theo. Grant, M. Y. Gilbert, R. D. Rix, Ely Gordon, C. F. Witt, C. H. Avery, W. S. Webster, B. P. Patten. Up to this date the Board of Supervisors was composed of eight members, one from each township, but the Belvidere special charter went into operation, and by virtue of it the President of the Town Board was made ex-officio a member of the Board of Supervisors, increasing the number to nine members.

1859.—Theo. Grant, Thomas Brown, Geo. Dean, Cephas Gardner, J. J. Bogardus, C. F. Witt, C. H. Avery, M. C. Bentley, B. F. Patten.

1860.—Theo. Grant, M. Y. Gilbert, Cephas Gardner, E. L. Tisdell, Stephen Lambert, Geo. Chafee, L. W. Lawrence, James Alexander, B. F. Patten.

1861.—Theo. Grant, Cephas Gardner, H. J. Doolittle, Stephen Lambert, George Chafee, L. W. Lawrence, James Alexander, B. P. Patten, M. Y. Gilbert.

1862.—B. P. Patten, Theo. Grant, M. Y. Gilbert, George Chafee, S. P. Lane, Cephas Gardner, E. H. Reynolds, J. R. Bogardus, W. S. Webster.

1863.—Cephas Gardner, Mark Ramsey, Stephen Curtis, I. R. Bogardus, W. S. Webster, B. F. Patten, A. H. Manley, Wm. Corning, I. T. Witbeck.

1864.—A. H. Manley, M. Y. Gilbert, Cephas Gardner, M. M. Boyce, I. T. Witbeck, George Reed, I. R. Bogardus, W. S. Webster, B. P. Patten.

1865.—L. W. Lawrence, John W. Stow, Stephen Lambert, M. Y. Gilbert, George Reed, G. W. Woodward, J. S. Hildrup, A. H. Manley, B. P. Patten.

1866.—A. H. Manley, B. P. Patten, George Chafee, I. R. Bogardus, E. H. Talbott, Daniel E. Foote, Isaac Sewell, J. Alexander, Stephen Lambert.

1867.—George Chafee, F. P. Low, T. S. Bartholomew, H. E. Fox, Clark Heath, B. P. Patten, P. J. Garcelon, M. Y. Gilbert, Asa Lawrence.

1868.—H. E. Fox, Geo. Chafee, C. W. Heath, C. Gardner, B. P. Patten, C. H. Wilson, F. I. Hall, M. Y. Gilbert, W. R. Dodge.

1869.—Ezra May, H. E. Fox, C. Gardner, Alex. McNair, F. I. Hall, Silas DeMunn, Geo. Reed, C. W. Heath, C. H. Wilson.

1870.—Charles H. Wilson, Alex. McNair, E. May, H. E. Fox, John J. Foote, C. F. Witt, C. W. Heath, F. I. Hall, B. F. Langdon.

1871.—C. F. Witt, J. J. Foote, M. Y. Gilbert, H. W. Pier, Silas DeMunn, C. W. Heath, I. A. Cornell, Frank Tanner, W. F. Hovey.

In April, 1872, an Assistant Supervisor for Belvidere was elected, making ten members.

1872.—J. J. Foote, I. R. Bogardus, Henry Willard, William D. Boies, Henry Porter, Ezra May, Silas DeMunn, F. I. Hall, I. A. Cornell, Abram Drake.

1873.—M. Y. Gilbert, Silas DeMunn, H. W. Pier, I. T. Witbeck, I. V. Draper, I. A. Cornell, W. D. Boies, H. R. Willard, Samuel Wood, Stephen Lambert.

1874.—H. R. Willard, I. A. Cornell, Geo. Chafee, M. K. Avery, Philo Conyes, I. V. Draper, L. Whiting, S. Lambert, C. L. Smith, I. T. Witbeck.

1875.—George Chafee, H. R. Willard, O. S. Nichols, Frank Tanner,

P. Conyes, L. Whiting. I. A. Cornell, S. Lambert, John Greenlee, George W. March.

1876.—George Chafee, H. R. Willard, I. V. Draper, I. A. Cornell, P. Conyes, James Montgomery, S. Lambert, John Greenlee, G. W. Robinson, O. S. Nichols.

1877.—George Chafee, P. Conyes, James Montgomery, I. V. Draper, H. R. Willard, I. A. Cornell, John Greenlee, O. S. Nichols, John Hannah, George W. March.

POLITICAL AND PERSONAL RECOLLECTIONS, ETC.

The pioneers of '35 came to Boone County bold, fearless, industrious men. Full of enterprise and fixedness of purpose, they planted a little colony of thirty-seven persons, all told (in October, 1835), that, growing year by year in numbers and intelligence, until now (1877) the population equals forty-seven persons to the square mile. Each and all of these pioneers of '35, as well as those of the other early years of the settlement of the Kishwaukee country of the Pottawattomies, had their peculiarities and their humors, antipathies and preferences, politics and prejudices. To note some of these and preserve them in this volume is our purpose, hoping that, though snatched from the dim, distant past, they will serve to kindle afresh the memories "O' auld lang syne."

In those days the people were divided between the Whigs and Democrats. Coming to and settling on the unbroken wilds of Illinois, then in the far West, did not emancipate them from their political preferences or prejudices, and in the presidential election of 1836 the party lines were as clearly defined and as tightly drawn, although only twenty-three votes were polled in the Belvidere precinct, as if there had been as many thousands. The poll-book of that election, preserved among the records of the county clerk's office at Rockford, shows the names of these twenty-three voters. Of these only Simon P. Doty and David Caswell are living, the latter now a resident of Iowa.

As long as the Whig party preserved its organization, the contest between them and the Democrats was close. When an important national question was to be voted upon, the Democrats (in later years as the population increased) would usually carry the county by from fifty to one hundred majority. In local contests, the Whigs (always putting up their best men as candidates to be voted for) would usually succeed by small majorities. They never nominated any man for office that he might be sacrificed on the altar of some other man's ambition.

In the August election of 1838, party candidates were first presented to the people for their suffrage. Simon P. Doty was the Whig candidate for sheriff, and H. C. Walker was the candidate of the Democratic party. Walker was elected by six majority, but resigned in 1839.

The Whigs held their nominating convention that year at the house of Simon P. Doty. A public house, and the only public house in Belvidere at that time, it was a place of resort for Democrats as well as Whigs. On this particular occasion, there being a good deal of interest in the result of the convention, nearly all the voters of the precinct were gathered in and about the house. Just as the convention adjourned, the Democratic candidate for Congress in this district—then embracing nearly all of northern Illinois—arrived in town, and the Democrats at once determined to have a

Democratic rally and a Democratic speech. (The name of the candidate for Congressional honors and Democratic votes in that campaign has escaped the memory of our informant, but we think it must have been Stephen A. Douglas.) Dr. Molony was then an active Democrat, and he soon had the Democrats all mustered in a store-room adjoining Doty's hotel, and called the meeting to order by nominating a gentleman for chairman who was in nowise familiar with parliamentary usages, and withal very bashful and particularly noted for his economy of words. When he had taken the chair, a dry goods box or a nail keg being improvised for the occasion, Dr. Molony made the further motion that, as the Democratic candidate for Congress had visited their midst, and was then present in the house, that he be requested to make them a speech. Full of trepidation, the chairman attempted to put the motion, but the words would stick in his throat. Three or four times he essayed to get the question before the house, but as often failed. Dr. Molony seeing and appreciating the situation, sought to relieve the chairman, and said that the meeting understood the motion, and all that was necessary was to call for the ayes and nays. Making another desperate effort, the chairman said: "It has been motion-ded and seconded that the Democratic candidate for Congress be requested to make a Democratic speech to the meeting. All in favor of the motion *sanctify* it by saying I." This sanctification brought down the house in a roar, in the midst of which the Democratic candidate stepped forward, doffed his coon-skin cap, mounted a convenient barrel, and proceeded to comply with the *sanctified* request of the meeting. That, says our informant, was the first speech from a Democratic candidate for Congress delivered in Boone County.

An anecdote is told of Simon P. Doty in connection with the log cabin and hard cider campaign of 1840, when the Whigs sang of "Tippecanoe and Tyler too," as well as of "Tom Corwin, the wagon boy," that may not be out of place in this connection. Mr. Doty, in those days, was a man of wonderful physical development—tall, muscular, and as straight as an arrow, lithe and active as a cat, of great strength and fearless as a lion, there were not many men his equal in strength or daring; yet always a mild and courteous gentleman, but full of humor and ready to perpetrate a joke or "play a trick" on any occasion that offered. A leading Whig, he was chosen a delegate from Boone County in 1840 to attend the State convention at Springfield that year, to select delegates to the National Whig convention. There were neither railroads nor stage coaches in the direction of the State capital then. The only conveyance was by ox wagons. Fitting out one of these, laying in a supply of provisions, cooking utensils, etc., Doty and those who accompanied him, started out for the State convention. Scarcely a day out, they fell in with other teams, and still others and others, until they strung out over a mile or two in length. Camping out at night, they sang Whig songs, told Whig jokes, drank Whig cider, and bet on Whig majorities and the election of Gen. Harrison. Nearing Springfield, and when only a short distance out they stopped to dress up a little—to change their camp apparel for clothes a little more becoming president-makers. One man out of the crowd with whom they had fallen in company, a little "*nicer*" than the others, had provided himself with a pocket mirror, and wishing to "scrape his countenance," he got out his mirror, fastened it up against a tree, and proceeded to "scratch his face." Noticing his extreme fastidiousness, Doty went to a wagon, procured an axe, went to a white-oak

BELVIDERE.

tree and chipped or "blazed" off a piece of the bark, then got his razor and proceeded to shave himself thereby, much to the amusement of those who saw the joke. Some years later, Doty had occasion to travel through Michigan, and at one of his stopping places, incurred, by some means, the displeasure of a rough sort of fellow, who proposed, in back-woods parlance, to "eat Doty up." Ignorant of having given occasion for such an outburst of rage on the other's part, Doty took the matter quite coolly. But the man raged on, and began stripping for the fray. Another personage present, a hitherto silent spectator, volunteered a little friendly advice to the belligerent, but for a time his advice was unheeded. Eat Doty up, he would. He had made up his mind to do it, and he was a man that never went back on his mind or his word. At last the man of peace told him that Doty was not made to be eaten up by wolverines; that he was an Illinoisan, and a man who always shaved himself by the light reflected from a "blazed" place on a white-oak tree! and that he had seen him do it! That quieted the rage of the wolverine, and he put on his clothes, ordered "hard cider" for the crowd, and for the balance of the evening Doty was the lion and the observed of all observers.

As early as December, 1835, a political meeting was held in Belvidere. Dr. Whitney's letters locate that meeting at the Belvidere Hotel. The Belvidere Hotel, as we gather from Mr. Doty, was not built until 1836. The first house occupied by Mr. Doty was perhaps regarded as a hotel, and it was probably in that house the meeting referred to was held. It was a Whig meeting, and Mr. Doty was the presiding officer; Dr. Whitney the secretary, and E. A. Nixon and Mason Sherman made up the rank and file. With a unanimity worthy of imitation by all political conventions, they adopted resolutions and sent them to the Chicago *American*, the predecessor of the Chicago *Journal*, and published to the world their determination to elect General Harrison to the presidency in 1836. This, however, was not accomplished until 1840. In speaking of this convention in his reminiscences, Dr. Whitney grew poetical and concluded with these lines:

"From wild Madawaska's dark forest of pine,
To the far fertile glades where the Kishwaukee flows,
True sons of their fathers, the heroes combined,
And shook off the yoke of their tyrants and foes."

In the same letter from which the above is quoted, referring to the Fourth of July, 1836, Dr. Whitney said:

"Young morn shook from her purple wings as glorious a Fourth as ever kissed Aurora's cheek when she unbarred the gates of light, and no more patriotic and grateful hearts beat in American bosoms on that glorious day than did those of the settlers of Boone, as with all the artillery at our command, an old rifle, a tolerable shot gun, and a pocket pistol, the old settlers took their position on the mound, raised a liberty pole from which fluttered in the breeze a *pocket handkerchief* having the portraits of the presidents around its border, and being the nearest approach to a national flag of anything in these 'diggings.' We read the Declaration of Independence, fired a national salute, gave three times three that frightened the Indian from his wigwam and the red deer from his covert. And then, with Charley Watkins leading, we joined in singing:

'Strawberries and cream in the morning—
I'll deck her with pearl,
If she'll be my girl,
And follow me over the mountain.'

We tramped to the edge of the timber on the northwest side of the prairie, and in a few hours returned with our pails filled with strawberries, and closed the first national jubilee in this far off land in the spirit of the poet who wrote:

> 'Thy spirit, Independence, let me share,
> Lord of the lion heart and eagle eye;
> Thy steps we'll follow with our bosoms bare,
> Nor heed the storms that howl along the sky.'"

In another letter the same writer says that the most magnificent event that transpired in this country in those days was the burning over of the prairies in the fall of the year. The flames would spread in time of high wind with such rapidity that the fleetest horse could not keep in advance of them; and it is said that persons have been overtaken by them and perished in the flames. "In traveling over the country in those days, we carried matches with us in order to burn the prairie before us if we were likely to be overtaken by the fire. Late in the fall of 1835, I rode until the shades of night came on, and then dismounted, tethered my horse and turned him loose to graze. I had stopped on a little burr oak ridge, surrounded by sloughs and a vast extent of low lands, overgrown with an immense burden of vegetation. I wrapped myself in my cloak, and with the ground for a bed and the sky for a covering, I stretched myself at the root of a tree, and curtained with more than Egyptian darkness I endeavored to compose myself to sleep. The fall had been unusually dry, and the weeds and grass were like tinder. I had not lain long when my ear caught a heavy, jarring sound that made the earth tremble; and the dark clouds that lay piled up at the west put on a deep crimson hue, that was soon succeeded by a brilliant light that ascended from the earth; suddenly, for miles in length, the fire spread rapidly over the rolling prairie that intervened, and the "prairies on fire" shook beneath the angry tread of this volume of flame, that, careering before the gale, approached with inconceivable rapidity. I had no time to look for my horse, but, lighted a match and set fire to the grass. My horse, affrighted by the fiery element that now nearly surrounded us, came to me with all the speed he could bring into requisition, and with such seeming confidence did he approach me for succor that he came well-nigh running over me. I took up my saddle, my horse sticking close by me, and followed the fire I had set on the ground over which it had passed, to a safe distance from the all devouring flames that had now reached the more exuberant growth of the lowlands, from which the deer, aroused from his covert, bounded off among the scattering trees, and the wild geese arose from the ponds of the sloughs, and flew screaming in every direction, and the wolf, affrighted from his hiding place, ran howling from the approaching ruin. The fire caught the deep-tangled vegetation of the lowlands, and driven madly on by the winds that it had called up from their caverns, rolled its billows in no conceivable sublimity over many thousands of acres on either side, the sight of which would have confirmed Parson Miller, for the time being at least, in his prophecies, if he had but stood that night where I stood and gazed as I gazed on this vast tempest-tossed and troubled ocean that seemed to enwrap the earth in one continuous sheet of flame. But it soon swept on over the adjacent hills, sending back the distant roar of its thunder, leaving all behind in gloom, and too vividly impressing me with the power of the elements unchained to lose myself in slumber again that night."

Not to men alone belongs the credit of making this country what it is—of reducing it from uncivilized wilds to a garden of beauty. Women's bravery in turning their backs upon old homes and their comforts—the scenes and incidents of their girlhood—and traveling thousands of miles in jolting, jostling wagons—to find homes by camp fires until rude cabins could be built, demands equal commendation. Of the pioneer mothers who abandoned friends and comfortable surroundings in the eastern states forty-two years ago, to find homes on the prairies of the Kishwaukee, Mrs. John K. Towner is the only living representative. Forty-two years ago, at midnight of the last day of July, 1877, a journey of thousands of miles, made in a wagon drawn by two horses, was ended, and, in the midst of these wilds and the children native to the soil, that brave woman reined in her team, and by a camp fire, kindled in the grove on the south side of the Kishwaukee, a little below town, was cooked the first meal ever cooked by a white woman on these "Elysian Fields." There was a courage that prompted this undertaking akin to heroism, and had the task of caring for eight children, preparing their food by camp fires, depended upon men alone it is very questionable whether the journey would have been undertaken.

When the Towners came the Pottawattomies were encamped here—on or in close proximity to the fair grounds. There were several hundred of them, having assembled here for the last time previous to their removal, from whence to go to Chicago to receive their payments, presents, etc., and their wigwams made quite a little Indian village. They had a council house, made of poles and bark, old and partially decayed at that time, near the present crossing of the river below Martyn's mills. In a few days after the Towners were settled, an Indian dance, the "green corn dance," was held in this council chamber, and to show courtesy to these red men, Mr. Towner and his wife attended. The belles and beaus were dressed in their best paints, feathers and other Indian gew-gaws. One of the belles of the occasion was the wife of one of the leading Indians, a "capitain." She was dressed a little better than the rest of the "ladies" in attendance, the skirt of her dress being gaudily trimmed with short strips of narrow ribbon of all shades of color. During a favorable opportunity, Mrs. Towner took occasion to direct her attention to this "belle" and her dress, in a way that at once caused her to know that her "style" was admired by the "pale-faced" visitor, and after that she lost no opportunity to "show off" as she whirled in the "giddy mazes of the dance." The next day, in the same dress, but with the addition of a fine broadcloth shawl, handsomely trimmed, she "called" upon Mrs. Towner, with the evident intention of showing her "new shawl," which, of course, was much admired, as what well-bred woman would refuse to compliment the aristocracy in whose midst was her humble home. Mrs. Towner is of the opinion that this woman was of white origin, and cites as her reasons the following little episode: During one of her "calls" upon Mrs. Towner, she was toying with her youngest child, then quite a young babe, when, as most women will do, she was tickling its cheeks and chin, and employing "pet names," she seemed to forget her Indian tongue, and several times enunciated in good English, "Bubby," "Bubby," "Bubby." Hearing her use this term, Mrs. Towner turned to her and remarked: "You must be a white woman as you seem to know and understand the treatment of white babies so well." From that time her lips were sealed, and no artifice could draw her out. Soon after they were moved beyond the Mississippi, and Mrs. Towner never knew whether her suspicions as to her being a white woman were well founded or not. The Indian women were much opposed to the removal, and were often heard saying, more to themselves than to each other: "Me don't want to cross Mississippi; me don't want to cross Mississippi."

The incidents narrated above relate to the social features of Mrs. Towner's experience with the Pottawattomies while she lived in their midst, and with the recital of a little incident, and one which was not so pleasant, and calculated to try strong nerves, we dismiss the Indians, following them only in memory.

At one time Mrs. Towner was left alone with her children in their house, which was situated in the midst of the village. One of the Indians had become intoxicated, and in that condition entered the house, and declared he had come to kill her. She replied that she would kill him. One of her little girls, aged about ten years, said to her mother that a gun in the house was loaded. At this the Indian jerked a knife from his belt that looked, as Mrs. Towner expressed it, as long as a sword. By some means, she don't know how, she ejected him from the house, and closed and barred the door with a long, heavy wooden bench, determined to "hold the fort." The door was made of basswood puncheons, and between the pieces there were cracks or interstices large enough to admit a man's hand. Ejected by a pale-faced squaw only added fury to his rage, and he made thrust after thrust through cracks of the door with his knife. Finding he could effect nothing that way, he next essayed to gain admission to the house by climbing upon the roof and descending through the mud and stick chimney. But here he was again foiled by the brave woman within, who ripped open a straw bed, and threw part of the contents on the smouldering embers on the hearth. This raised a smoke that drove the Indian to the ground. By this time the white men belonging to the house had been alarmed, and came to her rescue. The Indian was taken away, and soon after the whole tribe removed west of the "Mississippi." It is but due to the memory of the Pottawattomies then encamped here to say that they repudiated Mrs. Towner's drunken and savage visitor as a "bad Indian," and one who did not belong to their people—an interloper who had fastened himself to them.

Another careful, economical, ingenious, provident woman was Mrs. Christopher Payne, whose husband, in the late fall of 1835, located a claim on Squaw Prairie, a part of which is now the beautiful and productive farm of Oliver Hale, in Bonus township. The incident referred to occurred before they removed to Boone County. A school was to be commenced in their neighborhood, and Mrs. Payne was anxious that her children should attend. Poor in purse, and money scarce, with nothing on which they could realize, their wardrobes ran down till they became quite scanty. Indeed, the children were but little better dressed than were the children of the Indians. To quote Flora McFlimsey, they had "nothing to wear." But Mrs. Payne had set her heart on giving her children an education, and go to school they must. But how to clothe them for the occasion—that was the question. But where there is a will there is a way, and Mrs. Payne was equal to the emergency, and the bottom lands along the Fox river promised the "raw material." Nettle weeds grew there in great abundance, and these she utilized. Going there, she pulled a sufficient quantity for the purpose, and spread them out to rot, as our fathers and mothers used to spread flax. When they had rotted sufficiently, they were "broke," "scutched" and "hackled." From the "hackle," the fibre thus obtained went to the "rock," and from the "rock" her fingers guided it to the "flyers" and the "spindle" of an old-fashioned, little wheel, the "treadle" of which was worked with her feet, and thus manufactured into thread. From the wheel to a hand "reel" and the "warping bars," and then to the old hand and foot-worked loom, where the thread was woven into cloth, and the cloth made into clothes that enabled her to send her children to school in respectable apparel. This, to some, may sound a little *nettly*, but that it is a true story can be vouched for by some who were fully cognizant of the circumstance, and who at this date (September, 1877,) are still living. Of such stuff were the women pioneers of this county made. All honor to the memory of those who have passed away, and to the names of those who have been spared to see the wigwams and camp fires of the Indians give way to palatial dwellings.

The memory of Dr. Daniel Hilton Whitney, who died Feb. 17, 1864, aged fifty-seven years, is held in high esteem by the people of Boone. One of the early pioneers, a man full of energy, soul and thought, of large experience among men, of quick perceptions and keen judgment, and a ready talker, he was that style of man calculated to win friends anywhere, especially among pioneers. He was tall, and of commanding appearance, dark, almost swarthy complexion, coal black hair and eagle-like eye. Of general intelligence and genial nature, he was prepared for a speech at any time and on any occasion, no matter whether it was at a religious meeting, a funeral, a pole raising, a Whig barbecue, a state or county convention. Ever ready to espouse the cause of the poor as against the rich—of the weak against the strong—he was known as the poor man's friend. In his professional practice, he was known far and near. No sick person within his reach was allowed to languish and suffer because of their inability to purchase medicine or pay doctors' bills. Volumes might be filled with recitals of his good deeds, but no words that we can employ would add any new lustre to the character he bore in the community where he lived so long. These traits of his nature, added to his rich fund of humor and aptness at repartee, always secured a place and a warm welcome for Dr. Whitney in every assembly.

A great many anecdotes are related of the subject of this sketch, and, as his name has often occurred in these pages, it is due alike to those who knew him not and those who knew him well, to spread on this record an incident or two illustrative of his character.

On one occasion, there was a Masonic gathering, and being a member of that order—always charitable and full of good deeds—he was the orator of the day. The meeting was held in the open air, in a grove adjacent to Belvidere. A stand had been erected, and seats arranged for the accommodation of the audience. The stand was not of the most substantial kind, and the combined weight of those who gathered upon it proved too much for its strength. During one of his happiest perorations, the forward supports gave way, and the speaker was thrown forward to the ground, alighting full length on his face. But he never lost a word. Gathering himself up, first upon his hands, then to his knees, still talking, and finally to his feet and an erect position, his speech was not interrupted by the loss of a single word. Only a gesture or two were missing, and these were more than compensated for by the *great force* with which he ended the period upon which he was entering when the treacherous stand gave way.

As a writer for the press, he was, perhaps, more rapid in thought than correct in diction—not for the want of language, however, but rather because of his rapidity of thought and great store of language. Words dropped from the end of his tongue like snow-flakes from an overcharged winter's cloud. They came so fast he had no time to choose between them. Yet in all his writings there was something to admire—something to claim and hold the reader's attention. In other places we have culled some of his memories as preserved in letters to the Belvidere press, that are well worth perusal. These selections are from letters numbered four, five and six. There were other contributions before and after the ones from which we quote, but they were not preserved—a neglect to be regretted. Relating particularly to the scenes incident to the early settlement of the country in which he was so conspicuous a character, they would have proved valuable adjuncts in preserving the country's history. What Stephen A. Douglas and Abraham Lincoln were to their respective political parties in Illinois, Dr. Whitney seems to have been to the earlier settlers of Boone County.

Returning to the series of letters relating to the early settlement of the county, to which we have repeatedly referred, and so liberally quoted, we copy number five of the series almost entire. In that letter Dr. Whitney wrote:

"Late in the fall of 1835, Gen. James Sayers made the claim on which Newberg was subsequently laid out, and in 1836 built a saw mill, and soon after fixed up a grist mill in the same building, and continued to operate it for several years. That was the first mill built in the north counties, and was of incalculable benefit to the early settlements.

"In these days it was not unfrequent that we had to depend on our guns for meat, and the number of prairie hens or ducks that we had the fortune to kill was the precursor of a day of high living, or the less comfortable assurance that we should go to bed on light suppers.

"Pope says 'the birds of heaven shall vindicate their grain,' and unless he meant they should take the whole, they didn't do as fairly by me as they intended. I purchased and sowed, with my own hands, ten bushels of wheat in the fall of 1835 (36?) (being the first sown in the county) on a strip of late broke prairie, on which now stands the barn of D. W. Read, and the prairie chickens and birds left 'nary a kernel.'

"The exorbitant price of provisions at Chicago, and the great difficulty of getting loads through the unbridged creeks and sloughs, and the near approach of winter, admonished us to bestir ourselves and provide for the long and rigorous months before us. The writer, with Rev. J. L. Towner (then a lad of about seventeen years), and Charley Watkins, went south about 250 miles, in the fall of 1836, and brought up and drove into the settlement some eight or ten hundred dollars worth of fat hogs and cattle, and notwithstanding pork was selling in the Chicago market at from $12 to $15 per cwt., and beef at from $8 to $12 per cwt., I sold the pork to this and surrounding settlements at from $6 to $8 per cwt., and the beef at from $3 to $4 per cwt.

"But little was done through the winter of 1835 towards making farms. The spirit of making land claims to sell again, that has always raged over the new territories of the West, broke out, ruining the settlers of northern Illinois, and greatly retarded the permanent improvement of the country. I have known claims of 160 and 320 acres without improvement, and the fee (title) yet in the government and the land unsurveyed, to sell all the way from $100 to $2,700, the consequence of which was that when the lands were hurried into market, these dupes were without money, and were obliged to get their lands entered by 'money shavers,' the pre-damned of mankind in all climes and ages, at from 25 to 40 per cent., the result of which was that many lost their farms in the end. Others struggled on, knowing nothing but 20, 25 and 30 per cent., and this extortion and acquiescence entailed upon us more than all things else the embarrassments under which the country has ever since struggled, and that now (18) rests like a frightful incubus upon our people, prostrating and paralyzing every energy and almost crushing out hope.

"There was one feature of this 'claim mania' that I could never understand. A very large proportion of the settlers who came in after the fall of 1835 could not be induced to take up claims for themselves; they would either buy or 'jump' (take forcible possession) a claim, although the lands contiguous were just as good, and they could have made their own claims; yet, if they could neither buy nor 'jump' claims here, they would pass on to other settlements where claims could be either bought or 'jumped.'

"Early in 1836, Col. Mack informed us that at the north, near the State line, was a beautiful prairie surrounded by fine groves of timber, and being anxious to induce settlements in the north part of the county, and knowing the propensities of the new settlers to 'jump' claims, Lewis A. Doolittle, Esq., and Dr. J. Briggs, who had just settled here, and myself started in search of Round Prairie, supplied with blankets, horse feed, etc., our hatchets in our belts, fully prepared for camping out. After wandering about all day, we came upon the southwest corner of Round Prairie about sundown. Drenched with rain and chilled with the northwest wind, we soon kindled a fire in a ravine near the late residence of Rev. S. Walker, built a hasty shanty of brush, and passed the night as best we could. The next morning we went to work 'claim making.' We made claim of Round and Long Prairies, blazed our trees, set our stakes, wrote our own names and any names that we happened to first think of, and where we had room wrote vengeance against any and all who should 'jump' them. Well satisfied with our day's toil we started for home. We had our accomplices in Belvidere who would inform the immigrants of this beautiful region, and who were sure to tell them it was claimed by 'land sharks' who never intended to occupy the claims, but were holding them for sale. In a short time we had the satisfaction of hearing that our claims were jumped, when we sent all the threats possible, which induced, as we anticipated, the effort on the part of the 'jumpers,' to hold the claims. The ruse was a successful one, and we soon had the pleasure of knowing that they were permanently occupied."

The severity and duration of the winter of 1842-3 will long be remembered by the people of that period in Boone County. October 6th snow began to fall, continuing for two or three days, until it had attained a depth of more than two feet. The stage-coaches, then running between Chicago and Galena, were abandoned about the 9th for four-horse sleighs. The cold continued to grow in intensity, and the surface of the snow, as well as beaten tracks, became a glare of ice. Wagons and other wheeled vehicles were useless, and runners came into general use. Preparations for such a winter had not been made, and there was much suffering among the people. One-third of the stock, it is estimated, either froze or starved to death. From the 6th of October, 1842, to near the middle of April, 1843—six months—the earth was covered with snow, packed by repeated falls, and solid enough to bear any ordinary horse. The use of four-horse sleighs, commenced on the 8th or 9th of October, was continued until the 5th of April—the last "sleighing party" passing through Belvidere on that day. There was thanksgiving and joy among the people when the last snow-drift had melted away beneath the rays of that April's sun, and the green carpet of spring time succeeded the white robes of the longest winter ever known before or since.

With only a few more brief paragraphs, and we will close this book. Its compilation has been a pleasant undertaking, but such pleasures can not always last, and "the best of friends must part."

The *first* marriage solemnized from Boone County was that between Dr. D. H. Whitney and Sarah Caswell, December 10, 1836—and this while Boone was a part of Winnebago County. This was his second marriage. His first wife was Elizabeth P. Hazard, a relative of Commodore Perry, to whom he was married July 5, 1828, in the State of New York. This wife died September 7, 1835, a short time after he had bade her adieu to find a new family home in Illinois. His second wife died September 15, 1870. From his last marriage six children were born, only two of whom grew to manhood and womanhood. The daughter, Addie, is the wife of W. S. Jones, merchant, of Belvidere. The son, Lieutenant Beverly Waugh Whitney, died in the army, for the maintenance of the Union, near Vicksburg, aged 20 years and 9 months. His remains were brought home to Belvidere for burial.

Of the first births, we can find no written record, but Judge L. W. Lawrence, who is a kind of local encyclopedia, tells us that the first child born in the county was John Haskins, son of Ira Haskins and wife, and that the event occurred in the winter of 1836–7. How he knows is this: Mr. Haskins lived at that time in a small cabin over the mound beyond the court-house. Their house was used as a house of worship, where meetings were held every Sabbath. The house would generally be crowded, and "Johnny" would be tucked away in his little cradle, and the cradle shoved under the table to economize room. The parents are both dead, and "Johnny," grown into John, is a resident of Vermont. George H. Hartwell, born in the old town of Newburg, and Henry Sweet, of the Belvidere post-office, son of Benjamin Sweet, have sometimes been disposed to contest the honors with Mr. Haskins, but Judge Lawrence's evidence is received as conclusive, although Messrs. Hartwell and Sweet are generally recognized as the only representatives of the first births now living in the county.

A RECORD OF THE OLD PEOPLE.

What more fitting close for a volume entitled the PAST AND PRESENT can be offered, than the names and ages of a few old people, whose lives are not only a part of the past and present of Boone County, but also of the country at large?

Father Petre, of Caledonia township, is said to be in his 108th year. He is in full possession of all his faculties, and able to walk around the house and door yard without help. *Older than the union of the States.*

Theophilus Rix, Belvidere, is in his 99th year. On his 96th birthday, his photograph was taken by J. Haynes.

Honor Plane, mother of John Plane, Belvidere, is in her 94th year. She was born May 2, A. D. 1783.

Mrs. Hannah Towner was born in the town of Elmira, New York, Jan. 19, 1797, and is consequently in her 80th year.

Mrs. Polly Lillibridge was born in Wayne County, Penn., Aug. 26, 1791, and is in the 87th year of her age. She was the first white child born in Mount Pleasant, in that county.

Martin Murch, father of Geo. W. Murch, merchant, South Belvidere, celebrated his 88th birthday in December, 1876.

James B. Martyn, born in England, has passed his 76th birthday, and on the 20th day of January, 1877, was presented with a healthy babe to bless his old age.

John Greenlee, father of the Greenlee Brothers, Belvidere, was born in Argyleshire, in the Parish of South End, Scotland, August 16, 1791, and celebrated his 86th birthday Aug. 16, 1877. He settled in Boone County, Dec. 24, 1836. He retains a clear memory, and remembers the scenes and incidents of the "long ago" as clearly as those of more recent occurrence.

Mrs. Clarissa Rockwell has passed her 83d birth day. Margery Collier is likewise in her 84th year. Susan Wellington is 84.

Mrs. Ray was born in May, 1800, and was 77 years old in May, 1877.

Mrs. Nancy Webb was born in Salem, New York, in 1800, and is now in her 77th year.

Mrs. Polly Mordoff is in her 81st year.

Green Terwilliger, father of J. S. and Dr. Simmons Terwilliger, was born in 1798, and is therefore 79 years of age.

N. T. Ingalls is 76 years old.

John Murphy is 79 years of age.

Enos Tomkins was born in the city of New York, February 1, 1795, and was 82 years old in February, 1877.

Charles McDougal, born in Canada, is in his 83d year. He settled in Boone County in 1836.

S. P. Doty is in his 81st year, and as straight as an Indian.

Cephas Gardner is 77.

Oliver Hale is 79.

Mrs. Sarah Hoar Holmes was born at New Ipswich, New Hampshire, June 24, 1787, and was 90 years old the 24th of June, 1877. She has always been able to read without the use of eye-glasses, and is able to do the finest kind of embroidery. Mrs. Holmes is a relative of the Hoars of Massachusetts.

Mrs. Rebecca L. Carver, a native of Pennsylvania, is 72 years of age.

Elijah Watson is 75 years of age, and his wife 73.

Joseph Harrington was 88 years of age March 14, 1877. He was born in Washington county, New York.

Mrs. Zada Shattuck, Spring township, was born in Connecticut, July 9, 1788, and is consequently in her 90th year since July 9, 1877.

Mrs. Olive Shattuck, Spring township, was born in Litchfield, Connecticut, November 10, 1788, and will be 89 years old the 10th of November, 1877.

Joel Davis, Spring township, was born in Somersetshire, England, June 16, 1798, and is in his 79th year.

Joseph Harrington is in his 89th year. He was born in Washington county, New York, March 14, 1789.

Baptist Young was born in Iniskilin, Ireland, April 1, 1793, and is in his 85th year.

Mrs. Candace Fuller, the mother of General A. C. Fuller, was born at New Britain, now Farmington, Conn., May 19, 1801, and was 76 years old May 14, 1877. This lady is well preserved and quite active in mind and body. Of strong likes and dislikes, she is either a very warm and ardent friend, or the directly opposite. From her the General inherited those sterling qualities and traits of character that enabled him to arise from the obscurity of a poor boy to a position among the first men of Illinois.

Uriah Hill is 88 years of age.
Erastus Shepardson is 77 years of age.
Marcus Linsley is 76 years of age.
Dyer Pierce is 85 years of age.
Phœbe Pierce is 77 years of age.
Mrs. Smith is in her 78th year.

Mrs. Electa Taylor, a native of Berkshire, Mass., is 70 years of age. Although this lady has not reached our standard (75 years and upwards), we consider her a subject eminently worthy of notice. She has been totally blind for ten years. She lives entirely alone, discharges all her domestic duties, such as cooking, etc.; conducts her own correspondence, manages her own financial affairs, and singularly, does all that the smartest and more fortunate of her sisters, or brothers, even, for that matter, could do, and is thoroughly informed upon current events. She has always possessed a most remarkable memory, and her early and middle-aged associations were with such men as William H. Seward and his contemporaries. She is as blithe and cheerful as any bright-eyed girl of twenty, and her heart just as young. The order and neatness that prevail in her home ought to be a reproach to thousands of her countrywomen from whose eyes God's sunlight has not been shut out. But, shut out from her eyes, it has entered her soul, and makes her cheerfully accept the decrees of the Great Omnipotent. "Socrates died like a philosopher." Electa Taylor lives the life of a true woman, that she may die like Socrates.

The united ages of the Old People whose names are given in the above list is equal to 3,014 years—an average of nearly 82 years each.

These are only a few who are known to have outlived the number of years allotted to man. The record might be extended, but time is pressing, and, in conclusion, we can but express the wish that the closing days of their declining years may be as calm and quiet as their own beautiful prairies in these autumnal days, loaded with bountiful harvest of grain and fruitage, ripe and waiting to be garnered.

OFFICIAL VOTE OF BOONE COUNTY, ILLINOIS.

The following is the Official Vote of Boone County, November 7, 1876.

NAMES.	Flora.	Belvidere.	Caledonia.	Manchester.	Spring.	Bonus.	Boone.	LeRoy.	Total.
President.									
Hayes	200	595	176	165	156	209	279	185	1965
Tilden	20	203	25	1	32	45	21	16	363
Cooper		1	16	20	1		5		45
Total	220	799	217	180	189	254	305	201	2373
Governor.									
Cullom	200	594	176	164	155	210	279	185	1946
Steward	20	206	42	22	34	44	26	16	460
Lieutenant Governor.									
Shuman	200	596	177	164	155	210	279	185	1908
Glenn	20	203	25	1	33	44	21	16	363
Pickerell		1	15	21	1		5		43
Secretary of State.									
Harlow	200	596	177	165	155	210	279	185	1967
Thornton	20	203	25	1	33	44	21	16	363
Houten		1	16	21	1		5		44
Auditor of Public Accounts.									
Needles	200	596	177	165	155	210	279	185	1967
Hise	20	204	41	22	34	44	25	16	406
Treasurer of State.									
Rutz	200	596	177	165	155	210	279	185	1935
Gundlach	20	203	25	1	33	44	21	16	363
Aspen		1	16	21	1		5		44
Attorney General.									
Edsall	200	596	177	165	155	210	279	185	1967
Lynch	20	204	25	1	33	44	21	18	362
Coy		1	16	21	1		5		44
Congressional Rep.									
Lathrop	173	227	163	142	86	122	189	48	1150
Hurlbut	29	403	31	39	70	89	91	138	890
Farnsworth	17	108	24	5	33	42	25	14	328
Curry				1					1
State Board of Equalization.									
Hunt	199	597	182	186	157	210	281	184	1996
Dean	20	204	35	1	33	44	23	16	376
Rep. State Legislature.									
Avery	588	1731	552	561	462	586	845	555	5880
Ashton	63	642	102	46	102	117	69	48	1149
Budlong		12				89			101
Hollister						15			15
County Attorney.									
Fuller	187	475	152	120	146	167	195	18	1505
Wood	35	316	65	65	42	78	110	123	844
Clerk Circuit Court.									
De Munn	33	257	101	94	35	110	145	113	898
Sawyer	185	538	117	93	154	142	160	78	1467
Sheriff.									
Lanning					4				4
Covey	219	796	217	187	183	253	305	201	2365
Albright					2				2
Coroner.									
Whitman	204	507	132	162	157	74	268	159	1663
Williamson	15	274	84	24	32	179	35	42	685

A TABULAR STATEMENT

Showing the Totals of Personal and Real Property of Boone County, for the year 1877.

Compiled by W. N. Bennett, Deputy County Clerk.

ITEMS.	Number	Average Value.	Assessed Value.
Horses of all ages	5,951	$46 64	$276,607
Cattle of all ages	16,248	17 48	283,816
Mules and Asses of all ages	70	56 93	3,985
Sheep of all ages	14,702	1 97	28,526
Hogs of all ages	12,747	4 16	52,907
Steam Engines, including Boilers	5	131 60	655
Fire or Burglar-Proof Safes	43	55 11	2,370
Billiard, Pigeon Hole, Bagatelle or other similar Tables	7	125 71	880
Carriages and Wagons of whatsoever kind	2,436	27 14	66,122
Watches and Clocks	2,214	4 68	10,362
Sewing or Knitting Machines	1,076	16 60	17,869
Piano Fortes	84	75 42	6,335
Melodeons and Organs	262	42 52	11,140
Patent Rights	2	202 50	105
Merchandise on hand			134,335
Material and Manufactured Articles on hand			4,950
Manufacturers' Tools, Implements and Machinery (other than Engines and Boilers, which are to be listed as such)			4,052
Agricultural Tools, Implements and Machinery			59,679
Gold and Silver Plate and Plated Ware			2,317
Diamonds and Jewelry			1,000
Moneys of Bank, Banker, Broker or Stock Jobber			6,707
Credits of Bank, Banker, Broker or Stock Jobber			5,584
Moneys of other than Bank, Banker, Broker or Stock Jobber			80,529
Credits of other than Bank, Banker, Broker or Stock Jobber			477,187
Bonds and Stocks			2,000
Shares of Capital Stock of Companies and Associations not incorporated by the laws of this State			3,000
Household or Office Furniture and Property			102,684
Investments in Real Estate and Improvements thereon (see Sec. 10)			350
All other Personal Property required to be listed			49,085
Shares of Stock of State or National Banks			97,494
Total Value of Personal Property			1,793,022
LANDS.			
Improved Lands, in acres*	173,727	25 26	4,388,280
Unimproved Lands, in acres	2,148	20 61	44,269
Total Value of Lands			4,432,549
TOWN AND CITY LOTS.			
Improved Town and City Lots	2,518	453 69	1,142,381
Unimproved Town and City Lots	250	75 06	18,765
Total Value of Town and City Lots			1,161,146
PROPERTY BELONGING TO RAILROADS.			
Lands other than "Railroad Track"			1,895
Personal Property other than "Rolling Stock"			910
Total Value of Railroad Property			2,805
Total Value of all Property as Assessed			7,389,522

*Acres of Wheat, 1,198; of Corn, 32,632; of Oats, 24,244; of Meadow, 24,557; of other Field Products, 10,182; of Inclosed Pasture, 41,318; of Orchard, 2,127; of Woodland, 16,361.

BIOGRAPHICAL DIRECTORY.

ABBREVIATIONS.

Co.	company or county	P. O.	Post Office
farm	farmer	prop.	proprietor
I. V. I.	Illinois Volunteer Infantry	S or Sec.	section
I. V. C.	Illinois Volunteer Cavalry	st.	street
I. V. A.	Illinois Volunteer Artillery	supt.	superintendent
mkr	maker	treas.	treasurer

BELVIDERE TOWNSHIP.

[P. O. Belvidere.]

ABBOTT WILLIAM, laborer.

ABBE AMZI, Farmer; Sec. 9; born in Berkshire Co., Mass., July 15, 1806; came to Belvidere, Boone Co. in 1842, and has lived here 35 years; he ran a saw mill for several years; he has carted grain to Chicago, and sold wheat for 50c per bushel, taking thirteen days to make the trip; owns 310 acres land, and what is unusual, owns all the land he wants; has held office of Road Commissioner twelve years; has also been School Trustee and School Director; married Sybil Bates, of Pittsfield, Mass., in 1829; she died Oct. 30, 1864; he married Mrs. Susan Collins, of N. Y., May 9, 1866; has five children by first wife, George H., Charles E., John D., Ellen M., Mary J.; John D. was Lieutenant and Acting Adjutant in 95th Regt. I. V. I; was in Red River campaign, and was sunstruck at battle of Guntown; Mrs. Collins had five children.

Abbott W. W. farmer; Sec. 2.

Adams E. W.

Ainsworth George, laborer.

Allen Charles, merchant.

ALLEN D. W. Retired; born in Oneida Co., N. Y., Nov. 15, 1817; lived in that State 33 years, and was engaged in Farming and Dairy business; came to this Co. Sept. 21, 1850, and has lived here 27 years; has held office of Town Trustee; married Mary Rix, of Conn., in 1838; she died in 1860; married Ruth F. Foster, of Maine; have two children, Francis A., and John R.

Allen Erastus, farmer.

Allen George, laborer.

Allen W. G.

Alwell Frank, barber.

Ames A. T. stock dealer.

Ames Baker, farmer.

AMES GEO. B. Dealer in Dry Goods, Carpets, etc.; born in Westfield, Chautauqua Co., N. Y., Feb., 1837; removed to Belvidere, 1853; opened the first Drug, Book and Paper Store on south side Nov. 1854, being the only store on that side. in these branches, for several years; added Dry Goods, etc. in 1864; he sold the Book and Paper business in 1868, and the Drug department in 1870; he is also of the firm of Ames, Lowry & Burnside, Boone, Ia.; he owns 1,500 acres of land in Iowa; married Miss Eva S. Watson, of Nashua, N. H., Feb., 1861; the children of this union are Cora E., Genevieve, Minnie, Atta Maud and George B. Ames, Jr.; Minnie died Oct. 8, 1867.

ANGELL ABNER, M. D., Physician; born in New Berlin, Chenango Co., N. Y., Jan. 6, 1816; lived in that State until 27 years of age, and came to this State in 1843, to Genoa, DeKalb Co.; came to this Co. in 1845, and has lived here 32 years; has practiced his profession 34 years; was Surgeon in the army; was at Camp Douglas, Chicago, and had charge of the Post Hospital there; married Miss L. Augusta Caulkins, July 8, 1841; have three children, Mrs. Cornelia A. Winne, born May 15, 1843; Mrs. Ellen M. Sager, Jan. 25, 1845; Mrs. Frances Addie Smith, June 20, 1850.

Anderson Clark, painter.

Andrews H. G. farmer; Sec. 13.

Andrews Mervin, carpenter.

Andrus D. A. K.

Ashton Seneca, farm; Sec. 34.

Ashton L. farmer; Sec. 34.

Askins Patrick, laborer.

AVERY EGBERT H. Carpenter and Bridge Builder; born in Groton, Conn., Jan. 1, 1816; lived in that State 40 years, engaged in Building business; came to Belvidere, Boone Co., Oct. 4, 1854; has lived here 23 years, engaged in Building and Bridge Building; married Sarah L. Cogshall, of New London, Conn., Nov. 9, 1840; have four children, Mrs. Mary Blakesley, Mrs. Louisa Sykes, Charles and Colby; lost one daughter.

Avery Sidney, retired farmer.

Avery W. D. merchant.

BADGER JOHN, mechanic.

Bailey Daniel, farmer.

Bailey Spencer, farmer; Sec. 13.

Baker J. H. farmer.

BALLARD EDWARD, Proprietor of old Newberg Saw-mill; Sec. 30; born in Oswego, N. Y., Oct. 23, 1831; lived in that State 23 years; came to Illinois, Boone Co., in 1853; has lived here 24 years; married S. E. Sheldon, of Mich., in April, 1855; she was daughter of F. S. Sheldon, one of the earliest settlers of Boone Co; they have two children, M. E., born in 1856; Addie E., Feb, 1874; lost one son, Frederick E.

Ballentyne Alex, laborer.

BALLIET J. R. Music Dealer and Dealer in Sewing Machines; South State st.; born in town of Riley, McHenry Co., Ill., Feb. 26, 1848; lived in that Co. 19 years, and came to city of Belvidere in 1867, and has been engaged in business of Music Dealer and Sewing Machines for the past five years; married Miss Mary L. Detrick, of this city, Dec. 24, 1874.

Barker Alpheus.

BARKER S. G. Farmer; Sec. 16; born in Chenango Co., N. Y., Aug. 7, 1821; lived in that State 23 years; came to Illinois, Boone Co., in 1844, and has lived here 33 years; owns 190 acres of land; has held offices of School Director and Road Master; his first wife was Louisa Spencer, of N. Y.; she died June 2, 1872; married Miss McMichael in 1874; he has six children, five by his first wife and one by his present wife; three sons and three daughters.

Barney H. P. farmer; Sec. 8.

Barney John, farmer; Sec. 18.

Barney S. C. farmer; Sec. 8.

Barnes Calvin, farmer; Sec. 10.

Barnes Jas. farmer; Sec. 27.

BARNES JOHN, Farmer; Sec. 23; born in Oneida Co., N. Y., Oct. 20, 1847; lived there about 18 years; came to Illinois, to Boone Co., in 1865, and has lived here 12 years; rents farm of 230 acres from M. S. Molony; married Miss Jessie Wrate, of Belvidere, Boone Co., Nov. 5, 1872; she was born in Westfield, Vt., Sept. 23, 1853.

Barnes Orrin, farmer; Sec. 11.

Barnes Richard, farmer; Sec. 27.

Barr Andrew, mechanic.

Barr Wm. mechanic.

Barrett Pat. laborer.

Barrett W. H.

BARRINGER MARTIN, Retired; born in Rensellaer Co., N. Y., July 19, 1806; lived in that Co. 23 years, and in Genesee Co. 10 years; came to Illinois, DeKalb Co., in 1843; has lived in Belvidere eight years; engaged in Farming many years; has held office of Road Commissioner; married Mary Ann Ives, of Rensellaer Co., N. Y., July 3, 1827; she was born Dec. 11, 1810, and died June 27, 1874; married Mrs. Lunah Sage, of Genesee Co., N. Y., Aug. 12, 1874; has five children, Edward, Alidah, Mary E., Fidelia, Susan J.; lost one daughter.

Bartlet John G. laborer.

Basnies Charles, laborer.

Bassett Simon, retired.

Bassett S. B. mechanic.

Beck John, wagon maker.

Beckington O. auctioneer.

Bement F. B. retired farmer.

Bement George, jeweler and dentist.

Benedict F. retired clergyman.

Bennett A. F. farmer; Sec. 10.

Bennett H. D. mechanic.

Bennett J. A. farmer; Sec. 25.

Bennett J. H. farmer; Sec. 1.

BENNETT MRS. MARY S. born Groton, Mass., May 25, 1805; lived there thirty-four years, and came to this State and Co. in 1839; has lived here thirty-eight years; one of few early settlers now living that were here when she came; married Jas. Bennett, Jan. 5, 1839; he was born in Groton, Mass., Nov. 25, 1802; he was a large land owner in this Co.; died Aug. 20, 1868; children: Jas. A., born Nov. 25, 1830; Samuel, born Nov. 14, 1832, died Nov. 25, 1875; John H., July 7, 1835; Sarah J., April 12, 1838; Geo. S., May 25, 1843; Charles, Oct. 8, 1845; Joshua, Sept. 25, 1848, died March 23, 1850; George was in army, Co. B, 95th I.V.I., and was taken prisoner for one year and fourteen days and released.

BENNETT WILLIS H. Deputy County Clerk, Belvidere; born Erie, Pa., Aug. 24, 1851; lived there 8 years, and came to Ills., to Boone Co., in 1859; was salesman in hardware house in Chicago for 4 years; has occupied his present position for past 3 years; his parents reside here; his father, Henry D. Bennett, was native of N. Y. State, and came here over 30 years ago; one of the early settlers.

BENTLEY MARTIN C. Farmer; born in Franklin Co., Vt., Jan. 1, 1805;

lived in that State seventeen years, and came to Illinois, Boone Co., in 1844; has lived here thirty-three years; engaged in farming many years; used to cart his grain to Chicago and Milwaukee, sold his wheat for 50½c to $1.00 per bushel; held office County Commissioner before the town was organized; has held offices of Supervisor, Assessor and School Trustee; married Sallie M. Woodruff, Feb. 7, 1832; she was born Erie Co., N. Y., Aug. 2, 1810; have five children: Mrs. Julia Ann Foote, Mrs. Frances G. Phoenix, Mrs. Alice J. Sherrill, Helen J. Bentley, Mrs. Georgie E. Witbeck; lost three children.
Benway Edw. laborer.
Berman John, clerk.
Best Rev. E. C. clergyman.
Bidwell Hiram, mechanic.
Bigelow J. grocer.
Bishop E. R. merchant.
Bishop J. J. R. R. employe.
Blaisdell Jas.
Blakey Wm. shoemaker.
Boardman H. W. farmer; Sec. 22.
BOGARDUS ELI, Farmer; born Onondaga Co., N. Y., Aug. 16, 1812; lived there twenty-three years; came to Branch Co., Mich.; lived there fifteen years; came to Boone Co., to Belvidere, in 1850, and has lived here twenty-six years; cultivates broom corn to large extent, and has raised as much as 800 acres in one year; he is the pioneer in broom corn business in this State; owns two farms, 273 acres; married Maria Griffin, from Onondaga Co. N. Y., April 1, 1834; have three children: Mrs. Emeline Bunker, Mrs. Elizabeth Shaw, Mrs. Etta Adams.
Born A. W. barber.
BOWLEY HENRY F. Dry Goods Merchant; born in Sussex, England, Sept. 27, 1837; came to this country in 1855; came to Belvidere same year; went to California in 1861, and returned in 1866; in 1875 he succeeded Mr. Jas. Rider in the Dry Goods business, J. G. Stevens becoming associated with him; married Miss Hannah Rider of Belvidere, June 27, 1866. James Rider, father of Mrs. Bowley, came to Belvidere in 1851; he opened the first store on the south side of the river July 4, 1852; he died in 1875; his widow, Mrs. A. Rider, resides here.
Bowley M. E. jeweler.
Boyce Wm. M. shoemaker.
Boyle C. farmer; Sec. 7.
Braden Wm. mechanic.
Brady J. J. merchant tailor.
Brennan Edw. saloon keeper.
Brennan M. F. saloon keeper.
Brooks B. J. farmer; Sec. 2.
Brown J. D. attorney.

Bruce E. R. farmer; Sec. 4.
Bruce John, farmer.
Bruner Geo. laborer.
Brundridge F. mechanic.
Buchanan A. photographer.
Bucklin S. D.
Burnside A. W. physician.
Bush A. farmer; Sec. 10.
BUSH A. C. Carpenter; born St. Lawrence Co. N. Y., March 15, 1826; lived there seventeen years, and came to this town and Co. in 1843; has lived here thirty-three years; only one log house in town, on South Side; married Laura E. Hall, from Erie Co., Penn., in Feb., 1849; have four children: Emerson, Ira, Bennie and May.
Butler Mike, shoemaker.
Butler Nicholas, mechanic.
Butler Pat. farmer.

C ARNEY JOHN, laborer.
CAMPBELL GEORGE W. Farmer; Sec. 19; born in Otsego Co., N. Y., Aug. 11, 1820; lived in that State sixteen years; came to Illinois, to Boone Co., in 1836, and has lived here forty-one years; one of the few early settlers now living that were here at that time; plenty of Indians here when he came; used to cart his grain to Chicago; no cash market here; has sold wheat at 75c a bushel; owns 208 acres land; has held office of School Director; married Cornelia Marsh, from Plainfield, Otsego Co., N. Y., in 1850; they have five children: Ellen, Mary, George, Frank and Georgiette; lost one daughter.
Carpenter Chas. mechanic.
Carpenter Frank A. mechanic.
CASE E. W. Groceries and Provisions; was born in Bark Hamsted, and came from there to city of Belvidere in 1868, and engaged in the grocery trade and is doing an extensive business; he has two stores, one on north side, corner State and Mechanic streets, and one on south side on State street; he sells more goods than any merchant in Boone Co., his sales amounting in 1876 to $75,000, and in 1877 will amount to $100,000.
Case Eliphalet, shoemaker.
Chamberlin Frank, farmer.
Chamberlin T. M. farmer.
Cheeney John, laborer.
Church Alanson, cooper.
Church Chas. cooper.
Clark H. E. musician.
Coffin Isaac, gardener.
COVEY S. L. See end of this Tp.
CRARY M. E. (Mrs.) See end of this Tp.

Coleman Otis, nurseryman.
Collier John, marble cutter.
Collier Thos. carpenter.
Collins Edw. farmer; Sec. 9.

CONGER JEFFERSON, Farmer; Sec. 36; born in Westerlo, Albany Co., N. Y., March 30, 1837; lived there eighteen years; came to Boone Co., Ills., in 1854, and has lived here twenty-three years; has been engaged in Lumber business in Michigan for past ten years; owns farm of 160 acres just outside city limits; his mother, Mrs. Eliza Conger, lives with him; his father, John Conger, died March 25, 1874; they were from Albany Co., N. Y.; he has two brothers, one here and one in Iowa; he has four sisters, two in this Co., one in Michigan, and one in Iowa.

Conley C. laborer.
Conley Jas. laborer.
Conley M. J. mechanic.
Cook Jas. mechanic.
Cook Jas. harness-maker.

COON R. W. Publisher of Belvidere *Northwestern*; born in Frankfort, Clinton Co., Ind., May 31, 1842; came to this State, to Peoria Co., in 1850; went to Alton, Madison Co., in 1855, and went to Pana in 1851; came to this town and Co. in 1870, and has published the Belvidere *Northwestern* seven years; married Miss Susan Bacon, from New Hampshire, in 1866; she died in 1868; married Miss Mary A. Keeler, of this city and Co., in 1872; has three children, Emma M., Edith M., and Blanche M.

Cooper D. D. constable.
Cornell W. H. mechanic.
Coultrup David, mechanic.
Coultrup Wm. mechanic.
Courtney D. G. student.
Courville Chas. mechanic.
Covey George, laborer.
Covey S. L. sheriff and stock dealer.

CRANDALL LUCIAN L. Born in Cazenovia, Madison Co., N. Y., Aug. 11, 1815; lived in that State twenty-nine years, and came to Boone Co., to Belvidere, July 4, 1845, and has lived here thirty-two years; one of the earlier settlers; married Serena C. Stevens, from Allegheny Co., N. Y., Jan. 15, 1840; they have one child, Mary F.; lost one daughter, Adelle E.

Crary F. R. druggist.
Crinklaw James, butcher.

CRONK ENOCH, Farmer; Sec. 13; born in Dover, Dutchess Co., N. Y., March 11, 1805; lived in that State seventeen years, and came to Boone Co. in 1842, and has lived here thirty-five years; one of the early settlers; only a few shanties in the town of Bonus at that time; used to cart grain to Chicago, and has sold his wheat at 30, 35 and 40c a bushel; took seven days to make trip; married Mary Denny, from Dover, Dutchess Co., N. Y., in December, 1826; she was born June 28, 1806; they have been married fifty-one years; have three children, Richard, Abbie Jane, and Joel; lost two children.

Cross S. L. farmer.
Cunningham H. merchant.
Cunningham M. laborer.
Curtis Peter, laborer.
Curtis Stephen, merchant.

DALE JAMES, painter.

Danforth G. H. grocer.
Darnaelle J. W. retired merchant
Darville J. C. hotel-keeper.
Dawson James F. farmer; Sec. 15.
Dawson John, mechanic.
Dawson Wm. mechanic.
Dawson Wm. M. farmer; Sec. —.
Dean C. B. attorney.

DEAN GEORGE, Retired, born in Ireland, December 18, 1803; lived there twenty-nine years; came to Lower Canada in 1832; lived there twelve years; came to this country in 1844, and to this Co. the same year; has lived here thirty-three years; engaged in farming many years; has carted grain to Chicago and sold his wheat at 40c a bushel; held commission of Coroner in 1853, under administration of F. Pierce; has held offices of Supervisor, and Road Commissioner; married Matilda J. Willis, in Ireland, in 1832; she died in 1846; married Elizabeth Smith, formerly Elizabeth Davis, Sept. 30, 1858; she was born in Maine, Sept. 27, 1816; two children, George W. and Mary Jane Martyn.

Dean G. W. farmer; Sec. 14.
Dellas Peter, laborer.
DeMunn Geo. clerk.

DeMUNN HORATIO C. Born in Genesee Co., N. Y., Nov. 12, 1824; lived in that State twenty-one years; came to Belvidere, Boone Co., in 1845, and has lived in this Co. thirty-two years; has been engaged in farming and teaching school; was appointed Deputy Circuit Clerk in 1856; was appointed Circuit Clerk in 1863; was elected County Clerk in 1864, re-elected in 1868, and again re-elected in 1872; was elected County Treasurer in 1859; married Miss Abagail A. Stackpole, Nov. 22, 1849; she was from Maine, and born Nov. 24, 1830; they have four children: George M., born Aug. 4, 1852; Ella J., February 14, 1854; Kittie A., April 10, 1860; M. Gertrude, Jan. 4, 1866.

Dennison D. A. mechanic.

BELVIDERE TP.

DERTHICK DUDLEY, Butcher and Meat Business; born in Chicago, Nov. 20, 1847; lived there two years, and came to this Co., to Belvidere, in 1849, and has lived here twenty-eight years; was in a printing office three years, and has been engaged in butcher business sixteen years; married Miss Martha Sisk, of Paris, Edgar Co., Ill., Aug. 19, 1872; they have two children: Grace Dudley, born June 10, 1874; Walter M., Nov. 28, 1875.

Derthick Nelse, mechanic.
Derthick Wm. H. mechanic.
Devlin Arthur, laborer.
Devlin Thomas, laborer.
Dickerman O. farmer.
Dingman Joseph, farmer; Sec. 32.
Dingman S. farmer.
Dodge W. R. justice of peace and attorney.
Dolan John, laborer.
Donnelley Francis, laborer.
Donohue James, laborer.
Donohue Thomas, laborer.
Donovan T. farmer; Sec. 9.

DOOLITTLE MRS. MARY, Sec. 25; born in Essex Co., N. Y., Nov. 20, 1823; lived in that State twenty-six years, and came to Belvidere, Boone Co., in 1849, and has lived here twenty-eight years; married Rival Doolittle, in January, 1858; he was born in Vermont, in 1820, and removed to New York when about 18 years old, and came to this Co. in 1836; one of the early settlers; they have one son, John R., born Aug. 18, 1863; he had one son, Fred. H., born March 6, 1859.

Doran H. constable.

DOTY SIMON P. Proprietor Belvidere Hotel; born in Dutchess Co., N. Y., May 9, 1797; lived in that State and was sailing on coast for a number of years; came to this Co. in July, 1835, and has lived here over forty-two years, and he is the oldest male settler now living in this Co.; the Pottawattomie Indians were here when he came; he helped pull down their wigwams, and burned them in 1836; he still owns the lands he first camped on when he came, in 1835; has kept hotel over forty years; he has held office of Sheriff of this Co., and also Commissioner; he married Elizabeth Brewster, of New York; she died in 1855; married Matilda Stiles, of St. Lawrence Co., N. Y.

Dow H. L. insurance agent.
Downs G. W. retired farmer.
Downs James, laborer.
Downs Mike, laborer.
Doyle Garnett, farmer.
Doyle Peter, laborer.
Doyle Wm. laborer.

DuBOIS CORNELIUS, Retired; born in Franklin Co., N. Y., April 3, 1813; lived there twenty-two years, and came to Belvidere in 1836, and has lived here forty-one years; one of the earliest settlers; only very few now living here that were at that time; engaged in farming many years; used to cart his grain to Chicago, and has sold wheat at 50c a bushel, taking five to eight days to make trip; has held office of School Director and Roadmaster; married Mary Sheldon, from New York, in the spring of 1838; she died in 1849; they had one son, Frederick S.; married again to Mrs. Julia Watkins, formerly Julia Brink, of Genesee Co., N. Y., March 2, 1852; have one son, Lewis A., born June 22, 1854; Mrs. Watkins had one son, Nathan. W.

DuBOIS FRED. S. Farmer; Sec. 18; born in Belvidere, Boone Co., on the place where he now resides, Oct. 3, 1842; has lived here thirty-five years; only a few persons born in Boone Co. now living here older than he; is engaged in farm and dairy business; owns a farm of 130 acres; married Celestia M. Gleason, April 25, 1867; she was born in the town of Guilford, Winnebago Co., Ill., April 30, 1844; they have one child, Mary Eunice, born Sept. 8, 1873.

Dunbar W. W.; clerk.
Dunlavy Frank, laborer.
Dunton G. B. farmer; Sec. 24.

DUNTON WM. S. President First National Bank.

Dupuy D. D. farmer.
Dupuy G. laborer.
Durham Wm. H.; agent.

EASTON REV. T. C. Presbyterian clergyman.

Edgecomb D. J. blacksmith.

EISSFELDT REV. CHAS. F. TH. Pastor Evangelical Lutheran Immanuel Church; born Milwaukee, Nov. 29, 1854; lived there 16 years; entered the Preparatory there and spent 2 years; then entered the Northwestern University at Watertown, Wis., and spent 4 years, and went to St. Louis and studied 3 years in Theological Concordia Seminary; passed examination June 15, 1877; he received a call to the Evangelical Lutheran Immanuel Church, Belvidere, and also to the German Lutheran Church, Pecatonica, Winnebago Co., Ills.

Ellick George, farmer.
Ellis D. E. physician.
Erdlmeyer F.; laborer.
Erwin G. L. farmer.
Erwin Wm. S. farmer; Sec. 4.
Estell D. G. mechanic.
Escalt Henry.

FARRAR & QUACKENBOSS, Livery and Boarding Stable, opposite Julian House, Belvidere; J. H. Farrar was born in Oxford Co., Maine, March 28, 1848; came to this Co. in 1867; married S. J. Decosta, from Oxford Co., Maine; they have three children.

Farrar J. M. laborer.

Fay D. A. farmer; Sec. 13.

Feakins Charles, butter dealer.

Fellows J. H. mechanic.

Fewins Eli, mechanic.

Fish Garnett, pump maker.

Flaack I. H. mechanic.

Flynn M. J. merchant tailor.

FOOTE DANIEL F. Physician; born in Chenango Co., N. Y., April 7, 1828; studied medicine with Dr. Frederick Hyde, of Cortlandville, N. Y., Prof. Syracuse University and Dean of Medical Faculty; graduated University of Buffalo in 1851; practiced in Tioga Co., N. Y.; came to Belvidere in May, 1854, and has practiced his profession here 23 years; has held office Board of Town Trustees and Coroner; is member American Medical Association, State Medical Society, and one of its vice presidents in 1876; was member International Medical Congress held in Philadelphia in 1876; married Miss Martha E. Updegraff, from Tioga Co., N. Y., July 19, 1855; three children, daughters, Stella E., Hattie L., Mary I.

Foote J. C. druggist.

FOOTE HON. JOHN J. It has ever been a subject of debate whether grand occasions give rise to our celebrated men or that our celebrated men occasion the grand and important epochs in history. It allows the largest amount of argument on both sides, for it may be shown that without certain events transpiring there would have been nothing to develop the genius, enterprise and skill of our celebrated men; while, on the other hand, it can be argued that many of the most brilliant occasions might have arisen and passed unnoticed had not the genius of the hour seized upon them and made them serve the good of their generation and universal humanity. The truly great man is not made so by the mere elevation to important positions of civil or sacred responsibilities. The man who can discharge duty in despite of opposition—the man who can reverence his conscience so greatly as to preserve it unharmed—the man who can wield the largest amount of benevolent power for his fellow men—bringing tact and executive and administrative ability to his post of duty and honor—may be truly classed as exhibiting that type of greatness so much needed to meet the exigencies of our times. That the subject of the present sketch merits all this noble and generous distinction, will appear in the following brief synopsis of his life and official career.

John J. Foote was born in Hamilton, Madison County, N. Y., on the 11th of February, 1816. He was educated at Hamilton Academy, and there pursued his classical course, and received the honorary degree of Master of Arts from Madison University, in 1837. In 1858, he embarked in the mercantile trade, and continued in the same until his removal West. In his business career he was marked for strict integrity and financial success. He became early identified with the educational institutions of his native town, and maintained a deep and abiding interest in their rise, growth, and prosperity. At an early period he took an active and prominent position in both local and State politics. As a mark of the high esteem in which he was held by all citizens, irrespective of party, he was elected to important offices in his native town when the opposite party was largely in majority—frequently holding the office of Supervisor and Chairman of the County Board. Repeatedly, offices of great trust were offered and declined, such as Canal Commissioner, and, in 1853, the unanimous nomination of the Whigs of the Twentieth District, composed of Madison and Oswego counties, for a seat in the Senate. But, in the fall of 1857, the Republican party, of which he was one of the prominent founders, brought him forward and elected him to a seat in the Senate, representing the counties of Madison, Chenango and Cortland, by the largest majority ever given to any member from that district.

Senator Foote, during his senatorial career, introduced what is known as, and has become a part of our national history, "The Personal Liberty Bill," which enlisted the most active sympathies and keenest debate among the leading men in the New York Legislature. While in the senate he was associated and taken into counsel with the most prominent minds in the state, among which might be named his Excellency, Gov. Morgan, Hon. Thurlow Weed, Vice President Wheeler, and others, and was always admired for his qualities as a statesman, and especially for his noble, independent and severe honesty. A man who in the support and vindication of true principles, was as inflexible as Cæsar, as just as Aristides, and as pure as Cato!

In 1860 he represented in the electoral college of New York, the counties of Oswego and Madison. Owing to failing health, he relinquished business and came to Belvidere, Boone Co., Illinois, in the fall of 1865, to take charge of his large and thrifty farm, located near to the town, and has been twice elected President of the Boone County Agricultural Society, and repeatedly Supervisor of the town and Chairman of the County Board.

So wide and extensive was his range of influence among the leading official men of the state and city of New York, that upon the heavy defalcations in the Post-office of New York city during the administration of General Jones as Post-master, the result of an utter want of system, which characterized his and previous administrations, and want of executive ability to eradicate existing evils of maladministration, that Mr. James, who had received the appointment of Postmaster, and who was required to give bonds to the amount of $400,000, was requested by his bondsmen and other leading men, to induce Mr. Foote to take charge of the financial department of the Post-office. Owing to the critical state of his health, he only consented, after repeated and urgent solicitations, to accept the position temporarily, as Auditor. Such, however, was his executive ability and administrative tact, that he was enabled to recover the office from its long disintegrated and demoralized state of affairs, to the most rigid system and order, so as to command the admiration of all the officials at Washington; the plan of whose operations is now adopted in several large cities of the United States! During his term in the New York city Post-office, he had entire charge of the financial arrangements of the Post-office, including the construction of the new Post-office and Court-house building, costing several millions of dollars. The business of the New York Post-office is enormous; the transactions of one department—the money order—reaches the sum of $35,000,000 per annum. There are twenty branch Post-offices, all comprised under the New York city Post-office. As a sample of the immense business of this Post-office, the mail matter of one department of Mr. Foote's division—the newspaper and periodical department delivered in the course of one year, would make a train of 76 miles long of wagons, each wagon containing one ton!

Mr. Foote was Auditor in charge of the first division, and acting Post-master during the absence of the Post-master. The assignment of duties of his division we find as follows: "The supervision and keeping of all accounts between the office and Post-office at Washington, and the Custodian Division and the U. S. Treasury Department; the supervision of all official matters envolving the disbursements and receipt of money, including the auditing accounts of Cashier and of all the divisions and departments and branches of the office, of all pay-rolls and of all vouchers, bills and requisitions for construction, services, supplies and repairs; the supervision of the Unpaid Postage Department, and of the payment of postage by stamps, or otherwise, or mailable matter deposited or received for delivery at the office; and supervision of the depository for mail locks and mail pouches, and sacks received for distribution or repairs, and the department for repairs of the same, and care and preservation of the Post-office and Court House building, heating apparatus, machinery, furniture and fixtures; construction, repairs, changes in building and furniture, or fixtures; and service and material for the same; and supervision of the Engineers' Department."

Upon Mr. Foote's retirement from the office, the most flattering testimonials from Post-master James and the several heads of the varied departments were presented, all expressing regret at his withdrawal from the high and distinguished position he had so successfully occupied, and also expressing the kindest wishes for his future happiness and restored health. The following letter was presented to Mr. Foote from Post-master James, on tending his resignation:

POST-OFFICE, NEW YORK CITY }
OFFICE OF THE POSTMASTER. }
April 7, 1876. }

My Dear Senator—I have the honor to acknowledge the receipt of your letter tendering your resignation as Auditor of this office, to take effect the 30th instant.

The friendship that has existed between us for more than a quarter of a century, and my knowledge of your personal worth, rare executive and financial ability, together with your unflinching courage and sterling integrity, would impel me to ask the withdrawal of your resignation but for the fact stated in your letter—that your private business is suffering from want of your attention, and that your health is giving way under the great strain placed upon it by your untiring labors in your division of the work of this office.

In thus reluctantly accepting your resignation, I desire to thank you for the zeal and fidelity with which you have discharged the varied duties of your division, and to express the hope that your private life in the future may be as pleasant to you and yours as your past official life has been beneficial to the public whom you have so faithfully served.

I shall, however, fill the office of Auditor temporarily, in the hope that, after a few months' rest, your health and private business will permit you to resume its duties.

I am, my dear Senator,

Very truly yours,

THOMAS L. JAMES, *Post-master*.

THE HONORABLE JOHN J. FOOTE,
Auditor New York Post-office.

The following resolutions, elaborately and artistically executed, were handsomely framed and presented on his retirement from official duties:

POST-OFFICE, NEW YORK CITY, }
April 8th, 1876. }

HON. JOHN J. FOOTE, *Auditor New York Post-Office:*

Dear Sir: As the official relations which for nearly three years have existed between yourself and the undersigned, are, as we understand, shortly to be terminated by your resignation, we desire to express to you the regret which each of us experiences at parting with one whose personal qualities and official conduct have, during that time, secured at once our friendship and respect. Entering the service, as you did, without previous knowledge of the details of its operations or of the complicated regulations which govern them, your persistent industry and untiring perseverance soon enabled you to acquire a familiarity with postal affairs equal to that possessed by those of long experience, while the business talents which had so well served you in your previous mercantile career enabled you to introduce, and to put in successful operation, improvements the effect and benefit of which are now apparent to all, and will long be felt and appreciated hereafter. While you have been strict and unswerving in your own adherence, and in requiring the adherence of others, to the rules and principles which, in fulfillment of the duty assigned to you by the Post-master as supervisor of the financial affairs of this office, you have found it necessary to prescribe, your intercourse with us in regard to those matters has been marked by a courtesy and consideration which will leave none but pleasant remembrances in connection therewith.

In taking leave of you we beg to offer our congratulations on the relief from the cares of official life which your retirement will afford, and to tender our best wishes for your happiness and prosperity up to and beyond that time when the final accounts of all shall be audited, with errors and omissions excepted.

Very truly your friends, H. G. Pearson, Wm. H. Wareing, H. Major, Wm. M. Heagerty, Geo. F. Hopper, J. Gayler, Levi Blakeslee, Wm. Phinley, E. Y. Ten Eyck, Hugh Gardner, Anthony Yeoman, John Richards, Charles Forrester, R. C. Jackson.

Thus terminated his official relations with the New York post-office, commanding the highest respect and praise from many in the metropolis who had learned of his able and efficient administration as Auditor. The press tendered him, also, unqualified commendations for his efficient fulfillment of all the duties assigned to that responsible position.

Here in his own town and among all the citizens of Boone County, both himself and family are universally beloved.

Foote Wm. S. dentist.

Fosage Fred, laborer.

FOSTER LEIGHTON, Retired; born in Limerick, Maine, April 19, 1810; lived in New Portland, Dover and Bangor 43 years; came to Belvidere in 1852, and has lived in Boone Co. 25 years, and was engaged in farming many years; has held office of Town Trustee; married Miss Clarissa Ricker, March 7, 1833; she was born in New Portland, Maine, April 6, 1813; they have three children, Mrs. Ruth Fallen, John R., Seth L. Foster.

Fox W. I. manufacturer (shoemaker).

FRANCIS JAMES, Farmer; Sec. 33; born in Sussex Co., Eng., Nov. 18, 1838; came to this country in 1853; came to Boone Co., Belvidere, the same year, and has lived here 24 years; he married Miss Sallie E. Moore, from Cortland Co., N. Y., June, 1863; have one child, Celona Frances, born March 11, 1869; have lost two daughters, Anna Belle, Mary Jane.

FREEMAN JOHN D. Carpenter; born in Allegheny Co., N. Y., June 26, 1825; went to Pennsylvania when nine years of age, lived there twenty-one years; came to this town and Co. in 1855, and has lived here twenty-two years; married Pollie Northrup, of Schoharie Co., N. Y., Dec. 24, 1846; she was born July 12, 1813; they have two children; James, born Nov. 20, 1848; Clara, May 9, 1854.

Fritz Chas. mechanic.

FROOM ELIJAH G. Farmer; Sec. 16; born in Ogdensburg, N. Y., July 14, 1812; lived there and in Canada twenty years, came to this Co. Aug. 12, 1840; only had 9 cents in his pocket when he arrived; has lived here 37 years; one of the early settlers; he used to cart grain to Chicago, also pork; has taken 6,500 lbs. of pork at one load to Chicago; has sold winter wheat at 44 cents, corn 10 cents, and potatoes 5 cents a bushel; owns farm of 109 acres; married Mrs. Rhoda Cross, formerly Rhoda Eggleston, July 24, 1842; she was born in Washington Co., N. Y., June 13, 1813, and came to Chicago in 1837; an early settler; she had one child, S. L. Cross.

Froom George, grocer.

Froom P. S. grocer.

FULLER GEN. ALLEN C., Whose portrait appears in this work, was born in Farmington, Hartford Co., Conn., on Sept. 24, 1822; he studied law with Judge J. R. Doolittle, of Warsaw, N. Y., now of Chicago, and was admitted to the practice of law in the Supreme Court of the State of N. Y.; he came to Belvidere in 1846, a young lawyer, with nothing but industry, integrity, and capacity, to recommend him to the people—how well they have served him his present enviable reputation shows; he was elected Judge of the Circuit Court, and discharged the duties of that high office with marked ability; the breaking out of the rebellion found him upon the bench; he was tendered the position of Adjutant General; the members of the bar opposed his resignation, and urged him to accept the appointment temporarily; he entered upon its duties Nov. 11, 1861, and in July following resigned his seat on the bench. The following extract from a report of a Legislative Committee appointed to inspect the Adjutant General's office tells how faithfully he performed the arduous duties pertaining to his trust:

"That we have thoroughly examined the office of the Adjutant General and find it a model in completeness, one that preserves in all its glory the proud records of our soldiery, and reflects infinite credit upon the great state whose sons they are:

"That in the judgment of this committee the thanks of every patriotic citizen of the state are due to Gen. Fuller for the able and efficient manner in which he has discharged the duties of the office, and for his indefatigable efforts in collecting and preserving the glorious record of a glorious state."

Gov. Yates thus refers to his invaluable services: "I acknowledge myself deeply indebted to Gen. Fuller in the management of the military affairs of the state. He has been a most able, faithful and energetic officer, and is entitled to the gratitude of the state." In 1864, he was elected to represent Boone Co. in the General Assembly, and on the first of January resigned the position of Adjutant General and was chosen Speaker of the House of Representatives. He has filled the office of State Senator with credit to his constituency and honor to himself.

With the exception of Gov. Yates, no other name is mentioned so frequently and favorably in state military matters as that of Gen. Fuller. The boys in blue remember him as a true friend, and will ever extend to him a cordial place in their memories. Wherever Illinois and her gallant sons are mentioned, Gen. Fuller will be among her *Brightest Jewels* or *Noblest Heroes.*

FULLER CHARLES E. Attorney and Counsellor at Law; born in Flora, Boone Co., Ill., March 31, 1849; son of Seymour and Eliza A. Fuller, who came to Illinois from Genesee Co., N. Y., and settled in Flora Tp., Boone Co., in 1845, where they still reside; attended district school until 12 years of age; in 1861 to 1863, clerked in store in Belvidere for uncle, Mr. J. C. Mordoff; afterwards, until 1867, was employed at clerking in Cherry Valley, Ill., Independence, Ia., and Wataga, Ill.; in 1867-8, carried on a book store at Waverly, Ia., in connection with brother, J. A. Fuller; afterwards, until spring of 1869, traveled through Iowa and Minnesota as agent for a wholesale book house, in Dubuque; in 1869 commenced the study of law, in the office of Hon. Jesse S. Hildrup, Belvidere, Ill.; was admitted to the bar Aug. 17, 1870, at the age of 21 years; has since practiced profession at Belvidere, practice rapidly increasing until it is second to that of no attorney in the county; practice also extends into the neighboring counties of Winnebago, DeKalb, McHenry and Kane; was leading attorney for the defense in the Donnell murder case at Geneva, Kane Co., May, 1877; has taken a somewhat active part in politics, as a Republican; made several active political canvasses for the Republicans in 1870, 1872 and 1876, gaining considerable reputation as a stump speaker; is now Chairman Republican County Committee, and member Judicial Committee 12th Circuit; in 1875 was elected Corporation Attorney of Belvidere, and re-elected in 1876; at the fall election of 1876 was elected State's Attorney, which office he now holds; was married April 24, 1873, to Miss Sadie A. Mackey, daughter of Hon. Hugh Mackey, of Cherry Valley, Ill.; after the death of Judge M. M. Boyce in 1873, purchased the law office and library of the old firm of M. M. Boyce & Bro., and with large additions thereto since, has now one of the finest offices and largest law libraries in the West.

Fuller D. P. farmer; Sec. 4.
Fuller Major, farmer; Sec. 4.
Fulligar James, laborer.
Fulligar Thomas, saloon keeper.

GAGE E. T. clerk.

Gahlbeck John, laborer.
Galligher Hugh, laborer.
Gannon J. farmer; Sec. 1.
Garcelon E. E. stock dealer.

GARDNER CEPHAS, Retired; born in Grafton Co., N. H., Oct. 9, 1800; removed to Bennington Co., Vt., at early age; lived there and in Mass. six years; removed to Lower Canada and lived there eighteen years, and came to this Co. in 1836, and is one of the earliest settlers—only one man here now (Mr. S. P. Doty) that was here then; was in Minnesota in mercantile business two years, and represented town of St. Anthony in State Legislature; has held office County Treasurer for four years, and Supervisor for several terms, and Justice of the Peace for four years; married Pamelia Bodwell, of Stansed, Lower Canada, in 1824; she died in May, 1862; four children, Mrs. Emeline Maloney, Mrs. Jane Waterman, Mrs. Pamelia Moulton, Mrs. Mary Ann Tripp.

Garweth R. retired farmer.

Gawath R. farmer; Sec. 5.
Gibson J. W. teacher.
GILMAN COL. L. O. Deputy U. S. Marshal; born in Province of Quebec, Jan. 28, 1831; lived there 21 years; came to U. S. and lived in Mass. 7 years; came to Boone Co. 1860; was in the army, Colonel 15th I. V. I.; was wounded at battle of Atlanta, July 22, 1864; was at battle of Pittsburg Landing, siege of Corinth, siege of Vicksburg; was in Gen. Sherman's campaign in 1864 until wounded; was elected Sheriff of this Co. in 1866; was elected County Treasurer in 1870, and was appointed Deputy U. S. Marshal in 1870, office at Chicago; married Miss Elotia I. Garland, Jan. 10, 1855; she was from Province of Quebec; have five children, Maria E., William T., Cora L., Nellie M., Alfred L.
Gilman Thomas, gardener.
Gilman W. H., Jr., jeweler.
Gilman Wm. H., Sr., retired.
GILSON GEORGE, Retired; born Isle of Man, Aug. 12, 1795; came to America in 1825; came to this State and Co. in 1835; one of oldest settlers, only few living were here then; was engaged in farming many years; his farm of 188 acres was one of the first settled in Boone Co.; has held office of School Director and Path master, hauled some of the first loads of wheat from this Co. to Chicago, and sold it for 32 cents per bushel, dug the first cellar in Rockford; married Elizabeth Hurst, from Cambridgeshire, Eng., born in Lincolnshire; she died June 25, 1872; seven children, Thomas, William, Henry, Mary Ann, Eliza Jane, living; lost two children
Gimson S. shoemaker.
Glasner J. M. merchant.
Glass E. E. farmer; Sec. 3.
Glass E. T. farmer; Sec. 3.
Gleason A. H. attorney.
GOODRICH JOSEPH, Retired; born Somerset Co., Me., Feb. 6, 1813; lived there twenty-two years; went to Ohio and lived there four years; came to this State in 1839; he brought the first threshing machine in this State; he lived in Alabama, Mississippi and Louisiana sixteen years; came to this Co. in 1858; he married Mrs. Harriet L. Ticknor, (formerly Harriet L. Luce,) of Prattville, Ala., June 5, 1855; she was born in Conn.; they have one child, Mrs. Leonard Longeor; lost one son, Joseph, born in Conn., Feb. 17, 1857, died Aug. 5, 1863.
Goodspeed Jas. farmer.
Gorman Patrick, farmer.
GOUGH THOS. Farmer; Sec. 34; Belvidere P. O.; born Newcastle, Eng., Aug. 26, 1846; and came to this country 1867, and to this Co. same year; lived here 10 years; owns farm 50 acres in town Bonus, 1¾ miles from Belvidere; married Carrie Shippey from Elkhorn, Wis., April 2, 1876; they have one child, James William, born Jan. 2, 1877   James W.Gough, brother of above, was born in Ireland, 1848; came to this country 1869, and came to Boone Co. same year; rents farm of his brother, Thomas, in town Bonus.
Gould J. H. sewing machine agent.
Grady John, laborer.
Gray H. R. farmer; Sec. 24.
Gray Hartwell, farmer.
Gray John, livery stable.
Gray Richard,
Gray Wm. livery stable.
GRAY BROS. Livery, Sale and Boarding Stable.
Gritzbaugh W. tailor.
Greenlee Chas. merchant.
Greenlee Geo. merchant.
Greenlee John, Jr. merchant.
Greenlee John, Sr. retired.
Guilbault M. laborer.

HALE OLIVER, retired farmer.
Halloway Edw. clerk.
Hall J. B. laborer.
Halleck E. H. 'bus driver.
HAMMOND D. H. Farmer; Sec. 18; born in Cortland Co., N. Y., March 2, 1832; lived in that State twenty years; came to Boone Co. in 1854; was in the army over three years, 65th I. V. I., Co. E; was at the surrender of Harper's Ferry, and through the Atlantic campaign; was in the battles of Knoxville, Franklin, and others; was promoted to Sergeant of Co. E; has held office of Collector of the town of Caledonia; married Elizabeth M. Shanks, in Wis., Feb., 1868; she was from Ohio; they have one child, Nora Maud, born Jan. 14, 1871.
Hannah John, stock dealer.
Happer Geo. farmer; Sec. 8.
Harder Geo. laborer.
Harder Peter, farmer.
Harder Wellington, laborer.
Harding C. B. produce dealer.
Harrison John, mechanic.
HARTWELL GEO. H. Carpenter and Builder; born in Belvidere, Feb. 8, 1837; he has lived in this Co. forty-one years, and is the first white child born in Boone Co. now living here; married Miss Alice M. Rix, from Utica, N.Y., in 1862; she died Feb. 23, 1877; children: Frank, George and Eddie; lost one son, Terry; Thos. W. Hartwell, father of Geo. H., was born in Mass., and came to Boone

Co. in 1835; was one of the earliest settlers; held office of Justice of the Peace before the Co. was organized; he died in 1847.
Harvey Robert.
Haskins Henry, mason.
Haskins Ira, physician.
Haskins Morris R.
Hathorn Nathan.
Hayes A. merchant.
HAYNES JOHN, Photographer; born in Steubenville, Ohio, Nov. 12, 1833; lived in that city; he studied and engaged in his profession in New York city; was in Chicago twelve years; came to Belvidere in 1873; he married Miss Lucy A. Bonbright, from Philadelphia, in March, 1863; they have two children, Mary and William Haynes.
HAYWOOD WM. Dealer in Agricultural Implements; born Chautauqua Co., N. Y., May 4, 1823; lived there twenty-four years, and came to this State and Co. June 4, 1846; has lived here thirty-one years; one of the early settlers; was in Mexican War; was Second Lieutenant 5th I. V. I.; was in several skirmishes; was in the army during the late war, Captain Co. B, 15th I. V. I., the first regiment in the U. S. mustered in the service for the war; has held office of Justice of the Peace for a number of years; married Miss Lydia E. Rix, from Herkimer Co., N. Y., in 1849; two children, Mary E. and Henry L.
Hedges C. E. retired.
Herbert J. H. retired farmer.
Herrick Geo. blacksmith.
Hersey M. B. carpenter.
HEYWOOD JONATHAN, Farmer; Sec. 8; born in Lancashire, Eng., Aug. 4, 1813; came to this country in 1838; worked in Sprague's Print Works, Rhode Island; he came to this Co. in April, 1840, walking most of the way here; he entered 80 acres of his present farm of 132 acres from the government; in 1850 he went to California, walking most of the way there; was gone four years; he married Jane Worthington, from Lancashire, Eng., in 1842; they have ten children, seven sons and three daughters, and have lost two daughters.
Heywood Z. V.
Hicks J. M. farmer.
Hicks S. J. farmer.
HILDRUP JESSE S. United States Marshal Northern District of Ill.; born Middletown, Conn., May 14, 1833; lived there fifteen years; removed to State of N. Y., and from there to Harrisburg, Penn.; came to Belvidere, Boone Co., in 1860, and has practiced law here since; he has held offices of Corporation Trustee, Supervisor,

Deputy Provost Marshal, and Master in Chancery; was member of the Constitutional Convention of 1870; he represented this district in the State Legislature during the Twenty-seventh and Twenty-eighth General Assemblies; he was appointed United States Marshal for Northern District Ill. by President Hayes, March 16, 1877; married Nellie Brinkerhoff, from Mansfield, O., Feb., 1858; they have four children; Hattie S., James J., Nellie S. and Fred. W.
Hill Harvey, dealer.
Hill Henry, laborer.
HILL IRA D. Carpenter; born Putnam Co. N. Y., Dec. 25, 1823; lived there thirty years, and came to this State and Co. in 1853; was engaged in farming and carpenter business; was in army, Co. B, 95th I. V. I.; was in battles of Vicksburg, Nashville and Spanish Fort; was on detached duty part of the time; married Mrs. Phœbe Case, formerly Mrs. Phœbe Miller, of Putnam Co., N. Y., July 25, 1844; two children: Jane Ophelia and Sarah Adelia.
Hill Uriah.
Hill Orlando, shoemaker.
Hill S. W. mechanic.
Hill Josiah, shoemaker.
Hines Bertrand, farmer.
Hodges Pat. farmer; Sec. 17.
HOLLENSHEAD G. C. Carpenter; born in Tompkins Co., N. Y., Feb. 19, 1813; lived in that State 43 years, and came to this Co. in 1856; he lived in Forreston ten years; married Sophronia Johnson, from Orange Co., N. Y., Sept. 12, 1844; have three children, DeWitt Clinton, Ella S., Grace A.
HOLLISTER LUTHER, Retired; born in Green Co., N. Y., Sept. 7, 1807; lived there 25 years; lived in Schoharie 6 years, Montgomery Co. 15 years, Greene Co. 10 years; came to this State and Co. in 1865; engaged in Farming; has held office of Justice of the Peace six years, and Town Trustee; married Jane Onderdonk, of Albany Co., N. Y., in 1829; have four children, Samuel, now in Atchison, Kan.; Abram, now in Austin, Minn.; Wm. H., physician in Austin, Minn.; Sarah J. Lane, now in Port Byron; lost one son, Lansing, Captain in 120th Regt. N. Y. V. I., and killed at battle of Gettysburg; lost one daughter, Mrs. Alice M. Brealy.
HORAN ANDREW, born in Co. Antrim, Ireland, Nov. 27, 1819; came to Quebec in 1841; lived there six years; arrived in this country, at Chicago, Oct. 10, 1847; came to Belvidere in Sept., 1848, and has lived here twenty-nine years; was in the employ of the old Chicago & Galena R. R. eight years; has been in the employ of American Express Co. ten years; mar-

ried Catherine Johnston, Nov. 26, 1839; she was born in Co. Antrim, Ireland, May 24, 1821; they have four children, Robert, born in Ireland, Sept. 3, 1840; John, in Canada, April 10, 1843, was wounded before Vicksburg, June 12, 1863, and died at Memphis; Mary Jane, in Canada, April 16, 1846; Charles E., in Belvidere, Aug. 8, 1857; Robert was in the army, Co. G. 95th Regt. I. V. I., three years; was with the regiment in all its battles and skirmishes.

Horan Robert, painter.

HOPKINS D. Dealer in Harness, Saddlery, Hardware and Carriages; born in Oneida Co., N. Y., Feb. 22, 1834; lived there thirteen years; came to McHenry Co. and lived there eight years; lived in Rockford eight years, and came here in 1864; been in business here thirteen years; married Miss Frank A. Smiley, from Erie Co., Penn., Dec. 9, 1866; she was born Nov. 4, 1844, and came here in 1854; they have one son, Charles E. Hopkins, born August 27, 1877; lost one son, Harry C.; he was born Sept. 20, 1868, and died in infancy.

Hopkins George, mechanic.
Houghtailing Wm. gardener.
Hovey A. T. clerk.
Hovey Calvin, laborer.
Hovey H. C., R. R. employee.
Hovey S. B., R. R. employee.
Hovey Wm. F. merchant.
Hovey W. W., R. R. employee.
Howard H. B. laborer.
Howard H. W. mechanic.
Howe W. E. produce dealer.
Hubbel Ezra, carpenter.
Hubbell F. E. mechanic.
Hudson Samuel.
Hull F. A. machinist.

HULL H. Farmer; Sec. 13; born in Putnam Co., N. Y., Nov. 17, 1834; lived in that State twenty-one years, and came to Boone Co. in 1855; has been engaged in farming in the towns of Bonus and Belvidere; owns 138 acres land; has held office of Road Master; married Calista M. Stockwell, Feb. 9, 1860; she was born in Livingston Co., N. Y.; they have three children, Alice A., born Dec. 7, 1861; Annie E., April 18, 1862; Clara I., Dec. 18, 1864; lost one son, Freddy, born Aug. 17, 1869, died 1871.

Hull W. B. retired farmer.
Humphrey I. A. jailor.

HUMPHREY J. M. born Knox Co., Ohio, Aug. 31, 1840; educated at Beloit, Wis.; was in army; was Captain Co. C, 142d Regt. I. V. I.; engaged in Farming and Breeder of Fine Stock; married Rosira Newton, from Binghampton, N. Y., in December, 1862; have five children, one son and four daughters.

Huntington L. S. carpenter.
Huntington M. farmer; Sec. 13.
Hurd F. E. farmer; Sec. 22.
Hurlbut Geo. H. civil engineer.

HURLBUT STEPHEN A., Whose portrait appears in this work, was born at Charleston, South Carolina, Nov. 29, 1815; was thoroughly and liberally educated; studied Law and was admitted to the Bar in 1837; removed to Belvidere, Illinois, Sept., 1845, where he has since resided, practicing his profession when not engaged in public duties; was a member of the Constitutional Convention of Illinois, in 1847; was Presidential Elector on the Whig ticket in 1848; was a member of the State Legislature in 1859, 1861 and 1867; was Presidential Elector at large on the Republican ticket in 1868; Mr. H. raised the first company in the state of Illinois for the regular U. S. service for three years, which afterwards became Co. B. of 15th Regt. I. V. I.; was appointed Brigadier-General of Volunteers, June, 1861, to rank from May 17, 1861; commanded the 4th Division at Pittsburg Landing; Gen. Hurlbut has the credit of forming the best line of battle and saving the day to the Union Army at the battle of Shiloh, and for meritorious service on that occasion was promoted Major-General in September, 1862; was assigned to the command of the Sixteenth Army Corps at Memphis, and to the command of the Department of the Gulf in 1864 and 1865; was honorably mustered out in July, 1865; was appointed, by President Grant, Minister Resident to the United States of Columbia from 1869 to 1872; was elected to the Forty-third Congress as a Republican, receiving 15,532 votes against 5,134 votes for his opponent, S. E. Bronson; re-elected to the Forty-fourth Congress; married Sophronia Stevens, of Alleghany Co., New York, in 1847; they have one son, George H.; Mr. H. is living quietly at his beautiful home in Belvidere, wearing with becoming modesty his well-earned laurels in both military and civil life.

INGALLS O. B. farmer.

Insley John, retired merchant.
Irish Leonard, farmer.
Irvin W. S. farmer; Sec. 4.

JACOBS J. J. laborer.

Jaffray Jas. merchant.
Jarvis Frank, farmer.
Jarvis Henry, laborer.
Jarvis Richard, farmer; Sec. 33.
Jarvis Robert, laborer.

Jasper F.

JENNER ASHER E., Justice of the Peace; born in Essex Co., N. Y., April 10, 1818; lived in that State twenty years, and came to this State and Co., to Belvidere, in 1838, and has lived here thirty-nine years; one of the earliest settlers; only eleven buildings here when he came, and he knew every man in this county for several years; he has held office of County Clerk and also County Treasurer, and has been Justice of the Peace for the past sixteen years; married Mary J. Cook, of N. Y., in 1840; she died in 1854; two children; married Emmeroy E. Lyon, of Burlington, Vt., in 1856; had two children; Kittie H., Nellie A., Charlie J., George C.

Johnson A. W. retired physician.
Johnson A. W. farmer; Sec. 10.
Johnson O. T. laborer.
Johnson Theodore, farmer.
Johnson Thomas, gardener.
Johnson Wm. W. retired physician.

JONES A., Farmer; Sec. 15; born in Albany Co., N.Y., May 6, 1822; lived in that State 35 years; came to Illinois, to Boone Co., in April, 1857, and has lived here 20 years; was engaged in Lumber business in Belvidere six years; has held office of Road Master; owns farm of 32 acres, and other property; married Mary A. Vanatten, from N. Y., in 1846; they have two children, Betsy Ann, born in 1855; Sarah, 1858; lost two daughters.

Jones W. S. merchant.
Judd Albert B.

KAHLER FRED. farmer.

Kahler John, farmer; Sec. 7.
Kane John, Sr., laborer.
Keeler A. printer.

KEELER WARREN, Farmer; Sec. 12; born in Cortland Co., N. Y., June 12, 1822; lived in that State 27 years, and came to Illinois, to Boone Co., in 1849, and has lived here 28 years; owns farm of 222 acres; has held offices of Road Commissioner and School Director; married Delotia Keeney, of Onondaga Co., N. Y., Jan. 11, 1844; she was born July 21, 1818; they have five children, Felicia B., Horatio, Mary A., Alson H., Emma L.; lost one daughter, Harriet.

Kehoe Michael, laborer.
Keller John, farmer.

KELSEY C. E. Music Dealer and Printing; born in Clinton, Conn., April 4, 1831; lived in that State for thirty years; he edited a paper in that State during the war; came to Belvidere in 1864; has been engaged in music business twenty-six years; is organist in First Presbyterian Church in this city; he is local correspondent of the Belvidere *Standard*, and correspondent Chicago Evening *Post*; married Miss Ellen E. Tompkins, of this city, Oct. 4, 1859; she was born in the State of Pennsylvania.

Kendall J. H. farmer; Sec. 4.
Kennedy John, clerk.
Kerdin Pat. mechanic.
Kief Francis O. laborer.
Kieley Patrick, mechanic.
King Amasa.
Kimble John B.

KING FRANCIS, Dealer in Hardware and Lumber; born in Tioga Co., N. Y., Feb. 15, 1842; lived in that State six years, and came to this State, to Belvidere, in 1848, and has lived here about thirty years; was engaged in farming, and has been engaged in business for twelve years; has held office of Constable; married Miss Anna Dean, from the State of Maine, Dec. 11, 1868; they have one child, Cora Clare, born Jan. 9, 1877.

KING FRED. H. E. Agent C. & N. W. R. R.; born Oneida Co., N. Y., April 24, 1827; lived in that State thirty years, and came to this State in 1857; lived in McHenry five years; came to Belvidere in 1862, and has been here sixteen years; he has been connected with the railroad for fourteen years, and has been agent of the American Express Co. for seven years; married Miss Frances W. Mack, of McHenry Co., Aug. 21, 1860; five children, two girls and three boys, Winnie E., Emma J., Albert E., Willie P., and Charles F.

King Leander, shoemaker.
King Leander, 2d, mechanic.
Kinney Pat. laborer.
Kinzie Joseph, farmer.
Kinzie M. H. farmer; Sec. 21.
Kinzie T. W. farmer; Sec. 11.

KINYON JOB, Retired; born in Chittenden Co., Vermont, May 23, 1820; lived there twenty years; removed to St. Lawrence Co., N. Y.; lived there seven years; came to Belvidere, Boone Co., and has lived here over thirty years; engaged in farming in town of Flora; has carted grain to Chicago, and sold winter wheat from 40 to 75c a bushel; married Miss Hannah Ellis, of Vermont, in December, 1841; have two children, Chastina and Lydia; lost three, Sylvester A., Mary, and Eliza.

Kirkland G. W. farmer.
Kraft August, painter.

KNIGHT C. C. Blacksmith; born in Baltimore, Maryland, March 18, 1826; lived there twenty-five years; came to this State, and has lived in Belvidere twenty-one years; has been engaged in business six years; worked for C. & N. W. R. R.

for fifteen years; married Miss Mary Rosacrans, from New York State, in 1857; they have three children, Ida, Charles, and Nellie.

LaBARR B. B. merchant.

LaBarr Wm. mason.
Lacy D. W. farmer; Sec. 25.
Lacy W. H. farmer; Sec. 19.
Laden John, saloon-keeper.
Laidley Jas. farmer; Sec. 18.

LAKE LEONARD L., M. D. Physician; born in Erie Co., N. Y., Sept. 26, 1821; lived there sixteen years; came to this Co. in 1837; one of the early settlers; he studied medicine and graduated at Rush Medical College, Chicago; he has practiced his profession here twenty-nine years; he is quite a horticulturist, and has forty varieties of grapes on his grounds; has held office of Coroner for ten years, and one of the Board of Town Trustees; was Asst. Surgeon 13th Ill. Cavalry; was at Camp Douglas, Chicago; was Asst. Surgeon 15th Regt. I. V. I., and shared the campaigns of the regiment till the fall of Vicksburg; married Miss Asenath Marvin, from Erie Co., N. Y., Feb. 13, 1843; two children, Prof. L. N. W. Lake, and Hattie May; lost one daughter.

Lake L. N. W. music teacher.

LAMBERT STEPHEN, Retired; born in Dover, Piscataquis Co., Maine, March 22, 1814; lived in that State thirty-eight years, and came to this State and Boone Co. May 18, 1852, and has lived here twenty-five years; engaged in farming in town of Flora many years; owns a farm of 160 acres; has held office of Supervisor town of Flora several terms, also Assessor same town; has held office of Supervisor of Belvidere three years; married Lydia Crowell, from Maine, May 15, 1836; they have one child, John C., born Dec. 31, 1841.

Lambert Wm. farmer.
Lambert Frank, mechanic.
Lane D. C.
Lathrop Andrew, wagon maker.
Laurence A. J. farmer.
Lawrence John, carpenter.
Lawton A. farmer; Sec. 27.
Laying G. W. laborer.

LEACH E. J. Carriage and Wagon Maker; born in Bennington Co., Vt., Nov. 17, 1823; lived there fourteen years; lived in New York ten years; came to this town and Co. in 1847, and has lived here thirty years; was in the army, 95th Regt. I. V. I., Co. B; was Regimental Steward; married Martha C. Campbell; she died in 1862; they had three children, Chester C., Walter J., and Alice A.; married Eliza J. Gillson, from Caledonia, in December, 1866; have one daughter, Bessie May.

Leary Thomas, laborer.
Leonard J. R. produce dealer.
Leonard M. G. produce dealer.
Leonard Orin, tinner.
Leonard S. E.
Letto Edward, farmer; Sec. 6.
Lewis John, mechanic.
Lewis L. C. druggist.
Lewis Timothy, farmer; Sec. 21.
Lindsley M. retired farmer.
Linnell Lester, farmer.

LINNELL THOS. J. Retired; born in Jefferson Co., N. Y., Oct. 18, 1815; lived in that State thirty years; came to Rockford, this State, Nov. 9, 1845; lived there six years; came to Boone Co., town of Caledonia, in 1851; he is a mason by trade, and engaged in farming for many years; has held offices of School Director and Roadmaster; married Mary Thorn, Jan. 31, 1841; she was born in Jefferson Co., N. Y., May 1, 1824; seven children, Lester J., Selwyn C., Amy Ann, Jane E., Lucena D., Maryette, and Jesse F.; lost four sons, Henry W., Melville, Nathan, and Charles.

List John, mechanic.
Litts C. H. shoemaker.

LIVINGSTON ALEX. L. Of Livingston & Humphrey, Hardware Dealers, State st.; born in Glasgow, Scotland, Oct. 1, 1841; came to this country in 1855; came to this Co. in 1861, and has lived here sixteen years, engaged in hardware business; married Maggie L. Cunningham, from Rhode Island, Feb. 3, 1866.

LIVINGSTON & HUMPHREY, Hardware and Stove Dealers, South State street.

Lobatien Geo. gardener.
Longcor J. C. druggist.
Longcor L. S. broker.

LONGCOR SAMUEL, Plow Manufacturer; born in Dundee, Yates Co., N. Y., Oct. 25, 1813; learned the blacksmith trade in town of Bath, Steuben Co.; came to Belvidere in the spring of 1839, and has lived here over thirty-eight years; one of the earliest settlers, and only a few persons here when he came; he was engaged in blacksmithing and wagon making business for a long time, but for past twenty-five years has confined his business to the manufacture of plows; he took the first premium at the Mechanics' Institute, Chicago, in 1852, for the superiority of his plows over all others, and was awarded a silver medal; he was among the first to manufacture scouring plows in this State; he married Malinda Smith, of Steuben Co., N. Y., Jan. 7, 1835; eight children.

LONGCOR ADDISON, Was born in N. Y., in 1835; was in the army; 1st Lieut., and commanded Co. B, 15th Regt. I. V. I.

LONGCOR LEONARD S. Real Estate and Loan Business; born in Belvidere, Aug. 22, 1845; at the age of 25 he was an accomplished Plow Maker, having learned the business of his father; married Miss Juliet G. Ticknor, of Plattsville, Alabama, June 23, 1870; she was born in same place, and is a step-daughter of Joseph Goodrich, of this town; have two children living. Willard Ticknor Longcor, born Aug. 17, 1872, and Harriet Goodrich Longcor, Sept. 21, 1877.

LONGCOR JOHN C. Druggist; was born Aug. 8, 1847; engaged in drug business.

LOOP CHAS. B. Postmaster; born Steuben Co., N. Y., Oct. 12, 1835; came to this State and Co., to Belvidere, at an early age, and has lived here about forty years; one of the early settlers; was in army, 95th I. V. I.; went out Captain Co. B, and was promoted to Major; was in many severe engagements—Port Gibson, Champion Hills, Vicksburg, Kenesaw Mountain, Peach Tree Creek, Siege of Atlanta, Jonesboro and Nashville; was on staff duty of Generals Leggett and Blair; was elected Clerk of this Co. in 1865; re-elected in 1869, and re-elected in 1873; was appointed Postmaster here in 1877; married Maria J. Pierce, from Washington Co., N. Y., in 1858; they have four children.

Loop M. mechanic.

Loop Mordacai, shoemaker.

LOVEJOY SAMUEL, Farmer; Sec. 14; born in Washington Co., New York, May 4, 1830; lived in that state about twenty-one years; removed to Illinois, to Winnebago Co., in 1851; he went to Iowa in 1860, and was engaged in Mercantile trade at Cedar Falls; returned to Boone Co. in 1864; rents farm of Wm. McBride, Esq.; married Miss Clara R. Perry, from New York, Dec. 6, 1855; they have three children, Dwight S., Eliza Hettie, Clara.

LOVELESS S. Grocer; born Bay Fundy, Feb. 13, 1815; lived there sixteen years; went to sea; was in West India trade for six years; sailed from Buffalo to Chicago six years; came to this Co. and town in 1847, and has lived here thirty years; run the Big Thunder Flouring Mills here for ten years; has been engaged in grocery business for many years; married Hannah M. Russell, from Vermont, in 1854.

Lovett S. retired farmer.

Lucas Moses, clerk.

LUCE A. R. Farmer and Carpenter; born in Tolland Co., Conn., Sept. 26, 1829; he lived in that State for forty-four years; came to Boone Co., Belvidere in 1873; married Mary French, from Conn., in 1860; she died April 1, 1870; married Emily V. Baker, from N. Y. State, Sept., 1874; have three children; Ida E., born Dec. 27, 1861; Frank H., Aug. 30, 1863; Wilbert R., June 17, 1865.

Luce Geo. L., farmer; Sec. 23.

Lyon John, shoemaker.

McLAIN CHAS. mechanic.

McBRIDE WM. Was born in Alleghaney Co., N. Y., July 5, 1816, and came to Boone Co. to Belvidere, Sept. 20, 1837; he owns 600 acres of land, one mile north of Belvidere; bought the claim of Mr. Churchill for $400; was engaged in farming until two years ago, when he went to the mountains, and engaged in mining, making Lake City, Colorado, his home; value of his property, about $25,000; his first wife was Miss Elizabeth Reynolds; she lived about seven years; they had two children; his second wife was Mrs. Sarah Haight, of McHenry Co, this State; they have five children, all living; Robt. McBride came here Oct. 1836; James McBride came here, May, 1837; early settlers.

McDOUGALL CHAS. Retired; born Canada East, April 10, 1795; came to Chicago June 14, 1836, and to this Co. in July, same year; has lived here forty-one years; one of the earliest settlers; only few houses here at that time; he owns the same land he entered when he first came here, 222 acres; has held the office of Road Commissioner, and was Path Master for some years; married Fanny Terry, of Canada, April 8, 1822; she was born June 17, 1799; they have been married over fifty-five years; children: Mary, born Feb. 19, 1823, died May 10, 1825; Mrs. Miranda Merchant, Feb. 5, 1825; Lorenzo S., March 6, 1827; Charles, March 5, 1832, died Feb. 21, 1833.

McLaurie Geo. S. manufacturer.

McMaster Alfred T. laborer.

McMillan N. farmer; Sec. 6.

McMullen J. E. merchant.

McNallis Francis.

McNamara M. laborer.

Macklin Beverly, farmer.

MAREAN MARVIN CLARK, Justice of the Peace; born in Broome Co., N. Y., June 8, 1827; lived in the State of N. Y. twenty-seven years, and came to this Co. in 1854; is stone mason by trade; is engaged in farming; has held office of Town Clerk of the town of Flora, and Justice of the Peace for eight years; has held office of Justice of the Peace here for four years; married Miss Olive Howard, from Broome Co., N. Y., May 7, 1851; two children: Willie M., born May 16, 1853; Harry, Oct. 15, 1858.

Markham Wm. farmer.

Marske C. merchant.

Martin Anthony, laborer.

Martin Dominick, laborer.

Martin Geo. farmer.

Martin L. C. farmer.

MARTYN JAS. B., Proprietor Baltic Mills; born in County Cornwall, England, Dec.28,1801; lived in England twenty-eight years, and came to this country in 1829; came to New Orleans; removed to Huntsville, Ala., and lived there five years, when he came to Galena, in this State; came to Midway (which is now Rockford, Winnebago Co.) in the fall of 1835, and lived there until 1852; removed to Cherry Valley and engaged in milling business; came to Belvidere in 1854 and engaged in same business; has held office of Magistrate in Rockford; married Elizabeth Brewer, from County Cornwall, Eng., in 1824; she died in 1870; they had one son, who died at the age of thirty-one; married Miss Elizabeth Rightor, from Rockford, Winnebago Co., Feb. 10, 1876; they have one child, James R., born Jan. 20, 1877.

Martyn Thos. clerk.

MASON JOHN, Tailor; born Newcastle, Staffordshire, Eng., Dec. 1, 1827; came to this country in 1849; came to Belvidere in 1851, and has lived here twenty-six years; married Miss Caroline Owen, Aug. 23, 1855; she was born in Chautauqua Co., N. Y., Nov. 2, 1828; they have had three children: Emma Jane, born June 3, 1856, died Jan. 25, 1862; Clara Belle, June 7, 1859, died Feb. 22, 1864; Mary Louise, Jan. 5, 1869.

Masters Wm. laborer.

MAY EZRA, born in Eastern Tp., Lower Canada, Nov. 6, 1813; lived there until twenty-three years old; came to U. S. in 1836, to Michigan City, Ind.; came to this State, to Boone Co., in 1839, and has lived here thirty-eight years; one of the early settlers; has been engaged in farming, mercantile business and distilling for some years; he has carted wheat to Chicago and sold it for 37½c a bushel, taking five and six days to make the trip; he is one of the largest, if not the largest, land owner in Boone Co.; he has held the offices of School Director, Town Trustee, and has represented the town in Board of Supervisors and President of Agricultural Society, for some years; married Miss Louisa N. May, Feb. 24, 1841; she was from Orleans Co., N. Y.; she died Sept. 16, 1862; have seven children, three sons and four daughters.

May G. A. farmer.

MAY HUGH, Farmer; Sec. 28; born in Crawford Co., Pa., Sept. 6, 1824; lived in Pa. twenty years; came to Ill., to De Kalb Co., in 1844; lived in that Co. twenty-two years, and came to this Co. in 1866; has lived in this State thirty-three years; has held office of School Director; he married Catherine Hart, from Pa., Dec. 31, 1846; she died in 1860; married Julia Harper, from Ohio, in 1861; they have four children: Geo. A., Seth Thomas, Estella C., and Ulysses Grant; have lost two sons.

Mead W. M. canvasser.

Meier E. F. mechanic.

Merchant N. H. grain dealer.

MEYER J. GEORGE, Carpenter and Builder; born in Baden, Germany, Sept. 29, 1848; lived in Baden about nineteen years; came to this country in 1867; came to Belvidere same year; has been engaged as carpenter and builder; married Theodora Zimmerman, July 31, 1873; she was born in Baden, Germany, Dec. 6, 1852; they have two children, Wm. Fred., born Sept. 2, 1875; Baby, May 14, 1877; lost one son.

Mill Jas.

Millard Geo. laborer.

Minter Ernst, Sr. butcher.

Minter Ernst, Jr. laborer.

Mitchell Stephen, furniture dealer.

Moore Geo. farmer; Sec. 31.

Moore J. A.

Moore W. W. farmer; Sec. 33.

Mordoff G. J. farrier.

Mordoff J. C. hotel keeper.

Morley Ephraim, retired farmer.

Morley F. C. butter dealer.

Morse B. J. farmer.

Morse Civilian, merchant.

MORSE F. Farmer; Sec. 24; born in Mass., Nov. 14, 1812; removed to Orleans Co., N. Y.; lived there twenty-five years; came to Belvidere, Boone Co., in 1837, and has lived here forty years; one of the early settlers; used to cart his grain to Chicago, has sold wheat for 45c a bushel; owns farm 80 acres; married Cordelia Knowlton, from Mich., in 1853; have four children: Seymour, Stephen, Willis, Frank Leslie; lost one son.

Morse Jas. mechanic.

Morse Junia, pump maker.

Mott Lott, farmer.

Morse P. farmer; Sec. 24.

Morse Putnam, laborer.

Morse Seymour.

Morse Stephen, farmer; Sec. 24.

Morse T. farmer; Sec. 24.

MOSS ASA, Farmer and Dairyman; Sec. 21; born in Washington Co., N. Y., Dec 21, 1818; lived in that State eighteen years; came to Ill., to Boone Co., in 1836, and has lived here forty-one years; one of the earliest settlers; used to cart grain to Chicago, taking five and six days to make the trip, and has sold wheat at 40c per bushel; has seen pork sell at $1.00 per hog in Chicago; owns farm of 100 acres; has held office of Assessor in the town of Spring, Road Commissioner, Town Collector and Poor Master; married Alvira Stewart, from Erie Co., N. Y., in 1845; have seven children: Ellen H., Ann E., Carrie P., Harvey S., Judson C., Myra J. and Warren C.

Moss A. F. farmer; Sec. 35.

MOSS CHAS. S. County Surveyor; born in Belvidere, Boone Co., Jan. 9, 1848, and has lived in this Co. twenty-nine years; engaged in Farming and Surveying; studied Civil Engineering, and graduated at Chicago University; was elected Surveyor of Boone Co. in 1871, and re-elected in 1875; married Miss Mary C. A. Brown, Nov. 6, 1876; she was born in Weston, Mass.

MOSS EDWARD E. Farmer; Sec. 23; born in Cortland Co., N. Y., March 17, 1815; lived in that State twenty-one years; came to Illinois, to Boone Co., in July, 1836, and has lived here over forty-one years, and is one of the few early settlers now living that were here when he came; only two log houses in Belvidere; he was a carpenter by trade; engaged in Building for several years, then bought a farm; used to cart his grain to Chicago, as there was no cash market here for it; has sold wheat for three shillings per bushel; owns farm of 70 acres; he helped organize the first school district on the south side of the river; built the first school house on the south side; has held offices of Road Commissioner, Assessor and Town Collector, School Trustee, and School Director; married Sarah Cates, from Chautauqua Co., N. Y., May 23, 1838; they have four children, S. H. Moss; Mrs. Malissa Caldwell, wife of C. W. Caldwell; Mrs. Eva Bristol, wife of H. P. Bristol, of Iowa; Mrs. Hattie Lincoln, wife of W. P. Lincoln, of Linn Co., Iowa; lost four children, two sons and two daughters.

Moss G. B. farmer.

MOSS W. S. A., Farmer; born Windsor Co., Vt., Feb. 24, 1816; lived there 40 years, and was engaged in the mercantile business, cattle drover, etc.; came to Ills. in 1856, and to Boone Co. in 1859, and engaged in manufacturing agricultural implements; is now engaged in farming, here and in Iowa; owns farm of 140 acres here, and 960 acres in Iowa; married Miss Eliza Cady, from Vermont, in 1837; they have two children, Harriet L. and Byron J.

Moulton D. E. retired merchant.

Mulloy A. grocer.
Mundy Frazy, farmer.
Murch E. L. merchant.
Murch G. W. merchant.
Murch L. H. merchant.
Murch Martin, retired.
Murin James, laborer.
Murin Pat. laborer.
Murphy Daniel, farmer; Sec. 5.
Murphy John, laborer.
Murphy J. A. farmer; Sec. 20.

NASH ALFRED, laborer.

Nash E. J. mail carrier.
Nelson L. carpenter.
Nelson Smith, carpenter.
Newton Wm. retired farmer.
Norton E. C. attorney.
Norton R. G. retired farmer.

O'BRIEN MARK, laborer.

O'Brien Martin, laborer.
O'Brien Michael, mechanic.
O'Brien Peter, mechanic.
O'Kief Cornelius, laborer.
Oaks E. S. farmer.
Oaks G. A. mechanic.

OSGOOD MAJOR R. E. Livery Stable; born in Jefferson Co., N. Y., Nov. 11, 1827; went to Ohio at an early age, and lived there until 1865; was in the army, in the 6th O. V. C.; enlisted as Private, and won his promotion to rank of Major; was wounded slightly at Shenandoah Valley and at Culpepper C. H.; was with Gen. Sheridan in Wilderness campaign; was elected Sheriff of this Co. in 1870; married Miss Eliza J. Russell, of Ohio, May 10, 1849.

Ott Joseph, mechanic.
Outcault W. W. laborer.

PALMATIER A. farmer.

Palmer David, mechanic.
Park Oliver, farmer.
Park Wm. carpenter.
Parkhill Robert, agricultural implements.
Pass Frank, laborer.
Pease Sylvester, musician.
Peck C. H. farmer; Sec. 9.
Peck C. H. dealer.
Peck C. W. farmer; Sec. 4.
Pedlar Edmund W. miller.

PEPPER SAMUEL, Florist; born in Nottinghamshire, Eng., Aug. 20, 1827; came to this country in 1848; lived in

Rochester, and came to Belvidere in 1840; was in the army in Co. G, 95th Regt. I. V. I.; was in battle of Yellow Bayou, Mobile Bay, and Red River campaign; has been Sexton of Cemetery for past seven years; married Mary Jane Powell, March 21, 1854; she was born in Franklin Co., N. Y., Feb. 11, 1834: six children, Mary E., Samuel E., Martha A., Emma Gertrude, William C., Jessie A.; lost one son.

Perkins A. H. S. printer.
Perkins M. D. ice dealer.
Perry G. W.

PETTIT DANIEL B. Book, Stationery, Notions and Wall Paper; born in Wayne Co., Penn., Dec. 9, 1822; lived there fifteen years, removed to Delaware Co., New York, and lived there eight years; then started on foot and alone from Delaware Co. to Boone Co., Illinois, and reached Belvidere Sept. 25, 1845, and has lived here over thirty-two years; there was very little improvement here when he came; he taught the only school there was in this town in 1845 and 1846, and continued teaching for eight years; he was engaged in farming for fifteen years; has been engaged in business here for four years; has held the office of Assessor and Corporation Trustee, and various Church offices; married Mary E. Doyle, in Hancock, New York, June 18, 1846; they have just returned from a visit of eleven weeks to their old home in the East; they have four children, Edward E., jeweler, Belvidere; Daniel B., Jr., in business with his father; Dr. William H., Physician, Cedar Falls, Iowa; Mrs. Mary E. Dean, Buffalo, New York.

Petit D. W. cheese factory.
Pettit E. E. jeweler.
Pettit Frank, student.
Phelps M. farmer; Sec. 6.
Phillips J. dentist.
Pickard A. N. carpenter.
Pickard I. H. carpenter.
Pierce E. D. post-office clerk.
Pierce Geo. E. merchant.
Pierce John L.
Pierce Martin, retired.
Piel John, laborer.
Piel Joseph H.
Piel R. T. drayman.
Pinkham J. K. marble cutter.
Piper M. mechanic.
Pitkin L. miller.
Pitkin W. L. miller.
Plane E. B. merchant.
Plane F. W. merchant.
Plane John, merchant.
Pluke George, butcher.

Pratt J. T. mechanic.

PORTER THOS. W. Retired; born in County Norfolk, England, Dec. 13, 1803; came to this country Dec. 10, 1833; lived in New York State five years; came to this Co. Sept. 12, 1838, and has lived here 39 years; only one store here; has carted grain to Chicago, and sold wheat at 50 cents per bushel; owns 160 acres of his land, the same he first entered; married Charlotte Lane, May 26, 1825; she was born in County Norfolk, England, Aug. 5, 1800, and she died Nov. 20, 1873, in 74th year of her age; nine children, Thos. W., born in England, Nov. 26, 1826; Henry, born in England, March 9, 1828; Charlotte L., born in England, March 6, 1832; Anna M., born in England, Aug. 11, 1833; Robt., born in Erie Co., N. Y., May 2, 1835; Jas. W., born in Erie Co., N. Y., July 25, 1838; Elizabeth P., born in Boone Co., April 18, 1841; Washington, born in Boone Co., Oct. 26, 1843; Fred, born in Boone Co. Feb. 13, 1846.

Poulton J. J. printer.
Powell J. farmer; Sec. 10.
Powell John, farmer.
Powell M. farmer; Sec. 10.
Powell M. L. farmer.

QUACKENBOSS A. Livery, Sale and Boarding Stable, opposite Julian House; born Canada East, Oct. 17, 1821; came to the states in 1838; came to Boone Co., Belvidere, in 1845, and has lived here over thirty-two years; engaged in business with Mr. Farrar; his first wife was Miss Amelia Slusser; his present wife was Julia Martin, from State New York; married July 15, 1865; they have three children, Fanny A., Jennie M., Arthur W.; lost one son.

Quinn James.

RAMSEY JOHN, mechanic.

RAMSEY MARK, Vice-President First National Bank.
Rands Chas. farmer; Sec. 36.
Ransom E. D. druggist.
Ray M. S. retired farmer.
Ray T. L. photographer.
Redell John, laborer.
Reed William, mechanic.
Reinhardt Thos. clerk.
Reynolds D.
Reynolds E. H. farmer.
Reynolds John, laborer.
Reynolds L. H. farmer.
Rhulman F. cabinet maker.
Rice G. W. 'bus driver.
Rice Nelson, laborer.
Rice O. W. merchant.

Richardson Geo. laborer.
Richardson John, carpenter.
Richardson Wm. laborer.
Ristan S. S.
Ritzart Henry, laborer.
Ritzert Ludwig, farmer.
ROBERTS R. Publisher *Belvidere Standard;* born East Hartford, Conn., Dec. 24, 1824; lived in that State some years, and served his apprenticeship in New York City; came to Chicago in 1843; published the *Woodstock Democrat* in 1850; came to this Co. 1854; he has published the *Belvidere Standard* over 25 years without change; has held office of Corporation Trustee; married Miss P. L. Cowdrey, of Ashtabula, Ohio, in Sept., 1856; have three children, daughters, Anna, Bertha, Jessie.
Robertson C. A. clerk.
Robinson Charles, clerk.
Robinson E. R. retired farmer.
Robinson George W. painter.
ROBINSON WM. H. Blacksmith; born in County Kent, England, March 3, 1850; came to this country at an early age; lived in New York two years; came to Belvidere in 1854, and has lived here 23 years; has been engaged in blacksmith business for 8 years; his parents are living here in this town.
ROLLINS JOHN A. Sec. 11; born in Belvidere, Ill., Oct. 31, 1839; pursued his academical studies at the Preparatory Department of Beloit College, Wis., and at the Ann Arbor High School, Mich.; entered Michigan University in Oct., 1860, and remained there until shortly after the breaking out of the civil war, in 1861, when he enlisted as a Private in the 45th I. V. I.; was detailed as Clerk at General Grant's Headquarters, in Jan., 1862; promoted to 2d Lieut. in June, 1862, and to 1st Lieut. the following October; was in the battles of Pittsburg Landing, Medon Station, Port Gibson, Jackson, Champion Hills, and Siege of Vicksburg; resigned in July, 1863; resumed his collegiate studies in 1864, and graduated at Michigan University in 1867; entered the Law School at Albany, New York, in Nov., 1867, and was admitted to the Bar in 1868; received the Degree of Master of Arts from his *Alma Mater,* in 1879; has since traveled somewhat extensively in the Western States and Territories, besides attending to his large farming interests in this County.
Rood A. N. laborer.
Root Richard, laborer.
Rose G. A. clerk.
Rote Henry, farmer.
ROWEN W. C. Retired; born in Batavia, Genesee Co., N. Y., March 2, 1826; lived in that State 16 years; came to Racine, Wis., lived there 1 year; came to DeKalb Co. 1843, lived there 17 years; came to Belvidere 1860; went to California 1873; has held office Town Trustee for 7 years, and also Town Collector in DeKalb Co.; married Miss Lovina Caswell, Oct. 8, 1861; she was born in Orleans Co., N. Y., Nov. 25, 1835; have three children, J. W., born Jan. 13, 1864; Perry C., Feb. 18, 1867; Lovina C., March 28, 1875.
Rutger Francis, clerk.
Ryerson A. F.

SABIN D. D. merchant.
Sage J. horse dealer.
Sage O. N. clerk.
Sager A. farmer; Sec. 11.
Sager Moses, retired farmer.
Sanford A. J. sewing machine agent.
Sargent O. J. produce dealer.
SAWYER JAMES W. Circuit Clerk; born in Windsor Co., Vermont, Nov. 9, 1835; came to this state, to Cook Co., Nov., 1836, and has lived in this state over forty-one years, his father and mother being early settlers; he removed to Wisconsin in 1860; was in army in 1st Wisconsin Battery; was in several battles and skirmishes—Chickasaw Bayou, Arkansas Post; was left at James Plantation, below Vicksburg, on account of sickness, during that memorable siege; came to Belvidere, Boone Co., 1870; has held office School Trustee; was elected Clerk of Circuit Court of Boone Co. Nov., 1876; married Miss Rule D. Fisher, from Washington Co., New York, May 30, 1866; they have one child, Willie M., born in Carondolet, Mo., Oct. 6, 1869.
Sawyer W. J. farmer; Sec. 22.
Saxton J. C. clerk.
Saxton John, furniture dealer.
SAXTON JOY H. Furniture Business; born Buffalo, N. Y., Feb. 16, 1841; came to Belvidere in 1846; has lived here 31 years; was in army, Co. G, 95th Regt. I. V. I.; was on detached service at headquarters Gens. McPherson and Howard; married Matilda Herbert, from this town and Co., May 5, 1875; one child, Gertie C., born Feb. 9, 1876. John Saxton, father of the above, was born State of New York, 1813; came to this town and Co. in 1846; lived here 31 years; held office of P. M. here 5 years; married Almeda V. Handy, from N. Y., in 1837; have two children, sons.
Schemerhorn Chas. farmer.
Schemerhorn E. C. speculator.
Schemerhorn R. J. livery.
Schofield G. W.
SCOTT CHARLES, M. D., Physician; born in Lycoming Co., Penn., May

26, 1849; lived in that State 14 years, and came to Winnebago, Co., this State; studied medicine and graduated at Rush Medical College, Chicago, in 1874; spent one year in hospital; came to Belvidere and has practiced his profession here since; married Miss Clara E. Towsley, of Portage Co., Ohio, May 24, 1877.

Scott J. T.

Scott W. W. laborer.

Sellard Geo. farmer; Sec. 11.

Sergent Eli, butter dealer.

Sewell Frank.

SEWELL ISAAC, Retired; born in Suffolk Co., Eng., Oct. 10, 1817; came to Canada at an early age, and to this country in 1839; came to Rockford, and removed to Boone Co., town of Caledonia, the same year, and has lived here thirty-eight years; has held office of Town School Trustee; also been School Director for many years, has also held office of Supervisor; he used to cart his grain to Chicago; married Mary Godwin, in Detroit, May, 1839; she was born in England, they have six children, Joseph, William, Sutton, Edson, Frank, Alice V.; lost one daughter, Maria.

Sewell William, mechanic.

SEYMOUR C. H., M. D., Homeopathic Physician; born in Avon, Livingston Co., N. Y., May 2, 1828; lived in that State sixteen years; removed to Milwaukee, Wis., and lived there eight years; graduated at Carroll College, Waukesha, Wis.; studied medicine, and graduated at Jefferson College, Philadelphia; attended lectures and graduated at Hahnemann Medical College, Chicago; was in California and Colorado several years; came to Belvidere in 1877; married Mary A. Rogers, of Albany Co., N. Y., March 10, 1855; she studied medicine and graduated at St. Louis College, received Diploma, and is practicing medicine here with her husband.

Shannon Edward, laborer.

Shaw Daniel, laborer.

Shaw E. J. student.

Shaw H. B. laborer.

Shaw J. L. laborer.

Shaw S. T. mechanic.

Shean John, laborer.

Sherman E. B. grain dealer.

Sherman H. O. lumber dealer.

Sherman J. O. lumber merchant.

Sherrell H. J. teacher.

Sherrell John, farmer.

SHERRILL PROF. HENRY J., Principal Public School of North Belvidere; Sec. 34; born in Madison Co., N. Y., April 23, 1834; lived in that State for forty-two years, engaged in Teaching; commenced teaching at the age of sixteen; came to Belvidere, Boone Co., in 1865, and is Principal of the North Belvidere Public School; he has taught in two schools twenty-two years, and has been engaged in teaching since 1846; owns farm of 80 acres; married Jennie A. Briggs, of Chenango Co., N. Y., July 31, 1854; she died in 1870; had one son, Frank A., born Nov. 19, 1862; lost one son, Willie, born July 19, 1857, died June 27, 1861; married Mrs. Alice J. Seaver, formerly Miss Alice Bentley, of Aurora, N. Y., Dec. 23, 1875; have one child, Jennie, born July 22, 1877.

Siebert Jacob, manufacturer.

Siebert Valentine, laborer.

Simons A.

Simons H. H. mechanic.

Simons P. B. mechanic.

Simpson Thos. O. laborer.

Slafter A. A. farmer.

Slater Wm. musician.

Soost Wm. saloon-keeper.

Smedley Ephraim, mason.

Smedley Jas. E. laborer.

Smedley Nathan, physician.

Smiley Edward, photographer

Smiley F. R. clerk.

Smiley R. farrier.

Smith A. M. farmer; Sec. 22.

Smith C. L. farmer.

Smith F. J. farmer.

Smith F. S. grain dealer.

Smith Frank.

Smith H. F. farmer; Sec. 21.

Smith Montgomery, farmer; Sec. 22.

Smith S. farmer; Sec. 5.

Smith Samuel, farmer; Sec. 13.

Smith Wm. farmer; Sec. 7.

Smith Z. W. farmer.

Spackman C. attorney

Spencer C. farmer.

Spencer D. farmer; Sec. 3.

Spencer S. mechanic.

Spencer Simeon, farmer; Sec. 3.

Spoor Jas. farmer.

Starr H. G. dealer.

Starr J. C. manufacturer.

Stearns H. H. farmer.

STEPHENSON JOHN, Farming and Stone Quarrying; Sec. 5; born in Cumberland Co., Eng., Sept. 16, 1818; lived in England twenty-nine years; came to Belvidere, Boone Co., in 1847; went to California in 1850, and was there five years; owns 213 acres land; has been engaged in Stone and Lime business; has been married twice; his first wife was Elizabeth Tyson, of Cumberland Co., Eng.; she died in 1847; married Martha

POPLAR GROVE

Telford, from north of Ireland, in 1857; have four children, Hannah Jane, John, Mary E., Martha A.; lost one daughter.

Stevens J. G. merchant.

Stewart George, merchant.

Stockwell F. S. farmer; Sec. 13.

Stockwell M. F. farmer; Sec. 13.

Stockwell P. F. farmer.

Stoner Frank, mechanic.

Stone W. S.

Storms L. S. laborer.

Storms T. laborer.

Stow C. L. retired merchant.

Streeter O. C. carpenter.

Strong L. L. laborer.

Strong M. E. laborer.

Styles J. W. laborer.

Styles John C. mechanic.

Styles Wm. H. clerk.

Sullivan Cornelius, laborer.

Sullivan Dennis, mechanic.

Sullivan J. J. saloon keeper.

Sullivan Jeremiah, mechanic.

Sullivan Jerry, wagon maker.

Sullivan John, saloon keeper.

Sunderland W. farmer.

Sullivan M. farmer; Sec. 11.

Swail W. D. broker.

SWASEY SAMUEL, Retired; born in Newberry, Vt., Feb. 22, 1804; removed to N. H. at an early age; lived there until 1843; came to this State that year, and returned to N. H. in 1836; held office of Register Probate for ten years; represented the town of Haverhill in the State Legislature for six or seven years, and was chosen Speaker of the House for three sessions; was member of the Constitutional Convention in 1850; came to this State in 1857; lived in Chicago nine years; came to this Co. in 1867; married Edith Holmes, of Petersborough, N. H., in 1842; they have four children: Chas. J., Samuel, Jr., Edith A. and Edward H.; lost two: Frank Pierce and Katie; Mrs. Sallie Holmes, mother of Mrs. Swasey, was born in New Ipswich, N. H., June 24, 1767, and was ninety years of age last June.

Sweatman Geo. W. farmer; Sec. 32.

Sweatman John, farmer; Sec. 32.

Sweet H. M. clerk.

Sykes H. B. merchant.

Sylvius Dan, farmer.

T AYLOR W. S. mechanic.

TAYLOR MRS. ELECTA, Formerly Miss Electa Burghardt; born in Berkshire Co., Mass., June 8, 1808; lived there twenty years; removed to Ontario Co., N. Y., and lived there 15 years; came to Belvidere in 1843, thirty-four years ago; she married Dr. C. VanBrunt, from Orange Co., New York, in 1844; he died in 1851; on the 17th day of Sept., 1862, she married the Rev. Hutchins Taylor, the first pastor of the First Presbyterian Church of Syracuse, N. Y., the first church organized in that city; he came to this state in 1844; died Aug. 31, 1868; in 1865 Mrs. Taylor's eyesight began to fail, and she has been totally blind for ten years, living all alone, performing all of her household duties, and making her home pleasant and attractive to all who enter it by her cheerful, hopeful disposition; she has three sisters, Mrs. Avaline Younglove, of Buffalo; Mrs. Maria Sears, of Belvidere; Mrs. Annie Kirby, of Detroit. Mrs. Maria Sears was born in Berkshire Co., Mass., Nov. 25, 1818; lived there nine years, and in New York state ten years; married Brownell Sears, from Ontario Co., New York, in 1839; they came to Boone Co. in 1839, thirty-eight years ago; he died June 3d, 1864; they had three children, Louisa M., Addie C., Irving C.; lost one son, Horace B.; he was in army, 45th Regt. I. V. I.; died April 9, 1862.

Teeple E. farmer.

Teeple Edgar E. farmer; Sec. 30.

Teeple Luke, farmer; Sec. 30.

Terry E. K. clerk.

Terwilliger G. retired.

Terwilliger Irving, bank clerk.

TERWILLIGER JAS. S., Cashier First National Bank; born in Cortland Co., N. Y., March 26, 1822; came to this Co. in 1847, and has lived here over thirty years; has held office of Justice of the Peace for some years; married Miss Emily Mitchell, from Petersburg, N. H., in 1848; they have one child, Florence M.

Terwilliger Jas. banker.

Terwilliger P. A. merchant.

Terwilliger S. retired.

THOMAS DEXTER S. Farmer; Sec. 32; born in Me., Oct. 26, 1835; lived in that State twenty years; came to Boone Co. in 1855, and has lived here twenty-two years; was engaged in the grocery business and was burned out in 1858; was in the army, 15th I.V.I.; married Miss Ellen M. Blake, from N. H., in May, 1857; they have four children: Chas. W., Mary Frances, Georgie B., Willie.

Thomas J. H. laborer.

Thomas Jerome, laborer; Sec. 32.

Thomas Lafayette, farmer.

Thompson E. S. laborer.

Thompson J. C. broker.

Thompson W. S. merchant.

Thurston W. H. farmer; Sec. 28.

Tibbets T. W. farmer.
Tisdale Grove, laborer.
Tobine H. W. farmer; Sec. 19.
Tobine H. W. farmer; Sec. 18.
Tobine Wm. farmer; Sec. 22.

TOMKINS ENOS, Was born in New York City, Feb. 1, 1795; at the age of eighteen he participated in the war of 1812, enrolling in a city militia company, under Capt. Hugh Maxwell; from this company he was transferred to a company called the Sea Fensibles, under Capt. Shoemaker, with headquarters at Mill Rock, on which they erected a block house and a fort. At this time New York City was under martial law. At the expiration of his term of service he was honorably discharged. Learning that a number of government vessels were being fitted out in New York harbor for the purpose of annoying the British blockading squadron, which was then off Sandy Hook, and being anxious to be at the front, he enlisted for six months, but before the expiration of that time peace was proclaimed, and he enlisted as carpenter's mate on board the United States brig, Flambeau, John B. Nicholson Commander, which was sent up the Mediterranean to fight the Algerines, against whom we had declared war, and to whom our government, as well as all Europe, was paying tribute for the use of those waters. Under command of Commodore Decatur, the squadron arrived off the harbor of Algiers, and so unexpected was their appearance Decatur found the Algerine Commodore's ship off on a collecting trip. Our fleet immediately started in pursuit, and after a hot running fight of one hour and twenty minutes the enemy was brought to bay. Out of her crew of 800 men, 180 were killed, among whom were her Commodore and several of her officers, so that on the surrender of the ship, that duty devolved upon the boatswain, he being the highest officer on duty. The ship's armament consisted of sixty-four brass guns, and she was considered the flower of the Algerine navy. The Flambeau was detailed to take the prize into Carthagena, a Spanish port. On the return of the brig to the beautiful harbor of Algiers, she found the U. S. squadron in line of battle, awaiting her arrival, with "bows on and matches lit," ready for shelling the city. When the brig had taken her position, Commodore Decatur sent his terms to the Dey and gave him twenty minutes for an answer. His terms were accepted. They compelled the Algerines to forever renounce their claim to tribute from our shipping, and also secured the release of all Christians of every nationality held in bondage by them. This accomplished, the squadron sailed up the Mediterranean on a pleasure trip and returned to New York in October, 1815. For the part Mr. Tomkins took in this war he is now receiving a pension from the United States government. Soon after his discharge from the navy, Mr. Tomkins went to Georgia, and spent most of his time in the Southern States, until the year 1824, when he visited Farmington, Conn., and married Miss Rebecca Newell, with whom he returned to North Carolina, where he continued in the manufacture of clock cases, in which he was quite extensively engaged, owning factories in the states of Virginia, North Carolina, Tennessee, Pennsylvania and New York, and in Canada. In the year 1828, he moved with his family to Pennsylvania, where he lived twenty-three years, during which time his manufactories turned out clock cases, chairs and bedsteads. In September, 1851, he moved to Illinois, and settled in Belvidere, Boone Co., where he has since resided. He was for several years senior member of the firm of Tomkins & Fuller, Bankers, the first institution of the kind ever started in Boone Co. This firm also opened a bank in Rockford, the second of the kind in that city. On leaving the banking business, he retired from active life. He cast his first vote for Andrew Jackson for President, and has voted for every democratic President since, and still adheres strongly to democratic principles; he has been for many years a member of the Presbyterian Church, and held the office of elder throughout the existence of the Second Presbyterian Church of Belvidere. The old gentleman's family now consists of his wife, Rebecca; N. C. Tomkins, of Salt Lake City, U. T.; William H. Tomkins, of San Francisco, Cal.; Ellen E., wife of C. E. Kelsey, a well-known music dealer of Boone Co., and Anna M., wife of J. B. Collins, of Chicago.

Tomlinson A. D. bank clerk.

TOUSLEY R. J. Proprietor Julian House; born in Portage Co., Ohio, Nov. 28, 1835; left there and went to Wis. in 1847, and lived there eight years; came to Belvidere in 1865, and has conducted Julian House for past twelve years; married Miss Augusta Traver, daughter of Robert Traver, Dec. 12, 1865; she was born in Cortland Co., N. Y., April 11, 1845; have two sons: Herbert T., born Aug. 9, 1867; Frank R., April 18, 1869.

Traver Robt. retired hotel keeper.
Tripp S. farmer; Sec. 29.

TRUESDELL EUGENE E. P. Real Estate and Loan; born in Hampden Co., Mass., Sept. 24, 1845; lived in that State twenty-two years, and came to Belvidere July, 1867; is engaged in Real Estate and Loan Business; married Miss Fannie T. Page, Jan. 25, 1871; she was born in Belvidere, Nov. 26, 1846; they have two children, Ernest P., born June 2, 1873; Lucy Frances, Nov. 20, 1875; Mrs. Frances T. Page, mother of Mrs. Truesdell, was born in Montpelier, Vt., and came to Belvidere in 1843; one of the early settlers; she married Dr. David Page, of Mass.; he was one of the early settlers of this Co. and identified with its interests; he died Jan., 1868.

Turneaune T. S. shoemaker.

Turner A. D. stock dealer.

Tuttle Geo. laborer.

TUTHILL ISAAC W. Blacksmith; born Orange Co., N. Y., Aug. 25, 1847; lived in that State nine years; came to Rockford, this State, in 1856, and learned his trade there; he has been engaged in business here three years; married Miss Lizzie G. Wallace, from Poplar Grove, in this Co.; born Dec. 12, 1851; they were married Oct. 8, 1874.

Tyman Patrick, farmer; Sec. 12.

UPDEGRAFF W. D. carpenter.

VAN NATTER A. farmer; Sec. 2.

Van Epps J. S. farmer.

Vanderwacker H. farmer; Sec. 18.

Vanderwacker John, farmer.

Vanderwacker R. farmer.

Veeder Robt. farmer.

Vickery R. farmer; Sec. 2.

Vickery Robt. miller.

Vorus John, mechanic.

Vorus Fred, mechanic.

WADDLES J. S. farmer.

Wait Valorus, farmer.

WALDOCK JOHN, Brewer; born in Bedfordshire, Eng., Jan. 16, 1844; came to this country in 1856; came to Rockford; lived there several years; came to Belvidere in 1860; was engaged in bakery business; is now running Belvidere Brewery; served in the Crimean war, and was at the seige of Sebastapol; was in the army over three years, Co. D, 15th I. V. I.; enlisted as private, and was promoted to First Lieutenant; was in battle of Pittsburg Landing, Seige of Corinth, Vicksburg, and a number of others; married Eliza Dupuy, from Rockford, Jan. 1, 1860; they have four children: Julia, Arthur J., Walter A. and Geo. N.

Walker Byron, farmer; Sec. 3.

Walker Edgar, farmer.

Walker Frank, farmer.

Walker F. H. merchant.

WALKER HOUGHTON C. Merchant; born Town Peacham, Caledonia Co., Vermont, Oct. 23, 1815; lived in that state twenty-one years; came to Chicago Sept., 1836, and came to Belvidere in April, 1837, and has lived here over forty years; only very few living here now that were here when he came; he is engaged in the dry goods business, and is the oldest merchant in Belvidere; his father built store on N. W. corner State and Mechanic streets, in 1839; he engaged in mercantile business with his father at an early day, and it took him a month to go to Boston and buy his goods and return, and he was obliged to walk large part of the way from Dunkirk to Buffalo; he was elected Sheriff of Boone Co. in 1838, and was called the Boy Sheriff; has also held office of Town Clerk; married Miss Emeline A. Frost, of Brooklyn, New York, July 5, 1843; they have two sons, Francis H., born July 13, 1844; in business with his father; Charles F., born Aug. 14, 1846, now in Chicago.

WALKER THOMAS D. Farmer; Sec. 4; born in Chenango Co., N. Y., Jan. 29, 1811; lived in that state twenty-seven years; came to Illinois, to Boone Co., in 1838, and has lived here thirty-nine years; one of the early settlers; was engaged in quarrying stone and burning lime; used to cart grain to Chicago; has sold wheat at 60 cents a bushel; owns 160 acres land; has held office of School Director and Path Master; married Sarah Smith, Aug. 18, 1830; she was born in Chemung Co., N. Y., June 18, 1812; have five children, Sarah E., Edgar, Cornelia, Frank, Phœbe; lost three children.

Walker Wm. farmer.

WALLACE JOHN, Retired; born in Wishaw, Lanarkshire, Scotland, Oct., 1823; lived in Scotland twenty-five years; came to this country in 1848; came to Belvidere same year, and has lived in this Co. twenty-nine years; engaged in Farming in towns Manchester, Caledonia, and Boone; has held offices School Director and Path Master; married Elizabeth Gibb, of England, 1854; she died in 1857; married Agnes Ray, from Scotland; she was born in Scotland; he has three children, Jane, Elizabeth, Susan.

Ward L. farmer; Sec. 32.

Warren D. A. mechanic.

Warren Edwin W. farmer; Sec. 14.

WARREN HENRY, Farmer; Sec. 14; born in Devonshire, England, March 6, 1828; came to this country in 1831; lived in Genesee Co., N. Y., twenty-two years; came to Boone Co in 1853, and has lived here twenty-four years; owns 111 acres land; has held office School Director and Road Master; married Rebecca Roach, from Devonshire, England, in May, 1852; have four children, Eliza A., Edwin W., Nellie M., Alice R., lost two children.

Warren J. W. laborer.
Washburn L. butcher.
Watkins Allen.
Watkins J. B. farmer.
Watson David, farmer; Sec. 7.
Watson D. M. farmer.
WATSON ELIJAH, Retired; born in New Hampshire, April 16, 1803; lived in Nashua eighteen or twenty years, and in that state fifty-seven years; came to this state, to Boone Co., 1860; engaged in Farming many years; married Miss Eliza Palmer, Feb. 28, 1827; she was born in Kensington, New Hampshire, Jan. 29, 1806; they were married fifty years last February; they have six children, Eliza, Jennie, Josiah, Emma, Eva, Charlie; lost two children; Charlie was in army, 35th Regt. Wisconsin V. I., Co. F.; was in Mobile Campaign, at siege Spanish Fort; they were under fire of enemy thirteen days.
Watson John, farmer; Sec. 7.
Watson Wm. farmer; Sec. 7.
Webb Wm. W. clerk.
Weekley Chas. saloon keeper.
WELSHER REV. WILLARD A., Pastor First Baptist Church; born in Monroe Co., N. Y., May 8, 1837; lived in that state twenty-six years; entered Rochester University and graduated there in 1862; his first Pastorate was at Litchfield, Ohio, in 1864; from there went to Troy, Ohio; came to Illinois; was Pastor successfully at Toulon, Chillicothe, and Cambridge; was called to Pastorate First Baptist Church of this city in June, 1874, the largest house of worship here; married Miss Sarah J Wood, from Monroe Co., N. Y., May 8, 1852; have three children, Arthur G., born May 31, 1855; Ina L., Jan. 18, 1870; Lewis Henry, July 10, 1875.
Westfall John T. farmer.
Weston Hiram, clerk.
Weston Wm laborer; Sec. 27.
Whelden Jabez, farmer; Sec. 7.
Whelden Philip G. farmer; Sec. 7.
Whelden P. G., Jr., Sec. 7.
Wheeler A. H. farmer.
Wheeler G. S. laborer.
WHEELER LEWIS E., Farmer; Sec. 24; born in Madison Co., N. Y., Aug. 19, 1830; lived in that state twenty-five years; came to this Co. in 1855, and has lived here twenty-two years; owns 252 acres land; has been married three times; his first wife was Sarah Sheffield, of Madison Co., N. Y.; his second wife was Margaret Saxton, of Belvidere; had two sons and two daughters, Frank, Clara, Sarah, Ernest; married his present wife, Mary Ames, of Belvidere, Dec. 10, 1873; they have one child, Walton A. Wheeler, born Feb. 27, 1877.
White Alonzo.
Whitehead Harry, merchant.
WHITEHEAD REV. J. M. Pastor South Belvidere Baptist Church; borne Wayne Co., Ind., March 6, 1823; lived in Indiana forty-one years; entered the ministry in 1844, his first pastorate being at Rolling Prairie; he preached in that county twenty years; was in the army two years, Chaplain of the 15th Ind. V. I., Army of the Cumberland; was pastor First Baptist Church, Kankakee, seven years; also pastor North Star Baptist Church, Chicago, six years; every member of this church but two was burned out in the great fire of 1871; he has built a church in every pastorate he has presided over before coming here; he was called to his present charge in 1876; married Miss Mary J. Patterson, from Ky., July 4, 1847; she was brought up in Ohio; they have three children: John W., Eliza O. and Nellie E.; have lost five children, two sons and three daughters.
Whitehead Wm. merchant.
WHITMAN CHAS. S. Retired; born in Bennington Co., Vermont, Jan. 4, 1800; lived there twenty-five years; removed to New York state; he is one of the earliest settlers Boone Co. now living that was here when he came; carted grain to Chicago for many years, taking from six days to two weeks to make a trip; sometimes they would have twenty yoke of oxen to pull one load through slough, taking all day to get through; married Mary Ann Jakway, of Fort Miller, New York, in 1824; she died in 1857; he married Mrs. Diana Hartwell, of Boston; she died Oct. 1, 1876; six children, three sons and three daughters; buried first child ever buried in this Co.
Whitman F. S. physician.
Whitman R. T. farmer.
Whitmore Abijah, laborer.
Whitmore Alonzo, laborer.
Whitworth Ernest.
WILCOX DANIEL, County Treasurer; born in Herkimer Co., New York, Sept. 14, 1814; lived in that state thirty-five years; came to this Co. to Belvidere, in 1855; was connected with C. & N W. R. R. for nineteen years; he was elected County Treasurer; married Miss Sarah A. Rix, of Herkimer Co., New York, in Feb., 1853; they have one child, Ralph T. Wilcox, born Dec. 1, 1854.
Wilbur George W. attorney.
Wilds G. W.
Williams A. O. druggist.
Williams D. wood dealer.

WILLIAMS JOSEPH R., Meat Market; born in Cumberland Co., Penn., Aug. 14, 1810; lived in that state twenty-two years; lived in Perrysville, Ohio, sixteen years; went to Warsaw, Ind., 1838; lived there seven years; came to this town and Co. July 20, 1845, and has lived here thirty-two years; his only brother, William Williams, now of Washington, D. C., was member of Congress, from state of Indiana, for six years; married Tabitha Doolittle, from Vermont, in March, 1845; have four children, two sons and two daughters, William R., Albert, Mrs. Helen Leonard, Blanche Williams; his sons are at Sioux Falls, Dakota Territory.

Williams John, laborer.

Williams Wm. H. mechanic.

WILLIAMSON G., M. D., Physician; born in Meadville, Penn., May 3, 1844; lived there eleven years; came to Marengo, this state, 1855; studied medicine and graduated at Rush Medical College, Chicago, season 1867; he has practiced his profession here for seven years; was in the army, member 17th Illinois Cav., under Col. Beveridge, now ex-Governor this state; married Miss Susie Bunker, of Woodstock, McHenry Co., Oct. 7, 1868.

Wilson Robert, mechanic.

Wing F. J. painter.

WING JOSEPH V., Carriage Manufacturer; born in Sherburn, New York, Oct. 14, 1813; lived in that state thirty-six years; came to Belvidere in 1849; has lived here twenty-eight years; has been engaged in business since he came; married Sarah A. Johnson, from Virgil, Cortland Co., N. Y., in 1840; they have four children, Fred, Eugenia, David, Frank; lost three children.

Winters Isaac, laborer.

WINNE FRANCIS I., Street Commissioner; born in Albany Co., N. Y., April 12, 1832; lived in N. Y. State twenty-one years; came to Boone Co., to Belvidere, in 1853; has lived here twenty-four years; engaged in Farming number of years; married Miss Keziah Sager, Aug. 30, 1860; she was born in Greene Co., N. Y., in 1830.

WITBECK ISAAC T. Retired; born in Green Co., New York, June 14, 1810; lived there forty-four years; came to Chicago in spring of 1854; lived there four years; was engaged in the manufacture of wagons and plows, of the firm of H. Witbeck & Co.; removed to Boone Co., June, 1858; has lived here nineteen years; engaged in farming five years; removed to Belvidere, 1861, and on account of ill-health retired from active business; has held office of Supervisor Town of Flora, and Assistant Supervisor of Belvidere; also Corporation Trustee; married Miss Miranda Onderdonk, from Albany Co., New York, Nov. 4, 1855; they have two children, Luther John, Abram O.; lost two, one son and one daughter.

Wicon Ansel, farmer; Sec. 19.

Wolverten D. C. butter dealer.

WOOD SAMUEL, Proprietor City Scales; born in Gloucestershire, England, February 25, 1812; was engaged in the furniture business there; came to this country in 1850; lived in New York State and Canada, and came to Belvidere, Boone Co., in October, 1855, and has lived here twenty-two years; was engaged in produce business here for some years; he was one in company with W. H. Gilman and others in building the stores under Adelphi Hall, and erected most of the buildings on the southwest end as far as the scales; has held office of Corporation Trustee for three terms, and was elected President of the Board; owns a farm of 80 acres in town of Flora; married Lucy A. Stiles, his present wife, from Hamilton Co., N. Y., Feb. 9, 1854; they have three children: Joseph, born in England, Oct. 10, 1852; Frederick, in England, Feb. 12, 1858; Mary A. in England, July 31, 1845; their daughter, Mary A. Wood, married Rev. A. A. Newhall, of Woburn, Mass., July 19, 1876; they are both missionaries in Southern India.

WOOD WALES W. Attorney; born in Cattaraugus Co., N. Y., April 25, 1837; attended Genesee College two years, and then entered Union College, Schenectady, and after two years graduated there, class of 1857, one of the few who received honor of election to "Phi Beta Kappa Society;" came to this city and Co. in 1857, and entered law office of "Fuller & Wood," and was admitted to the Bar in 1860; enlisted in army, and was appointed Adjutant 95th Regt. I. V. I.; was Assistant Adjutant General on General McArthur's staff; was on similar duty and took part battle Nashville, Mobile, and other campaigns; at close war, he wrote the history of the 95th Regt.; resumed his profession; was appointed Master in Chancery in 1865; served eight years; was elected States Attorney this Co., 1872; served four years; married Miss Alice E. Humphrey, from Smithport, McKean Co., Penn., June 13, 1866; have one child, Gertrude C. Wood, born June 20, 1869.

Woods William, laborer.

Woodruff C. W. mechanic.

WRANCH JOSIAH. Farmer; born in England, June 1, 1834; came to this country in 1843; lived in New York State twelve years; came to this Co. in 1855, and has lived here twenty-two years; owns 37 acres of land just outside of corporation, and 172 acres in Nebraska; married Miss Amelia L. Benjamin, Dec. 7, 1865; she was born in Cazenovia, N. Y., Jan. 12, 1845; have four children: Fanny, born Sept. 3, 1866; Alice, Oct. 1, 1868; Fred, June 19, 1871; Belle, Sept. 8, 1873.

WRATE F. S. Farmer and Dairyman; Sec. 28; born Cambridgeshire, Isle of Ely, England, Aug. 9, 1831; came to this country in 1853; lived in Vermont four years; came to Illinois, to Kewanee, Henry Co., in 1857; was in grain business; was Sutler of 124th Regt. I.V.I., during the war; was trading down the Mississippi River for two years; came to Belvidere, Boone Co., in 1864, and is engaged in farming and dairy business; owns farm of 165 acres; married Jane Jackson, of Cambridgeshire, England, in April, 1852; have four children, Jessie, Franklin, Lydia, and Albert.

Wrate Frank W. farmer; Sec. 28.

WRIGHT OMAR H. Attorney; born in Durham, Greene Co., N. Y., May 23, 1827; at the age of 25 was elected Principal of Greeneville Academy, Greene Co., N. Y., and afterwards Professor of Fort Plain Seminary, which he resigned on account of ill health; he prepared for college at Union Academy, Knoxville, Pa.; entered Alfred University and graduated in 1850; he has lived in Belvidere since 1856; was Principal of Public Schools; has held office of Magistrate several years, and also City Clerk; was Government Assessor eight years; has practiced his profession here for many years, and is Master in Chancery of Boone Co. Circuit Court; in 1858, he married Miss Helen M. Williams, of Belvidere, formerly of Oswego, N. Y.; they have two sons, Robert W. and Omar H.

WYMAN CHARLES, (Deceased.) born in Granville, N. Y., September 15, 1815; lived in New York State twenty years; then a party of four, consisting of himself, his brother Alfred, and two Mr. Bartletts, came to Boone Co., town of Caledonia, in the fall of 1835, locating on Sec. 8; they dug a hole in the ground and covered it over, where they passed the winter, and lived on corn cake and molasses; the two Mr. Bartletts had to borrow twenty-five cents of their companions in Chicago to get through; they went to Rockford, and became among the wealthiest people there; the Wyman brothers took up land here; Charles married Miss Matilda Steele, from Vermont; they remained where he first located until April, 1875, when he departed this life, leaving a wife and six children, who are still living in Boone Co.; children are, Mrs. Martha Sherman, Mrs. Maria Ball, Edwin, Mary, Emma, and Justin.

Wyman E. C. broker.

YOUNG E. L. P. policeman.

Youts Henry, farmer.

Yourt John, broker.

ZEIGLAR W. F. baker.

COVEY SIMEON L. Sheriff Boone Co.; Belvidere; born in Chautauqua Co., N. Y., Feb 1, 1834; came to Belvidere in 1837, one of the early settlers; has been engaged in Farming, Grocery trade, and Stock business; owns farm of 204 acres in town of Boone; has held office of Deputy Sheriff; was elected Sheriff of Boone Co. in 1872, re-elected in 1874, and again re-elected in 1876; his first wife was Miss Eliza Webster, of Hamburg, N. Y.; had one son, Geo. H. Covey, born May 8, 1855; married Miss Elizabeth Porter, daughter of Thos. W. Porter, Esq., of this city, Nov. 8, 1876.

CRARY MRS. MARY E. Superintendent of Schools Boone Co.

BOONE TOWNSHIP.

ADAMS M. A. dentist; Capron.

ALEXANDER JAMES, Retired Farmer; Sec. 24; P. O. Capron; was born in Fayette Co., Ind., Aug. 28, 1816; owns 215 acres, valued at $10,750; left there and came to this Co. in the fall of 1840, and is one of the oldest settlers; Mr. A. was Supervisor five years, and Assessor five years; have four children, E. S., F. M., Serena and E. J.; wife was Miss Sarah Mitchell; she was born in Fayette Co., Penn., July 12, 1814; they were married Sept. 1, 1836; she died Aug. 25, 1875.

Alexander S. grain merchant; Poplar Grove.
Allen Watson, mechanic; Capron.
Anderson A. O. farmer; Sec. 10; P.O.Capron.
Anderson A. farmer; Sec. 28; P.O. Capron.
Anderson J. T. farmer; Sec. 11; P.O.Capron.
Anderson N. farmer; Sec. 22; P.O. Capron.
Andrews R. farmer; Sec. 1; P.O. Capron.
Andrews Wm. merchant; Capron.
Andrus Lyman, farmer; Sec. 33; P.O.Bonus.
Anonson Anon, laborer; Capron.
Anonson Kittle, retired; Capron.

BALL EDWARD, farmer; Sec. 20; P. O. Poplar Grove.
Ball E. B. farm; Sec. 20; P.O. Poplar Grove.
Ball Horace, laborer; Capron.
Ball J. B. farm; Sec. 20; P.O. Poplar Grove.
Ball O. farmer; Sec. 20; P.O. Poplar Grove.
Bates Benj. farmer; Sec. 15; P.O. Capron.
Bates Chas. farmer; Sec. 15; P.O. Capron.
Bates Fred, mechanic; Capron.

BATES ISAAC, Farmer and Stock Raiser; Sec. 15; P. O. Capron; born in Birmingham, Eng., Nov. 16, 1818; owns 334 acres, valued at $16,700; left there and came to the U. S. and to this Co. in 1845, and is one of the oldest settlers; have six sons and one daughter, Wm. H., born in England, June 30, 1841; Charles, born in England, March 29, 1843; Frederick, born in England, Feb. 18, 1845; Samuel, born in Boone Co., May 6, 1847; Benjamin, born in Boone Co., May 11, 1851; Ellen, born in Beloit, Wis., April 30, 1854; Albert E., born in Boone Co., June 19, 1858; wife was Miss Phœbe A. Tongue; she was born in England, Aug. 18, 1821; they were married July 27, 1840; he was Township Trustee and Township Clerk a number of years.

Bates Samuel, mechanic; Capron.
Bates Wm. H. farmer; Sec. 15; P.O.Capron.
Bean Knute, farmer; Sec. 23; P.O. Capron.

Becker H. farmer; Sec. 29; P.O. Bonus.
Beebe L. M. farm; S. 5; P.O. Poplar Grove.
Benson B. L. farmer; Sec. 11; P.O. Capron.
Benson J. L. farmer; Sec. 11; P.O. Capron.
Berry T. F. mechanic; Capron.
Bounds A. F. farmer; Poplar Grove.
Bounds Wm. farm; S. 30; P.O.Poplar Grove.
Briggs Albert.

BRIGGS M. C. Physician and Surgeon; Poplar Grove; was born in Chenango Co., N. J., Dec. 16, 1833; commenced the study of medicine under Dr. Henry M. Crawford, of St. Charles, Kane Co., Ill.; he served four years in the late rebellion as Assistant Surgeon; has family, seven children, Allison M., Salen S., Lizzie W., Edwin J., Nellie C., Owen M. and Mary E.; wife was Miss Mary J. Weld; she was born in Orford, N. H., Oct. 24, 1834; they were married Oct. 25, 1852.

Brown H. D. farmer; Sec. 32; P.O. Bonus.
Brown M. O. farmer; Sec. 33; P.O. Bonus.
Brown Thomas, laborer; Capron.

BURNSIDE EDWARD, Station Agent of the C. & N. W. R. R.; Poplar Grove; born in McHenry Co., June 27, 1853; came to this Co. in 1874; not married.

CADDICK ISAAC, Farmer; Sec. 17; P. O. Poplar Grove; was born in Worcestershire, Eng., June 5, 1822; owns 100 acres, valued at $3,500; left there and came to the U. S. and to this Co. in 1850, and is one of the oldest settlers; has two children, Catherine J. M., born in Boone Co., March 17, 1852; Walter A., born May 10, 1856; wife was Catherine J. Bowder; she was born in Penn., June 4, 1820; they were married in May, 1851; she died in November, 1876.

Carpenter C. farmer; Sec. 28; P.O. Capron.
Carroll H. M. merchant; Capron.
Casterline Gilbert, laborer; Capron.

CHAMPLIN I. H. Farmer; Sec. 36; P. O. Bonus, born in Windom Co., Conn., Nov. 13, 1800; came to this Co. in 1853; owns 100 acres, valued at $5,000; have four children, Samuel, Mary F., James H. and Chas. H.; wife was Miss Lavina Gifford; she was born in Columbia Co., N. Y.; married Jan. 15, 1840.

Cinnaman H. farm; Sec. 13; P.O. Chemung.
Clark Nels.
Cole A. J. retired; Capron.
Coleman Frank, mechanic; Capron.
Coleman J. B. mechanic; Capron.

Coleman P. farm; Sec. 6; P.O. Poplar Grove.
Coleman Wm. farm; S. 6; P.O. Poplar Grove.

COLVIN J. V. Farmer and Stock Raiser; Sec. 33; P. O. Bonus; was born in Bradford Co., Penn., April 30, 1837; came to this Co. July 1, 1846; owns 120 acres, valued at $6,000; is one of the oldest settlers; have two children, Jesse, born Jan. 10, 1865; Ruth, Aug. 2, 1874; wife was Miss E. M. Williams, born in the same Co., Sept. 8, 1835; married April 18, 1860.

Conley Harrison, laborer; Capron.
Conley Henry, laborer; Capron.
Conley John N. painter; Capron.
Conley A. L. Justice of the Peace; Capron.
Conrad Wm. farmer; Sec. 2; P. O. Capron.
Cook James, farmer; Sec. 8; P. O. Capron.
Cook M. farm; Sec. 7; P. O. Poplar Grove.
Covey H. J. farm; S. 30; P.O. Poplar Grove.
Covey S. farm; Sec. 30; P. O. Poplar Grove.
Cowen R. farm; S. 17; P. O. Poplar Grove.
Cramer Wm. Postmaster; Capron.

CORNWELL BARNEY, Lumber Dealer and Station Agent, Capron; born near Toronto, Canada, Jan. 6, 1828; came to this Co. in 1844; owns 330 acres, valued at $14,250, and is one of the oldest settlers; wife was Miss Margaret Ann Day; she was born in Canada; married March 1, 1854; he was Road Commissioner one term; has been Station Agent on the C. & N. W. R. R. for the past seventeen years; have had five children: Thos. Milton, born Jan. 15, 1855, died Dec. 6,1868; Jas. Leonard, born June 12, 1857, died Oct. 6, 1866; Barney Emery, born Feb. 22, 1859, Geo. Oct. 4, 1861, died Oct. 18, 1862; Clara Etta, born Jan. 13, 1869.

CORNWELL MRS. PHŒBE, Farmer; Sec. 7; P. O. Poplar Grove; born in Canada, Dec. 24, 1823; owns 100 acres, valued at $5,000; widow of Gabriel Cornwell; he was born in Canada, Sept. 6, 1821; he came to this Co. in 1845; was one of the oldest settlers; he died May 22, 1863; Mrs. C's maiden name was Coleman; they were married March 19, 1842; have three children, Sarah E., married Wm. H. Belt, and lives in Delaware Co., Iowa, Melvin E., and Wm. A., at home.

Cornwell Thomas, mechanic; Poplar Grove.
Cornwell Wm. mechanic; Poplar Grove.
Cornwell M. farm; S. 7; P. O. Poplar Grove.

DAY SYLVESTER, farmer; Sec. 9; P. O. Capron.
Day Edward, laborer; Capron.
Dean G. S. farm; S. 6; P. O. Poplar Grove.
Dickerson C. A.
Dickerson Daniel.
Dunn John.

EDGELL C. S. farmer; Sec. 7; P. O. Poplar Grove.
Edson Charles, farmer; S. 2; P. O. Capron.
Edson Peter, farmer; Sec. 2; P. O. Capron.
Egleston W. F. farmer; S. 23; P. O. Capron.
Ellam J. farm; Sec. 21; P. O. Poplar Grove.
Ellingson E. farmer; Sec. 22; P. O. Capron.
Ellingson Jno. farm; Sec. 15; P. O. Capron.
Ellingson Ole, farm; Sec. 22; P. O. Capron.
Emmons Jos. farmer; P. O. Poplar Grove.
Everts H. F. mechanic; Capron.

FORD JOHN, farmer; Sec. 25; P. O. Capron.
Fenton Charles, laborer; Capron.
Freeman Charles, cheese maker; Capron.
Fross Charles W. peddler; Poplar Grove.
Fross J. S. meat market; Poplar Grove.
Frye Pascal, farm; Sec. 26; P. O. Capron.
Frye Walter, farm; Sec. 26; P. O. Capron.
Furgeson R. farmer; Sec. 23; P. O. Capron.

GEORGESON JOHN, farmer; Sec. 15; P. O. Capron.
Georgeson Ole, farm; Sec. 14; P. O. Capron.
Goodrich Nathan, mechanic; Capron.

GOODSELL LEWIS, Miller; P. O. Capron; was born in Norway, October, 1829; left there and came to the U. S. and to McHenry Co. in 1850; has been a resident of this Co. fourteen years; wife was Miss Elizabeth Bean, born in Boone Co., Jan. 5, 1843; they were married in December, 1863; have four children: Henry, born Sept. 29, 1864; Ellen, April 23, 1867; Julia, April 4, 1869; Lewis F., Dec. 24, 1871.

Green Philomon, laborer; Poplar Grove.

HAGER BENJAMIN, railroad laborer; Capron.
Hannah R. laborer; Sec. 30; P. O. Capron.
Hanson Hans, farm; Sec. 12; P.O. Capron.
Hanson Knute, farm; Sec. 11; P. O. Capron.
Hanson Ole K. farm; Sec. 10; P. O. Capron.

HANSON OLIVER K. Farmer and Stock Raiser; Sec. 11; P. O. Capron; was born in Norway, July 12, 1830; came to the United States and to this Co. in 1842, and is one of the oldest settlers; owns 170 acres, valued at $6,800; has eight children, Hannah, Knute, Edward, Christina, Thomas, Maria, Olena, and William; wife was Miss Toma Edward, born in Norway; married in 1852.

Harmond M.N. farm; S.20;P.O.Poplar Grove.
Hart George.
Haskins Ed. farm; S. 34; P. O. Russellville.
Hawley Edw. hardware store; Poplar Grove.
Hazen Jos. farmer; Sec. 9; P. O. Capron.
Head Marion, farmer; P. O. Poplar Grove.

HEATH C. W., Farmer and Stock Raiser; Sec. 27; P. O. Capron; was born in New Jersey, March 31, 1824; came to this Co. Oct. 12, 1845; owns 316 acres, valued at $12,640; Mr. H. is one of the oldest settlers; has five children, Clara, Lelia, Stanley, Ina, and William; has been married twice; first wife was Jane Miller; she was born in New York; married Oct. 12, 1847; she died in March, 1854; he married again, to Cynthia Stevenson, April 12, 1856; was Supervisor four years, and held other town offices.

HELGESON OLE, Farmer; Sec. 10; P. O. Capron; born in Norway, Nov. 3, 1821; came to this Co. in 1843, and is one of the oldest settlers; owns 60 acres, valued at $2,400; wife was Miss Christina Olson; she was born in Norway; they were married Jan. 26, ——; have six children, Cornelia, Maggie, Rossia, Bertie, Helga, and Bella; lost one, Olena.

HINMAN STEPHEN, Farmer; Sec. 21; P. O. Poplar Grove; was born in Montgomery Co., N. Y., Aug 16, 1799; owns 110 acres, valued at $5,500, and is one of the oldest settlers; has three children living; lost four; Stephen, born Feb. 6, 1827, deceased; Jerusha, Sept. 17, 1830, deceased; David M., Nov. 19, 1834; Rosaltha, Oct. 19, 1838; Calirna, June 30, 1840; Helen M., May 4, 1842, deceased; John W., Nov. 10, 1845, deceased; wife was Phylinda Goodell; she was born in Ontario Co., N. Y., July 26, 1802; married Oct. 16, 1823; was Town Clerk, School Treasurer, and School Trustee, a number of years.

Hinman D. farm; S. 21; P.O. Poplar Grove.
Hermanson A. farm; Sec. 11; P.O. Capron.
Hermanson Andrus, farm; S.11; P.O.Capron.
Hermanson H. farm; Sec. 11; P.O. Capron.
Hermanson I. farmer; Sec. 11; P.O. Capron.
Hill Henry, farmer; Sec. 26; P.O. Capron.
Hooper Benj. laborer; Capron.
Hopkins P. C. mechanic; Capron.
Hoppersted J. O. farm; Sec. 12; P.O.Capron.
Hovey E. farmer; Sec. 13; P.O. Capron.
Houck E. S. farmer; Sec. 25; P.O. Bonus.
Hurley Geo. W. farmer; Sec. 2; P.O.Capron.
Hutchinson A. farmer; Sec. 25; P.O.Capron.
Hutchinson Arch. farm; S. 25; P.O. Capron.
Hutchinson J. farmer; Sec. 25; P.O. Capron.

IVERSON IVER.

IVERSON JOHN, Farmer; Sec. 21; P. O. Capron; born in Norway, June 8, 1831; left there the 12th of May, 1853, and landed in Chicago; came to this Co. in March, 1854; owns 158 acres, valued at $6,320; have five children, Julia A., Embert, Irving, Nels A. and Bertie; wife was Miss Christie Nelson; she was born in Norway, March 8, 1843; they were married May 21, 1861.

Irvin G. farmer; Sec. 34; P.O.Poplar Grove.

JACKSON LEONE.

Johnson A. farmer; Sec. 15; P.O. Capron.
Johnson A. L. farmer; Sec. 2; P. O. Capron.
Johnson E. farmer; Sec. 2; P.O. Capron.
Johnson H. L. farmer; Sec. 12; P.O. Capron.
Johnson H. farmer; Sec. 2; P.O. Capron.
Johnson L. farmer; Sec. 12; P.O. Capron.
Johnson O. E. farmer; Sec. 14; P.O.Capron.
Johnson O. L. farmer; Sec. 1; P.O. Capron.
Johnson Wm.O. farmer; Sec.13; P.O.Capron.
Jury Henry, laborer; Capron.

KELLOGG J. E, Lumber Dealer and Farmer; P. O. Capron; was born in Rensselaer Co., N. Y., Feb. 4, 1820; came to this Co. in 1844; owns 225 acres, valued at $10,115; have four children, George A., born Dec. 31, 1845; Ada, June 1, 1855; Herbert E., Feb. 28, 1861; Kittie, April 3, 1877; wife was Miss A. J. Townsend; she was born in the same Co.; married Dec. 3, 1840.

KENDIG W. H. Miller; Capron; born in Erie Co., Penn., Nov. 8, 1840; came to this State in 1867, and to this Co. in 1875; one daughter, Lizzie, born Jan. 20, 1871; wife was Miss E. A. Crawford; she was born in Allegheny Co., N. Y., April 29, 1838; they were married March 3, 1860.

Kerr John, farmer; Sec. 35; P. O. Capron.
Kimble Elias A. laborer; Capron.

KIMBLE JOHN, Farmer and Stock Raiser; Sec. 32; P. O. Russellville; born in Morris Co., N. J., May 11, 1821; came to this Co. in 1862; owns 159 acres, valued at $7,950; has ten children living, lost one, Betsy J., Melvina, Jacob, John, Susan, Wm., Anne, Corabell, Margaret (deceased), Carrie and George; wife was Miss Caroline Bueller; she was born in N. Y.; they were married in 1844.

Kirk Geo. farmer; Sec. 3; P.O. Capron.
Knuteson C. laborer; Capron.
Knuteson Neri, farmer; Sec. 12; P.O.Capron.

LAMB E. G. farmer; Sec. 33; P.O.Bonus.

Lamb Pason, farmer; Sec. 33; P.O. Bonus.
Langhechr Fred, farm; Sec. 3; P.O. Bonus.
Lascelles John, mechanic; Capron.
Lattimer S. R. laborer; Capron.
Lewis B. S. laborer; Capron.
Lines Austin.
Linderman A. farmer; Sec. 8; P.O. Capron.
Linderman G. W. mechanic; Capron.
Linderman John C. farmer; Capron.

Linscott Wm. farmer and preacher; Sec. 3; P. O. Capron.
Lloyd Wm. farmer; Sec. 13; P.O. Capron.

LOING WALTER, Farmer and Stock Raiser; Sec. 35; P. O. Bonus; was born in Allegheny Co., N. Y., Sept. 2, 1829; came to this Co. in June, 1859; owns 170 acres, valued at $8,500; is one of the oldest settlers in the Co.; have one daughter, Eliza, born May 3, 1860; wife was Miss Orpha Curtis; she was born in London, Canada, April 10, 1830; they were married July 7, 1858; he was Town Commissioner a number of years.

Loveless Elijah, mechanic; Capron.
Loveless Nathan, laborer; Capron.

McCLURE JAMES, farmer; Sec. 35; P. O. Capron.
McCluskey J. farmer; Sec. 9; P. O. Capron.
McCluskey R. farmer; Sec. 9, P. O. Capron.

McINTYRE DONALD and PETER, Farmers and Stock Raisers; Sec. 6; P. O. Capron; Donald was born in Scotland, Jan. 17, 1857; came to the United States and to Winnebago Co. in 1857; Peter was born in Scotland in 1846, and came the year following; they own 320 acres, valued at $16,000; Donald not married; Peter has one daughter, Mary A., born May 10, 1876; wife was Miss Mary Sillars; she was born in Scotland in 1852; they were married Feb. 18, 1875.

McIntyre P. farm; Sec. 6, P.O. Poplar Grove.
McQuaid Geo. railroad laborer; Capron.
Magill Wm. farm; S 7; P. O. Poplar Grove.
Manley A. B. teacher; Capron.
Mann James, Jr. laborer, Capron.
Mann James, farm; Sec. 4; P. O. Capron.
Maskey Ernest, farm; Sec. 9; P. O. Capron.
Merrill Geo. H. painter, Capron.
Merrill J. W. attorney at law; Capron.
Milliken Chas. farm; Sec. 27; P. O. Capron.
Milliken Geo. farm; Sec. 27; P. O. Capron.

MILLIKEN JAMES S. Farmer; Sec. 27; P. O. Capron; was born in Cheshire Co., N. H., Oct. 9, 1819; owns 150 acres, valued at $8,000; came to the State and to McHenry Co. in 1841, and to this Co. in 1842, and is one of the oldest settlers; has five children, Arvilla, George, Vina, Parthena, and Orris, wife was Miss Rachel Mitchell; she was born in Fayette Co., Penn., July 16, 1826; they were married Jan. 4, 1843; Mrs. M. came to this Co. in 1857; he was Town Constable four years.

Moore A. K. farmer; P. O. Poplar Grove.
Moore Green, farmer; P. O. Poplar Grove.
Moore John, laborer; P. O. Poplar Grove.
Moore Thomas, farmer; P. O. Poplar Grove.

NELSON KNUTE, farmer; Sec. 15; P. O. Capron.
Nelson I. farmer; Sec. 13; P. O. Capron.
Nelson Nels K. farmer; P. O. Capron.
Nelson Ole, farmer; Sec. 3; P. O. Capron.

NESMITH M. S. Of the firm of Nesmith & Stevenson, Druggists, Capron; born in Henry Co., Ill., May 28, 1843; came to this Co. in 1869; has two children: Myrtle A., born Jan. 8, 1871, George T., Oct. 25, 1872; wife was Miss Paulina, daughter of George and Mary A. Steele; she was born in Erie, Whiteside Co., Ill., Dec. 25, 1842; they were married Oct. 5, 1869; he served two years and one month in the late war, in Co. B., 34th I.V.I., and in Co. G., 156th I. V. I.; is Town Clerk.

NICHOLS F.A., M.D., Physician and Surgeon; Capron; was born in Erie Co., Penn., July 11, 1829; commenced the study of medicine with Dr. Green, of Marengo; attended the medical department of the university of Penn.; graduated in 1864; was assistant surgeon in the late rebellion, for three years; commenced practice in Capron in 1870, where he has since been engaged; married Miss S. Deette Hoyt, of Woodstock, McHenry Co., in Feb., 1867; they have one son, Dillon, born in Dec., 1868

Nichols John, farmer; P. O. Capron.
Nichols W. W. laborer, Capron.
Nutting S. lab; Sec. 8; P. O. Poplar Grove.
Nygard Ole, mechanic; Capron.

OLESON ANDRUS T. farmer; Sec. 11; P. O. Capron.
Oleson Enan, laborer; P. O. Capron.
Oleson Ole T. farmer; P. O. Capron.

OLSON THOR, Farmer; Sec. 24; P. O. Capron; born in Norway, Oct. 14, 1811; owns 40 acres, valued at $2,000; left Norway May 3, 1843, and came to this Co. the following spring, and was the first Norwegian that settled in the Co., and among the first to emigrate from Norway; has two sons, Ole T. and Stoner T.; has been married three times; first wife was Rosa T. Olson; she was born in Norway; she died in this Co. in 1852; he married again to Margie Olson; she died in 1855; married again to Anne Olson, who is now living with him.

Onderdonk L. farm; S.30; P.O. Poplar Grove.
Osman C. A. trader; Capron.
Ostrom A. D. farmer; Sec. 17; P. O. Poplar Grove.
Ostrom George, farm; P. O. Poplar Grove.
Ostrom G. farm; Sec. 17; P.O. Poplar Grove.
Ostrom J. E. laborer; Poplar Grove.
Ostrom Luther, laborer; Poplar Grove.

PARSON SAMUEL, farmer; Sec. 25; P. O. Capron.

Patten James, mechanic; Poplar Grove.
Patten T. farm; S. 30; P. O. Poplar Grove.
Phinney W. R. farm; Sec. 36; P. O. Bonus.
Pickard David, mechanic; S.5; P.O.Capron.
Pollgreen Wm. pork buyer; Capron.
Powell Horace, mechanic; Capron.
Powell Reuben, mechanic; Capron.

RAE GEORGE, farmer; Sec. 20; P. O. Poplar Grove.
Rae John, farm; S. 20; P. O. Poplar Grove.
Reed Gerd, farmer; Sec. 23; P. O. Capron.

REID ANNE, Farmer; Sec. 6; P. O. Capron; born in the Co. of Armaugh, Ireland, Jan. 6, 1830; widow of Thomas Reid; he was born in the same Co., Jan. 1, 1823; they were married Nov. 22, 1847; he died Jan. 6, 1855; left a family of five children, Maria E., James W., Sarah A., Robert B., and Thomas W.; he left an estate of 120 acres, which has been divided, leaving Mrs. R. 40 acres, valued at $1,800.

Reid James, farmer; Sec. 6; P. O. Capron.
Reynolds Henry.
Ridge George, laborer; Capron.
Ridge Robert, merchant; Capron.
Robbins G. F. laborer; Capron.
Robbins J. H. farm; Sec. 27; P. O. Capron.
Robinson J. farm; S. 6; P. O. Poplar Grove.
Rolansen John, laborer; Capron.
Rowe James, restaurant; Capron.
Rollingson Ole. farm; Sec. 12; P.O. Capron.

SANDS CLARENCE, farmer; Sec. 27; P. O. Capron.
Sands Elling, farm; Sec. 1; P. O. Capron.

SANDS GEO. Farmer, Stock and Dairyman; Sec.27; P. O. Capron; born in Delaware Co., N. Y., Oct. 7, 1818; came to this Co. in 1839; owns 206½ acres, valued at $10,300; Mr. S. is one of the oldest settlers in the Co.; wife was Miss Betsy, daughter of Obadiah Sands, the first settler of Bonus township; he settled in Oct., 1836, she was born in Delaware Co., N. Y., April 2, 1826; they were married Jan. 18, 1844; have three sons, George H., Clarence O., and Edward F., Mr. S. has one of the best improved places in the Co.

SANDS WM. Farmer and Stock Raiser; Sec. 3; P. O. Capron; was born in Forfarshire, Scotland, Jan. 22, 1828; left there and came to the U. S. and to Cook Co., Ill. in 1851; owns 160 acres land, valued at $8,800; has two sons and three daughters; Wm., Nellie, Jennie, Rudolph, and Mary; wife was Miss Helen Milve; she was born in the same Co., Feb. 28, 1834; they were married April 7, 1860; has been School Director about fourteen years.

Scott Francis, farmer; Sec. 22; P.O. Capron.
Scott John, farmer; Sec. 27; P. O. Capron.

SCOUGALL LAUGHLIN, Farmer and Stock Raiser; Sec. 28; P. O. Poplar Grove; born in Scotland, Jan. 26, 1839; owns 115 acres, valued at $5,750; left there and came to the U. S. in 1850, and to this Co. in 1852; have eight children: George, Belle, Frank, Clara, Ella, Frederick, Kate and Hattie; has been married twice; first wife was Miss Mary Anne Cornwell; she was born in Canada; married in 1857; she died in 1868; married again to Nancy Jane Wagner; she was born in 1839, and married in 1869; is School Director, and has been for twelve years.

Shackett T.W.farm; S.19; P.O.Poplar Grove.
Shackett Thos.farm; S.19; P.O.Poplar Grove.
Shackett Wm. farm; S.19; P.O.Poplar Grove.
Shannon Geo. farmer; Sec. 10; P.O. Capron.
Shannon M. A. laborer; Capron.
Skeel H. F. clerk; Capron.
Skeel Rockwell, laborer; Capron.
Smith Geo. farmer; Sec. 5; P. O. Capron.

STEVENSON EDWARD Was born in Baltimore, Md., Feb. 8, 1795; Sarah Watson, his wife, was born in Burlington, N. J., Oct. 9, 1803; they were married in Warren Co., O., Nov. 4, 1819; moved to this Co., Boone township, in the spring of 1837; in the fall of the same year they bought 160 acres of government land, in Sec. 24, where they now live; they have eight children, all married and living close by, except one son in Iowa.

STEVENSON H. B. Attorney at Law and Druggist; Capron; born in McHenry Co., May 6, 1850; came to this Co. in 1855; not married; studied law at the Union Law College at Chicago, and received his diploma in June, 1875; was admitted to the bar and commenced practice the same year at Capron; he is also the junior partner of the firm of Nesmith & Stevenson, druggists; has his office in Capron, and is prepared to practice in all Courts.

STEVENSON JAMES. Farmer; Sec. 3; P. O. Capron; born in Delaware Co., Penn., Dec. 22, 1839; owns 80 acres, valued at $2,800; came to the State with his parents when very young, and went to McHenry Co.; came to this Co. in 1866; has four children: Lillie Bell, born March 7, 1870; Jennie L., July 3, 1873; Mary M., Oct. 11, 1874; Annie L., March 25, 1877; wife was Miss Belle Nelson, born in Pittsburgh, Sept. 8, 1845; married May 31, 1866; he served three years in the late war, in Co. E., 95th I. V. I.

Stevenson O. farmer; Sec. 24; P.O. Capron.
Stevenson S. L. speculator; Capron.

STEVENSON SILAS R. Farmer and Stock Raiser; Sec. 24; P. O. Capron; born in Warren Co., Ohio, Jan. 31, 1821; came to this Co. May 6, 1857; owns 200 acres, valued at $10,000; Mr. S. is one of the very oldest settlers; he married Miss Eliza J. Penwell; she was born in Fountain Co., Ind., Sept. 11, 1825; have three sons and three daughters; Sanford, lives in California; Orlando, Harriet, Lillian, Almond and Delphia M.; he has served as Road Commissioner, School Trustee, and County Superintendent of the Poor.

STEVENSON WM. R. Farmer; Sec. 24; P. O. Capron; born in Boone Tp., Boone Co., Nov. 28, 1841; owns 86 acres, valued at $4,300; Mr. S. was about the first white child born in the Co.; his father came to the Co. in May, 1837, and was one of the first settlers; wife was Miss Emma J. Whipple; she was born in McHenry Co.; have one son; Mr. S. served over three years in the late Rebellion, in Co. B, 95th I. V. I., and received five different wounds.

Stimes Ole, farmer; Sec. 15; P. O. Capron.
Stow H. H. clerk; Capron.
Stow Hiram, farmer; P. O. Capron.
Stow Jas. H. farmer; Sec. 35; P. O. Bonus.
Stockwell David, laborer, Capron.
Streeter Alonzo, mechanic; Capron.
Streeter Wm. laborer; Capron.
Stuff G. L. S. clergyman; Poplar Grove.

THOMPSON CHAS. farmer; Sec. 11; P. O. Capron.
Thompson Eric, farmer; Sec.4; P.O. Capron.
Thompson Ole, miller; Sec. 5; P.O. Capron.
Thornton A. butcher; Capron.
Thornton T. R. meat market; Capron.
Tolverson Stall, farmer; Sec. 4; P.O. Capron.
Torgson Torgs, farmer; Sec. 1; P.O. Capron.

TRIPP G. I. Merchant; Capron; born in Boone Co., Nov. 12, 1840; has one son, Everet H., born June 13, 1867; wife was Miss E. J. Stowe; she was born in Boone Co. in 1840; they were married in Sept., 1868; he served three years and nine months in the late war; was Sergeant two years in Co. I, 37th I. V. I., and then was promoted to First Lieutenant in the 92d Regt. Colored Volunteers.

VANALSTINE NEWELL, lives in Caledonia; P. O. Capron.
Vance Thos. farmer; Sec. 23; P. O. Capron.
Vickers Robt. blacksmith; Poplar Grove.

WAGENER ISAAC, farmer; Sec. 29; P. O. Poplar Grove.

WAGNER DAVID, Retired Farmer; Sec. 29; P. O. Poplar Grove; born in Maryland, forty miles from Baltimore, April 9, 1804; came to this Co. in 1855; owns 30 acres, valued at $1,200; has three sons and one daughter, William, Isaac, Richard and Nancy Jane; wife was Hannah Gurnea; born in N. Y., Aug. 9, 1808; they were married June 3, 1830.

Wagener R. farm; S. 19; P.O. Poplar Grove.
Wagener Wm. farmer; Sec. 34; P.O. Capron.
Waren Geo. laborer; Capron.
Wares Andrew, mechanic; Capron.
Wares A. F. farmer; P. O. Capron.
Warn Stephen, retired; 107 y'rs old; Capron.
Webster W. H. merchant; Poplar Grove.
Wellbay J. farm; S. 29; P. O. Poplar Grove.

WHEELER MRS. ELIZA E. Farmer; Sec.19;P.O.Poplar Grove; born in Addison, Vt., Feb. 19, 1819; owns 300 acres, valued at $15,000; widow of Obediah, who was born in Erie Co., N. Y., May 9, 1820; left there and came to this Co. in 1844, and was one of the oldest settlers; they were married in 1840; he died Aug. 8, 1876; left four sons and one daughter, and lost one daughter; Mrs. Wheeler's maiden name was Wolcott.

Wheeler Thomas, Jr., farmer; Sec. 19; P. O. Poplar Grove.
Wheeler Thomas, farmer; Sec. 30; P. O. Poplar Grove.
Wheeler W. farm; Sec.19; P.O.Poplar Grove.
White O. S. farmer; Sec. 26; P. O. Capron.
Wicks D. W. farm; S. 29; P.O.Poplar Grove.
Wilcox George J. peddler; Capron.

WILLARD H. R. Farmer and Stock Raiser; P. O. Bonus; Sec. 36; was born in Ulster Co., N. Y., Feb. 17, 1823; came to this Co. in 1844; owns 240 acres, valued at $9,600; Mr. W. is one of the oldest settlers; has been Supervisor four terms; have seven children living and lost two; wife was Miss C. M. Morse, born in Cortland Co., N. Y., Oct. 3, 1829; they were married Nov. 13, 1847; he is Township Trustee.

Willet S. farmer; Sec. 17; P. O. Poplar Grove.
Williams W. G. hotel keeper; Capron.
Wolfram H. farmer; Sec. 2; P. O. Capron.
Wood P. J. physician; Capron.
Woodward A. O. merchant; Poplar Grove.
Woodward A. S. merchant; Poplar Grove.
Woodward M. F. merchant; Poplar Grove.
Wooster John W. laborer; Capron.
Wooster N. H., Jr., farmer; P. O. Capron.

WOOSTER N. H. Justice of the Peace; Capron; was born in Oxford, New Haven Co., Conn., Dec. 25, 1821; came to this Co. in 1840, and is one of the oldest settlers; have three sons and three daughters, Laura E., married John L. Conley; Mary J., married John H. Landon; George J., John W., W. H., Jr., and Minnie; wife was Miss Abigail A. Hovey; she was born in N. H., on May 30, 1826; they were married Oct. 4, 1844; has been Justice sixteen years; served eight months in the late rebellion, in Co. C, 137th I. V. I.

WORTHINGTON GEO. W. Farmer; Sec. 30; P. O. Poplar Grove; born in DuPage Co., Ill., June 12, 1843; owns 176 acres, valued at $5,280; came to this Co. with his parents the following March, and is one of the oldest settlers; he served three years in the late rebellion, in Co. B, 15th I. V. I.; has three children, Mary E., Alvira and Wm. A.; wife was Miss Lizzie Van Valkenburg; she was born in Columbia Co., N. Y., March 26, 1847; they were married March 17, 1870.

Wright Henry.

YATES A. E. Hardware Merchant; Capron; born in Bonus Tp., this Co., Jan. 1, 1851; have no children; wife was Miss Alice Tripp; she was born in the same Tp.; married March 31, 1876; value of estate, $3,000.

Young Babtist, laborer; Sec. 15; P.O.Capron.

Younges J. G. farmer; Sec. 4; P. O. Capron.

Youngs Robert, laborer; Capron.

BONUS TOWNSHIP.

ANDERSON E. Sec. 3; P. O. Garden Prairie.
Andrews Adelbert, farmer; Sec. 11; P. O. Garden Prairie.
Andrews Asel, farmer; P. O. Belvidere.
Andrews Ansel, farm; P.O. Belvidere.
Andrews Frank, farmer; Sec. 11; P. O. Garden Prairie.
Andrews J. H. farm; S. 11; P. O. Belvidere.
Andrews Melvin, farmer; P. O. Belvidere.
ANDREWS WARREN, Farmer; Sec. 11; P. O. Belvidere; born in N. Y., 1821; came to this Co. 1850; owns 270 acres land; has held office of School Director; married Louisa Keeler in Feb., 1847; she was born in N. Y., have five children, Adelia, Adelbert, Ellen, Alda J. and Frank.
Andrus D. R. farm; Sec. 8; P. O. Belvidere.
Atwood N. P., P. O. Belvidere.
AVERY MYRON K. Farmer; Sec. 11; P. O. Garden Prairie; born in Penn., Aug. 20, 1834; came to this Co. July 9, 1858; owns 280 acres land; has held offices of Supervisor, School Trustee, and was member of the 29th General Assembly of the State of Illinois; married Miss Abigail M. Tongue in 1854; have six children, Cyrus d., Florence L., Stella E., Clara E., Myron A. and Mabel E.

BANE W. C. retired; P. O. Garden Prairie.
BAILEY THEODORE, Farmer; Sec. 9; P. O. Belvidere; born in N. Y., 1845; came to this Co. 1854; owns 150 acres land; married Miss E. Powers in 1868; she was born in N. Y.; have three children, Carrie, Fred and Frankie.
Barber H. H. farmer; P. O. Belvidere.
Barmore H. H. farmer; P. O. Belvidere.
BARTON FRED L., Farmer; Sec.16; P. O. Belvidere; born in N. Y., Sept. 17, 1855; came to this Co. in 1869; owns 40 acres land.
Bassett P. farm; S. 2; P. O. Garden Prairie.
BENNETT GEO. W. Wagon Maker; Garden Prairie; born in N. Y., 1853; came to this Co. in 1876; married Miss Hattie Baxter in 1876; she was born in Boone Co.
BICKNELL B. R. Farmer; Sec. 9; P. O. Belvidere; born in Maine, 1817; came to this Co. 1865; owns 120 acres; married Miss Rebecca Hawes in 1855, who was born in Maine; have two children, Fred J. and R. Cena.
Bills J. W. farm; S. 23; P.O. Garden Prairie.
BILLS O. Farmer; Sec. 23; P. O. Garden Prairie; born in Tioga Co., N. Y., Sept. 26, 1825; came to this Co. 1844; owns 160 acres land; married Miss M. Winegar in 1854; she was born in N. Y.; has held office of School Director; have nine children, James, Charles, Frank, Lillie, Fred, Ettie, Belle, May and George.
Bogardus H. B. farmer; Sec. 5; P.O. Bonus.
Bogardus I. R. farm; S. 14; P.O. Belvidere.
Boomer B. F. farmer; P. O. Garden Prairie.
Bounds A. J., P. O. Belvidere.
BOYCE HUGH, Farmer; Sec. 23; P. O. Belvidere; born in Vermont in 1800; came to this Co. in 1852; owns 120 acres; wife was Maria Post, born in N. Y.; have five children.
Brady Joseph.
Brown N. B., P. O. Belvidere.
Brown T. J. farmer; Sec. 20; P.O. Belvidere.
Brownell A. farm; S. 36; P.O. Garden Prairie.
Brush C. farm; S. 12; P. O. Garden Prairie.
Brush Frank, farmer; P. O. Garden Prairie.
Brush Geo. farmer; P. O. Garden Prairie.
Brush I. R. farm; S. 12; P.O.Garden Prairie.
Bnell Wilmot, farmer; P. O. Belvidere.
Burton Daniel, P. O. Garden Prairie.
Burton H. farm; S. 23; P.O. Garden Prairie.
Burton N. Y. teamster; P.O. Garden Prairie.
BURTON THOMAS, Farmer; Sec. 27; P. O. Belvidere; born in Ireland, in 1827; came to this Co. in 1857; owns 133 acres; married Miss M. Walker, in 1854; she was born in Ireland, have six children, Lizzie, George, Walker, Sarah, John, and Mary; lost two.

CAMP BENJAMIN, farmer; Sec. 2; P. O. Bonus.
Camp Chester, Jr., farm; S. 2; P. O. Bonus.
Camp James, farmer; Sec. 2; P. O. Bonus.
Carpenter Jos. farm; Sec. 28; P.O.Belvidere.
Cleveland E. A. farm; Sec. 4; P. O. Bonus.
Cleveland Henry, farm; Sec. 4; P. O. Bonus.
Collar J. S. farmer; P. O. Bonus.
Collar J. V.; P. O. Bonus.
CONGER ENOCH, Farmer; Sec. 31; P. O. Belvidere; born in New York, in 1834; came to this Co. in 1866; owns 75 acres; married Miss Eleanor F. Martin, in 1857, who was born in New York.
Conger F. P. P. O. Belvidere.
Cook Almond, farm; P. O. Garden Prairie.
Cook E. A. farm; S. 12; P.O.Garden Prairie.
Cook Egbert, farmer; P. O. Garden Prairie.
Cramer Lewis.
Crane H. P. farm; S. 1; P.O. Garden Prairie.

Crawford And., Sr., Sec. 34; P. O. Belvidere.
Crawford And., Jr., farm; S.33; P.O.Belvidere.
Crawford James, farm; P. O. Belvidere.
Cronk Abram, farmer; P. O. Bonus.
Cronk Festus, farm; Sec. 22; P.O.Belvidere.
Cronk Geo., farm; Sec. 22; P. O. Belvidere.
Culbertson A. J. farm; P. O. Garden Prairie.

DAVEY G. railroad employe; P. O. Garden Prairie.

DECKER LEWIS, Farmer; Sec. 3; P. O. Bonus; born in New York, in 1826; came to this Co. in 1854; owns 105 acres; married Miss Betsy Williams, in 1848; she was born in Penn.; have one child, Lewey.

Doran Patrick, Sec. 10; P. O. Belvidere.
Drake C. B. farm; Sec. 22; P. O. Belvidere.
Drake C. E. farm; Sec. 28; P. O. Belvidere.
Drake L. A. farmer; Sec. 3; P. O. Belvidere.
Dreelan Andrew, farmer; P. O. Belvidere.

ENGLEBRECHT A. P. O. Garden Prairie.

FASSETT (A. C.) & ROSEKRANS (J. D.) Merchants, Garden Prairie; the former was born in New York, and came to this Co. in 1876; married Miss A. Hopkins, in 1866; she was born in New York; have one son, Willie; the latter was born in New York, and came to this Co. in 1856; married Miss H. A. Simpkins, in 1866; she was born in McHenry Co.; have four children.

FEELEY ABIGAIL C. Wife of Thomas Feeley; Sec. 23; P. O. Garden Prairie; born in Oxford Co., Maine, in 1816; came to this Co. in 1856; owns 140 acres of land; she married Tilden Jones, in 1840; he was born in Maine, and died in March, 1875; married C. Feeley in 1876.

Feeley C. Sec. 34; P. O. Garden Prairie.
Flemming John, farm; S. 22; P.O.Belvidere.
Flood George, P. O. Belvidere.
Fox H. E. farm; S. 34; P.O.Garden Prairie.
Fox S. C. farm; S. 34; P. O. Garden Prairie.
Franz J. farmer; Sec. 9; P. O. Belvidere.

GARDNER ALFRED, farmer; P. O. Bonus.

HALL JOHN S. farmer; Sec. 7; P. O. Belvidere.

HALE A. D. Farmer; Sec. 6; P. O. Belvidere; born in Delaware Co., N. Y., June 22, 1834; came to Boone Co. in Oct., 1836, and has lived here 41 years; only very few (four or five) now living that were here then; there were plenty of Indians; he learned the Indian language playing with them, and still understands it; he used to cart grain to Chicago, and has sold his wheat there at from 50 cents to $1 per bushel; he married Mary Hall, of Putnam Co., N. Y., in Dec., 1855; they have five children, John P., Ada C., Frank D., Meeker O., Freddie; lost one daughter, Abbie A. Oliver Hale, father of A. D. Hale, was born in Delaware Co., N. Y., in 1799; came to Boone Co. 1836; was one of the earliest settlers; the nearest neighbor or house north of him was at Geneva Lake, 34 miles distant; he and his wife used to visit there, going with ox team; used to go to Ottawa, 80 miles, to mill; at one time he got in a slough with a load of potatoes and had to take off his overcoat and carry all of the potatoes in the coat to hard ground, then took his wagon apart and carried that out one part at a time; he married Susanna Bradt, Feb. 26, 1826; she was born in Delaware Co., N. Y., Jan. 9, 1802; they have lived together over 51 years, have two children, A. D. Hale, Mrs. Cassie Lambert; lost five.

Harrell John A.

HASKINS ALONZO, Farmer; Sec. 3; P. O. Bonus; born in N. Y., 1815; came to this Co. 1861; owns 123 acres land; married Miss Lovina McKinney, Sept. 10, 1835; she was born in N. Y.; have four children, Theresa M., Lydia L., Edgar D. and Mary J.

Havens Harrison, farmer; P. O. Belvidere.
Hawes B. farmer; Sec. 21; P. O. Belvidere.
Heaton S. S., P. O. Belvidere.
Heaton T. farmer; P. O. Garden Prairie.
Hendrickson John, railroad man; P. O. Garden Prairie.
Hendrickson Wm. railroad laborer; P. O. Garden Prairie.
Herbert B. farmer; Sec. 17; P.O. Belvidere.
Herbert John H., P. O. Belvidere.
Herbert Wm. R. farm; S. 17; P.O.Belvidere.
Herriton A. farmer; Sec. 8; P.O. Belvidere.
Herriton C. farmer; Sec. 8; P.O. Belvidere.
Herriton J. farmer; Sec. 8; P.O. Belvidere.
Hollenbeck A., P. O. Garden Prairie.
Hoppen G. farm; S. 1; P.O. Garden Prairie.
Hoppen R. farm; S. 1; P.O. Garden Prairie.
Howard E. farmer; Sec. 21; P. O. Belvidere.
Huber J. farmer; Sec. 28; P.O. Belvidere.
Hull J. D. farmer; Sec. 7; P.O. Belvidere.
Huntington F. A. farm hand; P.O. Belvidere.

HYDE F. D. Farmer; Sec. 25; P. O. Garden Prairie; born in Chautauqua Co., N. Y., 1839; came to this Co. in 1844; owns 171 acres land; has held office of School Director; married Miss Mary A. Bennett in 1859; she was born in N. Y.; have five children, Marietta, Byron F., Mertie A., Bertie A. and Lucia P.

Hyde J. A. farm; S.35; P.O. Garden Prairie.

HYDE MRS. PARMELIA, Widow; Sec. 35; P.O. Garden Prairie; born in

Essex Co., N. Y.; she married O. Hyde, July 12, 1837; he was born in Erie Co., N. Y., July 28, 1819, and died Aug. 28, 1871; has six children, Fletcher D., Deette, William, Alice, Julius A. and Lucia; lost three.
Hyde Wm. farm; S. 35; P.O. Garden Prairie.

JACKSON CHARLES D., Miller; P. O. Garden Prairie; born in Miss., Oct 7, 1810; came to this Co. in 1838; he has shaken hands with LaFayette; has held office of School Director; he owns 161½ acres land, and is associated with Mr. Brown in the milling business; they are proprietors of the Garden Prairie Mills, and own jointly 76 acres of land; he married Miss Mary A. Stowe in 1844; she was born in N. Y.; have two children, Nathan and Lucy.

JACKSON NATHAN D. Farmer; Sec. 1; P. O. Garden Prairie; rents of his father; he was born on this farm in 1845.
Johnson Charles, P. O. Belvidere.
Johnson J. F.

KEELER ENNIS, farmer; P.O. Belvidere.

KEELER MILTON F. P. O. Belvidere; born in Cortland Co., N. Y., Oct. 4, 1833; lived in that State eighteen years, and came to Belvidere in 1851, and has lived in this Co. twenty-six years; he owns Cheese Factory, and is engaged in manufacturing Cheese at this place; was in the army, in 95th Regt. I. V. I., and was in siege of Vicksburg and in a number of engagements; married Louisa Owens, of Canandaigua, Ontario Co., N. Y., Jan. 3, 1853; have eight children, four sons and four daughters, George H., Charles M., Willie E., Frank H., May, Helen, Grace, and Emma C.

KEELER WM. Farmer; Sec. 18; P. O. Belvidere; born in N. Y., in 1829; came to this Co. in 1849; owns 260 acres; has held offices of Assessor, School Director and Highway Commissioner; he married Miss Viola Stockwell in 1852, who was born in N. Y.; has three children, Ennis, Nettie and Fronie, and also an adopted son, a nephew, Freddie; lost one son, Charlie.
Kellogg G. A. farmer; Sec. 4; P. O. Capron.

KELLY THOS. Farmer; Sec. 16; P. O. Belvidere; born in Ireland, in 1836; came to this country in 1847; lived in Colerado about twelve years, and came to this Co. in 1875; owns 160 acres; he married Mary A. Keys, in 1863; she was born in Ireland; has five children, Catherine, Thomas F., Robert E., Lilla May, Maggie, lost one son, John A.

KIPP A. Farmer; Sec. 2; P. O. Bonus; born in N. Y., in 1825; came to this Co. in 1856; owns 120 acres; has held office of School Director; married Miss C. Hill, in 1852; she was born in N. Y.; have three children, Ida R., Carrie E., and Amie A.
Konika Philip, P. O. Garden Prairie.

LAMPERT FREDERICK, farmer; Sec. 29; P. O. Belvidere.
Lampert W. farmer; Sec. 29; P.O. Belvidere.
Lanning Frank, farmer; P.O. Belvidere.
Lanning J. M. farm; Sec. 31; P.O. Belvidere.
Lawrence E. C. farm; S. 28; P.O. Belvidere.

LAWRENCE FRANKLIN, (Deceased); Farmer; Sec. 32; was born in Groton, Mass., in 1814; came to this Co. in 1839, and was one of the earliest settlers; married Miss Anna Blood, in 1837, who was born in Mass.; he died in 1877, leaving his wife and five children, Andrew J., Charles H., Luther, Frances A., and Mary C., still surviving.
Lawrence L. farm; Sec. 32; P. O. Belvidere.

LAWRENCE JOHN, (Deceased) Was born in Ashby, Middlesex Co., Mass., March 8, 1788; removed with parents to Onondaga Co., N. Y., 1802; on his nineteenth birthday was married to Miss Lydia Sweet; they soon removed to Chenango Co., which was then a wilderness; came to Bonus, Boone Co., Ill., in 1837; on dividing the county into precincts, he was elected the first Justice of the Peace, which office he held for nineteen consecutive years, when he was obliged to resign on account of deafness; in 1855, being 67 years of age, he took the state census for Boone Co., alone, on foot; he has always been active as a religious man, having been baptized into the Baptist church in 1816; he had eleven children; ten grew to maturity, nine still living; his wife died in Oct., 1873; he died Nov. 20, 1876, aged nearly 89 years; they had lived together, as husband and wife, nearly 67 years.

LAWRENCE LUTHER W. Judge of County Court; born in Chenango Co., N. Y., April 19, 1808; lived in that State twenty-eight years, and came to this Co. in 1836, and has lived here forty-one years; for twenty-five years he was an itinerant preacher in the Baptist Church, and knew every man within twenty miles of Belvidere; he was elected Judge of Boone Co. in 1865; held the office twelve years; he has represented this district in the State Legislature three terms; was a member of Constitutional Convention in 1862; held office of Superintendent of Schools of this Co.; married Miss Elvira Chamberlain, Jan. 22, 1829; she was from Cazenovia, Madison Co., N. Y., six children, three sons and three daughters, Alonzo D., Edwin L., Harriet E. Sturtevant, Sarah Wyckoff, Esther M., Luther C.
Lincoln J. E. farm; Sec. 30; P.O. Belvidere.
Love M.

CALEDONIA TP.

BONUS TOWNSHIP.

Loveridge Jas. farmer; Sec. 22; P.O. Garden Prairie.
Lyons G.S. farm; S.35; P.O. Garden Prairie.

McCABE WM. D. farmer; Sec. 1; P. O. Garden Prairie.
McCane Jas. farmer; Sec. 27; P.O. Belvidere.
McCay Jas. miller; Sec. 8; P. O. Belvidere.
McClaron Jas. farmer; P. O. Bonus.
McDougall L. S. farmer; Sec. 36; P. O. Garden Prairie.
McLane Jas., Sr., farmer; P. O. Belvidere.
McMaster D. W. farm; S.29; P.O. Belvidere.

MABIE AARON, Farmer; Sec. 8; P. O. Belvidere; born in Delaware Co., N. Y., 1807; came to this Co. in 1842; owns 120 acres of land; has held office of School Director; married Miss Amy Turneaure, in 1828; she was born in N. Y.; has six children, Charles, Lydia, Edward, Ira, Jacob and Julia; his son, Jacob Mabie, enlisted in the Elgin Battery, in the late war, and served until discharged on account of disease contracted in the army.

MABIE D. Farmer; Sec. 19; P. O. elvidere; born in Delaware Co., N. Y., in 1846; came to this Co. in 1843; owns 66 acres of land; has held office of Supervisor; married E. F. Veness, June 9, 1869; she was born in England; have three children, Henry C., Fannie E., and Nellie.

Mabie Jacob, farmer; Sec. 9; P.O. Belvidere.
Markey E.
Marvin R. V. P. O. Garden Prairie.
Meehan J. farmer; Sec. 20; P.O. Belvidere.
Mersereau S.M. farm; Sec.19; P.O.Belvidere.

MILLER ALFRED J. Farmer; Sec. 9; P.O. Bonus; born in Penn., 1837; came to this Co. in 1841; owns 90 acres; married Mrs. Arletta Stevens, in 1869; she was born in Vt.; has one child by former marriage, Elmer A.

MILLER I. D. Farmer and Miller; Sec. 16; P. O. Belvidere; born in Penn., 1828; came to this Co. in 1842; owns 170 acres land; he is associated with McKay in the milling business and proprietors of Little Thunder Mill, built in 1852; he married Caroline Akin, in 1852; she was born in Penn.; has three daughters, Lilla, Ida and Nellie.

MOAN DENNIS, Farmer Sec. 3; P. O. Belvidere; born in Ireland, in 1824; came to this Co. in 1852; owns 204 acres; he married Miss Margaret Ryan, in 1854; she was born in Ireland; has five children: John, Katie E., Dennis, Francis D., and James; lost one daughter, Margaret.

Moan Jas. farmer; Sec. 10; P.O. Belvidere.
Moan John, farmer; P. O. Belvidere.
Morey Myron, P. O. Garden Prairie.
Morgan R. W. farmer; Sec. 5; P. O. Bonus.

Morris Henry, farmer; P. O. Garden Prairie.
Morris Robt. farmer; P. O. Garden Prairie.
Moss A.
Munger E. farmer; Sec. 29; P. O. Belvidere.

NEWELL G. W. lumber dealer; P. O. Garden Prairie.

NEWMAN JAS. A. Farmer; Sec. 10; P.O. Belvidere; born in N. Y., April 24, 1824; came to this Co. in 1869; owns 300 acres land; lived fourteen years in Kenosha Co., Wis., and two years in Lake Co., Ill., previous to his removal to this Co.; he married Betsey Andrews, in 1846; she was born in N. Y., and died June 10, 1850; his second wife was Sarah A. Cook, who was born in N. Y.; has two children by first marriage, Jas. L. and John A.; one daughter by second marriage, Nellie L.

NICHOLS O. S. Farmer; Sec. 23; P. O. Garden Prairie; born in N. Y., in 1830; came to this Co. in 1859; owns 200 acres; holds office of School Director, and is serving his fourth term as Supervisor; he married Miss Emma Koon, in 1859; has two children, Nellie and Eugene.

Nutt H. S. farmer; P.O. Belvidere.

ORR R. F. P. O. Belvidere.

PANGBORN JAS. renter; P. O. Belvidere.

Parle John, Sr. R. R. hand; Garden Prairie.
Parle John, Jr. P. O. Garden Prairie.

PAYNE D. R. Retired, Sec. 24; P. O. Garden Prairie; born in N. Y., June 20, 1798; came to this Co. May 14, 1856; he married Miss Mahala Sweet, in Jan., 1823; she was born in Dutchess Co., N.Y., Oct. 8, 1799; have five children: Festus, Minerva, Jira, Dodgy, Hemes; lost three children.

Pease Calvin, farmer; Sec. 1; P. O. Garden Prairie.
Perverse John, P. O. Garden Prairie.

PETTIS THOS. T. Retired; Sec. 2; P. O. Garden Prairie; born in N. Y., Jan. 10, 1809; came to this Co. in 1838; owns 24 acres land; in 1830 he removed to Michigan, and lived there seven years; while there, was Justice of the Peace and Collector three years, and assisted in taking the census of Michigan previous to its admission in the Union as a State.

Pier H. W. farmer; Sec. 23; P. O. Belvidere.
Polk Wm.

PORTER HENRY, Farmer; Sec.24; P. O. Garden Prairie; born in England, 1828; came to this Co. in 1858; owns 26 acres land; has held offices of School Director and Supervisor; married Miss Anna E. Roper, in 1858; she was born in England; have three children: Frank H., Fred. W. and Thos. W.

PORTER JAS. W. Farmer; Sec. 25; P. O. Garden Prairie; born in Buffalo, N. Y., 1838; came to this Co. in 1848; owns 320 acres; married Miss Martha J. Keith, in 1863; she was born in Vt.; have four children: Walter W., Lottie E., Clark A. and Laura A.

Porter Robt. farmer; Sec. 25; P. O. Garden Prairie.

Powers C. C. farm, Sec. 31; P. O. Belvidere.

Price W. L. P. O. Belvidere.

Pritchard C. H. P. O. Belvidere.

Pritchard W. W. P. O. Belvidere.

PRYOR ROGER, Farmer; Sec. 21; P. O. Belvidere; born in Ireland, in 1827; came to this Co. in 1853; owns 80 acres of land; married Lizzie Burchell, in 1869; she was born in Ireland; have four children, Mary Ellen, Maggie, Annie, and Thomas.

R ANDALL A. F. P. O. Garden Prairie.

Randall D. S. P. O. Garden Prairie.

RANDALL J. W. F. Garden Prairie; Dealer in Dry Goods, Groceries, Boots and Shoes, Notions, Hardware, and Agricultural Implements; was born in New York, April 6, 1815; came to this Co. in 1842; married Miss C. O. Sutherland, who was born in Edgar Co., Ill.; have four children, Carlos B., Ida B., Mary S., and Aaron F., 3d.

Rhapstack C. R. R. land; P. O. Garden Prairie.

Rhodes I. shoemaker; P. O. Garden Prairie.

Roderick J. blacksmith; P.O.Garden Prairie.

Roper J. J. farm; S. 24; P.O.Garden Prairie.

ROPER SION, Retired Farmer; Sec. 24; P. O. Garden Prairie; born in England, in 1809; came to this Co. in 1834; owns 80 acres of land; married Miss Mary C. Clark, in 1832; she was born in England; have eight children, Julia M., Horace H., Anna E., John J., Spencer I., Elizabeth L., Fannie, and Rosa J.; lost one son, Edwin.

Rosekrans J. D. merchant; P. O. Garden Prairie.

Rosekraus J. O. farm; Sec. 34; P. O. Garden Prairie.

Rulison Frank. farm; Sec. 10; P. O. Bonus.

Rulison Geo. farmer; Sec. 3; P. O. Bonus.

RULISON RALPH, Farmer; Sec. 10; P. O. Bonus; born in New York, in 1818; came to this Co. in 1845; owns 354 acres; has held offices of Assessor, School Director, and School Trustee, and holds the office of Justice of the Peace; married Maria Passage, in 1842; she was born in New York; have seven children, George B., Ella F., Alice L., Herman M., Frank A., Elsie J., and Grant U.

Ryan John, farm; Sec. 11, P. O. Belvidere.

SACKET CLARENCE E. Printer; Garden Prairie; born in this town, in 1848.

SACKET DANIEL H. Post-master, Garden Prairie; born in Vermont, Aug. 9, 1804; came to this Co. in 1837; owns 70 acres land; came to Chicago in 1833, and being a Millwright built the first mill in Illinois north of Ottawa, and at Geneva built the first mill that made flour for the eastern market; married Caroline Ames, Jan. 1, 1832; she was born in Vermont; have four children, Eliza J., George W., Emma C., and Clarence E.; he has held office of School Director, and holds office of Post-master.

Sacket J. S. money loaner; P. O. Garden Prairie.

Sanford S. D. farmer; Sec. 5; P. O. Bonus.

SANDS FRED. Farmer; Sec. 8; P. O. Belvidere; born in N. Y., 1834; came to this Co. in May, 1836, and has lived on the same farm since that time; owns 200 acres, valued at $60 per acre; married Miss Henrietta Brooks, in 1857; she was born in New York; have two children, Beecher and Betsey; he has held offices of School Director and Road Commissioner.

Scott William, P. O. Capron.

Sears C. A. farm; S. 36; P. O. Grand Prairie.

Sears E. C. farm; S. 26; P. O. Grand Prairie.

SEARS H. O. Farmer; Sec. 36; P. O. Garden Prairie; born in Bristol, Ontario Co., N. Y., 1820; came to this Co. Oct., 1839; owns 415 acres land; married Miss Harriet A. Ames, in 1841; she was born in Vermont; have three children, Edward C., Charles A., and Theron M.

Sherburne G. N. farm; S.32; P.O. Belvidere.

Sherburne J. H. farm; S.32; P. O. Belvidere.

Shafter M. C. farmer; Sec.28; P.O. Belvidere.

Smith C. H. Sec. 4; P. O. Bonus.

Smith Harlon.

Smith J. M. P. O. Bonus.

Smith R. D. farmer and blacksmith; Sec. 5; P. O. Bonus.

Smith Simeon, farmer; Sec. 4; P. O. Bonus.

Smith W. B. farmer; Sec. 5; P. O. Bonus.

Smith William, P. O. Bonus.

STAPLETON EDWARD, Farmer; Sec. 23; P. O. Garden Prairie; born in Ireland, in 1823; came to this Co. in 1855; owns 150 acres; married Miss Mary Prior, in 1851; she was born in Ireland; have six children, Margaret, John, James, Maria, Julia, and Edward; lost three.

Stapleton Jas. farm; P. O. Garden Prairie.

Stapleton J. farm; S.23; P.O. Garden Prairie.

Stevenson T. S. farm; Sec. 12; P. O. Capron.

STOCKWELL FRANK S. Farmer; Sec. 7; P. O. Belvidere; born in this town in 1850; owns 115 acres of land; married Miss Fuller, in 1874; she was born in Flora township; have one child, Maudie.

STONE A., Farmer; Sec. 19; P. O. Belvidere; born in Mass., in 1807; came to this Co. in 1837; owns 187½ acres of land; he married Miss E. H. Ellis, who was born in Mass.; have five children, Daniel B., Charles A., May Elizabeth, Martha E., and Hattie E.

Stone Chas. physician; S. 29; P.O.Belvidere.

Stott D. station agent; P. O. Garden Prairie.

Stow J. D. farmer and doctor; Sec. 4; P. O. Bonus.

Stow F. J. P. O. Garden Prairie.

Sweet L. K.

Sweezy Whiting, Sec. 1; P. O. Bonus.

TRIPP H. P. farmer; Sec. 36; P. O. Garden Prairie.

TRIPP JAMES D., Farmer; Sec. 18; P. O. Belvidere; born Columbia Co., N.Y., Dec. 26, 1807, and removed to Madison Co. at an early age; lived in that State 44 years, and was engaged in Farm and Dairy business; removed to Ills., Boone Co., in 1851, and has lived here 26 years; owns farm of 200 acres; has held office of Assessor of this town, also Road Commissioner; married Miss Angelina Maxom, from Madison Co., N. Y., Oct. 4, 1829; she was born in Rensselaer Co. Jan. 4, 1809; they have six children: Mrs. Kate W. Stockwell, Mrs. H. Caroline Mather, Mrs. Celia A. Woodward, Julia A., John G., and Joseph E.; have lost seven children: Stephen W., James H., Mary A., Stephen O., and three who died in infancy.

Tripp John G. farmer; P. O. Belvidere.

Tongue Geo. T. farm; P. O. Garden Prairie.

TURNABE URIAH B., Farmer; Sec. 17; P. O. Belvidere; born in N. Y., 1825; came to this Co. 1844; owns 160 acres of land; married Miss Laura Cline in 1850; she was born in N. Y.; have nine children, Hattie, Marion, Georgeanna, Elnora, Howard P., Lucia, Laura, Eva and Phœbe E.; has been School Director six years.

Tynan J. farm; Sec. 22; P. O. Garden Prairie.

WALKER G. F.

Walters George, P. O. Belvidere.

Walters W. W., P. O. Belvidere.

WATKINS A. L., Farmer; Sec. 14; P. O. Garden Prairie; born in N. Y., 1827; came to this Co. in 1872; owns 240 acres land; married Eliza A. Swain, who was born in N. Y.; have five children, Merit, Lora, Lott, Fred and Alida.

Wells B. B.

Westfall H. farm; S. 28; P.O.Garden Prairie.

Whipple N. G. farmer; P. O. Belvidere.

White Henry, P. O. Belvidere.

Wilbur Harrison, farmer; P. O. Belvidere.

WINIGAR JAMES G., Farmer; Sec. 28; P. O. Belvidere; born in N. Y., 1830; came to this Co. in Oct., 1839, and has resided in the same Section since that time; owns 160 acres; married Sarah A. Henton in 1854; she was born in N. Y.

WIXOM ANCIL, Farmer; Sec. 19; P. O. Belvidere; born in Putnam Co., N. Y., May 24, 1837; lived there 18 years, and came to Belvidere, Boone Co., in 1855; has lived here 22 years, engaged in farming; owns farm of 160 acres; married Miss Julia Hart, from Carmel, Putnam Co., N. Y., Nov., 1860; have three children, Noah, born Feb. 8, 1861; Nellie, Sept., 1873; Lilly, Dec. 8, 1875; lost three children. B. H. Wixom, father of the above, was born in Putnam Co., N. Y., in 1805; lived there 50 years; came to this Co. in 1855; married Easter Hill, of Putnam, N. Y.; she died 1869; had three children: Noah, he died in 1856; Smith, was in army; Ancil.

Wixom B. farmer; Sec. 19; P. O. Belvidere.

Woodruff E. D. farmer; Sec. 4; P.O. Bonus.

WOODRUFF JOHN, Merchant; Sec. 5; P. O. Bonus; born in New Haven Co., Conn., 1814; came to this Co. 1849; owns 20 acres land; holds offices School Director, Justice of the Peace and Post-Master at Bonus; married Lucinda Dimmick in 1834; she was born in N. Y.; have five children, Russell D., John D., Mary K., Edward D. and Charles D.; his son, Russell D., enlisted in the spring of 1861 in the 15th I. V. I.; served three years, and re-enlisted as a Veteran; he was a prisoner seven months at Andersonville, and one of the last released.

YOURT A. farmer; Sec. 34; P. O. Garden Prairie.

CALEDONIA TOWNSHIP.

ANDREW JOHN, farmer; P.O. Caledonia Station.
Atkinson E. Y. farmer; P. O. Poplar Grove.
Atkinson J. farm; S. 2; P. O. Poplar Grove.
Atkinson R. farm; S. 2; P.O. Poplar Grove.

BAILEY THROOP, farmer; Sec. 23; P. O. Poplar Grove.
Baker Wm. A. mechanic; Caledonia Station.
Balch Orin, laborer; Poplar Grove.
Berg Frank, farmer; P. O. Belvidere.
Bigerstaff C. farmer; P. O. Caledonia Station.
BROOKS W. H. Merchant; Poplar Grove; born in Erie Co., N. Y., March 7, 1827; came to this Co. in 1851; have four children, Lottie E., Gertie E., Howard S. and Albert W.; wife was Miss Harriet Strong, born in Erie Co., N. Y.; was Collector one term, and Constable one term.
Brown C. farm; S. 7; P.O. Caledonia Station.
Brown D. farm; S. 9; P.O. Caledonia Station.
Brown T. farm; S. 8; P.O. Caledonia Station.
Brown Wm. farmer; Sec. 36; P.O. Belvidere.
Bruner I. farm; S. 10; P.O. Caledonia Station.
Bruner P. farm; S. 10; P.O. Caledonia Station.
Budish James.
Burdick J. S. farmer; P.O. Caledonia Station.

CASSADY JOHN, teacher; Caledonia Station.
Cassady P., R. R. laborer; P.O. Poplar Grove.
Cassidy P. farm; S. 27; P.O. Caledonia Sta.
Chappell J. B. farm; S. 1; P.O. Poplar Grove.
Chappell J. B., Jr., farmer; Sec. 12; P. O. Poplar Grove.
Chappell T. G. mechanic; Caledonia Station.
Church J. M. farm; S. 2; P.O. Poplar Grove.
Clark A. farm; S. 14; P.O. Poplar Grove.
Clay J. farm; S. 9; P.O. Caledonia Station.
Cleveland H. W. farm; S. 28; P.O. Caledonia Station.
Cleveland T. W. farm; S. 28; P.O. Caledonia Station.
Cochran Gilman, Caledonia Station.
Colwell Jas. farmer; P. O. Argyle.
Cook A. farmer, Sec. 35; P.O. Belvidere.
Cornwell D.D. farm; S.36; P.O. Poplar Grove.
Cornwell H. farm; S. 12; P.O. Poplar Grove.
Covey E. H. farm; S. 25; P.O. Poplar Grove.
Covey S. farm; S. 25; P.O. Poplar Grove.
Crouse S. H. preacher; Caledonia Station.
Cummins A. farm; S. 17; P.O. Caledonia Sta.
Curtis A. F. farm; S. 36; P.O. Poplar Grove.

Curtis L. E. farm; S. 36; P.O. Poplar Grove.

DAWSON WILLIAM, laborer; Poplar Grove.
Day Hiram, farmer; P. O. Capron.
Dean M. T. farmer; P. O. Poplar Grove.
Dimond R. farm; S.25; P.O. Poplar Grove.
DRAKE ABRAM, Farmer and Stock Raiser; Sec. 27; P. O. Caledonia, born in the town of Pittsfield, Rockingham Co., N. H., Jan. 2, 1811; owns 270 acres, valued at $13,500; Mr. D. is one of the oldest settlers, no family; wife was Miss Sophia Storey; she was born in the city of Boston, Oct. 31, 1825; they were married July 11, 1844; was Justice of the Peace about ten years, was Post-master at Caledonia ten years, and held the office of Supervisor two years.
Dymond A. T. farm; S. 13; P.O. Poplar Grove.
Dymond J. farm; S. 13; P.O. Poplar Grove.
DYMOND ROBERT, Farmer and Stock Raiser; Sec. 15; P. O. Poplar Grove; born in England, Jan. 17, 1815; came to this Co. in 1845; owns 120 acres, valued at $6,000; has one daughter, Elizabeth; she married Lorenzo Spencer; had one son, James, who served three years in the late war, in Co. K, 95th Ill. Regt.; he died just after returning home; wife was Miss Elizabeth Clark, born in England.
Dymond S. farm; S. 25; P. O. Poplar Grove.

EARLY WILLIAM, farmer; Sec. 27; P. O. Caledonia Station.
Edgall S. M. farm; S. 13; P.O. Poplar Grove.
Emerson H. H. farmer, P. O. Caledonia Sta.
Erwin S. V. farmer; P. O. Poplar Grove.

FORD RICHARD, farmer; Sec. 10; P.O. Poplar Grove.

GORHAM STEPHEN.
Gorman Peter, farmer; Sec. 14; P.O. Caledonia Station.
Gorman Philip, farmer; Sec. 14; P.O. Caledonia Station.
Greenlee J. farm; S. 6; P.O. Caledonia Sta.
Greenlee T. farm; S. 6; P.O. Caledonia Sta.
Greenlee W. farm; S. 6; P.O. Caledonia Sta.
GRINNELL H. S. Post-master; Caledonia Station; born in Litchfield Co., Conn., April 29, 1809; came to this Co. in 1857, and to Caledonia Station in 1859; have two children living, Wm. E., born Jan. 28, 1837, in Canada; Sarah A., born in Canada, Nov., 1841; wife was Miss Harriet A. Pier, born in Vermont, July 16, 1814; they were married Jan. 23, 1833; value of estate, $800.

Grow Edgar, farmer; P.O. Caledonia Station.

HALEY PAT. railroad employe; Poplar Grove.
Halliday A. J. laborer; Caledonia Station.
Ham J. J.
Hammond H. Parks Corner.
HAMMOND H. A. Proprietor Caledonia Cheese Factory; Sec. 35; P. O. Belvidere; born in Boone Co., Aug. 3, 1848; owns 200 acres, valued at $7,000; has two children, Myron, born June 4, 1874; Wm., born June 8, 1877; wife was Melvina Stevens, born in this Co.; married Sept. 21, 1870.
Hammond H. L. mechanic; Belvidere.
Hanson E. farm; Sec.5; P. O. Caledonia Sta.
Hanson J. farm; Sec.5; P. O. Caledonia Sta.
Hanson J. A. farm; S.5; P. O. Caledonia Sta.
Hanson N. E. farm; S.4; P. O. Caledonia Sta.
Hanson S.M.S. farm; S.5; P.O.Caledonia Sta.
Hart W. farmer; Sec.23; P. O. Caledonia Sta.
HAZLEWOOD WM. Farmer; Sec. 36; P. O. Poplar Grove; born in Canada, Aug. 1, 1832; came to this Co. in 1845; owns 80 acres, valued at $3,400; has four children, Albert, James H., Annie and Nettie; wife was Miss Elizabeth Brown, born in England; married Oct. 3, 1866.
Head J. N. farm; Sec.11; P.O. Poplar Grove.
Henderson J. farm; S.28; P.O.Caledonia Sta.
Henderson R. farm; S.21; P.O.Caledonia Sta.
Herrington P. farm; S.17; P.O.Caledonia Sta.
Howard W. farm; Sec.11; P.O.Caledonia Sta.
Hill George, farmer; P. O. Belvidere.
Hines L. farmer; P. O. Caledonia Station.
Horner George, farmer; P. O. Hunter.
Hostroser J. farm; S. 14; P.O. Poplar Grove.
Hyer W. mechanic; P. O. Caledonia Station.

JACKSON J. F. laborer; P. O. Caledonia Station.
Johnson Ole, laborer.
Jory James, mechanic; P. O. Poplar Grove.

KELLEY CAMPBELL, farmer; Sec. 4; P. O. Caledonia.
Kelley C. farmer; S. 20; P.O. Caledonia Sta.
Kelley D. S. farm; S. 16; P.O. Caledonia Sta.
Kelley Jas. farm; Sec. 16; P.O. Caledonia Sta.
Kelley Jno. farm; Sec.16; P.O. Caledonia Sta.
Knox L. farmer; Sec. 14; P.O. Poplar Grove.
Knox W. T. farm; S. 14; P.O. Poplar Grove.

LANE S. P. farmer; Sec. 26; P. O. Belvidere.
Lang S. P. mechanic; Caledonia Station.
Lawler M. farm; S. 28; P. O. Caledonia Sta.
LEACH C. C. Farmer and Stock Raiser; Sec. 33; P. O. Belvidere; born in Bennington Co., Vt., Feb. 28, 1820; came to this Co in 1845; owns 197 acres, valued at $6,895; Mr. L. is among the oldest settlers; has three sons, Frank M., born July 15, 1850; Fred. G., April 16, 1855; Grant S., June 29, 1863; wife was Miss Cynthia Smith, born in Chenango Co., N. Y., March 4, 1829; married April 22, 1847.
Leach Fred. farmer; Sec. 33; P.O. Belvidere.
Lidster Ralph, shoemaker; Caledonia Sta.
Linnell Selwin, farmer; P. O. Argyle.
Long J., Jr., farm; S. 15; P.O. Caledonia Sta.
Lovering Wm., Jr., mechanic; Poplar Grove.

McALLEE JOHN. farmer; P. O. Argyle.
McEachran Archie, farmer; Sec. 17; P. O. Caledonia Station.
McEachren Geo. farmer; Sec. 18; P. O. Caledonia Station.
McEachran Hugh, mechanic; Argyle.
McEachran Jas. farmer; Sec. 16; P. O. Caledonia Station.
McEachran John, farmer; Sec. 9; P. O. Caledonia Station.
McEachran John; farmer; Sec. 8; P. O. Caledonia Station.
McMillan Mat. farmer; P. O. Caledonia Sta.
McNAIR ALEXANDER. Farmer and Stock Raiser; Sec. 7; P. O. Caledonia Station; born in Campbelltown, Scotland, June 7, 1828; came to this Co. in 1842; owns 285 acres, valued at $14,250; Mr. McNair is one of the oldest settlers; has six children, Elizabeth, Catherine, Mary, Jeannette, James and Alexander; wife was Miss Mary Armour; she was born in the same place; married Oct. 20, 1853; was Supervisor two years, and Assessor one term.
McNeilage Wm. mechanic; Caledonia Sta.
Mahoney Cornelius, laborer; Caledonia Sta.
Marriett T. G. farmer; Sec. 16; P. O. Caledonia Station.
Marshall W. farm; S. 14; P.O. Caledonia Sta.
Merritt R. farm; Sec. 23; P.O. Poplar Grove.
Merriett T. farm; S. 15; P.O. Caledonia Sta.
Mitchell Jas. laborer; Caledonia Station.
Mitchell R. farm; S. 17; P.O. Caledonia Sta.
Montanye Chas. laborer; Caledonia Station.
MONTANYE J. D. Proprietor of Hotel; Caledonia Station; born in Orange Co., N. Y., Feb. 9, 1820; came to this Co. in 1854; have eight children, Mary E., Inda A., Charles, Kate, Isaac V., John N., Clarence H., and Della; wife was Miss Parmelia Brown; born in Sullivan Co., N. Y., Jan. 20, 1828; married Dec. 25, 1845; value of estate $4,000.
MONTGOMERY JAMES, Farmer and Stock Raiser; Sec. 1; P. O. Poplar Grove; born in Argyleshire, Scotland,

July 4, 1834; came to this Co. March 17, 1870; owns 160 acres, valued at $8,000; left Scotland in 1842, and went to Guilford, Winnebago Co., and remained there till March, 1870, then came here; have five children, Albert F., Arthur C., James E., Jennie E., and Allen R.; wife was Miss Lavinia Tofflemire; born in Canada, April 25, 1836; married Nov. 20, 1860; she died March 10, 1877; is Supervisor, and has been for two years, and has held other Township offices.

Moore D. A. farmer; P. O. Poplar Grove.

Moore J. farm; Sec. 36; P. O. Poplar Grove.

MOORE WM. Farmer; Sec. 8; P. O. Caledonia Station; born in Canada, Sept. 18, 1842; came to this Co. in April, 1871; has two children, James F., born Aug. 15, 1867; William H., Oct. 17, 1871; wife was Miss Mary J. Atkinson; born in Canada, April 4, 1843; married March 20, 1864.

Murphy David, Sr., laborer; Caledonia Sta.

Murphy David, Jr., farm; P.O. Caledonia Sta.

Murphy Dennis, laborer; Argyle.

NEAL DENNIS, farmer; P. O. Poplar Grove.

O'BRIEN JOHN, farmer; Sec. 31; P. O. Argyle.

Olmes William.

Outcalt Otis, farmer; P.O. Caledonia Station.

PARKER GEORGE, laborer; Poplar Grove.

Pearsall S. M. farm; S.24; P.O. Poplar Grove.

Petrie Francis, farmer; P. O. Belvidere.

Petrie P. farmer; Sec. 36; P. O. Belvidere.

Picken Archie, farmer; P. O. Caledonia Sta.

Picken J. A. farm; S.18; P.O. Caledonia Sta.

Picken John, farmer; Sec. 18; P. O. Caledonia Station.

Postlewaite Thos. farmer; Sec. 12; P. O. Poplar Grove.

Postlewnite W. H. farmer; Sec. 12; P. O. Poplar Grove.

RALSTON ALEX. farmer; Sec. 20; P.O. Caledonia Station.

RALSTON JNO. Farmer and Stock Raiser; Sec. 6; P. O. Caledonia Station; born in Scotland, Aug., 1818; came to this Co. in 1852; has nine children; George, Peter, John, Charles, Jane, Martha, Elizabeth, Jeannette and Margaret; wife was Miss Elizabeth Picken, born in Scotland.

RALSTON A. J. Farmer; Sec. 29; P. O. Caledonia Station; born in the south end of Cantire, Scotland, Jan. 14, 1820; owns 190 acres, valued at $7,600; left there and went to Canada in May, 1849; remained there seven years and then came to this Co.; have six children, and lost three; wife was Margaret McKerrell; she was born Jan. 14, 1825; married Dec. 28, 1843.

Ralston Gavin, farmer; Sec. 20; P. O. Caledonia Station.

Ralston George, farmer; Sec. 6; P. O. Caledonia Station.

Ralston Robt. farmer; Sec. 30; P. O. Argyle.

Ralston Wm. A. farmer; Sec.18; P.O. Argyle.

Ramsey E. farm; Sec.3; P. O. Caledonia Sta.

Ramsey J. farm; Sec.3; P. O. Caledonia Sta.

Ramsey T. farm; Sec. 3; P.O. Caledonia Sta.

Ramsey W.G.farm; S.10; P.O.Caledonia Sta.

REID W. H. Farmer and Stock Raiser; Sec. 31; P.O. Argyle Station; born in LaSalle Co., Ill., Sept. 27, 1837; his father left Scotland the year previous and went to LaSalle Co.; remained there about one year and then went to Winnebago Co., where he remained until 1865, when he came here; has four children: Mary A., born Jan. 3, 1868; Margaret, April 21, 1870; Hugh, Jan. 13, 1873; Elizabeth A., Oct. 8, 1875; wife was Mary Andrew, born in Harlem, Winnebago Co., Aug. 27, 1843; married Feb. 16, ——.

Reymore B.F. R.R. employe; Poplar Grove.

SANDERS W. H. farmer; Sec. 35; P. O. Caledonia Station.

Sage Menzo.

Schure Jno. farmer; P.O. Caledonia Station.

Seeley Chas.

SEWELL SUTTON, Farmer and Stock Raiser; Sec. 34; P. O. Caledonia Station; born in this Tp., Boone Co., May 15, 1847; rents farm of his father; has two children: Minnie, born April 10, 1873; Charley, April 4, 1875; wife was Miss Maryette Linnell, born in this Tp., May 17, 1855; married May 30, 1872.

Sherman E. farm; S. 13; P.O. Poplar Grove.

Sibley D. M. farmer; P. O. Caledonia Sta.

Simonds Geo.

Slowey Thos. laborer; Caledonia Station.

Spencer A. farm; S. 23; P. O. Poplar Grove.

Spencer E. farm; S 23; P. O. Poplar Grove.

Spencer E. L. farmer; P. O. Poplar Grove.

Spencer J. farm; S. 26; P. O. Poplar Grove.

Spencer L. farm; S. 15; P. O. Poplar Grove.

Stapleton Edw. R.R. laborer; Caledonia Sta.

Stephens W. L. R. R. laborer; Caledonia Sta.

Steward Rev. W. W. minister; Caledonia Sta.

Suhr Jno. farmer; P.O. Caledonia Station.

Suher Jos. farmer; P. O. Caledonia Station.

Sullivan J. farmer; Sec. 29; P. O. Argyle.

TAYLOR MALCOLM, laborer; Caledonia Station.

Thompson Geo. farmer; Sec. 9; P. O. Caledonia Station.

Thompson John, farmer; Sec. 15; P.O. Caledonia Station.
Thompson Robt. farmer; Sec. 15; P.O. Caledonia Station.
Thornton F. A. laborer; Hunter.
Tofflemire Andy, farmer; Sec. 10; P. O. Caledonia Station.
Tofflemire F. farm; S.16, P.O. Poplar Grove.
TOFFLEMIRE J. J. Farmer and Stock Raiser; Sec. 31; P. O. Argyle Station; born in Harlem Tp., Winnebago Co., March 12, 1842, about one-half mile from where he now lives; owns 131 acres, value $6,550; has five children: Cora L., born Oct. 21, 1866; Warren E., Feb. 14, 1869; J. Verner, June 1, 1871; Roy, April 19, 1874; Benjamin, May 20, 1877; wife was Miss Amy A. Little, born in Watertown, N. Y., Feb. 7, 1843; they were married Jan. 1, 1866.
Tucker Chas. H. mechanic; Poplar Grove.
Tucker L. S. laborer; Poplar Grove.
Turner A. J. laborer; Argyle.

VICKERS G. W. farmer; P. O. Poplar Grove.
Vickers Geo., Sr. farmer; Sec. 11; P. O. Poplar Grove.
Vickers Geo., Jr. blacksmith; Poplar Grove.
Vickers J. S. farm; S.11; P.O. Poplar Grove.
Vickers Jos. farmer; P. O. Poplar Grove.
Vickers Robt. farm; S.11; P.O. Poplar Grove.
Vickers Robt. mechanic; Poplar Grove.

WAKEFIELD A. farmer; Sec. 29; P. O. Caledonia Station.
Ware B. H.
Warren I. H. farmer; P. O. Poplar Grove.
Warren J., Sr., farm; S. 2; P.O.Poplar Grove.
Warren J. W. farm; S. 2; P.O. Poplar Grove.
Webster J. W. farm; S. 35; P.O. Belvidere.
Webster W. S. lumber merchant; Poplar Grove.
Wellington S. farm; P.O. Caledonia Station.
Whalen Jos. P. farmer; P.O. Argyle.
Wheeler D. farm; S. 13; P.O. Poplar Grove.
Wheeler G. farm; S. 14; P. O. Poplar Grove.
Wheeler W. B. farm; S.14; P.O.Poplar Grove.
Whitcomb L. C. retired; Poplar Grove.
WHITING ANDREW, Farmer and Stock Raiser; Sec. 27; P. O. Caledonia Station; born in Kennebeck Co., Me., Nov. 9, 1846; owns 118 acres, value $4,720; left there and came to this Co. with his parents in the fall of 1858, and is one of the oldest settlers; have three sons, Chas. O., born Nov. 3, 1858; Wm. A., Aug. 3, 1860; Ephraim A., May 13, 1863; wife was Miss Mary A. Kyes, born in Ohio, May 9, 1847; married Sept. 10, 1854; was Assessor one term, and Road Commissioner three years.
Whiting C. farmer; P. O. Caledonia Station.
Whiting F. farm; S. 22; P.O.Caledonia Sta.
WHITING LUTHER, Farmer and Stock Raiser; Sec. 22; P. O. Caledonia Station; born in Caledonia Tp., this Co., Nov. 28, 1841; owns 136 acres, valued at $5,460; have three children: Nellie, born May 2, 1868; John H., Oct. 24, 1870; Ira, Aug. 18, 1875; wife was Miss Mary E. Sabin, born in Schenectady Co., N. Y., May 28, 1845; married May 28, 1866; he served four years and three days in the late war in Co. A., 12th I. V. I.; was Supervisor two years and Road Commissioner five years.
Whittle J. farm; S. 20; P. O. Caledonia Sta.
Willott G. railroad employee; Poplar Grove.
Wilson R. merchant; Caledonia Station.
Winne Garrett, farmer; P.O. Belvidere.
Wright G. C. farmer; P.O.Caledonia Station.

FLORA TOWNSHIP.

ADAMS FRANK E. farmer; Sec. 18.

Adams O. farm; Sec. 19; P.O.Cherry Valley.
Albright Wm. H. farm; S. 13; P.O.Belvidere.
Aldrich A. C. farm; Sec. 1; P. O. Belvidere.
Alexander J. farm; S. 4; P.O.Cherry Valley.
Allen A. H. farmer; Sec. 10; P.O. Belvidere.
Allen A. H., Jr., farmer; P. O. Belvidere.

ALLEN BERNARD B. Farmer; Sec. 3; P. O. Belvidere; born Oxford Co., Me., March 26, 1831; lived in Maine about 32 years; engaged in farming and clerk in store 8 years; removed to Boone Co. 1863; has lived here 12 years; owns farm 117¾ acres; has held offices School Director and Road Surveyor; married Mary C. DeCosta, from Oxford Co., Me., Sept. 6, 1857; they have three children: Fred L., born Aug. 25, 1858; Guy, April 15, 1863; Grace May, June 6, 1874; lost one little girl, Lettie, twin sister of Grace May.

Allen W. F. farmer; P. O. Belvidere.

ALLEN W. W. Farmer; Sec. 15; P. O. Belvidere; born in Oxford Co., Me., May 21, 1841; lived in that State 25 years, and worked as clerk in store for a long time, and brought up there; learned bootmaker's trade, and worked at trade in Abington, Mass., 4 years; came to Boone Co. in 1866; engaged in farming and stock dairy; owns 100 acres land; married Miss Mary A. Bonney, from town of Sumner, Oxford Co., Me., fall of 1862.

Anderson A. G. farmer; P.O.Cherry Valley.
Anderson F. laborer; S. 15; P. O. Belvidere.
Atkins D. farmer; Sec. 20; P. O. Belvidere.

ATKINS MICHAEL H. Farmer; Sec. 17; P. O. Cherry Valley; born Somersetshire, England, Aug. 23, 1836; lived in England 31 years; came to this country in Aug., 1869; came to Cherry Valley, Winnebago Co., same year; rents farm of Mr. Farley of 100 acres; married Miss Charlotte Atkins, of Somersetshire, Eng., May 30, 1859; they have seven children, four sons and three daughters: Florence, Augusta, Douglass, William, Rosa, Thomas, Walter.

AVERY HENRY W., Jr., Farmer; Sec. 5; P. O. Belvidere; born in New London Co., Conn., May 31, 1823; lived there 21 years; came to Boone Co. in 1844, and has lived here 33 years; but very little improvement here when he came; has held offices of Justice of Peace, Road Commissioner, Assessor and School Trustee; owns farm 240 acres; married Lydia J. Avery, from Chenango Co., N. Y.; she died in 1847; had one child, Mrs. Elizabeth D. Thompson, born June 24, 1846; married Rachel P. McCord, from Carlisle, Penn., in Sept., 1848. Henry W. Avery, Sr., father of the above, was born in New London Co., Conn.; came to Illinois, Boone Co., in 1853, and is now 83 years old; married Betsy Dennison, from same place, in 1817; she died in 1866; had two children, Rev. F. D. Avery, of Conn., and H. W. Avery, Jr.

BASSET PERRIS, farmer; P. O. Cherry Valley.

BANKS SEBASTIAN S. Farmer; Sec. 9; P. O. Belvidere; born Piscataquis Co., Me., Feb. 24, 1837; lived there 9 years, and came to DeKalb Co., Ill., in 1846, and has lived on this Prairie 31 years; came to Boone Co. in 1868; owns farm of 142 acres; went to California in 1859; crossed the plains with oxen, only four of them in the party, returning on horseback; married Miss Jeannette Bucklin, from Canandagua Co., N. Y., March, 1871; they have two children: Annie Stella, born Jan. 15, 1872; Irving, Jan., 1874.

Basiner Chas., Sec. 19.
Bennett A. farmer; Sec. 33; P. O. Belvidere.

BENNETT CHARLES, Farmer; Sec. 17; P. O. Belvidere; born in Belvidere, Oct. 8, 1845; has lived in this Co. 32 years; attended school in Chicago and Poughkeepsie, N. Y.; among the early native born of this Co.; farm and dairy; owns farm of 200 acres; married Miss Ellen C. Reynolds in Belvidere, Dec. 1, 1868; she was born in Waukesha Co., Wis., July 9, 1847; they have six children, Herman James, Edward Joseph, born Feb. 14, 1870; Ellen Gertrude, June 10, 1871; Jennie M., Dec. 14, 1872; Stella, March 26, 1875; Charles, Dec. 8, '76.

Bennett Chester, farmer; P.O.Cherry Valley.
Bennett O. farmer; Sec. 33; P. O. Belvidere.
Benson Chas. farmer; Sec. 3.
Bixler Ira, farmer; Sec. 34; P. O. Belvidere.

BLAKE WILLIAM, Farmer; Sec. 9; P. O. Belvidere; born in Cornwall, Eng., Aug. 19, 1826; lived in England 27 years; came to America in 1853; came to Rockford, Winnebago Co., same year; lived there 11 years; lived in Lee Co. 10 years; came to Boone Co. 1875; owns 220 acres land; married Susan Hucknen, from England, Jan. 1854; they have eight children: Mary E., James, George, Fanny, Charlie, Annie, Frank, Freddie; lost two children.

Blank C. farmer; Sec. 7; P.O.Cherry Valley.
Bliss E. farmer; Sec. 26; P. O. Belvidere.
Bliss P. A. peddler; P. O. Belvidere.
Bowen H. L. farmer; Sec. 25; P.O.Belvidere.
Brody J. laborer; Sec. 7.
Brodt A. laborer; Sec. 7; P.O.Cherry Valley.

FLORA TOWNSHIP.   391

Brown E. D. farmer; Sec. 27; P.O.Belvidere.
Brown E. F. farmer; Sec. 27; P.O.Belvidere.
Brown M. laborer; Sec. 22; P. O. Belvidere.
Brown N. B. farmer; P. O. Belvidere.
Brown W. B. farm; Sec. 11; P.O. Belvidere.
Buck C. farmer; Sec. 18; P.O.Cherry Valley.

CANDIDO THOMAS, farmer; Sec. 8; P. O. Belvidere.

Case C. farmer; Sec. 36; P. O. Belvidere.
Case C. C. farm; S. 19; P. O. Cherry Valley.

CASE DAVID L. Farmer; Sec. 8; P. O. Cherry Valley; born in Winnebago Co., Ill., July 29, 1850; lived there about 22 years, then removed to Boone Co. in 1872, and has lived here 4 years; has a farm of 160 acres; has held offices of Constable and Road Master; married Miss Emma A. Wheeler, of Cherry Valley, Feb. 22, 1877; she was born in Massachusetts, and removed to Winnebago Co. in infancy.

Casey Geo. farmer; P. O. Cherry Valley.
Casey Jas. farmer; P. O. Cherry Valley.
Casey Wm. farmer; P. O. Cherry Valley.

CHAMBERLAIN DANIEL S. Farmer; Sec. 22; P. O. Belvidere; born in town of Flora, May 15, 1854; has lived in this town and Co. 23 years, except while traveling in Iowa and Missouri for a short time; was engaged in fruit and confectionery business in Belvidere; married Ella M. Lawson, Aug. 27, 1873; she was born in New York State, March 11, 1856; rents farm of 40 acres.

CHENA CHAS. E. Farmer; Sec. 21; P. O. Belvidere; born in Jefferson Co., Sept. 7, 1840, and lived there 25 years; went to Michigan in 1865, and lived there 10 years; held office of Secretary of Lapeer Co. Grange; came to Boone Co., Ill., in 1875; has held office of Path Master; married Miss Jane Clark, from Jefferson Co., N. Y., in March, 1863; they have two children: Helen H., born 1865; Fred. G., 1871.

Clark Edward, farmer; P. O. Belvidere.
Clark Wm. farmer; Sec. 25; P. O. Belvidere.
Cline A. farm; Sec. 31; P. O. Cherry Valley.

CLINITE JACOB, Farmer; Sec. 31; P. O. Cherry Valley; born in Wertemberg, Germany, April 13, 1827; came to this country in 1832; came to the State of Ohio and lived there about 20 years, then removed to Illinois, Boone Co., in 1851, and has lived here 26 years; has held offices of School Director and Overseer of Roads; married Miss Caroline Ernst, Aug. 4, 1850; she was born in Penn. and brought up in Ohio; owns farm of 80 acres, 30 acres in Winnebago Co., 80 in Ogle Co., 320 in Kansas; they have nine children, six sons and three daughters: William A., George F., Charles W., Albert L., Edward, Frank, Emma, Ida, Ettie; lost one daughter, Mary.

Cochran John, farmer; P. O. Belvidere.
Cochran S. C. farmer, P. O. Belvidere.
Cochran Wilson, farmer; P. O. Belvidere.

COE GEO. W. Farmer; Sec. 27; P. O. Belvidere; born Lycoming Co., Penn., Sept. 28, 1845; removed to Ogle Co., Ill., when three years of age; lived there about 25 years, and came to Boone Co. in 1873; engaged in farming and stock raising; owns farm of 80 acres; has held office of Overseer Highways; married Miss Mary McKee, from Boone Co., in Feb., 1875; she was born in this town June 27, 1849.

Cohoon John, farmer; P. O. Belvidere.

COHOON ORVILL S. Farmer; Sec. 12; P. O. Belvidere; born Erie Co., Penn., Oct. 29, 1833; lived in that State about 18 years; went to Indiana, lived there 18 months, and removed to Illinois, Boone Co., June 17, 1853, and has lived here 24 years; was engaged in mercantile business two years; lived in car house, about where Baptist church stands, south side, and it was the only house on 40 acres; he is engaged in farming, dairy and stock raising, and owns farm 148 acres; he was on committee to raise funds and recruits during war; married Miss Juliette R. Wood, from Wisconsin, in 1857; she died 1864; married Miss A. H. Field, from Michigan, in January, 1865.

COMPTON HENRY P. (firm of Pike & Compton) Broom business; Sec. 5; P.O. Cherry Valley; born in Somerset Co., N. J., Feb. 17, 1834; came to Winnebago Co. in 1853; has lived in Boone Co. twenty years; is engaged in the manufacture of Brooms; owns farm of forty acres; married Harriet N. Pike, from Maine, in 1857; they have four children, three sons and one daughter.

CRAIG GEO. Farmer; Sec. 29; P. O. Cherry Valley; born in Co. Armagh, Ireland, July 9, 1831, being one of family of seventeen brothers and two sisters; he was the seventeenth brother and the seventeenth child of the family; two of his brothers were born on the same day of the month, July 9; came to this country in 1855, and lived in Philadelphia two years, engaged with his brothers in manufacturing; he has seven brothers in Philadelphia; married Miss Martha Gibson, from Co. Armagh, Ireland, Jan. 17, 1854; they have five children, four sons and one daughter, William, Robert, George A., Lizzie and Benjamin.

Craig Robt. farmer; P. O. Cherry Valley.
Cramer A.farm laborer; S.5; P.O. Belvidere.

CUNNINGHAM BRADFORD L. Farmer; Sec. 36; P. O. Belvidere; born in Delaware Co., N. Y., Oct. 30, 1825; lived there 11 years, and came to Boone Co. by team, being six weeks on the road, in May, 1837, and has lived here over 40 years; is one of the earliest settlers, and there is not a person here now who was here when he came; only two or three log houses on the prairie when he came; he carted his grain to Chicago, and has carted wheat there for others, and got 25 cents a bushel for hauling, and sold it at same price; entered land from government; owns 127 acres; married Ellen Newton, July 20, 1851; she was from Chenango Co., N. Y.; born Dec. 26, 1853; they have three children, Wilber N., born June 11, 1854; Harley W., Feb. 15, 1856; Florence E., Jan. 17, 1868; parents were early settlers here and are both dead.

Cunningham Chauncy, farm; P.O. Belvidere.
Cunningham H. farm; S. 26; P.O. Belvidere.
Cunningham H. C. farmer; Sec. 24; P.O. Belvidere.
Cunningham H. farm; S. 26; P.O. Belvidere.
Cushman H. H. farm; S. 25; P.O. Belvidere.

DAWSON HERBERT, Sec. 26; P. O. Belvidere.

DEAN EDWIN, Farmer; Sec. 35; P. O Belvidere; born in Oxford Co., Maine, Jan. 16, 1821; lived in that State 22 years; removed to Illinois, Boone Co., Oct. 22, 1843, and has lived here 34 years; one of the early settlers, only few here now who were here when he came; used to haul grain to Chicago, and has sold winter wheat at three shillings per bushel; owns farm of 180 acres; entered part of farm from government; has held offices of Road Commissioner and School Director for some years; married Rebecca B. Low, of Guilford, Maine, April, 1843; have four children, Orville E., was in army, in 15th Regt. I. V. I.; Henry E. lives in Minnesota; Clarissa E.; and William E., studying law in Iowa City.

DEAN ORVILLE E. Farmer; Sec. 35; P.O. Belvidere; born in Boone Co., Jan. 17, 1844 and has lived in this Co. 33 years, except 4 years he lived in State of Missouri; was in the army, in 15th Regt. I. V. I. Co. B, the first company raised in Boone Co.; was in the battle of Shiloh, and discharged on account of sickness; enlisted again in 142d Regt. I. V. I., Co. C; has held offices of School Director and Constable, owns farm of 78 acres; married Miss Huldah L. Crosby, of New York, Dec. 5, 1866; they have three children, Stella L., Ira L., and baby; have lost two children, Wyatt O., and Almeda.

Dean Thos. farmer; Sec. 34; P.O. Belvidere.

DECOSTA JACOB, Farmer; Sec. 24; P. O. Belvidere; born in Oxford Co., Maine, July 6, 1811; he lived in Maine and Massachusetts about 55 years; was engaged in making Boots and Shoes in Mass., about 40 years; removed to Illinois, Boone Co., in 1866; owns farm of 40 acres; married Miss Selina Record, from Oxford Co. Maine, in Feb., 1836; they have five children, Mrs. Mary C. Allen, Mrs. Sylvira J. Farrar, William Henry, Mrs. Azubah E. Allbright, Mrs. Malzena Allen; lost three daughters in Maine.

DELAVERGNE GEO. W. Farmer; Sec. 22; P. O. Belvidere; born in Jefferson Co., N. Y., Feb. 17, 1828; lived in New York State 40 years, engaged in Farming; came to Boone Co. in March, 1868; has lived here 10 years, engaged in Farming; owns farm of 30 acres; has held office of Overseer of Roads; married Miss Roxey A. Clark, Oct. 14, 1865; she was born in Jefferson Co., N. Y., June 6, 1843; they have two children, Clark, born March 11, 1866; Esther, June 14, 1868.

DELAVERGNE HUSTED, Farmer; Sec. 34; P. O. Belvidere; born in Herkimer Co., N. Y., April 18, 1820; removed to Jefferson Co., and lived there until 1869; came to Boone Co., Ill., and has lived here 8 years; married Sarah Wescott, of Vermont, in 1852; they have one adopted child, Franklin, born Sept. 14, 1852; came to this Co. in 1869, and has lived here since; owns farm of 80 acres; married Miss Clarissa Ellen Dean, of this town and county, Sept. 21, 1874; they have one child, daughter, Myra E., born November, 1875.

Dixon G. R. farmer; Sec. 4; P. O. Belvidere.
Dixon Jas. farmer; Sec. 4; P. O. Belvidere.
Dixon F. W. farmer; Sec. 4; P.O. Belvidere.
Donnelley E. J. farmer; P.O. Cherry Valley.
Draper I. V. farmer; Sec. 3; P. O. Belvidere.
Drummond S. L. farmer; Sec. 18.

EDWARDS HENRY, farmer.

Erickson P. laborer; Sec. 7.
Erwin R. A. farmer; P. O. Belvidere.

FAKE GEO. H. farmer; Sec. 7; P. O. Cherry Valley
Fake J. H. farm; Sec. 7; P.O. Cherry Valley.

FANCHER G. W. Farmer; Sec. 8; P. O. Cherry Valley; born in Warren Co., N. Y., June 3, 1820; lived there 31 years, came to this State, to Cherry Valley, in 1851; is a Carpenter by trade; married Sarah Adams, of Washington Co., N. Y.; she died in 1854; they had three children, Cynthia, Sarah and Mary; married Maria R. Edson, from Ashfield, Mass., June 8, 1855; they have two children, Lily May, born March 6, 1865; Eugene Nov. 28, 1867

Farley Thos. farm; S. 29; P.O. Cherry Valley.
Fitzgerald P. farm; Sec. 24; P.O. Belvidere.

FOOTE ELI, Farmer; Sec. 11; P. O. Belvidere; born in Chenango Co., N. Y., Oct. 18, 1822; lived there 22 years, came to Belvidere, Oct. 17, 1844; came by carriage most of the way; snowed very hard the night they arrived, also the next day; has lived here 33 years; used to cart his grain to Chicago, and has sold wheat at 50 cts. a bushel; owns farm of 80 acres; has held office of Town Treasurer of the School Fund; married Julia A. Milmine, formerly Miss Julia A. Bentley, of Aurora, N. Y., Sept. 19, 1871; she had two children, Willie A. and Helen L.

Fowler L. farmer; Sec. 13; P. O. Belvidere.

Fox Geo. Sec. 32; P. O. Belvidere.

French D. C. farm; Sec. 14; P.O. Belvidere.

Frint N. H. farmer; Sec. 36; P.O. Belvidere.

Fuller D. A. farm; S. 6; P.O. Cherry Valley.

Fuller G. farm; Sec. 6; P. O. Cherry Valley.

FULLER S. Farmer; Sec. 6; P. O. Cherry Valley; born in Bennington Co., Vt., July 8, 1817; lived there 18 years; removed to N. Y. State; came to Illinois, Boone Co., in 1846, and has lived here 32 years; used to cart his grain to Chicago, and has sold wheat for 30c to 40c per bushel; owns farm of 240 acres; has held offices of Justice of the Peace, Road Commissioner, School Trustee and School Director; married Eliza A. Mordoff, from Wyoming Co., N. Y.; have five children, James A., of Rockford; George N., Chas. E., Dufay A., Mrs. Mary Stockwell; Geo. N. was born Oct. 14, 1845; married Miss R. E. Mason, from Dayton, Ohio, March 23, 1873; she died in December, 1875; D. A. Fuller was born Feb. 21, 1852; married Miss Jennie Robinson, of Cherry Valley, March 24, 1875; he holds office of Justice of Peace.

GATES D. W. farmer; Sec. 1; P. O. Belvidere.

GRAVES ANDREW J. Farmer; Sec. 27; P. O. Belvidere; born in Guilford, Piscataquis Co., Me., Nov. 23, 1831; lived there 13 years, and came to Boone Co., town of Flora, in October, 1845, and has lived here 32 years; among the early settlers, not many here now who were here then; he carted grain to Chicago before any cash market here; owns 79 acres land; has held offices of School Director and Overseer of Roads; married Miss Lydia Rice, from State of New York, Feb., 1854; have five children, Washington Irving, Julius Albert, Howard Wilber, Mary Josephine, Eugene Carlton.

Graves Geo. H. farmer.

Graves Irving W. farmer; P. O. Belvidere.

GRAVES SAMUEL S. Farmer; Sec. 26; P. O. Belvidere; born in Hancock Co., Me., Feb. 28, 1806; lived in that State 39 years; came to Boone Co., town of Flora, Oct. 3, 1845, and lives on same farm, 40 acres, he entered from government; it was most all government land around here then; used to cart his grain to Chicago, and sold wheat for 90c per bushel when his neighbors only got 70c; married Hannah Young, from Somerset Co., Me., Aug.

28, 1830; they have had five children, Andrew Jackson, Helen M. Ward, Theodore W., was in army, Co. I, 9th I. V. C., died at Lagrange, Tenn.; George H., was in army, Co. B, 15th I. V. I., was in battles of Pittsburg Landing, Corinth and others; Huldah J. and Julia.

Green G. C. farmer; Sec. 2; P. O. Belvidere.

Greenmon G.H. farm; S. 23; P.O.Belvidere.

GRIGGS CALVIN, Farmer; Sec. 34; P. O. Cherry Valley; born in Oneida Co., N. Y., Feb. 25, 1816; moved to Indiana at an early age; came to this State about the year 1826, and has lived in this State over 50 years; came to Cherry Valley, August, 1835; has lived in this vicinity over 42 years; there were plenty of Indians when he came; only very few now living who were here when he came; no improvements of any kind, and only one house in Rockford; used to pound corn in a mortar and pestle from a hole burned in a log; used to grind wheat and buckwheat in a coffee-mill; used to go to Ottawa, 70 miles, to mill; carted grain to Chicago, sold wheat for 40c per bushel, no market for it here; has paid $3 a bushel for spring wheat; he made the first beef barrel ever made in this Co., in 1835, hewed out of a log, has it in his possession now; he has counted 43 deer at one time from the mound east of Cherry Valley; owns 259 acres land; married Hannah Smith, of Ohio, April 2, 1844; have nine children, Maria, Joseph, Daniel, George, Lucy, Eli, William, Fred, Mary; Joseph P. Griggs, father of above, was one of the earliest pioneers of the West; born 1789 and died in 1845.

GRIGGS HORACE, Farmer; Sec. 20; P. O. Cherry Valley; born in Terre Haute, Ind., Dec. 26, 1825; came to Illinois in August, 1835, to Cherry Valley, Winnebago Co., and has lived here over 42 years, and is the only settler here now who was here when he came; used to pound corn with an old pestle made out of iron wood, 42 years ago, and has it in his possession yet; the mortar was a log with a hole burned in the end of it; he used to haul grain to Chicago.

GRIGGS LANDON, Farmer; Sec. 21; P. O. Cherry Valley; born in Princeton, Ind., May 25, 1820; came to Cherry Valley, Winnebago Co., in August, 1835, and has lived in this vicinity over 41 years; one of the oldest settlers; there were plenty of Indians, and only one house in Rockford when he came; they used to grind their buckwheat in a coffee-mill, and pound corn in a mortar made in the end of a log; used to cart grain to Chicago, and has sold wheat at 40c a bushel; has held offices of School Director and Road Master; owns farm of 80 acres; married Martha Smith, of Cuyahoga Co., Ohio, in Dec., 1844; they have two children, Sarah

L., born June 5, 1858; Nancy Maria, May 20, 1860; have lost two children, Charles W., was in the navy during the war, was on the monitor Osage, and died in Memphis, Tenn.

Groff A. F. carpenter; S. 36; P.O. Belvidere.

Grummons G. H. farm; P.O. Cherry Valley.

Grummons H. B. farmer; Sec. 26; P. O. Cherry Valley.

Grummons S. L. farm; P. O. Cherry Valley.

HALE JAS. farmer; Sec. 13; P. O. Belvidere.

Hale Wallace, farmer; P. O. Belvidere.

HALL F. I. County Clerk; Sec. 23; P. O. Belvidere; born Monroe Co., N. Y., May 22, 1836; lived in that State eight years; removed to Walworth Co., Wis., in 1844; lived there twenty-two years; came to Boone Co., town of Flora, 1866; owns farm of 70 acres; has held office of Superintendent of Schools; held office of Supervisor for some years, and School Trustee; is Master of the Flora Grange, also Master of the Boone Co. Grange; is President of Flora Vigilant Society, organized in 1873; received the appointment of County Clerk of Boone Co. by Board of Supervisors, in March, 1877; married Miss Abbie M. Lovett, from Maine, in March, 1858; they have four children: Fred, born Feb. 4, 1859; Addie M., Sept. 25, 1860; Emily R., Aug. 3, 1872; Mark, March 22, 1875.

Halquist Chas.

Hannah Thos. farm; Sec.11; P.O. Belvidere.

Hawkey R. farmer; Sec. 31.

Holmes Chas. farmer; Sec. 20.

Hovey F. H. farm; Sec. 22; P. O. Belvidere.

HOWARD A. Farmer; Sec. 5; P. O. Belvidere; born Chenango Co., N. Y., Sept 24, 1824; lived there 10 years, and lived in Madison Co., 15 years; removed to Ill., to Boone Co., and has lived here 27 years, on the same farm he first bought; owns farm of 200 acres; has held office of Assessor of this town, also Road Commissioner; married Miss Lavina Sexton, from Earlville, Chenango Co., N. Y., Jan. 24, 1848; they have five children, two sons and three daughters: Emory L., Frank L., Addie L. Adelia J., Gertrude J.; lost two daughters: Eva R. and Ida.

Howard A. farmer; Sec. 12; P. O. Belvidere.

Howard Frank L. farmer; Sec. 5; P. O. Cherry Valley.

IRISH D. farmer; Sec. 36; P. O. Belvidere.

JARVIS JAMES, farmer; Sec. 8; P. O. Belvidere.

Jenkins Chas. P. O. Belvidere.

JENKS ALONZO M. Farmer; Sec. 6; P.O. Cherry Valley; born in Covington, Genesee Co., N. Y., March 7, 1818; lived there and in Wyoming Co. about 24 years; came to Boone Co., Ill., Nov. 18, 1842; came by lake and cars to Ann Arbor, Mich., and walked from there; has lived here 36 years; only few persons here now that were here when he came; could go to Belvidere and not see a fence, also for eight miles south; carted grain to Chicago for ten years after coming here; was thirteen days making one trip to and from Chicago; has sold wheat at 15c a bushel; owns 244 acres land; 400 acres in Iowa; entered 80 acres from government; married first, Mary M. White, from N. Y., in 1842; she died in 1855; two children; married Abbie Ann Fuller, of Washington, Co., N. Y., in Jan., 1856; two children by first wife: Frank S. and Mrs. Marion A. Lake, of Story Co., Iowa; lost two children.

JOHANSSON C. Farmer; Sec. 31; P. O. Cherry Valley; born March 7, 1845; came to this country in 1869; came to Ill., to Winnebago Co., same year; lived there four years, and came to Boone Co. in 1873; owns farm 40 acres; married Hannah Johansson, from Sweden, April 4, 1869; they have two children: Lottie, born Sept. 20, 1871; Gustavus, June 8, 1875. A. G. Johansson, brother of the above, was born in Sweden, Nov. 26, 1851; lived there 21 years and came to this country in 1872; came to Cherry Valley; came to Boone Co. in 1876.

Johnson O. farmer; Sec. 20.

Jordan E. T. farmer; Sec. 29.

Jordan J. R. farmer; Sec. 30.

Jordan T. S. farmer; Sec. 29; P. O. Cherry Valley.

Jordan W. E. farmer; Sec. 19.

Jordan Z. farm; S. 24; P. O. Cherry Valley.

KELLEY DENNIS, farmer; Sec. 13; P. O. Belvidere.

Kelley John, farmer; P. O. Cherry Valley.

KEATOR GEO. T. Farmer; Sec. 9; P.O. Belvidere; born Binghampton, N.Y., June 27, 1844; removed to Penn. at an early age; lived there until eighteen years of age; returned to Binghampton and lived there 5 years; came to Ill., to Boone Co., in 1869; has lived here eight years; owns farm of 80 acres; married Miss Emma P. Dodge, of Binghampton, N. Y., April 15, 1869; she graduated there, and taught school for four years; they have one child (son), William Albert, born in February, 1870.

Keith A. J. farmer; Sec. 31.

KEITH LEWIS, Farmer; Sec. 31; P. O. Cherry Valley; born Morgan Co., O., May 2, 1826; lived in that State for 9 years; went to Indiana in 1835; then removed to Ill., to DeKalb Co., which was not then surveyed (March, 1857), has lived in this vicinity over forty years; no improvements of any kind when he came; his uncle and grandfather were on the first jury ever drawn in Rockford; he then carted grain to Chicago; no market for it here; sold a great deal of wheat at 31c a bushel; owns 1,400 acres of land in this vicinity and 1,000 in Iowa; his first wife was Catherine Brown, from Ohio; she died in 1862; had three children; Lewis W., Luther L., Roswell C.; married Miss Louisa M. Farley, from Ohio, in 1864; she was born Feb. 2, 1840; they have two children: Julia Florence, born July 14, 1869; Estella, born March 31, 1871.

KING ORIGIN, Farmer; Sec. 22; P. O. Belvidere; born in Tioga Co., N. Y., May 8, 1833; lived in that State 24 years, and was engaged in brick making; came to Boone Co., Ill., in 1856, and has lived here ever since, 21 years; owns 40 acres land; has held offices of Town Collector of Flora and School Director; married Hannah A. Loring, from Tioga Co., N. Y., March, 1861; she died December, 1862; they had one son, Ernest L.; married Amanda Hastings, of Belvidere, March 18, 1875; she was from Vermont.

KINGSBURY DANIEL B. Farmer; Sec. 34; P. O. Cherry Valley; born DeKalb Co., Ill., Oct. 20, 1850, and lived there until 1876—25 years; his parents were early settlers, came there 37 years ago; only one house between his father's and Belvidere when they came; has held office of Town Collector; owns farm of 22 acres; married Miss Elvira Dean, from DeKalb Co., Jan. 27, 1870; she died Aug. 20, 1875; he married Miss Laura Young, from DeKalb Co., Jan. 17, 1877; he had two children by first wife: Frank Leslie and Myrtie Alvira.

Koch G. W. farmer; P. O. Belvidere.

Lambert A. farmer; Sec. 26; P. O. Belvidere.
Lambert J. C. farm; Sec. 26; P.O. Belvidere.
Lane M. farmer; Sec. 15; P. O. Belvidere.
Leonhart C. farmer; Sec. 10; P.O. Belvidere.

LEAMAN GEO. Farmer; Sec. 29; P. O. Cherry Valley; born in Licking Co., O., July 5, 1820; lived there 23 years; came to Ill., Boone Co., in September, 1843, and has lived here 34 years; only a few here now that were here when he came; he is a carpenter and joiner, and worked at his trade 15 years; is engaged in farming, and owns farm of 110 acres; has never had a lawsuit; has held office of Path Master, and is now School Director; married Deborah Bennett, Jan. 1, 1846; she was born in State of N. Y., 1826; have seven children, two girls and five boys: Charles W., Charlotte, Silas, Frances, Mary, Willie, Freddie; lost two daughters.

Leaman S. farm; S. 29; P. O. Cherry Valley.

LEE WILLIAM, Farmer; Sec. 34; P. O. Cherry Valley; born Clearfield Co., Penn., Dec. 3, 1823; lived in Penn. 20 years; came to Boone Co., August, 1844; has lived here over 33 years; only few here that were here when he came; there were no fences between here and Belvidere; used to haul his grain to Chicago, and 56c was the highest price he ever got for winter wheat in Chicago; he entered the land on which he now lives from the government; owns farm of 160 acres; has held offices of Road Commissioner and School Director for some years; married Miss Rebecca McKee, from Penn., in 1843; she died in 1865; they had four children: Thos. M., Mary C., Joseph B., and Miller D.; married Miss Harriet Taylor, May 1, 1866; she was from Noble Co., O., and born Jan. 30, 1843; they have two children: Emory U. and Oscar E.

Lincoln E. N. farm; Sec. 3; P. O. Belvidere.

LINCOLN JEDEDIAH, Retired; Sec. 2; P. O. Belvidere; born Middlesex Co., Conn., Oct. 28, 1805; lived in that State 25 years; lived in Dunkirk and Erie about 8 years, and came by team to Boone Co., Feb., 1839; was three weeks on the way; has lived here 38 years; one of the earliest settlers here; very few here in this town that were here when he came; used to cart his grain to Chicago; no cash market here then; owns farm of 20 acres; his first wife was Mary Belden, of Conn.; one child, Mrs. Mary B. Gillette, of Kansas; his present wife was Miss Mary Nichols, of Chautauqua Co., N. Y.; they were married Sept. 26, 1836; she was born Chenango Co., N. Y., July 6, 1812; they had five children: [Phœbe E., born in Erie; Oscar J., born Boone Co., lives in Iowa; Edgar N., born Boone Co.; Mrs. Alice N. Sisson, born Boone Co., lives in Iowa; William P., born Boone Co., lives in Iowa; Phineas Nichols, father of Mrs. Lincoln, came here at an early day and bought large tracts of land, and divided among his children; has owned 350 acres of land and has divided it among his children, and now owns 20 acres.

Longgreen J. laborer; Sec. 7; P. O. Cherry Valley.

LUCAS O. F. Farmer; Sec. 36; P. O. Belvidere; born Boone Co., town of Flora, Nov. 9, 1840; has lived in this Co. 37 years, except 3 years he lived in De Kalb Co.; he owns farm of 74 acres; he married Miss Almira Lawton, at Fort Scott, Kan., Jan. 13, 1862; she was from Potter Co., Penn.; born March 14, 1842; she came to Boone Co. in 1855, and from there removed to Kansas; they have one son, Wilmar H., born in this town, July 15, 1863; Horace and Elizabeth Lucas, parents of Walter and O. F. Lucas, came to Boone Co. from Ind. in 1841; he died July 26, 1852; Mrs. Lucas is still living in Belvidere; they had five children: Walter, born June 7, 1839; Oscar F., Nov. 9, 1840; Catherine E., Dec. 17, 1844; Olive, Feb. 26, 1847; Moses, June 23, 1849.

LUCAS WALTER, Farmer; Sec. 25; P. O. Belvidere; born town of Flora, June 27, 1839, and has lived in this town for 38 years, is the oldest person now living here that was born in this town; has held offices of Justice of the Peace and Assessor of this town; owns farm of 30 acres; married Miss Edna Cushman, March 11, 1862; she and her husband were both born in the same house, her birthday being Feb. 15, 1837; they have two children: Myra, born April 14, 1865; Earl, June 16, 1873; the parents of both Mr. and Mrs. Lucas were among the earliest settlers of Boone Co.

McCHESNEY JOHN, farmer; P. O. Cherry Valley.

McCARTNEY ADDISON S. Farmer; Sec. 35; P.O. Belvidere; born in Bedford Co., Penn., Feb. 6, 1845; lived there about 12 years, and came to Boone Co. in 1857; has lived here 20 years; engaged in farming and stock raising; owns farm 160 acres; his mother, Mrs. Jane McCartney, is living with him; his father, John McCartney, died Feb. 18, 1871; they were from Bedford Co., Penn.; came to this Co. in 1857.

McGee J. L. farmer; P. O. Belvidere.

McKEE SAMUEL, Farmer; Sec. 32; P. O. Cherry Valley, born Washington Co., Penn., March 17, 1814; lived in that State 22 years, and came to Ill., Boone Co., June 24, 1846; has lived here over 31 years; only two small fences between his house and Belvidere; used to cart his grain to Chicago and St. Charles; owns 175 acres land; has held offices of Collector, Assessor, Overseer of Poor, and Road Commissioner; was appointed Supervisor; married Elizabeth Neff, from Washington Co., Penn., Nov. 11, 1835; they have eight children: Jonathan N., Thomas, John C., Milton, Carrie E., Mrs. Martha E. Neff, Mrs. Mary J. Koch, Mrs. Sarah J. Eustis, of Iowa; Alfred, died of disease contracted in army; was in 105th I. V. I.

McMann Geo. laborer; S. 22; P.O.Belvidere.

Mackey L. farmer; P. O. Cherry Valley.

Mackey T. farmer; P. O. Cherry Valley.

MACCONNOUGHEY OTIS, Farmer; Sec. 22; P. O. Belvidere; born in Cuyahoga Co., Ohio, Oct. 4, 1819; lived there about 30 years, and came to this State, Boone Co.; no improvements on prairie at that time; only few here that were here when he came; owns farm of 100 acres, and property at Cherry Valley and Capron; has held office Path Master; married Laura Ann Stevens, from Jefferson Co., N. Y., January, 1854; she came to Boone Co. two years after her husband came; they have five children: Ira, George, Charles, Annie, Myra, lost three children, two sons and one daughter.

Magee J. L. farmer; Sec. 24; P.O. Belvidere.

MAGEE GARRET, Farmer; Sec. 14; P. O. Belvidere; born in Albany Co., N. Y., March 11, 1848; lived in that State 19 years in same county and same district; came to Boone Co. in 1867, and has lived here 10 years; engaged in farming and stock raising; owns 60 acres land; has held office of Road Master; married Ardelia Hersey, from this Co. and town, Nov. 18, 1869; they have one child, son, Wentworth Magee, born Oct. 2, 1872.

MAREAN ALONZO, Farm and Dairy; Sec. 11; P. O. Belvidere; born in Broome Co., N. Y., Sept. 25, 1822; lived there 24 years, and came to Illinois, Boone Co., March 4, 1846; came by team from New York State, and was 22 days making the trip; has lived here 31 years; was engaged in teaming from Chicago to Galena; owns 170 acres land; has carted winter wheat to Chicago and sold for 60 cts. a bushel; has held offices of School Director and Road Master; married Statira Robinson, Me., Oct. 1, 1855; they have four children: Jennie, John E., Clara, Fred. A.

Meehan John, P. O. Belvidere.

Meeker A. A. farm; S. 8; P.O.Cherry Valley.

Minar Christopher, P. O. Belvidere.

Mitchell T. laborer; Sec. 5.

Money Chas. farmer; Sec. 13; P.O.Belvidere.

Mornessey James, Sec. 19.

Moore Frank, farmer; P. O. Belvidere.

Moore Samuel, farmer; P. O. Belvidere.

MOREHEAD WM. Farmer; Sec. 20; P. O. Cherry Valley; born North of Ireland, May 27, 1827; lived there 20 years, and came to this country in 1847; went to State of New York and lived there 5 years; came to Boone Co. in 1852, and has lived here 25 years; owns 160 acres land; has held offices of Road Master and School Director; married Margaret Gibson, from County Armagh, Ireland, in 1852; they have five children, three sons, two daughters: Mary Jane, Annie, William J., Henry, Frank.

Morrissey Jas. farmer; Sec. 8; P.O.Belvidere.

Moss Judson, farmer; P. O. Belvidere.

MUNN ALFRED, Farmer; Sec. 12; P. O. Belvidere; born in Oneida Co., N. Y., Nov. 5, 1828; lived in that State 25 years, then came to Illinois, Boone Co., in 1853, and has lived here 24 years; owns farm 132 acres; has held office of School Director; married Alvira Knapp, of Oneida Co., N. Y., in 1848; she died Aug. 14, 1866; married Rhoda Spinning, from Oneida Co., N. Y., Feb., 1867; they have three children: Frank, John and Alice; have lost two children.

FLORA TOWNSHIP.

MUNN FRANK E. Proprietor Flora Creamery; Sec. 12; P. O. Belvidere; born Oneida Co., N. Y., June 30, 1851; removed to Boone Co., Ill., at an early age, and has lived here 24 years; he established the Creamery in 1876, and makes from 500 to 1,000 pounds a week during the year, which has already reached a high reputation, all of his butter being shipped to the St. Louis market, commanding the highest market price; he was awarded the first premium of $100 at the St. Louis Exposition Fair in 1876; he has held office of School Director; married Miss Julia Spinning, N. Y., Sept., 1873.

Munn G. farmer; Sec. 24; P. O. Belvidere.
Munn John, P. O. Belvidere.
Munn Wm. H. farmer; P. O. Belvidere.
Myres W. farm; Sec. 20; P.O. Cherry Valley.

NAUMAN CHARLES A. laborer; Sec. 30.

Neff J. farmer; Sec. 27; P. O. Belvidere.

NEFF MARTIN B. Farmer; Sec. 27; P. O. Belvidere; born in Blair Co., Penn., Oct. 31, 1812, lived there 19 years, and came to Boone Co. in 1861, and has lived here 15 years; owns farm of 80 acres; has held office of Town Collector, and has been School Director for 12 years; married Miss Martha McKee, of this town and Co., they have five children; Zilda, Mary, Bernice, Gertie, Wallace.

Nelson J. laborer; Sec. 25; P. O. Belvidere.

NORTON E. C. Attorney; Sec. 25; P. O. Belvidere; born in Flora, April 7, 1844; he has lived in this Co. thirty-three years; only few native born now living here older than he; he studied law, and has been engaged in practicing his profession in Belvidere some years; is of the firm of Norton & Speekman, Belvidere; married Miss Abbie J. Eggleston, from New Lebanon, N. Y. Jan. 23, 1868; they have two children, Carrie E., born Dec. 31, 1871; Robbie G., Dec. 10, 1873.

Norton J. G. farmer; Sec.25; P.O. Belvidere.
Norton S. H. farm; Sec. 25; P. O. Belvidere.

OBERHAUSER H. W. Sec. 9.

OAKS ELDRIDGE G. Farmer; Sec. 21; P. O. Belvidere; born in Piscataquis Co., Maine, Aug. 19, 1812; lived there 33 years; came to Illinois, to Boone Co., in 1845, and has lived here over 32 years; only one house between here and Belvidere when they came; he has raised wheat and sold it for 30 cents per bushel; has held office School Director; he preempted his farm, on which he lives, from Government; married Liberty Leighton, from Kennebec, Maine, in June, 1832; they have four children living, Cyrus, Marshall, John F., Abbie; lost two girls, Susan and Amy.

OAKS JOHN F. Farmer; Sec. 22; P. O. Belvidere; born in Piscataquis Co., Maine, Nov. 7, 1839; lived there until 7 years of age; removed to Boone Co., Ill., and has lived here over 30 years; he has been engaged in threshing for past 20 years; commenced when 18 years of age; has held office of Constable; owns farm of 80 acres of land; married Miss Olivia Wattles, of this Co., in 1867; she died in 1869; married Miss Maria H. Law, in Iowa, in December, 1875; she was from state of Indiana.

Oaks M. W. farmer; Sec. 24; P.O. Belvidere.
Ongrin A. laborer; Sec. 30; P. O. Belvidere.

PATTERSON EUGENE C. Sec. 2; P. O. Belvidere.

PAINE B. F. Farmer; Sec. 24; P. O. Belvidere; born in Orleans Co., N. Y., Nov. 20, 1820; lived in New York 11 years; moved to Erie Co., Penn.; lived there 13 years; came to this state July 3, 1845, to Boone Co., and has lived here over 32 years; engaged in farming, owns farm of 40 acres of land; has held office of Assessor of Flora, also office of Collector, and has held office of Town Treasurer 5 years and Town Clerk 7 years; married Amanda M. Hovey, from Broome Co., New York, July 4, 1855; they have one son, Charles A., born Nov. 8, 1859.

PARTLOW DANIEL, Farmer; Sec. 11; P. O. Belvidere; born near Freeport, Ill., Jan. 19, 1848; removed to Wisconsin at an early age, and from there to state of Iowa, where he lived 4 or 5 years; returned to Boone Co. in 1862, and has lived here 15 years; married Miss Delia Norcross, of Glens Falls, New York, December, 1869; they have three children, two sons and one daughter, Charlie, Frank and Nellie.

Patterson J. H. farm; Sec. 2; P.O. Belvidere.
Peel J. farmer; Sec. 15; P. O. Cherry Valley.
Perrin N. M. laborer; Sec.20; P.O. Belvidere.
Perry H. farmer; Sec. 36; P. O. Belvidere.
Perry Olias, farmer; P. O. Belvidere.
Philbrick H. A. farm; S.14; P. O. Belvidere.
Philbrick H. W. farm; S.14; P. O. Belvidere.
Pierce Frank P. farmer; P. O. Belvidere.
Pike C. W. farmer; P. O. Cherry Valley.

PIKE CHAS. W., Sec. 5; of the firm of Pike & Compton, was born in Piscataquis Co., Maine, Sept. 5, 1835; came to Illinois, to Boone Co., Dec. 31, 1854, and has lived here twenty-three years.

PRIEST GEORGE W. Farmer; Sec. 6; P. O. Cherry Valley; born in Madison, Oneida Co., New York, Oct. 14, 1851; removed to Cherry Valley, Winnebago Co., when 4 years of age; removed to Boone Co. in 1875; has 151 acres of land, and is interested largely in cultivating broom corn; married Miss Florence Mackey, daughter of Hugh Mackey, Esq., one of the oldest settlers of Cherry Valley; they have one child, Edna Priest, born Aug. 15, 1874.

Pryor Robert, P. O. Belvidere.

RANDALL ALBERT, farmer; Sec. 24; P. O. Belvidere.

Randall H. farmer; Sec. 15; P. O. Belvidere.

ROACH WILLIAM, Farmer; Sec. 35; P. O. Cherry Valley; born in Ohio, Oct. 12, 1849; lived in that state 14 years; removed to Illinois, to Boone Co., in 1865, and has lived here 12 years; he owns farm of 56 acres in DeKalb Co.; married Miss Ella E. Witter, from this town and Co., in Aug., 1871; they have two children, Ida May, Estella.

Robbins H. farmer; Sec. 23; P. O. Belvidere.

ROBINSON A. M. Farmer; Sec. 23; P. O. Belvidere; born Cumberland Co., Maine, May 3, 1809; removed to Boone Co. in 1841, came by team, and was 8 weeks on the way; has lived here 33 years; among the early settlers; used to haul his grain to Chicago; married Zophira Cochran, from Maine, in 1837; she died 1854; married Susan Whitney, of Maine, in 1855; had seven children: Samuel, born in Maine; James G., born Maine, was in army, 1st Colorado Cavalry, 3 years; William, born Maine, Fred A., born Maine, was in army, 9th Ill. Cav., died at Helena, Ark.; Walter A., born Boone Co.; Arthur P., born Boone Co.; Frank, born Boone Co.; Nathan Whitney, son of Mrs. Whitney, enlisted in Drosser's Battery, and was wounded at Holly Springs, was in battles of Ft. Donelson, Ft. Henry, Pittsburg Landing and Corinth. Samuel Robinson was born in Piscataquis Co., Me., Dec. 29, 1836; came to Boone Co. 1844, and has lived here 33 years; owns 115 acres land; married Miss Sarah Cochran, of this Co., Nov. 3, 1869; she died Jan. 21, 1875; they had one child, died in infancy.

ROBINSON A. W. Farmer; Sec. 14; P. O. Belvidere; born in Piscataquis Co., Me., Oct. 7, 1830; lived in Maine 11 years, and came to Boone Co., town of Flora, Oct. 7, 1841; came by team 1,600 miles, and was 7 weeks coming; there are very few here now that were here when he came 36 years ago; no cash market here for grain; used to cart it to Chicago; he carted a load of wheat to Chicago when 13 years of age, carried it up two pair of stairs and sold it for 40 cts. a bushel; owns farm of 120 acres; married Miss Mary Russell, Jan. 16, 1852; she came to Boone Co. 1835, and is one of the oldest settlers of this Co.; her parents used to grind corn in coffee mill after breaking it up in a mortar, it was so far to go to mill; they had two children: Freddie E., born Nov. 28, 1854, died July 23, 1856; Lydia Ann, born May 27, 1857, died Oct. 15, 1858.

Rochime F. farm; S. 7; P. O. Cherry Valley.
Rogers J. B. Sec. 12; P. O. Belvidere.

ROYAL ALLEN S. Farmer; Sec. 34; P. O. Belvidere; born Piscataquis Co., Me., Nov. 5, 1820; lived there 24 years, and came to Boone Co. May 9, 1844, and has lived here over 33 years; one of few early settlers in this town now living that were here when he came; only one piece of land broken between here and Belvidere; he entered his land from government; owns 130 acres; used to haul his grain to Chicago before there was any cash market here; he used to teach school; has held offices Road Commissioner and Overseer of Poor; he holds office of Justice of Peace; married Miss Lucy J. Robinson, from Maine, June 2, 1847; she was born Oct. 25, 1828; she has been an invalid for 30 years and bed-ridden for past 8 years; they have four children: Solon, born Sept. 22, 1849, teaching school; Leroy, Sept. 26, 1852, lives in Iowa; Tira, June 24, 1855; Lilian, April 28, 1860.

Russell C. farmer; Sec. 26; P.O. Belvidere.
Ryan Alb. farm; Sec. 33; P.O.Cherry Valley.
Ryan And. farm; Sec. 33; P.O.Cherry Valley.

SAWYER FRANK, farmer; P. O. Belvidere.

Sergeant H. W. farm; S. 34; P.O.Belvidere.
Shannon H. farmer; Sec. 36; P.O.Belvidere.
Shannon P. farmer; Sec. 33; P.O.Belvidere.
Shattuck H. farmer; Sec. 14; P.O Belvidere.

SHATTUCK H. A. Farmer; Sec. 14; P. O. Belvidere; born in Boone Co., town of Flora, Feb. 18, 1852; has lived in this Co. 25 years, his father and mother were among the earliest settlers of this Co.; his father used to cart grain and pork to Chicago and Milwaukee the nearest markets; his grandmother is still living, 88 years old; owns farm of 80 acres; married Miss Maria Stone, Nov. 19, 1774; she was born in Wisconsin, June 22, 1853, and came to this Co. when 4 years of age; they have two children: Louis L., born Sept. 4, 1875; Mathias T., Nov. 19, 1876.

Shipe J. A. laborer; Sec. 30.
Shirley G. B. farmer; Sec. 7; P.O.Belvidere.

SHIRLEY LEWIS, Farmer; Sec. 7; P. O. Cherry Valley; born in Morgan Co., Ohio, March 1, 1820; lived in Ohio 18 years; lived in Indiana 2 years; came to Illinois, to Winnebago Co., in 1840; removed to Boone Co., and has lived here over 30 years; he has carted his grain to Chicago and sold wheat at 50cts. a bushel; he pre-empted the farm on which he now lives from government; he owns 1,500 acres land; married Miss Lucinda Keith, from Ohio, Jan., 1842; she was one of the early settlers here; they have six children, three sons and three daughters: Silas W.,

Charles F. Witt
SPRING TP.

George Benjamin, Louis E., Elizabeth, Lucretia and Jane.

SHIRLEY LEWIS, Jr., Farmer; Sec. 30; P. O. Cherry Valley; born in Indiana, Jan. 12, 1841; removed to this State when 3 years of age, to Winnebago Co.; went to California in 1859, and was there 3 years; returned to this State, to Boone Co., in 1863; he has carted hundreds of loads of grain to Chicago; has sold wheat at 43 cts. a bushel; has seen price of wheat 25 cts. a bushel in trade here; owns 380 acres land here and 640 acres in Kansas; has held offices of School Director and Road Master; married Leah Reams, from Hampshire, Kane Co., Ill., in Nov., 1864; she died Feb. 28, 1876; has six children: Celestia, Flora E., Carrie, Gertrude, Roswell, Bertie.

SILVIUS HENRY, Farmer; Sec. 36; P. O. Belvidere; born in Luzerne Co., Penn., Oct. 10, 1822; lived in that State 32 years; engaged in carpenter business; came to Illinois, Boone Co., 1854, and has lived here 23 years; owns 122 acres land, and 13 in DeKalb Co.; has held offices of School Director and Path Master; married Melissa E. Dimmick, from Penn., Sept. 30, 1845; they have seven children, six sons and one daughter: Orrin M., Lyman W., Thomas Burr, Urias H., Marion M. C. G., Irving H., Ida W.

Smith Thos. farmer; Sec. 10; P.O.Belvidere.
Spencer James, P. O. Belvidere.
Spencer Jos. farmer; P.O.Cherry Valley.

SPENCER JABEZ I. Farmer; Sec. 28; P. O. Cherry Valley; born Otsego Co., N. Y., Oct. 10, 1804; lived in that State 40 years; came to Boone Co. June 8, 1844, and has lived here over 34 years; no improvement here on prairie at that time; only few here now that were here when he came; used to cart his grain to Chicago; the last load of wheat hauled there sold at 33 cts. a bushel; owns 400 acres land; has held offices School Director and Road Master; he was the first Assessor in the town of Flora; married Loraina Thompson, from Cherry Valley, Otsego Co., N. Y., Feb. 8, 1829; she was born Feb. 1, 1813; they have had four children: Jabez, was murdered in Nevada; Addison, died, was Lieut. 9th Reg. Kansas Cavalry; Avery, killed in skirmish with Guerrillas on Spring River; Milton, born Oct. 30, 1836, only son living.

Sprague J. farm; S. 22; P. O. Cherry Valley.
Spoor A. B. farmer; Sec. 36; P.O. Belvidere.
Spoor Charles, farmer; P. O. Belvidere.
Spoor D. farmer; Sec.21; P. O. Belvidere.
Sutherland J. farmer; P. O. Belvidere.
Sternborn F. laborer; P. O. Belvidere.
Stiles D., Jr., farmer; Sec.23; P.O. Belvidere.

SWAIL ROBERT, Farmer; Sec. 3; P. O. Belvidere; born in Longueuil, Canada, near Montreal, November 1, 1835; lived in Canada 24 years; came to the United States in 1860; came to Illinois, Boone Co., in same year, and has lived here 17 years; engaged in farming and stock raising; has held office of Path Master; owns 80 acres land; married Miss Harriet Feakins, in this town, Nov. 27, 1861; she was from Cherry Valley, Otsego Co., N. Y., born May 19, 1841; they have 7 children, Sarah, Ettie, Alice, Charles F., William C., Mabel, Frank C.; lost one daughter.

Sweeney Cornelius, farmer; P. O. Belvidere.
Sweeney W. farmer; Sec. 31; P.O. Belvidere.

TAYLOR CHAS. farmer; Sec. 28; P. O. Belvidere.

TANNER FRANKLIN, Farmer; Sec. 16; P. O. Belvidere; born in Genesee Co., N. Y., Sept. 10, 1819; lived there and in Chautauqua Co. 24 years; removed to Illinois, to Boone Co., July, 1843, and has lived here over 34 years; among the early settlers here; only few now living who were here when he came; used to haul his grain to Chicago with ox teams, there being no cash market here; all he had from the sale of one load of wheat after paying expenses was three dollars and a half, and a grind stone; owns farm of 120 acres; has held office of Supervisor, and has held office of School Treasurer for 21 years; his first wife was Abagail Wilcox, from N. Y.; married Sept. 13, 1840; she was born in Conn., 1816, died June 10, 1874; married Miss Julia Wilcox, May 31, 1875; she was born in Chautauqua Co., N. Y., Nov. 19, 1827; he has one adopted son, Albert Tanner, living in Iowa. Abel and Electa Tanner, parents of Mr. Tanner, came to this Co. in 1839; were early settlers; have both passed away.

Tayler J. L. farm; S. 28; P.O. Cherry Valley.
Taylor J. laborer; Sec. 7; P. O. Belvidere.
Taylor W. farm; Sec 28; P.O.Cherry Valley.
Terry D. laborer; Sec. 8; P. O. Belvidere.
Thomas D. F. farmer; P. O. Cherry Valley.
Thompson J. C. farm; Sec.5; P.O. Belvidere.

THOMPSON JNO. C., Jr., farmer; Sec. 5; P. O. Belvidere; born in Franklin Co., Mass., June 14, 1838; removed to Illinois; went to Kansas, and lived there 8 years; was in Government service there; returned to Illinois, to Boone Co., in 1874; owns farm of 80 acres; was in the army, 92d Regt. I. V. I.; married Miss Elizabeth D. Avery, June, 1874; she was born in this Co., June 24, 1846; they have one child, Edward Avery Thompson, born Aug. 20, 1876; they have lost two children.

Thompson N. farm; Sec. 18; P.O. Belvidere.
Thorn S. farmer; Sec. 23; P. O. Belvidere.

Tripp H. J. farmer; P. O. Belvidere.
Tucker F. W. farm; Sec.12; P. O. Belvidere.
Tucker C. farmer; Sec. 12; P. O. Belvidere.
Tucker P. H. farm; Sec. 12; P.O. Belvidere.
Turner Wm. H. farm; S.24; P. O. Belvidere.

UTING J. laborer; Sec. 30; P. O. Belvidere.

VANDOREN W. H. minister; Sec. 21; P. O. Belvidere.

Vincent G. A. farm; Sec. 18; P.O. Belvidere.

WAITE C. G. farmer; Sec. 23; P. O. Belvidere.

Walker J. M. farmer; P. O. Cherry Valley.
Walsted J. farm; Sec.7; P.O. Cherry Valley.

WEBBER F. S. Farmer; Sec. 26; P. O. Belvidere; born in Piscataquis Co., Maine, Feb. 21, 1834; lived there 12 years, and came to Boone Co., Ill., with team, 1,500 miles, in September, 1845; was very little improvement here on prairie then; used to cart grain to Chicago; owns 110 acres land; has held office Town Collector in Ogle Co.; also Collector for town of Flora; School Director for ten years; married Frances Arvilla Watkins, from N. Y., May 13, 1857; she was born July, 1838; they have had two children, Charlie L., born June 7, 1864, died Oct. 16, 1873; Frankie S., May 7, 1865.

Weber A. farmer; Sec. 27; P. O. Belvidere.
Weed Mahlon O. farmer; P. O. Belvidere.

WEED W. H. Farmer; Sec. 1; P. O. Belvidere; born in Delaware Co., N. Y., July 18, 1838; lived in that State 16 years, and came to Illinois, to Boone Co., in 1854, and has lived here 23 years; is engaged in Farm and Dairy business; has held office of Road Master; owns farm of 160 acres; Mahlon O. Weed, brother of above, was born in Delaware Co., N. Y., June 29, 1850; came to this Co. in 1854; is attending Industrial School, at Urbana, Ill.; Jas. Weed, father of above, was born in Delaware Co., N. Y., Feb. 6, 1803, and brought his family here in 1854; died June 5, 1869; married Abigail Terry, from Delaware Co., N. Y., in 1837; they had four children, three sons and one daughter.

Welty J. laborer; Sec. 30.
Westfall J. T. farmer; Sec.36; P.O. Belvidere.
Wheeler F. farmer; Sec. 24; P. O. Belvidere.
Wheeler G. G. farmer; P. O. Cherry Valley.

WHIPPLE W. Farmer; Sec. 10; P.O. Belvidere; born in Herkimer Co., N. Y., Feb. 6, 1833; lived in that State 34 years; came to Illinois, Boone Co., in 1867, and has lived here 10 years, engaged in Farm and Dairy business; owns farm of 80 acres, the old Barney Smith place, one of the oldest farms in the Co.; married Elizabeth M. Brown, from England, Nov. 14, 1854; they have two children, Jessie F., born Oct. 2, 1861; Clayton C. W., born Sept. 4, 1871; lost one son, Russell, born Aug. 2, 1855; he died in 1857.

Whitney R. E. farm; Sec. 2; P.O. Belvidere.

WILCOX HENRY A. Farmer; Sec. 16; P. O. Belvidere; born in Chautauqua Co., N. Y., Dec. 24, 1837; lived there 7 years, and came to Boone Co. in 1844, and has lived here 33 years, within three miles of where he now lives; only few improvements here then; runs threshing machine and corn sheller; he has shelled 100 bushels corn in 22 minutes, and 840 bushels in 4½ hours; has held offices of School Director and Overseer of Roads; owns farm of 24 acres; married Susan Oaks, from Maine, Oct. 30, 1861; they have six children, Cora E., Nathalie, Luella, Mary, Jay, Annette.

WILLIAMS JAMES, Farmer; Sec. 2; P. O. Belvidere; born Tioga Co., N. Y., June 23d, 1803; lived in that State 41 years, and came to Illinois, to Boone Co., in 1844, and has lived here 33 years; is engaged in farming; owns farm 150 acres and 90 acres in De Kalb Co.; he married Emma Royce, from Tioga Co., N. Y., June 19, 1838; she was born Dec. 17, 1820.

Williams R., farmer; Sec. 2; P.O. Belvidere.
Wilson J., farmer; Sec. 29.
Witbeck A. O., farm; S. 1; P. O. Belvidere.
Witbeck L. J., farm; S. 10; P. O. Belvidere.
Witter Joseph, farmer; Cherry Valley.
Witter O. P., farmer; S. 34; P. O. Belvidere.

WITTER WILLIAM, Farmer; Sec. 28; P. O. Cherry Valley; born in Orange Co., O., Feb. 21st, 1821; lived in that State 18 years, and lived in Mich. 8 years and came to Ill., Boone Co., fall 1843, and has lived here 34 years; only little improvement here when he came, and not a fence on the prairie; has carted wheat to Chicago and got 25c bushel for hauling; he entered 40 acres of the farm on which he now lives from government; owns 170 acres, and 26 acres timber; has held office School Director; married Julia Ann Shirley, from Ohio, Nov. 18, 1846; they have three children, Joseph C., Ellen, Mary A.

Woodman A., farmer; S. 21; P.O. Belvidere.
Worf A., farmer; Sec. 15; P.O. Belvidere.
Worf John, farmer; Sec. 14; P.O. Belvidere.
Wright J. M., farmer; S. 13; P.O. Belvidere.

ZUBLER DAVID, Farmer; Sec. 21; P.O. Cherry Valley.

Zubler Wm. H., farmer; P.O. Cherry Valley.

LEROY TOWNSHIP.

ANDERSON ANDREW, farmer; P. O. Capron.
Anderson Peter, farmer; P. O. Capron.
Ardery J. farm; Sec.30; P.O. Parks Corners.

BAILEY ABRAM, farmer; Sec. 12; P.O. Sharon.
Bailey J. A. farmer; Sec. 12; P. O. Sharon.
Bailey Oliver, farmer; P. O. Sharon.
Bird John, farmer; P. O. Parks Corners.
Blodgett Alonzo, farmer; P.O. Sharon.
Blodgett A. F. farmer; P. O. Sharon.
Blodgett Frank, farmer; P. O. Sharon.
Blodgett H. J. farmer; P. O. Sharon.
Blodgett J. S. farmer; P. O. Sharon.
Blodgett R. F. farmer; Sec. 22; P.O. Sharon.
Bogardus W. J. farmer; P. O. Capron.
Bowman Benj. farmer; Sec. 28; P. O. Parks Corners.
Bowman Benj., Jr. farm; P.O.Parks Corners.
Bowman Elijah, farm; Sec. 20; P. O. Parks Corners.
Bowman Geo. C. farm; P.O. Parks Corners.
Bowman T. L. farmer; P.O. Parks Corners.
Brooks P. M. farmer; P. O. Parks Corners.
Brown Jas. farmer; P. O. Chemung.
Brown Jos. farmer; P. O. Chemung.
Brown Robt. farmer; P. O. Sharon.
Burch Jacob, farmer; P. O. Parks Corners.
Burch John, farmer; P. O. Parks Corners.
Burch Rev. O. E. minister; P. O. Parks Corners.
Burns Levi, farmer; P. O. Sharon.
Burton Chas. farmer; Sec. 13; P. O. Sharon.

CAMPBELL DAVID, farmer; Sec. 35; P. O. Capron.
Carr Bethel, farmer; Sec. 24; P. O. Sharon.
Carr Chas. farmer; Sec. 24; P. O. Sharon.
Chamberlain Jos. farm; S. 33; P.O. Capron.
Chamberlain Leroy, farmer; P. O. Capron.
Chester John, farmer; P. O. Sharon.
Chester Lawrence, farm; S. 3; P.O. Sharon.
Chester Segar, farmer; Sec. 9; P. O. Sharon.
Chilson J. farmer; Sec. 27; P. O. Capron.
Clark Wilbur.
Conyes Philo, farmer; P. O. Capron.
Cornell D. D.
Coughran W. farmer; Sec. 34; P.O. Capron.
Cramer H. farm; S. 28; P.O. Parks Corners.
Cramer J. farm; S. 28; P. O. Parks Corners.
Cramer Peter, blacksmith; Sec. 20; P. O. Parks Corners.

Croft H. B. farmer; Sec. 9; P. O. Sharon.
Culver H. M. farmer; P. O. Sharon.
Culver Leroy, farmer; P. O. Sharon.

DANIELS DAVID, farmer; Sec. 20; P. O. Parks Corners.
Dean John W. farm; Sec. 35; P. O. Capron.
DeMunn F. farmer; Sec. 27; P. O. Capron.
DeMunn L. farmer; Sec. 27; P. O. Capron.
DeMUNN SILAS, Farmer; Sec. 27; P. O. Capron; born in Alexander, Genesee Co., N. Y., March 4, 1826; came to this Co. in 1866; married Miranda Palmer, Feb.12, 1850; she was born in Batavia, N. Y., Aug. 9, 1828; they have six children: Jennie, Frank, LeVant, Sumner, John and Fred.
Densmore Clark, farm; Sec.23; P.O. Sharon.
Dixon J. H. farmer; Sec. 15; P. O. Sharon.
Dodge A. farmer; Sec. 26; P. O. Capron.
Dorn F. D. farmer; P. O. Sharon.
Downing S. farmer; P. O. Parks Corners.
Dugall T. H. farmer; Sec. 1; P. O. Sharon.
Dullam Geo. farmer; P. O. Parks Corners.
Dullam Jno. farmer; P. O. Parks Corners.
Dullam Thos. farmer; P. O. Parks Corners.
Dullam Wm. farmer; P. O. Parks Corners.
Duryea Millard, farmer; P. O. Capron.

EDWARDS HIRAM.

Ellis Jas. teacher; P. O. Capron.
Ellis Wm. farm; S. 17; P. O. Parks Corners.
Elwanger J. farmer; Sec. 27; P. O. Capron.
Emery H. farmer; Sec. 32; P.O. Capron.
Emery J. B. farm; S.32; P.O. Parks Corners.
Englehart M. farmer; Sec. 13; P.O. Capron.

FARMER FRED, farmer; P. O. Parks Corners.
Frayer Miles, farmer; Sec. 12; P.O. Sharon.
Funnell Geo. farmer; P. O. Sharon.

GILMORE JOHN, farmer; Sec. 33; P.O. Capron.
Goodall R. farm; S. 21; P.O. Parks Corners.
Goodall Thos. farmer; P.O. Parks Corners.
Goodall Wm. farmer; P. O. Parks Corners.
Griffin Henry, farmer; P. O. Capron.
Groesbeck D. farmer; Sec. 9; P. O. Sharon.
Groesbeck E. H. farmer; Sec. 9; P.O. Sharon.
Groesbeck G. farmer; Sec. 9; P. O. Sharon.

HAMMOND H. B. farmer; Sec. 29; P.O. Capron.

HAMMOND HENRY, Farmer; Sec. 19; P. O. Parks Corners; born in England, March 14, 1819; came to this Co. in 1854; first wife was Elizabeth Keating; present wife was Sarah Armstrong; married Aug. 16, 1869; six children, Mary, Lydia, George William, Sarah A. and Joseph.
Hammond S. W, farmer; Sec. 20; P.O. Parks Corners.
Hayden Omer, farmer; Sec. 28; P.O. Capron.
Head J. P. farm; S. 29; P. O. Parks Corners.
Hortier John, farmer; P. O. Sharon.
Hovey Eugene, farm; Sec. 33; P.O. Capron.
Hovey T. R. farmer; Sec. 33; P. O. Capron.
Hunt B. farmer; Sec. 32; P.O. Parks Corners.
Hunt W. farm; Sec. 32; P.O. Parks Corners.
Hutchinson David, farmer; P.O. Capron.
Hyndman R. farmer; Sec. 26; P. O. Capron.

JOHNSON HENRY, farmer; P. O. Capron.

KEEFE B. farmer; Sec. 10; P. O. Sharon.

Keefe Jas. farmer; Sec. 10; P.O. Sharon.
Kenyon J. T. farmer; Sec. 3; P.O. Sharon.
Kenyon W. C. farmer; Sec. 3; P. O. Sharon.
Klumph Ebez. farmer; Sec. 8; P. O. Sharon.
Klumph J. farmer; Sec. 17; P. O. Sharon.
Klumph Jos. farmer; Sec. 17; P. O. Sharon.

LAMBERT D. M. farmer; Sec. 27; P. O. Capron.

Lambert Melvin, farmer; P. O. Capron.
Lambert Morris, farmer; P. O. Capron.
Langdon B. F. farmer; Sec. 13; P.O. Sharon.
Langdon M. F. farmer; Sec. 14; P.O. Sharon.
Landon Jno. farmer; Sec. 4; P. O. Sharon.
Landon Levi, farmer; Sec. 7; P. O. Sharon.
Lawshee W. C. farm; Sec. 14; P. O. Sharon.
Leach C. C. mechanic; P. O. Parks Corners.
Leavett Oscar, farmer; P. O. Sharon.
Lillie Harry, farmer; P.O. Parks Corners.
Lilley Jos. farmer; P. O. Parks Corners.

McCOLLAM WATSON, farmer; Sec. 27; P. O. Capron.

McDonald David, farmer; P.O. Sharon.
Markle B. farmer; P. O. Parks Corners.
Markle J. B. farmer; Sec. 30; P. O. Parks Corners.
Marshall D. farmer; Sec. 25; P. O. Capron.
Marshall Jno. farm; Sec. 36; P.O. Chemung.
Marvin Jno. farmer; P.O. Capron.
Mayberry F. P. farmer; Sec. 7; P. O. Parks Corners.
Mayberry G. W. farmer; Sec. 7; P. O. Parks Corners.
Mayberry H. R. farm; Sec. 7; P. O. Sharon.
Mayberry L. C. farmer; Sec. 7; P. O. Parks Corners.
Mayberry R. farm; S. 7; P.O. Parks Corners.
Maxworther George.
Miles G. N. farmer; P. O. Sharon.
Millard Emer, farmer; Sec. 27; P.O. Capron.
Millard W. farmer; Sec. 35; P.O. Capron.
Morrison John, carpenter; P. O. Capron.

NELSON JAMES, farmer; Sec. 10; P. O. Sharon.
NELSON N. J. Farmer; Sec. 10; P. O. Sharon; born in Norway, June 28, 1844; came to this Co. in 1845; Republican; Lutheran; married Anna Newton, born in Boone Co.; have had five children, Oscar, James, Nellie, Bertha, and have lost one.
Nettleton D. farmer; Sec. 36; P. O. Capron.
Nettleton W. farmer; Sec. 36; P. O. Capron.
Nobles Jno. farmer; P. O. Parks Corners.
Nobles Sam'l, P. O. Parks Corners.

OLESON OLE, farmer; P. O. Capron.

PETERSON H. farmer; P. O. Capron.

Pierce A. farm; Sec. 19; P.O. Parks Corners.
Pierce A. S. farm; S. 19; P.O. Parks Corners.
Pierce E. farm; Sec. 19; P.O. Parks Corners.
Piper E. farmer; P.O. Sharon.
Piper M. farmer; Sec. 17; P. O. Sharon.
Potter G. W. farmer; Sec. 12; P. O. Sharon.
Prindle E. F. farmer; Sec. 15; P. O. Sharon.
Prindle G. W. farmer; P. O. Sharon.

RAYMOND SELVEY, farmer; Sec. 14; P. O. Sharon.

Reaser H. M. post-master; Sec. 20; P. O. Parks Corners.
Reed Jas. farmer; Sec. 36; P. O. Capron.
Rhodawalt H. farmer; Sec. 11; P.O. Sharon.
Rhodawalt J. farmer; Sec. 11; P. O. Sharon.
Rhodawalt S. farmer; Sec. 11; P. O. Sharon.
Robbins M., Farmer; Sec. 20; P. O. Parks Corners.
Robbins T., farm; S. 20; P.O. Parks Corners.

SALESBURY O. A., Farmer; P.O. Sharon.

Schellenger A., farmer; P.O. Parks Corners.
Schums Rob. E.
Shunk Jacob, farmer; Sec. 1; P. O. Sharon.
Shunk John, clk.; Sec. 1; P. O. Sharon.
Sizer Thos., farmer; Sec. 27; P.O. Capron.
Smith Ira, farmer; Sec. 13; P. O. Sharon.
Smith J., farmer; Sec. 34; P. O. Capron.
Smith R. W., farmer; P. O. Capron.
Smith William, farmer; P. O. Capron.

Spooner M. T., farmer; Sec. 13; P.O.Sharon.
Stall Philip, farmer; Sec. 35; P. O. Capron.
Stott John, farmer; Sec. 36; P.O. Chemung.
Swort A. C., farmer; Sec. 3; P. O. Sharon.

TEETER JAMES, Farmer; Sec. 8; P. O. Sharon.
Teeter Smith, farmer; Sec. 8; P. O. Sharon.
Todd S, farmer; Sec. 20; P. O. Parks Corners.
Tongue John, mechanic; P. O. Sharon.
Tripp Thos. J., farmer; P. O. Capron.
Tuttle Loren, farmer; Sec. 34; P. O. Capron.

VANANWERP JOHN, Farmer; P. O. Capron.
Vandyke Cornelius; Sec. 10; P. O. Sharon.
Vandyke Oscar, farm; Sec. 10; P. O. Sharon.
Vanocker J., farmer; Sec. 13; P. O. Sharon.
Vanocker P., farmer; Sec. 13; P. O. Sharon.

WARD C., Farmer; Sec. 28; P. O. Capron.

Warren C., farm; S. 31; P. O. Poplar Grove.
Warren Steven, farmer; P. O. Poplar Grove.
Warren W., farm; S. 31; P.O. Poplar Grove.
Webster D. G., windmill; Sec. 20; P. O. Parks Corners.
Weeks A., farmer; Sec. 12; P. O. Sharon.
Wise Francis, farmer; Sec. 14; P.O. Sharon.
Witter Lewis, farmer; Sec. 34; P.O. Capron.
Witter Sanford, farmer; Sec. 34; P.O.Capron.
Wolcott Byron, farmer; Sec. 11; P.O.Sharon.
Wolcott'C. W., farmer; Sec. 12; P.O.Sharon.
Wolcott E. B., farmer; Sec. 2; P. O. Sharon.
Wolcott Fred, farmer; Sec. 2; P. O. Sharon.
Wright G., farm; S. 19; P.O. Parks Corners.
Wright J., farm; S. 19; P. O. Parks Corners.

YOEMAN CHARLES W. Farmer; Sec. 31; P. O. Parks Corners.
Young Herbert, farmer; P.O. Parks Corners.
Young Oscar, farmer; P. O. Sharon.
Young Prescott, farmer; P.O. Parks Corners.

MANCHESTER TOWNSHIP.

ABELL M. B. farmer; Sec. 34; P. O. Hunter.

ADAMS DAVID, Farmer; Sec. 16; P. O. Hunter; born in N. Y., June 22, 1817; Republican; came to this Co. in 1846; owns 320 acres of land, valued at $10,600; married Mary Mapes, Feb. 1, 1838; she was born in N. Y.; children are: Lorinda, Ezra (who enlisted in the 12th I. V. C., in 1862; was stationed at Napoleonville, where he died through the effects of being sun struck; lost his life in defence of his country); next are: Willis A., Merritt, Elizabeth M., Ira C., George R., Elmer and Clarence.
Adams Merritt, farmer; Sec. 16; P.O.Hunter.
Adams W. farmer; Sec. 22; P. O. Hunter.
Anderson O. farmer; Sec. 15; P. O. Clinton.
Atkinson J. O. farm; Sec. 22; P. O. Hunter.

BALL J. G. farmer; Sec. 29; P. O. Caledonia.
Ball W. T. farmer; Sec. 29; P.O. Caledonia.
Bamlet T. farmer; Sec. 17; P. O. Hunter.
Bason Lewis, farmer; Sec. 4; P. O. Clinton.
Bemis John, farmer; Sec. 18; P. O. Beloit.
Bennett Albert, farmer; Sec. 8; P. O. Beloit.
Bennett Mason, farmer; Sec. 8; P. O. Beloit.
Bennett W. farmer; Sec. 8; P. O. Clinton.
Blake Andrew, farmer; Sec. 7; P.O. Roscoe.
Blake James, farmer; Sec. 8; P. O. Beloit.

Bowles J. C. farmer; Sec. 31; P. O. Roscoe.
Brayton G. farmer; Sec. 22; P. O. Caledonia.

BRAYTON R. C. Farmer; Sec. 32; P. O. Caledonia; born in Canada, Aug. 7, 1805; came to this Co. in 1864; Republican; Baptist; owns 137 acres of land, valued at $6,850; married S. Gorner, Dec. 24; came to Chicago in 1835; to Winnebago Co. in 1836; to Ogle Co. in 1847; to Boone Co. in 1864; children are: George B., Russell B., Stephen B., and eight girls; George enlisted in Co. I, 110th Regt. I. V. I., in 1864; served to the end of the war, and was honorably discharged; Russell enlisted in 74th Regt. I. V. I., in 1862; was in the battle of Stone River, Lookout Mountain, and Kenesaw Mountain; served to the end of the war; Stephen enlisted in 34th Regt. I. V. I., in 1861; served under Col. Kirk about one year; was in the battle of Corinth and Shiloh, where he was taken sick and had to leave the battle field.
Burgerson K. farmer; Sec. 11; P.O. Clinton.
Burgerson T. farmer; Sec. 11; P.O. Clinton.
Bullard B. M. farmer; Sec.31; P. O. Roscoe.
Burlingame J. J. farm; Sec. 27; P.O.Hunter.
Burlingame S. J. farm; Sec. 27; P.O.Hunter.

CAMPBELL J. E. Yankee Notions peddlar; Sec. 34; P. O. Hunter.
Carr Frank, farmer; Sec. 19; P. O. Beloit.
Cass C. B. farmer; Sec. 17; P. O. Beloit.

CASS LUKE, Farmer; Sec. 17; P. O. Beloit, Wis.; born in Vermont, Sept. 11, 1811; came to this Co. in 1863; Independent; Methodist; owns 140 acres land, valued at $6,500; has been Assessor 1 year and Collector 4 years; married Miss Lucy Fisher; children are: Amanda E., Hollis H., Wm. M. Welcom and Henry H.; Mrs. Cass died Sept. 1, 1830; married again Abigail A. Blinn, Aug. 1, 1832; had three children, Chas. B., now living, and two deceased.
Cass W. M. farmer; Sec. 17; P. O. Beloit.
Clement E. W. farmer; Sec. 22; P.O. Hunter.
Clement J. mail carrier; Sec. 22.
Coats E. farmer; Sec. 1; P. O. Sharon.
Cornell J. A. farmer; Sec. 7; P. O. Beloit.
Cosper W. renter; Sec. 8; P. O. Beloit.
Cutler R. farmer; Sec. 8; P. O. Beloit.

DANIELS A. P. farmer; Sec. 17; P. O. Beloit.
Daniels J. P. farmer; Sec. 8; P. O. Beloit.
Dunn S. renter; Sec. 28; P. O. Hunter.
Duxstad K. B. farmer; Sec. 9; P.O. Clinton.

ELLINGSON ELLING, farmer; Sec. 12; P. O. Clinton.
Ellingson J. farmer; Sec. 12; P. O. Clinton.
Elliott Jedediah, farmer; Sec. 28; P. O. Hunter.
Elliott John, farmer; Sec. 28; P. O. Hunter.
Elliott W. S. farmer; Sec. 28; P. O. Hunter.
Ellis B. farmer; Sec. 20; P. O. Hunter.
Ellis G. H. farmer; Sec. 18; P. O. Beloit.
Ellis Newton, farmer; Sec. 19; P. O. Beloit.
Ellis Osro, farmer; Sec. 18; P. O. Beloit.
Ellsworth E. D. farm; S.29; P. O. Caledonia.
Ellsworth J. B. farm; Sec. 29; P. O. Hunter.
ELLSWORTH S. A. Farmer; Sec. 29; P. O. Hunter; born in N. Y., June 1, 1814; came to this Co. in 1845; Republican; owns 190 acres land, valued at $7,600; married M. Steel; she was born in N. Y.; have three children living and one deceased; she died Dec. 28, 1849; buried at Roscoe Cemetery; married again S. J. Sherman, born in Vermont, May 12, 1852; have one son living; John L. enlisted in the 4th Wis. Bat. in 1861; taken sick shortly after; died July 7, 1862, losing his life in defense of his country; G. O. enlisted in Co. K, 95th I. V. I., in 1861; was in the battle of Vicksburg; was wounded and discharged at the close of the war; married J. O. Veel; lives at Rockford.
England R. farmer; Sec. 28; P. O. Hunter.
ERWIN R. A. Teamster; Sec. 32; P. O. Caledonia; born in Boone Co., May 24, 1853; Republican; Methodist; is at present at work in the stone quarry of Mr. Brayton.

FILES W. farmer; Sec. 15; P. O. Hunter.
Fish B. F. farmer; Sec. 10; P. O. Clinton.

GIFFORD E. farmer; Sec. 38; P. O. Hunter.
Gilley Chas.
Goldthwait A. farmer; Sec. 20; P. O. Beloit.
Graham H. farmer; Sec. 11; P. O. Clinton.
Grant R. F. farmer; Sec. 11; P. O. Clinton.
Grant T. W. farmer; Sec. 31; P. O. Clinton.
Gray R. G. farmer; Sec. 20; P. O. Beloit.
Griffis A. farmer; Sec. 29; P. O. Roscoe.
Griffis O. farmer; Sec. 29; P. O. Roscoe.

HANSAS ROBERT, farmer; P. O. Caledonia.
Hazzlewood E. farmer; Sec. 23; P. O. Parks Corners.
Hazzlewood J. farmer; Sec. 23; P. O. Union Corners.
Hazzlewood J. farmer; Sec.23; P.O. Hunter.
Hazzlewood R. P. O. Union Corners.
Howard F. farmer; Sec. 22; P. O. Caledonia.
Howard R. farmer; Sec. 22; P. O. Hunter.
Hill Chas. farmer; Sec. 6; P. O. Beloit.
Hill Horace, farmer; Sec. 7; P. O. Beloit.
Hill Melvin, farmer; Sec. 7; P. O. Beloit.
Hill Nelson, farmer; Sec. 6; P. O. Beloit.
Hinkley M. E. farmer; Sec. 7; P. O. Beloit.
Horner Frank, farmer; Sec. 21.

ISAACSON CLAUS, farmer; Sec. 4; P. O. Clinton.
Isaacson O. farmer; Sec. 10; P. O. Union.
Iverson Nels, farmer; Sec. 10; P.O. Clinton.
Iverson Stark, farm; Sec. 10; P.O. Clinton.

JOHNSON JOHN, farmer; Sec. 35; P. O. Parks Corners.
Johnson O. H. farmer; Sec.28; P. O. Poplar Grove.
Johnson Sever; farm; Sec. 15; P. O. Hunter.
Jones L. M. farm; S.34; P. O. Poplar Grove.

LARSON BAR, farmer; Sec. 14; P. O. Clinton.
Larson Hans, farmer; P. O. Clinton.
Larsen Henry, farm; S. 30; P. O. Caledonia.
Lee A. O. farmer; Sec. 10; P. O. Clinton.
Lee L. O. farmer; Sec. 10; P. O. Clinton.
Lee Ole, farmer; Sec. 10; P. O. Clinton.
Linderman Bennett,farm; S.16; P.O.Clinton.
Linderman B. F. farm; Sec. 16; P.O.Clinton.
Linderman C. A. farm; Sec. 8; P.O. Beloit.
Linderman J. F. farm; Sec.16; P.O. Clinton.

MANCHESTER TOWNSHIP. 407

Linderman J. W. farm; Sec.16; P.O.Clinton.

LINDERMAN L. D. Farmer; Sec. 16; P. O. Clinton, Wis.; born in N. Y., March 15, 1813; came to this Co. in 1838; Republican; Methodist; owns 160 acres land, valued at $8,000; married Sarah A. Olmstead, Oct. 3, 1833; she was born in Conn., Aug., 1809; children are: Ralph B., born March 3, 1835 (married); Louisa Casber, John W. and James L., born Jan. 29, 1841; Mary E., May 8, 1837 (all married).

Little C. farm; Sec. 36; P. O. Poplar Grove.
Little E. B. farm; Sec.36; P.O. Poplar Grove.

LIVINGSTON ARTHUR, Farmer and Carpenter; Sec. 27; P. O. Hunter; born in N. Y., Feb. 10, 1832; came to this Co. in 1853; Republican; owns 21 acres land, valued at $1,050; married M. Gibbs, May 8, 1856; she was born in N. Y.; children are: Elmer L., born Feb. 3, 1857; Marvin E., in 1859; Jane, 1860; James, 1862; Julia M., 1866; William, 1868; Frank, 1870; Lorenz, 1875.

Livingston A. H. farm; Sec.35; P.O. Hunter.
Livingston J. H. farm; Sec. 34; H.O.Hunter.
Lovesee H. farmer; Sec. 30.
Luce Israel, farmer; Sec.18; P.O. Caledonia.
Lufkin G. W. farmer; Sec. 18; P. O. Roscoe.
Lufkin Sidney; farm; Sec. 20; P. O. Beloit.

McGEACHY JAS. farmer; Sec. 34; P.O. Hunter.

McLean Angus, farm; Sec.21; P.O. Hunter.
McMillan Dan'l, farm; Sec.34; P.O. Hunter.

MANLEY A. H. Farmer; Sec.7; P.O. Beloit; born in Vt., Feb. 6, 1826; came to this Co. in 1849; Independent; Free Church; owns 85 acres land, valued at $5,100; has been Supervisor, School Trustee and Town Clerk for several years; married Jane E. Brookins, Feb. 28, 1848; she was born in N. Y.; children are Adelmorn B. and Jessie M.

Manley M. C. farmer; Sec. 8; P. O. Beloit.
Mason Chris. farmer; Sec. 8; P. O. Beloit.
Mason John, farmer; Sec. 8; P.O. Beloit.
Merchant S. B. farmer; Sec 31; P.O. Roscoe.
Morgan H. S. farmer; Sec. 18; P. O. Beloit.
Morgan H. farm; Sec.36; P.O. Poplar Grove.
Munson Thos. farmer; Sec. 15; P. O. Clinton.

NASH S. L. farmer; Sec. 22; P. O. Hunter.

NASH CHAS. A. Farmer and Postmaster; Sec. 22; P. O. Hunter; born in N. Y., March 14, 1837; came to this Co. in 1869; Republican; owns 80 acres land, valued at $4,000; has been Town Clerk for five years; married M. J. Wright, Jan. 3, 1867; children are: Anna M., born Sept. 30, 1867; Sidney L., March 16, 1869, and Minnie A., March 11, 1867; S. L. Nash,

his father, also his mother, are living with him on the place.

Nomtand O. T. farm; Sec. 10; P. O. Clinton.
North Wm. E. farmer; Sec.28; P.O. Hunter.

OLESON HOLVER, farmer; Sec. 24; P. O. Parks Corners.

PALSON HOGAN, farmer; Sec. 12; P.O. Clinton.

Parker B. L. farm; S.35; P.O. Poplar Grove.
Parker Edw. farm; Sec. 35; P.O. Caledonia.
Partch D. L., Sec. 35.
Patrick Daniel, farmer; Sec. 26.
Patrick R. R. farmer; Sec. 35; P.O. Hunter.
Patterson Arch. farm; Sec. 27; P.O. Hunter.

PETERS WM. Farmer and Mason; P.O. Beloit, Wis.; born in England, April 16, 1834; came to this Co. in 1870; Independent; owns 120 acres land, valued at $5,000; Mr. P. was employed by the government during the war; married Eliza Daniels, Feb. 21, 1857; she was born in N. H., Nov. 12, 1830; children are: Estella C., born Dec. 1, 1858; Arthur B., Dec. 6, 1860; William J., Nov. 26, ——; B. F., Aug. 10, 1866; Mary E., Nov. 19, 1868; Lucy A. and Lucy E., June 1, 1871; Ebbie C., Jan. 9, 1875, (died Jan. 10, 1877).

Peterson P. C. farmer; Sec.21; P.O. Clinton.

RALSTON PETER, farmer; Sec. 38; P. O. Caledonia.

Rainols P. M., Sec. 31.
Ralston T. farmer; Sec. 33; P. O. Caledonia.
Ramsey N. farm; S. 24; P. O. Poplar Grove.
Rathbone Chas. A. farm; Sec. 6; P.O.Beloit.
Reeser Joseph, farmer; Sec. 8; P. O. Beloit.

ROBARDEZ C. J., Carpenter; P.O. Hunter; born in France, July 15, 1842; came to this Co. in 1876; Republican; has made a trip across the plains; lives with Mr. N. H. North.

Rounds Thos. farmer; Sec. 20; P. O. Hunter.

SAMPSON LEWIS, farmer; P. O. Hunter.

Schellenger Ansel, farm; Sec. 24; P.O.Parks Corners.
Scofstad O. J. farmer; Sec. 1; P. O. Clinton.
Seaver Wm. farmer; Sec.3; P.O.Clinton,Wis.
Seaverson S. farmer; Sec. 26; P. O. Hunter.
Sehring J.V. farmer; Sec.35; P.O.Caledonia.
Secoy Elisha, farmer; Sec.34; P.O.Caledonia.
Secoy Simon, farmer; Sec.34; P.O.Caledonia.
Severt Lewis, farmer; Sec. 2; P. O. Clinton.
Smith H. H. farmer; Sec. 32.
Smith Patrick, farm; Sec. 31; P.O.Caledonia.
Snow N. E. farmer; Sec. 20; P.O.Caledonia.
Stevenson Knudt. farmer; Sec. 13; P.O.Parks Corners.

STOLL RUDOLF, Farmer; Sec. 8; P.O. Beloit, Wis.; born in Switzerland in Aug., 1836; came to Co. in 1857; Republican; enlisted in Co. K, 2d Wis. V. I. in 1861; was in the battles of second Bulls Run, South Mt., Gettysburg, Wilderness, Spottsylvania, Chancellorsville, Weldon Railroad, Gainsville, Antietam, Cedar Mountain, and about six more; served as Sergeant to the close of the war, and was honorably discharged; married Christina Zilley, June 7, 1868; she was born in Prussia; children are William, Harry, Edward, Fred and Alice.

Stowell C. M. farmer; Sec.20; P.O.Caledonia.

THOMPSON LEWIS, farmer; P. O. Clinton.

Thompson Ole, farmer; Sec. 3; P.O.Clinton.
Thornton W.H. farmer; Sec. 28; P.O.Hunter.
Tiffany D. N. farmer; Sec. 19; P. O. Beloit.
Tiffany D. W. farmer; Sec. 19; P. O. Beloit.
Tillerson Lewis, farmer; Sec.23; P.O.Hunter.
Tillerson O. R. farmer; Sec. 23; P.O.Hunter.
Tisdal N. blacksmith; Sec. 7; P. O. Beloit.
Tolefson T. farmer; Sec. 4; P.O.Clinton,Wis.
Tongen Ole, farmer; Sec. 14; P. O. Clinton.
Tongen O. O. farmer; Sec. 14; P. O. Hunter.

Turner R. M. mason; Sec. 10; P. O. Hunter.

UTTON W. S. farmer; Sec. 20; P. O. Hunter.

Utton Wm. farmer; Sec. 20; P. O. Beloit.

VANANTWERP G. H. farmer; Sec. 36; P. O. Poplar Grove.

WADDELL WALTER, farmer; Parks Corners.

Wadsworth J. farmer; Sec. 20; P.O. Hunter.
Ward A. farm; Sec. 35; P.O. Parks Corners.
Watts C. E. farmer; Sec. 30; P. O. Roscoe.
Ward C. farmer; Sec. 25; P.O.Poplar Grove.
Watts G. W. farmer; Sec. 30; P.O. Caledonia.
Watts I. N. farmer; Sec. 35; P. O. Hunter.
Weller W. B. farmer; Sec. 35; P. O. Poplar Grove.
Witter A. D. farmer; Sec. 12; P. O. Clinton.
Witter L. farmer; Sec. 12; P. O. Clinton.
Wright A. farmer; P. O. Poplar Grove.
Wright J. C. farmer; Sec. 36; Poplar Grove.
Wyman Samuel, farm; Sec. 33; P.O. Hunter.

YOUNG O. C. Farmer; Sec. 21; P. O. Hunter.

SPRING TOWNSHIP.

ABBOTT HORATIO, farmer; Sec. 14; P. O. Garden Prairie.

Abbott J. farmer; Sec. 14; P. O. Belvidere.
Abbott P. T. farm; S.14; P.O. Garden Prairie.
Abbott W. farm; S. 4; P. O. Garden Prairie.
Albright George D. farmer; P. O. Belvidere.

ALBRIGHT N. J. C. Farmer; Sec. 5; P. O. Belvidere; born in Vermont, June 24, 1834; came to this Co. in 1845; owns 105 acres land, valued at $6,000; married Miss Adeliza Jayne in Belvidere, in 1858; she was born in Ohio, Aug. 30, 1838; have five children, Emma Eliza, Delos G., Zermira A., Cora Belle, Gertrude Maude.

Alderman L. B. laborer; S.25; P.O.Belvidere.

ASHCRAFT J. C. Farmer; Sec. 16; P. O. Belvidere; born in Penn., Jan. 24, 1852; came to this Co. in 1869; Republican.

ATKINSON JAMES, Farmer; Sec. 23; P. O. Belvidere; born in England, Feb. 19, 1803; came to this Co. in 1849; owns 40 acres land; has been Justice of the Peace seventeen years; Commissioner Highways six years; married Margaret McLatchie, in Canada, Jan. 20, 1829; she was born in Canada, Oct. 21, 1807; have had eleven children, the names of those living are: Sarah Ann (now Mrs. Curtis), John, James E., Maria (now Mrs. J. Thomas); Eli enlisted in army in 1861, died in the service, Aug. 17, 1862; Robert enlisted in 9th I. V. C.; was honorably discharged Oct., 1865; Mary E. (now Mrs. Landers, born Sept. 30, 1848; married Dec. 31, 1874; has one child, Francis H., born Dec. 30, 1875.

BARKER EDMOND H. Farmer; Sec. 12; P. O. Garden Prairie.

Barker Edward H. farmer; Sec. 12; P.O. Garden Prairie.

Barr James, farmer; P. O. Belvidere.

BARRINGER LAWRENCE, Farmer; Sec. 17; P. O. Belvidere; born in Germany, Aug. 10, 1825; came to this Co. in 1857; owns 44 acres land; is Commissioner Highways; married Miss Theresa Keeler, in N. Y., on Nov. 4, 1854; she was born in Germany, Jan. 20, 1832; have six children, Edward, born Sept. 5, 1856;

SPRING TOWNSHIP 409

John, July 17, 1858; Helen Jane, Sept. 29, 1860; Caroline, April 7, 1865; Walter, July 10, 1868; Minnie, June 27, 1870.

BAXTER JOHN, Farmer; Sec. 10; P. O. Belvidere; born in England, June 28, 1807; came to this Co. in 1846; owns 240 acres land; married Miss H. Smithson, in Montreal, Canada, July 23, 1832; she was born in England, July 27, 1815; have had twelve children, Jonas, born Sept. 30, 1834; Elizabeth, Jan. 11, 1837, died Feb. 20, 1844; Mary Ann, May, 1839; Emeline, July 1, 1841; William, May 30, 1843; John D., Oct. 19, 1845; Elizabeth, March 1, 1848; Thomas J., Dec. 21, 1849; Harriet T., May 3, 1852; Charles W., March 23, 1854, died Oct. 20, 1867; Albert F., Dec. 10, 1855; Rosanna, June 2, 1861.

Beckington Henry, farmer; Sec. 1; P. O. Garden Prairie.

Beckington M. farmer; P.O.Garden Prairie.

Beckington T. farm; S.1; P.O.Garden Prairie.

BISHOP D. W. C. Carpenter and Joiner; Sec. 16; P. O. Belvidere; born in New York, March 2, 1818; came to this Co. in 1851; owns 57 acres land; married Miss L. Crittenden, in this Co., July 3, 1852; she was born in Ohio, Nov. 16, 1836; have ten children living.

BLACKFORD FRANCIS, Farmer; Sec. 3; P. O. Belvidere; born in England, July 20, 1819; came to this Co. in 1833; owns 142 acres land, valued at $7,000; has held the office of School Director; married Miss Jane Atkinson, in this Co., Nov. 29, 1853; she was born in Canada, May 1, 1833; have had eight children, Francis, born Oct. 22, 1856; William Ross, Nov. 2, 1858; Maggie, Oct. 30, 1860; Eli Robert, April 19, 1863; Jane, Jan. 2, 1867, died Jan. 13, 1867; Steven Daniel, Jan. 13, 1868; Harvey James, July 21, 1870; Albert, March 16, 1873.

BLACKFORD JAMES, Farmer; Sec. 3; P. O. Belvidere; born in England, Aug. 30, 1815; came to this Co. in 1833; owns 140 acres land; is School Director; first wife was Miss Abbott; present wife was Louisa Morey; they were married in this Co., Dec. 30, 1859; she was born in England, Nov. 4, 1840; have eight children, Eva, born Nov. 9, 1860; Emma, Aug. 19, 1862; Carrie, Feb. 2, 1865; James, March 5, 1867; Jennie, April 4, 1869; May, Feb. 4, 1871; Fredrick, Oct. 21, 1872; Leon, Nov. 27, 1873.

Blackford S. farmer; Sec. 3; P. O. Belvidere.

Blakesley F. S. farmer; P. O. Belvidere.

Borroughs C. farm; S. 34; P. O. Belvidere.

Bowers E. S. farm; Sec. 17; P. O. Belvidere.

Brainard Eli, farmer; P. O. Belvidere; 3.

Brooks Benj. farmer; S. 23; P. O. Belvidere.

Brooks J. farmer; Sec. 34; P. O. **Belvidere.**

Brooks P. E. farm; Sec. 23; P. O. Belvidere.

Burnett M. A. farm; S. 15; P. O. Belvidere.

Burroughs Jno. farm; S. 24; P. O. Belvidere.

CATES GEORGE H. Farmer; Sec. 12; P. O. Belvidere.

CATES GEORGE S. Farmer; Sec. 3; P. O. Belvidere; born in Salem, Mass., Nov. 2, 1816; came to this Co. in 1845; owns 214 acres land; married Miss Marilla Heaton, in this Co., March 5, 1853; she was born in New York, Aug. 16, 1821; have had two children, George H., born Oct. 18, 1855; James S., June 3, 1858, died March 24, 1860; Mr. Cates has been Justice of the Peace eight years.

CHAFEE GEORGE, Farmer; Sec. 6; P.O. Belvidere; born in N.Y.,Aug.16, 1811; owns 170 acres land, valued at $8,500; has been Supervisor six years; married Miss Anita Smith, in Belvidere, in 1857; have one child, Lillie; Mrs. Chafee was born in Madison Co., N. Y.

Chamberlain M. farm; S. 5; P. O. Belvidere.

CHAMBERLIN MRS. SARAH, Farming; P. O. Belvidere; Sec. 5; born in Conn., Jan. 22, 1818; Baptist; owns 690 acres land, valued $35,000; husband was Wm. H. Chamberlin; they were married in Conn., March 23, 1843; he was born in Mass., April 16, 1818; died in this Co., Sept. 29, 1873; they have had eleven children, six of them are living, Charles H., born March 17, 1849; William M., June 8, 1851; Mary E. (now Mrs. Kirk), Dec. 19, 1853; Sarah Belle, May 15, 1856; Kate Louisa, April 30, 1859; Jennie V., May 8, 1861.

COOPER JOHN, Farmer; Sec. 35; P. O. Genoa; born in Middlesex Co., N. J., March 3, 1839; came to this Co. in 1860; owns 120 acres land.

Cohoon Wilford, farmer; P. O. Belvidere.

Colvin H. farmer; Sec. 35; P. O. Belvidere.

COLVIN JEFFERSON, Farmer; Sec. 35; P. O. Belvidere; born in Erie Co., N. Y., Jan. 22, 1832; came to this Co. in 1875; owns 135 acres land, valued at $8,750; married Mrs. Parks, in N. Y., March 30, 1876; she died Nov. 3, 1876.

CURTIS CHARLES, Farmer; Sec. 11; P. O. Belvidere; born in England, Aug. 30, 1814; came to this Co. in 1836; owns 460 acres land; married Miss Mary Ann Mounsey, Feb. 22, 1841; she was born in Canada, Jan 1, 1824; have had eleven children, George Fredrick, born April 10, 1842; Lucy Louisa, March 24, 1844, died July 12, 1863; Horatio Nelson, Aug. 26, 1846; Winfield S., April 5, 1849; Franklin Albert, Aug. 16, 1851; Emma Jane, Dec. 18, 1853; Walter Chas., March 7, 1856; Clara Melissa, Aug. 9, 1858; Jessie Elizabeth, Sept. 3, 1861;

Alice Mary, March 8, 1864; William Henry, Jan. 28, 1867.

CURTIS HENRY, Farmer; Sec. 10; P. O. Belvidere; born in England, March 30, 1813; came to this Co. in 1836; owns 160 acres land; married Mrs. Mounsey (maiden name, Miss Atkinson), in Canada, April, 1855; she was born in England, July 26, 1804; have five children, William H. H., born Aug 26, 1840; Thomas, June 6, 1843; George, Nov. 26, 1845; Elizabeth (now Mrs. Williams) March 11, 1858; Mrs. Curtis' children by first husband are, Mary Ann Mounsey (now Mrs. Chas. Curtis), born Jan. 1, 1824; Maggie S. (now Mrs. Stevens), May 1, 1829; Rebecca C. (now Mrs. Kough) Oct. 27, 1831.

Curtis Patrick, rents farm; Sec. 1; P. O. Garden Prairie.

Curtis S. farmer; Sec. 11; P. O. Belvidere.

Curtis Walter, farmer; P. O. Belvidere.

DAVIS JOEL, Jr., farmer; Sec. 27; P. O. Belvidere.

DAVIS JOEL, Sr., Farmer; Sec. 28; P. O. Belvidere; born in England, June 16, 1798; came to this Co. in 1850; owns 132 acres land; has been School Director three terms; married Eleanor Howell, in England, July 19, 1827; she was born in England, June 2, 1802; have four children living.

Davis S. farmer; Sec. 28; P. O. Belvidere.

DeWane J. farmer; Sec. 29; P. O. Belvidere.

DeWOLF MIRON, Farmer; Sec. 15; P. O. Belvidere; born in Pa., Nov. 26, 1820; came to this Co. in 1847; owns 87 acres of land; married Matilda Taylor, in Pa.; she was born in Pa., Jan. 31, 1828; have four children living, Collins A., born Jan. 26, 1857; Adell, Dec. 23, 1859; Eleanor, Oct. 4, 1854; Mahala, Aug. 1, 1867

DeWOLF W. C. Farmer; Sec. 14; P. O. Belvidere; born in Erie Co., Pa., Feb. 8, 1830; came to this Co. in 1854; owns 120 acres land; has held various offices; is at present Town Trustee; married Huldah J. Strong, in Erie Co., Pa., March 22, 1854; she was born in Erie Co., Pa., Feb. 16, 1832; have had five children, Nancy E. (now Mrs. E. L. Woodruff) born Dec. 25, 1855; Hiram S., Oct. 10, 1858 died May 27, 1876; Frank L., born April 23, 1862; William C., Jr., Nov. 4, 1865; Nettie A., Aug. 19, 1868.

DUNHAM MRS. N. M. Sec. 15; P. O. Belvidere; born in Madison Co., N. Y., March 4, 1816; came to this Co. in 1869; husband was Daniel H. Dunham; he was born in Madison Co., N. Y., Oct. 26, 1812; he died in this Co., May 26, 1874; have two children, DeLeon, born Dec. 23, 1850; Edward K., Aug. 22, 1858.

Dunham R. farm; S.24; P.O.Garden Prairie.

FORD FRANK, farmer; Sec. 29; P. O. Belvidere.

FOORD JOHN, Farmer; Sec. 29; P. O. Belvidere; born in Maine, Dec. 21, 1810; came to this Co. in 1853; owns 210 acres land; first wife was Hannah G. Martin; four children by this first marriage; present wife was Mrs. Gould; have three children by present wife.

GIBBS MR. farmer; Sec. 32; P. O. Belvidere.

GLEASON E. L. Farmer; Sec. 21; P. O. Belvidere; born in Franklin Co., Mass., April 7, 1806; came to this Co. in 1840; owns 225 acres land; married Miss P. A. Spink, in N. Y., June 2, 1835; she was born in Vermont, April 5, 1815; have six children, Leonard E., born Sept. 15, 1836 (he married Miss Julia M. Crittenden, in Iowa, Jan. 7, 1876; she was born in this Co., Sept. 29, 1847); Adeliza J. (now Mrs. Albright), Aug. 31, 1838; Mary E. (now Mrs. Gibbs), May 6, 1840; Amos H., May 2, 1846; Eila, born Dec. 16, 1847; Zerneria, Oct. 31, 1851.

Gooch T. farm; Sec.13; P. O. Garden Prairie.

Gooch T.W. farm; S.13; P.O.Garden Prairie.

GOULD J. B. Farmer; Sec. 5; P. O. Belvidere; born in Warren Co., N. Y., May 26, 1820; came to this Co. in 1837; Republican; Episcopal; owns 404 acres land, valued at $35 per acre; married Miss Charlotte Blackford, in this Co. in 1845; she was born in England, Jan. 10, 1824; have had ten children, Harvey A., Oct. 8, 1847; Nellie B., Nov. 11, 1850; Alice J., June 1, 1852; Fannie F., Oct. 14, 1853; Ira J., Nov. 1, 1851, died Feb. 22, 1854; Alfred, Sept. 12, 1849, died, aged eleven months; Alice, Aug. 8, 1846, died, aged two months; Frank, July, 1847, died, aged two years; Lucius, Feb. 21, 1863; Blanche C., April 16, 1868.

GRETTON SAMSON, Farmer; Sec. 4; P. O. Belvidere; born in N. J., Sept. 19, 1844; came to this Co. in 1850; Republican; Episcopal; owns 142 acres land, valued at $7,000; married Miss Sarah Lawman, in Belvidere, in 1869; she was born in England, Dec. 30, 1850; have two children, Alice, May 22, 1871; Wallace, May 3, 1875.

HAKES HARRISON H. Farmer and Stock Raiser; P. O. Belvidere; owns farm 185 acres; born Cattarangus Co., N. Y., April 2, 1841; lived there 13 years; went to Wis. 1854; came to this Co. and settled in Spring Tp. in 1857, and has lived there 20 years; was in army 4 years in Co. B. 8th Ills. Cav.; married Miss Ann Davis, Jan. 16, 1866; she was born in England, Aug. 15, 1837; have three children, Ella L. born July 11, 1866, Mary L. born Aug., 1872, George H. born Oct., 1874.

Hammond F. A. farmer; P. O. Belvidere.
Hammond J. M. farm; S.20; P. O. Belvidere.
Hannah R. farm; S. 11; P.O. Garden Prairie.
Hansaw T. farmer; Sec. 31; P. O. Belvidere.

HEWER JOSEPH, Farmer and Stock Raiser; Sec. 35; P. O. Belvidere; born in England, Aug. 14, 1843; came to this Co. in 1867; owns 280 acres land, valued at $11,500; married Miss Martha Pinegar, in 1868; she was born in England, have two children; Wm. Francis, born Nov. 8, 1870; Gracie, Jan. 1, 1869; Mr. Hewer is Importer of Berkshire swine.

Hewitt James, farmer; P. O. Belvidere.
Hollembeak F. farm; Sec.21; P.O.Belvidere.
Hollembeak G. farm; Sec.21; P.O.Belvidere.

HOLLEMBEAK WM. L. Farmer; Sec. 21; P. O. Belvidere; born in Stafford Co., N. Y., June 7, 1823; came to this Co. in 1844; owns 120 acres land; has been Town Collector two terms; Commissioner Highways three years; Town Trustee three years; married Myra Shattuck, in this Co., Feb. 7, 1850; she was born in Ohio, Sept. 13, 1829; have three children, George, born in this Co., Dec. 5, 1850; Frank, Nov. 23, 1852; Abraham, March 9, 1855.

Horton Thomas D. farmer; P. O. Belvidere.
Hull P. A. laborer; Sec. 6; P. O. Belvidere.

HUGHES H. C. Farmer; Sec. 15; P. O. Belvidere; born in Wales, March 4, 1825; came to this Co. in 1839; owns 120 acres land; married Sarah A. Britt, in this Co., in 1864; she was born in Ohio, Jan. 28, 1841; have three children, Ernest Henry, born Sept. 11, 1865; William H., April 11, 1869; Silas L., March 1, 1874.

HUGHES LEWIS, Farmer; Sec. 16; P. O. Belvidere; born in Wales, April 23, 1821; came to this Co. in 1839; owns 100 acres land; married Mrs. Murrin, in this Co., April, 1872; have two children, Edward, Jan. 16, 1873; William H., April 11, 1877.

ISLES RICHARD, rents farm; Sec. 23; P. O. Belvidere.

JOHNSON ALFRED, farmer; P. O. Belvidere.
Johnson Joseph W. farmer; P. O. Belvidere.

JOHNSON THEODORE, Farmer; Sec. 5; P. O. Kingston; born Schleswig, Holstein, Germany, Aug. 24, 1843; came to this country 1867; has followed sailing for some years, on the lakes, on the ocean and on the coast; came to Boone Co. in February, 1875, and is engaged in Farming; he married Miss Nona Johnson,Nov., 1874; she was born in Prussia; he owns Farm of 42 acres.

KAHOY THOMAS, Farmer; Sec. 22; P. O. Belvidere; born in Ireland, in 1831; came to this Co. in 1867; owns property valued at $1,200; married in 1858; have six children, five boys and one girl.

Kelley J. farmer; Sec. 22; P. O. Belvidere.
Kelley L. farmer; Sec. 22; P. O. Belvidere.
Kimmey R. farmer; Sec. 29; P. O. Belvidere.

KING WILLIAM B. Farmer; Sec. 23; P. O. Belvidere; born in England, May 11, 1822; came to this Co. in 1846; owns 120 acres land; married Matilda Huline, in this Co., March 11, 1856; have three children, Mary Ann, born May 15, 1857; Wm. Henry, Oct. 18, 1859; Ellen, Feb. 7, 1862; Emma, Feb. 6, 1868, died Feb. 12, 1869.

LANDER EDWARD P. farmer; Sec. 23; P. O. Belvidere.

LANDER EDWIN, Farmer; Sec. 15; P. O. Belvidere; born in England, April 26, 1815; came to this Co. in 1849; owns 143 acres land; is School Director and Commissioner of Highways; married Mary Skittery, in England, Jan. 5, 1837; she was born in England, Sept. 14, 1812; have four children living, William E., born Oct. 22, 1837; Edward, Feb. 2, 1843; has been Town Collector two terms; Town Clerk and Town Trustee several terms; enlisted in 9th Ill. Cav., Sept. 12, 1861; served three years; was honorably discharged; Eliza, born Jan. 21, 1848; Susan A., Jan. 31, 1852.

Lander W. E. farm; Sec.23; P. O. Belvidere.

LANE T. E. Farmer; Sec. 13; P. O. Garden Prairie; born in Maine, March 10, 1840; came to this Co. in 1846; owns 80 acres land; married Miss Celinda Sergant, in this Co., Oct. 11, 1865; she was born in N. Y., on March 5, 1849; have two children, Charley Leroy and Luther P.

LANNING A. B. Farmer; Sec. 17; P. O. Belvidere; born in N. Y., March 10, 1816; came to this Co. in 1842; owns 42 acres land; has held the office of School Director and Commissioner Highways; married Miss Stroud, in N. Y., on Feb. 6, 1839; she was born in N. J., July 19, 1818; have had two children, Sarah J. (now Mrs. Bowers), born Dec. 14, 1847; Daniel R., July 6, 1849. Erwin S. Bowers, son-in-law of Mr. Lanning, was born in Wisconsin, June 24, 1845; he enlisted in 2d W. V. I., Dec. 28, 1863; served until close of war; was honorably discharged.

Lanning H. farmer; Sec. 7; P.O. Belvidere.

LANNING JOHN S, Farmer; Sec. 7; P. O. Belvidere; born in New York, Aug. 15, 1824; came to this Co. in 1842; Republican; Baptist; owns 91 acres land, value $4,000; married Miss Mary Rich, in Cook Co., Ill., May 29, 1846; she was born in New Jersey, June 2, 1825; have three children living, Henry, born Aug. 6, 1851; Albertie, March 19, 1853; Charley, Sept. 20, 1860.

Lanning J. L. farm; Sec. 4; P. O. Belvidere.
LANNING U. R. Farmer; Sec. 15; P. O. Belvidere; born in Ontario Co., N. Y., Feb. 11, 1818; came to this Co. in 1842; Baptist; owns 80 acres land; married Enretta Lawrence, in this Co., March 13, 1844; she was born in New York, May 18, 1824; have three children, Mary, born Jan. 5, 1845; Noel R., Feb. 19, 1848; J. Lawrence, July 1, 1850.
Lawman Wm. farm; Sec. 9; P. O. Belvidere.
Lobdell F. K. farm; Sec. 22; P.O. Belvidere.
Lobdell J. M. farm; Sec. 22; P.O. Belvidere.
Lobdell W. F. farm; Sec. 22; P.O. Belvidere.
Lord C. B. farmer; Sec. 20; P.O. Belvidere.
Lord O. farmer; Sec. 20; P.O. Belvidere.
Lucas R. farmer; Sec. 21; P.O. Belvidere.

McKEOWN FELIX, farmer; Sec. 24; P. O. Garden Prairie.
MACK WM. M. Farmer; Sec. 7; P.O. Belvidere; born in Canada, May 23, 1822; came to this Co. in 1864; owns 80 acres land; has been School Director and Road Commissioner; married Susana Reed, in Vermont, in 1851; she was born in Canada; have had ten children; eight of them are living.
Martin J. farmer; Sec. 14; P.O. Belvidere.
Martin O. farmer; Sec. 14; P.O. Belvidere.
May J. F. farmer; Sec. 16; P.O. Belvidere.
MAYBURRY J. Farmer; Sec. 28; P. O. Belvidere; born in Pa., April 18, 1830; came to this Co. in 1853; owns 26 acres land; married Miss Desdemona Wells, in Crawford Co., Pa., July 2, 1853; she was born in Pa., Sept. 22, 1833; have seven children, three boys and four girls.
Mawer C. A. farmer; Sec. 11; P. O. Garden Prairie.
Mawer Wm. farmer; Sec. 11; P. O. Garden Prairie.
Merchant H. farmer; Sec. 6; P.O. Belvidere.
Merrill A. farmer; Sec. 7; P.O. Belvidere.
Merrill T. S. farmer; Sec. 7; P.O. Belvidere.
Meyers Geo. farmer; Sec. 32; P.O. Belvidere.
MOORE RICHARD, Farmer; Sec. 31; P. O. Belvidere; born in Pa., May 25, 1826; came to this Co. in 1855; owns 90 acres land; married Miss Maggie Gordon, in this Co., Oct. 25, 1855; she was born in Pa., May 24, 1832; have six children, John A., born Dec. 2, 1856; Lizzie, May 4, 1858; William A., Oct. 30, 1859; George G., April 4, 1862; J. P., Sept. 16, 1869.
Mullen M. farmer; Sec. 22; P. O. Belvidere.
Murphy J. W. farm; Sec. 19; P.O. Belvidere.
Myers Geo. farmer; Sec. 33; P.O. Belvidere.

NEWMAN JNO. A. farmer; Sec. 12; P. O. Garden Prairie.

PAGE ARTHUR, farmer; Sec. 14; P. O. Belvidere.
PAGE THOS. Farmer; Sec. 14; P. O. Garden Prairie; born in England, Dec. 21, 1838; came to this Co. in 1852; owns 320 acres land; married Miss Jane E. Hammond in England, in 1859; she was born in England, April 9, 1830; have had five children, Emily E. (now Mrs. Halleck), born May 12, 1851; Arthur T., Jan. 6, 1853; Franklin J., Oct. 23, 1857; Herbert C. Sept. 22, 1859; Bertha, Sept. 22, 1860, died Aug. 12, 1867.
Parker Thos. farmer; P. O. Belvidere.
PAYN JIRA, Farmer; Sec. 4; P. O. Belvidere; born in N. Y., April 17, 1828; came to this Co. in 1855; Republican; Episcopalian; owns 96 acres land, valued at $5,000; has held the office of Town Assessor for two years; married Miss Elizabeth Arnold in New York, Jan. 2, 1853; she was born in Saratoga, N. Y., Aug. 22, 1832; have had six children, Mary, born Nov. 28, 1853; Delmere, Sept. 18, 1856; Fred, March 16, 1859; Henry, Dec. 30, 1861, died Feb. 20, 1862; Cora, Sept. 16, 1865; Frank, March 27, 1870.
Peirce W. H. farmer; Sec. 14; P. O. Garden Prairie.
Percy Robert, farmer; P. O. Belvidere.
PETERS GEO. Farmer; Sec. 28; P. O. Belvidere; born in England, May 20, 1824; came to this Co. in 1850; owns 200 acres land; married Miss Martha Davis in England, in 1848; she was born in England, Aug. 15, 1827.
Pinegar H. farmer; Sec. 25; P. O. Belvidere.
Pinegar W. farmer; Sec. 26; P.O. Belvidere.
Powers Herbert, farmer; P. O. Belvidere.
Pratt F. K. farmer; Sec. 7; P. O. Belvidere.
PRATT M. K. Farmer; Sec. 7; P. O. Belvidere; born in N. H., Jan. 11, 1813; came to this Co. in 1854; Republican; owns 125 acres land, valued at $6,250; married Miss Louisa Dagget, in N. H., in 1841; she was born in N. H., Dec. 10, 1812; have two children, Frederick K., born May 25, 1843; Eliza D. (adopted), Nov. 8, 1855.

RANDOLPH E. K. F. farmer; Sec. 26; P. O. Genoa.
Ransley G., Sr. farm; Sec. 9; P.O. Belvidere.
Reed Chas. farmer; Sec. 17; P. O. Belvidere.
Reed Frank P. farmer; P. O. Belvidere.
Reed Fred. farmer; Sec. 35; P. O. Belvidere.
REED GEO. Farmer; Sec. 35, P. O. Belvidere; born in Westfield, Mass., May 26, 1824; came to this Co. in 1848; owns 515 acres land, valued at $20,600; has been Supervisor three years; married Miss Eliza A. Wait, Oct. 10, 1849; she was born in Warsaw, N. Y., Aug. 23, 1828; have had four children, Fannie E., born

SPRING TOWNSHIP. 413

Sept. 6, 1850; Franklin P., Nov. 9, 1852; Frederick A., Jan. 8, 1855; Albert E., July 9, 1857, died May 9, 1863.

Rix Chester, farmer; Sec. 19; P.O. Belvidere.

Roberts A. L. wagon-maker; Sec. 33; P. O. Kingston.

Robinson J. farmer; Sec. 10; P.O. Belvidere.

ROGERS JOHN, Jr., Farmer; Sec. 19; P. O. Belvidere; born in England, May 26, 1839; came to this Co. in 1848; owns property to value of $5,000; married Miss Carrie Peniger, in Belvidere, Oct. 18, ——; she was born in England, in 1847.

Rogers J., Sr., farm; S. 20; P. O. Belvidere.

Rogers Thos. farm; Sec. 19; P. O. Belvidere.

Rowen G. C. farmer; Sec. 36; P. O. Genoa.

S ANDALL I. C. farmer, Sec. 30; P. O. Belvidere.

Sawyer S. H. B. farm; S. 7; P. O. Belvidere.

SCRIVEN JAMES, Farmer; Sec. 30; P. O. Belvidere; born in England, July 10, 1824; came to this Co. in 1848; owns 97 acres land; married Miss Elizabeth Scriven in England, April 12, 1854; have children.

Shattuck A. farmer; Sec.17; P.O. Belvidere.

SHATTUCK F. H., Farmer; Sec.32; P. O. Belvidere; born in Ohio, June 22, 1823; came to this Co. in 1836; owns 160 acres land; has held the office of Township Collector one term; Township Treasurer two years; married Miss Harriet Britt, in this Co., Aug. 30, 1847; she was born in Ohio, Nov. 6, 1827; they have five children, two girls and three boys.

Shattuck G. E. farm; Sec.17; P.O. Belvidere.

SHATTUCK HARLYN, Farmer; Sec. 22; P. O. Belvidere; born in Madison Co., N. Y., March 3, 1815; came to this Co. in 1845; owns 200 acres land; has held several different offices; is now Township Assessor; first wife was Miss Ruth E. Murray; they were married March 31, 1842; she was born in Ohio, Dec. 26, 1818; died July 19, 1864; had ten children, five of whom are living; present wife was Mrs. Hall, (maiden name was Lucretia Orton); they were married on July 29, 1865; she was born in N. Y., Dec. 21, 1830; have had four children by this marriage, three of whom are living.

SHATTUCK LOOMIS, Farmer; P. O. Belvidere; born in N. Y., Jan. 6, 1803; came to this Co. in 1839; owns 200 acres land; has held various town offices; wife was Lydia Brown; have five children living.

Shattuck L., Jr. farm; S. 16; P.O. Belvidere.

Shattuck M. farm; Sec. 17; P. O. Belvidere.

Shattuck Wm. L. farmer; P. O. Belvidere.

Shepardson A C.farm; S. 17; P.O. Belvidere.

Shepardson E.carpntr.; S.17; P.O.Belvidere.

Sherburne J. H. rents farm; Sec. 10; P. O. Belvidere.

Sellard Jas., Sr. farm; Sec. 5; P.O. Belvidere.

Sellard Jas., Jr. farm; Sec. 5; P.O. Belvidere.

Silvius S. I. farmer, Sec. 31; P. O. Belvidere.

Simpkins G.farm; S.11; P.O.Garden Prairie.

Simpkins Geo. W. farmer; Sec. 11; P. O. Garden Prairie.

Smith G.W. rents farm; S.32; P.O. Belvidere.

SMITH MASON, Farmer; Sec. 4; P. O. Belvidere; born in N. Y., Nov. 2, 1806; came to this Co. in 1848; Republican; Presbyterian; owns 196 acres land, valued at $10,000; has been Justice of the Peace eight years; married Miss Philomela Bartlett, Jan 31, 1854; she was born in N. Y., July 11, 1819; have four children; Caroline, born Dec. 7, 1854; Jessie Fremont, Aug. 24, 1856; Elmer Mason, Feb. 18, 1859; Lucy Theodosia, April. 23, 1861.

SMITHSON BENJAMIN, Farmer; Sec. 10; P.O. Belvidere; born in England, June 8, 1826; came to this Co. in 1858; owns 80 acres land; has been School Director; married Miss Jane Blackford, in this Co., April 4, 1848; she was born in England, in 1826; came to this Co. 1853.

Stanley Dyer, farm; Sec. 25; P.O.Belvidere.

Stanley Thos. C. farm; Sec.25; P. O. Garden Prairie.

STEVENS T. M. Farmer; Sec. 36; P. O. Belvidere; born in Canada, Aug. 6, 1846; came to this country when 2 years of age; came to Cherry Valley, Winnebago Co., same year; lived in that Co. some years; also lived in DeKalb Co., Town of Milford; came to Boone Co., in 1858, and has lived here 19 years; he and his brothers, G. F. Stevens and A. C. Stevens, are engaged in Farming and own 75 acres land; two of the brothers were born Aug. 5, and one Aug. 6, of different years; their mother lives with them.

Stockwell C. E. carpenter; S. 4; P. O. Belvidere.

Stockwell J. carpenter; S. 4; P.O. Belvidere.

STOCKWELL P. R. Carpenter; Sec. 4; P. O. Belvidere; born in New York, on the 11th of June, 1820; came to this Co. in 1869; owns 14 acres of land, 4 in this Co. and 10 in McHenry Co.; married Caroline P. Arnold, in New York, on the 2d of February, 1841; she was born in N. Y., on the 12th of July, 1824; Mr. Stockwell enlisted in the 151st Penn. Vols., on the 22d of September, 1862; served as Drum Major; was honorably discharged July 2, 1863; there are seven of Mr. Stockwell's children living; two of them served in Penn. regiments from the commencement until the close of the war.

Stockwell S. B. farm; S. 4; P. O. Belvidere.

Sweeney —. farm; Sec. 24; P. O. Belvidere.

THURBLY CHARLES, rents farm; Sec. 30; P. O. Belvidere.
Thurbly T. farmer; Sec. 26; P. O. Belvidere.
Tripp Chas., Sr., farm; S. 8; P.O. Belvidere.
Tripp E. L. farm; Sec. 18; P. O. Belvidere.
Tripp John P. farm; S. 18; P. O. Belvidere.
Tripp John P. farm; S. 7; P. O. Belvidere.
Tripp Oliver, farm; Sec. 8; P. O. Belvidere.

WAITT CLARK M. farmer; P. O. Belvidere.
Wait M. C. farmer; Sec. 18; P.O. Belvidere.
Wattles Luther, farm; S. 31; P.O. Belvidere.
Waugh John, farm; S. 32; P. O. Belvidere.

WHITE J. M. Farmer; Sec. 34; P. O. Belvidere; born in this Co., Sept. 9, 1845; Republican; owns 120 acres land, valued at $4,800; married Miss Stanley, in Belvidere, March 2, 1864; she was born in New York, July 18, 1838; they have five children.
White John, farmer; P. O. Belvidere.

WIFFIN ROBERT, Farmer; Sec. 11; P. O. Garden Prairie; born in England, March 15, 1807; came to this Co. in 1856; owns 290 acres of land; married Miss Lawson, in England, May 24, 1835; she was born in London, in 1804; have two children living: Mary (now Mrs. Theobald), born Aug. 8, 1837; Jeremiah, born Dec. 14, 1842; he married Miss Mary Gooch, in this Co., March 13, 1877; she was born in this Co., Oct. 10, 1853.
Wilbur B. F. rents farm; S.19, P.O.Belvidere.

WILLIAMS MRS. ELIZABETH, Farmer; Sec. 10; P. O. Belvidere; born in this Co., March 11, 1838; Episcopalian; owns 60 acres land; husband was George Williams; he was born in England, Oct. 10, 1827; died Jan. 30, 1874; he held many offices in the town until time of his death; they were married March 11, 1858; had five children: Sarah Elizabeth, born Dec. 9, 1858; Mary Jane, Nov. 12, 1860; Charles Henry, Jan. 4, 1863; George Curtis, Nov. 22, 1865; Lucy Louisa, Feb. 13, 1870.
Winne Francis, farm; S. 20; P.O. Belvidere.

WINNE G. F. Farmer; Sec. 20; P. O. Belvidere; born in Albany Co., N. Y., April 7, 1827; came to this Co. in 1854; Baptist; owns 204 acres land, valued at $8,000; married Miss Esther Kendall, in Albany Co., N. Y., Aug. 31, 1850; she was born in Kendall Co., N. Y., Sept. 20, 1828; have had three children: Esther Louisa, born May 21, 1852, died Nov. 3, 1865; Francis A., July 15, 1855; Homer R., Oct. 7, 1857; Sarah (adopted when eight weeks old), born Sept. 26, 1869.
Winegar George W. farm; P. O. Belvidere.

WITT C. F. Farmer; Sec. 29; P. O. Belvidere; born in Chesterfield, Hampshire Co., Mass., Sept. 20, 1811; came to this Co. in 1844; owns 290 acres of land; Mr. Witt has held various important offices in the early settlement of the Co.; has held the office of County Justice sixteen consecutive years; has represented the township, in which he resides, in County Board eight years; been Assessor four years, Town Clerk two years; is at present Town Justice; has held the office of School Trustee and Township Treasurer a number of years; married Miss Eliza A. Brown, in Warren Co., N. Y., 1836; she was born in Warren Co., N. Y., Feb. 9, 1814; have had nine children; five of them are living.
Witt Henry C. farm; Sec. 32; P.O.Belvidere.
Witt Isaac N. farm; Sec. 32; P.O.Belvidere.

WOLCOTT WM. Farmer; Sec. 9; P. O. Belvidere; born in Penn., November, 1855; came to this Co. in 1869; Republican; owns property to the value of $2,000; married Miss Pluma L. Barton, in New York; she was born in Oswego, N. Y., Jan. 2, 1842.
Wylde Saml. farm; Sec. 27; P. O. Belvidere.

J. D. EASTER & CO.

The developing of this great western country has brought to the front a few representative men in each of the leading branches of industry. To develop the state, and cause it to blossom like the rose, necessitated farmers; and farmers could do nothing without tools and machines, and the result was far-seeing men, with energy and enterprise, laid the foundation of the great industries that, by the aid of capital, have been developed into mammoth institutions.

Among the manufacturers engaged in producing machinery and implements for the farmers, there is probably nowhere to be found a firm more widely and favorably known, than that of J. D. Easter & Co., Chicago. They are recognized as the originators and introducers of the celebrated Marsh Harvester, the original of its class, and to-day the most successful Harvester made. The experience of each year suggests new ideas that are at once adopted and added to the machine, keeping it in advance of all the other machinery devised for grain gathering. Heeding the call for an Automatic Grain Binder, they have secured the most simple and satisfactory device yet invented, and attached it to the Marsh, and together they are the most complete machine for the farmer known for harvesting. Not content with a harvester of common size only, they also make one called the Harvester King; which is the Marsh, increased to a six foot cut, and has an immense capacity for work. In addition to these harvesters, they also make the Warrior Mower, the most perfectly working grass cutter in the field. With this, as with all machines they make, the very best material and workmanship is employed, and the Warrior is celebrated for its perfect work and durability.

The Corr Sulky Plow, also made by them, is a marvel of perfection in its work. It is almost amusing to see with what ease a small boy can manage it, and do as satisfactory work as an experienced man. The independent crank axle adjusts it to any condition or shape of surface, and it will work any where that a plow can be asked to run.

Their experience in the field, among the farmers and stock men, brought to their notice the need of automatic pumps that can be depended on. To meet this necessity they commenced the manufacture of the Marsh Wind Mill, to all intents and purposes the same as any other mill, save in one important feature, and that is its graduating crank, by which the amount of work done by the mill is wholly governed by the winds, the stroke to the pump being changed from about three inches to eight inches, so that it will work in a lighter wind than any other wind mill made, and in strong winds increases its work, by which means it will do more pumping, by half, than any other of the same size. These facts, we are assured, can be demonstrated at any time.

These are the leading machines they make. In addition to them, they also make the Easter Harvester, in two sizes—$6\frac{1}{2}$ and 5 feet cut; the Marsh Riding Cultivator; a Header Attachment for the Harvester, etc., making them the manufacturers of the largest assortment of large and useful farm implements and machines in the country. To have room in which to do all the work required in supplying these to the farmers, they built a substantial brick block at Nos. 14 and 18, South Canal Street, 50x150, three stories high, where they have a most complete and convenient warehouse and offices, and can transact their immense business without delay or confusion.

www.ingramcontent.com/pod-product-compliance
Lightning Source LLC
Chambersburg PA
CBHW022111290426
44112CB00008B/639